THE PHILOSOPHY OF PSYCHOLOGY

THE PHILOSOPHY OF PSYCHOLOGY

EDITED BY
WILLIAM O'DONOHUE AND
RICHARD F. KITCHENER

SAGE Publications
London • Thousand Oaks • New Delhi

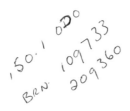

Preface, Introduction and Editorial selection ©
William O'Donohue and Richard F. Kitchener 1996
Chapter 1 © Harvey Siegel 1996
Chapter 2 © Harold I. Brown 1996
Chapter 3 © Steve Fuller 1996
Chapter 4 © Michael E. Gorman 1996
Chapters 5 and 8 © Richard F. Kitchener 1996
Chapter 6 © Max Hocutt 1996
Chapter 7 © Roger F. Gibson 1996
Chapter 9 © Ullin T. Place 1996
Chapter 10 © Richard Garrett 1996
Chapter 11 © Joseph F. Rychlak 1996
Chapter 12 © Herbert A. Simon 1996
Chapter 13 © Mark H. Bickhard 1996
Chapter 14 © C.A. Hooker 1996

Chapter 15 © Karl H. Pribram 1996
Chapter 16 © Aaron Ben-Ze'ev 1996
Chapter 17 © Ullin T. Place, Nick Chater, Mike
Oaksford, Barry C. Smith, Graham Richards, Elizabeth
R. Valentine 1996
Chapter 18 © Adolf Grünbaum 1996
Chapter 19 © Edward Erwin 1996
Chapter 20 © William O'Donohue and Jason S. Vass 1996
Chapter 21 © Hugh Lacey and Barry Schwartz 1996
Chapter 22 © Joseph Agassi 1996
Chapter 23 © Jon Ringen 1996
Chapter 24 © Karen Strohm Kitchener 1996
Chapter 25 © William O'Donohue and Richard Mangold
1996

First published 1996

 SAGE Publications Ltd
6 Bonhill Street
London EC2A 4PU

SAGE Publications Inc
2455 Teller Road
Thousand Oaks, California 91320

SAGE Publications India Pvt Ltd
32, M-Block Market
Greater Kailash - I
New Delhi 110 048

British Library Cataloguing in Publication data

A catalogue record for this book is
available from the British Library

ISBN 0 7619 5304 3
ISBN 0 7619 5305 1 (pbk)

Library of Congress catalog card number 96–070152

Typeset by TKM Productions, Boston MA 01960 USA
Printed in Great Britain by Hartnolls Ltd, Bodmin, Cornwall

CONTENTS

Preface   viii

The Contributors   x

Introduction   xiii

1 EPISTEMOLOGY, PSYCHOLOGY OF SCIENCE,   **1**
AND THE FOUNDATIONS OF PSYCHOLOGY

   1 Naturalism and the   Harvey Siegel   4
       Abandonment of Normativity

   2 Psychology, Naturalized   Harold I. Brown   19
       Epistemology, and Rationality

   3 Social Epistemology and   Steve Fuller   33
       Psychology

   4 Psychology of Science   Michael E. Gorman   50

   5 Genetic Epistemology and   Richard F. Kitchener   66
       Cognitive Psychology
       of Science

2 BEHAVIORISM, PSYCHOLOGY, AND PHILOSOPHY   **79**

   6 Behaviorism as Opposition   Max Hocutt   81
       to Cartesianism

   7 Quine's Behaviorism   Roger F. Gibson   96

   8 Skinner's Theory of Theories   Richard F. Kitchener   108

   9 Linguistic Behaviorism as a   Ullin T. Place   126
       Philosophy of Empirical Science

| 10 | Skinner's Case for Radical Behaviorism | Richard Garrett | 141 |
| 11 | Must Behavior Be Mechanistic? Modeling Nonmachines | Joseph F. Rychlak | 149 |

3 COGNITIVE SCIENCE AND PSYCHOLOGY   157

12	Computational Theories of Cognition	Herbert A. Simon	160
13	Troubles with Computationalism	Mark H. Bickhard	173
14	Toward a Naturalized Cognitive Science: A Framework for Cooperation Between Philosophy and the Natural Sciences of Intelligent Systems	C. A. Hooker	184
15	Neurobehavioral Science, Neuropsychology and the Philosophy of Mind	Karl H. Pribram	207
16	Typical Emotions	Aaron Ben-Ze'ev	227
17	"Folk Psychology" and Its Implications for Psychological Science		
	Introduction	Ullin T. Place	243
	The Falsity of Folk Theories: Implications for Psychology and Philosophy	Nick Chater Mike Oaksford	244
	Does Science Underwrite Our Folk Psychology?	Barry C. Smith	256
	Folk Psychology from the Standpoint of Conceptual Analysis	Ullin T. Place	264
	On the Necessary Survival of Folk Psychology	Graham Richards	270
	Folk Psychology and Its Implications for Cognitive Science: Discussion	Elizabeth R. Valentine	275

4 CLINICAL PSYCHOLOGY AND PHILOSOPHY   279

| 18 | Is Psychoanalysis Viable? | Adolf Grünbaum | 281 |

19   The Value of Psychoanalytic   Edward Erwin   291
         Therapy: A Question
         of Standards

20   What Is an Irrational Belief?   William O'Donohue   304
         Rational-Emotive Therapy and   Jason S. Vass
         Accounts of Rationality

5 ETHICS AND PSYCHOLOGY   **317**

21   The Formation and   Hugh Lacey   319
         Transformation of Values   Barry Schwartz

22   Prescriptions for   Joseph Agassi   339
         Responsible Psychiatry

23   The Behavior Therapists'   Jon Ringen   352
         Dilemma: Reflections on
         Autonomy, Informed Consent,
         and Scientific Psychology

24   Professional Codes of Ethics   Karen Strohm Kitchener   361
         and Ongoing Moral Problems
         in Psychology

25   A Critical Examination of the   William O'Donohue   371
         Ethical Principles of   Richard Mangold
         Psychologists and Code
         of Conduct

         Index   381

PREFACE

As both psychologists and philosophers know, the fields of psychology and philosophy hardly ever stand still (although, because of their natures and subject matters, philosophy tends to be slightly more fixed than psychology). Historically, the relation between these two fields has rarely been one of peaceful coexistence. Originally undifferentiated in antiquity, psychology was a branch of philosophy until recent times. Once having secured its independence, however, it became rather jealous of its new-found autonomy and insisted that its empirical status separated it from arm-chair philosophy. As we point out in our Introduction, this all changed with the Cognitive Revolution. Now, both fields seem willing to concede the other has something to offer (although precisely what that is has always been subject to dispute).

Being trained in both psychology and philosophy, both authors have always thought one could not separate the two fields (except for administrative purposes), and that they should become even more open and receptive to the contribution of the other. Of course, we have not always agreed on the precise relation between psychology and philosophy but we have agreed that this connection is broader than textbooks and anthologies in the field indicate.

Although there are several very good anthologies in the field of "Philosophy and Psychology," most of them, with few exceptions, center on issues related to Cognitive Psychology and Cognitive Science. Although securing a central place for these interdisciplinary relations, we also believe they are somewhat broader and incorporate several other areas. Consequently, we have tried to be more sweeping in our selection of contributions and to stress the rather unlimited ways in which psychology and philosophy are related to each other.

With the rise of naturalistic epistemology in the '60s, the question of the relations between psychology and epistemology have been much discussed typically in the context of "naturalistic epistemology." In this area, the interdisciplinary relation has usually run from psychology *to* epistemology (and not the other way around). Part 1 contains several discussions of these relations between psychology and philosophy, in particular, the autonomy of epistemology, the relevance of psychology and the cognitive sciences for epistemology and philosophy of science, and the psychology of science. Part 1 thus represents what has traditionally been called "foundational" issues in psychology and philosophy. Part 2 is devoted to such foundational issues in the context of what has been one of the most important "research programmes" in psychology and philosophy in the 20th century—behaviorism. Here, the lines of influence between psychology and philosophy go both ways. Although many individuals believe there are no longer any interesting or unresolved issues surrounding philosophical behaviorism and psychological behaviorism, we disagree. The contributions contained in this section illustrate, contrary to this widespread assumption, the many ways in which philosophical issues surrounding behaviorism continue to be of perennial issue.

The status of cognitive psychology and cognitive science is the theme of Part 3. Although the theme of 'philosophical issues in the cognitive sciences' continues to be discussed in a plethora of new journals and books, the contributions of our authors are not without originality and merit. Once again, we have encouraged authors from a variety of points of view and approaches to address selected aspects of contemporary cognitive psychology. The reader will note in these essays a bidirectional influence between psychology and philosophy.

In the past, there have been all too few discussions of the connections between psychology and philosophy in the "softer" areas, in particular, clinical psychology and related fields have been underrepresented in most textbooks and anthologies in the philosophy of psychology. (Here, it is philosophy which seems to have had a dominant role.) Part 4, therefore, is devoted to philosophical issues in clinical psychology, especially psychoanalysis and rational emotive therapy. We had hoped to include more contributions in this section, but alas we were not able to secure philosophical discussions of other aspects of the softer areas. Partly this is remedied in Part 5, which is concerned with ethical issues in psychology. Whereas the other sections, by and large, were concerned with epistemological and metaphysical issues in psychology, here moral philosophy and ethics loom large. Our experience has been that these issues have not been widely discussed by philosophers and psychologists. But this is precisely one central area where philosophical issues seem unavoidable. Part 5 thus contains a variety of contributions to questions surrounding the question of values in psychology, the nature of responsibility and autonomy, and issues of professional ethical conduct in the context of psychological practice.

All of the contributions to this volume are original; none have been previously published. Our thanks to the authors for their patience and understanding as we proceeded through the long and tedious process of soliciting manuscripts, reviewing and evaluating them, selecting and suggesting changes, etc. Our thanks also to two outside reviewers—George Howard (University of Notre Dame) and Arthur Houts (Memphis State University), who carefully read the entire manuscript and graciously offered extensive suggestions for improvement. Thanks also to Ziyad Marar and Sharon Cawood at Sage.

Bill would like to acknowledge his family, Jane and Katie, and Dick would like to acknowledge his family, Karen and Brian, for their understanding and support as we both spent more time away from our families than we had any right to. But as always they were understanding and supportive.

THE CONTRIBUTORS

Joseph Agassi has a joint appointment as Professor of Philosophy at Tel-Aviv University and York University, Toronto, and holds a PhD from the London School of Economics. He has authored or edited over twenty books in the areas of science, philosophy and psychiatry.

Aaron Ben-Ze'ev is Professor of Philosophy and Dean of Research at the University of Haifa in Israel. His main field of research is philosophy of psychology, and in particular the study of emotions and moral psychology. The author of The *Perceptual System: A Philosophical and Psychological Perspective* (1993), he is currently completing a book on the study of emotions.

Mark H. Bickard is Henry R. Luce Professor in Cognitive Robotics and the Philosophy of Knowledge at LeHigh University, Pennsylvania. His primary interests concern the nature of psychological processes, such as representation and language. He can be contacted by e-mail: mhb0@lehigh.edu or on the internet:
http://www.lehigh.edu/~mhb0/mhb0.html.

Harold Brown is Professor of Philosophy at Northern Illinois University in DeKalb. His main research interests are philosophy of science and theory of knowledge and he is the author of *Perception, Theory and Commitment: The New Philosophy of Science* (1979), *Observation and Objectivity* (1987), and *Rationality* (1988).

Nick Chater is Professor of Psychology at the University of Warwick and specializes in statistical modelling, connectionism and language and reasoning.

Edward Erwin is Professor of Philosophy at the University of Miami and his chief focus is philosophy and psychotherapy. The author of *A Final Accounting: Philosophical and Empirical Issues in Freudian Psychology* (1996), his *Philosophy and Psychotherapy: Razing the Troubles of the Brain* will be published by Sage in 1996.

Steve Fuller is Professor of Sociology and Social Policy at the University of Durham, UK. A philosopher of science by training, he taught in departments of philosophy, rhetoric and science studies in the USA, before his appointment to a chair in Durham in 1994. He is the founding editor of the journal *Social Epistemology* and the author of several books.

Richard Garrett is Professor of Philosophy at Bentley College in Waltham, Massachusetts. His publications and research interests cover a wide range of topics in ethics, philosophy of mind, metaphysics, epistemology, and philosophy of language.

Roger F. Gibson is Professor of Philosophy and Chair of the Department of Philosophy at Washington University in St. Louis. He has teaching and research interests in naturalized epistemology and the philosophy of language, and has written several books on Quine.

Michael E. Gorman is an Associate Professor in the Division of Technology, Culture and Communications at the University of Virginia, where he teaches courses on ethics, invention, discovery and communcation. His main focus is experimental simulations of science, described in his book *Simulating Science* (1992).

Adolf Grünbaum is Andrew Mellon Professor of Philosophy, Research Professor of Psychiatry, and Chairman of the Center for Philosophy of Science at the University of Pittsburgh. His writings deal with the philosophy of physics, the theory of scientific rationality, the philosophy of psychiatry and the critique of theism.

Max Hocutt has been Professor of Philosophy at the University of Alabama for thirty years. He is retiring editor of *Behavior and Philosophy* and was a visiting fellow at Oxford, Princeton and St. Andrews. He has written numerous articles on philosophy, psychology and pedagogy.

C.A. Hooker is Professor of Philosophy at the University of Newcastle, Australia. His research focuses on the nature of complex, self-organizing adaptive systems, their integration into a naturalist realist conception of reason and other norms, and their application to both individual and social cognitive processes.

Richard F. Kitchener is Professor of Philosophy at Colorado State University and has a special interest in philosophical issues in psychology. He is the author of *Piaget's Theory of Knowledge: Genetic Epistemology and Scientific Reason* (1986) and *The World View of Contemporary Physics: Does it Need a New Metaphysics?* (1988).

Hugh Lacey is the Eugene M. Lang Research Professor of Philosophy at Swarthmore College, Pennsylvania. In addition to writing numerous articles on the philosophy of science and the philosophy of psychology, he co-authored *Behaviorism, Science and Human Nature* (1982) with Barry Schwartz. He is currently working on a book about science and values.

Richard Mangold is a doctoral student in clinical psychology at Northern Illinois University.

Mike Oaksford is Professor of Experimental Psychology at the University of Wales in Cardiff. His main areas of interest are human thinking, reasoning and decision making.

William O'Donohue is Associate Professor of Psychology at the University of Nevada, Reno. His research specialisms include the study of human sexuality, behavior therapy and the philosophy of psychology. He is the author of many books and articles and is on the editorial board of several journals, including *The Journal of Mind and Behavior*.

Ullin T. Place is a retired psychologist and philosopher who holds two honorary lectureships, one in philosophy at the University of Leeds, and the other in psychology at the University of Wales, Bangor. His best known publication 'Is consciousness a brain process?' (1956) is the primary source for the Australian version of the mind–brain identity theory. His interests include conversation analysis, text analysis, learning theory, connectionism and the neuropsychology of consciousness.

Karl H. Pribram is widely known for his work in neurophysiology, neuropsychology and neurophilosophy and is currently the director of the Center for Brain Research and Informational Sciences at Radford University in Virginia. He is the recipient of numerous awards, notably the Lifetime Contribution Award from the Board of Medical Psychotherapists.

Graham Richards is a member of the faculty of Staffordshire University and is the author of *On Psychological Language* (1989).

Jon Ringen is Professor and Chair of Literature, Science, and the Arts at the University of Iowa. His current chief interest is in contemporary science studies and his publications include articles on topics in the philosophy of psychology, the philosophy of linguistics and the general philosophy of science.

Joseph F. Rychlak holds the Maude C. Clarke Chair of Psychology at Loyola University of Chicago. He is a past president of the Division of Theoretical and Philosophical Psychology of the American Psychological Association. He is the author of several books and papers on artificial intelligence and logical learning theory.

Barry Schwartz has been a member of the psychology department of Swarthmore College, PA, since 1971. He is presently the Dorwin P. Cartwright Professor of Social Theory and Social Action. Among his publications are *The Battle for Human Nature* (1986) and *The Cost of Living: How Market Freedom Erodes the Best Things in Life* (1994).

Harvey Siegel is Professor of Philosophy at the University of Miami. The author of *Relativism Refuted* (1987), *Educating Reason* (1988), *Rationality Redeemed?* (1996), and *Reason and Education: Essays in Honor of Israel Scheffler* (1997), his key areas of interest are epistemology, philosophy of science and philosophy of education.

Herbert A. Simon is Richard King Mellon University Professor of Computer Science and Psychology at Carnegie Mellon University. In 1978, he received the Alfred Nobel Memorial Prize in Economic Sciences, and in 1986 the National Medal of Science. The central focus of his work is his interest in human decision making and problem solving processes and their implications for social institutions.

Barry C. Smith is a lecturer in the Department of Philosophy at Birkbeck College, University of London. Specializing in the philosophy of language, the philosophy of mind, the philosophy of psychology and theoretical linguistics, he has a book coming out later this year entitled *Realism and Antirealism: An Inquiry into Meaning, Truth and Objectivity.*

Karen Strohm Kitchener is a member of the faculty at the University of Denver and has written

numerous articles on counseling psychology and ethics.

Elizabeth Valentine is Senior Lecturer in Psychology at Royal Holloway University of London and currently Chair of the History and Philosophy Section of the British Psychological Society. She is the author of *Conceptual Issues in Psychology* (1992) and is chiefly concerned with philosophical problems in consciousness and the psychology of memory and musical performance.

Jason S. Vass is a doctoral student in counseling psychology at Northern Illinois University.

INTRODUCTION

The relation between psychology and philosophy has had a long and checkered career, indeed a long past but a short history since the respective disciplines did not become separated, at least institutionally, until quite recently. But whenever we mark this great divide, it can certainly be said that the relations between the two fields have been one of 'love–hate' or 'approach–avoidance'. It was not too long ago that one could say (Harre & Secord, 1972):

> When a behavioural scientist reads philosophical writings, he often feels that the philosopher is being dogmatic and arbitrary, that he is legislating truth instead of leaving it to empirical investigation to discover. When a philosopher reads psychology, he often thinks that the conceptual basis of the study is naive and ill-secured, and developed in a haphazard manner without adequate critical thought, so that the empirical work is vitiated because it is ultimately confused, overlooking distinctions that seem to him obvious. (pp. 2–3)

Indeed, one need only recall Wittgenstein's famous remarks at the close of the *Philosophical Investigations*: "The confusion and barrenness of psychology is not to be explained by calling it a "young science" ... For in psychology there are experimental methods and *conceptual confusion* (Wittgenstein, 1953, p. 232e).

Historians of psychology sometimes pick the late 19th century (e.g., 1879), as the birth of psychology as a science—an empirical science set apart from philosophy both with respect to its methods and its subject matter (Boring, 1950). Many of the psychologists who championed the separation of psychology from philosophy proceeded, however, to write philosophical textbooks on a variety of subjects—here one need only think of Fechner, Wundt, Stumpf, Külpe, Helmholtz, James, Dewey, Ward, McDougall—on ethics, logic, metaphysics, the mind–body problem, philosophy of science, etc. (Boring, 1950). Apparently these psychologists felt it was perfectly appropriate for an individual to do both psychology and philosophy. Hence the breach was broader in theory than in practice.

With the rise of behaviorism in the 1920's, the separation between psychology and philosophy became more ideologically established as psychology became more professionalized. Indeed, Watson, Weiss, Hunter, Lashley, among others, were vocal and adamant about psychology being radically distinct from philosophy, once again in subject matter—mind vs. behavior—and method—empirical observation vs. introspection and unguarded speculation. On this view, psychology was to be an empirical, natural science—something some earlier psychologists hesitated to claim—investigating the (public) behavior of organisms via purely empirical, observational and experimental means. By contrast, philosophy consisted of pure armchair speculation about unobservable entities often based upon introspection, intuition, etc., and claming some type of transcendent or transcendental certainty. Here, then, was another battle cry of empiricism vs. rationalism, fact vs. theory, fact versus norm, etc. Hence, although philosophers had something to gain from psychology, most of these individuals (e.g., Watson) thought psychology could learn nothing from philosophy, indeed that philosophy should be avoided at all costs.

With the rise of classical neo-behaviorism and learning theory in the '30's and '40's (Hull, Spence, Guthrie, Skinner, Tolman), the situation changed from an undisguised hostility to a more cooperative endeavor as logical positivism (or logical empiricism) rose to a position of hegemony in the Anglo-American world. Although the standard or received interpretation, that logical positivism was the philosophical basis of neo-behaviorism (Koch, 1964) seems to be in need of serious qualification and revision (Smith, 1986), the neo-behaviorists and mainstream psychologists of this period looked to this philosophical school for philosophical inspiration and help in laying out the philosophical grounding of their psychology (Turner, 1965); reciprocally, logical positivists such as Carnap, Hempel, Feigl and Bergmann, looked to psychology for answers to the relevant empirical questions and illustrations of their prescriptive philosophical views. During this period (1930-1960), there was a kind of temporary marriage of convenience between mainstream experimental psychology, learning theory, motivation, meta-theory, and logical positivism. In particular, it was the metaphysics, epistemology, philosophy of science and meta-ethics of logical positivism that psychologists of this period eagerly read and it was the latest scientific results in psychophysics, learning, motivation, emotion, etc., that the logical positivists eagerly assimilated.

During this period of mutual harmony, the logical empiricists formulated what is surely the standard or received view concerning the relation between psychology and philosophy, one that still to this day lies tacitly behind the thinking of many psychologists and philosophers. On this view, inherited ultimately from Frege (1953), and staunchly championed by the logical empiricists, there is a fundamental dichotomy between psychology and philosophy: Psychology is an empirical, natural science, concerned with discovering empirical facts by means of standard empirical methods (observation and experimentation) and inference (induction, hypothetico-deductivism, model building). By contrast, philosophy was seen as a higher-order, meta-level discipline, one that could not compete with psychology over factual issues but a discipline that had taken "the linguistic turn": Instead of making claims about the world, philosophy was employed in making claims about the linguistic form in which such empirical claims were to be couched. Philosophy was concerned, therefore, with linguistic and conceptual matters, with getting clear about the logic of our (scientific) language, about what our empirical statements really meant, whether such things were really justified (meaningful) or not, etc. Psychology, therefore, made empirical discoveries about the world and philosophers helped psychologists to talk about their results more carefully and adequately. Because psychology operated on the object-language level and philosophy operated on the meta-language level, because psychology made empirical discoveries and philosophy engaged in linguistic, conceptual analysis, there was (and could be) no competition between the two; they were engaged in separate (but equal) tasks.

Of course, on this standard view, the question arose: How is psychology relevant to philosophy? and How is philosophy relevant to psychology? The short of it was that psychology was not relevant to philosophy (properly conceived), nor was philosophy relevant to psychology (properly conceived). Psychology was not relevant to philosophy because psychology was a factual discipline and philosophy was a non-factual (normative, conceptual) discipline. Properly conceived, philosophy had no empirical component, hence nothing empirical would be relevant to it. Of course, there were empirical components to be found in many accounts of traditional philosophy, but this was part of a philosophy improperly conceived and executed. But properly dressed, philosophy contained no empirical part.

On the other hand, philosophy had questionable relevance to psychology because philosophy was non-empirical, conceptual, analytic, normative, and a priori; and psychology was empirical, synthetic, naturalistic, factual and a posteriori. If philosophy was relevant to psychology, it would be because: 1) psychology as practiced tacitly contained philosophical components; and 2) philosophy could provide a conceptual analysis of the linguistic aspects of psychology (Ryle, 1949). However, scientific psychologists were interested in purging these philosophical components (as they were generally seen as unhelpful biases) and conceptual analysis was not regarded as a useful methodology (as compared to observational and experimental methods).

Of course, many philosophers welcomed the opportunity to point out that since the meta-level was superior (in some way) to the object level, philosophy got to call the shots and retain its hegemony about the lesser empirical science. Nelson Goodman (1972) put it this way:

> The scientist may use platonistic class constructions, complex numbers, divination by inspection by entrails, or any claptrappery that he thinks may help him get the results he wants. But what he produces then becomes raw material for the philoso-

pher, whose task is to make sense of all this: to clarify, simplify, explain, interpret in understandable terms. The practical scientist does the business but the philosopher keeps the books. (p. 168)

The alternative would have been to argue that psychologists could engage in the philosophical analysis just as well as philosophers could. This would have threatened the hegemony of philosophy as well as undercutting the claim that psychology was an empirical science. Psychologists might, on a rainy Sunday afternoon, with nothing else to do, engage in such philosophical (non-scientific) activity, but they should recognize this for what it was—amateur philosophy—certainly no part of psychology as a science. Hence, philosophy had no relevance for a properly conceived science of psychology.

This conception of the relative standing and aims of psychology and philosophy was part of a long-standing tradition in philosophy (going back at least to Kant) but articulated with great care and brilliance by Frege (1953) and Popper (1965). It was based upon the long-standing view that there is a fundamental dichotomy between the empirical and the philosophical:

Empirical	Philosophical
"is" (fact)	"ought" (norm)
observational	theoretical
synthetic	analytic
a posteriori	a priori
contingent	necessary

Along with this dichotomy went two correlative fallacies: *psychologism*—attempting to answer a philosophical question by empirical (psychological) means—and *logicism*—attempting to answer empirical questions by philosophical means. Typically, philosophers (e.g., Frege, Popper) charged psychologists (and some philosophers) with psychologism; psychologists (e.g., Piaget) charged philosophers (such as Popper, 1972) with the fallacy of logicism.

Three events occurred in the 1960's to change all of this: Quine, Kuhn, and the rise of cognitive science. Quine's (1961) article, "Two Dogmas of Empiricism," is suitably recognized as perhaps the most important article in 20th Century Analytic Philosophy. Although challenged and rebutted by several individuals, the verdict of history appears to be that Quine has shown there is no analytic–synthetic distinction, i.e., no distinction between

statements true by virtue of the meaning of their terms and those true by virtue of some extra-linguistic fact. Quine argued that a satisfactory account of analyticity could not be found because each of the key terms involved with the notion of analyticity—logical truth, synonymity, and analyticity—could only be defined in terms of the others. Thus, Quine argued that the notion of analyticity was circular or incompletely explicated. What is significant for our purposes is that the breakdown of the analytic–synthetic distinction led to the standard conception of the relation between philosophy and psychology being thrown into doubt, for if there is no analytic–synthetic distinction, what are the respective roles of psychology and philosophy? Once the analytic–synthetic distinction goes, so do the distinctions: a priori/a posteriori, normative/description, the necessary/contingent, etc., for each of the latter depend, in one way or another, on the analytic–synthetic distinction. It is not surprising, therefore, that Quine (1969) soon came to draw the obvious conclusion, viz., that traditional (normative) epistemology, which attempted to provide absolutely certain foundations for all knowledge—"first philosophy"—must be radically reconceptualized and in fact replaced by a *naturalistic epistemology* (Kornblith, 1994).

Of course, what naturalistic epistemology is supposed to be remains unclear and it may be questioned whether, according to Quine, "Epistemology ... simply falls into place as a chapter of psychology and hence of natural science" (1969, p. 82). But at the very least, it appears that psychology is relevant to epistemology. As Goldman (1986), for example, has argued, epistemologists must now pay attention to what is going on in cognitive psychology. But more than this, epistemologists must also look to other fields of psychology, e.g., social psychology, animal and human learning, developmental psychology, etc., which may also shed light on, say, epistemology, a point psychologists have argued for years (Campbell, 1974; Koch, 1964; Skinner, 1957). It is but a short step to claim that not only must epistemology be naturalized, so too must logic, philosophy of science, philosophy of language, philosophy of mind, ethics, and so forth. What all of this would involve remains, needless to say, very unclear.

So far, the breakdown of the analytic–synthetic distinction and the emergence of naturalistic epistemology can be interpreted in an asymmetrical way: Philosophy (e.g., epistemology) is to become naturalized (and perhaps replaced by psychology). But what about psychology? Isn't it in a similar situation? Should it become "normativized" (and replaced by philosophy)? In short, isn't philosophy as a traditional normative discipline relevant to psychology as an empirical science?

Such a conclusion has been drawn by several philosophers, especially those (e.g., Dennett, 1978) influenced by the views of Donald Davidson (1984) on the question of how one goes about interpreting the behavior, beliefs, and assent of others (especially when the other is a thoroughly alien speaker—"radical interpretation"). According to Davidson, the three components of belief, meaning, and holding something to be true are so inescapably bound together that the result is a (semantic) holism. In interpreting, say, what belief an individual holds, one must ascribe truth or falsity to such beliefs based upon certain environmental conditions. In doing so, one should employ "the principle of charity": The interpreter of a native speaker should assign "truth conditions to alien sentences that make native speakers right when plausibly possible, according, of course, to our view of what is right" (Davidson, 1984, p. 137). Hence to even identify what belief a speaker holds, one must assume that most of his utterances are true, most of her beliefs (and actions) are rational. This rules out, according to Davidson, global skepticism, incommensurability, and cultural relativism.

Furthermore, if rationality is a normative concept, as Davidson believes, then insofar as psychologists are concerned with desires and beliefs, which constitute the mainstay of folk-psychological theory, they will tacitly be immersed in normative claims about rationality. If this view is correct, then normative issues will be necessarily involved in the very construction of a psychological theory of belief. In short, cognitive psychology will have to contain a normative component. (According to Davidson, this would prevent psychology from becoming a natural science like physics.) In so far as the normative realm has traditionally been the province of philosophy, philosophy would be relevant to psychology.

In his "Two Dogmas of Empiricism" Quine criticized not only the analytic–synthetic distinction, he also criticized the empiricist dogma that *all meaningful statements are reducible to empirical observations*. Quine argued that statements do not face the court of experience individually but rather as a group. Due to this interdependency among statements, the meaning of an individual statement cannot be reduced to a unique set of empirical observations. Quine suggested that in a paradigmatic case of experience confronting belief—that of scientific experimentation—it is the entire web of belief that is involved in making the experimental prediction, not just an isolated statement. Thus, if the prediction turns out to be false, all the individual knows is that some adjustment needs to be made in his web of belief, but experience does not indicate how truth values should be distributed. "Any statement can be held true come what may, if we make drastic enough adjustments elsewhere in the system" (Quine, 1953, p. 27). However, the logical positivists and those influenced by them subscribed to this problematic kind of reductionism, and therefore held that theoretical terms could be eliminated since their meaning was completely dependent upon empirical observation terms (and not other theoretical terms). This was the classical idea, prevalent in the '30's, of operationalism and the intervening variable paradigm. However, once the idea became popular that the meaning of theoretical terms had "surplus meaning" and that one could not, therefore, eliminate theoretical terms, it was recognized that *theory is inescapable in psychology*, even in empirical psychology.

This same point was dramatically shown by the work of Thomas Kuhn (1970) who argued not only for the ineliminability of theoretical terms ("paradigms") but also that a static (synchronic) epistemology and philosophy of science must include or be replaced by a dynamic (diachronic) epistemology or philosophy of science.

In arguing for the essential ineliminability of theoretical terms, Kuhn (along with several others) argued that "observations are theory-laden," Hence, it became increasingly important in empirical research to be concerned with issues concerning the nature of a theory, theory-construction, theory-evaluation, and theory choice, issues that required criteria of evaluation. Such criteria—simplicity, quantitative precision, theoretical coherence, depth of explanation, power, plausibility, fertility, etc.—appear to be non-empirical (Kukla, 1994), criteria very much like those rationalists have traditionally employed in evaluating theoretical and philosophical ideas. This gave increasing credence to epistemological rationalism—the traditional home of philosophy. Hence, philosophy appeared to have an important and direct role to play in a science of psychology; it could contribute to issues of theory-evaluation and the correlative conceptual analyses required. (In suggesting that these criteria of theory-evaluation should be called *values* [Kuhn, 1977] was suggesting that norms—epistemic norms—had an essential role to play in science. See also Laudan, 1984.) This move towards rationalism was also championed in a somewhat different way by individuals instrumental in establishing the cognitive revolution, e.g., Chomsky (1966, 1972) and, more recently, Anderson (1990). (See also the recent discussions [Brown, 1991; Sorenson, 1992] of the important role of "thought-experiments" in science.)

Although even for the logical positivists, there was philosophical work to be done in science (e.g., constructing formal–logical languages for science, providing conceptual analyses of key constructs), contemporary post-positivistic analyses of science suggest to the psychologist that there is even a larger conceptual–philosophical component of scientific pursuits. Some of the chief extra-empirical concerns include:

- Analyzing the epistemological merits of research methodologies used by various scientists. After all, if the methodology is flawed on epistemic grounds, then the entire research program becomes suspect. Grünbaum's analysis (this volume) of Freud's clinical method is a case in point.
- Explicating and understanding the interconnections in the web of scientific belief. Of particular importance is to understand and identify the interconnections between observations and other elements in the web.
- Identifying problematic moves in the evolution of research programs, for example, the use of ad hoc stratagems (Lakatos, 1980) to save a favored view.
- Identifying and assisting in the resolution of the conceptual problems that arise in the theoretical/conceptual aspects of a scientific program. Laudan has argued:

"Even the briefest glance at the history of science makes it clear that the key debates between scientists have centered as much on nonempirical issues as on empirical ones ... When ... Newton announced his 'system of the world,' it encountered almost universal applause for its capacity to solve many critical empirical problems. What troubled many of Newton's contemporaries (including Locke, Berkeley, Huygens, Leibniz) were several conceptual ambiguities and confusions about its foundational assumptions. What was absolute space and why was it needed to do physics? How could bodies conceivably act on one another at-a-distance? What was the source of the new energy which, on Newton's theory, had to be continuously super-added to the world order? How, Leibniz would ask, could Newton's theory be reconciled with an intelligent deity who designed the world? In none of these cases was a critic pointing to an unresolved anomalous empirical problem. They were rather raising acute difficulties of a *nonempirical kind.*" (Laudan, 1977, p. 46)

For Laudan, scientific progress can occur when a conceptual problem is solved without an increase in the number of empirical problems solved. Laudan suggests that conceptual problems arise when a theory appears to be internally inconsistent, or when its concepts are vague, or when the theory conflicts with other theories that we also believe are true. Laudan suggests that science aims at maximizing the number of solved empirical problems, while minimizing the number of conceptual and anomalous problems.

- Finally, some (O'Donohue, 1989) have argued that in conducting research the psychologist inevitably becomes involved with philosophical commitments because: (1) problem statements (e.g., what developmental factors result in antisocial personality disorder?) presuppose an ontology in that these problem statements make reference to certain entities; (2) research is designed to rule out plausible rival hypotheses, but what is considered *plausible* is a judgment that is heavily influenced by philosophical beliefs; and (3) the scientists' problem choice is influenced by philosophical considerations. For example, ethical considerations influence the choice of whether to conduct research on autism or sport performance.

Many individuals claim there was a cognitive revolution in psychology that occurred in the '60's (Baars, 1986; Gardner, 1985), some even selecting the year—1957. This was part of a larger revolution—the cognitive revolution—and the rise of cognitive science. Cognitive science is an interdisciplinary field including cognitive psychology, artificial intelligence, philosophy, linguistics, neurology, anthropology, etc. Many of the revolutionary features ascribed to the impact of Quine and Kuhn continued during the cognitive revolution, e.g., an increasing stress on the ineliminability of theory (or paradigms) (de Mey, 1982), a renewed openness to rationalism (Gardner, 1985; Paivio, 1975), an insistence that philosophy is an essential part of cognitive science (Gardner, 1985), etc. Indeed, anyone reading current cognitive science will be struck by the fact that empirical cognitive scientists are knee-deep in philosophical issues, that they recognize this, and do not eschew philosophizing! Indeed, for many empirical cognitive scientists, core issues in cognition are philosophical issues: intentionality, representation, semantics, innate ideas, etc. In fact, many cognitive psychologists are deeply acquainted with issues in contemporary philosophy and do philosophy side by side with philosophers. Correlatively, many contemporary philosophers, in doing philosophy regularly and consistently, cite empirical studies to support their philosophical views about cognition.

That a new marriage of philosophy and psychology occurred in the '60's can be illustrated in an illuminating way by mentioning the important appearance of a two-volume work in 1980, edited by Ned Block (Block, 1980), entitled *Readings in the Philosophy of Psychology*. These volumes contain articles both by psychologists and philosophers on a variety of philosophical issues in cognitive science, e.g., mental representation, imagery, innate ideas. (This interdisciplinary trend has continued with the recent appearance of Goldman, 1993). As Block pointed out, the anthology was not intended to cover the entire field of philosophy of psychology but only that part related to cognitive psychology. It excluded several important areas: perception, memory, developmental psychology, social psychology, personality, emotion, etc. No doubt Block would have preferred his anthology to include these other areas since it would be a misnomer to equate *philosophy of cognitive psychology* with *philosophy of psychology*. Indeed, in an invited article ("Philosophy of Psychology") intended to summarize current research in philosophy of science, Block (1979) made this point. Block characterized the philosophy of psychology in a standard way as "the study of conceptual problems of theoretical psychology" (p. 450). Clearly, as Block pointed out, such conceptual problems extend far beyond the realm of cognitive psychology. What then should be included in 'philosophy of psychology'? How should it be conceptualized and delimited? A similar question arises about the field of philosophy of science: What should it cover? One can argue (Kitchener, 1992)

that it should cover the entire field of philosophy, viz., epistemology, metaphysics and ethics. Similarly, one can argue that the philosophy of psychology should be construed as the study of *the epistemology, metaphysics and ethics of psychology*. Most of the philosophy of cognitive psychology is focused on metaphysical issues, with lesser attention being paid to the epistemology and methodology of cognitive psychology. By contrast, in the heyday of logical positivism, epistemological issues were supreme. Both areas have systematically neglected ethical issues in psychology; we have tried to fill this gap somewhat by including articles on ethical issues in psychology.

If the philosophy of psychology is defined as the study of the conceptual problems in theoretical psychology, this should certainly include conceptual issues about foundational issues in theoretical psychology, in particular, conceptual issues about the adequacy of current approaches to theoretical psychology. In our view, this should include a more critical examination of the major competing theoretical approaches, including cognitive psychology, behaviorism, Piagetian psychology, Freudian psychology, etc.

Our aim in the present anthology, therefore, is to present a somewhat broader cross-section of work in philosophy and psychology. It is an attempt to build upon the classical anthology of Block but to take it a step further to include broader philosophical issues applied to a greater variety of areas in psychology. This is not meant to demean the importance of cognitive psychology, which clearly lies at the heart and makes up the bulk of current discussions about philosophy of psychology. It is rather to suggest that if there are important philosophical issues in cognitive psychology, there surely are additional philosophical issues in areas falling out of cognitive psychology.

As our historical aperçu has indicated, part of the rationale for the current interest in the relations between philosophy and psychology emerged from a breakdown of the received view concerning the respective roles of philosophy and psychology. In this post-positivistic era, therefore, how can they be demarcated, if at all?

As we have already suggested, one cannot make a sharp distinction between the empirical and the conceptual/theoretical/normative. Psychology qua empirical science ineluctably will be involved in conceptual, theoretical and normative issues; hence psychology will have to become immersed in these more traditional philosophical areas. Philosophy, which has usually been thought to be concerned with the conceptual/theoretical/normative, will have to play close attention to the empirical results of psychology. Naturally, philosophers will be unable to engage in empirical research because their training normally does not include the standard empirical research techniques and statistical knowledge necessary to carry out ordinary laboratory experimentation, field research, observational study, etc. Philosophers will be limited, therefore, to what they are characteristically good at—conceptual analysis.

Should psychologists limit themselves to empirical research methods? We have suggested this is not possible; hence, the answer is obviously, no. Psychologists must, therefore, per force engage in conceptual analysis. But doesn't conceptual analysis likewise require specialized training? Although our answer here can only be tentative, we would suggest the following: Every scientist with a certain minimum level of intelligence and scientific training can engage in conceptual analysis. This is because conceptual analysis is a general intellectual ability the exercise of which is necessary for a great variety of intellectual tasks; hence, it is domain-general, whereas the ability to do empirical research is more domain-specific. This does not mean, however, that this ability is equal in all scientists or that all scientists can do conceptual analysis equally well. Indeed, since it depends both on native intelligence and training, one would expect that those with a greater amount of intelligence would be better at it (ceteris paribus) whether they are philosophers or psychologists, and those with a greater amount of training and practice in it would also, ceteris paribus, be better at it. In short, psychologists can certainly do conceptual analysis (hence philosophy), just as philosophers can; however, for most psychologists, there is a need for professional training and practice in conceptual analysis. To do philosophy of psychology well, therefore, we are suggesting that psychologists have course work in conceptual analysis, e.g., analytic philosophy, philosophy of science, epistemology, philosophy of mind, philosophy of language.

Indeed, the last few years have seen an increasing number of psychologists taking formal course work in philosophy, e.g., philosophy courses relevant to cognitive psychology. Similarly, philosophers are increasingly turning to courses outside of philosophy to complete their education, especially courses in cognitive science. It is partly because of this new interdisciplinary style of education, that one can say the fields of philosophy of psychology, theoretical psychology, philosophical psychology are flourishing. For example, recent years have seen the appearance of half a dozen new journals in these areas: *Behaviorism, Journal of Mind and Behavior, Journal for the Theory of Social Behaviour, New Ideas in Psychology, Philosophical Psychology, Psychological Inquiry, Theory and Psychology*. It is in this new spirit of a rapprochement between philosophy and psychology that we publish this new, and we trust exciting, anthology in the philosophy of psychology.

REFERENCES

Anderson, J. R. (1990). *The adaptive character of thought*. Hillsdale, NJ: Lawrence Erlbaum.

Baars, B. J. (1986). *The cognitive revolution in psychology*. New York: Guilford.

Block, N. (1979). Philosophy of psychology. In P. D. Asquith & H. E. Kyburg, Jr. (Eds.), *Current research in the philosophy of science* (pp. 450–462). East Lansing, MI: Philosophy of Science Association.

Block, N. (Ed.) (1980). *Readings in the philosophy of psychology* (2 Vols). Cambridge, MA: Harvard University Press.

Boring, E. G. (1950). *A history of experimental psychology* (2nd ed.). New York: Appleton-Century-Crofts.

Brown, J. (1991). *The laboratory of the mind: Thought experiments in the natural sciences*. London: Routledge & Kegan Paul.

Campbell, D. (1974). Evolutionary epistemology. In P. A. Schilpp (Ed.), *The philosophy of Karl Popper* (pp. 413–463). LaSalle, IL: Open Court.

Chomsky, N. (1966). *Cartesian linguistics*. New York: Harper & Row.

Chomsky, N. (1972). *Language and mind* (2nd ed.). New York: Harcourt, Brace & Jovanivich.

Davidson, D. (1984). *Inquiries into truth and interpretation*. Oxford: Clarendon Press.

Dennett, D. (1978). *Brainstorms: Philosophical essays on mind and psychology*. Cambridge, MA: M. I. T. Press.

Frege, G. (1953). *The foundations of arithmetic* (J. Austin, Trans.). Oxford: Blackwell. (Original work published 1884)

Gardner, H. (1985). *The mind's new science: A history of the cognitive revolution*. New York: Basic.

Goldman, A. I. (1986). *Epistemology and cognition*. Cambridge, MA: Harvard University Press.

Goldman, A. I. (Ed.) (1993). *Readings in philosophy and cognitive science*. Cambridge, MA: M.I.T. Press.

Goodman, N. (1972). *Problems and projects*. Indianapolis, IN: Bobbs-Merrill.

Harre, R. & Secord, P. (1972). *The explanation of social behaviour*. Oxford: Blackwell.

Kitchener, R. F. (1992). Towards a critical philosophy of science. In D. Lamb (Ed.), *New horizons in the philosophy of science* (pp. 4–26). Hants: Avebury Publishing.

Koch, S. (1964). Psychology and emerging conceptions of knowledge as unitary. In T. Wann (Ed.), *Behaviorism and phenomenology* (pp. 1–45). Chicago: University of Chicago Press.

Kornblith, H. (Ed.) (1994). *Naturalizing epistemology* (2nd ed.). Cambridge, MA: M.I.T. Press.

Kuhn, T. (1970). *The structure of scientific revolutions* (2nd ed.). Chicago: University of Chicago Press.

Kuhn, T. (1977). Objectivity, value judgment, and theory choice. In *The essential tension* (pp. 320–339). Chicago: University of Chicago Press.

Kukla, A. (forthcoming). Amplification and simplification as modes of theoretical analysis in psychology. *New Ideas in Psychology*.

Lakatos, I. (1980). Falsifiability and the methodology of scientific research programmes. In J. Worrall & G. Currie (Eds.), *Imre Lakatos: Philosophical papers. Vol. I: The methodology of scientific research programmes* (pp. 8–101). Cambridge: Cambridge University Press. (Original work published 1970)

Laudan, L. (1977). *Progress and its problems*. Berkeley: University of California Press.

Laudan, L. (1984). *Science and values: The aims of science and their role in scientific debate*. Berkeley: University of California Press.

Mey, M. de (1982). *The cognitive paradigm*. Dordrecht: D. Reidel.

O'Donohue, W. (1989). The (even) bolder model: The clinical psychologist as metaphysician-scientist-practitioner. *American Psychology*, 44, 1460–1468.

Paivio, A. (1975). Neomentalism. *Canadian Journal of Psychology, 29*, 263–291.

Popper, K. (1965). *The logic of scientific discovery* (2nd ed.) New York: Harper & Row. (Original work published 1934)

Popper, K. (1972). *Objective knowledge*. New York: Oxford University Press.

Quine, W. V. O. (1953). *From a logical point of view*. Cambridge, MA: Harvard University Press.

Quine, W. V. O. (1961). Two dogmas of empiricism. Reprinted in W.V. O. Quine, *From a logical point of view* (2nd rev. ed., pp. 20–47). New York: Harper & Row. (Originally published in *Philosophical Review*, 1951, *60*, 20–43.)

Quine,. W. V. O. (1969). Epistemology naturalized. In *Ontological relativity and other essays* (pp. 69–90). New York: Columbia University Press.

Ryle, G. (1949). *The concept of mind*. New York: Barnes & Noble.

Skinner, B. F. (1957). *Verbal behavior*. New York: Appleton-Century-Crofts.

Sorensen, R. A. (1992). *Thought experiments*. New York: Oxford University Press.

Smith, L. D. (1986). *Behaviorism and logical positivism: A reassessment of the alliance*. Stanford, CA: Stanford University Press.

Turner, M. B. (1965). *Philosophy and the science of behavior*. New York: Appleton-Century-Crofts.

Wittgenstein, L. (1953). *Philosophical investigations* (G. E. M. Anscombe, Ed. & Trans.). Oxford: Blackwell.

PART 1

EPISTEMOLOGY, PSYCHOLOGY OF SCIENCE, AND THE FOUNDATIONS OF PSYCHOLOGY

As indicated in our general introduction, psychologists (at least since the late nineteenth century) have been interested in the underlying philosophical, theoretical, and conceptual bases of their discipline. Sometimes this set of questions has been termed 'philosophy of psychology', sometimes 'metatheory', but psychologists have invariably been drawn toward traditional philosophical issues: issues in (1) *epistemology*, including, in particular, issues in scientific methodology and philosophy of science, (2) *metaphysics*, especially the philosophy of mind and, more recently, semantic theory, and (3) *normative* issues, issues concerning ethics but also what we can call *epistemic values*.

Traditionally, methodological issues were taken to be primary since they were concerned with how to do psychology, and methodological issues are epistemological in nature. Similarly, issues in the philosophy of science have traditionally loomed large since these issues were also concerned with the question of the construction and evaluation of theories, the precise form a psychological explanation should take, the reduction of psychology to biology, and so on.

Concern about normative issues—especially moral ones—has traditionally taken a back seat in discussions of psychological metatheory; with the exception of the applied areas, where ethical issues related to psychotherapy are obviously unavoidable, psychologists have paid scant attention to normative questions, with many of them following the lead of the logical empiricists (Kitchener, 1992) and dismissing pseudoquestions or questions incapable of scientific resolution.

It is not quite so easy to dismiss such normative issues when it comes to epistemology, however; psychologists, engaged in the activity of theory choice, must obviously answer questions such as: What *should* an individual do if a theory T_1 is simpler than another theory T_2 but T_2 is more consistent with the rest of science? An answer to such a prescriptive question obviously presupposes an appropriate *normative standard* (criterion) for choosing between theories.

Psychologists are thus inescapably committed to issues involving *epistemic norms*. Indeed, on the canonical or "received" view concerning the nature of epistemology, this enterprise itself has been considered to be a *normative* enterprise. Epistemology, according to this standard view, is concerned with the question: Under what conditions is a person *entitled* to claim that he knows some theory to be true, well confirmed, corroborated or plausible? When is she *adequately warranted* in believing one theory or hypothesis to be better than another? When does the evidence constitute adequate *grounds* for a theory? Epistemic concepts such as *warrant*, *evidence*, and *grounds* are thus normative concepts, but epistemologically normative, not morally normative. On this view, epistemology is concerned with answering normative questions such as these.

Recently (roughly since the '60s) this traditional view has come under attack and a different conception of the nature and role of epistemology has arisen—*naturalistic epistemology*[1] (Kornblith, 1994). Although there are several varieties of naturalistic epistemology—evolutionary epistemology, psychological epistemology, developmental epistemology—all of them are united by a certain rejection of the received view of epistemology and the adoption of a countersuggestion: Epistemology should become naturalized, i.e., it should allow that empirical science has some role to play in the epistemological enterprise.

In his paper, "Naturalism and the Abandonment of Normativity," Harvey Siegel takes issue with this program of naturalistic epistemology as conceived by one of its founders—Quine (1969). In other places, Siegel has raised objections to the possibility of a naturalistic epistemology in the context of philosophy of science or developmental psychology. Here, he focuses on Quine's particular formulation of naturalistic epistemology. Quine's interpretation of naturalistic epistemology has been seminal in this new field and represents what many take to be a radical, nonnormative naturalism.

According to Quine's initial formulation of his program of naturalistic epistemology, traditional epistemology should be set aside since it has pursued an impossible task—providing the incorrigible foundations of knowledge; instead it is to be replaced by psychology (Quine, 1969, p. 82). Even if this view is too extreme—and other passages of Quine portend a much more moderate position—Quine is certainly endorsing the relevance of psychology for epistemology, something that psychologists have been claiming for years (e.g., Campbell, 1977/1988; Koch, 1964; Royce, 1974; Royce, et al., 1978; Skinner, 1957; Smith, 1986).

Clearly, therefore, the relation between psychology and epistemology needs to be spelled out more clearly. This task is undertaken in Brown's contribution ("Psychology, Naturalized Epistemology, and Rationality") in which he argues, contrary to Siegel, that epistemology should become naturalized and in so doing, psychology should come to play an important epistemological role. Brown is thus concerned to rebut the criticisms of individuals such as Siegel who believe a naturalized, psychological epistemology is not possible. Needless to say, even if a psychological epistemology were possible, its precise form remains to be seen.

As several writers have probed the possibility of a psychological epistemology, an issue that has arisen concerns what we can call the *unit of analysis*: Should an appropriate epistemology be based upon a biological or psychological unit? If the latter, should we construe the psychological in a narrow sense—the individual as solitary knower—or in a social sense—an individual as related to other individuals in a social setting? Some are convinced the latter approach is preferable, thus creating a social–psychological epistemology. Steve Fuller has been one of the main designers of this latter approach, arguing for a social epistemology (Fuller, 1988). In his present contribution ("Social Epistemology and Psychology"), not only does Fuller sketch out a program of social epistemology, he maintains that such an approach is *both* empirical and normative. Here he joins issue with Siegel's argument.

Fuller's program of a social epistemology can be seen as part of the new field of a *cognitive theory of science* (Fuller, et al., 1989; Giere, 1988, 1992). (See Part 3 on Cognitive Science and Psychology.) Fuller's social epistemology would play an important part in the new, multidisciplinary program as would the psychology of science and the sociology of science. A flourishing aspect of such a cognitive theory of science is the recent rise of empirical and theoretical work in the burgeoning area of *psychology of science*. There have been several recent contributions to this new field (e.g., Gholson, et al., 1989). Several theoretical approaches to the psychology of science, together with a wealth of empirical data, are insightfully summarized in Gorman's contribution ("Psychology of Science"), in which several interdisciplinary problems and responses between philosophy and psychology are discussed.

Gorman's contribution is written from a (broadly) cognitive approach to the psychology of science; such an approach has become of late something of an orthodoxy. There are, however, as Kitchener points out in his contribution ("Genetic Epistemology and Cognitive Psychology of Science"), other approaches to a cognitive psychology of science. In particular, he sets out what a genetic epistemological approach to the cognitive psychology of science would look like.

Most cognitive–psychological approaches to science studies and epistemology assume a naturalistic approach to cognition and epistemology. Most of them do not address, however, the issue raised by Siegel and others concerning the normative dimension of a cognitive psychology of science. In summarizing what contributions a genetic epistemology could make to the cognitive psychology of science, Kitchener returns us to these earlier issues and suggests that genetic epistemology is both normative and naturalistic. Like Fuller, therefore, Kitchener is advocating a position intermediate between that of Quine and Siegel. Needless to say, it is precisely this set of issues surrounding the nature of epistemology and philosophy of science and the relations between philosophy and psychology that will surely be the continued subject of much future discussion and debate; indeed, such issues have a direct bearing on the very nature, task and methodology of psychology.

ENDNOTE

1. The standard anthology on naturalistic epistemology is Kornblith (1994). It should be pointed out, however, that Kornblith does not provide a representative selection of the various approaches to naturalistic epistemology; for a summary of such approaches see Maffie (1990).

REFERENCES

Campbell, D. (1977). Descriptive epistemology: Psychological, sociological and evolutionary. William James Lectures, Harvard University. (Partially reprinted in E.

S. Overman [Ed.], *Methodology and epistemology for social sciences: Selected papers of Donald T. Campbell* [pp. 435–486]. Chicago: University of Chicago Press, 1988.)

Fuller, S. (1988). *Social epistemology*. Bloomington, IN: Indiana University Press.

Fuller, S., et al. (Eds.). (1989). *The cognitive turn: Sociological and psychological perspectives on science*. Dordrecht: D. Reidel.

Gholson, B., et al. (1989). *Psychology of science: Contributions to metascience*. Cambridge: Cambridge University Press.

Giere, R. N. (1988). *Explaining science: A cognitive approach*. Chicago: University of Chicago Press.

Giere, R. N. (Ed.). (1992). *Minnesota studies in the philosophy of science. Vol. XV: Cognitive models of science*. Minneapolis: University of Minnesota Press.

Kitchener, R. F. (1992). Towards a critical philosophy of science. In M. Lamb (Ed.), *New horizons in the philosophy of science* (pp. 4–25). Hants, England: Averbury Press.

Koch, S. (1964). Psychology and emerging conceptions of knowledge as unitary. In W. T. Wann (Ed.), *Behaviorism and phenomenology* (pp. 1–41). Chicago: University of Chicago Press.

Kornblith, H. (Ed.). (1994). *Naturalistic epistemology* (2nd ed.). Cambridge, MA: M. I. T. Press.

Maffie, J. (1990). Recent work on naturalized epistemology. *American Philosophical Quarterly, 27*, 281–293.

Quine, W. V. O. (1969). Epistemology naturalized. In *Ontological relativity and other essays* (pp. 69–90). New York: Columbia University Press.

Royce, J. (1974). Cognition and knowledge: Psychological epistemology. In E. C. Carterette & M. P. Friedman (Eds.), *Handbook of perception. Vol. 1: Historical and philosophical roots of perception* (pp. 149–176). New York: Academic Press.

Royce, J., et al. (1978). Psychological epistemology: A critical review of the empirical literature and the theoretical issues. *Genetic Psychology Monographs, 97*, 265–353.

Skinner, B. F. (1957). *Verbal behavior*. New York: Appleton-Century-Crofts.

Smith, L. S. (1986). *Behaviorism and logical positivism: A reassessment of the alliance*. Stanford: Stanford University Press.

CHAPTER 1

NATURALISM AND THE ABANDONMENT OF NORMATIVITY

Harvey Siegel

INTRODUCTION

Epistemology traditionally has been conceived as a *normative* discipline, concerned to develop and articulate criteria governing the appropriateness of belief. Ideally, it informs us of the warrant or justification that candidate beliefs enjoy and of the nature of warrant and justification themselves. That is, epistemology ideally helps us to determine which of our beliefs are justified and so *worthy* of belief (and why they are); insofar, it helps to determine what we *should* believe.

A large and growing body of work suggests that epistemology should be *naturalized*: reconceived as an empirical discipline and pursued in accordance with the techniques of natural science. One outstanding question this work raises is precisely that of the status of epistemology's supposed normativity. Can epistemology be naturalized in a way that preserves that normativity? If not, should naturalism be adopted at the cost of the abandonment of that normativity? This latter question is my central concern here.

According to the naturalized epistemologist, traditional epistemological questions concerning the nature of evidence, warrant, and justification can be solved (if at all) only by 'going natural', i.e., by scientifically studying the natural processes by which beliefs and theories are acquired, maintained, and altered in the light of experience. On this view, epistemology relinquishes its traditional autonomy from, and instead takes its place as part of, empirical psychology or cognitive science (or science generally); all epistemological questions are, to the extent that they are resolvable at all, in principle resolvable by empirical scientific investigation: "Epistemology, like science, is [according to the naturalist] an a posteriori enterprise. Epistemic issues are empirical and resolvable a posteriori" (Maffie, 1990, p. 283); "epistemology should be pursued as an empirical discipline" (Brown, 1988, p. 53); "[we must conceive] epistemology as an *empirical* science" (Boyd, 1984, p. 85, emphasis in original); "science itself is given a voice in matters of epistemology" (Kosso, 1991, p. 349). The naturalized epistemologist tells us that we should abandon our epistemological armchairs and do epistemology as a natural scientist might. Rather than spinning philosophical tales about knowledge and justification, we should study the way in which cognizers actually go about forming, holding, and changing their (scientific and other) beliefs. As Quine (1969a) vividly puts it:

> ...why all this creative reconstruction, all this make-believe? The stimulation of his sensory receptors is all the evidence anybody has had to go on, ultimately, in arriving at his picture of the world. Why not just see how this construction really proceeds? Why not settle for psychology? ...If all we hope for is a reconstruction that links science to experience in explicit ways short of translation, then it would seem more sensible to settle for psychology. Better to discover how science is in fact developed and learned than to fabricate a fictitious structure to a similar effect. (pp. 75–78)

The crucial point here is that naturalized epistemology involves the abandonment of traditional, armchair a priori epistemological theorizing, and the replacement of such theorizing with empirical inquiry. Such naturalistic inquiry takes epistemology as a subject to be pursued within science, utilizing the methods and techniques of natural science; rejects the possibility of some vantage point outside of science from which the epistemic status of science can be judged; and presupposes the epistemic legitimacy of both scientific theory and scientific method. For the naturalist, this legitimacy can be challenged, but only from within the ongoing course of scientific inquiry; there is no possibility of calling the entire substantive and methodological edifice of science into question.[1]

What are the implications of naturalism, so understood, for the normativity of epistemology? More generally, what is the relationship between naturalism and normativity? In particular, does naturalism force the abandonment of normativity?

One group of naturalists, whose views will occupy us in what follows—the 'nonnormative naturalists'—advocate this abandonment, and argue that epistemology, properly naturalized, must be reconceived as nonnormative. On this view, to opt for naturalized epistemology is to give up epistemology's pretensions to extrascientific normativity. If naturalized epistemology is correct, then traditional epistemology is given up and replaced by empirical psychology or, more generally, by cognitive science (or, more generally still, by science as a whole). Such a replacement represents a dramatic shift from traditional conceptions of epistemology, which take seriously the task of

accounting for the warrant enjoyed by scientific claims and theories. If epistemology is naturalized in this way, then the task of justifying our confidence in science is given up, since in appealing to science to settle epistemological questions, we are presupposing the legitimacy of that science. To attempt to question that legitimacy from some vantage point outside of science is, according to the nonnormative naturalist, to cling to a traditional but outdated and indefensible conception of the scope and power of epistemology. This is the view commonly attributed to Quine, who argues that there is no 'first philosophy', no 'cosmic exile' outside science from which science can be judged; no extra-scientific normative theory of evidence for the traditional epistemologist to construct.

In what follows I criticize nonnormative naturalism, i.e., versions of naturalized epistemology that embrace the abandonment of epistemic normativity.[2] Quine's naturalism is typically regarded as one such version. Since his version is widely known and is representative of the difficulties facing all versions of nonnormative naturalism, I concentrate on his version in what follows. I shall argue that any such nonnormative naturalism— whether advocated by epistemologists or by psychologists[3]—is untenable.[4]

NATURALISM AND THE ABANDONMENT OF NORMATIVITY

It is frequently said of Quine that "he rejects...the idea of a normative epistemology" (Antony, 1987, p. 243). He certainly seems to do so, if his frequent remarks concerning "settling for psychology" are taken literally, and he is generally interpreted in this way. Alvin Goldman, for example, says that while Quinean naturalism is "perfectly tenable, [it] neglects the evaluative strain pervading most of historical epistemology" (Goldman, 1986, p. 3). Jaegwon Kim (1988) claims that Quine "is asking us to set aside the entire framework of justification-centered epistemology. That is what is new in Quine's proposals. Quine is asking us to put in its place a purely descriptive, causal–nomological science of human cognition." Kim continues, in a passage worth quoting at length:

> Thus, it is normativity that Quine is asking us to repudiate. Although Quine does not explicitly characterize traditional epistemology as "normative" or "prescriptive", his meaning is unmistak-

able. Epistemology is to be "a chapter of psychology", a law-based predictive–explanatory theory, like any other theory within empirical science; its principal job is to see how human cognizers develop theories (their "picture of the world") from observation ("the stimulation of their sensory receptors"). Epistemology is to go out of the business of justification. We earlier characterized traditional epistemology as essentially normative; we see why Quine wants us to reject it. Quine is urging us to replace a normative theory of cognition with a descriptive science. (Kim, 1988, p. 389)

Hilary Putnam writes that

Taken at face value, Quine's position is sheer epistemological Eliminationism: we should just *abandon* the notions of justification, good reason, warranted assertion, etc., and *reconstrue* the notions [*sic*] of "evidence" (so that the "evidence" becomes the sensory stimulations that *cause us* to have the scientific beliefs we have)…

…the expression "naturalized epistemology" is being used today by a number of philosophers who explicitly consider themselves to *be* doing normative epistemology, or at least methodology. *But [Quine's] paper, 'Epistemology Naturalized', really does rule all that out.* (Putnam, 1982, p. 19, last emphasis added)

Many, indeed most, commentators interpret Quinean naturalism in this normativity-eschewing way.[5]

And small wonder: Quine's writings are full of suggestive recommendations of nonnormativism. In addition to the famous "why not settle for psychology?" passage already cited, Quine writes:

[E]pistemology still goes on, though in a new setting and a clarified status. Epistemology, or something like it, simply falls into place as a chapter of psychology and hence of natural science. It studies a natural phenomenon, viz., a physical human subject. This human subject is accorded a certain experimentally controlled input—certain patterns of irradiation in assorted frequencies, for instance—and in the fullness of time the subject delivers as output a description of the three-dimensional external world and its history. The relation between the meager input and the torrential output is a relation that we are prompted to study for somewhat the same reasons that always prompted epistemology; namely, in order to see how evidence relates to theory, and in what ways one's theory of nature transcends any available evidence. (Quine, 1969a, pp. 82–3)

[T]he impossibility of that sort of epistemological reduction [where every sentence is equated to a sentence in observational and logico-mathematical terms] dissipated the last advantage that rational reconstruction seemed to have over psychology; it conquered our last scruple against unbridled psychologism. (Quine, 1969b, p. 51)[6]

[W]e are seeking only the causal mechanism of our knowledge of the external world, and not a justification of that knowledge in terms prior to science. (Quine, 1970, p. 2; see also Quine, 1974, pp. 19–20, 136)

Quotations like these—from Quine himself, and from his various and varied commentators—could be multiplied indefinitely. They make it clear that Quinean naturalism is regularly and plausibly interpreted as involving the abandonment of the traditional normativity of epistemology. What can be said concerning that abandonment? I turn now to a consideration of arguments against it.[7]

ARGUMENTS AGAINST NONNORMATIVE NATURALISM

A variety of criticisms have been made of the project of replacing traditional, normativity-oriented epistemology with a nonnormative, descriptive/causal science of cognition. Some overlap with others, and no doubt they could be differently organized. Nevertheless, together they constitute a compelling case against the sort of nonnormative naturalism that Quine is typically taken as defending.

Is/Ought Confusion

This objection suggests that nonnormative naturalism commits the naturalistic fallacy in that it argues from facts concerning the formation, sustaining, and alteration of belief to conclusions concerning what ought to be believed. Abner Shimony (1987a) puts the objection this way:[8]

…the findings of the natural sciences concerning mental phenomena are relevant only to descriptive epistemology, which studies the way in which thought processes actually work. The essential part of the enterprise of epistemology, however, is not descriptive but normative, prescribing the thought processes which ought to be followed in order to make correct inferences and in general to achieve knowledge. The failure to discriminate normative from descriptive epistemology would be a conflation of *ought* and *is*, which has been shown by meta-ethics to be a fundamental error. (p. 2, emphases in original)

Insofar as nonnormative naturalism eschews any concern with the normative evaluation of inferences, processes, and beliefs, this objection misses the mark; for if nonnormative naturalism genuinely rejects normative concerns, it cannot be convicted of deriving normative conclusions from factual considerations. This objection is better conceived, therefore, as an objection to versions of naturalism that strive to retain at least some dimensions of epistemic normativity. Nevertheless, to the extent that nonnormative naturalism does, despite its proclaimed repudiation of the normative, attempt to establish normative conclusions on the basis of descriptive facts concerning cognition, it appears that it does commit the naturalistic fallacy. To the extent it does not—that is, to the extent that nonnormative naturalism genuinely eschews normativity—it ignores, and does not speak to, "the essential [normative] part of the enterprise of epistemology" (Shimony, 1987a). In short, this objection poses a dilemma for nonnormative naturalism: either it commits the naturalistic fallacy, or it ignores the distinctively normative core of epistemology. The second horn of the dilemma poses a problem for the nonnormativist and will be pursued further here; the first horn poses a problem for the normative naturalist and will be ignored in what follows.

Illicit Dismissal of Normative Questions Concerning Justification from Epistemology

This objection is closely related to the problem posed for nonnormative naturalism by the second horn of this dilemma. The objection has been made by several writers and is easily put: The nonnormative naturalist has produced no compelling reason for rejecting the normative dimension of traditional epistemology, or for reconceiving of epistemology as a nonnormative domain.

This objection admits of both a stronger and a weaker version. Some writers, articulating the stronger version, have suggested that it is incoherent to abandon normativity. Putnam (1982), for example, writes that "[t]he elimination of the normative is attempted mental suicide....there is no eliminating the normative, and no possibility of reducing the normative to our favorite science, be it biology, anthropology, neurology, physics, or whatever..." (pp. 20–21).[9] The problem Putnam's

discussion points to is this: Elimination of the normative is impossible, for any argument to replace normative conceptions in epistemology with (nonnormative) causal conceptions presupposes those very normative conceptions whose elimination is being sought. An argument for eliminating the normative must be an argument to the conclusion that it is in some sense more rational, or more reasonable, or better justified, to eliminate the normative from epistemology and to reconstrue the evidential relation as causal rather than as epistemic. But any such argument presupposes those very normative conceptions of rationality, reasonableness, or justification that it seeks to eliminate, and is consequently doomed to incoherence.[10]

This strong objection to eliminationism—that it is incoherent, and so must be mistaken—admits of a weaker version, according to which eliminationism, even if coherent, is nevertheless itself unjustified and so unworthy of our embrace. Haack (1993), for example, complains of Quine's naturalism[11] that it "lower[s] the aspirations of epistemology, and...trivialis[es] the question of the epistemic status of science" (p. 353); she argues that Quine has provided no good reason either to so lower traditional epistemological aspirations, or to trivialize the question of science's epistemic status. Others[12] have also criticized nonnormative naturalism for dismissing, without adequate reason, the traditionally central question of the epistemic status of science (the adequacy of which naturalism presupposes).

Both versions of this second objection to nonnormative naturalism are powerful. The first, stronger version suggests that abandoning normativity is incoherent. The second, weaker version suggests that, even if coherent, nonnormative naturalism has not justified its abandonment of the normative; in particular, it has not provided any compelling justification for its abandonment of traditional questions concerning the epistemic status of science—the very science it presupposes and relies upon in its pursuit and practice of naturalized epistemology.

A related difficulty is that nonnormative naturalism is not only incapable of addressing the epistemic status of science; it is incapable of addressing its own epistemic status, i.e., of establishing the epistemic merits of nonnormative naturalism itself.

Nonnormative Naturalism, in Eschewing Justification, Renders Itself Incapable of Being Justified

Here we encounter another self-reflexive difficulty accruing to nonnormative naturalism. There are, of course, a wide range of possible epistemic stances concerning naturalized epistemology; three such stances, of central concern to us here, are those of nonnormative naturalism, normative naturalism, and traditional, normative nonnaturalism. How are these rival (meta-) epistemological positions to be evaluated? Presumably, those debating the relative merits of these positions will construct arguments designed to establish the relative superiority of their favored position and the relative inferiority of its rivals. Consider, then, the predicament of the proponent of nonnormative naturalism. She favors nonnormative naturalism but, being committed to it, she cannot argue that her favored view is better justified than, or cognitively preferable to, its rivals. To do so would be to embrace and utilize the very normative conception of justification that her position rejects. Thus it appears that nonnormative naturalism cannot be coherently argued for or defended. Even if it is in fact the correct or most justified position, to argue for it seems ineluctably to embroil its defender in self-contradiction. It is thus incapable of rational defense.[13] As Stroud suggests, the defense of nonnormative naturalized epistemology "is not itself part of naturalized epistemology" (1981, p. 87).[14]

In fact, this problem for nonnormative naturalism can be seen to be even more imposing: It can be posed in such a way that it suggests the conclusion that nonnormative naturalism is *self-defeating*, in that the nonnormative naturalist must *assume* or *presuppose* the traditional, normative conception of justification in order to argue for the elimination of that very notion, which elimination is the cornerstone of her position. If she appeals to that traditional, normative conception of justification in order to argue that her nonnormative naturalism is itself justified, she undercuts that position by presupposing that which her position requires her to abandon;[15] while if she refuses to yield to the temptation to employ that traditional notion, she leaves herself unable to justify her own view. This is a very deep problem for the nonnormative naturalist (Siegel, 1984).

Related to this difficulty for the nonnormative naturalist is an additional difficulty, namely, that even by its own lights, nonnormative naturalism must, in carrying out its own project, engage in normative assessment.

Nonnormative Naturalism Is Incapable of Carrying Out Its Own Project

This inability stems from the fact that the nonnormative naturalist seeks, despite herself, to evaluate the products of natural processes; in doing so, she is compelled to engage in the very sort of normative inquiry she strives to avoid. Consider the following characterization of the Quinean naturalist's project:

> Indeed, what was once the philosophical study of epistemic norms—epistemology—becomes, on Quine's view, the *empirical* study of normative reasoning—psychology. Epistemology, fully naturalized, becomes descriptive—aiming not at a validation of scientific practice, but seeking instead to uncover the processes by which human beings arrive at *good* empirical theories. (Antony, 1987, p. 251, last emphasis added)

As Antony here suggests, the naturalized epistemologist is interested in the empirical, psychological study of "the processes by which human beings arrive at good empirical theories." But which empirical theories are the good ones? Will the psychological processes being studied divide into two sorts, those by which we arrive at good theories, and those by which we arrive at bad ones? This seems most unlikely, especially in view of the fact that the goodness/badness of theories is on most accounts a function not of the processes by which they were produced, but of the degree to which—once produced, by whatever processes—they account for the evidence in their domain, are explanatory, predictive, and so on; and, further, in view of the fact that that goodness/badness changes, after the theory in question has been arrived at, as a result of new evidence and theoretical insight—so that a theory's epistemic status typically changes after it is produced, which change cannot be accounted for in terms of the processes responsible for the theory's production. In short, naturalistic study of the psychological processes by which we produce theories, since these processes are those by which we produce bad as well as good theories, cannot aid us in the task of distinguishing the good from the bad. So if naturalized epistemology is to engage in the study of "the processes by which human beings arrive at *good* empirical theories," some preempirical, non-naturalistic determination of the goodness of theories is necessary. Such determination will of course be a normative undertaking. Consequently, the naturalized epistemologist cannot engage in her project without an unavoidable appeal to and reliance upon normative considerations. If she, as a nonnormative naturalist, cannot appeal to such considerations, she cannot carry out her project. Carrying it out, on the other hand, requires the abandonment of her nonnormative stance.[16]

This difficulty suggests that the goodness of theories, i.e., their normative, evaluative status, depends upon the evidence that can be mustered for and against them, where 'evidence' is understood as a normative, epistemic notion. Naturalized epistemologists, like their traditionalist counterparts, do speak of evidence and the relation between evidence and theory. However, this notion and relation are understood dramatically differently by traditional and naturalized epistemologists.

The 'Evidence' Relation of Naturalized Epistemology is Causal, Not Epistemic

Quine is sometimes clear that by 'evidence' he means that which *causes* the adoption, maintenance, and alteration of beliefs and theories. (See the passages cited above from Quine, 1969a, pp. 82–3; 1970, p. 2.) It is at least plausible that for Quine the evidence relation is causal rather than epistemic (although Quine frequently conflates these two conceptions of the evidence relation, e.g., Quine, 1974, p. 37; 1975, p. 78). As the previous objection suggests, however, causal relations will not suffice if the naturalized epistemologist means to study the causal processes by which *good* theories are produced, for the same causal processes will produce bad as well as good theories; causal considerations will not enable us to distinguish the good from the bad. To so distinguish, we need not a *causal* evidence relation, but the traditional, normative conception of evidence providing epistemic warrant or probative support for beliefs and theories. As Kim (1988) puts the point:

…the concept of evidence is inseparable from that of justification. When we talk of "evidence" in an epistemological sense we are talking about justification: one thing is "evidence" for another just in case the first tends to enhance the reasonableness or justification of the second. And such evidential

relations hold in part because of the "contents" of the items involved, not merely because of the causal or nomological connections between them.
…[Naturalized epistemology and traditional epistemology] both investigate "how evidence relates to theory". But putting the matter this way can be misleading, and has perhaps misled Quine: the two disciplines do not investigate the same relation…[N]ormative epistemology is concerned with the evidential relation properly so-called—that is, the relation of justification—and Quine's naturalized epistemology is meant to study the causal–nomological relation. (pp. 390–391)[17]

The important point here is not simply that the nonnormative naturalist has reconstrued the concept of evidence, rendering it a causal rather than a normative notion. It is rather that, so reconstrued, the nonnormative naturalist cannot take note of the way in which evidence can probatively support (or not) beliefs and theories, nor of the fact that the same causal, psychological processes can produce beliefs and theories that are and are not so supported by evidence. Consequently, she cannot differentiate those that are so supported from those that are not. But this distinction is central to her own project of studying the processes by which *good* theories are produced; it is also a necessary preliminary to addressing what Shimony (1987a) identified as "the essential [normative] part of the enterprise of epistemology." As Kim (1988) puts it, to take the evidence relation as causal is to give up epistemology's concern with justification, and "for epistemology to go out of the business of justification is for it to go out of business" (p. 391). In other words, insofar as naturalized epistemology is concerned to study the evidence relation causally rather than normatively, it is not rightly regarded as epistemology at all. To nonnormatively naturalize is simply to abandon the traditional epistemological projects of identifying and justifying criteria of justification, and of using them to determine what we in fact know (or are justified in believing), and indeed whether we know (or are justified in believing) anything at all.[18]

Circularity

A final difficulty facing naturalized epistemology, much discussed in the literature, is that of circularity. Shimony (1987a) characterizes the objection thus:

…the knowledge which the natural sciences provide concerning human beings is indirect and inferential and is therefore not trustworthy unless scientific methodology has been justified. But scientific methodology is a part of epistemology. Consequently, any program making essential use of the results of the natural sciences in epistemology, for the purpose of assessing claims to knowledge, is blatantly circular. (pp. 2–3)[19]

Since the epistemic status of science is itself an open question which epistemology must address, any appeal to putative scientific knowledge in an attempt to answer that question is circular—it utilizes the science whose status is itself at issue. This way of establishing the epistemic status of science, then, surely won't do; for in pursuing the matter naturalistically, the naturalist presumes the epistemic legitimacy of the very science whose legitimacy is at issue. This challenge to nonnormative naturalism is thus a fundamental one, for it suggests that the question at issue cannot, in principle, be decided naturalistically.

Given the fundamental nature of this objection, it is not surprising that both defenders and critics of naturalism have addressed it at length. Quine (1969a), for example, has long argued for the legitimacy of the naturalist's appeal to natural science in addressing epistemological questions:

> The stimulation of his sensory receptors is all the evidence anybody has had to go on, ultimately, in arriving at his picture of the world. Why not just see how this construction really proceeds? Why not settle for psychology? *Such a surrender of the epistemological burden to psychology is a move that was disallowed in earlier times as circular reasoning. If the epistemologist's goal is validation of the grounds of empirical science, he defeats his purpose by using psychology or other empirical science in the validation. However, such scruples against circularity have little point once we have stopped dreaming of deducing science from observations.* If we are out simply to understand the link between observation and science, we are well advised to use any available information, including that provided by the very science whose link with observation we are seeking to understand. (pp. 75–76, emphasis added)[20]

This famous passage is only one of many from Quine's writings that suggests the legitimacy of naturalistic circularity, i.e., of appealing to the results of scientific inquiry to resolve outstanding questions concerning the epistemic status of the very science appealed to. In suggesting here that it is "the epistemological burden" that is being "surrender[ed] to psychology," Quine is clearly suggesting that it is the traditional epistemological worry concerning the epistemic status of science that naturalism aims to address. However, as we have seen above and as has been pointed out elsewhere (Siegel, 1980, pp. 318–319), the naturalistic appeal to psychology "to understand the link between observation and science" is equivocal: It could mean either that psychology can help us understand the causal mechanisms by which scientific theories are produced, or that it can help us understand the way in which observation provides probative support for theories, and so the epistemic criteria by which we should judge scientific theories and in terms of which their epistemic status is properly determined. The former sense is unobjectionable, but, as argued above, such a causal account of theory production does not speak to the traditional worry about the epistemic status of science, especially in view of the fact that such a causal account will account for the production of bad or epistemically weak, as well as good or epistemically strong, theories. The latter sense does speak to the traditional epistemic worry, but, in doing so, it seems clearly to render naturalism open to the charge of (vicious) circularity—not because the traditionalist is still "dreaming of deducing science from observations," but because she sees a damning circularity involved in utilizing the results of scientific inquiry in order to establish or determine the epistemic standing of the very science being presupposed and utilized. It is unclear whether Quine intends his brand of naturalism to speak to traditional epistemic concerns. What is clear is that, if he does so intend, his remarks considered thus far do not disarm the worry concerning circularity. Of course, if he does not regard his naturalism as speaking to those traditional concerns, then he avoids problems concerning circularity; but he does so by rendering naturalism irrelevant to those concerns.

The problem of interpretation of Quinean naturalism we are now facing—that is, the problem of determining whether or not Quinean naturalism is best interpreted as speaking to traditional epistemological concerns, or as rejecting those concerns in favor of issues concerning the causal mechanisms responsible for the production of scientific theories—is a difficult one. Quine himself seems to be of two minds here, and his commentators have regularly noted the difficulty of interpreting Quine on this issue.[21]

Quine frequently suggests that his naturalism does speak to traditional epistemological concerns. In particular, he often suggests that the appeal to the results of scientific inquiry in the resolution of traditional epistemological issues must be seen as legitimate once one realizes that those traditional issues spring from within science, and therefore that one is free to appeal to science in resolving them:

This fear of circularity is a case of needless logical timidity, even granted the project of substantiating our knowledge of the external world. The crucial logical point is that the epistemologist is confronting a challenge to natural science that arises from within natural science. The challenge runs as follows. Science itself teaches that there is no clairvoyance; that the only information that can reach our sensory surfaces from external objects must be limited to two-dimensional optical projections and various impacts of air waves on the eardrums and some gaseous reactions in the nasal passages and a few kindred odds and ends. How, the challenge proceeds, could one hope to find out about that external world from such meager traces? In short, if our science were true, how could we know it? Clearly, in confronting this challenge, the epistemologist may make free use of all scientific theory. His problem is that of finding ways, in keeping with natural science, whereby the human animal can have projected this same science from the sensory information that could reach him according to this science.

Ancient skepticism, in its more primitive way, likewise challenged science from within. The skeptics cited familiar illusions to show the fallibility of the senses; but this concept of illusion itself rested on natural science, since the quality of illusion consisted simply in deviation from external scientific reality.

It was science itself, then as in later times, that demonstrated the limitedness of the evidence for science. And it would have befitted the epistemologist, then as now, to make free use of science in his effort to determine how man could make the most of those limited sources.

Once he recognizes this privilege,... [o]ur liberated epistemologist ends up as an empirical psychologist, scientifically investigating man's acquisition of science.

A far cry, this, from old epistemology. Yet it is no gratuitous change of subject matter, but an enlightened persistence rather in the original epistemological problem. It is enlightened in recognizing that the skeptical challenge springs from science itself, and that in coping with it we are free to use scientific knowledge. The old epistemologist failed to recognize the strength of his position. (Quine, 1974, pp. 2–3)

And again:

The positing of bodies is already rudimentary physical science; and it is only after that stage that the skeptic's invidious distinctions can make sense....

Rudimentary physical science, that is, common sense about bodies, is thus needed as a springboard for skepticism. It contributes the needed notion of a distinction between reality and illusion, and that is not all. It also discerns regularities of bodily behaviour which are indispensable to that distinction. The skeptic's example of the seemingly bent stick owes its force to our knowledge that sticks do not bend by immersion; and his examples of mirages, after-images, dreams, and the rest are similarly parasitic upon positive science, however primitive.

I am not accusing the skeptic of begging the question. He is quite within his rights in assuming science in order to refute science; this, if carried out, would be a straightforward argument by *reductio ad absurdum*. I am only making the point that skeptical doubts are scientific doubts....

Epistemology is best looked upon, then, as an enterprise within natural science. Cartesian doubt is not the way to begin. Retaining our present beliefs about nature, we can still ask how we can have arrived at them. Science tells us that our only source of information about the external world is through the impact of light rays and molecules upon our sensory surfaces. Stimulated in these ways, we somehow evolve an elaborate and useful science. How do we do this, and why does the resulting science work so well? These are genuine questions, and no feigning of doubt is needed to appreciate them. They are scientific questions about a species of primates, and they are open to investigation in natural science, the very science whose acquisition is being investigated. (Quine, 1975, pp. 67–68)

In both of these long and widely cited passages, Quine suggests (a) that skepticism arises from within science; (b) that, therefore, the epistemologist, concerned to answer the skeptical challenge and so to demonstrate the possibilty of knowledge, is free to appeal to and make use of the very science whose status as knowledge, whose epistemic status, is at issue; (c) that the epistemological problem of skepticism is itself a scientific problem, namely, the problem of (scientifically) explaining how the "meager input" of "stimulations at our sensory surfaces" gives rise to the "torrential output" amounting to "an elaborate and useful science"; (d) that the naturalized epistemologist is pursuing, in an "enlightened" way, the central problems of concern to traditional epistemology; and, nevertheless,

(e) that the naturalized epistemologist is not concerned with issues of justification, but rather with those of (scientific) explanation: in particular, of explaining how humans project science from sensory stimulations, and why that science works so well.

Now if the traditional problem of skepticism is understood as the scientific problem of explaining how scientific theory is produced by creatures like us from the meager input of sensory stimulation, it is uncontroversial that the scientist working on that problem is free to appeal to the very science whose production is under investigation. But it is far from clear that this problem—of explaining the production of scientific theory by members of our species on the basis of the sorts of sensory stimulations that that very theory tells us we are capable of experiencing—is the same one as the traditional problem of skepticism. Indeed, it seems very much like a "gratuitous change of subject matter" rather than "an enlightened persistence...in the original epistemological problem." For the challenge posed by skepticism is traditionally understood as that of accounting for the possibility of knowledge; of saying why we are entitled to claim of our beliefs (if we are) that at least some of them are justified, and at least some of them constitute knowledge. That is, the traditional epistemologist is not concerned to explain how scientific theory is produced or why it works, but rather to determine if, and if so why, we are justified in believing it. The first of these is Quine's scientific question; to answer it the naturalized epistemologist is surely free to make use of whatever science she can. But the second question is not a scientific one; it is rather a question concerning the epistemic status of science. This second question asks why we are entitled to regard our putative scientific knowledge as genuine, and why we are justified in believing it. To answer this second question by appealing to current science does seem to be problematically circular. For if the naturalized epistemologist argues that we are entitled to regard our scientific beliefs as justified because those beliefs are caused, scientific investigation shows, by psychological/biological/chemical/neurophysiological processes of certain types, the traditional epistemologist is surely within her rights to ask: (i) why beliefs caused by those processes are rightly regarded as justified; and (ii) why, until question (i) is answered, we are entitled to regard scientific pronouncements about the causal origins of such scientific beliefs as them-

selves justified. Question (i) is not itself a scientific question, but rather one concerning the nature of normative justification and the (naturalistic) properties of beliefs and theories upon which epistemic justification supervenes. Question (ii) is also not a scientific question, but rather one concerning the epistemic status of the scientist's scientific pronouncements. If the naturalist appeals to further scientific findings in order to answer it, she can surely be charged with arguing (viciously) circularly—for it is precisely the epistemic status of all such scientific findings that question (ii) queries.

Notice, moreover, that the fact—if it is a fact[22]—that skepticism arises from within science does not in the least establish that the naturalist, in answering questions (i) and (ii), can freely appeal to the results of scientific inquiry in answering those questions. As we saw earlier, Quine (1975) allows that the skeptic "is quite within his rights in assuming science in order to refute science; this, if carried out, would be a straightforward argument by *reductio ad absurdum*" (p. 68). But as Stroud (1984, pp. 224–229) compellingly argues, Quine's ceding this point undermines any force he might think accrues to his insistence that "skeptical doubts are scientific doubts." For if skepticism concerning science *arises* from within science, it is nevertheless clear that, once arisen, it cannot be defeated by the deliverances of the very science it calls into question. As Stroud (1984) puts the point:

> Suppose we ask, as Descartes does, whether we know anything about the world around us, and how any such knowledge is possible. And suppose we ask this question and find an answer to it difficult because of certain things we take at the outset to be true about the physical world and about the processes of perception which give us the only access we have to it. If we then reasoned as Descartes reasons and arrived by *reductio ad absurdum* at the conclusion that we know nothing about the physical world, and we found ourselves dissatisfied with that conclusion, clearly we could not go blithely on to satisfy ourselves and explain how knowledge is nevertheless possible by appealing to those very beliefs about the physical world that we have just consigned to the realm of what is not known. By our own arguments, despite their scientific origin, we would find ourselves precluded from using as independently reliable any part of what we had previously accepted as knowledge of the world around us. The scientific origin of our original question or doubts would therefore do nothing to show that the answer to our question or the resolution of our doubts can be found in an empirical study of human knowledge as an observable phenomenon

in the physical world. (p. 229; see also Stroud, 1981, pp. 84–85)

There are two points to note here. First, even if Quine is right that "skeptical doubts are scientific doubts," it hardly follows from this alleged fact about the origins of skepticism that it can be acceptably or usefully responded to by appealing to science. For once the skeptic calls the deliverances of science into question, then, even if her skepticism springs from within science, it cannot be resolved on the basis of further scientific pronouncements. For her skepticism calls all such pronouncements into question. The origin of her skepticism in science, even if genuine, is irrelevant here, and is unable to resolve her skeptical doubts in an acceptable, nonviciously circular way.

Second, despite Quine's frequent insistence that the naturalist is manifesting "an enlightened persistence...in the original epistemological problem," this seems clearly mistaken. For the original epistemological problem concerns not the causal explanation of our species' development of science, but rather the epistemic status of that self-same science. The causal/explanatory story the Quinean naturalized epistemologist wants to tell cannot be regarded as an answer to traditional questions concerning the justificatory status of putative scientific knowledge. The question of the Quinean naturalist—"How do we acquire our overall theory of the world and why does it work so well?" (Gibson, 1987, p. 62)—is a causal/explanatory question of a character far different from the traditional question concerning the epistemic status of that overall theory of ours.

Nevertheless, despite the seeming change of subject matter the Quinean naturalist brings to traditional epistemology, Quine frequently suggests that he has not changed the subject and that his brand of naturalism is "an enlightened persistence... in the original epistemological problem." What are we to say of Quinean naturalized epistemology here? While it is not clear from the texts whether Quinean naturalism is addressed to traditional epistemological problems, or rather abandons those problems for other, scientific causal/explanatory ones, it is clear what we should say in either case. On the one hand, Quinean naturalism fails to resolve the traditional problems, and the circularity involved in appealing to science in order to establish the epistemic status of the very science appealed to is a major reason for this fail-

ure. On the other hand, if the Quinean naturalist abandons the pursuit of those traditional problems in favor of scientific questions concerning the causal relationships between sensory stimulations and the production of scientific theory, then the circularity involved is benign, since it is surely unproblematic to appeal to science in order to resolve scientific questions; but this effort, however acceptable, cannot be seen as resolving traditional epistemological problems concerning the epistemic status of science or the possibility of knowledge.[23] In short: If Quinean naturalism is aimed at the resolution of traditional epistemological problems, it fails, and the circularity involved in appealing to science in order to establish the epistemic merits of science is a major reason for that failure; if it is not aimed at such problems, then its circularity is unproblematic, but naturalism so understood is irrelevant to the rational resolution of those traditional issues.

It should be clear that the conclusion just reached—that Quinean naturalized epistemology either fails to resolve traditional epistemological questions, or is irrelevant to those questions—applies whether or not such naturalism is construed nonnormatively. So construed, Quinean naturalism is irrelevant to traditional epistemology. Construed normatively, the conclusion reached is that Quinean naturalism fails to resolve the issues it is aimed at resolving. I have not discussed normative naturalism here. I wish simply to note that the circularity objection is powerful even against Quinean nonnormative naturalism, in that it helps to establish the irrelevance of nonnormative naturalism to the normative issues at the heart of traditional epistemology.

SUMMARY AND CONCLUSION

I have considered six objections to nonnormative naturalism of the sort frequently attributed to Quine.[24] First, nonnormative naturalism, insofar as it speaks to traditional epistemological concerns, harbors a deep is/ought confusion and commits the naturalistic fallacy; to the extent it is innocent of this charge it is irrelevant to traditional epistemology. Second, nonnormative naturalism illicitly dismisses normative questions concerning justification from epistemology. This objection admits of two versions: According to the strong version, such dismissal is incoherent; according to the weak version, such dismissal, while coherent, is nevertheless unjustified. Third, nonnormative naturalism, in eschewing justification, renders itself incapable of being justified. Fourth, nonnormative naturalism is incapable of carrying out its own project, which involves the scientific study of the psychological/biological/neurophysiological processes by which humans produce *good* scientific theories. Fifth, nonnormative naturalism distorts the evidence relation by construing it as causal rather than as epistemic. Sixth, nonnormative naturalism faces difficulties involving vicious circularity. Some of these problems with nonnormative naturalism are self-reflexive in nature. Some accrue to normative naturalism as well as to nonnormative naturalism. Obviously they overlap in various ways, reinforce each other in various ways, and could be individuated in different ways. Nevertheless, they provide a suggestive catalogue of the difficulties facing nonnormative naturalism.

These six objections to nonnormative naturalism are formidable. They are sufficiently strong, I hope to have shown, to warrant the rejection of this sort of naturalism. Elsewhere I argue that most naturalists, including Quine, do not advocate nonnormative naturalism, but instead seek to incorporate at least some dimension of normativity into their view. In the face of these objections, they had better do so. Nonnormative naturalism is a fatally flawed (meta-) epistemological stance.[25]

ENDNOTES

1. The account of naturalism just given emphasizes the naturalized epistemologist's rejection of a priori armchair speculation concerning matters epistemological, and her insistence that epistemology be reconceived as a subject within science, to be pursued empirically or scientifically. This is rightly regarded as the core of naturalism (see, e.g., Kosso, 1991, p. 349: naturalists "are advocating an empirical approach to epistemology, empirical in the sense that many epistemological questions are to be answered by the evidence of science. Questions relating to justification of scientific claims… are not to be answered by a priori philosophizing but by science itself"), but of course particular writers introduce special emphases and slants. See Ketchum (1991); Kitcher (1992, pp. 57–9); Lehrer (1990, p. 154); Uebel (1991, pp. 624–7); and Maffie (1990), which also systematically reviews the literature.

2. It is perhaps useful to draw a distinction between what might be called 'eliminative nonnormative naturalism' and 'noneliminative nonnormative naturalism'. The latter position does not reject or strive to eliminate

epistemic normativity, but rather proposes simply to *ignore* traditional normative epistemological issues—perhaps on the grounds that their pursuit has (historically) been unproductive—and to pursue other, scientific issues. (Giere [1985, 1987, 1988] can perhaps be interpreted as holding this second position. See Siegel [1989, 370 ff.] for discussion.) All the arguments adduced below against nonnormative naturalism construe it in the first sense; it is this eliminativist position that I claim falls to the objections soon to be adumbrated. The second position, in recommending the ignoring of traditional normative epistemological questions, is not significantly challenged by these objections; on the other hand, it does not itself seriously challenge traditional normative epistemology. I am grateful to Ed Erwin for drawing this distinction and for discussion concerning it.

3. It is an interesting question whether major figures in psychology embrace the sort of nonnormative naturalism discussed below. While I cannot deal with this question seriously here, some brief remarks are perhaps in order. Jean Piaget's "genetic epistemology" is surely naturalistic; it is not nonnormative, for he explicitly argues for the epistemological superiority of later stage thinking. However, Piaget's arguments for that superiority, which are based upon his psychological research findings, do not in my view provide the kind of support needed; in that sense his naturalistic epistemology is problematic (Siegel, 1978). Donald Campbell, whose enthusiastic embrace of "evolutionary epistemology" might suggest a commitment to nonnormative naturalism, is in fact not so committed; he quite clearly recognizes that the validity of a scientific theory or conception cannot be read from the facts concerning its causal ancestry (Campbell, 1977; see Siegel, 1980, p. 298, for discussion). Finally, B. F. Skinner is plausibly interpreted as embracing nonnormative naturalism; whether or not that interpretation is correct might usefully be pursued by following the ins and outs of Quinean naturalism considered in what follows, since Quinean behaviorism is widely thought to rest on Skinner's behaviorism.

4. Elsewhere (Siegel, 1990, 1992, 1996) I argue that extant versions of *normative* naturalism—i.e., versions of naturalism that endeavor to acknowledge and account for epistemic normativity—face different but equally powerful difficulties.

5. The *locus classicus* of this interpretation of Quine is of course Quine (1969a). Many readers of Quine interpret him this way, including (in addition to those just cited) Almeder (1990), Antony (1987, pp. 249–251), Cohen (1986, pp. 44–45), Hooker (1987, pp. 361 n. 5, p. 409 n. 34), Kosso (1991, p. 350), Laudan (1987, pp. 24–5; 1988, pp. 347, 350), Ricketts (1982), Rorty (1979, pp. 220–230), Siegel (1980), and Steup (1992, p. 9). A penetrating analysis of Quine's naturalism and its embrace/rejection of normativity is that of Haack (1993).

6. Interestingly, this passage is reproduced verbatim in Quine (1969a, p. 82), but with the last clause deleted.

7. I refrain from rehearsing here the Quinean arguments *for* the abandonment of normativity in epistemology. They are most clearly presented in Quine (1969a), and can be found in many other Quine writings as well. Brief accounts of them may be found in Kornblith (1985), Kim (1988), and Siegel (1980, 1984, 1995). A detailed defense of them is presented in Gibson (1988). A nuanced analysis, partly critical and partly supportive, is developed in Haack (1993). Maffie (1990, p. 285) identifies Armstrong, Barnes and Bloor, Campbell, P. Churchland, P. S. Churchland, Dretske, Goldman, Nozick, Roth, and Stich as fellow travelers in the Quinean eliminationist program.

8. I do not mean to suggest that Shimony endorses the objection. For his consideration of it, see Shimony (1987a, p. 6).

9. Compare Putnam's remarks concerning naturalism and suicide with the following:

> To give up philosophy's traditional attempt to provide a systematic justification for human knowledge, especially for the fundamental principles of science, is to commit suicide on a grand level. And this is what naturalistic epistemology, or the naturalization of epistemology, is all about. (Sagal, 1987, p. 321)

10. This is one sort of self-reflexive difficulty that nonnormative naturalism faces. Almeder (1990, p. 275) is only one of many commentators who agree with Putnam that this difficulty renders naturalism "radically incoherent." We will see more self-reflexive difficulties below.

11. When construed 'scientistically' rather than 'modestly'. For discussion of these two varieties of Quinean naturalism and of Quine's conflating them, see Haack (1993).

12. See, e.g., Kosso (1991), Laudan (1987, 1988), Sagal (1987, pp. 322–323), Siegel (1980, 1984), Steup (1992), and Stroud (1981, 1984). Kim argues (quite plausibly in my view) that the naturalist's call to abandon normativity rests on confusing the idea that (a) epistemic justification, while normative, must have naturalistically specified criteria and that epistemically justified beliefs are so because that normativity supervenes upon naturalistic properties of the beliefs—i.e., because they meet the naturalistically specified criteria—with the idea that (b) "justification itself *is*, or is *reducible* to, a naturalistic-nonnormative concept" (Kim, 1988, p. 403, n. 34, emphases in original; see pp. 399–400). Armed with this distinction, Kim, who embraces (a) but rejects (b), forcefully argues that Quine has provided no good reason to abandon the traditional, normative/justificatory epistemological project, since normative justification's supervening on naturalistic properties does not entail that justification is itself nonnormative, or that normative justification cannot be had.

13. It is, one might say, *impotent* in that it is unable to argue coherently for itself. For a similar problem concerning epistemological relativism, see Siegel (1987, chap. 1).

14. While Stroud is here concerned with the ability of naturalized epistemology to deal with the traditional problem of skepticism, his point is easily recast as a point about the inability of naturalism to contribute to its own justification and defense. This criticism is also made in Siegel (1980, 1984) and in Sagal (1987), but see also Shimony's (1987c) reply to Sagal.

15. Notice that the presupposition in question is not of the *reductio ad absurdum* variety, in which the presupposition is abandoned at the end of the argument. On the contrary, if the nonnormative naturalist's position is to be justified and is to be seen as such, then at the end of the day that presupposition must still be available to her. So the difficulty cannot be avoided by construing it as a premise in a *reductio* argument that will ultimately be relinquished.

16. For an elaboration of this argument, with reference to Quine, see Siegel (1980, p. 319; 1984, especially p. 676). Essentially the same point is made, in Putnam's name, by Almeder (1990, p. 273).

17. Several writers have noted the radical shift involved in construing the evidence relation as causal rather than as normative and epistemic. In addition to Kim (1988, pp. 389–391), see, e.g., Putnam (1982, pp. 18–20), Sosa (1983, pp. 66–69), and Stroud (1984, pp. 251–252). Haack, however (1993, pp. 345–346), while accepting a sharp distinction between causal/descriptive and epistemic/normative conceptions of the evidence relation, rejects the view that for Quine the evidence relation is strictly causal and nonnormative; she interprets Quine as regarding the relation as normative, but as more narrow than it is traditionally taken to be. I enthusiastically endorse Haack's interpretive analysis of the relevant Quine texts. See also Stroud's discussion (1984, chap. 6) of the difficulty of interpreting Quine on this point.

18. Traditional epistemology can be characterized in various ways; the differences between them are sufficiently small that traditional epistemology, however so characterized, can be easily distinguished from nontraditional, nonnormative naturalized epistemology. Kim (1988, p. 381) characterizes traditional epistemology as concerned to "identify the criteria by which we ought to regulate acceptance and rejection of beliefs,...to determine what we may be said to know according to those criteria," and to "com[e] to terms with the skeptical challenge to the possibility of knowledge." Haack (1989, p. 111) characterizes it as consisting centrally in the projects of "the explication of epistemic concepts (central among which...is the concept of epistemic justification)" and of "the ratification of criteria of justification." Stroud (1981, 1984) characterizes traditional epistemology largely in terms of responding to the skeptical challenge to the very possibility of knowledge. While these and other authors emphasize different aspects of tradi-

tional epistemology, all are agreed that it involves identifying and spelling out criteria of epistemic justification;
justifying (or 'ratifying') those criteria; determining, by
reference to those criteria, what we know; and responding to the skeptical challenge to the possibility of our
knowing anything at all. It is clear that nonnormative naturalism rejects the first three of these; it is argued below
that, despite appearances, it rejects the fourth as well.

19. I do not mean to suggest that Shimony endorses
this objection to naturalized epistemology. On the contrary, he argues that it can be met, at least by his version
of normative naturalism (Shimony, 1987a, pp. 7–9,
1987b). I will not consider Shimony's position further
here. The question to be addressed is rather whether nonnormative naturalism can meet the circularity objection.

20. In Quine (1969b, p. 45), the last three sentences of
this passage appear verbatim. To them is appended a
fourth: "We should favor psychologism."

21. Stroud (1984, pp. 214–254) provides a detailed
analysis of Quine's many, seemingly conflicting remarks
on this question. See also Haack (1993, esp. pp. 343–
353).

22. I doubt that it is. See Goldman (1986, p. 57) and
Maffie (1995, p. 7).

23. As Stroud (1984, p. 221) puts it: "Any question
empirical science can answer could not be the traditional
philosopher's question. That is not to say that there can
be no such thing as a science of human knowledge, but
only that any such 'internal' investigation, however feasible, could never be expected to answer the traditional
question."

24. As the reader may have guessed, I do not think
that Quine is best understood as advocating nonnormative naturalism. Despite the impressive textual evidence
presented above for such an interpretation of Quine, I
argue elsewhere (as do Antony, 1987; Gibson, 1988,
1989; Haack, 1993; and Roth, 1983, 1987) that a more
defensible interpretation of Quinean naturalism understands it as instrumentally normative rather than as nonnormative. I cannot argue the point here. I hope to have
shown, however, that nonnormative naturalism, whether
Quine's view or not, falls to the objections just made.
(Instrumentally) normative naturalism is considered in
Siegel (1990, 1992, 1996).

I should point out that even if Quine is correctly interpreted as a normative naturalist, it is not the case that all
naturalists are properly so interpreted. Besides Quine and
some of his followers, Maffie (1995, p. 20, n. 4) cites as
eliminativists Churchland (1979), Churchland (1987),
Stich (1983), and Barnes and Bloor (1982). (See also
those mentioned in note 7 above.) I agree with Maffie
that there is considerable textual evidence for regarding
these authors as nonnormativists. [A harder case is Pollock. His naturalism (1988) embraces epistemic norms,
but these are understood as 'procedural' norms (1987,
pp. 372–373). It is at least arguable that this account of
epistemic norms eliminates the normativity of epistemol-

ogy as that is usually understood, and so Pollock is
rightly regarded as a nonnormativist (despite his concern
with epistemic norms), but I cannot argue the case in
detail here.] If so, the objections to nonnormative naturalism adduced above apply to their positions with full
force. See also Bealer (1987) and Haack (1990).

25. I am grateful to Harold I. Brown, Edward Erwin,
Roger F. Gibson, Susan Haack, Jaegwon Kim, E. R.
Klein, and David Stump for comments on an earlier draft.

REFERENCES

Almeder, R. (1990). On naturalizing epistemology. *American Philosophical Quarterly*, 27, 263–279.

Antony, L. M. (1987). Naturalized epistemology and the study of language. In A. Shimony & D. Nails (Eds.), *Naturalistic epistemology: A symposium of two decades*. (pp. 235–257). Dordrect: D. Reidel.

Barnes, B. & Bloor, D. (1982). Relativism, rationality, and the sociology of knowledge. In M. Hollis & S. Lukes (Eds.), *Rationality and relativism*. (pp. 21–47). Cambridge: M.I.T. Press.

Bealer, G. (1987). The boundary between philosophy and cognitive science. *The Journal of Philosophy*, 84, 553–555.

Boyd, R. (1984). The current status of scientific realism. In J. Leplin (Ed.), *Scientific realism*. Berkeley: University of California Press.

Brown, H. I. (1988). Normative epistemology and natu-ralized epistemology. *Inquiry*, 31, 53–78.

Campbell, D. (1977). Comment on "The natural selec-tion model of conceptual evolution." *Philosophy of Science*, 44, 502–507.

Churchland, P. (1979). *Scientific realism and the plas-ticity of mind*. Cambridge: Cambridge University Press.

Churchland, P. S. (1987). Epistemology in the age of neu-roscience. *The Journal of Philosophy*, 84, 544–553.

Cohen, L. J. (1986). *The dialogue of reason: An analysis of analytical philosophy*. Oxford: Clarendon Press.

Gibson, R. F. (1987). Quine on naturalism and episte-mology. *Erkenntnis*, 27, 57–78.

Gibson, R. F. (1988). *Enlightened empiricism: An exam-ination of W. V. Quine's theory of knowledge*. Tampa: Univ. Presses of Florida.

Gibson, R. F. (1989). Review of C. Hookway, *Quine: Language, experience and reality. The British Journal for the Philosophy of Science*, 40, 557–567.

Giere, R. N. (1985). Philosophy of science naturalized. *Philosophy of Science*, 52, 331–356.

Giere, R. N. (1987). The cognitive study of science. In N. J. Nersessian (Ed.), *The process of science* (pp. 139–159). Dordrecht: Martinus Nijhoff Publishers.

Giere, R. N. (1988). *Explaining science: A cognitive approach*. Chicago: University of Chicago Press.

Goldman, A. I. (1986). *Epistemology and cognition*. Cambridge: Harvard University Press.

Haack, S. (1989). Rebuilding the ship while sailing on the water. In R. Barrett & R. Gibson (Eds.), *Perspectives on Quine* (pp. 111–127). Oxford: Blackwell.

Haack, S. (1990). Recent obituaries of epistemology. *American Philosophical Quarterly, 27*, 199–212.

Haack, S. (1993). The two faces of Quine's naturalism. *Synthese, 94*, 335–356.

Hooker, C. A. (1987). *A realistic theory of science*. Albany: State University of New York Press.

Ketchum, R. J. (1991). The paradox of epistemology: A defense of naturalism. *Philosophical Studies, 62*, 45–66.

Kim, J. (1988). What is "naturalized epistemology"? In J. E. Tomberlin (Ed.), *Philosophical perspectives, 2: Epistemology, 1988*, (pp. 381–405). Atascadero, CA: Ridgeview Publishing.

Kitcher, P. (1992). The naturalists return. *The Philosophical Review, 101*, 53–114.

Kornblith, H. (1985). Introduction: What is naturalistic epistemology? In H. Kornblith (Ed.), *Naturalizing epistemology* (pp. 1–13). Cambridge: M.I.T. Press.

Kosso, P. (1991). Empirical epistemology and philosophy of science. *Metaphilosophy, 22*, 349–363.

Laudan, L. (1987). Progress or rationality? The prospects for normative naturalism. *American Philosophical Quarterly, 24*, 19–31.

Laudan, L. (1988). Methodology's prospects. *PSA 86*, Vol. 2, 347–354.

Lehrer, K. (1990). *Theory of knowledge*. Boulder: Westview Press.

Maffie, J. (1990). Recent work on naturalized epistemology. *American Philosophical Quarterly, 27*, 281–293.

Maffie, J. (1995). Naturalism, scientism, and the independence of epistemology. *Erkenntnis, 43*, 1–27.

Pollock, J. L. (1987). Epistemic norms. *Synthese, 71*, 61–95.

Pollock, J. L. (1988). Interest-driven reasoning. *Synthese, 74*, 369–390.

Putnam, H. (1982). Why reason can't be naturalized. *Synthese, 52*, 3–23.

Quine, W. V. (1969a). Epistemology naturalized. In W. V. Quine, *Ontological relativity and other essays*. (pp. 69–90). New York: Columbia University Press.

Quine, W. V. (1969b). Stimulus and meaning. *Isenberg memorial lecture series 1965–66* (pp. 39–61). East Lansing: Michigan State University Press.

Quine, W. V. (1970). Grades of theoreticity. In L. Foster & J. W. Swanson (Eds.), *Experience and theory*. (pp. 1–17). Amherst: University of Massachusetts Press.

Quine, W. V. (1974). *The roots of reference*. La Salle, IL: Open Court Publishing.

Quine, W. V. (1975). The nature of natural knowledge. In S. Guttenplan (Ed.), *Mind and language*. (pp. 67–81). Oxford: Oxford University Press.

Ricketts, T. G. (1982). Rationality, translation, and epistemology naturalized. *Journal of Philosophy, 79*, 117–36.

Rorty, R. (1979). *Philosophy and the mirror of nature*. Princeton, NJ: Princeton University Press.

Roth, P. A. (1983). Siegel on naturalized epistemology and natural science. *Philosophy of Science, 50*, 482–493.

Roth, P. A. (1987). *Meaning and method in the social sciences: A case for methodological pluralism*. Ithaca, NY: Cornell University Press.

Sagal, P. T. (1987). Naturalistic epistemology and the harakiri of philosophy. In A. Shimony & D. Nails (Eds.), *Naturalistic epistemology: A symposium of two decades* (pp. 321–332). Dordrecht: D. Reidel.

Shimony, A. (1987a). Introduction. In A. Shimony & D. Nails (Eds.), *Naturalistic epistemology: A symposium of two decades* (pp. 1–13). Dordrecht: D. Reidel.

Shimony, A. (1987b). Integral epistemology. In A. Shimony & D. Nails (Eds.), *Naturalistic epistemology: A symposium of two decades* (pp. 299–318). Dordrecht: D. Reidel.

Shimony, A. (1987c). Comment on Sagal. In A. Shimony & D. Nails (Eds.), *Naturalistic epistemology: A symposium of two decades* (pp. 333–336). Dordrecht: D. Reidel.

Siegel, H. (1978). Piaget's conception of epistemology. *Educational Theory, 28*, 16–22.

Siegel, H. (1980). Justification, discovery and the naturalizing of epistemology. *Philosophy of Science, 47*, 297–321.

Siegel, H. (1984). Empirical psychology, naturalized epistemology, and first philosophy. *Philosophy of Science, 51*, 667–676.

Siegel, H. (1987). *Relativism refuted: A critique of contemporary epistemological relativism*. (Synthese Library, Vol. 189). Dordrecht: D. Reidel.

Siegel, H. (1989). Philosophy of science naturalized? Some problems with Giere's naturalism. *Studies in History and Philosophy of Science, 20*, 365–375.

Siegel, H. (1990). Laudan's normative naturalism. *Studies in History and Philosophy of Science, 21*, 295–313.

Siegel, H. (1992). Naturalism, instrumental rationality, and the normativity of epistemology. Invited address, presented at Eastern APA, December 1992.

Siegel, H. (1995) Naturalized epistemology and 'first philosophy'. *Metaphilosophy, 26*, 46–62.

Siegel, H. (1996) Instrumental rationality and naturalized philosophy of science. *Philosophy of Science*, in press.

Sosa, E. (1983). Nature unmirrored, epistemology naturalized. *Synthese, 55*, 49–72.

Steup, M. (1992). Epistemological naturalism and naturalistic epistemology. Paper presented at 1992 Pacific Division meeting of the American Philosophical Association.

Stich, S. P. (1983). *From folk psychology to cognitive science: The case against belief*. Cambridge: M.I.T. Press.

Stroud, B. (1981). The significance of naturalized epistemology. In P. French et al. (Eds.), *Midwest studies in philosophy 6*. (pp. 455–471). Minneapolis: University of Minnesota Press. Reprinted in Kornblith (1985), pp.

71–89. Page references in the text are to the 1985 reprint.

Stroud, B. (1984). *The significance of philosophical scepticism*. Oxford: Oxford University Press.

Uebel, T. E. (1991). Neurath's programme for naturalistic epistemology. *Studies in History and Philosophy of Science, 22*, 623–646.

CHAPTER 2

PSYCHOLOGY, NATURALIZED EPISTEMOLOGY, AND RATIONALITY

Harold I. Brown

DESCRIPTIONS AND NORMS

The concept of rationality has both a descriptive and a normative component. The descriptive side is exemplified by Aristotle's account of human beings as rational animals—creatures that have a rational part of the soul in addition to the vegetative and sensitive parts that we share with other animals. The normative side of rationality stands out when we recognize that although human beings have a capacity to be rational, there are situations in which we fail to behave rationally. Our ability to recognize failures of rationality and to criticize individuals for such failures requires norms for the proper exercise of our rational capacities. Now once we note this dual nature of the concept of reason, it becomes especially important to understand the relation between the two components. Yet, to raise this question is to raise one of philosophy's most difficult traditional problems: the relation between norms and descriptions. Historically this problem has most commonly arisen in the context of ethics but it appears whenever we reflect on norms, including epistemic norms. Indeed, an account of the relation between norms and descriptions is particularly pressing for proponents of a naturalistic epistemology. I want to develop these issues in somewhat greater detail.

In ethics one aspect of the relation between norms and descriptions was first made explicit in Hume's (1978) dictum that we cannot deduce *ought* from *is*:

> In every system of morality, which I have hitherto met with, I have always remark'd, that the author proceeds for some time in the ordinary way of reasoning, and establishes the being of a God, or makes observations concerning human affairs; when of a sudden I am surpriz'd to find, that instead of the usual copulations of propositions, *is*, and *is not*, I meet with no proposition that is not connected with an *ought*, or an *ought not*. This change is imperceptible; but is, however, of the last consequence. For as this *ought*, or *ought not*, expresses some new relation or affirmation, 'tis necessary that it shou'd be observ'd and explain'd; and at the same time that a reason should be given, for what seems altogether inconceivable, how this new relation can be a deduction from others, which are entirely different from it. (p. 469)

Note that Hume is making a narrow logical point in this passage, but the point is extremely important because Hume does not allow for any legitimate inferences other than deductions—Hume is famous for arguing that there are no legitimate inductive inferences.[1] Note also that the key consequence he draws from his logical point is that our normative ethical decisions have no cognitive foundation. One possible response to Hume is that there is more to cognition than is captured in deduction, and this is a point that I shall pursue in the course of this paper. But for the moment it is important to be clear that a wider issue is at stake than just a point about deduction. For our central aim in seeking norms is to be able to decide the right thing to do in various situations, and we need norms exactly because people do not always do the right thing. But how are we to determine the norms for correct behavior? Hume's point is that we cannot arrive at an account of correct behavior solely from a description of the way people do in fact behave, even when this description is supplemented by an account of the nature of the universe and by deductive logic.

The argument thus far suggests that we must be able to establish norms quite independently of an account of how people actually behave; but this is only half the story. A short journey down the historical path—from Hume to Kant—will bring us to the other half. Also in the context of ethical theory, Kant maintained that *ought* implies *can*. We are dealing again with deductive implication and Kant's aim was to provide a principle that would undercut claims that we are unable to carry out the dictates of morality. But "ought implies can" is logically equivalent to "not-can implies not-ought," that is, that we are not obliged to do what is beyond our power. I shall be concerned here with Kant's dictum in this latter form and, in particular, with its significance for the case of epistemic norms. The effect of Kant's thesis is to counterbalance Hume's in a rather interesting way. For while Hume's thesis entails that we cannot derive epistemic norms *solely* from a description of cognitive abilities, Kant's thesis entails that we cannot establish epistemic norms *without* an account of cognitive abilities. If we attempt to proceed a priori we may well end up with norms that have no legitimate force for human beings because they make demands on us that we cannot possibly fulfill. In other words, we need an account of the *appropriate epistemic norms* for human beings; an account of what is normatively rational requires a prior

account of what is rational in the descriptive sense—an account of what cognitive abilities human beings have available.

Note especially that what is normatively rational may vary for different beings depending on their cognitive abilities. So, what is normatively rational for adult human beings may be quite different from what is rational for young children, or properly programmed computers, or perhaps for Martians. Moreover, we might even have to recognize different rational demands on different people in different circumstances. I will not be able to explore all of these variations here, but the general point is crucial; some terminology from Reiner (1993) will help clarify what is at stake. Reiner notes that the term "rational" has two quite different contraries—arational and irrational—and this verbal distinction marks the exact distinction that we need. An arational being lacks the ability to behave rationally; we can think of a descriptive scale capturing different degrees of rationality with arationality as its zero point. A scale running from irrational to rational will be a normative scale, one that seeks to capture what an individual ought to do given the available capacities. But we cannot begin to locate an individual on the normative scale until we have located that individual on the descriptive scale; we cannot decide which norms are appropriate for us until we have determined where we are on the descriptive scale.

The conclusion we have just arrived at directly contradicts a dominant view in mainstream contemporary epistemology. On this view, normative epistemology must proceed independently of any of the descriptive subjects exactly because people can put forth descriptive claims that are incorrect. Thus, it is argued, we must already have a set of epistemic norms in order to decide which proposed descriptions are correct. This contradiction is important because there are powerful arguments on both sides. I will attempt to resolve the contradiction later in this paper, but it will be useful to set the stage by pursuing some further historical reflections. In doing so we will find that descriptive epistemology has played a much greater role in the development of normative epistemology than many contemporary epistemologists have acknowledged. Moreover, we shall see that descriptive theses have been fundamental not only in providing the basis for specific norms, but also in determining what *kinds of norms* are appropriate for human knowers.

SOME PROBLEMS OF EPISTEMOLOGY

We can begin by noting an obvious feature of human cognition: We are not omniscient but we are capable of learning a great deal on a wide number of topics. Although the point is obvious, it has played a central role in determining the problems of epistemology and their possible solutions. If we were omniscient then tasks such as finding the appropriate rules for evaluating knowledge claims would have no point—nor would there be a point to this quest if we were incapable of expanding the body of our knowledge. Moreover, specific features of human beings have also determined how we pursue the epistemologist's tasks. To take another obvious example, much effort has been expended in trying to understand how reliable our senses are, how we can improve their reliability, and how we can use information derived from sense perception to evaluate hypotheses that go beyond the limits of what we have already sensed. If we were organisms of a very different kind, this particular problem-cluster would not have played a central role in epistemology. Indeed, the central role of the "problem of perception" in philosophy is one of the characteristic features of the modern period that begins (roughly) with Descartes. But this new problematic emerged largely because of changes in our understanding of the actual nature of human sense perception. It will be worth our while to sketch some of these changes.

According to the most widely held view of sense perception in the later Middle Ages, our senses typically show us the physical world exactly as it is. The basic picture of how this comes about is founded in Aristotelian metaphysics. Briefly, Aristotle conceived of a physical object as consisting of a form imposed on a material substrate; all of the properties that characterize an object are included in the form. One crucial motivation for this view is that it allows us to understand the sense in which, for example, two distinct dollar bills are items of the same kind: We have a single form that is instantiated in two different bits of matter. Now just as the same form can occur in different material objects, that form can also be instantiated in a human mind, and this is what happens when we perceive a physical object. Aristotle provided an account of the human mind that made sense of this proposal. One crucial feature of this account is that the mind has no internal structure of its own that

enters into the perceptual process and "distorts" the form of the perceived object. Several medieval thinkers sought to provide a more detailed account of how the form is imprinted on the mind but I will not pursue these details here (see Lindberg, 1976, for discussion). I want, rather, to consider some developments that led philosophers to question the Aristotelian account of perception. I note in passing that a challenge to the view of the mind as lacking any internal structure also develops and becomes central with Kant, but I will limit discussion here to an earlier stage at which doubts about the Aristotelian view developed while still assuming that perception is passive.

Consider first the existence of perceptual illusions ranging from the octagonal tower that looks round when seen from a distance to the phantom limb. That illusions occur was not news in the seventeenth century, but they shifted from being considered unimportant curiosities to central phenomena that had to be dealt with by an adequate account of perceptual knowledge. This change of emphasis was supported by several overlapping strands in the developing science–philosophy complex, but I will consider only one strand here: the demand for a purely causal account of physical phenomena.

One direct consequence of a purely causal account of the physical world is that we must now think of sensory experience as initiated by the impact of physical objects on our sense organs and further mediated by causal processes in our nerves and brain. Once this step has been taken, two further reflections make it problematic whether physical objects ever have the properties that they appear to have when we perceive them. The first of these comes from reflecting on pain—a major example in the seventeenth century. An interaction between my body and another physical object may cause me to feel pain, but it is generally recognized that when we feel pain we are not perceiving a property that was out there in the physical object waiting to be detected under appropriate circumstances. Yet the causal process that yields our perception of any property of a physical object is of the same as that by which we come to feel pain.[2] Thus the experience of pain served as an entering wedge for arguing that sensory experience need not provide an accurate image of the physical object that caused our experience. But once we begin paying attention to examples of this sort, one standard problem of the epistemology of perception immediately arises: By what criteria can we assess which, if any, of the properties that a physical object appears to have actually characterizes that object?

Let me stress the key point that I am after in reviewing this bit of history: *The central epistemological question that I have just formulated arises because we believe that our senses operate in a particular way. Given a different account of the nature of our senses, or a radically different view of how we acquire information about the physical world, then this particular problem of epistemology need not arise.*

This conclusion can be further illustrated by considering a second standard epistemological topic, the theory of meaning. Throughout the history of empiricism it has been maintained that meaningful language must somehow be tied to experience. In the twentieth century this doctrine has taken many forms. Among logical positivists it appeared as the thesis that a nonanalytic proposition is meaningful if and only if there is a procedure by which that proposition can be empirically verified or falsified. Among later logical empiricists this became the claim that there is an observation language consisting of terms (not propositions) that get their meaning directly from experience; all other terms—including theoretical terms of science—must be either defined or somehow introduced on the basis of this observation language.[3] Other empiricists, who were not primarily concerned with philosophy of science, sought to reduce claims about material objects to claims about colors, shapes, feels, and other qualia that are immediately available to our senses. But why should we accept this dependence of *meaning* on experience? In the writings of the classical empiricists the answer was clear: Locke, Berkeley, and Hume based their account of meaning on an empirical account of how people actually learn the meanings of words. Now many twentieth-century empiricists rejected this justification because they sought to establish a philosophical discipline of epistemology that is independent of empirical psychology. Yet it is difficult to find an explanation in the twentieth-century literature of why we should accept this account of meaning that does not require a foundation in psychology. The most detailed accounts consist of attempts to show that, with the aid of modern logic, we can define terms that refer to material objects on the basis of terms that refer only to sensible qualia. But even if the

project succeeded—and it did not—we could still ask why we should proceed in this direction rather than attempting to define terms referring to sensible qualia on the basis of material object language. I submit that the only plausible reason for preferring one direction to the other is some claim about human psychology. My point, again, is that the very way in which traditional epistemological problems have been formulated depends on empirical claims about human cognition.

THE ANTINATURALIST RETURNS

I have been arguing that an attempt to construct a normative epistemology that is to be relevant to human beings must itself be built on an account of human cognitive abilities, but now it is time to give antinaturalist epistemologists their due. For there remains a problem with our discussion thus far which will set the framework for the remainder of this paper. One task of normative epistemology is to establish principles for evaluating empirical claims against the available evidence. Now the body of psychology on which we must draw in order to arrive at an account of human cognition must be established empirically. But this requires that we already have a set of methodological rules that will allow us to evaluate empirical claims within psychology. We would appear to be caught in a vicious circle: We need a body of psychology in order to choose an appropriate methodology, but we need a methodology in order to evaluate psychological hypotheses. An example from recent psychology will underline the problem.

A number of psychological studies have led to the conclusion that human beings exhibit a confirmation bias: Given a preferred hypothesis, they seek evidence that will support this hypothesis and tend to ignore evidence that contradicts the hypothesis (e.g., Faust, 1984; Nisbett & Ross, 1980). Now consider two different ways of thinking about this result. We could accept confirmation bias as a universal feature of human cognition, take it as therefore normatively correct, and support the claim that confirmation bias is rampant by providing evidence that confirms this claim. If this seems unsatisfactory, we can note that the psychologists who report this result agree. They maintain that confirmation bias is normatively incorrect in spite of its widespread occurrence. Indeed, they hold that there are systematic reasons why we should seek and give priority to evidence that contradicts our favored hypotheses. Yet in making this latter claim our psychologists are committed to the view that there are epistemic norms that can be justified on grounds other than empirical studies of human reasoning. Presumably, their own studies of human cognitive behavior adhere to these norms and do not exhibit confirmation bias. Thus it would appear that there must be some nonempirical justification for these norms and that this justification must be in place before we accept any of their claims about actual human reasoning.

We have now returned to the point from which this paper began and we can perhaps see more clearly why opponents of a naturalistic epistemology maintain that epistemic norms must be established a priori. A priori norms would provide an anchor outside of the process of empirical investigation that would provide a noncircular foundation for empirical inquiry. Yet the argument that took us from the beginning of this paper to the present point also reasserts itself. For once it is proposed that we need an a priori justification for our norms, we must ask whether we human beings are capable of such a priori justifications and we are thrown right back into the circle, since it is difficult to see how we can answer this question about human capabilities other than empirically.

So how shall we proceed? I will work from this point in two main stages. First, I shall leave the question of the foundations of methodology in the background and explore, on purely empirical grounds, some features of human cognitive abilities that are relevant for assessing our cognitive capabilities. On the basis of this discussion, I will propose some epistemic norms. Second, I will return to the foundational issues, examine the problem of vicious circularity more systematically than I have done so far, and then consider whether the arguments for the specific norms I have proposed are in fact vitiated by a circle.

THE NATURALISTIC PERSPECTIVE

The single most important development leading to naturalistic epistemologies is the theory of evolution with its inclusion of human beings in the evolutionary process. The key points I want to make have been argued elsewhere by many people (cf. Halweg & Hooker, 1989; Radnitzky & Bartley, 1987) and I will limit myself here to summarizing the relevant results.

Once we have learned to think of human beings as denizens of the natural world produced by the evolutionary process, we must give up any view of human cognition that assumes magical insights into reality. As a species, we began from ignorance and have acquired what knowledge we have through a slow, uncertain, nonlinear process of trial and error with no guarantee of success. In one respect this thesis was already central to the empiricist tradition, which held that all of our substantive knowledge of the world depends on experience and that any generalizations that go beyond what we have experienced are falsifiable and subject to replacement. But twentieth-century empiricists have been quite insistent that while this fallibilist view of cognition applies to our substantive knowledge of the world, it does *not* apply to our understanding of methodology. Methodology was conceived of as an a priori achievement along the lines developed above. However, a more thoroughgoing naturalism holds that our understanding of methodology is also arrived at by the kind of tentative process of theory construction that leads us to our understanding of various aspects of the world. This idea is captured in a slogan that has been adopted by several advocates of a thoroughgoing naturalism: We must learn how to learn about the world; what methods work depends on what the world is like and on what kind of being we are. (See, for example, Hooker, 1987; Laudan, 1987; Shapere, 1984.) One consequence of this view is that our methodological and substantive research must interact because our methodological theory must at least be consistent with our best available understanding of the kind of cognitive equipment we have and the kind of world we are dealing with.

The basic epistemological lesson to be drawn from evolutionary theory, then, is that we should be rather modest about our knowledge-claims at every level—including methodology. And this lesson has been reinforced by developments in many fields. Gödel's incompleteness theorem is only one of a number of results that have led us to reexamine the epistemic status of mathematics, which has long stood as the pinnacle of certainty to which other subjects have aspired. (See Kline, 1980, for many more examples.) Other limiting results, such as Church's theorem and results from complexity theory in computer science, have brought out limitations of a universal Turing machine, which has provided the model of an ideal computer and often a model of human cognition as well (e.g., Cherniak, 1986; Reiner, 1993). Meanwhile, studies in the psychology of human reasoning and the limitations of human memory have suggested that human cognition is significantly less powerful than the best that we can expect from a digital computer. (cf. Cherniak, 1986, chap. 3; Kahneman, Slovic, & Tversky, 1982; Nisbett & Ross, 1980; Wason & Johnson-Laird, 1972.)

Still, we must not be modest to the point of error. For while we have excellent reasons for relinquishing some of the more grandiose pretensions of our intellectual tradition, we should not ignore the rather impressive evidence suggesting that we have a much wider range of cognitive abilities than any other species we have encountered thus far—and that there may even be respects in which we have abilities that are not shared by a universal Turing machine. Consider, here, our ability to develop complex systems of abstract mathematics, to design spacecraft to explore other planets, even though this has no direct relevance to our survival and reproduction on this planet, our ability to develop and improve a theory of evolution, and our ability to study the nature of our own reasoning and to develop normative theories of logic and probability that allow us to recognize the limitations of our spontaneous reasoning. An adequate account of human cognitive abilities must be able to account for these accomplishments. All of which leads me to the next step in my argument: I want to discuss a cluster of human abilities that I think are central to our epistemic accomplishments but that have been given too little attention in the naturalistic literature. But I want to work my way toward this discussion by reviewing yet another theme from traditional epistemology.

THE LOGIC OF JUSTIFICATION

One of the pervasive concerns of traditional epistemology was generated by a plausible view of the logic of justification. On this view we justify a proposition, P, by properly relating it to other propositions. Let us use $P*$ for the set of propositions invoked to justify P. Now for the proposed justification of P to succeed, each of the propositions constituting $P*$ must itself be justified and, on the standard model of justification, the members of $P*$ must be justified by their relation to some other set of propositions, $P**$. An infinite regress clearly threatens: Any proposed justification requires some prior justification, which requires other prior justifications, ad infinitum. Traditionally epistemologists responded by seeking regress stoppers: some set of propositions that are justified without reference to any other propositions. These privileged propositions have been variously described as "self-evident," "self-justifying," and "indubitable." Once these privileged propositions have been established, they then provide the foundation for all further justifications.

There is a second regress that this view of justification faces, although it has received less attention in the literature. Justification requires rules that specify the relation between the propositions being justified and those that provide the justification. But not just any rules will do; a successful justification requires that we use the correct rules and thus our choice of rules must itself be justified, and we are on our way again. Here too it would seem that we require some self-justifying foundational rules to stop the regress. Elsewhere I have reviewed the relevant history and argued that attempts to provide these foundations have regularly amounted to the claim that our cognitive abilities include a form of infallible intuition that, under appropriate circumstances, provides us with the required knowledge of the foundational propositions and rules. (See Brown, 1988b, chap. 1 for a more detailed account of the path to a foundationalist epistemology and chap. 2 for the historical review.)

Now this appeal to infallible intuitions has no place in a naturalistic epistemology. Moreover, we have excellent empirical grounds for concluding that our cognitive repertoire does not include any such ability. The historical landscape is littered with universal propositions that were put forward as self-evident but that turned out to be false. Contemporary studies of perception in both psychology and philosophy have cast serious doubt on the indubitability of our perception reports. And the history of logic provides us with a display of controversies and reconsiderations even within the realm of elementary deductive logic. (See Brown, 1988b, sec. 2.7 for examples from logic.)

Several responses are available at this point. One possibility that some philosophers will always find attractive is to hew to the traditional demands for a legitimate justification, accept the conclusion that such justifications cannot be produced, and adopt some form of skepticism. Another possibility is to argue that since no indubitable refutation of the traditional approach has been provided, we should continue the search for self-evident foundations.

Yet another approach is to take seriously the conclusion that we have no unchallengeable beliefs, apply this conclusion to the traditional framework itself, and look for other ways of understanding rational justification that are compatible with our current understanding of our cognitive abilities. This last approach opens up a number of possible paths and I will follow one of these here; this requires that we look again at our cognitive abilities.

Skills

There are two points from our discussion of justification that require clarification. First, my remarks about rules that relate propositions to other propositions and rules to other rules can be read in two different ways: as referring to objective relations among propositions or to processes taking place within the mind of a cognitive agent. I am concerned here with the latter situation—with what is required for a specific individual to arrive at a justified belief. From this perspective it is not enough that one proposition entail another proposition. If I am to use the first proposition as part of a justification for the second, I must recognize this entailment.

Second, we must distinguish two different senses in which a process may be rule-governed: a process may *conform* to a rule or it may proceed by *following* that rule. A falling stone conforms to rules but does not follow rules; cognitive behavior provides a paradigm of rule-following. Note one striking difference between the two cases: A cognitive agent can fail to follow a rule, either inadvertently or on purpose; the stone cannot fail to fall in accordance with its governing rules. Since our topic is cognition, I will only be concerned with processes that follow rules.

It is widely held that all cognition proceeds by following rules, but the traditional account of justification suggests that this need not be correct. For if we ask why intuition is capable of stopping an epistemic regress, one possible answer is that acts of intuition do not depend on rules. Now I noted above that *infallible* intuitions have no place in a naturalistic account of mind, but this leaves open the possibility that our cognitive repertoire includes processes that have the following characteristics: They do not operate by following rules, they are fallible but yield results that are more reliable than chance, and they can be included in a naturalistic epistemology. Such processes would be

sufficient to stop an epistemic regress, although in a fallible, and thus tentative, manner. I am going to argue that such processes do exist. I will refer to processes of this type as *judgments*, avoiding the term "intuition" because of its historical association with an infallible insight. Thus I am going to retain most of the traditional account of justification, eliminating only the demand that justifications must rest on a foundation that is never subject to reconsideration.[4] My next task, then, is to explain the concept of judgment in more detail and to provide reasons for holding that humans have this ability. The ability to exercise judgment is an example of a cognitive skill that is continuous with physical skills. Examples of physical skills include the ability to ride a bicycle, catch and hit a baseball, or use a carpenter's tools. I will work my way toward an account of judgment by considering four characteristics of physical skills.[5]

1. Skills are learned through demonstration and practice, rather than by learning and following a set of rules. Ability typically improves with practice and deteriorates with lack of practice, although relearning tends to be faster than initial learning. That we do not learn a skill just by memorizing a set of rules is particularly clear in the many cases in which no one is able to formulate a set of rules to successfully guide this activity. And even in those cases in which we can formulate such rules, being able to state the rules is not sufficient for carrying out the activity in a skillful manner. For example, a physicist who fully understands the mechanics of keeping a bicycle balanced, but who has never ridden, still has to practice in order to learn to ride.

Although we do not learn skills by memorizing rules that we then follow, it could be argued that skill learning is a process of extracting rules in some nonconscious manner and then following those rules. But on reflection this is not an especially plausible hypothesis. Consider how the process of skill improvement would look on this account. One possibility is that the more skillful practitioner will have learned a larger set of rules than the less skillful person in order to deal with a variety of special circumstances. Yet if the improvement of a skill requires the acquisition of a growing set of ever more specific rules to cover special cases, we would expect performance to deteriorate as the number of rules to be searched and evaluated at each stage increases. This is exactly the opposite of what we find.

Alternatively, it could be argued that in improving a skill we develop a better ability to apply the rules we have already learned. But how are we to understand this notion of "applying rules"? If this requires learning further rules for the application of rules we are back to the expanding set of rules just considered, and we may even be on the verge of another regress. If the proposal does not require learning new rules, but some other kind of process, then my main thesis has been accepted: Learning and exercising a skill cannot be completely captured in following rules. Moreover, it now seems that even our ability to follow rules is based on a more fundamental ability that does not require that we follow rules.

2. For most physical skills, and especially for the more complex skills, there is a substantial range in which most people can learn and improve. Still, some people learn much more quickly than others; some develop a skill to a higher degree than others; and some are unable to learn a particular skill at all. For example, most people can develop some skill at catching fly balls, but few achieve the level of a major-league ballplayer, and a few are unable to develop this skill at all.

3. The ability to exercise a physical skill is fallible in the sense that even the best practitioner does not always exercise that skill to the highest degree within her capability and in some cases may fail altogether. Yet an enormous variety of human accomplishments depends on physical skills. Note especially that the fact that even the most adept sometimes fail does not provide grounds for concluding that there is no such thing as a skill, nor any reason for refusing to invest greater confidence in those who have shown facility at a particular task than in those who have not.

4. The above discussion leads directly to the central feature that concerns me: The ability to exercise any skill at all requires that we have some basic abilities that are not themselves carried out by following rules. And once this point is recognized, the determination of these basic abilities becomes a central task in attempting to understand human cognition.

I want to spend a moment on one more attempt to account for skillful behavior wholly on the basis of following rules. In many cases we can examine a form of behavior, formulate a set of rules for that behavior, and then use these rules as the basis for designing machines that will carry out this behav-

ior. Often the machine will be more reliable than would a human actor. Moreover, this occurs not only in cases such as the construction of industrial robots, but also when we program a computer to carry out a task. There are, however, several points about this possibility that should be kept in mind if we are to avoid misunderstandings. First, the fact that we can study a form of human behavior and capture it in a set of rules does not show that the humans we have studied were following those rules. We engage in the same kind of analysis for falling stones, the motions of the planets, and myriad other phenomena that provide paradigm cases in which skill is *not* involved. Second, an industrial robot no more follows rules than does a falling stone. *We* may have designed the robot to act in accordance with a set of rules, but the robot's own behavior is strictly determined in the same sense that the velocity with which a stone hits the ground is determined once we select the height from which it is dropped. Third, the points just made about the robot apply equally to the digital computer. Whatever is involved in writing a program and entering that program into the computer, it is a mistake to think that a set of rules now exist in the computer and that the computer follows those rules. Entering a program amounts to changing the states of a number of circuit elements and thus creating an initial condition in the computer. The situation is analogous to that in which I might "program" a rock to hit the floor with a velocity of (roughly) sixteen feet per second by lifting it to a height of four feet and then dropping it.

Now let us consider cognitive skills. Paradigm examples include the ability to solve deduction problems in logic, play chess, invent algorithms, formulate the rules in accordance with which various processes take place, and invent new scientific theories. These abilities clearly share the first three characteristics of physical skills noted above: They are taught by demonstration and learned through practice; there is a range of talents in developing and exercising these skills; and the exercise of these skills is fallible. The remaining feature—that cognitive skills are not exercised by following rules—provides the crux of the issue before us.

Before we tackle this issue, a distinction is in order. Many activities are defined by an explicit set of rules, but once we enter into this activity, there are different degrees of skill among those who obey these defining rules. All chess players have learned the rules that define the game, but knowing these rules does not automatically generate skillful play. In a similar way, those who write computer programs are constrained by the syntax of their programming language, but these rules do not generate algorithms, let alone efficient algorithms. The question currently before us is whether *skillful* performance results from following rules.

There are, of course, some rules for generating a skillful performance: rules for good chess play, programming heuristics, and so forth. But, again, these rules are not sufficient to generate a skillful performance in these areas. Not only do we find considerable variations in skill among those who take guidance from these rules, but it is just at the point where available rules cease to be sufficient that differences of skill become apparent. The construction of proofs in deductive logic provides a useful example. If we are working within a specific deductive system every permissible step is governed by a finite set of rules, but there is no sufficient set of rules for deciding what step should be made at any given juncture. Moreover, we can easily formulate metarules for constructing proofs that are completely in accord with the laws of logic but that it would be utterly absurd to follow. Consider a typical textbook problem: We have a set of premises from which we must derive a specified conclusion. Suppose that two sentences, "*p*" and "*q*" are either among the premises or have already been derived, and consider the following procedure. First we use the rule of conjunction to derive the single sentence "*p&q*." Next we use simplification to deduce "*p*" again and "*q*" again. Then we apply conjunction once again, and so on until we drop. This would be a mindless application of a set of rules, but note that no law of logic is ever violated in the procedure. The example is enough to make the point that following an established set of rules—even elementary rules of logic—is not *sufficient* to assure that we are behaving in a skillful manner.

A more crucial question is whether following a set of rules is *necessary* for skillful behavior, but at this point the traditional regress argument comes into play. Consider our example from logic once again. Someone who is skilled at constructing deductive proofs will be able to make a sensible choice of which rules to apply at each stage. We can look here for some metarules, but not just any metarules will do. Here too we can formulate lots of silly rules for making the decision. So we face another choice among rules and the need for even

higher-level rules, and so forth. At some point the process must stop if we are ever to go forward and this stopping point cannot itself be chosen by yet another set of rules. In other words, if justified rules are necessary for every coherent cognitive choice, then no choices will be possible. Yet we do produce deductive proofs and my proposal is that the ability to end the regress—for example, by choosing the next step in the proof—is the exercise of a skill. Not every choice will be correct—skills are fallible—but the choices of a skillful logician will be more reliable than chance. In other words, skills are regress-stoppers, but tentative, fallible regress-stoppers.

I want to make one more point before applying this account to judgment. The argument thus far can be seen as attempting to establish a close analogy between physical and cognitive skills, but an evolutionary perspective suggests that more than an analogy is involved. If a human being is a complex but unified organism, we should find genuine continuity between physical and cognitive skills. And there are cases—perhaps best illustrated by activities such as painting, sculpture, and musical improvisation—in which the physical and cognitive aspects of a performance are so thoroughly integrated as to defy any clear separation.

JUDGMENT

Judgment is a generic notion that refers to a class of cognitive skills: the ability to make decisions in a specific domain without relying on a set of rules. We must rely on judgment in many situations, for example, when no appropriate rules are known, or when there are alternative rules among which we must choose, or when we recognize that established rules cannot be used within available time limits. Several points about the notion of judgment must be stressed. First, judgment is domain specific: One develops engineering judgment or chess judgment or logical judgment much as one develops specific physical skills—by studying available knowledge (including established rules and techniques) in a particular field and practicing in that field. Second, judgment is exercised with respect to specific problems and decisions and thus requires study of the available information relevant to the problem at hand. A chess master does not recommend a move without studying the game in question, or a physician recommend a treatment without studying the patient. Third, it follows from the first two points that not every choice made without following rules is an exercise of judgment. Judgment requires specific expertise and information and there is no more guarantee that we will actually be able to exercise judgment in a given case than that we will know a rule. Fourth, while the exercise of judgment is an individual ability, it is not "subjective" in any pejorative sense. Judgment is exercised in response to specific problems and in the light of information that typically comes from outside of the individual. In other words, the ability to exercise judgment is no more "subjective" than is the ability to drive a car or catch a fly ball.[6]

We must now ask whether judgment has a place in a naturalistic account of human beings. Even though judgment lacks the infallibility that was traditionally attributed to intuitions, what grounds are there for believing that natural systems can embody such abilities? Within the limits of this paper I can only point to one recent development that provides strong reasons for holding that physical systems are capable of such behavior. I refer here to neural net computers that can make distinctions and arrive at reliable results without having been programmed in accordance with a set of rules or built so as to embody some set of rules. Often these computers are "trained" to carry out a specific task in much the way that human beings are trained. The trainer begins with a set of inputs for which the correct outputs are known and the machine's internal structure is adjusted slightly when it gives a wrong result. The machine's accuracy improves over time as the training process continues and in the course of training the machine often makes mistakes of the same kind that people make as they learn a particular skill. Indeed, not only is a program never written to govern the machine's behavior, but in some cases the trainers do not even understand how the machine has arrived at its successful behavior.[7]

Finally, the claim that humans can develop and exercise judgment is an empirical thesis. I have offered some anecdotal evidence for this claim, but the claim should be susceptible to systematic empirical study; systematic evidence that the phenomenon does not exist will undermine my proposal.

From Judgment to Reason

Let us now consider how judgment is to be incorporated into a full-blown account of rationality. The key point is that while rationality must ultimately rely on judgment, there are means available for improving the reliability of our judgments. Full rationality requires making use of these means in order to move from an initial judgment to a more reliable, better founded judgment. All of these means of improving judgment share the following feature: They increase the objectivity of judgment by taking the individual outside the circle of her own reflections. There appear to be three major ways of pursuing this improvement of judgment: the use of formal methods, observation, and submission of one's results to others for critical debate. Only brief comment on each of these will be possible in the present paper; in each case I want to illustrate how we can impose additional constraints on individual judgments.[8]

Formal methods draw out consequences of our claims that are implicit in those claims but that are not obvious. For example, the result of a series of arithmetic operations on a specific set of numbers is already determined; doing the arithmetic allows us to discover this result. In a similar way, whether a set of propositions is consistent is a fact about that set—a fact about which we may be mistaken. The classic example is Cantor's set theory, which was assumed to be consistent until Russell's proved otherwise.

Observation is not relevant to all cognitive tasks, but where it is relevant it provides constraints on our theorizing by bringing us into contact with the items about which we are making claims and allowing those items to have their say. Note that I am *not* maintaining that observational claims are ipso facto more certain than other kinds of claims. Rather, observation provides special constraints on our beliefs because observation brings us into contact with a world that is independent of those beliefs.

Finally, we should submit our views to evaluation and criticism by others because other people have perspectives, information, and skills that we do not have. To be sure, decisions as to how much observational data we should collect and when to cut off the processes of inference and debate are ultimately dependent on individual judgments, but there is nothing pernicious in this as long as we are clear that having arrived at a rational conclusion does not guarantee that the conclusion is true or that we have achieved the last word on the subject. Reason is a means of arriving at reliable but fallible results, results that can be reexamined when reasons for doing so appear.

FROM DESCRIPTIONS TO NORMS

In the course of this discussion we appear to have moved quite naturally from descriptive claims about human cognitive abilities and about means that are available for increasing their reliability to a number of norms for rational evaluation of our views. Here are some of these norms:[9]

N1. Do not attempt to exercise judgment on matters in which you lack expertise.
N2. Even where you have expertise, study the details of the problem at hand before arriving at a judgment.
N3. Always consider your judgments to be fallible and subject to further evaluation.
N4. When evaluating the results of a judgment pay attention to the logical consequences of that result.
N5. Where appropriate, gather observational evidence and seek to extend the range of available evidence.
N6. Submit your results to others for suggestions and criticism.

Although these norms certainly have not been deduced from the preceding descriptions, there is still a sense in which these norms have been based on those descriptions. Assuming that my descriptive claims about human cognitive abilities are correct, I have put forward a number of hypotheses about how to pursue reliable beliefs given these abilities. These norms are hypotheses in the sense that they too are subject to evaluation. One point of evaluation has already been noted: If empirical studies were to show that human beings have no ability to exercise judgment that is more reliable than chance, then the motivation and a major part of the justification for these norms will have been removed. In a similar way, if one could show that submitting one's views for critical debate tends to confuse issues and reduce the reliability of our beliefs, then N6 would be brought into serious question.

Note also that I am pursuing these norms in a rational manner in exactly the sense that I seek to capture in these norms. I am working in an area in which I believe that I have relevant expertise, that view has received some support from others in the field, I have studied a significant portion of the relevant literature, and by publishing my ideas on the subject I am submitting them to others for critical debate. Thus my project exhibits an important kind of reflexivity and it would seem that this reflexivity is unavoidable. After all, I am attempting to provide an account of rationality and I wish to pursue this attempt in a rational manner. Therefore I will certainly work in terms of the account of rationality that I think to be correct. But at this point the traditional worries about a vicious circle reappear. I cannot find any vicious circularity in the procedure I have followed, but the charge of circularity is a general one and, if it could be sustained, then my failure to find a vicious circle in my own procedure would provide no more (and no less) than a comment on the limits of my vision. It is important, then, that we attack the charge of circularity head-on.

THE CIRCLE ARGUMENT

The major objection to using scientific results in order to justify the scientific enterprise is that any such attempt begs the question—it assumes the very conclusion that it seeks to establish (e.g., Stroud, 1985; Siegel, 1989; see also Siegel's chapter (1) in this volume). But while this may seem a devastating objection, I shall argue that it is far from conclusive. Some preliminary points will set the stage.

First, there are areas in which some form of circularity seems to be unavoidable. For example, an empirical study of our perceptual abilities will presumably make use of those abilities. Similarly, attempts to prove that the system of logic we currently accept is correct will require that we make use of some logic in the proof. Presumably we will use that system of logic that we believe to be correct, rather than some alternative system that we consider to be in error.

Second, there are situations in which self-reference is not only unavoidable, but mandatory. For example, if my theory of knowledge holds that human beings are only capable of fallible conjectures, then I must treat that theory as a fallible conjecture on pain of self-refutation. In the same way, a theory of our cognitive capacities that is so restrictive as to entail that it is impossible for us to have produced and defended that very theory is ipso facto unacceptable.[10] This is why charges of reflexive inconsistency are so devastating to the more extreme forms of relativism: Their proponents appear to claim that their view is correct in a sense to which they deny any significance and on grounds that they maintain are not determinative of rational belief.

Third, it is an odd feature of question-begging arguments that, as a matter of logical form alone, they are valid. Whatever is wrong with question-begging arguments, the problem must be located in something other than their logical form. Let us consider, then, just what is problematic about the class of circular arguments that concerns us here—those that assume a theory or a methodology as part of an attempt to justify that very theory or methodology. We can approach this question by returning to the phenomenon of confirmation bias and considering why this tendency should be avoided. The key point has been familiar since Popper: It is always possible to find some confirming evidence for any hypothesis. But even in the face of massive confirming evidence, our hypothesis may still be false. On the other hand, if a false conclusion has been deduced from a set of premises, then something is certainly wrong with those premises; and if a set of propositions is inconsistent, it is not possible that all of the propositions in the set are true. This asymmetry between confirmation and disconfirmation suggests a basic principle of methodology: A proposed test of a hypothesis is legitimate only if it is possible that the test results in rejection of that hypothesis.[11]

Now many of those who argue that a naturalistic justification of methodology will be viciously circular are worried about a particularly drastic kind of confirmation bias: They are concerned that a test of a hypothesis, H, that assumes H in an essential way could not possibly refute H. Any such test, it is maintained, would necessarily come out in favor of H, but this support would be illusory because H could not possibly have been challenged by the test. Some contemporary skeptics about reason have made exactly this point:

> The basic point is that justifications of deduction themselves presuppose deduction. They are circular because they appeal to the very principles of inference that are in question. In this respect the justification of deduction is in the same predicament as the justifications of induction which tacitly make inductive moves by appealing to the fact that induction 'works'. Our two basic modes of reasoning are in an equally hopeless state with regard to their rational justification. (Barnes & Bloor, 1982, pp. 40–41)

This is a seductive thesis but, I shall argue, it is no more than that. It seems plausible as long as we keep the discussion on a very high level of abstraction, but when we look at specific examples in suf-

ficient detail, we will see that there are in fact cases in which assuming the hypothesis being evaluated does not prevent us from arriving at a challenge to that hypothesis. I will develop this point here for a particularly important example, the case of elementary deductive logic.[12]

Consider a system of logic, L_1, which allows the argument form A: From a premise of the form "p or q" we may deduce "p". By definition, an argument form is invalid if there is an argument of that form that has all true premises and a false conclusion. Consider, then, the following argument in which A itself plays a central role. Let "p" be "A is invalid," which we are assuming to be false; let "q" be any true proposition that you like. Our argument is:

$$A \text{ is invalid or } q.$$
$$\text{Thus, } A \text{ is invalid.}$$

The premise is true and the conclusion is, by hypothesis, false. Thus the argument form we are examining is invalid. However one may respond to this result, one point is clear: The fact that our argument proceeded on the assumption that A is valid did not prevent the argument from yielding a challenge to the validity of A.

As a second example consider a system of logic, L_2, that is inconsistent although those who are using this logic do not know this. Suppose we set out to study the consistency of L_2 and, since we believe that L_2 is correct, we carry out our study in a metalanguage that uses L_2 as its logic. Given that *any proposition* can be validly deduced using an inconsistent logic, then it is certainly possible for us to arrive at the conclusion that L_2 is inconsistent.

The crucial point in both of these examples is that assuming a particular system of logic does not prevent us from deducing a conclusion that challenges the correctness of that very system. A moment's reflection suggests that neither of the examples we have just considered should be especially surprising. Logics that are internally inconsistent or that include invalid arguments share the feature that they are not sufficiently restrictive. Given their excess liberality in licensing inferences, they actually make it easier to construct self-refuting arguments than would be the case for a more restrictive logic.

Let me underline the moral of these examples. They show that a circular argument does not automatically embody a *vicious* circle. As a result, those who wish to reject an argument because it "assumes what it seeks to prove" must themselves prove that the specific circle in question is vicious. In the particular case of my attempt to offer an account of normative rationality that is normatively rational on its own grounds, I will rest with the point that I can find no vitiating circularity until someone points one out.

CONCLUSION

A naturalistic epistemology should seem attractive—even natural—to those of us who view humans as members of the natural world. It is, thus, an odd feature of contemporary philosophy that many philosophers who reject any appeal to the supernatural in giving an account of human beings also reject the attempt to construct a naturalistic account of scientific knowledge. The objections, we have seen, derive from two closely related concerns: the worry that science cannot provide epistemic norms since science is a descriptive endeavor and we cannot deduce norms from descriptions; and the claim that even if we could extract norms from science, the attempt to use these norms to justify scientific results would be viciously circular. I have responded to both of these concerns in the present paper. With respect to the first I have argued that deduction is not at issue in arriving at norms for knowledge. Rather, we can reflect on our best understanding of how human cognition operates and on our cognitive goals and make proposals as to how best to pursue those goals. Moreover, these proposals can be critically evaluated. There is more to critical evaluation than has been examined in this paper (cf. Brown, 1988b), but we have seen that one major form of evaluation derives from the account of human cognition that we accept. Epistemic norms that are based on a particular account of our cognitive abilities become suspect if that account is rejected, and norms that require us to do what is beyond our capabilities are surely unacceptable.

My response to the second concern was to argue that, once we look at details rather than at general pronouncements, we find that reflexive evaluations need not involve a problematic circularity. Claims of vicious circularity must be justified by demonstrating that the specific case in question does embody a vicious circle.

The main outcome of both lines of argument is to focus philosophical attention on the details. Whether a naturalistic account of reason is possible depends on what cognitive abilities can appear in the natural world and this question cannot be answered a priori. Rather, as we develop a better understanding of actual cognition we can also develop a better grasp of the appropriate norms for us and we can apply these norms to provide a more accurate evaluation of our cognitive theories. In metaphorical terms, we have a helix, not a circle, and the helix is anchored in studies of actual human knowers.[13] If there is something logically defective about this process, it will have to be shown by examining specific cases.

ENDNOTES

1. Let me remind the reader that philosophers and logicians use the term "deduce" in a much more precise and narrow sense than it is used in much common discourse. Sherlock Holmes, Mr. Spock, and most people most of the time use "deduce" as a synonym for "infer" and include everything from rigorous deductions to educated guesses in its scope. The narrow sense of the term limits deduction to inferences in which the truth of the conclusion is guaranteed by the truth of the premises. I shall use "deduce" only in this narrower sense.

2. Consider: I need sufficient light to see the color of the wall; I must rub my hand across the wall with a moderate degree of pressure to feel its inherent roughness; I must press fairly hard to feel its inherent solidity; I must slam my hand on the wall really hard to feel the wall's inherent pain.

3. See Hempel (1965) and Brown (1979, chap. 3) for discussion of the changing accounts of how nonobservation terms are to be introduced.

4. I want to emphasize that such processes are *sufficient* to end the regress. Other hypotheses as to how this occurs, and more radical departures from the traditional account of justification, are surely possible.

5. A sketch of a similar view will be found in Suppes (1984, pp. 215–219); see also Brown (1988b, chap. 4). Dreyfus and Dreyfus (1986, 1991) have proposed a detailed account of how skills are learned.

6. The ability to exercise judgment is typically learned in a social setting, although the early stages in the development of a new kind of skill may provide an exception. But this does not alter the point that each exercise of judgment is an individual act.

7. See, for example, Rumelhart, McClelland, et al. (1986) and Churchland (1989). See also Brown (1988b, sec. 4.3) for further discussion of the place of judgment in the natural world.

8. I have discussed the role of observation in Brown (1987, 1990) and of critical debate in Brown (1988b, ch. 5). A more recent discussion will be found in Brown (1994).

9. The norms that follow are not, of course, algorithms but maxims in Polanyi's sense of the term: "Maxims are rules, the correct application of which is part of the art which they govern" (1964, p. 31). Exactly how these norms are to be followed in a specific case must rely on the judgment of those who would apply them.

10. Siegel maintains that epistemological theories must be self-justifying (1989, p. 371).

11. This is another methodological rule that is suggested, but not entailed, by a set of facts, in this case facts about logical relationships.

12. See Brown (1993) for an example that makes the analogous point in the case of observational tests of a theory.

13. See Hooker (1987, p. 13) for another example of the image. I want to thank Professor Hooker and the editors of this volume for comments on earlier drafts of this paper.

REFERENCES

Barnes, B., & Bloor, D. (1982). Relativism, rationalism and the sociology of science. In M. Hollis & S. Lukes (Eds.), *Rationality and relativism*. Cambridge: MIT Press.

Brown, H. I. (1979). *Perception, theory and commitment: The new philosophy of science*. Chicago: University of Chicago Press.

Brown, H. I. (1987). *Observation and objectivity*. New York: Oxford University Press.

Brown, H. I. (1988a). Normative epistemology and naturalized epistemology. *Inquiry, 31*, 53–78.

Brown, H. I. (1988b). *Rationality*. London: Routledge.

Brown, H. I. (1990). Prospective realism. *Studies in History and Philosophy of Science, 21*, 211–242.

Brown, H. I. (1993). A theory-laden observation can test the theory. *British Journal for the Philosophy of Science, 44*, 555–559.

Brown, H.I. (1994). Judgment and reason. *Electronic Journal of Analytic Philosophy*, 2:5.

Cherniak, C. (1986). *Minimal rationality*. Cambridge: MIT Press.

Churchland, P. M. (1989). *The neurocomputational perspective: Philosophical essays on the mind, brain, and science*. Cambridge: MIT Press.

Dreyfus, H., & Dreyfus, S. (1986). *Mind over machine*. New York: The Free Press.

Dreyfus, H., & Dreyfus, S. (1991). Towards a phenomenology of ethical expertise. *Human Studies, 14*, 229–250.

Faust, D. (1984). *The limits of scientific reasoning*. Minneapolis: University of Minnesota Press.

Halweg, K., & Hooker, C. A. (1989). *Issues in evolutionary epistemology*. Albany: SUNY Press.

Hempel, C. (1965). Empiricist criteria of cognitive significance: Problems and changes, in *Aspects of scientific explanation*. New York: Free Press.

Hooker, C. A. (1987). *A realistic theory of science*. Albany: SUNY Press.

Hume, D. (1978). *A treatise of human nature* (2nd ed.), L. A. Selby-Bigge (Ed.), rev. by P. H. Nidditch. Oxford: Oxford University Press.

Kahneman, D., Slovic, P., & Tversky, A. (1982). *Judgement under uncertainty: Heuristics and biases*. Cambridge: Cambridge University Press.

Kline, M. (1980). *Mathematics: The loss of certainty*. New York: Oxford University Press.

Laudan, L. (1987). Progress or rationality? The prospects for normative naturalism. *American Philosophical Quarterly, 24*, 19–31.

Lindberg, D. (1976). *Theories of vision from Al-Kindi to Kepler*. Chicago: University of Chicago Press.

Nisbett, R., & Ross, L. (1980). *Human inference: Strategies and shortcomings of social judgment*. Englewood Cliffs, NJ: Prentice-Hall.

Polanyi, M. (1964). *Personal knowledge: Towards a post-critical philosophy*. New York: Harper & Row.

Radnitzky G., & Bartley, W. W. (1987). *Evolutionary epistemology, rationality, and the sociology of knowledge*. La Salle, IL: Open Court.

Reiner, R. (1993). *A framework for theories of bounded rationality*. Unpublished doctoral dissertation, York University.

Rumelhart, D., McClelland, J., et al. (1986). *Parallel distributed processing*, 2 vols. Cambridge: MIT Press.

Shapere, D. (1984). *Reason and the search for knowledge*. Dordrecht: D. Reidel.

Siegel, H. (1989). Philosophy of science naturalized? Some problems with Giere's naturalism, *Studies in History and Philosophy of Science, 20*, 365–375.

Stroud, B. (1985). The significance of naturalized epistemology. In H. Kornblith (Ed.), *Naturalizing epistemology*. Cambridge: MIT Press.

Suppes, P. (1984). *Probabilistic metaphysics*. Oxford: Oxford University Press.

Wason, P., & Johnson-Laird, W. (1972). *Psychology of reasoning*. Cambridge: Harvard University Press.

CHAPTER 3

SOCIAL EPISTEMOLOGY AND PSYCHOLOGY

Steve Fuller

OVERVIEW

In this chapter, I present a version of social epistemology that radically departs from classical theories of knowledge and their focus on a conceptual
analysis of the individual cognitive agent. My version of social epistemology exchanges conceptual
analysis for the empirical methods of the social sciences and replaces the autonomous individual with
an appropriately sized and shaped social formation.

In the first section, I sketch the normative scope
of this enterprise, which is to design norms that
enable knowledge to be pursued by a community of
finite inquirers according to standards to which
they agree to be held accountable. Here issues of
knowledge and power come together in the form of
the rhetoric by which epistemic norms are proposed.

The second section lays out the disciplinary
resources on which social epistemology critically
draws. To appreciate the sort of "naturalism" that
social epistemology espouses, the human sciences
need to be reconstructed. Certain episodes from the
histories of sociology, psychology, linguistics, and

anthropology are highlighted as elements of the
needed reconstruction. The biggest challenge here
is to reconstruct robust normative and empirical
sensibilities within a framework that declares
norms and facts to be, in some significant sense,
"constructed" between the inquirer and the
inquired.

In section three, I sketch a research program that
addresses this challenge. It treats experiments as
sites for simulating sociohistorical variation. Affinities with evolutionary epistemology and counterfactual and comparative historiography are
explored, culminating in an analysis of the differences between the natural and social sciences,
based on differences in their knowledge production
ecologies.

The fourth and final section confronts the constructivist charge that social epistemologists simply do not have the credibility to enable their
findings to cause scientists to change their practices. My response to this legitimate complaint is
that if the social epistemologist is actually in a
position to argue with the scientist about this point,
then it would quickly become clear that the scien-

tist's credibility rests on his or her ability to rhetorically manage the uneasy claim that scientific knowledge is somehow both "personal" and "universal." Hopefully, the social epistemologist will contribute to a deconstruction of that rhetoric.

INTRODUCTION

"Social epistemology" is a naturalistic approach to the normative questions surrounding the organization of our knowledge enterprises. The subject matter corresponds to what the pragmatists used to call "the conduct of inquiry" and what may appear to today's readers as an abstract form of science policy. Social epistemology advances beyond other so-called naturalized epistemologies (as elaborated in, say, Kornblith, 1985) by taking seriously the fact that knowledge is produced by agents who are not merely individually embodied but also collectively embedded in certain specifiable relationships that extend over large chunks of space and time. Epistemologists and philosophers of science increasingly have been forced to treat social epistemological themes as they come to accept the findings of historical, sociological, and psychological studies of science as constraints on the advice they issue about the pursuit of knowledge.

Social epistemologies may be compared by the answers they provide to the following questions:

- Are the norms of inquiry relatively autonomous from the norms governing the rest of society?
- Is there anything more to a "form of inquiry" than the manner in which inquirers are arranged?
- Do truth and the other normative aims of science remain unchanged as particular forms of inquiry come and go?
- Is there anything more to "the problem of knowledge" than a matter of *whose* actions are licensed on the basis of *which* claims made under *what* circumstances?
- Is the social character of knowledge reducible to the aggregated beliefs of some group of individuals?
- Is the empirical purview of social epistemology limited to the identification of mechanisms and institutions that meet conceptually satisfying definitions of knowledge?

The more inclined the social epistemologist is toward offering a positive answer to each of these questions, the closer he or she remains to the Car

tesian starting point of classical epistemology. Goldman (1991) is the purest case in point, as he does not even turn to the social (or, for that matter, psychological) factors relevant to knowledge production until the relevant definitions of knowledge and related concepts have been established by a priori means. Meanwhile, Kitcher (1993) occupies the middle ground between Goldman and Fuller (1988, 1993a, 1993b), who, in turn, offers a program of research and policy based on negative answers to the above questions. The full spectrum of positions is represented in Schmitt (1987). In order to stress the departures that social epistemology is capable of making from traditional theories of knowledge, this article will presume negative answers to the above questions.

THE NORMATIVE SCOPE OF SOCIAL EPISTEMOLOGY

Philosophers have been pushed in the direction of social epistemology by the increasing resistance they have met from scientists who balk at norms of inquiry that presuppose reasoners who are either too perspicuous or too selfless. How does one deal with the embarrassing fact that scientific reasoners typically lack the requisite virtues? Wayward scientists simply no longer feel the guilt and remorse that they did fifty years ago when philosophers found fault with their practices. But instead of continuing to castigate the scientists, the social epistemologist proposes a twofold strategy for tackling the inevitable discrepancy between philosophical norms and scientific practice:

> **either** the norms really pertain to some form of group interaction or computer android, but not to the activity of any individual human;
> **or** the norms could govern the activity of individual humans, provided that the individuals are instructed or, in some way, motivated to adopt the norms.

As an example of what is at stake between these two options, consider the difference in psychologies implied by the following ways in which the Popperian norm of falsificationism may be instantiated in science:

> **either** each scientist is expected to offer her own bold conjectures, but to rigorously refute her neighbor's;
> **or** each scientist is expected both to boldly conjecture and to rigorously refute her own claims.

A credit to his training in pedagogy under Karl Buehler at Vienna (Bartley, 1974), Popper realized that the first option is psychologically more realistic than the second. And insofar as falsificationism is essential for the growth of knowledge, science would seem to be—for all practical purposes—an irreducibly social activity. Here Popper contributes a seminal insight to social epistemology.

Alternatives like the ones above drive home the point that, contrary to the pretensions of classical epistemology, the normative mission of social epistemology is not ended once the philosopher or methodologist constructs a conceptually satisfying model of how inquiry ought to proceed (e.g., definitions of knowledge that enjoin the inquirer to seek only "justified true beliefs"). On the contrary, that is the easy part. The hard part is to determine the unit of analysis to which the norms could be reasonably thought to apply and then the means by which those norms may be instantiated in that unit.

Virtually all of the norms of inquiry proposed by modern philosophers of science—including formulations of inductive logic (Carnap), the falsification principle (Popper), paradigms (Kuhn), disciplines (Toulmin), research programs (Lakatos), and research traditions (Laudan)—are better seen as governing some supraindividual unit of inquiry than the behavior of any particular inquirer who might be part of that unit. The founder of pragmatism, Charles Sanders Peirce, first realized this point when he observed that the rationality of induction as a method of science presupposed a potentially infinite and continuous community of inquirers. The exact dimensions of that supraindividual unit—how many people, what sort of interactions, over what chunk of space–time—is open to empirical determination, specifically by comparative historical and experimental social psychological studies of science.

To presume that the norms of inquiry could be straightforwardly instantiated in a particular scientist or that a scientific community is typified by any one of its members (a "normal scientist") is to court what logicians call the "fallacy of division," or what sociologists dub the "oversocialized" individual (Wrong, 1961). Historians will recognize this presumption as one of two sides of an argument that American psychologists had at the turn of the century about how to understand individual differences: Should they be seen as deviations from an ideal individual or as statistically normal variation within a functioning social organism (Boehme,

1977)? Despite the fact that experimental psychology has tended to presume the former paradigm, only the latter is true to the mission of social epistemology.

But what happens once a putatively idealized individual is itself part of the social context of inquiry? Such would be the situation of a programmed computer android that was capable of executing the reasoning required of formalized scientific norms (e.g., Bayesian inductive logic) better than any group or individual human could (Glymour, 1987). On the one hand, if there is sufficient commitment or incentive for applying the norm governing the machine's performance, then the community may prefer to cut the risk of human error by deferring to the machine's authority on the relevant occasions. On the other hand, the epistemologist may have background normative commitments—such as to individual accountability to the group or to the value of attempting to approximate a norm regardless of individual success—that would steer her away from the path of least resistance, which would be simply to let the computer do what it does best. In that case, she may want to make resistant individuals conform to the proposed norms of inquiry.

A politics, and especially a rhetoric, would then be needed to motivate the relevant changes in practices that are needed for the epistemologist to get her way. Exactly how to negotiate this situation is the social epistemologist's toughest assignment, as she must now assume the mantle of policymaker and pedagogue. Moreover, this situation is the most "normative," strictly speaking, in that it forces the epistemologist to consider the foundations of government: To what standards can people's actions be legitimately held, and under what circumstances may they legitimately resist the imposition of such standards?

At this point, the social epistemologist becomes reflexively implicated as a social agent, and—as Bacon, Comte, and Foucault would have it—questions of knowledge and power become one (Rouse, 1987). If this identification of knowledge and power seems authoritarian, that is only because relatively few people currently see it as their business to propose norms that would cover more than their own activities. This is the excess to which defenders of "local knowledge" have sometimes been driven (Geertz, 1983). Consequently, it is easy to cast the run of humanity into the roles of evaders, opponents—if not servants and victims—of the social epistemologist's schemes. However, contrary to postmodernist scruples, the solution is not to cease all normative pronouncements, but rather to make as many people as possible see that even if they are not directly involved in a particular form of inquiry, they have a stake in its conduct. Given the penetration of science into all spheres of life, the empirical case for public stakeholdership in science is easy to make. And as will become clear in what follows, social epistemology's own empirical base in the most recent incarnation of the sociology of knowledge, science and technology studies (STS), implies a strong democratizing impulse that is nourished by encouraging more people to make normative pronouncements for themselves and to contest those of others.

SOCIAL EPISTEMOLOGY'S NATURALISTIC RECONSTRUCTION OF THE HUMAN SCIENCES

Social epistemology is a radical version of naturalized epistemology (Fuller, 1992a). This implies, in the first instance, a denial that knowledge has any conceptually necessary (or a priori) component. More precisely, the features of knowledge that a classical epistemologist is inclined to consider conceptually necessary, the social epistemologist takes to be default hypotheses that are subject to revision in light of further inquiry. For example, the social epistemologist may find the correspondence theory of truth a *prima facie* plausible account of knowledge. But what if it turns out, upon further investigation, that inquirers appeal to this theory in ways that can be better explained (or predicted) in terms of political factors than by traditionally epistemological ones? Might we not then want to reconsider the adequacy of the correspondence theory as an account of knowledge, or for that matter, whether the distinction between knowledge and politics obscures more than clarifies?

Given the radical changes that have taken place in humanity's first-order accounts of nature, even over the last two centuries, is there any reason *not* to think that second-order conceptions of inquiry are themselves susceptible to change on a similar scale? Here social epistemologists are one with Popper (1963) and Quine (1985), except for being more willing than most naturalists to challenge the current self-understandings of the special sciences. Thus, social epistemologists retain the critical scruples that are emblematic of philosophy, for there is

no reason to presume that, simply out of their own accord, the findings of the special sciences will eventually add up to a coherent overall account of the knowledge system.

This last point raises a delicate issue. The need for stable first-order inquiries has traditionally inhibited second-order impulses to study the nature of inquiry. In Kuhnian terms, the demands of normal science limit the incentives for revolutionary change only to those periods in which a paradigm has accumulated enough anomalies to place it in a state of crisis. As Kuhn (1970) himself realized, scientists who applied their first-order methods to a second-order study of the grounds of their inquiries typically undermined their commitment to the first-order inquiries. At the very least, they came to realize the sociohistorical contingency of their discipline happening to follow one research trajectory rather than some other. Consequently, Kuhn held that it is just as well that scientists acquire an "Orwellian" (or Whiggish) sense of disciplinary history that masks the contingency that would be otherwise revealed by a more empirically informed account of that history (p. 167). However, a thoroughgoing naturalism of the sort promoted by social epistemology cannot afford the perverse luxury of Orwellianism.

Unfortunately, most contemporary forms of naturalized epistemology (especially those following Quine, 1985) presume the ontological shell of classical epistemology—the Cartesian knower—and then work within that framework to locate empirical correlates for such classical epistemic entities as "beliefs." Thus, there is a tendency to think that the naturalist must be committed to a kind of psychophysical reductionism, specifically to the expectation that an epistemic concept like "my belief that there is a chair in this room" will be replaced by empirical correlations between specific neural states (events, processes) and specific environmental conditions. With this understanding comes a certain view of the history of science, whereby the classical epistemologists (especially Descartes, Locke, and Kant) laid down the blueprints, experimental psychologists are surveying the construction site, and neurophysiologists will eventually erect the structure.

However, the social epistemologist is unimpressed by this naturalistic narrative because it fails to account for how an enterprise as sociologically complex as science ever could have emerged from such supposedly self-contained cognizers. As we saw in the last section, even philosophers of science have implicitly granted this point in their own units of analysis. A more comprehensive naturalism is promised by the sociology of knowledge and especially its latest incarnation, STS, which extends Mannheim's (1936) original insight into the "existential determination of thought" to the natural sciences (Bloor, 1991).

To appreciate the difference between sociology of knowledge and the forms of naturalized epistemology more familiar to philosophers and psychologists, consider two strategies for generating some philosophically interesting "problems of knowledge":

Strategy A

1. The thing I know best is the thing with which I have had the most direct acquaintance, namely, my own mind. After all, without it, I could not have made this very observation. But my mind is possibly not all that exists.

2. How, then, do I determine whether other possible things exist, and, if they exist, how can I know them, given that they seem quite different from my own mind?

Strategy B

1. We ordinarily experience everyone (and everything) as living in the same world. Yet, as people articulate their experience, it becomes clear that there are significant differences in the aspects of the world to which we have direct access.

2. What, then, accounts for these differences in access to our common reality, and what enables us to ignore them in everyday life, as we suppose that our own access is the one shared by all (right-minded) people?

Whereas Strategy A captures the tradition of inquiry that unites Descartes and Quine, Strategy B captures that of the sociology of knowledge. As Elster (1979) points out, the lineage of this latter tradition extends from Augustinian theodicy (How can divine harmony be compatible with day-to-day strife?), through Leibniz and Hegel, to Marx and Mannheim.

There are some important differences in the sorts of epistemological problems that the two strategies generate. Strategy A poses the problem of knowledge *inside-out*: How do we get out of our individual heads and into some common reality? Strategy B poses it *outside-in*: How do we get beyond our

common reality and into the mindsets that separate people? An important reason why self-described "epistemologists" and "philosophers of science" rarely draw on each other's accounts of knowledge lies in the difference between these two strategies.

All contemporary epistemologies—be they called "internalist" or "externalist"—operate within the inside-out strategy, in that knowledge is posed as a problem for each individual to solve on his or her own terms, namely, by approximating a standard to which the cognitive agent may or may not have conscious access (Pollock, 1986). In this construal of the problem of knowledge, there is no sense that epistemic access may be a scarce good, with one agent's access to knowledge perhaps impeding, competing with, or making demands on the epistemic access of some other agent. Such would be more in accord with the outside-in strategy, which is typically found in the problems posed by philosophers of science. Here the cognitive agent is portrayed as choosing between one of two or more alternative research trajectories, fully realizing that resources are limited and that other agents will be making a similar decision at roughly the same time (Fuller, 1985).

Both strategies operate with epistemological premises that are taken to be liabilities in advancing the search for knowledge. For Strategy A, a self-centered relativism is the initial liability that needs to be overcome: I am in my own head, but I suspect that there are other things out there different from me. How do I find out? Not surprisingly, this strategy stresses methods that are biased toward realism, such as looking for ("primary") qualities that remain invariant under a variety of observations and transformations. For Strategy B, on the other hand, a totalizing realism is the initial liability: We all live in the same world, therefore everyone must think like me, at least when they are thinking right. But why doesn't this seem to be the case? (Are they crazy?) The relevant corrective here is a dose of methodological relativism: Precisely *because* our reality is common, it cannot explain our palpable differences (cf. Barnes & Bloor, 1982, p. 34). We are thus better off regarding claims to common reality as disguised partial perspectives, or "ideologies," that may gain certain local material advantage by capitalizing on our weakness for thinking in terms of totalizing forms of realism.

The sociology of knowledge's adherence to Strategy B has led to no end of misunderstanding by philosophical opponents (cf. Brown, 1984). For example, most of the sociologists—certainly Mannheim and Bloor—have been epistemological realists and believe that most of the people they study are also realists, at least in the sense of believing that contact with reality is part of the "natural ontological attitude" (Fine, 1986). However, such a modest commitment to realism is bound to seem strange to philosophers wedded to Strategy A. For although sociologists of knowledge grant that there is a "fact of the matter" about the norms governing a given community of inquirers, because these norms govern *only* that community and no other (until demonstrated by studies of other communities), they conclude that the reality of the norms does not turn on their being generalizable across communities. In short, the sociologists are realists without being universalists.

Among the bad cognitive habits that universalism can breed, two stand out: (1) the tendency to minimize the differences in beliefs between people in different cultures, and (2) the tendency to exaggerate the pathology of those whose differences from our beliefs cannot be completely explained away. Thus, Bloor's (1991, chap. 1) four tenets of the Strong Programme in the Sociology of Scientific Knowledge—causality, impartiality, symmetry, reflexivity—are heuristics specifically designed to counteract these biases, which inquirers are prone to import when they study the knowledge produced by alien cultures. Bloor's philosophical critics err in interpreting these heuristics as unconditional epistemological principles.

However, it would be misleading to suggest that the sociology of knowledge has had benign designs on the future of epistemology and the philosophy of science. On the contrary, sociology has been at loggerheads with philosophy throughout most of its existence because of a profoundly historicist argument first made by the founder of sociology, Auguste Comte, which has since been repeated by Mannheim, Bloor, Latour (1987), and other sociologists of knowledge (cf. Meja & Stehr, 1990). The argument ties the emergence of sociology as a "positive science" with the withering away of philosophy—even of a philosophy that promotes the cause of science. Here are the steps of that argument:

1. Philosophy leads us to prefer science as the highest form of inquiry by getting us to develop theories of truth and rationality that force us to justify our knowledge claims by the rigorous standards of logical reasoning, which, in turn, reveal the inadequacies in our taken-for-granted habits of thought.
2. But once we start to do science, we realize that these philosophical theories are impediments to further inquiry, as they encourage us to rush to conclusions about the whole on the basis of knowing only a few of the parts. This tendency toward premature totalization is the result of trying to let reason do the work of empirical observation.
3. What this shows is that a mode of thought that persuades us of the value of science need not itself be of service to science, once we have been so persuaded. In fact, such a mode of thought may even be an obstacle and should be suspended, as it has outlived its usefulness.

Analytic philosophers have read this argument in the *Tractatus* (6.54), where Wittgenstein likens (his own) philosophy to the ladder that needs to be thrown away once it has been climbed. The history of science also reveals reasoning of this sort whenever a historian remarks, say, that Galileo's adeptness in revealing the artificiality and inconsistency of Aristotle's assumptions about physical motion —a philosophical virtue—was itself insufficient to establish the new paradigm, as that latter achievement required some empirically grounded first principles, "deductions from the phenomena," as Newton eventually put it. In short, philosophy benefits science only when science is not culturally dominant. Once science is dominant, however, it will spend much of its time purging itself of any philosophical residue. An example from Bloor (1991, pp. 40–41) illustrates this point.

In recounting Joseph Priestley's near-discovery of oxygen in the late eighteenth century, Bloor attempts to separate the wheat from the chaff in the concept of truth that is needed to explain what Priestley did and did not do. According to Bloor, to say that a particular belief of Priestley's is "true" or "false" may serve a perfectly legitimate function, namely, to distinguish between those views we share with Priestley (the "true" ones) and those we do not (the "false" ones). However, what Bloor finds illegitimate is to import a more "philosophical" conception of truth, whereby the set of beliefs we call "true" somehow better correspond to reality—independent of our interests in wanting knowledge—than the ones we call "false." By packing this philosophical encumbrance into the concept of truth, we are then able to strip Priestley of his interests, replace them with ours, and then judge his work by standards suited for promoting our interests. Since we are in fair agreement as to what those interests are, we rarely need to discuss them, and hence they do not appear to us *as interests*. Thus, the philosophical politics of truth rest on suppressing the voices of others with interests unlike our own.

Much as Comte had regarded the role of metaphysical abstractions—Liberty, Equality, and Fraternity—in the French Revolution, sociologists of knowledge tend to hold that philosophical notions—Truth and Rationality—are impediments to scientific inquiry because they politicize science unnecessarily. Of course, the sociologists are not so naive as to believe that science can purge itself of *all* politics. After all, don't sociologists of knowledge generally believe that science is interest-driven? Yes, but not just anybody's interests. The practices of scientists are presumed to have a historically based integrity of their own, which gives a particular community of practitioners authority to represent those practices (cf. Pickering, 1992). True, a scientific practice may be subject to legitimate change by its practitioners, and larger social and self-interested concerns may contribute to such change. But who decides, then, whether a practice is helped or hurt? That is an empirical matter to be settled by the scientists in a particular community, the result of which the sociologist is then in a position to discover. Philosophy can muddle the perspective of either the sociologist or the scientific agent, if either is led to believe that the interests at play have some special transcendent significance for inquiry that may go unrecognized by most of the practicing scientists. In that case, scientists would have relinquished their authority to represent science—at least so claim the sociologists of knowledge.

How valid is this claim of sociologists of knowledge to have rendered philosophy obsolete, if not downright atavistic? Obviously, the answer to this question bears decisively on the viability of social epistemology as a philosophical enterprise.

Recall at the outset that relativism functions *only* as a heuristic in sociological inquiry. In that case, we must take care not to overextend the heuristic to the point that the cognitive service performed by relativism turns into a liability. That point comes when the sociologist ignores the aggregated consequences of many locally monitored practices. The actions taken by a scientific community have consequences not only for the community's members but also for third parties who, whether they realize it or not, are stakeholders in the actions taken by

that community. These third parties may remain ignorant and silent because the language of science is quite unlike the language of their day-to-day concerns. But it takes only one course in philosophical semantics to realize that linguistic remoteness says nothing about causal relevance. People don't need to understand something for it to have impact on their lives. However, there must be ways of breaking down these linguistic barriers—both between disciplinary communities and between science and society more generally—if people are to respond intelligently to scientific impacts. Here we find new uses for some of the traditional preoccupations of philosophers, especially the development of procedural languages for facilitating normatively desirable social interactions concerning the production of knowledge (cf. Fuller, 1993b). In such cases, one needs to adopt a perspective—dare I say "global"—that transcends the viewpoints of particular communities of inquiry. A good resource for models of the perspective required is *intellectual property*, in which the law must ensure that an individual profits from his or her creativity without disadvantaging later innovators and inhibiting society's well-being (Fuller, 1991, 1992b).

Some readers may wonder how the sociology of knowledge could be left open to a line of objection as obvious as the one just raised. Yet, there is a sense in which sociological conceptions of knowledge production—and culture more generally—do presume a close correlation between linguistic difference and causal relevance: the greater the one, the less of the other. From the standpoint of historical linguistics, some of this is warranted: Language differences magnify or diminish, depending on the amount of interaction between groups. Indeed, Fuller's (1988) main thesis was that language differences magnify first to conceptual, and ultimately to world, differences as interaction diminishes. But of course one group may affect another through the material consequences of its actions even if no member of the first group actually has contact with any member of the second. Environmental pollution is a good case in point. (Economists generally call such effects *externalities*.) However, the point can be easily overlooked if a group is primarily identified with its language, and the language is presented simultaneously as the means by which the group is regulated and the vehicle by which its values are expressed. In that case, a society appears to be an organism whose anatomy is grammar (Saussure's *langue*) and whose physiology is discourse (Saussure's *parole*).

Indeed, late eighteenth- and early nineteenth-century studies of culture based on the philology of classical Indo-European and Semitic languages made just such connections, and, in retrospect, it is easy to see why they did. The communities under philological investigation were dead, and thus epistemic access was restricted to whatever order could be discerned from their written remains. Not to be underestimated here was the pre-Darwinian conception of life that informed the philologists' understanding of a "dead language" (Foucault, 1970). Each linguistic community was considered a species with its own unique vital principles. The German philological tradition had been influenced by recent advances in embryology that portrayed organic development as something completely internal to a species. This idea carried into the *Volkpsychologie* studies of the Romantic philosopher Herder and later to no less than Wilhelm Wundt. The main influence on the later Wittgenstein's conception of "language games," Fritz Mauthner, also drew on this tradition (Janik & Toulmin, 1973), as have such recent purveyors of the Wittgensteinian sociology of knowledge as Winch (1958) and Bloor (1983).

However, the pre-Darwinian conception of life was not limited to the German tradition. Although the early French practitioners of the human sciences tended to be more mechanistic than vitalistic in their orientation toward life, theirs was a medical vision of the organism in equilibrium with its environment. Consequently, pathology could be understood not as contact with a foreign element but only as an internally defined disorder occasioned by an environmental change (Canguilhem, 1978). Durkheim's account of social change was certainly in this vein. Not surprisingly, it was possible for someone trained in the German philological tradition to adopt Durkheim's research program and, in effect, provide the modern foundations for the human sciences, namely, Ferdinand de Saussure (Dineen, 1967, chap. 7).

The value of recounting this early history of the human sciences is that it suggests, counterfactually, that had these early practitioners operated with a notion of biological extinction—such as Darwin's—that did not attribute essences to species, then we might have been able to avoid the image of languages as well-defined entities that correspond to self-contained communities and

their "conceptual schemes" or "worldviews." Instead, we might have more quickly arrived at the nominalist view of language and social life portrayed in, say, Davidson (1986), where the boundaries between communities are eminently fluid and permeable, more a statistical drift of speech behaviors than incommensurable grammatical paradigms.

In any case, with the rise of field linguistics and ethnographic studies of living communities in the twentieth century (starting with Franz Boas and his student Edward Sapir), it became apparent at a practical level that "social order" is very much constructed by the inquirer as he or she compares multiple modes of epistemic access to the community: Do official accounts and explicitly stated norms count more or less than observed behavioral regularities? Should the inquirer consider a verbal response to a hypothetical situation a better or worse indicator of the native's normative sensibilities than what he or she does in practice? These questions are themselves normative ones for the inquirer, in that they compel judgments about what sets the standard for adequate performance in a community that seems subject to incommensurable standards. (One answer favored by the ethnomethodologists within sociology is simply that people live in many worlds [cf. Button, 1991].) Psychologists were thrown into the midst of these issues in the 1960s as they were forced to consider the relative merits of the behaviorist accounts of language provided by field linguists vis-à-vis the emerging innatist accounts provided by experimental psycholinguists influenced by Noam Chomsky—two alternatives that radically diverged on matters of epistemic access (Collett, 1977).

In the 1970s, an important line of research developed within cognitive and social psychology that implied a clear—some (e.g., Cohen, 1981) say crude—decision about how to weigh the different modes of epistemic access that inquirers have to people's activities. This research (summarized in Nisbett & Ross, 1980, and Faust, 1985) began by seeing whether people lived up to their own standards: Do their deeds match their words? From experiments done in this spirit, the psychologists discovered that both experts and lay people routinely violated their own professed norms of rationality. Moreover, as STS practitioners have moved away from their historical roots in the sociology of knowledge and into more ethnographically inspired observations of scientific communities, they have made similar discoveries, though these are more likely described as cases of "situational variability" than of "normative divergence" (Latour & Woolgar, 1986; Knorr-Cetina, 1981; Collins, 1985). Here is where social epistemology begins: What is a philosopher to do once he or she learns that scientists do not normally adhere to norms, even when they claim to be doing so?!

Admittedly, both the experimentalists and the ethnographers hedge on whether any of their findings imply that people in general—or scientists in particular—are deeply irrational. However, if it is true, as the evidence suggests, that human behavior is more a function of one's situation than of whatever "knowledge" one brings to the situation, then it would follow that what social psychologists call the "fundamental attribution error" is routinely at work in our knowledge production practices. The fundamental attribution error arises from an asymmetry in how people explain their own behavior vis-à-vis the behavior of others. People tend to explain their own behavior, when good, in terms of personal factors (e.g., "my expertise") and, when bad, in terms of situational factors (e.g., "unforeseen obstacles"); however, other people's behavior is explained, when good, in terms of situational factors (e.g., "her luck") and, when bad, in terms of personal factors (e.g., "his incompetence"). In that case, one would expect that the difference between human practices that are regularly explained in terms of personal (cognitive) factors vis-à-vis situational (social) factors will turn more on the authority of one's self-accounts than on any empirical correlations between attributions of knowledge and performance. Clearly, this conclusion has profound consequences for the advisability of acquiring credentials in an expertise, if, when watched closely, the experts perform no better than lay people (cf. Hammond & Arkes, 1986; Fuller, 1994).

The moral that the social epistemologist draws from the developments traced in this section is that politics is intertwined more tightly in the fabric of scientific inquiry than even sociologists of knowledge have allowed. For not only are the scientists' politics intertwined with their epistemic practices, but also the sociologists' own politics are intertwined with their own sense of an adequate account of the scientists' epistemic practices. In short, *there is no such thing as letting scientists speak for themselves because they may speak in any of a variety of tongues, depending on how one wants to hear them.*

It becomes of paramount importance, then, to know to what end one wants to understand a community of knowledge producers. This is currently a live concern among the majority of STS practitioners and the increasing number of psychologists (following Gergen, 1985) who operate from a broadly "constructivist" epistemological standpoint—though, as will be seen in the final section, perhaps the deepest criticism of social epistemology comes from this camp. At this point, simply note the difference in what the social epistemologist and the constructivist take as the "base line" or "brute fact" from which their respective inquiries into knowledge production then proceed.

Whereas constructivists typically start from the fact that science is already being done in certain ways and in certain places, the social epistemologist starts from the fact that the public is already—either directly (via taxes) or indirectly (via impacts)—paying for all this science to be done. From this difference in starting point flows divergent sensibilities about which perspectives are currently being given disproportionate attention and which ones remain underarticulated. In addition, one can even detect a difference in attitude toward the "contingent" character of knowledge production. Whereas the constructivist image of contingency is one of idiosyncratically embedded traditions and a presumption to local authority, the social epistemologist stresses the transitory side of contingency, the fact that knowledge production differs under different conditions and that special efforts need to be taken to prevent a variation of conditions from arising. This sense of contingency is intimately tied to the social epistemologist's predilection for experimentation (cf. Fuller, 1992c).

EXPERIMENTAL SOCIAL EPISTEMOLOGY AND THE SEARCH FOR THE SOCIAL ECOLOGIES OF SCIENCE

Happening upon the average conference in epistemology, an experimental psychologist would most naturally interpret what the philosophers are doing when they are trading definitions of knowledge as comparing recipes for producing knowledge in an imaginary laboratory. After all, epistemologists seem to say that if you put someone in a given situation, then the belief he or she is most likely to have about a given object will constitute knowledge. But having made this interpretation, the psychologist will then be struck by the extent to which the philosophers neglect two crucial validity questions, *especially* given their avowed normative aspirations (cf. Berkowitz & Donnerstein, 1982):

> *Ecological Validity*: What is made of the fact that these contrived situations are highly unrepresentative of the conditions under which people try to make sense of the world? Could it mean that we have a lot less knowledge than we thought, or that we need to have knowledge a lot less than we thought, or maybe that what the epistemological recipe for "justified true belief" gives us is not knowledge after all?
>
> *External Validity*: What steps could be taken to make our ordinary cognitive circumstances more like the artificial one (e.g., the philosopher's imagination or the psychologist's lab) in which knowledge is shown to be produced? Would the results be worth the effort? In short, can a real-world knowledge enterprise—a science—be improved by teaching its practitioners a particular theory of knowledge? If so, how? If not, why not?

In this volume (and also Gorman, 1992), Michael Gorman, a practicing experimental psychologist, has weighed the significance of these two validity claims for an experimental social epistemology. There is a sense in which the ecological/external distinction corresponds to the descriptive/prescriptive sides of the social epistemological project, and in which the two sides can be pursued in relative independence of each other. (In particular, one can try to reproduce desirable lab results outside the lab, even if one does not yet fully understand how the world outside the lab works.) But the point that needs to be stressed here is that *both* types of validity are routinely ignored by epistemologists. In effect, the epistemic predicament of the epistemologist vis-à-vis scientific practice is that of someone who grades classroom performance without ever having had any teaching experience: lots of finger-wagging at the students, but little improvement forthcoming in their behavior.

It is also worth noting that social epistemology's commitment to the experimental method is not limited to laboratory experiments, strictly speaking, but also covers methodologies that simulate experiments, such as comparative historical sociology. Because so much of metascientific debate in the social sciences today is still conducted under the influence of the century-old *Methodenstreit* between "positivists" and "interpretivists," we should perhaps return to a more innocent age for methodological inspiration, namely, when John Stuart Mill declared that the comparative method derives its epistemic power from its approximation of the experimental method, specifically its ability to show the difference that sociohistorical variation makes to observed behavior.

The experimental method has traditionally prided itself on the ability to elicit behaviors that would go unrealized in the normal course of events. Cross-cultural comparisons have also typically revealed unrealized possibilities for human action (namely, in others with whom we have not been in frequent contact), and hence have helped squelch any ethnocentric grounds for moral absolutism (cf. Sztompka, 1991). While positivists may continue to argue that the experimental method is a more scientifically rigorous way of achieving what historical sociology wants, nevertheless this is not to deny the sensed emancipatory power of comparative empirical inquiry that is shared by both sides. Let me now illustrate this "sensed emancipatory power" with a strategy for analyzing the history of science.

In 1905 Albert Einstein published three papers that are now said to have launched a revolution in the physical sciences. What made Einstein's papers revolutionary? Perhaps the most obvious response would be to point to Einstein's "genius" or "creative intellect" as having transformed the thinking of the physics community. To determine the uniqueness of Einstein's achievement, the historian would pose the following counterfactual:

> Would someone other than Einstein have come up with the Special Theory of Relativity?

The question presumes that something in the theory itself—its "content" perhaps—made it revolutionary. On the other hand, the social epistemologist would attribute the revolution that now goes under Einstein's name to the fact that *others* came to find his papers essential for lending credibility to their own work. The uniqueness of Einstein's achievement would therefore be measured in response to this historical counterfactual:

> Would it have been possible at the dawn of the twentieth century to mobilize a network comparable to the one surrounding the special theory of relativity that would have eventuated in the overthrow of Newtonian mechanics?

The question presumes that it was the effect that the theory had on the physics community (and elsewhere) that made it revolutionary, specifically, that it changed the norms by which physics research was subsequently legitimized.

One way of seeing the difference between these two historical counterfactuals is in terms of Campbell's (1988, chap. 16) evolutionary epistemology. Whereas the first counterfactual stresses the *variation* side of scientific evolution, the second counterfactual stresses the *selection* side. At its most extreme, the variationist view would presuppose a Lamarckian "orthogenetic" view of evolution, whereby scientific ideas develop through an internal logic that responds in optimally rational terms to environmental changes and diversity. This view, typically known as the "internal history of science," has been subjected to severe critique (e.g., Fuller, 1993a, chap. 2). Nevertheless, the view continues to exert considerable, albeit subtle, influence on science policymakers who want to design research environments that foster scientific creativity without clearly understanding which features or products of that creativity are likely to be retained by such environments and transmitted to the scientific community at large. What is missing, in other words, is the selectionist perspective, which looks at the scientific enterprise as a set of social ecologies for which the "unit of selection" is not necessarily theories or concepts (*pace* Toulmin, 1972), but whichever products of scientific practice *in fact* turn out to be retained by the scientific community. We shall now embed this social ecologies picture in the context of an experimental social epistemology.

A striking feature of the way the sciences are organized is that the perceived "hardness" of a science varies directly with the acceptance rate of articles for journal publication: the harder the science, the *easier* it would seem to get into print. The surface paradox of this claim quickly disappears, however, once it is recalled that, in graduate school, natural scientists learn to formulate issues according to the writing canons of their discipline. Moreover, natural scientists learn to associate quality work more with publication in specific journals than with the impact that their work actually has on the readers of those journals. While this practice consigns the natural scientist to a relatively small audience, it is an audience upon which she can depend for an appropriate level of attention and response. In marked contrast, what a natural scientist learns in graduate school, a social scientist only picks up haphazardly from the gatekeeping practices of the journals to which she submits her arti-

cles. I say "haphazardly" because the social scientist constantly gets mixed signals in her efforts to communicate with a potentially wide audience. As Cicchetti (1991) has observed, while rejection rates in the social sciences (and, interestingly, in interdisciplinary forms of natural science) are high, it is also true that eventually most articles find a place in some journal or other. Is this form of institutionalization good or bad?

Much depends here on whether one sees "science" primarily as a vehicle for each scientist's self-expression or as a collective enterprise issuing in knowledge products, the significance of which transcends any particular scientist's concerns. The expressive latitude permitted by the proliferation of social science journals clearly speaks to the former conception of science. But like most people who write about peer review, Cicchetti seems to believe that the fairer the system is to the individual scientist, the higher the quality of science that is likely to result. The key bridging concept is *innovation*, which he sees the natural sciences as systematically stifling. Indeed, the nearest Cicchetti comes to drawing prescriptive conclusions from his research is to say that good scholarship should not be lost to the world because of standards that are more stringent than they are reliable. Thus, he seems to prefer the social scientific mode of publication. But is this preference well grounded? To address this question, I will introduce the social ecology perspective, which has its roots in classical political theory.

Political theorists of the Enlightenment tended to agree that two conditions precluded the existence of society: Complete abundance renders society unnecessary, while extreme scarcity renders it impossible. The resource of concern to us here is access to publication. Given Cicchetti's analysis, the social sciences fail to optimize knowledge production because publication access is too abundant. Thus, each social scientist can diverge into her own separate niche (i.e., a unique discourse and audience) without fearing marginalization, mainly because there is no center, no forum in which all knowledge claims must be exchanged. Following Hawley (1950), we can project the consequences of resources becoming progressively scarcer, as measured in terms of a decline in publication possibilities. In particular, let us distinguish between *bounded abundance* and *moderate scarcity* as two intermediate states between abundance and scarcity in their pure forms.

In terms of a community of inquirers, pure abundance would be represented by an "anything goes" approach to knowledge, whereas pure scarcity would take the form of a radical skepticism. In the state of bounded abundance, however, possibilities have been cut sufficiently that each inquirer must take the behavior of other inquirers into account when judging how she herself should proceed. Simply repeating or reinventing what other inquirers have done will fail to merit publication. The best strategy under these circumstances is to carve out a niche within what others have done, using one's own work to complement theirs. It is a strategy that characterizes the natural sciences, one which instills a distinctly "market" mentality among scientific inquirers, especially if one imagines the market as a classical free trader like David Ricardo did, namely, as spontaneously generating an efficient division of labor on the basis of each party calculating the "comparative advantage" to be had by pursuing alternative paths of inquiry (White, 1981).

Yet, if Popper is right that the method of "conjectures and refutations" is the key to knowledge growth, then a state of moderate scarcity is to be preferred to that of bounded abundance. Here publication possibilities are tightened some more, to the point that some inquirers must be displaced in order for others to thrive. In that case, inquirers must adopt a more mutually critical attitude, which, while leading to the elimination of most inquirers in the long run, will also likely improve the quality of knowledge claims proposed by those who remain. Thus, every individual scientist's loss is potentially an overall gain for science.

The social ecology conception of scientific inquiry enables us to see the blind spots in a recent American debate over the progressiveness of the social sciences. The debate was occasioned by a list of "advances" that the political scientist Karl Deutsch and his associates compiled, which purported to show that the social sciences were just as much given to cumulative growth as the natural sciences (Deutsch et al., 1986). Deutsch then submitted this list to statistical analysis to discern the social conditions that fostered social scientific creativity. Deutsch (1986) saw many similarities between developments in the natural and social sciences, especially with regard to the delay between the introduction of an innovation and its widespread acceptance in one or more disciplines.

Daniel Bell (1986) countered that Deutsch would start seeing some sharp dissimilarities if he turned to the long-term survival rates of natural vis-à-vis social scientific innovations. To end the story, as Deutsch does, with the widespread acceptance of an innovation is to take for granted that the innovation has become a permanent part of the corpus of knowledge—at least as a basis for making subsequent innovations. While this probably holds for the natural sciences, Bell argued, it is hardly the case in the social sciences. From a long-term perspective, social scientific innovations appear to be little more than fads and fashions.

Part of the problem with assessing the merits of Deutsch's and Bell's claims is that they are concerned almost exclusively with what philosophers of science would recognize as the discovery and justification contexts of the scientific enterprise, which capture only the rhetorical surface of knowledge production. This is not to deny that the rhetoric has its uses. For example, any scientific innovation can be described as either a "discovery" or an "invention." To "invent" is simply to discover an application of real principles, whereas to "discover" is none other than to invent a new way of accessing real principles. Nevertheless, the rhetorical contexts in which these two descriptions work are quite different. Discovery-talk functions well when making a case before a university committee or a scientific forum, whereas invention-talk is essential to making claims to corporate funding and legal rights. Similarly, the rhetoric of justification, with its appeal to the logical unfolding of inquiry, is persuasive in contexts where one needs to muster up the past in a selectively memorable fashion, so as to highlight a preferred research trajectory. Classrooms and grant agencies come to mind as sites for such rhetoric. However, all this talk obscures the issues of social epistemology that are needed to resolve the Deutsch-Bell debate. In particular, we need to learn what governs the ways in which scientists direct attention to each other's work (cf. Collins, 1989).

What is it about the work of their colleagues that scientists find sufficiently compelling that they end up spending their time either building on it (cf. bounded abundance) or criticizing it (cf. moderate scarcity)? Recent historiographical models of the scientific inquirer drawn from cognitive psychology have failed miserably in coming to grips with this question, as historians simply take for granted that if a scientific community is working "rationally," its members reproduce in their own minds the innovation of a Faraday, Einstein, or some other "genius" (Fuller, 1993b, chap. 6). Social psychological research on the appropriation of ideas shows that the "contagion" model of knowledge transmission presupposed by these historians grossly oversimplifies the actual cognitive processes, even in children (Paulus, 1989, chap. 12). To propose a hypothesis for consideration, even one that has enough evidential support to merit publication in a mainstream forum, does not guarantee that it will be given any attention whatsoever. Deutsch's mistake in drawing parallels between the delays that, say, Newtonianism or Darwinism had to endure before being fully accepted by the community of natural scientists and the delays faced by today's social scientific innovators is that whereas there was continuous debate for the fifty-odd years from the time Newton and Darwin first proposed their views to the time of their general acceptance, very often social scientific innovations die stillborn, only to be reinvented years later in a more hospitable intellectual environment. It is only when the reinventors needed to distance themselves from other social scientific fashionmongers that they start looking for "precursors." (In this respect, Gregor Mendel's post-mortem fame as the "father of genetics" is the relevant analogue from the natural sciences; see Brannigan, 1981.) Thus, Bell's skepticism is probably warranted, insofar as Deutsch has confused the rhetorical contexts of discovery and justification with the actual transmission and institutionalization of epistemic practices.

In this section, four social ecologies have been implicated in the social epistemology of knowledge production. Each ecology consists of a selection mechanism that operates in a particular human environment. More plainly, it is a field of competition for the attention of an audience that is crucial for expediting the spread of science at a particular juncture:

1. *The ecology of the self or the workplace*: This is the self-editing of ideas and expressions, a process at which natural scientists become especially adept in the course of their professional training. It accounts for the high publication acceptance rates in natural science journals. This process is continued in the workplace through the mutual shaping of research team members, which includes brainstorming and transactive remembering, whereby team members remind each other of information or arguments that need to be taken into account before an acceptable scientific paper is produced (Paulus, 1989, chap. 11). Depending on whether one adopts a cognitivist or a behaviorist orientation, this mutual shaping may be seen as externalizing the self-editing process or self-editing may be seen as internally anticipating the response of colleagues.

2. *The ecology of the editorial office*: This consists of the often controversial "gatekeeping" practices of the peer review system, which covers both journal publication and such mechanisms of resource allocation as grant agencies (Chubin & Hackett, 1990). Such practices perform a much more pronounced selection function in the social sciences than in the natural sciences.

3. *The ecology of the university library*: This crucial ecology has been largely ignored, though it is here that the expansive tendencies of academic professionalism most intimately interface with those of commercial publishing: Who will buy the specialty journals, and how available will they be to potential readers? While the neglect of librarians may be partly explained by their lack of involvement in producing the scholarship of science, most of the neglect is probably traceable to a general failure to take seriously the *scale* of the scientific enterprise as a significant social psychological variable (Fuller, 1994). Consequently, it is still common to find even STS practitioners writing as if a scientific author communicates with a readership, if not directly, then only with the assistance (or impediment!) of an editor. It is too often forgotten that books and journals first need to be found on the library shelves.

4. *The ecology of the reading room*: The literature on the reception and spread of scientific ideas has markedly grown and improved with the emergence of the historical sociology of science (Shapin, 1982). Nevertheless, the presumptive psychology of readers leaves much to be desired. There remain two unresolved issues of major import: (1) How much of an author does one need to understand in order to put that work to use in one's own research? (2) Is the goal of scholarly reading really something like "persuasion" and "information," or is it something more self-serving and strategic? Answers to these questions will no doubt force a new conception of the sense in which scientists can be said to contribute to a cumulative body of knowledge (cf. Kaufer & Carley, 1993).

THE CONSTRUCTIVIST CHALLENGE TO EXPERIMENTAL SOCIAL EPISTEMOLOGY

Constructivists who otherwise would be inclined to support social epistemology are mystifed by its predilection for the experimental method, given that experimentation has been subject to more critical scrutiny by constructivists in both sociology and psychology than any other mode of inquiry (cf. Collins, 1985; Gergen, 1985). The social epistemologist's basic response is to say that the critics are simply not drawing sufficiently constructivist conclusions from their own findings, perhaps because they still think—in neo-Kantian fashion—that human beings cannot be studied by the methods used to study nonhuman beings.

Suspicions about a "human essence" are aroused whenever it is hinted that there are "natural" and "artificial" ways of studying humans. For example, when constructivists (e.g., Danziger, 1990) show that experiments embody certain power relations between experimenters and subjects, they often suggest that something essential about the subjects is suppressed that could be revealed in more "natural" settings. While the social epistemologist admits that experiments typically highlight certain behaviors at the expense of others, and that this trade-off is properly seen as having a political character, he or she denies that any of this is unique to experimentation as a methodology. After all, constructivist historians and ethnographers of science have yet to co-author their works with the people whose voices they have allegedly recovered!

The important question to ask here is *which* politics are appropriate to inquiry, and whether the epistemic virtues of the experimental method can be preserved in a less repressive political environment, say, one in which subjects can hold the experimenter accountable for the interpretation that he or she wishes to foist upon their behavior in the laboratory (cf. Fuller, 1992c). In this regard, the social epistemologist is very sympathetic to Donald Campbell's (1988, chap. 11) "experimenting society" thesis, which argues that it is in the experimenter's own *cognitive* interest to empower subjects to respond openly and critically to the experimenter's hypothesized account (in the case of social science) or proposed treatment (in the case of social technology). While such empowerment entails some relaxation of laboratory protocols, it nevertheless retains the idea that one can tell whether or to what extent a target standard has been achieved after an experiment has been performed, and, if not, one can open debate on whether the experimenter or the subjects need to adjust their behavior accordingly.

But now comes the deep objection to any experimental social epistemology, one that arises from both constructivist and historicist scruples. Campbell's experimenting society thesis sounds great when the "subjects" in question are, say, people living in poverty whom a sociologist is trying to understand or people afflicted with a disease who have a chance of being cured by a new drug. However, the thesis becomes less credible when the subjects are fellow knowledge producers who—in the case of natural scientists—are widely regarded as being much better at their jobs than the experimental social scientist is at his or hers.

The sociologist Stephen Turner (1993) observes that experimental psychology has been historically successful in areas where it has provided more rigorous accounts of phenomena that already appear in people's folk psychologies. However, the social psychology of science required by social epistemology (articulated in Shadish & Fuller, 1993) would not seem to offer the prospect of many such areas. Creativity may be one, Turner admits, since that is something that scientists already psychologize about (cf. Root-Bernstein, 1991). However, the concepts that seem to be central to a specifically *social* psychology of science—such as group decision making, consensus formation, and knowledge transmission—do not fit the bill so neatly, especially if social psychological concepts are used to explain things that scientists think are caused by the nonhuman stuff they interact with (i.e., "external reality"). Thus, the performance of experiments on student subjects working on tasks that are, only in the loosest sense, "analogues" to scientific ones would seem merely to beg the question that Turner wishes to raise. Just because the student subjects work on tasks that resemble scientific ones in certain specifiable respects, it hardly follows that scientists would accept the results of such experiments as telling them anything interesting about how their own psychologies work. Moreover, the psychologist who conducts these experiments bears the additional burden of having to explain to scientists why their folk psychological accounts won't explain their behavior just as well as the psychologist's appeal to social psychological concepts.

In effect, Turner is offering a Hobson's choice to experimental psychologists working on behalf of social epistemology:

> **either** the psychologist is going to have to explain the discrepancy with the scientist's account as well as why his or her account of the scientist's psychology is better than the scientist's own;
> **or** the psychologist is simply going to have to admit that he or she really wants the scientists to be doing something other than what they have been doing, which then leaves the psychologist with the even more daunting assignment of explaining why the scientists should listen to such advice.

Given these equally unappetizing alternatives, Turner advises that social epistemology scale down its ambitions.

In response, I grant Turner that a developed experimental social epistemology could turn the explanation of scientists' behavior into a site of contested authority. After all, the methods of science, *especially* experimentation, carry an authority that is independent of the people who practice those methods. And so, while people are fascinated by accounts of scientific genius, it is the appeal to universal method that ultimately enables a democratic society to put its faith in science (cf. Porter, 1992). One doesn't need to be an Einstein to get results by something called "the scientific method," and one can even contest Einstein from time to time by appealing to such a method. And if scientists complain too much that the social psychologist's laboratory does not capture the nuances of their work habitats, then the social epistemologist can rightfully ask the scientists what makes them think that, given such nuances, their work can have any currency outside their work sites.

The legacy of Michael Polanyi (1957) notwithstanding, science cannot be *both* personal *and* universal knowledge. The more that scientists appeal to the image of a personalized craft in the hope of escaping experimental scrutiny, the more they look like just another special interest group with restricted entry requirements, ones worthy of suspicion in a democratic society. But the more that scientists appeal to a scientific method the efficacy of which transcends the lab in which the scientist happened to train, the more they open themselves to the kind of abstraction and generalizability afforded by analogue laboratory experiments and, for that matter, computer simulations.

In short, what Turner presents as a liability is, in fact, a great virtue of experimentally studying knowledge production, namely, it challenges scientists to live up to their own rhetoric in a way that historical or ethnographic studies of science do not. However, assuming that the social epistemologist wants to go beyond mere deconstruction when she puts scientific rhetoric to the experimental test, the challenge remains of how to translate whatever changes can be made to scientific practices in laboratory settings into something that scientists will come to recognize as improvements in the scientific workplace, and hence something that they would want to adopt in their own practices. With a nod to Foucault, the ultimate question facing the social epistemologist, then, is not the manufacture of knowledge inside the lab, but the manufacture of desire outside.

REFERENCES

Barnes, B., & Bloor, D. (1982). Relativism, rationalism, and the sociology of knowledge. In M. Hollis and S. Lukes (Eds.), *Rationality and relativism.* Cambridge MA: MIT Press.

Bartley, W. (1974). Theory of language and philosophy of science as instruments of educational reform. In R. Cohen and M. Wartofsky (Eds.), *Boston studies in the philosophy of science XIV* (pp. 307–337). Dordrecht: D. Reidel.

Bell, D. (1986). The limits of the social sciences. In K. Deutsch, A. Markovits, & J. Platt (Eds.), *Advances in the social sciences, 1900–1980* (pp. 313–324). Lanham, MD: University Press of America.

Berkowitz, L., & Donnerstein, E. (1982). Why external validity is more than skin deep. *American Psychologist, 37,* 245–257.

Bloor, D. (1983). *Wittgenstein and the social theory of knowledge.* Oxford: Blackwell.

Bloor, D. (1991/1976). *Knowledge and social imagery* (2nd ed.). Chicago: University of Chicago Press.

Boehme, G. (1977). Cognitive norms, knowledge interests, and the constitution of the scientific object. In E. Mendelsohn et al. (Eds.), *The social production of scientific knowledge.* Dordrecht: D. Reidel.

Brannigan, A. (1981). *The social basis of scientific discoveries.* Cambridge: Cambridge University Press.

Brown, J. R., (Ed.). (1984). *The rationality debates: The sociological turn.* Dordrecht: D. Reidel.

Button, G. (Ed.). (1991). *Ethnomethodology and the human sciences.* Cambridge: Cambridge University Press.

Campbell, D. (1988). *Methodology and epistemology for social science.* Chicago: University of Chicago Press.

Canguilhem, G. (1978). *The normal and the pathological.* Dordrecht: D. Reidel.

Chubin, D., & Hackett, E. (1990). *Peerless science.* Albany: SUNY Press.

Cicchetti, D. (1991). The reliability of peer review for manuscript and grant submissions. *Behavior and Brain Sciences, 14,* 119–150.

Cohen, L. J. (1981). Can human irrationality be experimentally demonstrated? *Behavior and Brain Sciences, 4,* 317–370.

Collett, P. (Ed.). (1977). *Social rules and social behavior.* Totowa, NJ: Rowman & Littlefield.

Collins, H. (1985). *Changing order.* Sage: London.

Collins, R. (1989). Toward a theory of intellectual change: The social causes of philosophies. *Science, Technology, and Human Values, 14,* 107–140.

Danziger, K. (1990). *Constructing the subject.* Cambridge: Cambridge University Press.

Davidson, D. (1986). A nice derangement of epitaphs. In E. LePore (Ed.), *Truth and interpretation* (pp. 442–470). Oxford: Blackwell.

Deutsch, K. (1986). Substantial advances: Real but elusive. In K. Deutsch, A. Markovits, & J. Platt (Eds.), *Advances in the social sciences, 1900–1980* (pp. 361–372). Lanham, MD: University Press of America.

Deutsch, K., Markovits, A., & Platt, J. (Eds.). (1986). *Advances in the social sciences, 1900–1980.* Lanham, MD: University Press of America.

Dineen, F. (1967). *An introduction to general linguistics.* New York: Holt, Rinehart & Winston.

Elster, J. (1979). *Logic and society.* Chichester, UK: John Wiley & Sons.

Faust, D. (1985). *The limits of scientific reasoning.* Minneapolis: University of Minnesota Press.

Fine, A. (1986). Unnatural attitudes: Realist and instrumentalist attachments to science. *Mind, 95,* 149–179.

Foucault, M. (1970). *The order of things.* New York: Random House.

Fuller, S. (1985). *Bounded rationality in law and science.* Doctoral dissertation, University of Pittsburgh.

Fuller, S. (1988). *Social epistemology.* Bloomington, IN: Indiana University Press.

Fuller, S. (1991). Studying the proprietary grounds of knowledge. *Journal of Social Behavior and Personality, 6*(6), 105–128.

Fuller, S. (1992a). Epistemology radically naturalized. In R. Giere, (Ed.), *Cognitive models of science* (pp. 427–463). Minneapolis: University of Minnesota Press.

Fuller, S. (1992b). Knowledge as product and property. In N. Stehr and R. Ericson (Eds.), *The culture and power of knowledge* (pp. 157–190). Berlin: Walter de Gruyter.

Fuller, S. (1992c). Social epistemology and the research agenda of science studies. In A. Pickering (Ed.), *Science as practice and culture* (pp. 157–190). Chicago: University of Chicago Press.

Fuller, S. (1993a/1989). *Philosophy of science and its discontents* (2nd ed.). New York: Guilford Press.

Fuller, S. (1993b). *Philosophy, rhetoric and the end of knowledge: The coming of science & technology studies.* Madison: University of Wisconsin Press.

Fuller, S. (1994). The sphere of critical thinking in the post-epistemic world. *Informal Logic, 16,* 39–54.

Geertz, C. (1983). *The interpretation of cultures.* New York: Harper & Row.

Gergen, K. (1985). *Towards a transformation of social knowledge.* Berlin: Springer-Verlag.

Glymour, C. (1987). Android epistemology and the frame problem. In Z. Pylyshyn (Ed.), *The robot's dilemma.* Norwood, NJ: Ablex Press.

Goldman, A. (1991). *Liaisons.* Cambridge, MA: MIT Press.

Gorman, M. (1992). Simulating social epistemology: Experimental and computational approaches. In R. Giere (Ed.), *Cognitive models of science* (pp. 400–426). Minneapolis: University of Minnesota Press.

Hammond, K., & Arkes, H. (Eds.). (1986). *Judgement and decision making.* Cambridge: Cambridge University Press.

Hawley, A. (1950). *Human ecology.* New York: Ronald Press.

Janik, A., & Toulmin, S. (1973). *Wittgenstein's Vienna.* New York: Simon & Schuster.

Kaufer, D., & Carley, K. (1993). *Communication at a distance: The influence of print on sociocultural organization and change.* Hillsdale, NJ: Lawrence Erlbaum.

Kitcher, P. (1993). *The advancement of science.* Oxford: Oxford University Press.

Knorr-Cetina, K. (1981). *The manufacture of knowledge.* Oxford: Pergamon.

Kornblith, H. (Ed.). (1985). *Naturalizing epistemology.* Cambridge, MA: MIT Press.

Kuhn, T. (1970). *The structure of scientific revolutions* (2nd ed.). Chicago: University of Chicago Press.

Latour, B. (1987). *Science in action.* Milton Keynes, UK: Open University Press.

Latour, B., & Woolgar, S. (1986/1979). *Laboratory life* (2nd ed.). Princeton: Princeton University Press.

Mannheim, K. (1936/1929). *Ideology and utopia.* London: Routledge & Kegan Paul.

Meja, V., & Stehr, N. (Eds.). (1990). *Knowledge and politics.* London: Routledge.

Nisbett, R., & Ross, L. (1980). *Human inference: Strategies and shortcomings of human judgment.* Englewood Cliffs, NJ: Prentice-Hall.

Paulus, P. (Ed.). (1989/1980). *Psychology of group influence* (2nd ed.). Hillsdale, NJ: Lawrence Erlbaum.

Pickering, A. (Ed.). (1992). *Science as practice and culture.* Chicago: University of Chicago Press.

Polanyi, M. (1957). *Personal knowledge.* Chicago: University of Chicago Press.

Pollock, J. (1986). *Contemporary theories of knowledge.* Totowa, NJ: Rowman and Allenheld.

Popper, K. (1963). *Conjectures and refutations.* New York: Harper & Row.

Porter, T. (1992). Objectivity as standardization. *Annals of Scholarship, 9,* 19–60.

Quine, W. (1985/1969). Epistemology naturalized. In H. Kornblith (Ed.), *Naturalizing epistemology.* Cambridge, MA: MIT Press.

Root-Bernstein, S. (1991). *Discovering.* Cambridge, MA: Harvard University Press.

Rouse, J. (1987). *Knowledge and power.* Ithaca, NY: Cornell University Press.

Schmitt, F. (Ed.). (1987). Special issue on social epistemology. *Synthese, 73,* 1–204.

Shadish, W., & Fuller, S. (Eds.). (1993). *Social psychology of science.* New York: Guilford Press.

Shapin, S. (1982). The history of science and its sociological reconstructions. *Isis, 20,* 157–219.

Sztompka, P. (1991). Conceptual frameworks in comparative inquiry. In M. Albrow & E. King (Eds.), *Globalization, knowledge, and society.* London: Sage.

Toulmin, S. (1972). *Human understanding.* Princeton: Princeton University Press.

Turner, S. (1993). Making scientific knowledge a social psychological problem. In W. Shadish & S. Fuller (Eds.), *Social psychology of science* (pp. 345–351). New York: Guilford Press.

White, H. (1981). Where do markets come from? *American Journal of Sociology, 87,* 517–547.

Winch, P. (1958). *The idea of a social science.* London: Routledge & Kegan Paul.

Wrong, D. (1961). The oversocialized conception of man. *American Sociological Review, 26,* 184–193.

CHAPTER 4

PSYCHOLOGY OF SCIENCE

Michael E. Gorman

Psychology of science is an excellent area in which to explore the uneasy relationship between psychologists and philosophers. There have been a number of good, comprehensive treatments related to this issue in recent years. The "Bowling Green group," Tweney, Doherty and Mynatt (1981), edited *On Scientific Thinking*, which includes excerpts from scientists, philosophers, and psychologists and commentary by the editors. The "Memphis State group," Gholson, Shadish, Neimeyer and Houts (1989), edited *Psychology of Science: Contributions to Metascience*; as the emphasis on metascience in the title suggests, many of its chapters are devoted to the possible connections between psychology and philosophy of science. While the Bowling Green volume includes excerpts from previously published "classics," the Memphis volume contains original chapters by prominent current contributors to psychology of science, including the editors themselves.

The Memphis volume was based on a conference. Four other volumes have also emerged from conferences; each focuses on an aspect of psychology of science. Two are explicitly concerned with what Steve Fuller (1987) has called social epistemology. *The Cognitive Turn: Sociological and Psychological Perspectives on Science* (Fuller, Demey, Shinn, & Woolgar, 1989) emerged from a conference held in Boulder, Colorado, which focused particularly on the relationship between cognitive and sociological perspectives; chapters include many authors not represented in the Memphis volume. *Social Psychology of Science* (Shadish and Fuller, 1994) contains papers from a second Memphis conference and includes a number of prominent social psychologists among its authors.

Two recent edited books discuss psychology and philosophy from a cognitive perspective. The most recent volume in the Minnesota Studies in Philosophy of Science is *Cognitive Models of Science* (1992) edited by Ron Giere. Chapter authors include prominent psychologists and philosophers; again, there is some overlap in authorship with previous volumes, but all chapters are original and

The author wishes to thank Hilary Farris and David Klahr for their comments on an earlier draft.

many authors are not represented in the other edited books. One particular cognitive approach that receives emphasis in this volume is the focus of a separate book edited by Shrager & Langley (1990): *Computational Models of Scientific Discovery and Theory Formation.* Virtually every one of the computational simulations described in the chapters is based on an explicit or implicit philosophy of science and several chapters discuss the relationship between computational approaches and other psychological methods like experiments. Again, there are quite a few authors in this volume who do not appear in the other ones.

Other treatments are in the works, including a volume edited by David Gooding tentatively entitled *Sensation and Cognition,* which focuses on the role of hands-on techniques in shaping epistemology. To attempt to review anything approximating the content of all these volumes in a brief chapter would be hopeless. I content myself with recommending at the outset that any reader truly interested in psychology of science look carefully at these edited volumes; if nothing else, they will provide a valuable corrective for any biases presented in this chapter.

What I will do here is present a review and synthesis of much of the recent work on psychology of science. Consistent with what I assume are the interests of most philosophers, I will focus on scientific thinking. There is an important tradition of research into the way in which the personalities and motivations of scientists affect their careers and the progress of science; interested philosophers would do well to review the thorough treatments by Simonton (1988) and Feist (1991). Unfortunately, space does not permit a discussion here.

POPPER'S INFLUENCE ON PSYCHOLOGY OF SCIENCE

Let us begin our consideration of the relationship between psychology and philosophy of science by reviewing one of the oldest empirical research programs that combines these areas. Popper's idea that science progresses by falsification inspired three decades of experimental research. Ironically, Popper himself saw only a limited role for psychology. According to Barker (1989), Popper would "reject the use of psychology in any philosophically interesting context where questions about science are to be raised" and furthermore would "deny the appli-

cability of empirical methods to the study of science" (p. 89).

Despite Popper's views, Wason (1960) thought falsification raised questions that should be investigated empirically. He developed the "2-46 task," in which a subject was given the number triple '2,4,6' and told to discover a rule that determined which triples were correct or incorrect. Subjects conducted experiments by proposing triples; the experimenter told them whether each fit the rule.

Wason's (1960) original idea was to determine whether subjects would falsify their hypotheses about the rule. Subjects typically started with hypotheses like 'even numbers in order' and failed to propose triples that ought to be wrong if their hypotheses were right. (The actual rule was 'numbers ascend in order of magnitude'). Wason attributed this to a 'verification bias', and a long literature on this problem sprang up (see Klayman & Ha, 1987, for a good review).

Wason was not particularly interested in simulating scientific reasoning, but a group at Bowling Green took his task in that direction (see Tweney et al., 1980). They developed another, more sophisticated simulation in which subjects fired particles at shapes on a computer in an effort to discover the laws governing their interaction with these shapes (see Mynatt et al., 1977, 1978). To both of these tasks, the "Bowling Green group" added instructions to disconfirm, in an effort to combat the apparent bias that Wason had discovered. These instructions failed to improve performance, even when it was clear subjects were trying to follow them. Furthermore, Mahoney and Kimper (1976) ran scientists on the 2-4-6 task and found that they falsified less than Protestant ministers!

Did these results pose a problem for Popper's normative prescriptions regarding the importance of falsification? He no doubt would argue that the psychological results were simply irrelevant: The fact that subjects and scientists could not be trained to falsify on tasks that simulate scientific reasoning does not mean that falsification is not the way in which science ought to progress.

But it seemed to me that if falsification did not improve performance on simple, artificial simulations of science—bereft of the many confounding variables present in actual practice—that it was unlikely that falsification would constitute the sort of strategy that should be taught to young scientists. After all, scientists like Medawar and Eccles took Popper seriously enough to follow his prescriptions. What if empirical research showed these prescriptions did not work?

So I conducted a program of research designed to determine under what circumstances science and engineering students could effectively employ instructions to falsify. I used the 2-4-6 task and an analogous problem called "New Eleusis," which was designed to model the "search for truth"; a detailed account of these experiments can be found in Gorman (1992b). My results supported generalizations made by Klayman & Ha (1987): Falsification was an effective strategy when the target rule was more general than the subjects' initial hypothesis.

There were some paradoxes, however. On a very general rule—"the three numbers must be different"—subjects trained to falsify did no better than a control group. They were clearly trying to obtain evidence that would test the generality of their hypotheses, but they did not know what sort of evidence they were seeking. Following Tweney et al. (1980), I changed the task from a search for a single rule that would determine which triples were right and wrong to a search for two rules, one of which was "the three numbers must be different" and the other, "two or more numbers must be the same." In other words, subjects were now searching for separate rules governing which triples were correct and which were incorrect. This manipulation altered the way in which subjects represented the task, and resulted in greatly improved performance as compared with giving them instructions to falsify.

So falsification depended at least in part on what Johnson-Laird (1988) has called a 'mental model' of the task. Subjects who imagined they were searching for two complementary rules automatically searched the boundaries of each; subjects who thought they were searching for a single rule often ended up finding no negative evidence and proposing that it must be 'any number' or 'any number except O'. The importance of mental representations in science leads us to consider the philosopher who focused on the kinds of exemplars that form the basis for a scientist's worldview or 'paradigm'.

KUHN: A DIFFERENT ROLE FOR PSYCHOLOGY OF SCIENCE?

Kuhn thought that Popper's philosophy did a good job of describing what happened in times of crisis; what Popper missed was the importance of what Kuhn called 'normal science', when a result that

appears to contradict a paradigm falsifies the scientist, not the theory. Kuhn clearly saw the relevance of psychology to understanding the conceptual changes that occurred in times of crisis and revolution. His paradigm shift involved a radical shift in how scientists represent their area of study. He depended on research in Gestalt psychology to explain this shift, but work on mental models like the study noted at the end of the last section holds more promise for understanding these conceptual changes.

Kuhn's work has inspired both computational simulations and experimental studies. Langley, Simon, Bradshaw, and Zytkow (1987) described a series of computer programs designed to rediscover revolutionary scientific ideas like Kepler's laws of planetary motions; they argued that a few very general heuristics would suffice to make these discoveries because in a period of crisis scientists have to discard their familiar expert representations (cf. Simon, Langley, & Bradshaw, 1981). Kepler, for example, had to abandon the idea that planetary orbits form perfect circles.

The most sophisticated of these discovery programs is one developed by Kulkarni and Simon (1988). They used the detailed work of Holmes, a historian of science, to reconstruct Krebs's path to the discovery of the ornithine cycle. Then they built a program called KEKADA which simulated that path, treating falsifications as surprises that ought to be pursued. The power of such simulations is that they allow us not only to model Krebs's actual path, but to explore alternate paths he might have taken.[1] These programs, like the 2-4-6 task, model situations where discovery does not depend on a mental model (cf. Johnson-Laird, 1988) or on hands-on skills like Krebs's ability to slice tissues in a particular way.

Recent computational work on conceptual change includes simulations of anomaly recognition and resolution. For example, Rajamoney (1990) has developed a program called COAST that uses anomalies to trigger and guide theory revision. O'Rorke, Morris, and Schulenberg (1990) model a theory-driven form of abduction that derives explanations for anomalies. Other examples can be found in the excellent volume edited by Shrager and Langley (1990). Unlike Langley et al., these authors do not claim that their programs 'discover'; instead, they simulate aspects of scientific thinking. Such programs can provide models for processes like anomaly resolution;

these models can in turn be studied experimentally and used to shed light on historical cases.

The Shrager and Langley volume also includes pieces by two philosophers. Lindley Darden (1990) showed how anomalies encountered by Morgan and others early in the history of genetics could be diagnosed and fixed by using a model she developed; this model, in turn, could be implemented on a computer. Instead of making discoveries on its own, such a program could be used as a kind of 'expert assistant' by scientists.

Paul Thagard (Thagard & Nowak, 1990) developed a connectionist network to model the resolution of the sorts of conflicts between theories that result in paradigm shifts: Examples include the oxygen/phlogiston controversy and the acceptance of continental drift in geology. For Thagard, the computer appears to be a tool for sharpening his own theory of scientific progress.

Conceptual Change in Child and Scientist

Another area of psychology of science that is at least partly inspired by Kuhn compares conceptual change in children and adults, substituting more sophisticated analyses for Kuhn's original equation of gestalt shifts and paradigm shifts. Chi (1992) used a Kuhnian framework to review the literature on conceptual changes in children and adults. She argues that radical conceptual change often occurs before anomaly recognition, the point at which most of the computational programs begin. In other words, discovering that there is a problem or an inconsistency that cannot be assimilated into existing theory is itself a creative act that requires explanation. Her own analysis suggests that recognition and resolution of such anomalies requires an ontological shift to a new system of categories incommensurable with the previous one.

Kuhn's idea that the views of scientists who had gone through a paradigm shift were incommensurable with the views of those who had not is mirrored by the argument that children's thinking is fundamentally different from that of adults. Carey (1992) compared the problems children ages 3 to 5 have differentiating weight and density with the problem scientists before Black had differentiating heat and temperature. According to Carey, in both cases, the view before differentiation is incommensurable with the view afterward. In Chi's terms, an ontological shift has occurred. Neither Carey nor

Chi can completely account for the circumstances that lead to these shifts; both suggest the science classroom is the place to look for answers, where one can try a variety of interventions to produce such changes. For example, one can try to make students see that aspects of their view of the physical world embody ontological assumptions, analogous to the 'perfect circle dogma' that plagued cosmology before Kepler. A perfectly circular orbit was not seen as an assumption that could be changed; like all deep assumptions, it was seen as a fact.

Brewer and Samarapungavan (1991) "conclude that the child can be thought of as a novice scientist, who adopts a rational approach to dealing with the physical world, but lacks the knowledge of the physical world and experimental methodology accumulated by the institution of science" (p. 210). Their point is that the apparent differences in thinking between children and adults is really due to differences in knowledge, not reasoning strategies. For example, they studied second-graders and showed that those who had a flat-earth mental model could incorporate disconfirmatory information consistent with a Copernican view by transforming their model into a hollow sphere. They used this new mental model to solve a range of problems about the day/night cycle and the motion of individuals and objects across the earth's surface (see Vosniadou & Brewer, in press). These authors do not deal explicitly with the issue of incommensurability, but they do argue that before children can adopt the adult, spherical mental model of the earth, they have to change presuppositions like 'the ground around me is flat, so the earth must be flat'. Again, here is a set of assumptions that seem like unquestionable facts. Scientists involved in Kuhnian revolution learn to question such entrenched assumptions.

Brewer & Chinn (1991) have also explored the entrenched beliefs of adults by giving them brief readings on quantum theory or special relativity and asking them a series of follow-up questions. Both quantum theory and relativity make predictions that conflict with commonsense beliefs about space and time and cause and effect. Some subjects simply rejected the new information, resembling those scientists who cling to the old paradigm. Other subjects showed at least partial assimilation of the new material: They were able to give an answer that corresponded to what they had read, but they "sure didn't believe it" (p. 70).[2] Another move was to interpret the answer in terms of exist-ing beliefs, for example, by treating relativistic phenomena as optical illusions.

Lakatos (1978) would presumably argue that the 'entrenched beliefs' were analogous to the 'meta-physical hard core' of a research program, which is not subject to modification. If so, then one would predict that those subjects who gave the right answers for the wrong reasons might abandon their entrenched beliefs only with the greatest difficulty, and then only because they were not actually bound to a research program with all the commitment of active scientists who have staked their careers on its success.

However, it is also possible that those who gave correct answers are taking the first steps toward the kind of cognitive restructuring that Kuhn referred to as a 'paradigm shift'. Instead of happening in a sudden Gestalt flash, this research suggests such a shift is a process that could be studied. Future research should focus on what happens to such beliefs when they are contracted by more than a brief passage in a text.

Klahr, Fay, and Dunbar (1993) argue that studies like Vosniadou and Brewer's and Brewer and Chinn's do not give children or adults the opportu-nity to design new experiments and formulate and evaluate hypotheses, whereas experiments with simulations like the 2-4-6 task do. In a study using a task that permitted children and adults to generate experiments and hypotheses, Klahr, Fay, and Dun-bar (1993) found that superior adult performance "appears to come from a set of domain-general skills that go beyond the logic of confirmation and disconfirmation and deal with the coordination of search in two spaces" (p. 141). If so, this study, along with the other developmental[3] and computa-tional research cited in this section, raises the ques-tion that is the focus of the next section.

IS FALSIFICATION FINISHED?

A provocative new volume containing Popper's (1992) best lectures and essays has just appeared, so it may be premature to declare the master's work out of date. But in his introduction to *Simulating Science*, Ryan D. Tweney made the provocative claim that this book might be "one of the last major works in the intellectual tradition that flows from the ideas of Karl Popper" (p. xiii). Indeed, accord-ing to Tweney, experimental research showed that "falsification must take its place as *one* strategy

among others, one that can sometimes entail its own biases" (p. xiii). Certainly his view is consis-tent with the work of Klayman and Ha and others noted above.

At the same time falsification has fallen out of favor with psychologists, it seems to have suffered a similar fate among philosophers. It is common to speak of science studies as being in a 'post-Kuh-nian' phase, with the work of sociologists like Pinch (1985) undermining the traditional role of falsification. Philosophers like Lakatos, Feyera-bend, and Laudan have moved the debate beyond Popper. Their work has influenced psychology of science as well; for example, Tukey (1986) called for psychologists to make more use of Lakatos's philosophy in interpreting their experimental find-ings.

As Tweney suggested, falsification remains very much alive as one heuristic among many—to be employed in certain situations. One of the recent alternatives is counterfactual reasoning. According to Farris and Revlin (1989), a successful strategy on the 2-4-6 task is to propose a 'counterfactual hypothesis', which is one inconsistent with any previous hypothesis for which confirmatory evi-dence has been obtained. For example, if one thinks the rule on the 2-4-6 task is 'even numbers', one might propose the opposite hypothesis, 'odd numbers', and find out whether that is true by pro-posing a triple consistent with it.

Say the subject tries '3, 5, 7'. He or she now has evidence that triples which contain all even num-bers can be correct, and triples which contain all odd numbers can be correct. 'All even numbers' has been falsified; a different hypothesis that includes odd numbers is required.

Farris and Revlin cite original experimental evi-dence to demonstrate that counterfactual reasoning is superior to the sort of disconfirmatory heuristic used by Gorman and others. First, we have to be clear about the difference. Tweney, Gorman, and others equated disconfirmation with proposing tri-ples at variance with one's hypothesis. Farris and Revlin look for evidence that some subjects articu-late counterfactual hypotheses and then propose triples consistent with these counterfactual hypoth-eses. This strategy resembles what subjects do in the DAX-MED version of the 2-4-6 task discussed earlier; instead of looking for evidence that might disconfirm one hypothesis, in the DAX-MED design, subjects looked for positive evidence for two complementary hypotheses.

Farris and Revlin argue that their results demonstrate counterfactual reasoning is more effective than a disconfirmatory strategy, given that no study has shown a positive effect for disconfirmatory instructions. But my own research demonstrated that disconfirmation was effective in certain situations—specifically, when the target rule was more general than subjects' initial hypotheses and subjects were given no feedback on announced guesses (see Gorman, 1992a).

In Farris & Revlin's study, when subjects finally made an announced guess about the rule, they were told whether that guess was right or wrong. If the guess was wrong, the subject was allowed to continue proposing triples and hypotheses. Wason (1960), Tweney et al. (1980), and other 2-4-6 experimenters did the same. In my 2-4-6 and Eleusis studies, if a subject announced a guess, she was told that the experimenter could give no feedback on that guess until after the experiment was over—she had to decide whether to continue or not.

My 'no feedback' design models a situation in which scientists cannot ask 'God' whether their hypotheses are right: They have to determine the truth or falsehood of theories without appealing to outside authority. Farris and Revlin's design resembles a situation in which one can ultimately appeal to an outside authority—perhaps a funding agency, or a journal. This example illustrates the power of simulations to model different situations. A reasoning strategy that is effective in one context may fail in another. The question remains, would a counterfactual strategy be more effective than disconfirmation when subjects were encouraged to continue testing after they had made a rule announcement? This is a matter that can only be settled by further research.

The work on counterfactual reasoning illustrates that falsification is not dead as a research topic; it has been transformed. Instead of talking about a general disconfirmatory strategy, research is now focused on specific strategies like counterfactual reasoning that accomplish some of the goals of falsification in specific contexts. Much the same thing has happened to falsification in philosophy of science. As Kuhn said, falsification resembles what happens in periods of crisis and revolution, but not during periods of normal science.

Farris and Revlin's work also illustrates the way in which research into falsification has been transformed into a consideration of what part of a problem space subjects are searching in an effort to probe the limits of their hypotheses. This is a type of analysis that goes back to the classic work of Bruner, Goodnow, and Austin (1956) and is also reflected in the more recent work of Klayman and Ha (1987). Farris and Revlin's counterfactual heuristic directs subjects to search a space that includes instances inconsistent with their current hypothesis. This is a particularly useful strategy when the target rule incorporates evidence that lies beyond the scope of the current hypothesis. A rough analogy may be the wave–particle duality: Light can be made to behave like a particle or a wave. One is driven to find a more general rule that can explain this apparent paradox.

But the counterfactual strategy can also potentially lead to the discovery of other relationships between hypothesis and target rule. What if the two overlap? Consider our example again. A subject thinks the rule is 'even numbers', proposes 'odd numbers' as a counterfactual, discovers that odd-numbered triples are always wrong, and concludes the rule is 'all evens'. But suppose the rule were 'all evens or one odd'? Farris and Revlin direct subjects to use their counterfactual strategy iteratively, which means that the subject above should continue to search the space of counterfactual instances.

Perhaps the best work on search spaces in scientific reasoning has been conducted by Klahr, Dunbar, Shrager, and others at Carnegie-Mellon (cf. Shrager, 1990; Klahr & Dunbar, 1988; Klahr, Dunbar, & Fay, 1990). They asked subjects to learn how a device called a "Big Trak" functions by conducting experiments. Subjects had to generate and test hypotheses using strategies like confirmation and disconfirmation. The most successful subjects reacted to falsificatory evidence by developing new hypotheses that represented a 'shift in frame', which in turn suggested new areas of the problem space to search for evidence.

For example, in Klahr and Dunbar's study, subjects had to discover the function of an 'RPT' key. Most began with the idea that an instruction like RPT 4 meant 'repeat whatever program had been typed in four times' or 'repeat the last step in the program four times'. Typically, they began with confirmatory results and quickly obtained disconfirmatory information. In order to discover the rule, subjects had to change their representation of the role of the repeat key: It selected the step to be repeated, so that 'RPT 4' meant 'repeat step 4'. Subjects had to realize that the RPT key might serve as a *selector*, indicating which line was to be repeated, instead of a *counter*, indicating the number of times something was to be repeated. The shift from a counter to a selector frame directed subjects to a different part of the problem space to search for confirmations and disconfirmations. Klahr and Dunbar referred to this as switching between hypothesis and experimental spaces: A change in the type of hypothesis one is pursuing directs one to look for new kinds of evidence.

This is akin to how the DAX-MED version transforms the 2-4-6 task: Instead of looking for one rule with exceptions, subjects shift to hypotheses consisting of two mutually exclusive rules, and this also changes the type of experiments they conduct and how they interpret the evidence. Similarly, the counterfactual strategy involves generating two hypotheses that cover different parts of the problem space and then—depending on the result—iterating through the generation–experimentation cycle again, coordinating hypothesis and experimental searches until the rule is found.[4]

In a more recent study using a version of their RPT task, Klahr, Fay, and Dunbar (1993) established that third and to a lesser extent sixth graders had trouble with evidence that disconfirmed counter hypothesis, in part because they could not switch to a selector hypothesis. Klahr, Fay, and Dunbar (1993) interpret this as a failure to coordinate searches in hypothesis and experiment spaces, but their results also appear to support the idea that younger children had trouble processing falsifications: When children were trying to demonstrate that a counter hypothesis would work, "inconsistencies were interpreted not as disconfirmations, but rather as either errors or temporary failures to demonstrate the desired effect" (p. 140).

In conclusion, research on falsification continues in different forms. Nowadays, one rarely hears the questions that motivated the research, by Wason, Tweney, and others: "Can subjects falsify? If so, is it an effective strategy?" Instead, one hears discussion of strategies that involve shifts in the way subjects represent hypothesis and experiment spaces—shifts that enable them to attain the goals of falsification in specific situations.

Popper's criterion for a scientific theory was "criticizability by means of empirical tests or empirical refutation" (1992, p. 54). Therefore, falsification is not dead as a research program. Counterfactual reasoning, dual space searches, and a plethora of other strategies can be used to criticize

scientific theories—which of these heuristics is most effective depends on the nature of the task and the subjects' prior knowledge.[5]

What this research also shows is the intimate relationship between discovery and justification. Falsifications in Klahr, Fay, and Dunbar's studies were dismissed as errors unless subjects were able to come up with an alternate representation of the role of the RPT key. This resembles a Kuhnian model more than a Popperian: One's current hypothesis will not be abandoned until one can conceive of an alternative, a 'new paradigm' or set of exemplars. As Kulkarni and Simon's program shows, falsifications or surprises can motivate new discoveries. Psychology of science is no longer dominated by Popper; current work explicitly addresses concerns of other philosophers like Lakatos and Laudan (see Gorman, 1992a, for a discussion and examples).

INCREASING ECOLOGICAL VALIDITY IN EXPERIMENTAL SIMULATIONS

Philosophers should attend closely to this research because it shows how experiments can be used to translate normative prescriptions into specific strategies in a variety of contexts (cf. Fuller, 1989). This raises the question of the goals of a research program. Is one's research aimed primarily at determining whether a hypothesis about scientific conduct is correct or not, or is one more concerned with coming up with results that will generalize to actual scientific practice?[6] "Ecological validity" is the term used to describe how well experiments generalize to real situations and practices. Naturally, a study aimed primarily at testing a hypothesis will also be at least somewhat relevant to practice and vice-versa, but the two purposes can lead to very different sorts of studies.

For example, consider the experiments using Wason's 2-4-6 task mentioned above. This task is clearly not an ecologically valid representation of actual scientific activity. But it does attempt to simulate an important aspect of scientific reasoning that is relevant to a theoretical issue: whether falsification is an effective heuristic under *ideal, highly artificial circumstances*. As Berkowitz and Donnerstein (1982) have argued, artificiality is the strength of experiments; they allow one to abstract certain features of the "real world" and test the effect of variables under controlled conditions that eliminate much of the noise and confusion that exists in natural settings.

So, the 2-4-6 and other analogous tasks can tell us whether falsification is effective under ideal circumstances—on a relatively simple task whose solution does not depend on prior knowledge or sophisticated equipment, where results are easily obtained and always accurate. Naturally, one cannot generalize from such a situation to scientific practice without conducting additional research in more realistic contexts.

Laudan, Laudan, and Donovan (1992) agree that philosophical theories of scientific change should be subjected to empirical test, but disagree with the method I am advocating: "We deliberately chose a historical case-study (or more accurately a multi-case study) method rather than experiments... Given our lack of control over the events that constitute scientific change and the impossibility of creating a situation in which we could manipulate such events, an experimental study of scientific change was out of the question" (p. 11). I hope I have demonstrated that experiments can allow us to manipulate factors that affect scientific change. However, Laudan, Laudan, and Donovan would presumably object that the sorts of tasks and situations described above are simply too unrealistic for their purposes. But experiments can be modified to incorporate more ecologically valid features. What follows is a discussion of some ways in which this has been done in the psychology of science.

Adding Features of Science to Laboratory Tasks

The classic artificial universe research by Mynatt, Doherty, and Tweney (1977, 1978) was motivated, in part, by the desire to use a task that bore a stronger resemblance to science than problems like the 2-4-6 task. On their most complex computerized universe, in which subjects had to discover the laws governing the deflection of particles, these authors discovered that confirmation was most useful early in the inference process, and disconfirmation later. Tweney (1985) was able to extend these results to Michael Faraday.

Kevin Dunbar (1989) has created a computerized molecular genetics laboratory in which subjects were posed a problem similar to the one for which Monod and Jacob won the Nobel Prize in 1961. Dunbar did not intend to have subjects simulate the actual discovery path followed by Monod and Jacob; instead, he wanted "to use a task that involves some real scientific concepts and experimentation to address the cognitive components of the scientific discovery process" (Dunbar, 1989, p. 427).

Subjects were given elementary training in concepts of molecular genetics, using an interactive environment on a Macintosh computer. Then they were allowed to perform experiments with three controller and three enzyme-producing genes; they could vary the amount of nutrient, remove genes, and measure the enzyme output. The mechanism the subjects had to discover was inhibition, whereas the mechanism they had learned in training was activation.

Note that despite Dunbar's protestations to the contrary—"rather than inventing an arbitrary task that embodies certain aspects of science it is possible to give subjects a real scientific task to work with" (p. 427)—this task bears more resemblance to other artificial universes than it does to actual scientific problems. Subjects are given instructions that explain their little universe; these instructions, like the starting triple 2-4-6, bias them toward a hypothesis that is different from the one they are trying to find, and they are able to do a wide variety of mini-experiments to discover the rule—which, although it represents an actual scientific relationship, is as arbitrary to them as the numerical formulas discovered by subjects in the 2-4-6 task. There are none of the potential sources of error that occur in actual genetics experiments and no new techniques to be mastered.

All of which is to say that this simulation is a valuable complement to the reasoning experiments discussed earlier. Indeed, Dunbar relates his findings to the literature on disconfirmation. In this task, all subjects eventually disconfirmed their initial hypotheses about the role of the activator gene—no matter what genes were present or absent, there was always an output. What is interesting is what they did next: 6 groups reinterpreted activation to mean a search for the gene that facilitated enzyme production, 7 searched diligently for an activator gene and eventually gave up, and 7 set the goal of explaining their surprising results. Of the 7 groups in this category 5 actually found the inhibitor gene. Note that Dunbar's results support the thesis that successful disconfirmation depends on how subjects or scientists represent the task.

Using Scientists as Subjects

Theoretically, scientists could be used as subjects on any of the laboratory tasks used above, but in practice this rarely occurs (see Mahoney & Kimper, 1976, for an exception). Typically, scientists are used as subjects in studies of expert reasoning involving domain-specific problems that resemble those posed in textbooks. For example, Larkin (1983) found that experts represent problems in different ways than novices; the latter try to use weak or general heuristics to explore solutions, whereas the former try to re-represent a problem as an instance of a familiar class of problems that can be solved using appropriate equations. Interestingly, novices tend to try to apply equations early, whereas experts reason qualitatively until they arrive at a representation that suggests what set of equations to use.

Similarly, Clement (1991) has studied the way in which experts use informal, qualitative reasoning processes to solve problems like determining what happens when the width of the coils on a spring are doubled and the suspended weight is held constant. Experts in this situation often construct an analogous simpler case, e.g., imagining what happens if the coils are replaced by a U-shaped spring of the same length. Then the analogy has to be related to the case. Clement explains the subprocesses involved in analogical relations of this kind. Experts also use strategies like countefactual reasoning when pressed to justify their solutions more thoroughly.

These brief examples do not do justice to the long and interesting literature on expert and/or novice approaches to textbook problems. Results are applied to improving the way in which science is taught. The use of scientists and domain-specific problems makes these studies more ecologically valid than those using abstract tasks like the 2-4-6, save one feature: The abstract tasks permit us to study the processes by which new experiments are generated, whereas studies using textbook problems make subjects use qualitative reasoning independently of experimental manipulation. A logical follow-up would be to allow subjects to conduct—or at least propose—a variety of experiments in an effort to solve a complicated problem in a specific domain; one could then analyze their responses in terms of their reliance on strategies like counterfactual reasoning and dual-space search.

Dunbar (in press) has come close to realizing this goal by conducting a field study of four molecular biology laboratories. He collected data before, during, and after laboratory meetings and used protocol analysis to search for patterns.

In terms of falsification, he found that scientists quickly discarded hypotheses in the face of negative evidence. Individual scientists typically made small changes in features of their hypotheses, but in laboratory meetings, the group of scientists tended to consider alternate hypotheses. Indeed, Dunbar detected a 'falsification bias' among the senior scientists; they often discarded data that confirmed their hypothesis. Dunbar inferred that these senior scientists had frequently had the painful experience of being proved wrong, and therefore were more prone to adopt a critical stance toward their own work. This finding runs counter to Mitroff's (1974) observation that those scientists who were rated most successful by their colleagues stuck doggedly to their theories.

Dunbar listed three factors that were especially important in producing conceptual change:

1. Surprising findings, i.e., results that violated expectations. Often these were produced by the control conditions. Once again, serendipity favors the prepared mind; to design a good control condition, the scientist has had to consider alternate mechanisms that might produce a different result.
2. When other members of the research group challenged a scientist's interpretation of his or her data. This challenge was frequently accompanied by alternate explanations, including analogies. Research groups that included members with different but overlapping backgrounds were most likely to use analogies as an effective tool for conceptual change.
3. The scientist decides that these surprising findings are not due to error. "When the researcher believes that the findings are due to error, no amount of challenging, or suggestions of other explanations will result in conceptual change" (p. 14). This particular conclusion of Dunbar's is somewhat problematic in that he also argues that other members of a research group can refuse to accept that a scientist's inconsistent results are due to error and eventually force her/him to change her/his hypothesis.

Dunbar's goal is to shift iteratively between what he calls in vitro and in vivo studies, the former referring to experimental simulations and the latter to field studies. In the latter, it is hard to definitively settle issues like the role of error in conceptual change; the former allows us to study such issues carefully under controlled conditions, but does not guarantee that results will generalize to actual scientific practice. (We will have more to say about controlled simulations of scientific error in the next section.) The solution is to maintain a constant dialogue or dialectic between the two.

Adding Error

As Dunbar discovered, scientists are acutely aware of the possibility of error when they design and evaluate experiments, yet most of the simulations of scientific reasoning—whether experimental or computational—do not incorporate this important aspect of science. Apparent anomalies and falsifications are often the results of errors. To guard against this possibility, the 'methodological falsificationist' (Lakatos, 1978) advocates systematic replication. For example, Einstein's theory of special relativity was apparently falsified by the eminent physicist Kaufmann; Einstein himself remained undisturbed, and called for replication. Kaufmann's result was later found to be an error.

I conducted a series of studies to determine whether and under what circumstances the methodological falsificationist's advice worked (see Gorman, 1992a). To understand how error can be added to one of the problems that simulate scientific reasoning, let us once again use the 2-4-6 task as an example. In the usual version, every result is 100% reliable and unambiguous. In a possible-error version, I told subjects anywhere from 0 to 20% of their results might be erroneous, i.e., a triple that was classified as incorrect might be correct and vice-versa. Error would occur at random, as determined by a random number generator on a calculator.

Obviously, this simulates only one kind of error, labeled system-failure (SF) by Doherty & Tweney (1988) because this is the kind of error that occurs when a measuring device fails catastrophically, giving a result that is the opposite of the actual state of affairs. Doherty and Tweney contrast SF error with what they call measurement error, in which the device gives back results that vary from the true values by a small amount, usually distributed at random. Obviously, other types of error exist and should be simulated under controlled conditions.

To simplify our brief discussion of error, I will restrict myself to SF error and the 2-4-6 task.

(There is currently no way of simulating measurement error on the 2-4-6 task, but a wide range of other tasks can accommodate it.) Subjects working on the 2-4-6 task, given unlimited time and freedom to propose triples, used a strategy I called 'replication plus extension' to eliminate the possibility of SF error: They proposed triples that were similar to, but not exactly the same as, previous triples in an effort to replicate the current pattern and extend it slightly, e.g., following '1,2,3' by '4,5,6'. This looks much like the confirmatory strategy followed by some no-error subjects; the difference is now this strategy is used to eliminate error as well as corroborate one's hypothesis.

The methodological falsificationist said nothing about replication plus extension; logically speaking, this heuristic makes little sense, because if such a triple is wrong, one does not know whether to attribute the failure to the replication or the extension. But subjects used it robustly and well. Only when replication was made much more difficult and costly did this replication plus extension strategy interfere with disconfirmation; subjects end up adopting rules like 'numbers go up by ones' that were subsets of the actual rule.

Changing the rate of error from 0 to 20% greatly disrupted subjects' performance on even the simplest version of Wason's 2-4-6 task. The methodological falsificationist may be right in principle, but in practice, even on very simple artificial tasks, replication is not sufficient to isolate and eliminate errors. These studies raise more questions than answers, but that is the point—philosophers and psychologists can work together to sort out the effects of error and propose new strategies to cope with it.

Simulating Social Epistemology

Science is not simply a cognitive activity carried out by individuals in isolation. Dunbar (in press) documented the critical role of laboratory meetings in producing conceptual change. Proponents of the new sociology of scientific knowledge have done a particularly good job of emphasizing the way in which science emerges out of social interaction (e.g., Pinch, 1985; Latour, 1987). Therefore, another way to make experimental and computational studies of science more realistic is to simulate aspects of the social context in which science is embedded.

Robert Rosenwein and I (Gorman & Rosenwein, 1995; Rosenwein & Gorman, 1995) are currently outlining a program of research that could allow psychologists, philosophers, and others to simulate aspects of what Fuller (1987) has called 'social epistemology'. In the interests of simplicity, let us focus on an example. Funding agencies clearly play a major role in shaping scientific knowledge; sociological, historical, and other studies can shed light on this process.

But these methods can be complemented by simulation. Say one wants to study the differential effects of funding strategies, perhaps contrasting a peer review approach like that followed by a number of federal agencies to a "don't call us, we'll call you" approach favored by many private foundations. One can set up a complex simulation in which groups of subjects are working to solve a variety of problems that model aspects of scientific reasoning; in order to continue their work, subjects have to attract resources from funding sources. The peer review source could be open to all, whereas the private source could select a few research teams at random and pump resources into them. Would those teams supported by the private source marginalize other teams and eventually take over the peer review process? How would discoveries made by marginal teams fare?

Other issues obviously could be raised as well. The point is, experiments can be used to manipulate factors that might affect social epistemology, deliberately isolating variables like the influence of different types of funding sources. Results could be used to make normative or policy recommendations, but such recommendations would have to be checked carefully in even more ecologically valid settings. Simulation is a valuable complement to, but not a replacement for, studies of actual scientific practice.

COMBINING HISTORY AND COGNITIVE SCIENCE

Kuhn's revolutionary views also inspired the new sociology of scientific knowledge, which emphasizes field studies. Latour (1987), for example, argues that one should simply "follow scientists around," generating "thick descriptions" of their activities.[7] Popper (1992) has criticized this view, in part on the grounds that one always approaches a description from a perspective—there is no neutral "thick description."

A number of psychologists, historians, and philosophers have used cognitive science to provide frameworks for studying historical cases (see Tweney, 1989, for a discussion of the difference between a framework and a theory and Nersessian, 1993, for a good analysis of how cognitive science can be applied to history). Instead of thick descriptions, the results are analyses that resemble those done on the processes of experimental subjects, except that the historical cases are far richer and force expansions and alterations in the cognitive frameworks (see Gorman, 1992a, for a discussion).

Probably the most notable efforts to do cognitive studies of historical cases are Gruber and Barrett's (1974) work on Darwin, Tweney's (1985) and Gooding's (1990) work on Michael Faraday, Nersessian's (1993) work on James Clerk Maxwell, Carlson and Gorman's (1990) comparative studies of three telephone inventors, and Bradshaw's (1992) comparison of early airplane inventors. Space precludes a detailed description of all of these studies, but I will try to say a word or two about each, in hopes of enticing the reader to explore further.

Gruber originally expected to rely on the work of historians when he dove into the notebooks of Charles Darwin, but he found that his Piagetian framework enabled him to make original discoveries and see patterns that had eluded historians. In particular, he noticed that Darwin's apparently disparate activities were part of a "network of enterprises." Apparent "flashes of insights" usually have roots in earlier work that is part of this network.

Tweney used his own experimental work on confirmation and disconfirmation to frame and enrich his account of how Faraday used these strategies: Both Faraday and the experimental subjects preferred to confirm early in the inference process, and switch to disconfirmation only when they had well-corroborated hypotheses. But Faraday was not a perfect Popperian; when exploring the phenomenon of electromagnetic induction in 1831, he tended to abandon lines of inquiry that did not produce rapid confirmations. All of his later attempts to produce electricity from gravity were disconfirmed, but he felt this relationship might still be revealed by improved experimental techniques.

Tweney (1991) and Gooding (1990) constructed detailed problem–behavior graphs of Faraday's problem-solving processes. This is a method of analyzing protocols developed by Newell and Simon (1972). In the course of his research, Gooding has transformed the method into his own unique graphing system, which he thinks recaptures Faraday's experimental processes. In order to reconstruct these protocols, Gooding has had to replicate many of Faraday's experiments.

Nersessian has studied Maxwell's "method of physical analogy," using concepts from the cognitive literature, which includes detailed accounts of how material is transferred from an analogy to a target domain. Maxwell worked iteratively, transforming the analogy as he sought to fit it to his source; the cognitive literature has not dealt adequately with this kind of reiterative transformation. Therefore, Nersessian is working with the cognitive scientist James G. Greeno to clarify the process of analogical reasoning.

Similarly, the historian W. Bernard Carlson has collaborated with me in a comparative study of three telephone inventors: Alexander Graham Bell, Thomas Edison, and Elisha Gray. The goal of this project is to develop a set of concepts and tools that will allow for rigorous comparison of the cognitive styles of inventors and/or scientists. We have adopted a framework similar to the one outlined by Tweney (1989); like Gruber, we have found that this cognitive approach leads us to look at the historical data in a different way. For example, it is sometimes argued that Bell "stole" his idea for the telephone from Gray. But our work demonstrates that even though the two inventors produced devices that were physically similar at some stages of their invention processes, they had different mental models of how the devices functioned and pursued very different paths in developing them (see Gorman, Mehalik, Carlson, & Oblon, 1993; Gorman , 1995).

Gary Bradshaw has compared early airplane inventors, focusing more on differences in strategy than representation. He concludes that the Wright brothers succeeded because they searched in both design and function spaces, whereas other inventors searched only in design spaces. This dual-space search strategy is similar to the one advocated by Klahr and Dunbar (see above). The design space corresponds roughly to the experiment space; design parameters include the number, shape, and angle of wings; each of these parameters can produce a large number of variations. Therefore, to search the design space is inefficient. The function space resembles Klahr's hypothesis space, in that trying to maximize a particular function like lift directs one to consider certain designs,

just as a change in hypothesis directs one to do different experiments.

All these studies point to the way in which cognitive psychology of science can complement historical and philosophical studies, alerting scholars to look for relationships and patterns to which they would not ordinarily have been sensitive. Particularly noteworthy are the collaborations between disciplines: Gooding (philosopher) with Tweney (psychologist), Nersessian (philosopher) with Greeno (cognitive scientist), and Carlson (historian) with Gorman (psychologist).

IS PSYCHOLOGY OF SCIENCE A MARGINAL ENTERPRISE?

While psychology of science clearly can contribute to a multidisciplinary approach to science studies, it may be a marginal enterprise within psychology. At a recent symposium on Psychology of Science at the American Psychological Association's annual meeting in Washington, D.C. (August, 1992) a number of us discussed why psychology of science so often appears to be an avocation for psychologists—a secondary interest area, rather than a primary focus. What follows are my own speculations.

Psychology of science is practiced by a range of different research groups or "invisible colleges" in psychology. For example, an experimental psychologist who does studies of scientific reasoning using tasks like the 2-4-6 will find a ready audience in the *Quarterly Journal of Experimental Psychology*. Those psychologists who do computational and experimental work relevant to discovery programs like BACON and KEKADA will find a receptive audience in *Cognitive Science*. Referees for these journals quite reasonably expect to see specialized approaches appropriate to their audiences.

The danger, of course, is that such specialization can lead to balkanization, making it difficult for psychologists from different invisible colleges to keep up with one another's work. For example, studies involving abstract reasoning tasks are almost never cited in the literature involving textbook problems and vice-versa, even though there are important connections between these literatures and the approaches could be profitably combined. This balkanization makes it even harder for science studies scholars in areas like philosophy of science to keep up with the latest psychological work.

Fortunately, there are journals like *New Ideas in Psychology*, *Mind and Behavior,* and *Social Studies of Science* and organizations like the Society for Philosophy and Psychology that reach both philosophers and psychologists. A number of conferences and special volumes have arisen that span these audiences (see the beginning of this chapter). The question is, are these outlets taken seriously enough within psychology? Would an assistant professor publishing in such journals be able to get tenure?

The problem may be worse when it comes to obtaining funding for psychology of science research. Consider, for example, the NSF: Psychology of science work could be funded by Memory and Cognition, or History and Philosophy of Science and Technology. But while such research is relevant to both of these programs, it is central to neither.

It would be interesting to get some hard data on how articles and grant proposals on psychology of science fare.[8] The books cited at the beginning of this chapter suggest that interest in this area is growing rapidly, and scholars like Brewer, Klahr, and Tweney are focusing on psychology of science as a primary research area. Perhaps the sort of institutionalization that accompanied philosophy and sociology of science will have to accompany psychology of science.

ENDNOTES

1. In his recent autobiography, Simon (1991) concluded that his own discoveries stem from processes similar to KEKADA's.

2. This reminds me of an introductory psychology student who asked me before an exam whether I wanted him to answer the questions according to the textbook and what I had said in class or according to his Christian beliefs.

3. The developmental studies cited in this section are merely examples drawn from a long and rich literature relevant to the psychology of science. Another tack is to look at the way in which the presuppostions of adults— even some trained in physics—resemble a pre-Newtonian, Aristotelian worldview (cf. McCloskey, 1983). Children and many adults appear to have views consistent with earlier paradigms; therefore, the process by which their concepts change may be analogous to the change that occurs in scientists. The major difference, of course, is that these modern children and adults are changing to a culturally accepted view that is promoted by an educational system, whereas the change in working

scientists is to a theory or paradigm that represents a new direction.

4. Mike Oaksford, Michael Guanzon, and I recently compared DAX-MED and counterfactual instructions using an improved iterative counterfactual strategy, which emphasizes that subjects should propose a mutually exclusive, *complementary* hypothesis like 'at least one odd' if their original hypothesis is 'all evens'. Whenever subjects got a result consistent with this counterfactual hypothesis, they were expected to iterate through the strategy again, proposing a new hypothesis and a new complement. We tested this iterative counterfactual hypothesis on a complicated multidimensional version of the 2-4-6 task, where the problem space was much more complicated than in the traditional version. DAX-MED subjects were more successful at proposing complementary hypotheses and at solving the rule; in this situation, counterfactual instructions actually reduced performance.

5. The counterfactual and dual-space research traditions raise an issue that make Popper's warnings appear relevant again: Klahr's subjects always reason in two spaces, Farris's employ a counterfactual strategy, Gorman's disconfirm, etc. In part, this is because a good experimental researcher sets up conditions that make the desired response likely. Human cognition is remarkably plastic and can adapt to a wide range of contexts and situations (cf. Dennett, 1991, for a similar argument about self and consciousness). Psychologists tend to suffer from what I call 'overgeneralization disorder'; each psychologist tries to generalize the way people appear to act in her/his experimental context to a far wider range of situations than is justified. Sociologists and historians who work with cases often make a similar mistake.

Popper would not be disturbed by this tendency provided other researchers were criticizing these approaches: "*in the interest of the search for truth*, all theories—the more the better—should be allowed to compete with all other theories" (1992, p. 191; italics his). What Popper underestimated was the tendency of disciplinary divisions and invisible colleges to isolate scholars from this sort of competition. Even this isolation can be beneficial—it may allow new approaches a chance to grow before being exposed to competition. But eventually some kind of communication among different communities engaged in a common enterprise like psychology of science needs to occur. This volume represents an opportunity for such communication.

6. I have elsewhere (Gorman, 1992a) referred to these two types of validity as external and ecological, in order to connect them to the long psychological literature on validity. However, these terms have not always been used in consistent ways, and I find that without a very extensive discussion, even sophisticated readers become confused. I have therefore simplified my account in this chapter and omitted references to the exhaustive litera-

ture on this topic. See Gorman (1992b) and Fuller (1992) for further discussion.

7. Differences between cognitive and sociological approaches were highlighted in a recent symposium in *Social Studies of Science* (see Slezak, 1989, and the commentaries following his article).

8. In Gorman (1992a) I describe how a variety of journals reacted to my own research in psychology of science, but it is hard to generalize from such a sample. Informal conversations with colleagues suggest that at least some have had similar experiences. I invite other psychologists of science to correspond with me on this issue.

REFERENCES

Barker, P. (1989). The reflexivity problem in the psychology of science. In B. Gholson, W. R., Shadish, R. A., Neimeyer, & A. C., Houts (Eds.), *Psychology of science: Contributions to metascience* (pp. 92–114). Cambridge: Cambridge University Press.

Berkowitz, L., & Donnerstein, E. (1982). External validity is more than skin deep: Some answers to criticisms of laboratory experiments. *American Psychologist, 37,* 245–257.

Bradshaw, G. (1992). The airplane and the logic of invention. In R. N. Giere, (Ed.), *Cognitive models of science* (pp. 239–250). Minnesota Studies in Philosophy of Science, Vol. 25. Minneapolis: University of Minnesota Press.

Brewer, W. F., & Chinn, C. A. (1991). Entrenched beliefs, inconsistent information, and knowledge change. In L. Birnbaum (Ed.), *Proceedings of the 1991 International Conference on the Learning Sciences* (pp. 67–73). Charlottesville, VA: Association for the Advancement of Computing in Education.

Brewer, W. F., & Samarapungavan, A. (1991). Children's theories vs. scientific theories: Differences in reasoning or differences in knowledge? In R. R. Hoffman & D. S. Palermo (Eds.), *Cognition and the symbolic processes: Applied and ecological perspectives.* Hillsdale, NJ: Lawrence Erlbaum.

Bruner, J., Goodnow, J., & Austin, G. (1956). *A study of thinking.* New York: John Wiley.

Carey, S. (1992). The origin and evolution of everyday concepts. In R. N. Giere, (Ed.), *Cognitive models of science* (pp. 89–128). Minnesota Studies in Philosophy of Science, Vol. 25. Minneapolis: University of Minnesota Press.

Carlson, W. B., & Gorman, M. E. (1990). Understanding invention as a cognitive process: The case of Thomas Edison and early motion pictures, 1888–1891. *Social Studies of Science, 20,* 387–430.

Chi, M. T. H. (1992). Conceptual change within and across ontological categories: Examples from learning and discovery in science. In R. N. Giere, (Ed.), *Cognitive models of science* (pp. 129–186) Minnesota Studies in Philosophy of Science, Vol. 25. Minneapolis: University of Minnesota Press.

Clement, J. (1991). Experts and science students: The use of analogies, extreme cases, and physical intuition. In J. F. Voss, D. N. Perkins, & D. W. Segal (Eds.), *Informal reasoning and education.* Hillsdale, NJ: Lawrence Erlbaum.

Darden, L. (1990). Diagnosing and fixing faults in theories. In J. Shrager, & P. Langley, (Eds.), *Computational models of discovery and theory formation* (pp. 319–354). San Mateo, CA: Morgan Kaufmann Publishers.

Dennett, D. C. (1991). *Consciousness explained.* Boston, MA: Little Brown.

Doherty, M. E., & Tweney, R. D. (1988). The role of data and feedback error in inference and prediction. Final report for ARI Contract MDA903-85-K0193.

Dunbar, K. (1989). Scientific reasoning strategies in a simulated molecular genetics environment. *Program of the eleventh annual conference of the cognitive science society.* Hillsdale, NJ: Lawrence Erlbaum.

Dunbar, K. (in press), How scientists really reason: Scientific reasoning in real-world laboratories. In R. J. Sternberg & J. Davidson (Eds.), *Insight.* Cambridge, MA: MIT Press.

Farris, H., & Revlin, R. (1989). The discovery process: A counterfactual strategy. *Social Studies of Science,* 19, 497–513.

Feist, G. J. (1991). The psychology of science: Personality, cognitive, motivational and working styles of eminent and less eminent scientists. Dissertation, University of California at Berkeley.

Fuller, S. (1987). On regulating what is known: A way to social epistemology. *Synthese,* 73, 145–183.

Fuller, S. (1989). *Philosophy of science and its discontents.* Boulder, CO: Westview Press.

Fuller, S. (1992). Epistemology radically naturalized: Recovering the normative, the experimental, and the social. In R. N. Giere, (Ed.), *Cognitive models of science* (pp. 427–459) Minnesota Studies in Philosophy of Science, Vol. 25. Minneapolis: University of Minnesota Press.

Fuller, S., DeMey, M., Shinn, T., & Woolgar, S. (Eds.). (1989). *The cognitive turn: Sociological and psychological perspectives on science.* Dordrecht: Kluwer Academic Publishers.

Gholson, B., Shadish, W. R., Neimeyer, R. A., & Houts, A. C. (Eds.). (1989). *Psychology of science: Contributions to metascience.* Cambridge: Cambridge University Press.

Giere, R. N. (Ed.). (1992). *Cognitive models of science.* Minnesota Studies in Philosophy of Science, Vol. 25. Minneapolis: University of Minnesota Press.

Gooding, D. (1990). *Experiment and the making of meaning.* Dordrecht: Kluwer Academic Publishers.

Gorman, M. E. (1992a). *Simulating science: Heuristics, mental models and technoscientific thinking.* Bloomington, IN: Indiana University Press.

Gorman, M. E. (1992b) Simulating social epistemology: Experimental and computational approaches. In R. N.

Giere, (Ed.), *Cognitive models of science* (pp. 400–426). Minnesota Studies in Philosophy of Science, Vol. 25. Minneapolis: University of Minnesota Press.

Gorman, M.E. (1995). Confirmation, disconfirmation and invention: The case of Alexander Graham Bell and the telephone. *Thinking and Reasoning, I* (1), 31–53.

Gorman, M., & Rosenwein, R. (1995). Simulating social epistemology. *Social epistemology, 9* (1), 71–79.

Gorman, M. E., Mehalik, M., Carlson, W. B., & Oblon, M. (1993). Alexander Graham Bell, Elisha Gray and the speaking telegraph: A cognitive comparison. *History of Technology, 15*, 1–56.

Gruber, H., & Barrett, P. H. (1974). *Darwin on man.* New York: Dutton.

Johnson-Laird, P. N. (1993). *Human and machine thinking.* Hillsdale, NJ: Lawrence Erlbaum.

Klahr, D., & Dunbar, K. (1988). Dual space search during scientific reasoning. *Cognitive Science, 12*, 1–48.

Klahr, D., Dunbar, K., & Fay, A. L. (1990). Designing good experiments to test bad hypotheses. In J. Shrager, & P. Langley, (Eds.), *Computational models of discovery and theory formation* (pp. 355–402). San Mateo, CA: Morgan Kaufmann Publishers.

Klahr, D., Fay, A., & Dunbar, K. (1993). Heuristics for scientific experimentation: A developmental study. *Cognitive psychology, 25*, 111–146.

Klayman, J., & Ha, Y.-W. (1987). Confirmation, disconfirmation and information in hypothesis testing. *Psychological Review, 94*, 211–228.

Kulkarni, D., & Simon, H. A. (1988). The processes of scientific discovery. The strategies of experimentation. *Cognitive Science, 12,* 139–175.

Lakatos, I. (1978). *The methodology of scientific research programmes.* Cambridge: Cambridge University Press.

Langley, P., Simon, H. A., Bradshaw, G. L., & Zytkow, J. M. (1987). *Scientific Discovery: Computational Explorations of the Creative Processes.* Cambridge: MIT Press.

Larkin, J. (1983). The role of problem representation in physics. In D. Gentner, & A. L. Stevens, (Eds.), *Mental models* (pp. 75–98). Hillsdale, NJ: Lawrence Erlbaum.

Latour, B. (1987). *Science in action.* Cambridge: Harvard University Press.

Laudan, R., Laudan, L., & Donovan, A. (1992). Testing theories of scientific change. In A. Donovan, L. Laudan, & R. Laudan, (Eds.), *Scrutinizing science: Empirical studies of scientific change.* Baltimore, MD: Johns Hopkins University Press.

Mahoney, M. J., & Kimper, T. P. (1976). From ethics to logic: A survey of scientists. In M. J. Mahoney, (Ed.), *Scientist as subject: The psychological imperative* (pp. 187–193). Cambridge, MA: Ballinger.

McCloskey, M. (1983). Naive theories of motion. In D. Gentner, & A. L. Stevens (Eds.), *Mental models* (pp. 99–129). Hillsdale, NJ: Lawrence Erlbaum.

Mitroff, I. I., (1974). *The subjective side of science.* Amsterdam: Elsevier.

Mynatt, C. R., Doherty, M. E., & Tweney, R. D. (1977). Confirmation bias in a simulated research environment: An experimental study of scientific inference. *Quarterly Journal of Experimental Psychology, 29*, 85–95.

Mynatt, C. R., Doherty, M. E., & Tweney, R. D. (1978). Consequences of confirmation and disconfirmation in a simulated research environment. *Quarterly Journal of Experimental Psychology, 30*, 395–406.

Nersessian, N. J. (1993). Opening the black box: Cognitive science and history of science. Cognitive Science Laboratory Report 53, Princeton University.

Newell, A., & Simon, H. A. (1972). *Human problem solving.* Englewood Cliffs, NJ: Prentice-Hall.

O'Rorke, P., Morris, S., & Schulenberg, D. (1990). Theory formation by abduction: A case study based on the chemical revolution. In J. Shrager, & P. Langley (Eds.), *Computational models of scientific discovery and theory formation.* San Mateo, CA: Morgan Kaufmann Publishers.

Pinch, T. (1985). Theory testing in science—The case of solar neutrinos: Do crucial experiments test theories or theorists? *Philosophy of the Social Sciences, 15*, 167–187.

Popper, K. R. (1992). *In search of a better world: Lectures and essays from thirty years.* London: Routledge.

Rajamoney, S. (1990). A computational approach to theory revision. In J. Shrager, & P. Langley, (Eds.), *Computational models of discovery and theory formation* (pp. 225–254). San Mateo, CA: Morgan Kaufmann Publishers.

Rosenwein, R., & Gorman, M. (1995). Heuristics, hypotheses, and social influence: A new approach to the experimental simulation of social epistemology. *Social Epistemology, 9*, (1), 57–69.

Shadish, W. R. & Fuller, S. (Eds.). (1994). *Social psychology of science.* New York: Guilford Press.

Shrager, J. (1990). Commonsense perception and the psychology of theory formation. In J. Shrager, & P. Langley, (Eds.), *Computational models of scientific discovery and theory formation* (pp. 439–470). San Mateo, CA: Morgan Kaufmann Publishers.

Shrager, J., & Langley, P. (1990). *Computational models of scientific discovery and theory formation.* San Mateo, CA: Morgan Kaufmann Publishers.

Simon, H. A. (1991). *Models of my life.* New York: Basic Books.

Simon, H. A., Langley, P. W., & Bradshaw, G. (1981). Scientific discovery as problem solving. *Synthese, 47,* 1–27.

Simonton, D. K. (1988). *Scientific genius: A psychology of science.* Cambridge: Cambridge University Press.

Slezak, P. (1989). Scientific discovery by computer as empirical refutation of the strong programme. *Social Studies of Science, 19*(4), 563–600.

Thagard, P., & Nowak, G. (1990). The conceptual structure of the geological revolution. In J. Shrager, & P. Langley, (Eds.), *Computational models of scientific discovery and theory formation* (pp. 27–72). San Mateo, CA: Morgan Kaufmann Publishers.

Tukey, D. D. (1986). A philosophical and empirical analysis of subjects' modes of inquiry on the 2-4-6 task. *Quarterly Journal of Experimental Psychology, 38A*, 5–33.

Tweney, R. D. (1985). Faraday's discovery of induction: A cognitive approach. In D. Gooding, & F. James, (Eds.), *Faraday rediscovered: Essays on the life and work of Michael Faraday, 1791–1867*. New York: Stockton Press.

Tweney, R. D. (1989). A framework for the cognitive psychology of science. In B. Gholson, W. R. Shadish, R. A. Neimeyer, & A. C. Houts, (Eds.), *Psychology of Science*. Cambridge: Cambridge University Press.

Tweney, R. D. (1991). Informal reasoning in science. In J. F. Voss, D. N. Perkins, & D. W. Segal, (Eds.), *Informal reasoning and education*. Hillsdale, NJ: Lawrence Erlbaum.

Tweney, R. D., Doherty, M. E., & Mynatt, C. R. (Eds.). (1981). *On scientific thinking*. New York: Columbia University Press.

Tweney, R. D., Doherty, M. E., Worner, W. J., Pliske, D. B., Mynatt, C. R., Gross, K. A., & Arkkelin, D. L. (1980). Strategies of rule discovery on an inference task. *Quarterly Journal of Experimental Psychology, 32*, 109–123.

Vosniadou, S., & Brewer, W. F. (in press). Mental models of the earth: A study of conceptual change in childhood. *Cognitive Psychology*.

Wason, P. C. (1960). On the failure to eliminate hypotheses in a conceptual task. *Quarterly Journal of Experimental Psychology, 12*, 129–140.

CHAPTER 5

GENETIC EPISTEMOLOGY AND COGNITIVE PSYCHOLOGY OF SCIENCE

Richard F. Kitchener

INTRODUCTION

In recent years several psychologists (Fisch, 1977; Gholson & Houts, 1989; Gholson, Houts, Neimeyer, & Shadish, 1988; Grover, 1981; Mahoney, 1976; Singer, 1971; Tweney, Doherty, & Mynatt, 1981) have argued for the establishment of a psychology of science, a professional specialty analogous to the related professional disciplines of the philosophy of science, the history of science, and the sociology of science. Unlike these latter professional disciplines, however, which are relatively well established and can claim a distinct professional identity, a psychology of science has yet to reach this status and can, at best, be said to be in its incubation period. There is, for example, no standard textbook in this field, along with little agreement about its philosophical, theoretical, and methodological basis—a situation warranting our describing this field as being in its "preparadigm period."

As Kuhn's (1970) term suggests, there is little agreement among psychologists of science concerning the fundamentals of their field. Instead there are several distinct and competing theoretical approaches: (1) a *psychoanalytic* approach (Kubie, 1961), concerned with the psychodynamic processes underlying scientific activity and the neurotic processes distorting it; (2) a *behavioristic* approach (Skinner, 1948) in which one is concerned with delineating those environmental variables (e.g., reward) controlling the behavior of scientists; (3) a *Gestalt* approach (Wertheimer, 1945/1959) concerned with the perceptual structures at play underlying scientific creativity and problem solving; (4) a *psychodiagnostic* and *psychometric* approach (Cattell, 1954; Roe, 1953) concerned with constructing diagnostic tests and employing various statistical models to assess the capacities and mental abilities of scientists; and (5) a more strictly *cognitive* approach concerned with the underlying representations of scientists, how these representations change over time, what mechanisms are at work that explain these changes, and so on.

According to many individuals, this latter cognitive approach to the psychology of science, which is concerned with "the human cognitive processes and the cognitive constructions of knowledge"

(Faust, 1984, p. 31), holds out the greatest promise of becoming a paradigm for the psychology of science, constituting what can be called a *cognitive psychology of science (CPS)* (Fuller, de Mey, Shinn, & Woolgar, 1989; Gholson & Houts, 1989; Gorman, 1992; de Mey, 1982).

Recently there has also arisen what can be called a *social psychology of science* (Fuller, et al., 1989; Shadish & Fuller, 1994), with several possible theoretical bases: *social constructivism*, *experimental social psychology*, and the *"Strong Programme."* Not surprisingly, several individuals have suggested a combination of CPS and a social psychology of science although what such a combination would look like remains unclear.[1]

If the psychology of science has taken a cognitive turn, what kind of cognitive turn has it taken, i.e., what is the philosophy of cognitive psychology underlying the CPS? Several possibilities are available:

1. The most popular one surely would be an *information processing* approach, one wedded to artificial intelligence and computer simulation (Holland, Holyoak, Nisbett, & Thagard, 1986; Langley, Simon, Bradshaw, & Zytkow, 1987; Shrager & Langley, 1990; Simon, 1977, 1979; Tweney, et al., 1981).

2. A second approach to cognitive psychology would be a neural network, connectionist, or PDP approach (McClelland, Rumelhart, et al., 1986; Rumelhart, McClelland, et al., 1986), an approach still under active development.

3. A Gibsonian or ecological psychology of cognition would also be possible (Gibson, 1979), one involving a nonrepresentational conception of cognition.

4. A Gestalt or neo-Gestalt (Wertheimer, 1959) theory of cognition, although currently of historical interest only, has been applied to the psychology of science and could still be refurbished.

5. Finally, there is a *developmental* approach to cognition, historically the most important version of which is Jean Piaget's genetic epistemology (Piaget, 1950a, 1950b, 1950c, 1967; Kitchener, 1986).

Although other candidates are also available, it is Piaget's views about cognitive development that have attracted the most interest among contemporary cognitive psychologists of science. Indeed, several individuals have recognized the crucial relevance of Piaget's work for a cognitive theory of science (Faust, 1984; Giere, 1988; de Mey, 1982; Nowotny, 1973; Thagard, 1988; Tweney, et al., 1981). For example, Marc de Mey (1982, p. 260) says:

> …the pioneering studies in the cognitive approach to science are Jean Piaget's, whose monumental work and efforts to establish 'genetic epistemology'—combining cognitive psychology with philosophy of science—will prove to be the foundation for cognitive science in general as well as for its application to science in particular.

Likewise, Tweney, et al. (1981, p. 12) remark that, "The work of Piaget occupies a special position with regard to the psychology of science" since one of Piaget's ultimate goals has been the understanding of knowledge in general.

But if Piaget's genetic epistemology is to be (part of) the foundation of CPS, it remains unclear how it is supposed to do this, since seeing what a CPS based upon genetic epistemology would look like is little more than a promissory note and would seem to require two preliminary investigations: first, a conceptual clarification of its basic theoretical stance towards the psychology of science, and second, its detailed application to the history and practice of science. In this paper my task will be the former, along with sketching out several strands of what I take to be a Piagetian CPS.

SOCIOLOGY OF SCIENCE AND PSYCHOLOGY OF SCIENCE

Sociologists of science usefully distinguish the *sociology of knowledge*, the *sociology of scientific knowledge*, and the *sociology of scientists*. Likewise in the psychology of science, one can distinguish the *psychology of knowledge*, the *psychology of scientific knowledge* and the *psychology of scientists*. I will argue that a Piagetian CPS should be construed as a psychology of scientific knowledge and not as a psychology of knowledge or a psychology of scientists.

Some sociologists distinguish the sociology of knowledge from the sociology of scientific knowledge. Karl Mannheim (1968), for example, wanted to construct a general sociology of knowledge while, at the same time, excluding science from its relativistic implications. (Other sociologists of knowledge, however, include science under its program.)

In a similar vein, one can conceive of the possibility of a *psychology of knowledge* (which might or might not include scientific knowledge). Taking our clue from classical approaches to the sociology of knowledge, a psychology of knowledge would be an investigation into how psychological factors condition and limit the acquisition, representation, maintenance, and elaboration of knowledge in general. Among sociologists of knowledge, social class interests and ideological factors are usually thought to be crucial here, showing, for example, that knowledge is limited to historical contexts, involving particular and conflicting class interests. Likewise (one might suggest) there are psychological interests and ideologies that condition and limit the acquisition of individual knowledge. Although not yet in existence—but see Broughton (1987), Habermas (1965/1971), Holzkamp (1972), and Riegel (1976)—such a psychology of knowledge might be constructed on the basis of Freud's psychoanalytic theory: Motives and unconscious wishes condition and limit the acquisition and form of knowledge in the general sense that individuals would not be able to come to know certain kinds of things about themselves and others. Such a psychology of knowledge would largely be a psychology of the *deviant*: It would be a theory about how irrational factors prevent one from obtaining rational knowledge. Hence, it would be an externalist psychology of knowledge.

A *sociology of scientific knowledge* would be exclusively concerned with scientific knowledge, with those social conditions and social structures that influence the acquisition, maintenance, and change of scientific knowledge, e.g., replication practices, the peer review process, publication pressures, governmental funding, and so on. Similarly, a *psychology of scientific knowledge* might be concerned with those psychological conditions that control the acquisition, retention, and transmission of scientific knowledge in the individual. Although such psychological explanations might be externalist (noncognitive), following the lead of sociologists who believe that even the sociology of scientific knowledge must be cognitive (e.g., Whitley, 1972), one could argue for the importance of a *cognitive psychology of scientific knowledge*.

A *sociology of scientists* is a sociology concerned with particular features of individual scientists and their sociological explanation (e.g., how Newton's rivalry with Leibniz led him to do certain things). The counterpart in psychology would be a *psychology of scientists*, in which one would be concerned with understanding those particular idiographic traits of individual scientists (e.g., their personality, motivation, birth order, traumatic early experiences, sibling rivalry, etc.) that influenced them and carved out their unique life histories.[2]

Not surprisingly, much of contemporary psychology of science, even CPS, is concerned with the psychology of scientists. For example, if one consults the seminal work of Shadish, Houts, Gholson, and Neimeyer (1989), it seems clear that they are arguing for a psychology of scientists. A psychology of science, they say, is "the scientific study of scientific behavior and mental processes" (p. 9).[3] Likewise a concern with questions such as: "What early training experiences and personality characteristics are associated with becoming a highly creative scientist?" (Houts, 1988, p. 71) is clearly a question about the psychology of scientists. I will suggest, by contrast, that a quite different conception of the CPS can be maintained, one concerned not with the psychology of knowledge, nor with the psychology of scientists, but with the psychology of scientific knowledge.

Internalist vs. Externalist Psychology of Science

It is common among historians of science and sociologists of science to distinguish internalist and externalist approaches to the study of science and the explanation of scientific change. Roughly put, internalist approaches stress intellectual explanatory factors (e.g., beliefs about empirical evidence), whereas externalist approaches stress nonintellectual, socioeconomic factors (e.g., class interest). Many individuals would also argue (although this has not always been claimed) that internalist explanations involve logical and rational explanations of science whereas externalist explanations involve irrational factors. In a similar fashion, one can draw a comparable distinction between *externalist psychology of science* and *internalist psychology of science*, roughly equating these with the distinction between "cognitive" and "noncognitive" explanations. An externalist psychology of science would be concerned with explanations of scientific change involving noncognitive factors. Assuming one can identify 'cognitive' with 'rational,' external factors would be those psychological factors that produced nonrational or irrational behavior, e.g., why a scientist failed to make a discovery, why she discounted objective evidence and clung to an irrational theory, in short, *why a scientist failed to be objective and rational.* An internalist psychology of science, on the other hand, would be concerned with cognitive explanations of science, with explaining why a scientist adopted a correct theory and rejected a false one, how a scientist was able to solve a perplexing problem, create a novel and powerful theory based upon certain data, see problem areas in new ways, and so forth, in short, *why a scientist was objective and rational.* Perhaps the best example of externalist psychology of science might be a Freudian psychology of science, whereas internalist psychologies of science would include those varieties of psychology of science based upon genetic epistemology, information processing, cognitive psychology, Gestalt psychology, and so forth.[4] Quite clearly, therefore, a CPS based upon genetic epistemology would constitute an internalist psychology of science.

Epistemology vs. Psychology

Perhaps the most difficult problem facing the reader of genetic epistemology and cognitive psychology is the problem of distinguishing the psychological from the epistemological. Among epistemologists, for example, the psychological is thought to be the realm of the factual and empirical, whereas the epistemological is the realm of the normative and evaluative. The term 'cognition' effectively glosses over this very distinction. In some areas of psychology, it is possible to distinguish the psychological and the epistemological (e.g., personality theory, motivation, and emotion). But in cognitive psychology, this seems hardly possible, for 'cognition' has built into it certain epistemic notions; indeed the moment one speaks of 'representations', 'belief', 'memory', 'perception', one is drawn into questions about the *adequacy* of such cognitive states, of how well they match or correspond to the world, of their rationality, questions that are clearly epistemological in nature. Cognitive psychology is thus imbued through and through with epistemological strains. This is one of the reasons recent cognitive psychology and epistemology have experienced a cozy rapprochement and why some epistemologists (e.g., Goldman, 1986) believe cognitive psychology is relevant to epistemology. But this also means that epistemol-

ogy is relevant to cognitive psychology, or at least that cognitive psychologists cannot avoid dealing with epistemological issues.

This is nowhere more clear than in Piaget's genetic epistemology and his psychology of scientific knowledge. For example, his key theoretical concept of *equilibration,* in particular, *équilibration majorante* (Piaget, 1975/1985), is the basic explanation of developmental change and yet it is laden with normative notions. (See below.) Hence, Piagetian genetic epistemology may be a branch of *naturalistic epistemology* but it is a naturalistic epistemology that denies epistemic norms can be defined in terms of (or reduced to) brute empirical facts. What is provocative about the program is the notion that empirical, psychological facts about cognitive development are relevant—*epistemically relevant*—to epistemic norms (Kitchener, forthcoming). The situation is largely the same with respect to cognitive psychology in general.

One of the key questions for a CPS, therefore, concerns the question of the meaning of 'cognition' and 'psychology' and their relation to epistemology. Several sociologists speak of the cognitive *and* the social aspects of science (as if they were distinct); likewise (I would like to suggest), one can speak of the *cognitive and* the *psychological* aspects of science. The cognitive aspects of science can be restricted to the psychology of scientific knowledge, whereas the broader psychological aspects of science, those aspects, for example, involving a scientist's personality traits, motivation, early family experiences, and so on, would exclude cognitive psychological factors except insofar as these make a difference to the (general) development of scientific knowledge. A CPS should be primarily concerned with discovering the cognitive mechanisms at work resulting in the attainment of scientific knowledge. Consequently, such a CPS would not have much room left for a psychology of knowledge or for a psychology of scientists.

PIAGET'S COGNITIVE PSYCHOLOGY OF SCIENTIFIC KNOWLEDGE

The Program of Genetic Epistemology

Genetic epistemology would seem to have no room for the *psychology of knowledge* as a separate discipline. First, since (arguably) there is no knowledge except scientific knowledge, there is nothing for a psychology of knowledge to be about other than a psychology of scientific knowledge. Second, there is little reason to think that psychology can explain only the abnormal or deviant—why there fails to be knowledge or rationality. We seem to be left, therefore, with either a cognitive psychology of scientific knowledge or a cognitive psychology of scientists. The program of a genetic epistemological-based CPS can best be conceived, I would like to suggest, as being concerned with a cognitive psychology of scientific knowledge and not with a psychology of scientists. This is because it is the epistemic subject, not the individual person or the psychological subject, who is the subject of genetic epistemology.

The Epistemic Subject

Genetic epistemology has little interest in concrete flesh-and-blood individuals with all of their idiosyncrasies and features peculiar just to them. As Piaget put it in response to a question about why he had little interest in affectivity:

> ...I'm not really interested in individuals, in the individual. I'm interested in what is general in the development of intelligence and knowledge, whereas psychoanalysis is essentially an analysis of individual situations, individual problems, and so forth. (Bringuier, 1977/1980, p. 86)

In another context, Piaget admitted he had little interest in the subject of "lived experience" (Piaget, 1968/1970, p. 68), in "individuals or the individual" and hence in the problem of individual differences.

> I'm interested in what is general in the development of intelligence and knowledge whereas psychology is essentially an analysis of individual situations, individual problems, and so forth. (Bringuier, 1980, p. 86)

Insofar as a psychologist is interested in these idiographic features, Piaget is not a psychologist and has little interest in constructing a psychology of individual scientists. Hence, a Piagetian CPS would have little concern with individual scientists per se, even if such individuals happened to be Newton or Einstein. (This is not to say, however, that principles of genetic epistemology cannot be *applied* to individual scientists in an illuminating way—as Gruber (1981), de Mey (1982), and Miller

(1984) have done—nor is it to say that details about the life of individual scientists could not, suitably interpreted, provide evidence for or against a genetic epistemological account.[5] But as these two situations illustrate, we must distinguish the application of general principles and particular tests of these principles from a construction and theoretical defense of general theoretical principles.

In this regard, it is useful to draw upon Piaget's threefold distinction between the *epistemic subject*, the *psychological subject*, and the *individual person* (Piaget, 1981/1987, p. 153). The individual is unique and particular, characterized by idiographic features. The psychological subject, by contrast, consists of those abstract psychological properties (many of which are noncognitive factors) that are temporal and causal, tied up with the subject's history. The epistemic subject, by contrast, is nontemporal and implicational and consists of abstract cognitive structures and mechanisms. In short, a psychology of the individual would be concerned with a description of idiographic features; a psychology of the psychological subject would be nomothetic and causal; a psychology of the epistemic subject would be nomothetic and noncausal.

The *epistemic subject* is an abstract, idealized entity or set of structures common to individuals at a certain stage of cognitive development. As a *structuralist*, Piaget (1968/70) is interested in what we can call the Scientific Mind, Scientific Reason, or Scientific Rationality—the set of cognitive structures and mechanisms underlying the construction, development, and validation of scientific knowledge. This type of knowledge is *knowing-why* something is the case (theoretical comprehension) as opposed to *knowing-how* to do something. These underlying structures, constituting one's cognitive *competence*, are universal and shared by everyone belonging to the same stage of epistemic development.

Piaget's CPS would thus be concerned with the question, How does this scientific knowledge develop in the scientific mind? Hence, it would be a *psychology of scientific knowledge* (not a psychology of scientists). Since scientific knowledge consists of various theories, models, hypotheses, and so forth, a psychology of scientific knowledge would also have to be concerned with the question: *What are the cognitive mechanisms at work accounting for the ability of Scientific Reason to construct new theories, to modify old ones, to see data in new ways*? The basic explanation operating here, of course, is the notion of equilibration, which explains cognitive development. How it explains epistemic transitions is not particularly transparent in Piaget's theory, nor is the precise philosophical and conceptual status of this theory an open book. In fact, some individuals have written as if equilibration, the basic motor of development, is a causal, psychological concept, hence the province of psychology—the psychological subject. But this seems to be a conceptual exaggeration, since equilibration is not a brute psychological (causal) process but one infused with normative connotations. Hence it must belong to genetic epistemology as much as genetic psychology. But if so, then the notion of the epistemic subject must be broadened; it must constitute the locus of the dynamic mechanisms of cognitive development as well as its underlying structures. This will naturally involve a reconsideration and re-evaluation of the concept of the psychological subject.[6]

What is needed, in short, is an account of how epistemic structures are constructed. We know they are constructed (roughly) by the mechanism of reflective abstraction and the process of equilibration. Indeed, such a role was earlier explicitly given to the epistemic subject:

> Reflective abstraction starting from actions does not imply an empiricist interpretation in the psychologist's sense of the term, for the actions in question are not the particular actions of individual (or psychological) subjects: they are the most general co-ordination of every system of actions, thus expressing what is common to all subjects, and therefore referring to the universal or epistemic subject and not the individual one. (Beth & Piaget, 1961/1966, p. 238)

Hence, if equilibration plays the central role it appears to play in genetic epistemology, it must be the epistemic subject that is engaged in such a process.

Equilibration

It seems hardly controversial that Piaget's theory of equilibration (Piaget, 1975/1985) lies at the heart of his overall program, indeed constitutes part of the Lakatosian "hard core" of his research program. Equilibration is widely considered to be the fundamental explanation of cognitive development in Piaget's system. It constitutes his "epistemic dynamics" whereas his stage theory constitutes his

"epistemic kinematics" (Kitchener, 1991a). But if so, equilibration should not be construed as an ordinary causal account of cognitive development, on all fours with ordinary psychological explanations but a hybrid concept, at once both causal and epistemic.

Equilibration is a process, no doubt, but it is not an ordinary causal, psychological account of change, denuded of normative, epistemic implications. The concept *équilibration majorantes*, for example, is a clear-cut example of such a concept, characterized as "improving equilibration" or "optimizing equilibration". A system that proceeds via equilibration is a system that is thus improving or getting better at equilibrium, at solving problems and reaching goals. "Progress is produced by reequilibration that leads to new forms that are better than previous ones," Piaget says. "We have called this process 'optimizing reequilibration'" (1975/1985, p. 11):

> Optimization is manifested in two ways according to whether improvement simply results from the success of compensatory regulations and therefore from equilibrium momentarily achieved, or whether novelties are drawn by reflective abstractions from the mechanisms of the regulations in play. (1975/1985, p. 26)

Not only is equilibration laden with norms, so is the concept of reflective abstraction, creativity, and so forth. These are hardly ordinary, empirical, causal psychological constructs. The theory of equilibration may include such psychological components, to be sure, but in addition it must be seen as a normative epistemological theory, as an epistemological account of why the epistemic subject moves from one epistemic structure to the next, of why the epistemic subject abandons one epistemic structure and proceeds to construct another one, and so forth.

The answer in both cases is that this occurs because an earlier structure is less equilibrated and the subsequent structure is more equilibrated. Stage transitions occur, in short, because earlier stages are less adequate than later ones—less adequate epistemically—and this in turn is to be cashed out in terms of the notion of greater problem solving power, greater capacity to attain goals and satisfy needs, greater power to answer questions more adequately, and so on. These normative concepts motivate the subject to move on to something better in just the way that incoherence and inconsistency motivate the subject to move on and to remove such epistemic flaws. In short, it is precisely because these normative concepts can motivate the subject that they are hybrid concepts, at once both epistemic (normative) and psychological.

If this is the case, then it is surely a mistake to view the relation between epistemology and psychology in the way some individuals have, viz., as that between epistemic structures and psychological functions, for if I am correct then structures and functions are both epistemic and psychological. This would seem to have implications not only for what a psychology of scientific knowledge should be but also for what a CPS (in general) should be. The purely psychological will be of marginal interest to CPS and this is because a *cognitive* psychology of science should be interested in a psychology of scientific knowledge. Now, of course, a CPS might be interested in just a psychology of scientists (although such an account would be of marginal importance to my mind). Indeed, there is considerable evidence that much of contemporary cognitive psychology of science is concerned with the psychology of scientists, since according to Shadish, Houts, Gholson and Neimeyer (1989), "the bulk of past studies in psychology of science have focused on three topics: personality, creativity, and cognition" (p. 9). Issues of cognition and scientific creativity belong, I would suggest, to the psychology of scientific knowledge, whereas issues of personality clearly belong to the psychology of scientists. But what about creativity? Genetic epistemology, I would suggest, does have several suggestive things to say about scientific creativity and a brief examination of this topic will show that creativity has an epistemic dimension as well as a psychological one, an epistemic dimension not captured in the thinking of most of those working in the psychology of scientists.

Reflective Abstraction and Scientific Creativity

What is the question concerning scientific creativity and why is it important for CPS? In an article explicitly devoted to creativity, Piaget says:

> There are two problems involved in a discussion of creativity. One is the problem of the origins or causes of creativity. The second is the problem of the mechanism: how does it take place, what is the process of a creative act, how does one build something new, how can something new come out of what was not there before? (1981, p. 221)

Although the first of these problems is "wrapped in mystery," the second problem of the mechanism of creativity "is due to a process of reflective abstraction" (Piaget, 1981, p. 224).

Standard approaches to the psychology of creativity (e.g., Simonton, 1988) seem to be concerned with the question: what are the antecedent variables with which scientific creativity is correlated, e.g., family structure, role models, education, reinforcement history? Such an approach might appear to be similar to the first option mentioned by Piaget, viz., a study of the origins or causes of creativity (it turns out, however, that it really is not). But another question about creativity mentioned by Piaget concerns the how-possibly question: *How is scientific creativity possible*? How is it possible for something novel to emerge from something that is already existing? It is this question about creativity more than any other that has occupied Piaget's attention and is inextricably bound up with his stage theory, his theory of equilibration, and (in general) his theory of development. It turns out that such a preoccupation is as much epistemological as it is psychological (as the influential approach of Simonton [1988] also indicates).[7]

The problem of scientific creativity has a long history and is fraught with many conceptual problems, e.g., the problem of induction, the Meno paradox, the predictability of creativity, and so on. But one issue that confronts any theory of creativity is the following: The creation of a new scientific concept (problem solution, hypothesis, theory) is not totally unrelated to what has gone on before— whether an old theory or commonly accepted evidential data. Indeed, this background or problem situation sets constraints on what any adequate new hypothesis or problem solution can be. Such creative hypotheses are, in short, not random but *directed* by earlier knowledge. But neither is such a novel solution already contained in the old problem situation, except in the sense of a potentiality or possibility; otherwise, we would not speak of creativity and novelty. Furthermore, a later hypothesis is often more adequate than an earlier one and hence epistemically stronger. But how, in short, is it *possible* for new, more adequate epistemic structures to come from older, less adequate ones? Piaget's sketchy answer to these questions involves the notion of reflective abstraction.

There are two kinds of abstraction in Piaget's (1977a) theory—empirical abstraction and reflective abstraction—and several kinds of inductive generalization (Piaget, 1978). In *empirical abstraction*, a property is abstracted from an object or from some perceptual data (e.g., weight or color). But in *reflective abstraction*, the epistemic subject abstracts a property from its *actions* on the object, in particular, from the logical coordinations of action. For example, one can count objects by putting them in one-one correspondence. These kinds of action possess certain kinds of properties, relations or structure (e.g., addition, order). But properties like order, seriation, classification, sub-division, correspondence, etc., are properties of one's actions, not of properties of physical objects. Clearly to classify objects into a kind is to perform an action on them just as one does when one seriates them by, say, size. It turns out that certain kinds of actions have structural connections to other kinds of action. These structural connections constitute various possibilities existing between various kinds of action. Some of these properties of action can be abstracted and turned into higher-level cognitive entities—operations on operations—which occurs by reflective abstraction.

Reflecting abstraction has, Piaget claims, two inseparable aspects: a 'reflecting' in the sense of a projecting onto an upper level of what is happening on a lower level, and a 'reflection' in the sense of a cognitive reconstruction or reorganization (more or less conscious) of what has thus been transferred. Reflective abstraction is *reflecting*, i.e., "a *projection* (as by a reflector) onto a higher level of that which is drawn from an inferior level (e.g., from action to representation)" (Piaget, 1977a, p. 303), and it is reflexive, i.e., it involves "a mental act of reconstruction and reorganization on the higher level of that which is thus transferred from the lower."

In reflecting abstraction (*abstraction réfléchissement*), an operation is abstracted from one's action and projected or transposed onto a higher plane, with this projection leading to a reconstruction of earlier epistemic structures by reflexive abstraction (*abstraction réflexion*). On the higher level, the item abstracted from the lower level actions must be integrated into a new structure which requires a restructuring. This restructuring occurs by means of a twofold process of *constructive generalization* and *completive generalization* (Piaget, 1978). In an ordinary inductive generalization, new content is assimilated to old form, but in constructive generalization, a new structure is created. This may occur, for example, by the differentiation of older schemes, which must then be

integrated into a new structure. This integration can thus be called a completive generalization since it is a completion (or realization) of the possibilities latent in the operations found at the lower level. In this process, there is thus the creation both of new content and new form.

Empirical abstraction and reflective abstraction constitute, according to Piaget, "the method of construction of all physical concepts..." (Piaget & Garcia, 1983/1989, p. 205). This applies not only to observable data but also to the creation of novel theoretical ideas. Clearly, these dual reflective processes are central to issues of scientific creativity, problem solving, discovery, and reasoning. Although Piaget does not explicitly apply them to actual cases in the history of science, there is at least one (dense) passage in which he does point out their application—the case of Darwin and why Darwin took so long to develop his earlier ideas about evolution:

> There seem to be two reasons for this. One reason is that in order to solve a particular problem, one concentrates on the data so that empirical abstraction...and inductive generalization of an extensional (and hence limited) nature predominate. To achieve constructive generalizations and to overcome these limitations ("not only...but also"), however, a complete change in direction is needed and the use of reflective abstraction is required. This allows the discovery of the operations previously used instrumentally as objects of explicit thought. Such changes in direction and reversals are not easy, and they never happen all at once.
>
> A second reason for the length of time between discoveries and final achievements is that a set of possible intrinsic variations constitutes a structure, and it is well known that there is always a delay between the use of operations and their constitution as structures. The reason is that structures require a higher level of reflective abstraction and completive generalization because they require compositions between operations: what is involved here are operations "on" components, and this requires a new equilibrium between differentiations and integrations, including closure. (Piaget & Garcia, 1983/1989, p. 229; translation slightly amended)

Reflective abstraction is a mechanism that plays a crucial part in Piaget's psychology of scientific knowledge and genetic epistemology. Creativity is not completely *de novo*, since it builds upon earlier cognitive elements and structures drawn from one's actions—the locus of epistemic form or structure. But in building upon these abstracted properties, it creates new structures. How this restructuring occurs remains something of a mystery. In any case, what is clear is that creativity would be possible if something like reflective abstraction is working. It should also be clear that the mechanisms of reflecting abstraction and completive generalizations should not be viewed just as ordinary causal mechanisms—the province of the psychological subject; for although it is causal (in one sense), it is epistemic (in another). It is a process occurring in real time, but it is also a process directed by certain epistemic constraints. New cognitive stages are thus created by reflective abstraction but reflective abstraction operates according to the principle of improving equilibration.

Clearly there are numerous conceptual problems with the above account, not the least of which is the need to unpack the very concept of reflective abstraction in a more satisfactory way. Although Piaget has written a great deal on this notion, it still remains sketchy and vague, like many of his concepts (Haroutunian, 1984).

Second, there seem to be conceptual problems with the claim that reflective abstraction (and constructivism in general) can explain creativity. Fodor and Chomsky (Piatelli-Palmarini, 1980) have argued that Piaget's theory is inadequate because it cannot explain the creation of new concepts and that (contrary to Piaget) such concepts must somehow be innate. However, Piaget has argued that, although cognitive *functions* (e.g., autoregulation, equilibration, etc.) may be innate, not all *structures* and *concepts* (elements) are. Hence, these innate functions can explain the creation of new structures and concepts and can explain how more powerful epistemic structures can come from weaker ones. Of course, such a reply to the nativists' criticism needs considerably more clarification and defense, but I see no reason to conclude that such a reply cannot be constructed, nor that Piaget's theory of reflective abstraction is not a plausible, interesting theory of how scientific creativity is possible.

I have given only one example of how Piaget's genetic epistemology might be applied to the issue of scientific creativity. In so doing, I have tried to point out its complex and hybrid nature. It purports to answer the question, "How is the emergence of novelty possible?" and the answer provided is one in which the origin of novelty is severely constrained by what has gone before. These constraints are epistemic in nature. Indeed, the theory of reflective abstraction is one applicable to the question of whether there is a logic of discovery, of how plausible hypotheses are generated and antecedently evaluated. As such it maintains that there are "inductive" constraints operating from the beginning, a point of view apparently at odds with the currently popular model of blind variation and selective retention (Campbell, 1988; Popper, 1972) in which novel solutions are uncorrelated with antecedent problem solution efficacy. Piaget's theory of creativity might be wrong, of course, and it is certainly obscure in places. But it deserves considerably more attention than it has received by current cognitive psychologists of science.

CONCLUSION

In this paper I have attempted to sketch what implications Piaget's genetic epistemology has for contemporary CPS. That it is a cognitive approach is obvious and so is its developmental dimension. There needs to be considerably more discussion of Piaget's psychology of science than currently exists. In sketching out what I take to be such a CPS, I have focused upon his genetic epistemology. This is because Piaget has always contended that he is first and foremost a genetic epistemologist and only secondarily a psychologist. I have taken him at his word and hence may have underestimated the relevance of his genetic psychology for CPS. But, in addition, it is important to remember that psychologists of science are (or should be) interested in scientific *knowledge* and not just scientific behavior. There are lots of things interesting about science, but surely the distinctive thing is its claim to provide *knowledge* of the world, a claim that has been backed by a long history of successful products. There are psychological accounts of this scientific knowledge, so-called *psychological epistemologies*. Such psychological epistemologies should be fully integrated into contemporary psychology of science and science studies. But any psychological epistemology worth its name will be a psychological account of scientific knowledge, what I have called a psychology of scientific knowledge. A *psychogenetic* epistemology would therefore be an account of the genesis of scientific knowledge.

Piaget's genetic epistemology may not prove to be a promising approach to CPS. But whether it is or not, one must first be clear about what the program itself is. I might be entirely wrong of course about the nature of CPS and how genetic epistemology is related to it. But even if this is so, I hope I will have presented an argument that will provoke, in turn, a more adequate reading of the relevance of genetic epistemology to contemporary psychology of science.

ENDNOTES

1. For a sketch of what a genetic–epistemological approach to such a cognitive social psychology of science would look like, see Kitchener (1989).

2. Standard history of science is *idiographic*, concerned with the unique and unrepeatable particularities of the past, not *nomothetic*, concerned with general laws about the history of science. Nomothetic history was pursued by speculative nineteenth-century historians such as Hegel, Comte, and Spencer and twentieth-century figures such as Spencer and Toynbee and is currently out of fashion. It is possible, of course, to do *nomothetic history of science*, which might more accurately be called 'developmental' or 'evolutionary' history of science (Nisbett, 1969; Teggert, 1960). Elsewhere (Kitchener, 1987) I have argued that this is precisely what Popper and Lakatos are doing in their "historical reconstructions" of the history of science and what genetic epistemology is about.

3. However, Gholson and Houts (1989) suggest a different conception of CPS: It is concerned with "how the working practices of scientists lead to developments in scientific knowledge" (p.108).

4. The very distinction between internalist and externalist psychology of science needs to be analyzed much more fully. For example much of recent psychology of science is concerned with pointing out the irrationality of scientific behavior, the evidence for which comes from cognitive psychology itself (Faust, 1984; Mahoney, 1976; Thagard, 1988; Tweney, et al., 1981). This would be a kind of externalist CPS. Second, this distinction overlooks the possibility that sociological factors—things normally thought to belong to external psychology of science (e.g., Merton's [1973] norms of science)—can explain certain rational aspects of science. As I have argued elsewhere (Kitchener, 1989, 1993), Piagetian psychology of science holds out the prospect of being a sociology of science in addition to a psychology of science, one similar to those sociologies of science influenced by exchange theory and one concerned with social epistemology. Indeed, a crucial claim of Piaget's genetic epistemology (Piaget, 1977b) is that there is a logic to social interaction isomorphic to the logic of individual action (Kitchener, 1991b).

5. There are, however, problems with individual case studies providing an empirical test of Piagetian theory (Kitchener, 1993).

6. In some of Piaget's more recent writings (e.g., Inhelder & Piaget, 1979), and in the writings of his lifelong collaborator Bärbel Inhelder (1978; Inhelder, et al., 1976; Karmiloff-Smith & Inhelder, 1974) and the Genevan functionalists (Karmiloff-Smith, 1992; Leiser & Gillieron, 1990), there has been what appears to be a radical shift in the interpretation of the nature and activity of the psychological subject and a consequent shift away from the epistemic subject (Bullinger & Chatillon, 1983; Vuyk, 1981). As the present chapter indicates, I believe this to be a mistake, but I don't have the space or time to show this here.

7. One important way it is epistemological concerns the issue of the origin of ideas (concepts) and the historically important answers of nativism, empiricist learning theory, and Piagetian constructivism.

REFERENCES

Beth, E. W., & Piaget, J. (1966). *Mathematical epistemology and psychology* (W. Mays, Trans.). Dordrecht: D. Reidel. (Original work published 1961)

Bringuier, J-C. (1980). *Conversations with Jean Piaget* (B. M. Gulati, Trans.). Chicago: University of Chicago Press. (Original work published 1977)

Broughton, J. M. (Ed.). (1987). *Critical theories of psychological development*. New York: Plenum.

Bullinger, A., & Chatillon, J. F. (1983). Recent theory and research of the Genevan school. In J. H. Flavell & E. M. Markman (Eds.) [P. H. Mussen, series Ed.], *Handbook of child psychology. Vol. 3: Cognitive development* (4th ed., pp. 231–262). New York: John Wiley.

Campbell, D. (1988). *Methodology and epistemology for social sciences: Selected papers* (E.S. Overman, Ed.). Chicago: University of Chicago Press.

Cattell, R. B. (1954). *The personality and motivation of the research scientist*. New York: Academy of Sciences.

Faust, D. (1984). *The limits of scientific reasoning*. Minneapolis, MN: University of Minnesota Press.

Fisch, R. (1977). Psychology of science. In I. Spiegel-Rösing & D. de Solla Price (Eds.), *Science, technology and society* (pp. 277–318). London: Sage.

Fuller, S., de Mey, M., Shinn, T., & Woolgar, S. (Eds.). (1989). *The cognitive turn: Sociological and psychological perspectives on science*. Dordrecht: D. Reidel.

Gibson, J. J. (1979). *The ecological approach to visual perception*. Boston: Houghton-Mifflin.

Giere, R. N. (1988). *Explaining science: A cognitive approach*. Chicago: University of Chicago Press.

Gholson, B. & Houts, A. (1989). Toward a cognitive psychology of science. *Social Epistemology*, 3, 107–128.

Gholson, B., Houts, A. C., Neimeyer, R. A., & Shadish, W. R. (Eds.). (1988). *The psychology of science and metascience*. Cambridge: Cambridge University Press.

Goldman, A. I. (1986). *Epistemology and cognition*. Cambridge, MA: Harvard University Press.

Gorman, M. E. (1992). *Simulating science: Heuristics, mental models, and technoscientific thinking*. Bloomington: Indiana University Press.

Grover, S. C. (1981). *Toward a psychology of the scientist: Implications of psychological research for contemporary philosophy of science.* Washington, DC: University Press of America.

Gruber, H. (1981). *Darwin on man: A psychological study of scientific creativity* (2nd ed.). Chicago: University of Chicago Press.

Habermas, J. (1971). *Knowledge and human interest* (J. McCarthy, Trans.). Boston: Beacon Press. (Original work published 1965)

Haroutunian, S. (1984). *Equilibrium in the balance.* New York: Springer.

Holland, J., Holyoak, K. J., Nisbett, R. E., & Thagard, P. R. (1986). *Induction: Processes of inference, learning, and discovery.* Cambridge, MA: M.I.T. Press.

Holzkamp, L. (1972). *Kritische psychologie: Vorbereitende Arbeiten.* Frankfurt: Fischer.

Houts, A. C. (1988). Contributions of the psychology of science to metascience: A call for explorers. In B. Gholson, A. C. Houts, R. A. Neimeyer, & W. R. Shadish, (Eds.), *The psychology of science and metascience* (pp. 47–88). Cambridge: Cambridge University Press.

Inhelder, B. (1978). De l'approche structurale à l'approche procédurale: introduction à l'étude des stratégies. In *Actes du XXIe Congres International de Psychologie* (pp. 99–118). Paris: Presses Universitaires de France.

Inhelder, B., & Piaget, J. (1979). Procédures et structures. *Archives de Psychologie, 47,* 165–176.

Inhelder, B., Achermann-Valladao, E., Blanchet, A., Karmiloff-Smith, A., Kilcher-Hagedorn, H., Montangero, J., & Robert, M. (1976). Des structures cognitives aux procedures de decouverte. *Archives de Psychologie, 44,* 57–72.

Karmiloff-Smith, A. (1992). *Beyond modularity.* Cambridge, MA: M.I.T. Press.

Karmiloff-Smith, A., & Inhelder, B. (1974). If you want to get ahead, get a theory. *Cognition, 3,* 195–212.

Kitchener, R. F. (1986). *Piaget's theory of knowledge: Genetic epistemology and scientific reason.* New Haven, CT: Yale University Press.

Kitchener, R. F. (1987). Genetic epistemology, equilibration and the rationality of scientific change. *Studies in the History and Philosophy of Science, 18,* 339–366.

Kitchener, R. F. (1989). Genetic epistemology and the prospects for a cognitive sociology of science: A critical synthesis. *Social Epistemology, 3,* 153–169.

Kitchener, R. F. (1991a). Genetic epistemology. In J. Dancy & E. Sosa (Eds.), *A companion to epistemology* (pp. 151–154). Oxford: Blackwell.

Kitchener, R. F. (1991b). Jean Piaget: The unknown sociologist. *British Journal of Sociology, 41,* 421–442.

Kitchener, R. F. (1993). Piaget's epistemic subject and science education: Epistemological vs. psychological implications. *Science and Education, 2,* 137–148.

Kitchener, R. F. (forthcoming). *Genetic epistemology: Naturalistic epistemology and cognitive development.*

Kubie, L. S. (1961). *Neurotic distortions of the creative process.* New York: Noonday.

Kuhn, T. (1970). *The structure of scientific revolutions* (2nd Ed.) Chicago: University of Chicago Press.

Langley, P., Simon, H., Bradshaw, G. L., & Zytkow, J. M. (1987). *Scientific discovery: Computational explorations of the creative process.* Cambridge, MA: M.I.T. Press.

Leiser, D., & Gillieron, C. (1990). *Cognitive science and genetic epistemology.* New York: Plenum.

Mahoney, M. J. (1976). *Scientist as subject: The psychological imperative.* Cambridge, MA: Ballinger.

Mannheim, K. (1968). *Ideology and utopia* (L. Wirth & E. Shils, Trans.). New York: Harcourt, Brace & World. (Original work published 1929)

McClelland, J. L., Rumelhart, D. E., & PDP Research Group (1986). *Parallel distributed processing: Explorations in the microstructure of cognition. Vol. 2: Psychological and biological models.* Cambridge, MA: M.I.T. Press.

Merton, R. K. (1973). *The sociology of science: Theoretical and empirical investigations.* Chicago: University of Chicago Press.

Mey, M. de (1982). *The cognitive paradigm.* Dordrecht: D. Reidel.

Miller, A. I. (1984). *Imagery in scientific thought: Creating 20th-century physics.* Boston: Birkhäuser.

Nisbett, R. A. (1969). *Social change and history: Aspects of the Western theory of development.* New York: Oxford University Press.

Nowotny, H. (1973). On the feasibility of a cognitive approach to the study of science. *Zeitschrift für Soziologie, 2,* 282–296.

Piaget, J. (1950a). *Introduction à l'épistémologie génétique. Vol. 1: La pensée mathematique.* Paris: Presses Universitaire de France.

Piaget, J. (1950b). *Introduction à l'épistémologie génétique. Vol. 2: La pensée physique.* Paris: Presses Universitaire de France.

Piaget, J. (1950c). *Introduction à l'épistémologie génétique. Vol. 3: La pensée biologique, la pensée psychologique, la pensée sociologique.* Paris: Presses Universitaire de France.

Piaget, J. (Ed.) (1967). *Logique et connaissance scientifique.* Paris: Gallimard.

Piaget, J. (1970). *Structuralism* (B. Walsh, Trans.). New York: Harper. (Original work published 1968)

Piaget, J. (1977a). *Recherchers sur L'abstraction reflechissante. Vol. 2. L'abstraction de l'ordre des relations spatiale* (pp. 303–324). Paris: Presses Universitaire de France.

Piaget, J. (1977b). *Etudes sociologiques* (2nd ed.). Geneva: Droz.

Piaget, J. (1978). In *Recherches sur la generalisation* (pp. 219–243). Paris: Presses Universitaire de France.

Piaget, J. (1981). Creativity. In J. M. Gallagher & D. K. Reid, *The learning theory of Piaget and Inhelder* (pp.

221–230). Monterey, CA: Brooks/Cole. (Original work published 1972)

Piaget, J. (1985). *The equilibration of cognitive structures: The central problem of intellectual development* (T. Brown & K. J. Thampy, Trans.). Chicago: University of Chicago Press. (Original work published 1975)

Piaget, J. (1987). *Possibility and necessity. Vol. 1. The role of possibility in cognitive development* (H. Feider, Trans.). Minneapolis, MN: University of Minnesota Press. (Original work published 1981)

Piaget, J. & Garcia, R. (1989). *Psychogenesis and the history of science* (H. Feider, Trans.). New York: Columbia University Press. (Original work published 1983)

Piatelli-Pallmerini, M. (Ed.). (1980). *Language and learning: The debate between Jean Piaget and Noam Chomsky.* Cambridge: Harvard University Press.

Popper, K. (1972). *Objective knowledge: An evolutionary approach.* Oxford: Oxford University Press.

Riegel, K. (1976). *Psychology of development and history.* New York: Plenum.

Roe, A. (1953). *The making of a scientist.* New York: Dodd & Mead.

Rumelhart, D. E., McClelland, J. L., & PDP Research Group (1986). *Parallel distributed processing: Explorations in the microstructure of cognition. Vol. 1: Foundations.* Cambridge, MA: M.I.T. Press.

Shadish, W.R., & Fuller, S. (Eds.). (1994). *The social psychology of science.* New York: Guilford Press.

Shadish, W. R., Jr., Houts, A. C., Gholson, B, & Neimeyer, R. A. (1989). The psychology of science: An introduction. In B. Gholson, A. C. Houts, R. A. Neimeyer, & W. R. Shadish (Eds.), *The psychology of science and metascience* (pp. 1–16). Cambridge: Cambridge University Press.

Shrager, J. & Langley, P. (Eds.). (1990). *Computational models of scientific discovery and theory formation.* San Mateo, CA: Morgan Kaufmann.

Simon, H. (1977). *Models of discovery and other topics in the methods of science.* Dordrecht: D. Reidel.

Simon, H. (1979). *Models of thought.* New Haven, CT: Yale University Press.

Simonton, D. K. (1988). *Scientific genius: A psychology of science.* New York: Cambridge University Press.

Singer, B. F. (1971). Toward a psychology of science. *American Psychologist, 26,* 1010-1015.

Skinner, B. F. (1948). The operational analysis of psychological terms. *Psychological Review, 52,* 270–277.

Teggert, F. J. (1960). *Theory and processes of history.* Berkeley: University of California Press.

Thagard, P. (1988). *Computational philosophy of science.* Cambridge, MA: M.I.T. Press.

Tweney, R. D., Doherty, M. E., & Mynatt, C. R. (Eds.). (1981). *On scientific thinking.* New York: Columbia University Press.

Vuyk, R. (1981). *Overview and critique of Piaget's genetic epistemology* (2 vols.). New York: Academic Press.

Wertheimer, M. (1959). *Productive thinking.* (Enlarged ed.) Chicago: University of Chicago Press. (Original work published 1945)

Whitley, R. D. (1972). Black boxism and the sociology of science: A discussion of the major developments in the field. In P. Halmos (Ed.), *The sociology of science (Sociological Review Monograph,* No. 18) (pp. 61–92). Keele, England: University of Keele.

PART 2

BEHAVIORISM, PSYCHOLOGY, AND PHILOSOPHY

The next collection of papers depicts the considerable influence of behaviorism in both psychology and philosophy.

The influence of the behaviorisms of Pavlov, Watson, Tolman, Skinner, and Hull on twentieth-century psychology is uncontroversial (although the magnitude of its present influence—i.e., whether reports of its death are greatly exaggerated—is open to debate). It is important to note that behaviorism is not a single school of thought. There are various "behaviorisms." Skinner's radical behaviorism and Watson's methodological behaviorism are probably the best known in psychology. However, there are numerous others. Pavlov, Kantor, Tolman, and Hull all developed distinct brands of behaviorism. More contemporary behaviorism can be found in Rachlin's molar, teleological behaviorism or Staddon's biological behaviorism.

In philosophy early behaviorisms were associated with logical positivism, as evidenced, for example, in the behaviorisms of Wittgenstein and Hempel. Ryle's form of behaviorism was more associated with later ordinary language philosophy. Finally, Quine's behaviorism largely derives from naturalizing epistemology.

It is beyond the scope of this introduction to discuss the differences of these forms of behaviorisms—this alone would make an interesting book. While no doubt these behaviorisms share a certain family resemblance, the point here is that it is simplistic to think of behaviorism as a monolithic single school of thought. Some of the major forms of behaviorism will be discussed in the subsequent chapters.

Part of behaviorism's influence has been its empirical successes, but another part has been the persuasiveness (to some) of its claims regarding certain philosophical issues. (What is the mind? What is the proper way to conduct a science of behavior? What is knowledge? What is meant by "good"? etc.) Thus, psychological behaviorism has philosophical components and these need to be more clearly explicated (something that has rarely been done, considering all the grievous exegetical errors made regarding Skinner) and can then be evaluated for their adequacy.

However, many psychologists do not have an appreciation of the role of behaviorism in contemporary analytic philosophy (although many psychologists have some knowledge of the early twentieth-century behavioral philosophies of Wittgenstein and Ryle). Psychologists have had more exposure to philosophers who have had a mixture of interests in cognitive accounts of the philosophy of mind, philosophy of language, and artificial intelligence (e.g., Chomsky, Fodor, Minsky, Churchland; see Part 4 in this volume) and who have been highly critical of behaviorism. At times, part of the argument for an increased emphasis on cognition in psychology, given by psychologists, has been that behaviorism is out of vogue in contemporary philosophy and that there is a large degree of confluence between the consensus in philosophy and the "cognitive revolution" in psychology (e.g., Mahoney, 1989).

In the first paper, Hocutt traces the influence of Cartesian thought to contemporary theorists such as Chomsky, critiques the Cartesian framework, and argues for the superiority of the behavioral point of view.

Psychologists' exposure to the behavioral philosophy of Quine—arguably the most influential analytic philosopher of this century—has been much more limited. The next two papers illustrate the confluence that has not received enough attention—that between the views of Quine and Skinner. Professor Gibson provides an exposition of Quine's behaviorism, and Kitchener provides a description of important aspects of Skinner's behavioral account of psychological epistemology and its implications for Skinner's views on the roles of theories in science.

In the next piece, Professor Place suggests that insofar as all sciences depend on language and since behaviorism supplies the best account of language, then "linguistic behaviorism" is a good candidate for providing a philosophy of all empirical science.

The last two papers are largely critical of behaviorism. It is important to include papers that are critiques of behaviorism, because it is fair to say that the majority of what has been written about behaviorism is negative. Professor Garrett criticizes Skinner's philosophy of mind and Skinner's behavioral interpretation of these principles of reinforcement and examines the consequences of the rejection of these for Skinner's analysis of ethics and politics. In the final paper, Rychlak critically examines mechanistic accounts of human behavior such as often can be found in behavioral analysis. Professor Rychlak suggests these mechanistic accounts rely upon the citation of efficient causes. He suggests that experimental results do not entail that the hypothesized mechanism actually cause the observed effect, and that these results are also consistent with logical learning theory, which adopts teleological final causes in its explanatory framework.

REFERENCE

Mahoney, M. J. (1989). Scientific psychology and radical behaviorism. *American Psychologist, 44*, 1372–1377.

CHAPTER 6

BEHAVIORISM AS OPPOSITION TO CARTESIANISM

Max Hocutt

INTRODUCTION

Behaviorism is best regarded not as a positive doctrine but as a form of opposition to Cartesianism (Hineline, 1992, p. 1274).[1] That is what it was in the beginning; that is what it is now.

Cartesianism is the paradigm of what Wallace Matson calls an *inside-out* philosophy (Matson, 1987, p. 275). Its central thesis is that we perceive not things and events in the world outside us but ideas, signs, or other representations of these things inside us. Then we infer the existence of things outside us as causes of the ideas inside us. Thus, according to the Cartesian, I learn by introspection, reflection on my own ideas, that my idea of grass is green; then I suppose—not always correctly—that there may be something in the external world, viz., green grass, causing and corresponding to this idea. In short, according to the Cartesian, we start with the ideas inside us, then work outward, to the world outside us.

Behaviorists hold exactly the opposite view. The behaviorist believes that, because evolutionary selection favors adaptation to the environment, we know and understand best not what is going on inside us but what is going on outside us, in the world that is external to our skins. Thus, we know by means of the physical senses that the grass in our yard is green, that the sugar in our coffee is sweet, that the rock beside the road is hard, and that the tiger in the wild is dangerous. But because our senses mostly look outward, not inward, we do not know precisely what form our knowledge takes, or in any very exact way how we come to acquire, process, and store it. We know, however, that it results from interaction with the things in our environment. So we know that, in order to understand it, we shall have to start with external objects and work inside.

THE ORIGINS AND IMPLICATIONS OF CARTESIANISM

An outside-in view of things was standard until the sixteenth and seventeenth centuries, when it was struck severe blows by developments in astronomy and physics.

In astronomy, Copernicus had shown that the movements of the heavenly bodies are illusions; the reality is a moving earth. But if the motions that we see are not in the heavens, it seemed to follow that they must be in us. In physics, Galileo had shown that the seen color and felt solidity of material bodies are also illusions; the reality is clouds of invisible and intangible "atoms." But if the color that we see and the solidity that we feel are not in physical objects, then it seemed to follow that they too must be in us. In short, it began to appear that what we perceive are not things and events in the greater world outside our skins but the effects these things produce inside us, beneath our skins, on our minds (Matson, 1987, pp. 258–260).

Once accepted, this proposition was seen to have stunning implications. Some of these were made explicit by the great physicist and mathematician René Descartes, who said, in effect: The only things that one can know with certainty are the thoughts, feelings, emotions, perceptions, reasonings, and so forth, of one's own mind. Given suitable attention, these can be known unerringly by intro-spection, reflection of the mind on itself; but nothing else can be known with anywhere near the same degree of certainty (Ryle, 1949). Hence, I can know with certainty that I feel pain, desire a cold beer, seem to see a horse, and believe that $2 + 2 = 4$; but no person can know with assurance either the thoughts and feelings of other persons or the properties (shapes, sizes, colors, etc.) of material objects. Indeed, no one can know with certainty either that other people have thoughts or that there are material objects. Descartes, who was not insane, had no doubt that there were other minds besides his own, and bodies too; but believing that he could not prove either proposition, he took comfort in his faith that God would not let him be deceived about things so important (Matson, 1987, p. 275).

Other Cartesian Convictions

In keeping with this same religious faith, Descartes also had other metaphysical convictions. The most important was that the mind—which Descartes equated with the rational soul—is immaterial (Descartes, 1955, p. 434). In Descartes's opinion, this distinction enables the mind to survive the death of the body.

The use of the mind as Descartes saw it is to think (ibid.). For Descartes, thinking meant doing sums and syllogisms all but infallibly, in accordance with rigorously defined and eternally fixed rules (Descartes, 1955, p. 4). In Descartes's opin-

ion, beasts, which lack minds, have no comparable capacity for thought, good or bad. We know this from the fact that they have no capacity for intelligent speech (Descartes, 1955, p. 116). Your pet will not be in heaven with you.

Because thinking is immaterial, according to Descartes, so must be the ideas (i.e., the concepts) that the mind uses. This means that our ideas cannot have come into our minds by way of the physical senses. Instead, they must have been placed in us before our births by God. In other words, they must be innate.[2] The role of the physical senses is not to produce ideas but merely to activate them when they are needed (Descartes, 1955, p. 434). Thus, seeing the grass does not give me my idea of green. Instead, it merely elicits the idea that I already have—which explains why we have ideas of things that have never been seen or do not exist.

In Descartes's opinion, the body is a mere machine (Descartes, 1955, p. 250). Its actions are explicable mechanically in the terms of physics— except when they are being directed by a reasoning mind, which is able, with the assistance of an autonomous will, to guide the body toward previously determined ends. Hence, beasts, who have bodies but neither reason nor will, lack not only intelligent speech but also the capacity for purposive behavior. They are mere automata, whose actions are reflexes—automatic and unthinking responses to stimuli (Descartes, 1955, p. 434).

In summary, Cartesianism comprises belief in the following doctrines:

1. *Representationalism*: We perceive (and think about) not things but ideas.
2. *Nativism*: All our ideas are innate.
3. *Dualism*: The mind is a distinctly different thing.
4. *Rationalism*: Thinking is logical (i.e., rule-governed) reasoning.
5. *Mechanism*: The actions of bodies are purely mechanical.
6. *Speciesism*: Only human beings have minds.

Tying all of these doctrines together were Descartes's Christian faith in the immortality of the rational soul and his notion that the chief distinguishing mark of the soul's activity is consciousness, an ability not only to be in a certain state or condition but, by being in it, to recognize it for what it is. Psychology, as Descartes envisioned it, was therefore to be a study of the workings of the conscious, reasoning mind; and the chief method of the study was to be introspection, reflection of the mind on itself.

Why Cartesianism Entails Solipsism

The obvious trouble with this program is that it promises knowledge of one's own mind but rules out knowledge of both other minds and the external world.

Take just the first point. If introspection is the only way to know the mind, and if you can introspect only your own mind, not that of other people, then you cannot know their minds. For all you know, in fact, other people might not even have minds. You might be the only person there is. Solipsism.

Despite this clear logic, Cartesians have sanguinely believed that solipsism could be avoided by arguing from analogy. The idea is roughly this: I cannot directly observe your fear, as I can mine. But since I run away from things that I fear, then, it may be supposed, you must fear things from which you run away. So, although I cannot observe your fear, I can infer its existence from the fact that you run away. Ditto your other emotions and thoughts. That I cannot observe them does not prevent me from inferring their existence from your words and deeds. And this, Cartesians have generally supposed, should be enough.

Unfortunately, it isn't. If I cannot perceive your thoughts or feelings, then I have no way to tell what state of mind, if any, goes with your behavior. Hence, for all I can know, absolutely any state of mind might go with absolutely any form of behavior. Thus, you might run toward that which you fear, not away from it; and when you say "2 + 2 = 4" you might mean "I want a cold beer," or nothing at all. So inferences from conduct to corresponding states of consciousness are always extremely perilous, if they have any value at all.

Doesn't introspective testimony count for something? Not if Descartes was right. Given that introspection is supposed to be a virtually infallible source of knowledge about the mind, this may come as a surprise; but the reliability that Descartes attached to introspection does not transfer to the introspective report. Reports are forms of behavior; and, as we have just seen, one implication of Cartesianism is that any form of behavior might go with any state of mind. Thus, someone may not only act afraid when she feels courage but she may

also say that she is afraid, thereby misdescribing her emotion. Hence, inferences to consciousness from introspective reports are also highly dubious.

Things get even worse when we remember that, on Cartesian principles, we also cannot know the external (i.e., the physical) world, just the ideas of it that we have in our minds. But we shall put this vexed issue aside.

Other Problems with Cartesianism

Solipsism is trouble enough; but there is more. The Cartesian mind does not fit into the world as it is described by our best physical and biological science.

Like the other leading physicists of his time, Descartes believed that bodies are nothing but machines, whose actions are wholly determinate (i.e., precisely predictable) and automatic (i.e., necessary) reactions to physical forces. If this is so, however, there is no slack in the physical world to be taken up by the mind. For suppose, as Descartes uncritically did, that the mind could control the actions of the body. Then it could cause a machine to act in ways that were not wholly mechanical. Descartes never worried about this, but it certainly bothered his followers. They concluded that there can be no interaction between mind and body. Instead, there is only parallelism, preestablished harmony (Matson, 1987, p. 282).

An even more serious problem arose when, two centuries after Descartes, Charles Darwin proposed and all but proved his theory of biological evolution. An obvious implication of this theory, which holds that one species develops from another by a multitude of minuscule changes, is that there is no great divide between human beings and creatures very near them on the evolutionary scale. Contrary to Descartes's belief, we are not very different, biologically or behaviorally, from our cousins, the apes and chimpanzees. We are certainly cleverer; but the difference is small. By the end of the nineteenth century, then, it appeared that Cartesian metaphysics could be reconciled neither with mechanistic physics nor with evolutionary biology, two of the leading sciences.

In the twentieth century, a further problem came to the fore: reconciling Cartesianism with logic. It turns out that the acts of mind (beliefs, desires, etc.) so dear to Cartesian hearts are all infected by what Franz Brentano called *intensionality*, lack of existence of their objects. Thus, imagining or thinking about a horse counts as mental, while riding or feeding a horse counts as physical, because you can imagine or think about, but not ride or feed, a non-existing horse. As has been noted by Willard Quine and others, this also means that the mental violates the logical laws of identity, which require that different names of the same thing can be substituted for each other without changing any truths into falsehoods. Thus, if I hit Mark Twain in the nose, then I hit Samuel Clemens in the nose, for they are the same person and share the same nose; but if I think of Mark Twain, it does not follow that I also think of Samuel Clemens.[3]

Given, as Quine has said somewhere, that there is no entity without identity, this failure to satisfy the requirements of the logic of identity is cause to doubt whether, in the final analysis, the mental can be real. And, in fact, when we reflect (1) that the mental, as the Cartesian conceives it, exists only in the mind and (2) is, by Cartesian definition, private (i.e., unobserved by others), we see (3) that it cannot be real. For, judging by our usual standards, what exists only in the mind does not exist; and neither does what can be perceived in only one way or by only one person. Thus, pink elephants—which are seen but not smelled, and seen only by alcoholics suffering delirium tremens—do not exist. They exist in the alcoholic's mind; but they do not exist.

One further problem: Cartesian belief in the inherent logicality of human beings does not square with the behavioral evidence, and it never has. This has recently been documented in various ways by such observant social psychologists as Kahnemann, Tversky, Ross, and Nisbet; but it has never needed documentation. The fact is too obvious. Much of human behavior may be in some sense rational; but human beings are often not very logical, and they are often very illogical. Besides, there is good empirical reason to believe that empirical association is at least as important to human cognition as logical reasoning.

It turns out, then, that Cartesian doctrine suffers from a great many grave defects:

1. It entails solipsism.
2. It cannot be reconciled with mechanistic physics.
3. It cannot be reconciled with evolutionary biology.
4. It cannot be reconciled with logic.
5. Its a priori rationalism cannot be squared with obvious facts about human behavior.

HOW BEHAVIORISM WAS A REACTION TO CARTESIANISM

Behaviorism came into being in order to save psychology from these and related difficulties.

The rescue effort began in the late nineteenth century in the thinking of the American philosopher Charles Peirce. It came to full flower in the twentieth century in the work of, first, J. B. Watson, then B. F. Skinner. Philosophically, it took the form of denying both that the conscious mind is the subject of psychology and that introspection is its method (Ryle, 1949, pp. 11–15). Instead, behaviorists said, the "mind" may be supposed to exist and be in a given condition only insofar as the fact manifests itself in bodily responses to environmental changes.[4] Therefore, the proper method for psychology is not introspection of the conscious mind but empirical study of the behaving body (Watson, 1959, p. 6).

This study would be made possible, behaviorists believed, by the fact that, contrary to Cartesian theory, but consistent with workaday common sense, we can usually tell, without much difficulty, what other people are thinking, perceiving, and feeling. If behaviorists are right, however, we do this not by looking into invisible and intangible "minds" but by studying observable behavior. Thus, to discover that a man is angry, you do not have to get inside his mind. You can see the fact in his face, gestures, and bodily attitude. Then you can confirm it by discovering that he has been frustrated, insulted, or threatened and is undertaking to hurt somebody or destroy something.

How Behaviorists Came to Believe in Operational Definitions

How was this behaviorist program of studying the behavior of organic bodies to be carried out? Partly by means of what physicist Percy Bridgman called *operational definitions* (Bridgman, 1927).

Although the fact is not well known to psychologists, the idea for operational definitions was first conceived by Charles Peirce, the founder of pragmatism. Reflecting on methods that he regularly used as an experimental physicist for the Geodetic Coastal Survey, Peirce once formulated the following *pragmatic maxim*: "Consider what effects that might conceivably have practical bearings we conceive the object of our conception to have. Then our conception of these effects is the whole of our conception of the object" (Peirce, 1960, p. 258).

For a simple example of what Peirce had in mind when he wrote this carefully concocted but difficult saying, consider what is meant by describing an object O as *hard*. To give this meaning, Peirce said, we must specify some test for its truth—say, trying to scratch O. To do this is to define hardness pragmatically and empirically, so that everybody will know what is being discussed. That the definition may not exhaust all that there is to say about hardness is true; but it will at least have the virtue of making clear what we are talking about.

Hardness is a commonplace concept. Peirce believed, however, that pragmatic definition is also applicable to more esoteric ideas. Thus, for a second example, consider what we mean by the claim that object O has electrical charge C. According to Peirce, the explanation will refer to what this claim leads us to expect. Thus, suppose you expect that attaching O to a filament will make it produce light or that touching O will cause you to feel a shock. Then these expectations and others constitute your understanding of the claim that O has electrical charge C.

Peirce's maxim was suggested by his work in physics, but he saw no reason why it could not be used in psychology too. His reasoning was that, if there is a difference between one state of mind and another, then being in it will make a discernible difference. Therefore, he concluded, we can study states and traits of mind as we study hardness or electricity—by studying their effects and relating these to the circumstances that cause them.

For an illustration, suppose that someone is said to be angry. If Peirce was right, what this means can be ascertained by discovering how we expect the person who is angry to differ from the person who is happy, in love, or curious. Thus, suppose that we expect heightened blood pressure, increased muscle tension, rapid heartbeat, a flushed face, and physical assault or verbal abuse. Then these expectations define anger for us and distinguish it from other emotions or moods.

This insight inspired behaviorists tired of disputes about such airy abstractions as "mind" and "consciousness" to demand that psychological terms be defined pragmatically, so that all could know what was being discussed. By thus ensuring that everybody could know what was under discussion, behaviorists hoped to avoid both solipsism and verbal disputes.

Behaviorism and Reflexology

In the beginning, they hoped to reconcile psychology with physics by adopting the view that all behavior, including apparently purposive behavior, is just reflex, mechanically induced motion (Moxley, 1992). The salivation reflex studied by the Russian physiologist Pavlov was a simple reflex. More elaborate forms of behavior—e.g., eating an apple or reading a book—were thought to be complicated chains of simple reflexes. The problem was to figure out how to get complex reflexes by chaining together simple reflexes.

Unfortunately, reducing purposive behavior to complex reflexes turned out to be harder than anybody had anticipated. Consequently, some enterprising behaviorists began to look for another way. They soon found it in J. L. Thorndike's Law of Effect, the principle that behavior is modified by its consequences. Taking a cue from this principle, B. F. Skinner argued that the future likelihood of a given form of conduct (an operant) is a function of its past reinforcements. Thus, the rat runs purposively, rather than randomly, to the end of the maze, because that is where he has previously been fed. Believing that this explanation took the mystery out of purposive behavior, Skinner no longer felt constrained to restrict his studies to reflexes.[5] He abandoned what had come to be called S-R (stimulus-response) psychology in favor of study of the effects on behavior of various schedules and histories of reinforcement (Moxley, 1992).

To Skinner's everlasting chagrin, this fundamental change in the behaviorist program has not always been acknowledged by critics, who would rather attack a straw man; but it had great significance, because it enabled behaviorists for the first time to distinguish action, which is purposive, from mere motion, which is not. Thus, consider Skinner's most famous experimental device, the so-called Skinner Box. In this device, a rat is rewarded with food for pressing a lever. Whether the rat presses the lever with his foot, his nose, or his tail does not matter. The animal's physical motions are behaviorally irrelevant; their result is what counts. Purpose—direction toward ends—was thus neatly integrated into the world of physical motion.

How the Behaviorists Solved, or Avoided, the Remaining Problems of Cartesianism

Skinner's use of rats (and pigeons) as experimental animals is one symptom of another significant feature of behaviorism. Being Darwinians, behaviorists noticed that apes and chimpanzees not only resemble us in many ways but also behave much as we do. In fact, so do such inferior animals as dogs, cats, rats, and pigeons. Therefore, behaviorists concluded that studying animal behavior, both in the laboratory and in natural settings, can help us to understand human behavior too (Boring, 1950, p. 472).

Behaviorists dealt with Cartesian rationalism simply by giving it up. Instead of assuming a priori that human beings were rational, they would undertake to discover the facts by observation. While giving rationalism up, they also gave up the logically defective mentalist language that goes along with it. Mentalist language would be replaced by behaviorist language. Henceforth, we would talk not about what people believe and desire but about what they say and seek. Does Smith *believe* that the wine and the wafer are the body and the blood of Christ? Unanswerable question. What we know is that this is what he *says*. Does Jones *desire* a drink of water? Another unanswerable question. What we know is that this is what she *seeks*. In this way, unclear questions gave way to empirically determinate issues.

Behaviorist resolution to stick to empirically definite issues dominated thought and experimentation in the United States and elsewhere for nearly half a century, from about 1920 to about 1970. Although the fact is nowadays sometimes acknowledged only very grudgingly, this half century produced many great achievements. Among these were a highly varied technology, one that has been found useful in educational, industrial, domestic, commercial, and clinical settings. Behaviorists made valuable contributions to advertising, politics, teaching, management, and to the treatment of emotional and intellectual disorders.

THE DIFFERENCE BETWEEN CAUSES AND FUNCTIONS

Despite these achievements, behaviorism is not now much in favor. In fact, it is now more frequently an object of abuse.

The main cause of this abuse is behaviorist demand for pragmatic, or operational, definitions. This has caused both resentment and confusion. The resentment may be due to the fact that most people would rather use words than define them, especially if they are using words in indefensible ways. But this attitude should not be encouraged. Most people would rather spend money than earn it; but this is no reason to give them unlimited bank accounts. So let us turn from the resentment to the confusion, for which there is a better excuse.

Etymologically speaking, to define something is to draw boundaries around it. Therefore, definitions exist whenever we put any limits on the use of a term. In logic and mathematics, however, the term *definition* is sometimes used more strictly, to denote equations, statements of identity, licenses to substitute the *definiens* for the *definiendum*—what Quine calls conventions of notational abbreviation (Quine, 1966, p. 71).

This latter understanding of definition has caused the request for behavioral definitions to be interpreted as a demand that causes be identified with their effects.[6] Thus, it is supposed, an operational definition of hardness confuses the cause, the object's hardness, with resistance, its effect; an operational definition of electricity confuses the cause, electrical charge, with its effect, the glow; and a behavioral definition of anger confuses feelings of anger with their behavioral manifestations, red faces and shouting. Since one can have a red face or shout without feeling angry, and conversely, many Cartesians have concluded that demand for behavioral definitions is misguided.

Although influential, this criticism is defective. It assumes that there are such entities as hardness, electricity, and feelings of anger. But this need not be true. Because the words *hardness, electricity* and *anger* are names, it may seem to follow that they must name something; but not every name has something answering to it. The word *green* is a name, and so is the word *square*; but, although there are green colored and square-shaped things, there is no such thing as the color Green or the shape Square. Likewise, although there are hard objects, electrically charged filaments, and angry people, there is no such thing as hardness, electricity, or anger. Hardness, electricity, and anger are not things but conditions or characteristics of things.[7]

Although it may seem pedantic, this small point of logic makes an enormous difference to one's view of scientific explanation. Perhaps the simplest illustration from physics, the best developed science, is gravity. In some earlier views, gravity was a thing, viz., the force that caused objects to fall. Although this view is still favored by the scientifically uneducated general public, who love talk of mysterious powers and unseen forces, and even believe that such talk is scientific, philosophically sophisticated scientists now generally agree that there is no such *thing* as the force of Gravity. In the view of many good scientists, including Einstein, gravity is better regarded as a *function*, a relation between variables. This function cannot be pointed at, but it can be described by a formula: Bodies in isolated physical systems tend to move toward each other with a speed that is directly proportional to their masses and inversely proportional to the square of the distance between them. More simply: On the surface of the earth, gravity is the function described by the formula, "Dropped bodies tend to fall."

It follows that it is a mistake to think of gravity as the *cause* of things falling. The cause of things falling is their being dropped. What we call gravity is just the rule that, when the cause is in effect, so is the effect. Knowing this rule we may say:

> Bodies that are dropped tend to fall.
> This body was dropped.
> Therefore, this body fell.

So the rule, "Bodies fall when dropped," plays a part in our explanations of why things fall. But as the philosophers of science, Hempel and Oppenheim, observed a few decades ago, it plays the part of covering law, not the part of cause (Hempel and Oppenheim, 1948).

Reflections such as these seemed to show that much of science could be regarded as the search not for causes but for explanations—or rather, for the functional relationships (the covering laws) that enable us to provide explanations. What Peirce and Bridgman were proposing was to treat such physical properties as hardness and electrical charge not as things but functions, not as causes but rules relating causes to effects. Thus, hardness was to be regarded not as the cause of resistance but as the function that relates resistance to pressure. Similarly, electrical charge was to be regarded not as the cause of the glow but as that which relates the glow to such events as the rotation of magnets between coils of copper wire.

This having worked in physics, behaviorists proposed to try it in psychology too. They would undertake what B. F. Skinner was to call *functional analysis*, meaning an attempt to relate conduct to its circumstances and history (Moxley, 1992). Thus, anger would be treated not as a cause but as a function, one that relates irritating or frustrating stimuli and previous behavioral conditioning to increased heart rate, elevated blood pressure, red faces, shouting and destructiveness. The other emotions (fear, love, etc.) would be treated likewise (Derr and Thompson, 1992).

As this indicates, the answer to the charge that behaviorists confuse causes with effects is that those who say so are confusing functions with things.

Why Cartesians Are Not Satisfied with Functional Analysis

Unfortunately, these arguments do not persuade Cartesians. In their view, the business of psychology is to discover not the functions (or lawlike regularities) that relate circumstances to conduct but the states of mind that, the Cartesian believes, intervene between circumstances and conduct, causing one given the other. Thus, the Cartesian is interested not in the general relation between being insulted and shouting but in the particular feeling of anger that he knows, by introspection, to exist and that he believes, on principle, to have been caused by an insult and to be the cause of shouting. So the behaviorist, who searches for functional relations between observable kinds while neglecting introspectively known particulars, seems to the Cartesian to be fiddling while Rome burns.

What the Cartesian has in mind can be indicated by using our now familiar example once again. Suppose that we explain why Smith is shouting by saying, "Because he is angry." If the Cartesian is right, this will not be just a way of pointing out the existence of a function that relates insults or irritating circumstances to red faces and shouts; it will not just mean, "Smith is shouting in response to insult or irritation, because, other things being equal, he tends to shout when insulted or irritated." Instead, it will mean, "Something—let us call it anger—is going on inside Smith; and this internal but introspectively identifiable event, condition, or state of affairs connects an insult or an irritating event to Smith's shouting, by being the effect of the one and the cause of the other."

As the Cartesian sees it, the main business of the psychologist is to tell us about mediating events such as these (Fodor, 1979, p. 7). So the psychologist does not do his job as the Cartesian sees it if he merely relates circumstances to conduct, by telling us that the one frequently accompanies the other. In the view of the Cartesian, this kind of correlational science does not do what is wanted; it does not give us what used to be called the *proximal cause*. Granting, then, that insults and irritation tend to produce shouts, the Cartesian wants to be told how and why; he wants to know the mechanism. He wants, in other words, to know what goes on inside somebody when he is insulted and how this causes him to shout; and he does not mean to be put off by patient reminders that insults often lead to shouts.

For a physical analogy, consider hardness again. Grant that declaring an object to be hard is saying that it will resist pressure. We still want to know why this is so. What is there about hard objects that enables them to resist pressure? As it happens, the correct explanation refers to the bonds between the constituent molecules of hard objects. This account gives us a *structural* explanation of hardness. The Cartesian wants us to tell a similar story about the person who is angry. He wants a structural explanation for behavior.

Although behaviorists have sometimes resisted it, this Cartesian demand for structural explanations is not only legitimate but also unavoidable. There is no causation at a distance or across time. Instead, causation requires physical and temporal continuity. Furthermore, explaining why something sometimes happens also means explaining why it sometimes does not happen. Cartesians want the temporal and spatial gap between insult and shout filled by mention of what goes on in between; they want the filling to explain why insults sometimes lead to shouts but sometimes do not. In short, they want *continuity of cause* and *differentiation of effect*; and they do not believe that functions relating circumstances to behavior provide either.

In the view of the Cartesian, there is only one way to get what is wanted. We can get the continuity only by postulating or discovering an appropriate mental event, condition, or state of affairs; and we can get the differentiation only by postulating or discovering different mental events, conditions, or states of affairs. Thus, we can connect Smith's shouting to his being insulted only by discovering, or postulating, feelings of anger; and we can

explain why Jones does not shout when insulted by discovering or postulating that, unlike Smith, Jones does not easily get angry.

Why These Arguments Are Not Conclusive

The argument is powerful. In science, causal continuity and effect differentiation are reasonable requirements. So it is important to ask whether the behaviorist can satisfy them.

Differentiation is easy. As Skinner repeatedly said, we can always differentiate one effect from another by seeking, or postulating, differences in history. Thus, if Jones, who has a more placid temper than Smith, does not get angry quite so readily, perhaps it is because he has learned self-control; or perhaps it is because he inherited a different constitution or has had a better day. As this shows, to get differentiation, there is no need to discover, or to postulate, unobserved—much less unobservable—events, conditions, or states of affairs. Just look for different histories.

Continuity presents a greater difficulty. In my opinion, the honest behaviorist will admit that he does not provide it. Thus, consider the questions, "How, structurally speaking, does an angry person differ from one who is not angry? What is there about the angry person that makes him respond to insults or irritation by shouting and destroying things?" The behaviorist has no answer to these questions; he is unable to specify a mechanism. His self-selected job is describing the function. He regards the search for mechanisms as the job of the physiologist.

As all psychologists know, that job has been at least partly done. Thanks to the now classic researches of Cannon and his associates, we know that angry people tend to have higher blood pressure, elevated heart rates, increased adrenalin, and so on. The trouble is that these same physical symptoms are present in the case of sexual excitement, fear, and other states of arousal. So we do not yet know the full structural—just some of the functional—differences between the person who is angry and the person who is not. Nor, therefore, do we have a comprehensive account of how and why the structural state of anger leads to one form of behavior rather than another.

Here the Cartesian, who is ready to fill the gap by postulating a mental condition, the feeling of anger, appears to have the advantage. His advantage is, however, merely apparent. In the absence of an independent procedure for identifying it, talking about the mental but nonbehavioral feeling of anger is also not specifying the necessary mechanism. It provides that mechanism with a name but not with a distinguishing description.

As things stand, then, we know how to identify anger only by invoking the observed correlation between such circumstances as insults and such conduct as shouting. In other words, we can only identify anger functionally. But that is as much as to say that we cannot yet identify it structurally as an intervening mechanism. If there is such a distinctive mechanism—or, perhaps, two or three such mechanisms—we do not yet know what it is; and merely calling it a feeling of anger does not suffice to tell us. If we had another, more categorical way of identifying it, this would not be so. But, as things stand, we do not.

THE ISSUE JOINED: HOW BEHAVIORISTS AND CARTESIANS DISAGREE

Good Cartesians will protest that we do know how to identify and describe the state of mind that we call anger, because we can observe it by means of introspection and describe it by saying how it appears to those of us who feel it.

Looked at from a behaviorist point of view, the trouble with this reply is twofold. First, introspection does not involve use of any known sensory mechanisms. To put it crudely: We know that we see with the eyes and hear with the ears; but we do not know what we introspect with. Introspection is itself mysterious.[8] Second, it is notorious that the features of mental states discovered by means of introspection cannot be confirmed by other means or fitted into the world as it is described by physical science. Thus, unless you are willing to take my word for it, the fact that I feel anger cannot be confirmed by you; and there is no description for this feeling in the language of physics.

Why are these flaws? First, you do not dissolve one mystery by invoking another, deeper mystery. Instead, you just deepen the mystery. Thus, when you explain, in Cartesian fashion, how people are able to think and feel and choose by saying that they have minds that think and feel, and wills that choose, you do not advance our understanding. Instead, you just put the question off. Where before we had to ask, "How does a person think, feel, and choose?" we now have to ask, "How does the mind think and feel and the will choose?" No progress here.

Second, the fact is that, although real (i.e., physical) objects, events, and processes can always be detected by more than one person in more than one way, mental but immaterial objects, events, and processes cannot. In fact, public and variable detectability is our usual test and measure of the real. Thus, the physical elephants that we see in the zoo count as real, whereas the mental elephants that alcoholics see in delirium tremens do not. The latter exist in the alcoholic's mind, of course; but they do not exist. They have mental descriptions; but, because they lack physical descriptions, they count as unreal.

As behaviorists view them, then, Cartesian explanations are not explanations properly so-called, just familiar names for old mysteries. Thus, the Cartesian says that people shout and grow red in the face because they feel anger. The Cartesian may thereby name the condition that gives rise to the behavior in question; but he does not thereby identify it, much less say how it does the work that he attributes to it. So he makes little contribution to our understanding.

Cartesian Linguistics

Anger is, of course, just one example; and it is not one that much interests Cartesians, who have always cared more about the intellect than the passions. It is therefore not surprising that what brought behaviorism into its current disfavor, beginning some twenty years ago, was not so much its account of the emotions as its account of language and thought.

The attack on the most elaborate and sophisticated version of this account, Harvard professor Skinner's *Verbal Behavior*, was led by MIT professor of linguistics and philosophy Noam Chomsky, who argued that Skinner's discussion, which made reinforcement central to language learning, could explain neither how children learn language so easily and quickly nor how they come by the ability to construct novel sentences, utterances of which have not previously been reinforced (Place, 1992).

Chomsky's own explanation of these matters was distinctly Cartesian: The human brain comes innately endowed with a knowledge of the basic rules of grammar and logic—what Descartes would have called the rules of speech and thought.

These rules, which are essentially the same in the brains of all humans everywhere, are specifiable in formulas whose variables can be replaced by, or correlated with, suitable vocabulary, to produce sentences in any of the world's great variety of languages. The sentences can then be transformed or combined in accordance with similarly innate rules in order to produce new sentences—all in good logical fashion (Fodor, 1979, p. 58).

In other words, Chomsky held that the brains of suitably mature human beings are ready-built logic (i.e., syntax) machines, which need only to be provided with the requisite verbal (i.e., semantic) material in order to be able to generate an endless variety of correct sentences. Thus, because they already know the grammar and have only to learn the vocabulary, young children have no difficulty learning language or producing novel sentences.

How did Chomsky know this? He did not. He asserted it because it seemed to him to be the only hypothesis consistent with the available evidence. The chief task of the linguist, as Chomsky saw it, is to confirm this hypothesis by discovering and displaying the innate rules of grammar that, Chomsky presumed, underlie and underwrite all human speech and, thereby, all human thought. The program of research in Cartesian linguistics which Chomsky thus began is still in progress. It is an ongoing project, not a finished achievement.

While Chomsky was advancing his ideas about language, the electrical engineers at MIT, his home university, were working on another revolution: the two-valued digital computer. This device is essentially a machine for engaging in logical computation by electronic means. Composed of a complex of switched circuits, each of which is either on or off, as a sentence is either true or false, this machine has the capacity, when suitably wired and programmed, to effect logical and grammatical transformations in accordance with strict rules; and because logic is fundamental to much of arithmetic, it can also perform various arithmetical computations. In short, it can do sums and syllogisms, which Descartes, along with Aristotle, had taken to be the distinctive mark of intelligent thought.

Since the brain is itself composed of neurons, which make connections with each other by means of synapses, neuronal switching circuits, it did not take long for the people at MIT to venture the hypothesis that the human brain might itself be a two-valued digital computer, a machine for processing sentences, verbal expressions of thoughts. On the engineering side, the result was a program for artificial intelligence—constructing machines designed to do things that, up to now, only human beings have been able to do. On the philosophical side was a revival of the Cartesian theory of the mind as a built-in logic machine.

CARTESIAN MATERIALISM: THE NEW CARTESIANISM

There was, of course, one difference in this new theory: It was now not dualistic but materialistic. Unlike Descartes, who denied that thought is in any way physical, the new Cartesians insisted that states of mind are processes in the physical brain. It is just that we do not yet know their physical descriptions.

The fact that we do not yet know the requisite descriptions is, however, not supposed to matter, for two reasons. First, according to the new Cartesians, the very same mental state or operation could have two or more different physical embodiments (Hocutt, 1985). This possibility was suggested by thinking of the brain as a digital computer. As Hilary Putnam pointed out, two differently constructed or programmed computers can perform the same computation (e.g., adding 2 and 2) in quite different ways. Thus, Apple computers, which use different chips, work differently than IBM computers; but, so far as the user is concerned, the two can nevertheless do essentially the same things and get essentially the same results. Hence, the average computer user has no need to worry about how his machine works. For him, it is enough to know that it does work.

A second reason the Cartesian materialist feels no need for physical descriptions is this: He believes that, if the neurophysiologists will just do their job right, suitable physical descriptions will soon be forthcoming. Of course, the Cartesian knows that finding these descriptions will take time and ingenuity; but he is confident that it will be done. In the meanwhile, he believes that, just as we can leave it to computer engineers to worry about the structures and workings of computers, so we can leave it to neurophysiologists to worry about the structure and workings of brains.

This rationale enables the Cartesian materialist to eat his mentalist cake and keep it too. Now he can continue, as before, trying to discover how the mind functions while leaving it to others to discover how the brain makes this possible. In other words, he can continue to use the mentalist language and introspective technique of Cartesian psychology in the expectation that this dubious vocabulary will one day be couched in the more respectable diction of neural science.

To see how this might work in a particular case, suppose that a subject allowed to study a list of words is able to repeat it; and suppose that this is explained by saying that the subject "remembers" the list. Or suppose that the subject is able to close her eyes and count the number of windows on the front of her house; and suppose that this is explained by saying that she is viewing a "mental image" of her house. The Cartesian believes that the psychologist who offers these and like explanations has now done his job; and she can leave it to the neurophysiologist to do her job by discovering how changes in the subject's brain have made her memory, or mental image, possible. In short, the psychologist having identified the necessary cognitive operations, it is now up to the neurophysiologist to describe them and the computer scientist to "model" them by embodying similar operations in electronic machines.

Such, very crudely described, is the general idea behind some—although not by any means all—of what is now called "computational" or "cognitive" science.[9] According to this idea, we may one day know precise physical descriptions for mental states. In the meanwhile, our ignorance of these descriptions does not matter, because we can, as before, always identify the mental states in question, either introspectively, by looking into our own minds, or functionally, as the mental (i.e., computational) events that must be supposed to exist if we are to explain behavior.

Why Behaviorists Dislike the New Cartesianism Too

This new form of Cartesianism presents a serious challenge to behaviorism. The workings of the brain may not yet have been observed; but there is no reason to think that they will forever remain so. Although we do not yet know the physical descriptions of our various brain states, it is to be presumed that these can eventually be discovered. So Cartesians are no longer talking about things that cannot be publicly observed or fit into the world as it is described by physics. Now they freely acknowledge that even mental operations must

have physical descriptions. So, if behaviorists still dislike Cartesianism, it is fair to ask why.

The answer is that Cartesianism still has all the other problems remarked on earlier. One such problem is solipsism. Because the new Cartesians acknowledge that mental events are physical and, therefore, publicly observable, it may seem that this problem has also been solved. In fact, it has not. As Jerry Fodor, the leading expositor and exponent of the new Cartesianism, has insisted, the right method for psychology is "methodological solipsism," treating mental processes as if they were autonomous, independent of their surroundings (Buller, 1992). This follows from Fodor's Cartesian belief that the brain is essentially a logic machine, the computations of which are purely formal operations on internal representations (Fodor, 1979). So, to discuss how the brain thinks or reasons, we need not concern ourselves with what it thinks or reasons about (Fodor, 1981).

To appreciate the implications of this view, consider my belief that there are rabbits and my desire to eat rabbit stew. If Fodor is right, these are relations that I have, not to rabbits, but to whatever it is that, for the moment, happens to represent them in my brain. Likewise, imagining a rabbit is having a relation not to rabbits but to a representation (an image, perhaps, or a digitalization of an image?) in my own brain. Hence, Fodor believes with Descartes that all simple ideas (i.e., basic representations) are innate; complex ideas are just the results of recombining various simple ideas; and the brain is just an instrument for the recombination, which takes place in accordance with strict, antecedently given, and unalterable rules of logic.

As an account of the workings of man-made computers, this makes some sense.[10] It is easy to see that the computational operations of a computer are, in a sense, autonomous, functionally independent of the physical descriptions of the objects in its environment, if not the input through its peripherals. Indeed, as earlier noticed, these operations are, in a manner of speaking, independent of the physical description of the computer itself. It is, however, not obvious that the brain is such a computer, or that it enjoys such autonomy. In fact, this seems highly unlikely. Unlike the computer, which is a human artifact, the brain is a product of biological evolution, which favors organic structures that facilitate adaptation to their environments. Besides, human beings are not as rigidly logical as computers. Both facts are hard to reconcile with Cartesian belief that the brain is a logic machine that operates in splendid isolation, according to its own antecedently fixed rules and standards.

The Emptiness of Cartesian Explanations

Cartesian belief in innateness also bothers behaviorists, not because they have anything against innate knowledge but because they believe that postulations of such knowledge should be parsimonious, lest they border on seeming miraculous. No doubt we come readily equipped, or become so after suitable maturation, to make some rudimentary discriminations and perform some primitive operations; else we could never get going. But is it to be assumed that we come readily equipped for everything? That would be a very large claim.

Fodor has nevertheless defended something approaching this claim by arguing that it is an implication of the rest of his theory, which must be accepted because it is "the only game in town." In other words, we must adopt Fodor's Cartesian account because there is no better (Fodor, 1979, p. 42).

This is an *argumentum ad ignoratium*. Grant, for the moment, that one can readily explain any given form of behavior by postulating innate capacities and dispositions. Such postulates will be helpful only if we have some idea of how the innate mechanisms in question might have come into being; and, so far, the sad fact is that we do not. Descartes believed that our innate knowledge is God-given, but this explains a mystery by postulating a miracle. An evolutionary account would be better; but, so far, the Cartesians have made no effort to provide one.

Besides, despite Fodor's claim, there has always been an alternative: Most of what we know is learned by interaction with the environment. It is true that, until recently, no account of the workings of the brain has been able to explain how having one enables us to learn; so, here the Cartesians appear to have had a clear field. Recently, however, this situation has changed dramatically. Work on connectionist networks suggests an architecture for the brain that shows promise of coming closer to the facts in several ways (Bechtel and Abrahamsen, 1991; Churchland, 1989).

In the first place, connectionist networks employ parallel, rather than serial, processing. This means that they show better promise of modeling the workings of the cerebral cortex, which is built up in interconnected layers, which almost certainly work in parallel. In the second place, connectionist networks seem to have the capacity for learning. They start out with certain settings; but, given suitable feedback, they alter these initial settings so as to respond with more accurate discrimination to the objects in their environments. Thus, instead of following fixed rules, they appear to make up their own rules as they go along; and they can alter these rules to suit changes in their environments. In short, they learn; they are adaptive mechanisms. All of this is very good news to behaviorists.

Cartesians object that the connectionists have not yet shown in any detail how their machines model intelligent behavior, particularly human speech; but neither have the Cartesians.[11] Here we have two competing research programs. No one can be sure in advance which, if either, will prove successful; but the good behaviorist will put his money on the connectionist program.

Remaining Problems with the New Cartesianism

Even if the connectionist program fails, behaviorists will remain unwilling to bet on Cartesian philosophy, for several reasons.

One is the Cartesian's continued insistence on using mental terminology. As is well known to philosophers, nobody has yet been able to solve the logical puzzles that plague mentalist vocabulary; there is still no consistent and useful logic for belief, desire, or other mentalist terms. All such language remains not just empirically undefined but also logically unregimented. Its scientific legitimacy is still very much in question.

Despite this, Fodor has stoutly defended belief, desire, and other mentalist concepts on the grounds that using these concepts helps us to understand and predict each other's behavior (Fodor, 1979, p. 28). Unhappily, the premise is not true and the conclusion does not follow. Stick for the moment to belief. Let Smith accept, "Mark Twain wrote *Huckleberry Finn*." We cannot predict that he will also accept, "Samuel Clemens wrote *Huckleberry Finn*." He might if he accepts "Mark Twain is Samuel Clemens"; but there is no guarantee even of that.

This case is, of course, trivial; but there are plenty of important examples. Consider, again, the Catholic's sincere assertion that the wine and wafer are the blood and body of Christ. Does the Catholic truly believe this? Or does he just assert it very sincerely? The question is hopeless. What is to be the test of belief? How is it to be distinguished from sincere assertion? The epistemological and logical difficulties in answering this question are notorious; and attempts to overcome these difficulties just produce interminable verbal disputes.

It must be admitted, of course, that we folk psychologists are adept at making up combinations of beliefs and desires that will, together with antecedent assumptions about human rationality, enable us to predict or explain behavior with some degree of accuracy. Thus, we say "Smith is going to the grocer because he wants some meat and believes that the grocer has some." But this proves nothing to the point. Chemists once made more or less accurate predictions using the concept of phlogiston. Their success, such as it was, is attributable not to their understanding of the relevant mechanisms, which was very poor, but to their knowledge, which was considerable, of the relevant functions.

As the Cartesian says, talk of belief and desire certainly provides a useful, if opaque, shorthand with which to relate circumstances to conduct or future conduct to past. In fact, we wouldn't know how to get along without this shorthand, which works as well as it does only given the assumption that human beings are more or less rational. But although this shorthand and its attendant assumption are indispensable for the time being, using them still does nothing to identify the neural mechanisms that are involved. To invoke beliefs and desires is still to give functional, not structural, explanations.

Nothing wrong with that, of course. Behaviorists, who live in a glass house, cannot afford to throw stones at functional explanations. But the mental functions being invoked by the Cartesians do not satisfy the logical and empirical requirements of good science, and they are often falsely advertised as being not functional explanations but mental mechanisms. Besides, the assumption on which these functions are premised—that human beings are logical—does not square very readily with well-known facts. So, if behaviorists are living in a glass house, Cartesians are living in a house of cards.

CONCLUSIONS

If we exempt Aristotle's anticipation, behaviorism began three-quarters of a century ago as a reaction to Cartesianism, a moribund research program that, for religious reasons, had construed the human being, but no other living creature, as a material body possessed of an immaterial mind. The mind was believed to process God-given ideas using fixed rules of logic and to be knowable only by introspection. Behaviorists rejected this widely accepted view on several grounds. First, it invokes miracles and entails solipsism. Second, it cannot be reconciled with the Cartesian's view that bodies are machines. Third, belief that there is a great divide between men and beasts cannot be squared with evolutionary biology. Fourth, Cartesians use mentalist language, which is neither empirically well defined nor logically well regulated. Fifth, explaining how people think by saying that they have minds that do it for them (or that they remember by storing things in memory) does not help, although it may give us the illusion of understanding. Behaviorists, who prefer the reality, therefore demanded that all psychological terms be operationally defined and logically regimented. Furthermore, they gave up speculation about internal mechanisms in favor of functional analysis, the attempt to discover lawful relationships between circumstances and conduct.

Cartesians chafed under the restrictions inherent in behaviorism until Noam Chomsky successfully challenged behaviorist accounts of language and Jerry Fodor argued that bare functional analysis provides no account of mediating mechanisms. Proclaiming themselves to be materialists, these new Cartesians undertook to make their views scientifically respectable by suggesting that the human brain is a digital computer, a logic machine that operates with built-in ideas. Because nobody had a viable alternative theory until recently, this Cartesian hypothesis has inspired much interesting and useful work in cognitive psychology and artificial intelligence. But the new Cartesian hypothesis still postulates a virtual miracle by making everything innate; and it still makes a commitment to solipsism, while thumbing its nose at evolutionary biology, by supposing that the operations of the brain are autonomous, independent of the environment. Finally, it still makes essential use of illegitimate mentalist terminology, and it still invokes processes that are themselves in need of explanation—all decided defects. Work on connectionist networks promises an account that behaviorists should find more to their liking, if only because it eschews a priori assumptions and tries to stay close to the empirically known facts. But only time will tell which of these two philosophies, if either, is right; and there could be some little truth on both sides.[12]

ENDNOTES

1. Insofar as behaviorism is anything positive, it is just empiricism—insistence on talking about what can be observed (Gibson, 1988).

2. As Locke was to point out, it is, strictly speaking, necessary only that the simple ideas be innate; the compound ideas might result from the combination of simple ideas. Hence, the business of what was called analytical psychology, which was practiced by Wundt and his school, was to break compound ideas down into their simple, innately given, and introspectively known components.

3. So much literature has been devoted to this complex issue that I have not undertaken to provide documentation for these remarks, or to qualify them.

4. This has led some people to believe that behaviorists deny the existence of consciousness. In a manner of speaking, this is true. Behaviorists believe that there is no such thing as consciousness, as there is no such thing as color. But they believe like everybody else that some beings are conscious, as some things are colored.

5. The mystery referred to here is, of course, the question of how the future, which does not yet exist, can influence the present (Skinner, 1953).

6. The result of this was the disastrous view sometimes called logical, or analytical, behaviorism. According to this view, behaviorism is the thesis that mentalist vocabulary can be translated without change of meaning into behaviorist vocabulary. For comments on this view, see Hocutt (1985).

7. As philosophers from Aristotle to Quine have pointed out, the distinguishing mark of what we regard as a thing is that we talk about it. Insofar as we can talk about characteristics of things, these count as things in a secondary sense; but they are really only things by courtesy, for everything that we say by talking about them can be said by talking about the things of which they are characteristics. Thus, "Green is a color," seems to be about Green; but it is equivalent to "Green things are colored things," which is about things.

8. That is why behaviorists think that introspection ought, like observation, to be a subject for experimental investigation, not something to be taken for granted, still less regarded as privileged and infallible.

9. Let me enter a disclaimer here. I do not mean to imply that all cognitive psychology, or all research on memory and imaging, is Cartesian. Not so. But where the shoe fits, it must be worn.

10. By acknowledging this for the sake of the argument, I hereby ignore difficulties in the idea that computers contain, and perform computations on, representations. What computers contain are circuit boards and electrical currents. These count as computations over representations only given that we are prepared to impose a certain interpretation on what the computer is doing. I forego pressing this point because, I suppose, the same thing could be said about the brain if it turned out to be like the digital computer. It too could be said to contain representations and to compute only given that we, external observers, were prepared to interpret its processes in those terms, because of our interest in the connection between the brain's operations and the objects in its environment. All this would show, in the end, is that Ryle was right: Although people calculate, it is perhaps metaphorical in the extreme to say that either machines or brains do.

11. Actually connectionists have made progress even here. As Bechtel and Abrahamsen (1991) point out, connectionist networks make good pattern recognizers. But logic and grammar consist in patterns, which can be recognized by connectionist machines already in existence.

12. I want to thank Norm Ellis, Mark Rowlands, and Nick Thompson for helpful criticism and discussion.

REFERENCES

Bechtel, W., & Abrahamsen, A. (1991). *Connectionism and the mind: An introduction to parallel processing in networks.* Oxford: Basil Blackwell.

Boring, E. G. (1950). *A history of experimental psychology* (2nd ed.). New York: Prentice Hall.

Bridgman, P. W. (1927). *The logic of modern physics.* New York: Macmillan.

Buller, D. J. (1992). "Narrow"-mindedness breeds inaction. *Behavior and Philosophy, 20*(1), 59–70.

Churchland, P. M. (1989). *A neurocomputational perspective: The nature of mind and the structure of science.* Cambridge, MA: MIT.

Derr, P., & Thompson, N. S. (1992). Reconstruing hempelian motivational explanations. *Behavior and Philosophy, 20*(1), 37–47.

Descartes, R. (1955). In E. S. Haldane & G. R. T. Ross (Eds.), *The philosophical works of Descartes* (Vol. I). New York: Dover.

Fodor, J. (1979). *The language of thought.* Cambridge, MA: Harvard.

Fodor, J. (1981). *Representations.* Cambridge, MA: MIT.

Gibson, R. F., Jr. (1988). *Enlightened empiricism: An examination of W.V. Quine's theory of knowledge.* Tampa, FL: University of South Florida.

Hempel, C. G., & Oppenheim, P. (1948). Studies in the logic of explanation. *Philosophy of Science, 15,* 135–175.

Hineline, P. N. (1992). A self-interpretive behavior analysis. *American Psychologist, 47*(11), 1274–1287.

Hocutt, M. O. (1985). Spartans, strawmen, and symptoms. *Behaviorism, 13,* 87–97.

Matson, W. I. (1987). *A new history of philosophy,* Vol. II. New York: Harcourt Brace Jovanovich.

Moxley, R. A. (1992). From mechanistic to functional behaviorism. *American Psychologist, 17*(11), 1300–1312.

Peirce, C. S. (1960). In C. Hartshorne & P. Weiss (Eds.), *Collected papers of Charles Sanders Peirce* (Vol. V). Cambridge, MA: Harvard University.

Place, U. T. (1992). Eliminative connectionism: Its implications for a return to an empiricist/behaviorist linguistics. *Behavior and Philosophy, 20*(1), 21–37.

Quine, W. V. (1966). *The ways of paradox.* New York: Random House.

Ryle, G. (1949). *The concept of mind.* New York: Barnes & Noble.

Skinner, B. F. (1953). *Science and human behavior.* New York: Macmillan.

Watson, J. B. (1959). *Behaviorism.* Chicago: University of Chicago Press.

CHAPTER 7

QUINE'S BEHAVIORISM

Roger F. Gibson

"…I do consider myself as behavioristic as anyone in his right mind could be."
W. V. Quine, "Linguistics and Philosophy"

INTRODUCTION

Willard Van Orman Quine (b. 1908) is one of the most influential analytic philosophers of the twentieth century, placing him squarely in the company of Bertrand Russell, Ludwig Wittgenstein, and Rudolf Carnap. Beginning in the early 1930s, Quine has published countless journal articles and some twenty one books, including *Word and Object* (1960), *Roots of Reference* (1974), *From a Logical Point of View* (1980a), *Theories and Things* (1981c), *The Time of My Life* (an autobiography, 1985b), *Pursuit of Truth* (1992), and *From Stimulus to Science* (1995). He has made contributions to logic and set theory, philosophy of logic and set theory, philosophy of language, philosophy of mind, metaphysics, epistemology, and even ethics. However, it would not be amiss to say that over the past six decades Quine has been preoccupied with exploring the relations obtaining among mind, world, and language. Moreover, he has done so from a behavioristic point of view. In this essay, our chief concern is to ascertain the nature and scope of that point of view. But before doing so, we

would do well to set the stage by looking at some of the general features of Quine's philosophy, in particular at his naturalism, physicalism, empiricism, and fallibilism. As we shall see, Quine's empiricism and his behaviorism are intimately connected.

STAGE SETTING

Quine is a staunch advocate of *naturalism*, a view comprised of two theses: (1) *there is no adequate first philosophy*, i.e., no a priori *or* experiential ground outside of science upon which science can either be justified or rationally reconstructed, as was the wont of traditional epistemologists; (2) *science is the measure of what there is* as well as *the measure of how we come to know what there is*.

If there is no adequate first philosophy, as the naturalist maintains, then epistemologies as disparate as Descartes's and Carnap's fail of their purpose. While Descartes sought to deduce the truths of nature from a foundation of clear and distinct ideas, (early) Carnap sought to rationally reconstruct scientific discourse from a foundation of elementary experiences. Quine advances a series of philosophical arguments and considerations designed to establish the untenability of Descartes-like and Carnap-like epistemic programs. In short, Quine argues that Descartes-like efforts fail because not even the truths of arithmetic, let alone all the truths of nature, can be deduced from a foundation of clear and distinct ideas, and Carnap-like efforts fail because a theory's theoretical terms cannot be defined, even contextually, in observation terms.[1] Such reductionism is impossible if, as Quine maintains, many or most individual sentences of scientific theories do not possess their own observable confirming and infirming conditions in terms of which such reductive definitions must be framed.[2] The negative (naturalistic) conclusion Quine draws from all this is that traditional, foundationalist epistemology must be abandoned; the quest for a nonscientific epistemic ground for science is a will-o'-the-wisp.

However, all is not lost with the passing of first philosophy, for natural science remains, and, according to Quine, natural science offers not only the currently best theory of what exists (ontology), it also offers the currently best theory of how we come to know what exists (epistemology). In particular, the currently best theory of what exists supports physicalism, while the currently best theory of how we come to know what exists supports empiricism.

Quine's advocacy of *physicalism* means different things in different contexts. In philosophy of language it indicates his repudiation of mentalistic semantics; in philosophy of mind it indicates his repudiation of mind-body dualism; in ontology it indicates his acceptance of the doctrine that "nothing happens in the world, not the flutter of an eyelid, not the flicker of a thought, without some redistribution of microphysical states."[3] Still, Quine's ontological physicalism countenances more than physical states; it also countenances the abstract objects of applied mathematics, namely, classes. Quine's ground for admitting these abstract objects to his physicalist ontology is that science simply cannot proceed without them.

Quine's advocacy of *empiricism* endorses the following two tenets: "Whatever evidence there *is* for science *is* sensory evidence…[and] all inculcation of meanings of words must rest ultimately on sensory evidence."[4] These two tenets of empiricism are, according to Quine, findings of science: "Science itself teaches that there is no clairvoy-

ance; that the only information that can reach our sensory surfaces from external objects must be limited to two-dimensional optical projections and various impacts of air waves on the eardrums and some gaseous reactions in the nasal passages and a few kindred odds and ends."[5]

So Quine's commitments to physicalism and to empiricism are both based on current scientific findings. But Quine is also a *fallibilist* regarding science; he recognizes that science is changeable and, therefore, it conceivably might someday withdraw its support for physicalism and/or empiricism. Thus, Quine's commitments to physicalism and to empiricism are, at the same time, firm but tentative.

As we have seen, Quine rejects traditional epistemology (i.e., first philosophy). However, he does not abandon epistemology altogether. Rather, he advocates "an enlightened persistence . . . in the original epistemological problem,"[6] the problem of relating evidence to theory. Quine calls this enlightened persistence *naturalized epistemology*. The naturalized epistemologist is enlightened because, having given up the quest for a first philosophy outside of science, he/she recognizes the legitimacy of using the findings of psychology and allied sciences (e.g., neurology, genetics, psycholinguistics) for constructing an answer to the central question of epistemology, namely, 'How do we acquire our overall theory of the world and why does it work so well?'

One final bit of stage setting remains: It is very important to understand that, for Quine, natural science and empiricism reciprocally contain one another. Natural science *contains* empiricism on at least three grounds: (1) empiricists presuppose (they do not prove) the existence of the external world; (2) the two tenets of empiricism (noted above) are themselves findings of natural science; (3) sensory receptors, the human subject's contact points with the world (according to empiricists) are themselves physical objects belonging to the ontology of natural science, viz., to anatomy–physiology. Natural science *is contained in* empiricism in the sense that the ontology of natural science is a projection from the very same kind of sensory data (e.g., light rays, molecules, nerve endings, and so on) accorded to the human subject of the epistemologist's study. But this last reflection, Quine notes, "arouses certain logical misgivings: for is not our very talk of light rays, molecules, and men then only sound and fury, induced by irritation of our surfaces and signifying nothing? The world view [ontology] which lent plausibility to this modest account of our knowledge is, according to this very account of our knowledge [empiricism], a groundless fabrication."[7] Such a conclusion is nothing short of a reinstatement of the starting point of first philosophy (or the ending point of skepticism!), and nothing could be farther from the spirit of Quine's naturalism: "The recognition that it is within science itself, and not in some prior philosophy, that reality is to be identified and described."[8] Thus, in pursuing their account of the relation between evidence and theory, naturalized epistemologists are free to talk of light rays, molecules, nerve endings, and so on, for these things belong to the ontology of current science. Moreover, their epistemological findings regarding the sensory evidence for science do not as a matter of course repudiate the initial ontological lore within which those considerations are articulated: "On the contrary, our initially uncritical hypothesis of a physical world gains pragmatic support from whatever it contributes towards a coherent account of lorebearing or other natural phenomena."[9]

In sum, Quine repudiates foundationalist epistemology, rationalist or empiricist, traditional or contemporary. In its place he advocates the scientifically informed study of the acquisition of science. Thus, for the Quinian naturalist, science not only settles the question of what exists (ontology), it provides the evidential constraints for any account of how we come to know what exists (epistemology). Moreover, the currently best ontology is physicalism; the currently best epistemology is empiricism. Keeping this in mind, we are now prepared to explore the role that behaviorism plays in Quine's exploration of the relations obtaining among mind, world, and language.

QUINE'S BEHAVIORISM/ EMPIRICISM

Not only does Quine articulate more or less philosophical arguments and considerations in support of naturalism, physicalism, empiricism, and fallibilism, he goes on to sketch a more or less scientific (empiricistic) account of the relation of evidence to theory. It is in regard to this epistemological endeavor that he professes to be as behavioristic as anyone in his right mind could be. But what, precisely, does Quine mean by behaviorism?

As we shall see, he construes the term broadly; in particular, he does not define behaviorism in terms of conditioned response:

> When I dismiss a definition of behaviorism that limits it to conditioned response, am I simply extending the term to cover everyone? Well, I do think of it as covering all reasonable men. What matters, as I see it, is just the insistence upon couching all criteria in observation terms. By observation terms I mean terms that are or can be taught by ostension, and whose application in each particular case can therefore be checked intersubjectively. Not to cavil over the word 'behaviorism', perhaps current usage would be best suited by referring to this orientation to observation simply as empiricism; but it is empiricism in a distinctly modern sense, for it rejects the naïve mentalism that typified the old empiricism. It does still condone the recourse to introspection that Chomsky has spoken in favor of, but it condones it as a means of arriving at conjectures or conclusions only insofar as these can eventually be made sense of in terms of external observation.[10]

And what is this distinctly modern sort of empiricism to which Quine alludes?

> Empiricism of this modern sort, or behaviorism broadly so called, comes of the old empiricism by a drastic externalization. The old empiricist looked inward upon his ideas; the new empiricist looks outward upon the social institution of language. Ideas dwindle to meanings, seen as adjuncts of words. The old inner-directed empiricists—Hobbes, Gassendi, Locke, and their followers—had perforce to formulate their empiricist standard by reference to ideas; and they did so by exalting sense impressions and scouting innate ideas. When empiricism is externalized, on the other hand, the idea itself passes under a cloud; talk of ideas comes to count as unsatisfactory except insofar as it can be paraphrased into terms of dispositions to observable behavior.[11]

Quine's construal of behaviorism (broadly so-called) as externalized empiricism is closely connected to his views regarding the nature of the explanation of human behavior. He distinguishes "three levels of purported explanation, three degrees of depth: the mental, the behavioral, and the physiological."[12] Of these three, the mental is the most superficial, "scarcely deserving the name explanation. The physiological is the deepest and most ambitious, and it is the place for causal explanations."[13] But, for the present, it is the behavioral level that Quine thinks is the most useful in theorizing about language and mind:

Until we can aspire to actual physiological explanation of linguistic activity in physiological terms, the level at which to work is the middle one; that of dispositions to overt behavior. Its virtue is not that it affords causal explanations but that it is less likely than the mentalistic level to engender an illusion of being more explanatory than it is. The easy familiarity of mentalistic talk is not to be trusted.[14]

As this quotation makes clear, Quine regards behavioral explanation as a temporary measure which might hasten the day when (if ever) actual physiological explanation becomes available.

BEHAVIORISM AND PHILOSOPHY OF LANGUAGE

Competent in six languages and familiar with others, Quine has always had a passion for languages and for their study, antedating even his passion for philosophy. Even so, Quine's writings on meaning, synonymy, analyticity, language-learning, reference, and translation emanate more from his passion for epistemology than from his passion for languages and linguistics. Furthermore, his approach to the study of these topics is consistently behavioristic; indeed, he argues that one has no choice in the matter:

In psychology one may or may not be a behaviorist, but in linguistics one has no choice. Each of us learns his language by observing other people's verbal behavior and having his own faltering verbal behavior observed and reinforced or corrected by others. We depend strictly on overt behavior in observable situations. As long as our command of our language fits all external checkpoints, where our utterance or our reaction to someone's utterance can be appraised in the light of some shared situation, so long all is well. Our mental life between checkpoints is indifferent to our rating as a master of the language. There is nothing in linguistic meaning beyond what is to be gleaned from overt behavior in observable circumstances.[15]

The last sentence of this quotation from *Pursuit of Truth* expresses a behavioristic corollary of the equally behavioristic opening lines from the preface to *Word and Object*: "Language is a social art. In acquiring it we have to depend entirely on intersubjectively available cues as to what to say and when."[16] In *Word and Object* Quine set out to see just how much behavioristic sense can be made of meaning, synonymy, analyticity, language-

learning, reference, and translation. Thus, we can best glean a sense of the role that behaviorism plays in Quine's philosophy of language by surveying some of his findings.

Meaning, Synonymy and Analyticity

Prior to the publication of *Word and Object*, Quine scrutinized various intensional accounts of meaning, synonymy and analyticity in his celebrated "Two Dogmas of Empiricism" (1980b) and found them wanting. Therein he dismissed meanings construed as entities on the grounds that such posits are unexplanatory and even obfuscating. He went on to dismiss synonymy (sameness of meaning) and analyticity (true in virtue of meaning) because of their lack of clarity. True, synonymy and analyticity can be explained in terms of each other, but neither can be explained in terms of dispositions to verbal behavior. When critics complained that Quine's standard of clarity for analyticity and synonymy is unreasonably high, he responded by saying that he asks "no more, after all, than a rough characterization in terms of dispositions to verbal behavior."[17] Consistent with his brand of behaviorism, Quine insists merely on a rough characterization and *not* a full definition of analyticity or synonymy in terms of dispositions to verbal behavior.

Quine's treatment of semantics is not only negative, it is also constructive. In *Word and Object* (and in several subsequent writings), Quine articulates a scientific (behavioristic) semantics.[18] The cornerstone of this scientific semantics is the behavioristic method of querying sentences for a subject's assent/dissent. "Without this device there would be no hope of handing language down the generations, nor any hope of breaking into newly discovered languages. It is primarily by querying sentences for assent and dissent that we tap the reservoirs of verbal disposition."[19]

Quine calls the class of patterns of a person's activated nerve endings that would prompt a person's assent to a queried sentence the *affirmative stimulus meaning* (for that sentence, person, and time). The class that would prompt dissent he calls the *negative stimulus meaning* (for that sentence, person, and time). The ordered pair of affirmative and negative stimulus meanings for a sentence constitutes its stimulus meaning *simpliciter* (for a person, at a time). Note, too, that the affirmative and negative stimulus meanings for a sentence do not determine each other; there will be stimulus patterns belonging to neither; in other words, the query of some sentences, under certain stimulus conditions, would prompt neither assent nor dissent.

Quine divides, again along behavioristic lines, the class of declarative English sentences into standing sentences and occasion sentences. Roughly, *standing* sentences are those to which subjects would assent or dissent each time they are queried without their being accompanied each time by a prompting nonverbal stimulus. For example, most English speakers would assent to each query of 'There have been black dogs?' without being prompted each time by some black dog–presenting pattern of stimulation. Not so for the *occasion* sentence 'That dog is black'; here each elicited assent must be accompanied anew by a prompting, black dog–presenting pattern of stimulation.

Among the class of standing sentences are those Quine calls *eternal* sentences. The defining characteristic of such sentences is that their truth values remain permanently fixed. "An eternal sentence may be general in import, or it may report a specific local event. In the latter case it will gain its specificity through explicit use of names, dates, or addresses. The eternal sentences most characteristic of scientific theory are of course general."[20]

Among the class of occasion sentences are those Quine calls *observation* sentences. Quine has offered different characterizations of observation sentences at different times, but in *Word and Object* he wrote: "In behavioral terms, an occasion sentence may be said to be the more observational the more nearly its stimulus meanings for different speakers tend to coincide."[21]

Given his behavioristic notion of stimulus meaning and his behavioristic classification of sentences, Quine goes on to construct his scientific semantics. He fashions, so far as is possible, behavioristic parodies of the repudiated intensional notions of meaning, synonymy and analyticity. For example, Quine explains that two occasion sentences are cognitively synonymous for a person if whenever he would assent/dissent to the one he would do likewise to the other (i.e., when the two occasion sentences have the same stimulus meaning for that person). Two such sentences are cognitively synonymous for the entire linguistic community if found to be cognitively synonymous for each member of the community. Also, "a sentence is analytic if *everybody* learns that it is true by learning its words."[22] However, Quine is the first

to point out that none of these behavioristic parodies will bear the philosophical weight that some traditional epistemologists wanted the parodied intensional forerunners to bear. For example, Quine's behavioristic notion of analyticity cannot explain the putative necessity of mathematics—as the intensional notion of analyticity was thought by some logical positivists to do.[23]

As already noted, Quine has characterized observation sentences differently in different places. For example, in *Roots of Reference* he wrote: "A sentence is observational insofar as its truth value, on any occasion, would be agreed to by just about any member of the speech community witnessing the occasion…What is worth noticing is that we have here a behavioral criterion of what to count as an observation sentence."[24] In "On Empirically Equivalent Systems of the World" (1975c), he wrote: "The really distinctive trait of observation terms and sentences is to be sought not in concurrence of witnesses but in ways of learning. Observational expressions are expressions that can be learned ostensively."[25] In "Empirical Content" (1981a), he wrote:

> An observation sentence is an occasion sentence that the speaker will consistently assent to when his sensory receptors are stimulated in certain ways, and consistently dissent from when they are stimulated in certain other ways. If querying the sentence elicits assent from the given speaker on one occasion, it will elicit assent likewise on any other occasion when the same total set of receptors is triggered; and similarly for dissent. This and this only is what qualifies sentences as observation sentences for the speaker in question, and this is the sense in which they are the sentences most directly associated with sensory stimulation.[26]

Critics have claimed that some of these characterizations of observation sentences are inconsistent with one another. For example, Lars Bergström points out that according to Quine's 1981 characterization,

> a sentence may be observational for every speaker in a community, even though the speakers disagree about its truth value on many occasions. For example, some people may assent to "It's cold" and "That's a rabbit" on occasions when others dissent from these sentences. (People are not equally sensitive to cold, and many of us might easily mistake a hare for a rabbit.) In earlier writings, Quine had a different conception of an observation sentence: he required precisely that

"its truth value, on any occasion, would be agreed to by just about any member of the speech community witnessing the occasion." However, this requirement is hardly consistent with his examples, and he has since claimed that the "really distinctive trait of observation terms and sentences is to be sought not in concurrence of witnesses but in ways of learning. Observational expressions are expressions that can be learned ostensively."[27]

Getting clear on the nature of observation sentences is an important matter for Quine, since they play crucial roles in his scientific semantics and in his epistemology.[28] In his semantics, they are the kind of sentences that can be learned in isolation and whose meanings are pretty well captured by stimulus meaning ("all inculcation of meanings of words must rest ultimately on sensory evidence"). In his epistemology, they are the kind of sentences that state the intersubjectively appreciable evidence for science ("whatever evidence there is for science is sensory evidence").

Quine responded to Bergström in "Three Indeterminacies" (1990) and, more fully, in *Pursuit of Truth*, where he wrote:

As for the lacuna that Bergström noted…I retain my 1981 definition of observation sentence for the single speaker, and then account a sentence observational for a group if it is observational for each member *and* if each would agree in assenting to it, or dissenting, on witnessing the occasion of utterance. We judge what counts as witnessing the occasion…by projecting ourselves into the witness's position.[29]

This talk of projecting ourselves into the witness's position, i.e., talk of empathy or *Verstehen*, has always been a part of Quine's thinking about language-learning and the propositional attitudes. Only recently, however, has he emphasized the role that empathy plays in scientific semantics. This is a point to which we shall return in discussing language-learning and translation.

Language-Learning

According to Quine, "language is a social art. In acquiring it we have to depend entirely on intersubjectively available cues as to what to say and when."[30] In *Word and Object* Quine sketches a largely Skinnerian theory of early language-learning, wherein babbling, mimicry, conditioning, innate quality spaces, and ostension each play a role. When exposed to a linguistic environment, the normal child (who is endowed with instincts for babbling and mimicry, as well as a set of innate quality spaces needed for detecting and systematizing salient features of his environment, and who is motivated by stimulations encoded with pleasure and pain) begins learning his first language.

The initial method of his learning is *ostension*. Through babbling or mimicry, the child utters a sound, say that of 'mama', when Mama is present. Mama rewards this chance occurrence with a coo, a smile, or even a pat or a hug. The child is thus reinforced to repeat the performance. Such learning requires observationality. For example, in learning (or in teaching) ostensively the one-word sentence 'Fido', both the teacher and the pupil must see Fido's present ostended surface, and at least one of them must also see that the other sees Fido's surface at the time. Meeting this latter condition involves empathy, or *Verstehen*.

Before long, by observing his elders' overt behavior under intersubjectively appreciable environmental cues, the child catches on to the unconscious trick of associating sentences (as unstructured wholes) with his own appropriate nonverbal stimulations. In short, the child learns, inductively, the range of stimulus conditions governing the correct use of particular sentences. The psychological mechanism underlying the method of ostension approximates direct conditioning. However, the conditioning involved is not the simplest kind, for the child does not utter 'Mama' or 'Fido' whenever he sees, respectively, Mama or Fido. However, once having learned 'Mama' and 'Fido' he would assent to them when queried in Fido's or Mama's respective salient presences. "Once the child reaches this stage, his further learning of language becomes independent of operant behavior…; and then, with little or no deliberate encouragement on the part of his elders, he proceeds to amass language hand over fist."[31]

Quine acknowledges that, "Skinner, whose ideas the foregoing sketch is meant to follow in essential respects is not without his critics. But, at worst we may suppose that the description, besides being conveniently definite, is substantially true of a good part of what goes into the first learning of words. Room remains for further forces."[32] These further forces allow for a second general method for learning language, what Quine calls *analogic synthesis*. Sentences learned by this method are built up from learned parts by analogy with the ways in which those parts have previously been noticed to occur in other sentences—sentences which themselves may or may not have been learned as unstructured wholes. However, unlike the case of ostension, virtually nothing is known about the further psychological mechanisms underlying analogic synthesis.

In "Linguistics and Philosophy" (1976a), Quine emphasizes various features of the behavioristic theory of language-learning he had sketched in *Word and Object* eight years earlier. First, he emphasizes that behaviorism and nativism are not incompatible: "The behaviorist is knowingly and cheerfully up to his neck in innate mechanisms of learning-readiness. The very reinforcement and extinction of responses, so central to behaviorism, depends on prior inequalities in the subject's qualitative spacing, so to speak, of stimulations.... Innate biases and dispositions are the cornerstone of behaviorism, and have been studied by behaviorists."[33] Second, he reiterates features of his 1960 theory, namely, that quality space is innate, but that more innate structure is required to explain language-learning: "The qualitative spacing of stimulations is as readily verifiable in other animals, after all, as in man; so the language-readiness of the human infant must depend on further endowments."[34] These further "as yet unknown innate structures, additional to mere quality space, that are needed in language-learning, are needed specifically to get the child over the great hump that lies beyond ostension, or induction."[35] And what, according to Quine, is the fate of behaviorism should the processes involved turn out to be very unlike the classical process of conditioning? "This would be no refutation of behaviorism, in a philosophically significant sense of the term; for I see no interest in restricting the term 'behaviorism' to a specific psychological schematism of conditioned response."[36]

Six years after "Linguistics and Philosophy," in *Roots of Reference*, Quine further refines and extends his 1960 theory of language-learning. Talk of patterns of activated nerve endings gives way to talk of global episodes of activated nerve endings and of the receptual similarity of episodes; talk of quality spaces gives way to talk of the perceptual similarity and of the behavioral similarity of episodes. Moreover, Quine extends his 1960 theory by speculating on the psychological mechanisms underlying analogic synthesis, mechanisms by which a child could learn to refer to substances,

bodies, physical objects, and, eventually, to abstract objects. More precisely, he speculates on how a child, or the race, could acquire first-order predicate logic and set theory. First-order predicate logic encapsulates in pristine form the referential mechanisms of English, and sets are abstract objects (or universals) *par excellence*. In extending his theory in *Roots of Reference* in this way, Quine does not abandon his behavioristic scruples, but he acknowledges that in the final, speculative, third of the book "the behaviorism dwindles."[37] But he adds reflectively:

> Where I have insisted on behaviorism is in linguistics, because of how language is learned I would hope and expect that behavioristic rigor could also be brought in pretty much along the course of the story sketched in *Roots of Reference*, but I was struggling with what I felt were more significant problems. I expect also that some notions would resist full reduction to behavioral criteria. I would never, early or late, have aspired to the ascetic adherence to operational definitions that Bridgman envisaged. Science settles for partial criteria and for partial explanation in terms of other partially explained notions.[38]

Thus, Quine's speculations in *Roots of Reference* about how referential language emerges (for the individual or the race) do not represent a real retreat from his previous commitment to behaviorism in the study of language-learning.

Translation and Indeterminacy

In Chapter Two of *Word and Object*, Quine articulates his famous thought experiment of radical translation where a linguist is confronted with the task of translating a totally alien human language. All that the linguist has to go on in constructing his Native-to-English translation manual is the natives' behavior, verbal and otherwise. A rabbit scurries by, apparently prompting a native to utter 'Gavagai'. The linguist forms the tentative inductive hypothesis that 'Gavagai' can be translated as 'Rabbit'. Since it is assumed that the linguist has already ascertained the native expressions for assent and dissent, the linguist can query 'Gavagai' of the native as appropriate occasions present themselves. If, upon further testing, all goes well, then the linguist might learn that the native's stimulus meaning for 'Gavagai' is approximately the same as his own for 'Rabbit'. If, however, upon further testing they tend to diverge, then the linguist may have to give up his inductive hypothesis and try out some other candidate as translation of 'Gavagai'. It would appear that the question whether the stimulus meanings for a pair of observation sentences, like 'Gavagai' and 'Rabbit', are or are not approximately the same is an objective, empirical matter of fact. But there is a rub.

Let us assume that the translation of the sentence 'Gavagai' as 'Rabbit' has held up under testing. What theoretical sense can be made of the claim that the native's stimulus meaning for 'Gavagai' is approximately the same as the linguist's stimulus meaning for 'Rabbit'? In *Roots of Reference* Quine calls this the homology question. Answering this question is problematic because stimulus meaning is defined relative to each individual's own nerve endings and no two people's nerve endings are even approximately the same. In *Roots of Reference* Quine deals with the homology question as follows: "In practice, of course, psychologists find no difficulty in such intersubjective equating of stimulus situations; they simply see that there are no physical differences that are apt to matter. We shall do well to take the same line, having just noted in passing that there is more to the equating of stimulations than meets the eye, or indeed perhaps rather less than seems to do so."[39] But as theorists, what are we to do apart from practice? There the homology question continued to rankle until Quine addressed the issue in "Three Indeterminacies" (1990b) and, more fully, in *Pursuit of Truth*. In these recent writings Quine modifies his thought experiment of radical translation so as to avoid raising the homology question. Thus, instead of saying that the native's stimulus meaning of 'Gavagai' is approximately the same as the linguist's for 'Rabbit', one can make do with talking solely of the linguist's stimulus meaning:

> The observation sentence 'Rabbit' has its stimulus meaning for the linguist and 'Gavagai' has its for the native, but the affinity of the two sentences is to be sought in the externals of communication. The linguist notes the native's utterance of 'Gavagai' where he, in the native's position, might have said 'Rabbit'. So he tries bandying 'Gavagai' on occasions that would have prompted 'Rabbit', and looks to natives for approval. Encouraged, he tentatively adopts 'Rabbit' as translation.[40]

In short, the native's stimulus meaning for 'Gavagai' is dropped, and the linguist's empathy with the native's perceptual situation is added. The homol-

ogy question is rendered otiose. Moreover, this tact renders the linguist's imagined strategy in the thought experiment of radical translation both more realistic and more in tune with Quine's long-held view of the child's strategy in the normal language-learning context:

> Empathy dominates the learning of language, both by child and by field linguist. In the child's case it is the parent's empathy. The parent assesses the appropriateness of the child's observation sentence by noting the child's orientation and how the scene would look from there. In the field linguist's case it is empathy on his own part when he makes his first conjecture about 'Gavagai' on the strength of the native's utterance and orientation, and again when he queries 'Gavagai' for the native's assent in a promising subsequent situation. We all have an uncanny knack for empathizing another's perceptual situation, however ignorant of the physiological or optical mechanisms of his perception.[41]

Where does this new wrinkle, this talk of the role that empathy plays in radical translation, leave Quine's behaviorism? Recall that Quine has steadfastly maintained that his form of behaviorism (externalized empiricism) condones recourse to introspection as a means of arriving at conjectures or conclusions only insofar as these can eventually be made sense of in terms of external observation. Are the linguist's reliance on empathy to translate a native sentence and the parent's reliance on empathy to teach the child a sentence such forms of introspection? Can the linguist and the parent, even in principle, objectively test their respective conjectures? Each such "test" would seem always to rely on a further instance of empathy.

Be that as it may, soon in his task of constructing a Native-to-English translation manual, the linguist rises above such inductive hypotheses regarding translations of native observation sentences like 'Gavagai' and formulates analytical hypotheses that allow for translating native words and theoretical sentences that are remote from stimulus meanings. Quine maintains that, unlike inductive hypotheses (*real* hypotheses), analytical hypotheses are nonfactual. Still, it is empathy, again, that guides the linguist in formulating his analytical hypotheses: "Though there he is trying to project into the native's associations and grammatical trends rather than his perceptions. And much the same must be true of the growing child."[42]

With the advent of these nonfactual analytical hypotheses, translation of theoretical sentences

becomes indeterminate. Different linguists formulating different sets of analytical hypotheses could
construct different Native-to-English manuals of
translation such that the "manuals might be indistinguishable in terms of any native behavior that
they give reason to expect, and yet each manual
might prescribe some translations that the other
translator would reject. Such is the thesis of indeterminacy of translation."[43]

As Quine makes explicit, there is a behavioristic
source of the indeterminacy thesis:

> Critics have said that the thesis is a consequence
> of my behaviorism. Some have said that it is a
> *reductio ad absurdum* of my behaviorism. I dis-
> agree with this second point, but I agree with the
> first. I hold further that the behaviorist approach is
> mandatory. In psychology one may or may not be
> a behaviorist, but in linguistics one has no choice.
> Each of us learns his language by observing other
> people's verbal behavior and having his own fal-
> tering verbal behavior observed and reinforced or
> corrected by others. We depend strictly on overt
> behavior in observable situations.
>   …
>   There is nothing in linguistic meaning, then,
> beyond what is to be gleaned from overt behavior
> in observable circumstances.[44]

Since "the only facts of nature that bear on the correctness of translation are speech dispositions,"[45]
then "even a full understanding of neurology
would in no way resolve the indeterminacy of
translation."[46]

And not only is there indeterminacy of theoretical sentences, there is also indeterminacy of reference (or inscrutability of reference). The point here
is that stimulus meaning does not fix reference.
Knowing that the native's occasion sentence 'Gavagai' is translatable into English as the occasion
sentence 'Rabbit' does not settle the question
whether 'Gavagai' is a native term, and if it is, what
it refers to. The only way to settle these issues is
against a background of some nonunique set of
analytical hypotheses (which, as already noted, are
by their very nature nonfactual). Thus, consistent
with the speech dispositions of all concerned, one
linguist might translate 'Gavagai' as a concrete
general term denoting rabbits, while another linguist translates 'Gavagai' as an abstract singular
term designating rabbithood. And, just as with the
indeterminacy of translation of theoretical sentences, both of these translations of 'Gavagai' are
fully correct. The question of which (if either) of
these translations captures what the native intended

by 'Gavagai' is spurious; there is simply no fact of
the matter.

In sum, Quine's behaviorism permeates his
philosophy of language. It shapes his treatment
of meaning, synonymy, analyticity, language-
learning, reference, and translation. Moreover, it
shapes his general epistemology. We have noted
that he rejects foundationalist epistemology (first
philosophy), but he remains interested in the
empirical study of the epistemological relation of
evidence to theory. Breaking with the empiricist
tradition, though, Quine calls for externalizing that
study, i.e., for construing the relation of evidence to
theory as a relation between observation sentences
and theoretical sentences. For the externalized
epistemologist, the theory of language-learning
takes on added significance:

> We see, then, a strategy for investigating the rela-
> tion of evidential support, between observation
> and scientific theory. We can adopt a genetic
> approach, studying how theoretical language is
> learned. For the evidential relation is virtually
> enacted, it would seem, in the learning. This
> genetic strategy is attractive because the learning
> of language goes on in the world and is open to
> scientific study. It is a strategy for the scientific
> study of scientific method and evidence. We have
> here a good reason to regard the theory of lan-
> guage as vital to the theory of knowledge.[47]

Hence my earlier claim that Quine's writings
on meaning, synonymy, analyticity, language-
learning, reference, and translation emanate more
from his passion for epistemology than from his
passion for languages and linguistics.

PHILOSOPHY OF MIND

If Quine's interest in epistemology shapes his philosophy of language, so his philosophy of language
shapes his philosophy of mind. Quine says in
"Mind and Verbal Dispositions" (1975a) that he
believes in the affinity of mind and language,
though he wants to keep the relation right side up.
John B. Watson's theory of thought, viz., that most
thought simply is incipient speech, however inadequate, has matters right side up: "A theory of mind
can gain clarity and substance, I think, from a better understanding of the workings of language,
whereas little understanding of the workings of
language is to be hoped for in mentalistic terms."[48]
And, after surveying his theories of language-
learning and linguistic meaning, Quine concludes

"Mind and Verbal Dispositions" with an endorsement of the identity theory of mind:

> mind consists in dispositions to behaviour, and these are physiological states. We recall that John B. Watson did not claim that quite *all* thought was incipient speech; it was all incipient twitching of muscles, and *mostly* of speech muscles. Just so, I would not identify mind quite wholly with verbal disposition; with Ryle and Sellars I would identify it with behavioural dispositions, and *mostly* verbal. And then, having construed behavioural dispositions in turn as physiological states, I end up with the so-called identity theory of mind: mental states are states of the body.[49]

Quine's philosophy of mind can be briefly summarized as follows: Most everyday uses of mentalistic terms (e.g., 'belief', 'desire', and so on) have empirical content, though many uses of the same terms do not. We apply mentalistic terms having empirical content to persons other than ourselves largely (but not always) on the basis of those persons' behavioral symptoms. This follows from the way such terms are learned: "Such terms are applied in the light of publicly observable symptoms: bodily symptoms strictly of bodily states....Without the outward signs to begin with, mentalistic terms could not be learned at all."[50] However, such behavioral symptoms are neither necessary nor sufficient for ascribing mentalistic terms to other persons in particular instances, since mental states do not always manifest themselves in behavior and since mentalistic terms are vague. "Other grounds for ascribing beliefs [for example] may be sought unsystematically by probing the subject's past for probable causes of his present state of mind, or by seeing how he will defend his purported belief when challenged."[51] On the other hand, in ascribing mentalistic terms to ourselves we can rely on introspection: "Introspection may be seen as a witnessing to one's own bodily condition, as in introspecting an acid stomach, even though the introspector be vague on the medical details."[52] (Thus does Quine's brand of behaviorism reserve a role for introspection in both his philosophy of language and his philosophy of mind.)

When mentalistic ascriptions (grounded on either behavioral symptoms or introspection) have empirical content, they do *not* refer to behavior; rather, they refer to dispositions, mostly verbal ones. And, since Quine construes such dispositions as physiological states of the organism, "it is these

states that the [contentful] mental terms may be seen as denoting."[53]

Quine has called this theory of mind the identity theory, but he has also referred to it as the repudiation theory. What is the difference? None, according to Quine: "In either case the states of nerves are retained, mental states in any other sense are repudiated, and the mental terms are thereupon appropriated to states of nerves."[54] Even so, Quine prefers the repudiation theory over the identity theory. He does so because the identity theory is so easily abused:

> For, product though the identity theory is of hardheaded materialism, we must beware of its sedative use to relieve intellectual discomfort. We can imagine someone appealing to the identity theory to excuse his own free and uncritical recourse to mentalistic semantics. We can imagine him pleading that it is after all just a matter of physiology, even if no one knows quite how. This would be a sad irony indeed, and the repudiation theory has the virtue, over the identity theory, of precluding it.[55]

However, even accepting the repudiation theory there are some dispositions to behavior that are more explanatory than others. "The ones that we should favor, in explanations, are the ones whose physiological mechanisms seem likeliest to be detected in the foreseeable future."[56]

Even though Quine accepts the repudiation theory, where contentful mental states refer to physiological states, "[t]here is no presumption that the mentalistic idioms would in general be translatable into anatomical and biochemical terminology of neurology, even if all details of the neurological mechanisms were understood."[57] The uniform structure of the idioms of the propositional attitudes, for example, mask the great heterogeneity of the empirical evidence and neural mechanism. Thus, Quine concludes that "[e]ven those of us who do not acquiesce in a metaphysical dualism of mind and body must take the best of what [Donald] Davidson has called anomalous monism."[58]

CONCLUSION

Quine's brand of behaviorism is less rigorous than some. For example, he rejects any definition of behaviorism that limits it to conditioned response. He is even willing to give up the term as descriptive of his methodology in epistemology, philosophy of language, and philosophy of mind in favor of the term 'externalized empiricism'. Terminology aside, what matters to Quine is that theorists maintain empiricist discipline, couching all criteria for ascribing intensional terms in observation terms—terms that can be taught by ostension. As a further departure from stricter behaviorism, Quine admits roles for instrospection and empathy to play in his philosophies of language and mind.

As Quine remarks, one may or may not choose to be a behaviorist in psychology, but one has no choice but to be a behaviorist in linguistics.[59] The reason he believes that one has no choice is based on the empirical claim that people learn their language by observing the behavior of other people amid intersubjectively appreciable circumstances. The corollary to this empirical claim about language-learning is the semantical claim that there is nothing to linguistic meaning that cannot be manifested in behavior. But if this is so, then ascriptions of intensional terms generally can sometimes extend vacuously beyond the behavioral facts. This can happen in theoretical as well as in practical contexts. And when theories of language-learning, or of semantics, or of mind routinely incorporate such lapses of empiricist discipline, Quine regards them as unscientific. Such is the chief moral of Quine's right-minded behaviorism.

ENDNOTES

1. See Quine and Ullian (1978, pp. 42–46).
2. See Quine (1980a, pp. 42f).
3. Quine (1981b, p. 98).
4. Quine (1969, p. 75).
5. Quine (1974, p. 2).
6. Ibid., p. 3.
7. Quine (1976b, p. 229).
8. Quine (1981d, p. 21).
9. Quine (1976b, p. 230).
10. Quine (1976a, p. 58).
11. Ibid.
12. Quine (1975a, p. 87).
13. Ibid.
14. Ibid., p. 95.
15. Quine (1992, pp. 37–38).
16. Quine (1960, p. ix).
17. Ibid., p. 207.
18. Quine (1981e, pp. 43–54).
19. Quine (1975a, p. 88).
20. Quine (1974, p. 63).
21. Quine (1960, p. 43).
22. Quine (1974, p. 79).
23. See Quine (1992, p. 55).
24. Ibid., p. 39.
25. Quine (1975c, p. 316).
26. Quine (1981a, p. 25).
27. Bergström (1990, p. 39).
28. See Quine (1993, pp. 107–116).
29. Quine (1992, p. 43).
30. Quine (1960, p. ix).
31. Ibid., p. 82.
32. Ibid.
33. Quine (1976a, p. 57).
34. Ibid.
35. Ibid., p. 58.
36. Ibid., p. 57.
37. Quine, "Comment on Parsons," in Barrett and Gibson (1990, p. 291).
38. Ibid.
39. Quine (1974, p. 24).
40. Quine (1992, p. 42).
41. Ibid.
42. Quine (1992, p. 43).
43. Quine (1987, p. 8).
44. Ibid., p. 5.
45. Quine (1986a, p. 429).
46. Quine (1986b, p. 365).
47. Quine (1975b, pp. 74–75).
48. Quine (1975a, p. 84).
49. Ibid., p. 94.
50. Quine (1985a, pp. 5–6).
51. Ibid., p. 7.
52. Quine (1960, pp. 264–265).
53. Quine (1985a, p. 6).
54. Ibid.
55. Quine (1975a, p. 95).
56. Ibid., p. 95.
57. Quine (1985a, p. 6).
58. Ibid., p. 7.
59. See note 15 above.

REFERENCES

Barrett, R., & Gibson, R. (Eds.). (1990). *Perspectives on Quine*. Oxford: Basil Blackwell.

Bergström, L. (1990). Quine on underdetermination. In R. Barrett & R. Gibson (Eds.), *Perspectives on Quine* (pp. 38–52). Oxford: Basil Blackwell.

Quine, W. V. (1960). *Word and object*. Cambridge, MA: M.I.T. Press.

Quine, W. V. (1969). Epistemology naturalized. In *Ontological relativity and other essays* (pp. 69–90). New York: Columbia University Press.

Quine, W. V. (1974). *Roots of reference*. La Salle, IL: Open Court.

Quine, W. V. (1975a). Mind and verbal dispositions. In S. Guttenplan (Ed.), *Mind and language* (pp. 83–95). Oxford: Clarendon Press.

Quine, W. V. (1975b). The nature of natural knowledge. In S. Guttenplan (Ed.), *Mind and language* (pp. 67–81). Oxford: Clarendon Press.

Quine, W. V. (1975c). On empirically equivalent systems of the world. *Erkenntnis*, *9*, 313–328.

Quine, W. V. (1976a). Linguistics and philosophy. In *The ways of paradox and other essays* (Rev. ed., pp. 56–58). Cambridge, MA: Harvard University Press.

Quine, W. V. (1976b). The scope and language of science. In *The ways of paradox and other essays* (Rev. ed., pp. 228–245). Cambridge, MA: Harvard University Press.

Quine, W. V. (1980a). *From a logical point of view* (2nd ed., Rev. ed.). Cambridge, MA.: Harvard University Press. (Original work published 1953)

Quine, W. V. (1980b). Two dogmas of empiricism. In *From a logical point of view* (pp. 20–46). Cambridge, MA: Harvard University Press.

Quine, W. V. (1981a). Empirical content. In *Theories and things* (pp. 24–30). Cambridge, MA: Harvard University Press.

Quine, W. V. (1981b). Goodman's ways of worldmaking. In *Theories and things* (pp. 96–99). Cambridge, MA: Harvard University Press.

Quine, W. V. (1981c). *Theories and things*. Cambridge, MA: Harvard University Press.

Quine, W. V. (1981d). Things and their place in theories. In *Theories and things* (pp. 1–23). Cambridge, MA: Harvard University Press.

Quine, W. V. (1981e). Use and its place in meaning. In *Theories and things* (pp. 43–54). Cambridge, MA: Harvard University Press.

Quine, W. V. (1985a). States of mind. *The Journal of Philosophy*, *82*, 5–8.

Quine, W. V. (1985b). *The time of my life*. Cambridge, MA: M.I.T. Press.

Quine, W. V. (1986a). Reply to Hilary Putnam. In L. Hahn & P. Schilpp (Eds.), *The philosophy of W. V. Quine* (pp. 427–431). La Salle, IL: Open Court.

Quine, W. V. (1986b). Reply to Robert Nozick. In L. Hahn & P. Schilpp (Eds.), *The philosophy of W. V. Quine* (pp. 364–367). La Salle, IL: Open Court.

Quine, W. V. (1987). Indeterminacy of translation again. *The Journal of Philosophy*, *84*, 5–10.

Quine, W. V. (1990). Three indeterminacies. In R. Barrett & R. Gibson (Eds.), *Perspectives on Quine* (pp. 1–16). Oxford: Basil Blackwell.

Quine, W. V. (1992). *Pursuit of truth* (Rev. ed.). Cambridge, MA: Harvard University Press.

Quine, W. V. (1993). In praise of observation sentences. *The Journal of Philosophy*, *90*, 107–116.

Quine, W.V. (1995). *From stimulus to science*. Cambridge, MA: Harvard University Press.

Quine, W. V. & Ullian, J. S. (1978). *The web of belief* (2nd. Ed.). New York: Random House.

CHAPTER 8

SKINNER'S THEORY OF THEORIES

Richard F. Kitchener

INTRODUCTION

Consider the following comment by a distinguished 20th century psychologist:

> Whether particular experimental psychologists like it or not, experimental psychology is properly and inevitably committed to the construction of a theory of behavior.

Such a view might be attributed to various psychologists, for example, to Clark Hull or Donald Hebb. But few people would ever suggest that such a theoretical approach to psychology came from the pen of B. F. Skinner (1947/1972, p. 302). In the face of Skinner's insistence that theories of learning are not necessary (1950/1972), the only way to avoid a patent contradiction is to assume he is using 'theory' in two different senses. Not surprisingly this is precisely the case. Actually there are at least six different kinds of theory that Skinner (implicitly) recognizes, only one of which he rejects. On balance, therefore, Skinner seems to be decidedly protheory. Since Skinner is widely reputed to be antitheoretical or atheoretical (e. g., Scriven, 1956),

I will attempt to redress this widespread view by discussing Skinner's theory of theories. Second, in regard to the kind of theory he does reject, I will attempt to show that Skinner's criteria for what constitutes a theory (in this bad sense) are somewhat vague and inadequate, and that, on various interpretations, Skinner's views themselves must be counted as being theoretical after all. Finally, I will suggest that Skinner's theory of theories (and especially his objection to hypothetical mechanisms) is based upon a particular view about the aim of science, namely, that science attempts to predict and control. This view, in turn, derives from Skinner's positivism and radical naturalism, both of which need to be critically evaluated.

KINDS OF THEORIES

I do not know how many different senses of 'theory' one can find in the writings of Skinner, but there are at least six different varieties:

1. Theory as a set of basic assumptions
2. Theory as a proposition yet to be verified

3. Theory as conceptual analysis
4. Theory as the interpretation of behavior
5. Theory as a convenient summary of empirical data
6. Theory as a hypothetical mechanism[1]

Theory as a Set of Basic Assumptions

By a theory in this first, relatively harmless sense Skinner means just what one would naturally expect. "That nature is orderly rather than capricious" (1950/1972, p. 69) is an example that Skinner gives and other examples might also be cited, viz., basic assumptions about the goals of science (e. g., prediction and control), the appropriate methods to be employed (e. g., a single subject design rather than a statistical analysis), the nature of reality (e. g., physicalism). A theory[1] thus constitutes a set of metatheoretical or philosophical commitments and there seems to be no reason to suggest Skinner rejects or should reject a theory[1] of behavior. Indeed, every scientist would seem to be committed to such theories[1].

Theory as a Proposition Yet to be Verified

In the passage just mentioned Skinner proceeds to mention what seems to be a second kind of theory:

> Certain statements are also theories simply to the extent that they are not yet facts. A scientist may guess at the result of an experiment before the experiment is carried out....No empirical statement is wholly nontheoretical in this sense because evidence is never complete, nor is any prediction probably ever made wholly without evidence. (1950/1972, p. 69)

This sense of theory is somewhat more interesting, but unfortunately Skinner has little to say about it (no doubt because it seems harmless). As examples of Skinner's commitment to theory[2] we would cite his theory of punishment: Punishment is ineffective in extinguishing a response; it merely temporarily inhibits it. Such a theory, which seems now to be somewhat questionable (Azrin & Holz, 1966) is legitimate and necessary to any science since science is fallible and the truth of scientific conjectures or hypotheses awaits the verdict of subsequent experience. Scientists clearly use theory[2] and need to, but no more or no less than Sherlock Holmes uses a theory when he supposes "the butler did it"

or a weatherman would in reporting: "rain is likely tomorrow." In short, Skinner rightly accepts the legitimacy of this kind of theory.

Theory as Conceptual Analysis

A third sense of 'theory' can be called 'theory as conceptual analysis'. In Skinner's early experimental articles, he introduced several theoretical distinctions and conceptual clarifications. He argued (1931/1972) that a reflex can be interpreted in two distinct ways: as the underlying reflex arc—the physiological or structural notion of a reflex—or as the correlation between an environmental stimulus and a response—the functional notion of a reflex. For the behavioral psychologist, Skinner suggested, a reflex must be taken in the second, functional sense. When Skinner went on to argue that the concepts of stimulus and response must be taken as class concepts (1935a/1972) he was also engaging in this kind of theorizing, as he was when he introduced the distinction between respondent and operant conditioning (1935b/1972, 1937/1972).

Skinner's views about the proper definition of learning, extinction, punishment, or a reflex were offered as conceptual distinctions or conceptual analyses (although not in the standard philosophical sense).[2] Skinner's particular bent toward conceptual analyses derives from his commitment to a radical operationalism in which concepts are to be redefined or analyzed in terms of operations performed and results observed.[3] The goal of these operationalizations seems to be to clarify concepts from a behavioristic point of view so as to allow one to predict and control behavior more successfully. Because Skinner's version of operationalism is not widely known and is often misunderstood, and because it rests upon Skinner's firm rejection of a philosophical approach to epistemology, a brief discussion of Skinner's psychological epistemology may prove to be of value in understanding his views about theory.

Skinner's Psychological Epistemology[4]

Quite early in his writings (1945/1972), Skinner advanced a bold and controversial claim: Epistemology, from the behaviorist's point of view, must be thoroughly naturalized; echoing the later views of Quine (1969), *philosophical epistemology must be replaced by psychological epistemology*. As Skinner put it:

...a scientific analysis of behavior has yielded a sort of empirical epistemology. The subject matter of a science of behavior includes the behavior of scientists and other knowers. The techniques available to such a science give an empirical theory of knowledge certain advantages over theories derived from philosophy and logic. (1964, p. 84)

The nature of such an empirical, psychological epistemology was not elaborated in any detail but the general lines of such an approach can be pieced together from scattered remarks (Kitchener, 1979a; Ringen, 1993).

The rationale of such an empirical epistemology springs from Skinner's desire to be thoroughly naturalistic in his philosophy. For such a consistent radical naturalist, all nonnaturalistic categories and concepts must be interpreted as properties of the natural world, and this applies as much to logic as it does to anything else. But logic naturalized is just psychology.

Skinner's *Psychologism* (the identification or reduction of logic to psychological processes) took a unique form, however, for unlike earlier thinkers such as John Stuart Mill (1872; Skorupski, 1989), who also advocated psychologism, psychological processes are not to be interpreted as being mentalistic in nature, but rather behavioristic. This version of psychologism led to Skinner's radical operationalism, an operationalism that does not give operational definitions—at least not in the philosopher's sense of definition—but replaces or identifies a concept with test operations and behavioral results. Test operations are typically interpreted as stimulus occasions and behavioral results are operant responses (often verbal in nature). As Skinner (1945/1972) puts it: "The question 'What is length?' would appear to be satisfactorily answered by listing the circumstances under which the response 'length' is emitted (or, better, by giving some general description of such circumstances)" (p. 372). In general, terms, concepts and constructs should be dealt with "in the form in which they are observed—namely, as verbal responses" (*ibid.*). If so, terms such as 'definition' and 'meaning' must also be treated in precisely the same way, namely, as verbal responses occurring under stimulus conditions and subject to reinforcing contingencies. Thus the concept 'definition' is replaced by the verbal (emitted) response "definition" and an operational analysis would consist of determining how such a response is learned and currently being controlled. Similar behavioral

translations apply to other semantic notions such as meaning and synonymy.[5]

The rationale behind this radical operationalism stems, in part, from Skinner's concern with learning. Given that operant behavior is acquired under certain stimulus occasions, Skinner concludes that we must focus on the reinforcing practices of the community, in particular, on *contingencies of reinforcement*—relations between a stimulus occasion, a response, and a reinforcing stimulus. On this view, therefore, meaning, synonymy, and so forth turn out to be naturalistic contingencies of reinforcement: "...meaning is not properly regarded as a property either of a response or a situation but rather of the contingencies responsible for both the topography of behavior and the control exerted by stimuli" (Skinner, 1974, p. 90).

Skinner's psychologism, therefore, is just good psychology and it absorbs not only ethical values but all other normative concepts as well (Kitchener, 1979a, 1979b), including logic and epistemology. All normative concepts are to be identified, therefore, with naturalistic ones, in particular descriptions of reinforcement contingencies (Skinner, 1974, p. 115). Since a description is itself just a verbal response, norms, in turn, are transformed into verbal responses to reinforcement contingencies.

As applied to logic, this psychologism is just radical operationalism:

> To be consistent the psychologist must deal with his own verbal practices by developing an empirical science of verbal behavior. He cannot, unfortunately, join the logician in defining a definition, for example, as a "rule for the use of a term" (Feigl); he must turn instead to the contingencies of reinforcement which account for the functional relation between a term, as a verbal response, and a given stimulus. This is the "operational basis" for his use of terms; and it is not logic but science.
>
> The philosopher will call this circular. He will argue that we adopt the rules of logic in order to make and interpret the experiments required in an empirical science of verbal behavior. But talking about talking is no more circular than thinking about thinking of knowing about knowing...Eventually we shall be able to include, and perhaps to understand, our own verbal behavior as scientists. If it turns out that our final view of verbal behavior invalidates our scientific structure from the point of view of logic and truthvalue, then so much the worse for logic, which will also have been embraced by our analysis. (1945/1972, p. 380)

As applied to epistemology, this simply transforms normative (philosophical) epistemology into empirical (psychological) epistemology. What such a psychological epistemology would be remains unclear, but it would certainly be necessary to provide a naturalistic analysis of central epistemic concepts, such as truth, confirmation, justification, and so on.

Skinner began such analyses by claims such as "A proposition is 'true' to the extent that with its help the listener responds effectively to the situation it describes" (1974, p. 235). Confirmation is handled in a similar way: "We confirm any verbal response when we generate additional variables to increase its probability" (1957, p. 425). Skinner's theory of theories depends upon such a psychological epistemology.

Theory as the Interpretation of Behavior

A different sense of 'theory', although one that overlaps with the preceding one, is perhaps an equally revolutionary aspect of Skinner's theory of theories and it certainly is one that has been insufficiently stressed. Much of the goal of Skinner's program can be said to be the attempt to *interpret* ordinary behavior in terms of the operant paradigm (1957; 1971, p. 149; 1974, p. 19). In fact most of Skinner's so-called extrapolations involving verbal behavior, education, psychopathology, and the design of cultures are examples of theory$_4$. What he is doing here can be described as providing an *analysis* or *interpretation* to a complex form of behavior. He is in effect saying: "See behavior in this way, viz., as an operant response shaped by reinforcement, under the control of antecedent stimuli, etc....!" With regard to language, for example, Skinner (1957) is quite explicitly offering a behavioral interpretation in terms of mands, tacts, autoclitics, etc., an interpretation that rests upon basic facts "well known to every educated person," facts that "do not need to be substantiated statistically or experimentally at the level of rigor here attempted" (1957, p. 11). Likewise with regard to many mental concepts he is offering a similar kind of interpretation. The *purpose* of an act, for example, is to be analyzed or interpreted in terms of reinforcing stimuli; "a person *wants* something," Skinner suggests, "if he acts to get it when the occasion arises" (1971, p. 37), and a person *knows* there is gold in the Klondike (nonverbally) "if, when he needs gold, he goes to the Klondike" (1957, p. 364). This appears to be some kind of *log-ical* or *analytical behaviorism*, but a version different from the more familiar philosophical versions of Carnap (1932/1959), Hempel (1935/1949) and Ryle (1949).[6]

What Skinner means by an 'analysis' or 'interpretation' has not been systematically discussed. It can, however, be characterized in something like the following way:

> [In an experimental analysis of behavior] principles derived from research conducted under the favorable conditions of the laboratory are used to give a plausible account of facts which are not at the moment under experimental control. [Such analyses cannot] at the present time be proved, but...are to be preferred to treatments which lack the same kind of experimental support. (1969, p. 100)

To give a "plausible account of facts" is to indicate what variables might be controlling the response.

In offering such interpretations, Skinner's operant conditioning paradigm is the lens through which one can see the phenomena in question. In fact if one approaches behavior in this way, one can begin to see discriminative stimuli and reinforcers operating everywhere. One must be trained to do this, of course (Skinner admits), but this training is part of his overall strategy. Furthermore, Skinner admits such operant interpretations are not natural ways of looking at behavior, but ones requiring training. A naive observer, for example, reporting what he sees in a Skinner box, does not naturally see contingencies of reinforcement. Since he is naive and untrained, he "will find it hard to make any sense of these scattered facts" (1969, p. 9). Why? Because *direct observation, no matter how prolonged, tells him very little about what is going on?"* (1969, p. 9). Skinner proceeds:

> When we recall how long it took to recognize the causal action of the environment in the simple reflex, we should perhaps not be surprised that it has taken us much longer to see contingencies of reinforcement. The traditional homocentric view of human behavior discourages us from looking at the environment in this light, and the *facts themselves are far from obvious.* (1969, p. 9, my emphasis)

Our observer needs to learn to see the facts in a different way: He needs to learn to see contingencies of reinforcement. After doing so she can then apply this theory to various aspects of human behavior.

It is only when we have analyzed behavior under known contingencies of reinforcement that we can begin to see what is happening in daily life. Things we once overlooked then begin to command our attention, and things which once attracted our attention we learn to discount or ignore. (1969, p. 10)

Such a view about observation seems to be similar to those views of philosophers (e. g., Feyerabend, 1965; Hanson, 1959; Kuhn, 1970) who claim empirical observations are "theory-laden." According to these philosophers, our theory literally determines how we see the world; no sense can be given, therefore, to 'observation without a theory' or 'direct observation from all theory'. One is tempted to construe Skinner's remarks in a similar way. (Later I will suggest such a construal of Skinner is implausible, given his underlying epistemology and philosophy of science.)

According to Skinner certain theories are both important and necessary since they provide the basis for correctly interpreting behavior. But, according to him, we should not expect too much from these interpretations or analyses: They do not, for example, purport to give exact behavioral *translations*. The ideal translations of the phenomenalist and physicalist, in which an equivalence or identity sign would be flanked by two expressions such that there was a semantic or logical connection of some kind between them, is clearly not what is meant. In analyzing, translating, and interpreting, Skinner is covering only *part* (at best) of what we ordinarily mean by certain expressions (1974, p. 19). This, presumably, is the part valid for psychology. The remaining aspects may be ignored (at least for now) without serious loss but subject to future revision as our behavioral knowledge increases.

Theory as a Convenient Summary of Empirical Data

In his famous paper "Are Theories of Learning Necessary?" (1950/1972) Skinner introduced two further kinds of theory. After rejecting the notion of theories as hypothetical mechanisms (theory$_6$), he went on to say:

This does not exclude the possibility of theory in another sense. Beyond the collection of uniform relationships lies the need for a formal representation of the data reduced to a minimal number of terms. A theoretical construction may yield greater generality than any assemblage of facts.

But such a construction will not refer to another dimensional system and will not, therefore, fall within our present definition. It will not stand in the way of our search for functional relations because it will arise only after relevant variables have been found and studied. (1950/1972, pp. 99–100)

This latter type of theory, theory$_5$, Skinner believes to be essential in psychology, since it is the type of theory to which all psychologists are (properly) committed! It represents a type of theory ignored by many of his critics and though Skinner has not extensively discussed its details, he has consistently referred to it (1938, 1947, 1969). For want of a better term, I will call the sense of theory *theory-as-a-summarizing-device*. It is, I think, what positivistic philosophers have always understood a legitimate scientific theory to be. For them, as for Skinner, a theory is legitimate only as a convenient summary of observable, empirical data. In a paper written several years before his classic antitheoretical piece, Skinner defined this positivistic kind of theory:

A theory, as I shall use the term here, has nothing to do with the presence or absence of experimental confirmation. Fact and theories do not stand in opposition to each other. The relation, rather, is this: theories are based upon facts; *they are statements about organization of facts.* The atomic theory, the kinetic theory of gases, the theory of evolution, and the theory of the gene are examples of reputable and useful scientific theories. *They are all statements about facts,* and with proper operational care they need be nothing more than that. But they have a generality which transcends particular facts and gives them a wider usefulness. Every science eventually reaches the stage of theory in this sense. (1947/1972, p. 302; my emphasis)

Such a view was present even in his earlier book (1938): After characterizing his system as "positivistic," which "confines itself to description rather than explanation," he says:

Its concepts [e. g., reflex, drive, and extinction] are defined in terms of immediate observation and are not given local or physiological properties... Terms of this sort are used merely to bring together groups of observations, to state uniformities, and to express properties of behavior which transcend single instances. They are not hypotheses, in the sense of things to be proved or disproved, but convenient representations of things already known. (1938, p. 44)

In order to construct such a theory, one must proceed purely *inductively* (in a manner reminiscent of Bacon). Such an inductive method, as contrasted with the classical hypothetico–deductive method, involves three steps. First, one must identify the basic data—the basic independent and dependent variables. This is fundamentally the stage of collecting and describing particular facts concerning, say, rate of response, deprivation level, and reinforcement schedule, the result of which is a collection of particular facts. The second stage consists of discovering the laws or lawlike relations between these experimental variables. (For a discussion of this distinction, see Kitchener, 1976.) For example, on the basis of the data collected in stage one, we inductively arrive at the lawlike conclusion that strength of operant response is a function of reinforcement level. Here we have inductively established a scientific generalization or law.

The third stage is the crucial one, for at this stage one introduces *new concepts*. Sounding like the hypothetico–deductivist, Skinner claims these concepts "are something more than the second-stage laws from which they are derived. They are peculiarly the product of theory-making in the best sense, and they cannot be arrived at through any other process" (1947/1972, p. 307). What then are these third-stage concepts and how do they relate to second-stage lawful regulations? In the passage under consideration, the only help Skinner gives is through an example from physics—Galileo. After demonstrating the lawful relation between position and time (Skinner's second stage), Galileo proceeded (according to Skinner) to introduce a third-stage concept—acceleration. "Later...other concepts appeared—mass, force, and so on" (1947/1972, p. 307). (The best example of a Skinnerian third-stage concept is perhaps reflex reserve).

Now, presumably a concept such as acceleration is theoretical in the (positivist's) sense of being a "conceptual shorthand device" (Pearson, 1892) for representing a complex set of data in an economical way. Such concepts will be statements about facts and empirical regularities, convenient and economical representations of facts and nothing more. Their function will be economical and pragmatic in nature. These theoretical concepts differ from laws only in their degree of generality and in their ability to descriptively represent in a simple but abstract way. "The mere accumulation of uniformities is not a science at all. It is necessary to organize facts in such a way that a simple and convenient description

can be given, and for this purpose a structure or system is required" (1947/1972, p. 45). This structure or system would consist of these new concepts but they would be completely definable in terms of lower-level facts and laws. In short, they would be what Tolman (1936/1966) called an "intervening variable" but not a "hypothetical construct" (MacCorquodale & Meehl, 1948).

Here, Skinner seems to be following the classical positivist position concerning the nature of theoretical entities.[7] Skinner quite explicitly admits his debt to Mach and Poincaré (1931/1972, p. 431; cf. also 1938, p. 432; 1953, p. 13; 1969, p. 95) and consciously labels his system "positivistic." His philosophical allegiance to positivism is neither new nor surprising of course. But it has not been sufficiently stressed, nor fully understood (see, however, Smith, 1986).

Positivism: Mach and Skinner

Although a full discussion of Skinner's positivism would require a discussion of the many similarities between his views and those of Mach, Pearson, Poincaré, and pragmatism, perhaps it will be sufficient to note some of the relations between Skinner's philosophical views and those of an individual who explicitly influenced him—Ernst Mach.

According to Mach the aim of science is to give a convenient description of experience. Such descriptions enable one to predict phenomena and hence to anticipate them. This view of the aim of science stems from Mach's biological theory of knowledge.

From the point of view of evolutionary theory, all knowledge has survival value: It allows individual organisms to adapt to their environment. Knowledge, Mach says,

is a product of organic nature. And although ideas, as such, do not comport themselves in all respects like independent organic individuals, and although violent comparisons should be avoided, still, if Darwin reasoned rightly, their general imprint of evolution and transformation must be noticeable in ideas also. (1896/1943, p. 217)

As Dewey was to put it later, ideas are "instruments (tools) of action," whose function (ultimately) is to satisfy psychological and biological needs. Hence, science, as a codified system of such knowledge, has primarily a practical aim: to assist us in coping with the environment (Mach, 1883/1907, p. 4).

Science fulfills this task of prediction and anticipation of future phenomena by describing recurrent regularities in nature. These descriptions are known as scientific laws; they are summaries of functional relations between observable phenomena. For Mach (and other positivists) metaphysics—as the search for "things-in-themselves"—has no place in science. Instead, the ultimate subject matter of science consists of sensations.

> Again, to save the labor of instruction and of acquisition, concise, abridged description is sought. This is really all that natural laws are. Knowing the value of the acceleration of gravity, and Galileo's laws of descent, we possess simple and compendious directions for reproducing in thought all possible motions of falling bodies. A formula of this kind is a complete substitute for a full table of motions of descent, because by means of the formula the data of such a table can be easily constructed at a moment's notice without the least burdening of the memory. (Mach, 1895, p. 190)

Causality is just a functional relation between observable variables (Mach, 1886/1959, p. 89) and laws are general descriptions of these functional relations. Because laws are such general descriptions, they are economical summarizing devices; they are "rules for reconstructing facts." "This rule of derivation, this formula, this 'law' has, now, not in the least more real value than the aggregate of the individual facts. Its value for us lies merely in the convenience of its use: it has an economical value" (Mach, 1872/1911, p. 55).

Explanation has no mysterious qualities surrounding it since it consists merely of redescribing a phenomenon (one that we find puzzling) in simpler and more familiar terms (terms drawn from our experience). Explanation, in short, is always reduction to the familiar (Mach, 1883/1907, p. 6).

Mach's treatment of theories and theoretical entities—Skinner's stage 3 concepts—is much more difficult to summarize, but generally he considers theoretical terms (constructs) to be mental symbols standing for complex sets of sensations. This is true of all physical object terms (1886/1959, p. 29) and, a fortiori, of theoretical concepts such as atoms and molecules (1886/1959, p. 311). The meaning of these theoretical terms is completely given by the corresponding set of observations (Mach, 1872/1911, p. 57; 1886/1959, p. 42). 'Force', for example, "is not something that lies latent in the natural

processes, but a measurable, actual circumstance of motion, the product of the mass into the acceleration" (Mach, 1883/1907, p. 246). The function of such thought symbols is purely economical: They aid us in representing and describing phenomena, for example, by likening them to other phenomena with which we are more familiar. Hence, theories often function as models and analogies. Mach is quick to point out, however, that such models have only a heuristic function. "Once an hypothesis has facilitated, as best it can, our view of new facts, by the substitution of more familiar ideas, its powers are exhausted. We err when we expect more enlightenment from an hypothesis than from the facts themselves, (1883/1907, p. 498). Theoretical entities are tools or instruments of thought; they are *memoria technica*; they have no other function than an economical and heuristic one, and their complete cognitive value consists of the observations they represent. Ultimately, therefore, they are eliminable. As Mach picturesquely puts it: "The object of natural science is the connexion of phenomena; but the theories are like dry leaves which fall away when they have long ceased to be the lungs of the tree of science" (1872/1911, p. 74).

The similarities between Mach and Skinner are immediately evident. Of course, in place of Mach's 'sensations', one must substitute Skinner's concepts of 'stimulus occasion', 'response', and 'reinforcing stimulus'. But once this switch has been made, Mach's philosophy of science becomes, *mutatis mutandis*, difficult to distinguish from Skinner's.

Most of these similarities are obvious enough and require little defense; for example, Skinner's conception of the aim of science as prediction and control has its roots explicitly in Mach (Skinner, 1953, p. 14), and Skinner's biological (i.e., psychological) theory of knowledge takes its inspiration, like Mach's, from Darwin.[8] Knowledge for Skinner consists of operant responses to the environment, which, if they have survival value, are reinforced. This is obviously analogous to certain characteristics of biological species, which are reinforced or extinguished by the evolutionary process. Hence in both areas there occurs selection by consequences (Skinner, 1981).

Skinner's psychologizing of logic also has its roots in positivism (Mach, 1886/1959, pp. 49, 183): For both Mach and Poincaré (1902/1952), mathematical and logical concepts are equivalent to certain mental operations (Mach, 1886/1959, p. 332). In the hands of Skinner these mental operations are transformed into behavioral operations; consequently, mathematics and logic become descriptions of contingencies of reinforcement— what Skinner calls rules.

Furthermore, like Mach, Skinner (1938, p. 443; 1953, p. 23) believes causality to be just a functional relation between experimental variables and explanation redescription (Skinner, 1931/1972, p. 448; 1947/1972, p. 301; 1964, p. 102).

Finally, positivism is clearly at the basis of Skinner's views concerning third-stage concepts. These are symbolic ways economically representing complex relationships and ultimately are completely definable in terms of observables. Skinner believes 'acceleration' falls into this category, as presumably do his early (but later rejected) concepts of reflex *reserve* ("It is a convenient way of representing the particular relation that obtains between the activity of a reflex and its subsequent strength" [1938, p. 26]), *filter* ("a convenient device for representing the observed dependence of the rate upon external discriminative stimuli" [1938, p. 229]), and *drive* ("a device for expressing the complex relation that obtains between various similarly effective operations and a group of co-varying forms of behavior" [1938, p. 368]).

In sum, Skinner's insistence on the importance and necessity of theory₅, seems to stem from his philosophy of science, a version of classical nineteenth-century positivism.

Theory as a Hypothetical Mechanism

By 'theory as a hypothetical mechanism,' I mean the kind of theory criticized by Skinner in his famous paper "Are Theories of Learning Necessary?" (1950/1972). As Skinner defines this kind of theory, it refers to "any explanation of an observed fact which appeals to events taking place somewhere else, at some other level of observation, described in different terms, and measured, if at all, in different dimension" (1950/1972, p. 60; cf. 1947/1972, pp. 304–305). Skinner has three kinds of theories in mind: physiological mechanisms, mentalistic explanations, and explanations involving "the conceptual nervous system."

Physiological Mechanisms

Under *physiological mechanisms*, Skinner includes a variety of heterogeneous physiological explanations, but in particular the theoretical entities or processes postulated by Sherrington and Pavlov.

(Presumably he was thinking of the theories of Köhler and Hebb also.) These physiological mechanisms include synaptic connections, electric fields, concentration of ions, nervous breakdown, "nerves on edge," circuits, centers, and cell assemblies, as well as processes such as Pavlov's "cortical irradiation."

As this list suggests, Skinner seems to be concerned with "hypothetical" neural explanations epitomized perhaps by Pavlov's notion of the "irradiation" of cortical energy, or Sherrington's notion of a synapse as the hypothetical link between neurons. One might paraphrase Skinner's objections to these entities by saying that he is opposed to those postulated physiological entities that, *at the present time*, are unobserved and unobservable. Consequently, although a synapse was a hypothetical entity, say, in 1905, it is not one and, therefore, Skinner does not *now* reject synapses, neurons, acetylocholine, etc., but rather only such things as cell assemblies or brain fields. However, although this reading of Skinner is natural and plausible, it confronts certain problems, for Skinner also seems to reject these other physiological entities. After mentioning synaptic connections, electrical fields, and ionic concentration as examples of the sort of thing he had in mind, Skinner goes on to say:

> In a science of neurophysiology statements of this sort are not necessarily theories in the present sense. But in a science of behavior... all *statements about the nervous system are theories in the sense that they are not expressed in the same terms and could not be confirmed with the same methods of observation as the facts for which they are said to account.* (1950/1972, pp. 69–70, my emphasis)

Although in some places Skinner (1953, pp. 27–28) seems prepared to retract the above claim, he appears to be suggesting that for the operant behaviorist, the nervous system is theoretical.

Mentalistic Explanations

Under *mentalistic explanations* Skinner cites examples such as pleasure, the superego, and personality traits. Such explanations are theories "because the methods and terms appropriate to the events to be explained differ from the methods and terms appropriate to the explaining events" (1950/1972, p. 70). (Presumably, mental states are to be considered theoretical even if they are directly observable to the introspective psychologist.) The fact that the level of observation is different or that the terms

employed belong to a different system seem sufficient to make such a term theoretical.

Conceptual Nervous System

Finally, explanations in terms of the *conceptual
nervous system* include such things as habits, hunger, instincts, intelligence, abilities, as well as concepts such as expectancy, reaction potential, and so
on. In the case of these concepts (unlike the preceding two categories) there is no possibility of direct
observation here at all. Obviously Skinner is here
focusing primarily upon the learning theory of Hull
and others, who postulate theoretical constructs
that are neither neurological nor mental, but which
qualify as hypothetical constructs nevertheless.
Indeed, virtually all of cognitive psychology would
fall into this class (Skinner, 1977).

SKINNER'S CRITERIA FOR
A 'HYPOTHETICAL MECHANISM'

On an intuitive level what Skinner has in mind by
a theory$_6$ seems to be fairly clear. But when one
begins to examine his criteria more closely, they
prove to be somewhat vague and unhelpful in correctly categorizing proffered explanations as theoretical or nontheoretical.

His four criteria for an explanation being
theoretical$_6$ are the following: (1) They take place
somewhere else, (2) they occur at some other level
of observation, (3) they are described in different
terms, and (4) they are measured, if at all, in different dimensions.[9] I want to consider each of these in
turn and to show why they seem inadequate.

1. *Somewhere else.* What does it mean to say
that such theoretical explanations (and/or these
entities) take place "somewhere else"? Skinner
seems to have in mind here some kind of spatial
model, one in which there are different regions. A
Cartesian, for example, might argue that the activity of the mind takes place somewhere else than the
body, namely, in a special nonphysical place called
the mind. But those who countenance mentalistic
explanations are not always and in fact need not be
Cartesian. One contemporary school, for example,
maintains that mentalistic concepts are embedded
in action, and earlier thinkers such as Tolman and
Lashley (together with the early Carnap and
Hempel) attempted to define mentalistic terms in
terms of behavior. On these views, mentalistic con-

cepts do not refer to what occurs somewhere else at
all, since mental states are merely complex patterns
of behaviors, dispositions to behave, and so on.

Furthermore, it remains unclear why electrical
brain fields take place somewhere else, since presumably they take place in the physical world of
the brain. More importantly, are we to classify
covert, internal stimuli and responses (e.g., autonomic responses) as taking place somewhere else
or not? Exactly what constitutes a region is not
clear, nor is the boundary separating them. No
doubt in observing overt behavior one can give
some sense to the notion that brain events are
occurring somewhere else, namely, in the region
beneath the skin or in one of the nervous systems.
But these boundaries are, as Skinner himself maintains, somewhat arbitrary and not impregnable to
an operant account. This criterion, therefore, does
not seem to be very helpful; what sense one can
make of it seems to be better captured by Skinner's
second criterion.

2. *At some other level of observation.* What
Skinner means by this phrase is subject to several
possible interpretations. It might mean:

> 2a. Anything that cannot be observed by the
> naked eye takes place at some other level of
> observation.

If one must use, say, a microscope to observe
some internal process, then what is observed is
occurring at some other level of observation. Likewise, if one must use introspection to observe a
mental state, then it too is occurring at a different
level of observation.

As several thinkers have pointed out, however,
this type of demarcation seems to be implausible,
since there is no nonarbitrary way to draw a distinction between unaided observation (i.e., observation with the naked eye) and observation aided
with some artificial means, e.g., glasses, microscopes, electron microscopes.

On the other hand this claim might be:

> 2b. Anything that cannot be observed by the
> naked eye or by means of some instrument takes
> place at some other level of observation.

On this interpretation, however, the sense of
"some other level of *observation*" is lost (except
perhaps for introspection), since nothing can be
observed (at a different level of observation) unless
one presumably uses *some* perceptual means.

Hence, on this view, *nothing* could be observed at some other level of observation.

More importantly, this criterion will not help us to evaluate the status of theory$_6$. For suppose a physicist tells us she is observing an electron passing through a cloud chamber, or suppose a freshman student in psychology (told to report what she observes the rat to be doing) reports that "the rat is over in the corner deciding what he wants to do next." All of these observations would, I think, be objectionable to Skinner, although they do not seem to be ruled out by criterion 2b. But do they really? Can a physicist, for example, really be said to observe an electron?

Direct Observation

In order to decide that issue, Skinner must give us some account of what he means by 'observation'. One account of observation running throughout his writings is a positivistic one. In scientific observation, according to this account, observation must always be *direct* observation (as opposed to interpretation and inference). Criterion 2b, therefore, can be replaced by a slightly different interpretation:

2b'. Anything that cannot be directly observed takes place at some other level of observation.

'Directly observe' would have to mean something like: "observe without making any inference or interpretation," "observe only what is immediately there," "observe only what is incorrigible," etc. Such an account of observation can be found running throughout Skinner's writings (1931/1972, p. 449; 1938, p. 442; 1953, pp. 27–28, 33; 1954/1972, p. 122; 1969, pp. ix, xi, 111, 262; 1974, p. 212). For example, in one place he claims:

The sole criterion for the rejection of a popular term is the implication of a system or of a formulation extending beyond immediate observations. We may freely retain all terms which are descriptive of behavior without systematic implications. Thus, the term 'try' must be rejected because it implies the relation of a given sample of behavior to past or future events; but the term 'walk' may be retained because it does not. The term 'see' must be rejected but 'look toward' may be retained, because 'see' implies more than turning the eyes toward a source of stimulation or more than the simple reception of stimuli. (1938, pp. 7–8)

In his "Behaviorism at Fifty" (1964), Skinner relates an incident in which students "were asked to write an account of what they had seen" while observing the behavior of a pigeon. Their accounts were replete with terms such as 'expect', 'hope', and the like. Skinner then remarks that "the observed facts" could be stated in nonmentalistic terms.

The expressions "expect," "hope," "observe," "feel," and "associate" go beyond them [contingencies of reinforcement] to identify effects on the pigeon. The effect *actually* observed was clear enough: the pigeon turned more skillfully and more frequently; but that was not the effect reported by the students. (1964, p. 91, my emphasis: see also 1969, p. 182, for another example)

Such a view about direct observation was a major tenet of positivism and it is not surprising that Skinner would endorse it. Assuming a sharp theory versus observation distinction, this view maintains that to report an observation is to report whatever is *immediately* there; consequently observation reports will be *certain*.

On the other hand, several remarks by Skinner suggest a different view concerning the nature of observation. Skinner is quite prepared to say that the direct observation of a phenomenon is inadequate, that our observational abilities must be developed along different lines, and that we must come to see phenomena as exemplifying operant principles.[10] To *interpret* behavior is to presuppose an operant theory; to see contingencies of reinforcement in behavior is to insist that observations once again are heavily ladened with operant theory. But all of this theoretical interpretation is flatly opposed to Skinner's 'direct observation' criterion, and the conclusion seems inescapable that Skinnerian interpretations are theoretical in the pejorative sense, since they do go beyond direct observation. By the criterion of "some other level of observation," a Skinnerian interpretation (theory$_4$) seems to be an *observation at some other level*, at a level different from "direct observation."

Of course, once one has learned Skinner's theory, one can directly observe contingencies of reinforcement, rate of responding, etc. (1956/1972, p. 117; 1969, p. 111). But this makes direct observation a *relative* notion (relative to a particular theory) and opens the possibility that another theory (e. g., mentalism) could legitimately talk about directly observing mental states. For if indirect observation is relative to a theory, we need only say that the mentalist can distinguish, *in his theory*, between direct observation and nondirect observation. In sum, then, the status of 'direct observation' is unclear. If Skinner's rejection of theories as hypothetical mechanisms rests upon the criterion of direct observation, then Skinner's account must also be labeled theoretical$_6$. On the other hand, if Skinner's account is not theoretical, then his criterion of "some other level of observation" cannot be interpreted in terms of 'direct observation.'

Skinner is quite prepared to make inferences to what seem to be events occurring "somewhere else," namely inferences to events occurring inside the body of the observed subject—private events. (If these events are not "somewhere else," we need to be told why they are not.) To infer the existence of private events in others is obviously to go beyond what is immediately observed. Indeed, Skinner admits: "In studying behavior we may have to deal with the stimulation from the tooth as an inference rather than directly observable fact" (1953, p. 258; cf. also 1953, pp. 282, 373). Indeed, several papers are concerned precisely with the problem of how to handle private events in a functional analysis of behavior (1945/1972, 1957, 1972). For example, in his important paper on operationalism (1945/1972), Skinner suggests several ways in which we may be taught to report on (read: respond to) private events: (i) There may be public stimuli that accompany private stimuli and the presence of such public stimuli (e. g., tissue damage or a blow to the head) may lead us to infer the existence of private stimuli. (ii) A private stimulus may produce public behavior and on the basis of such collateral responses (e. g., groans, facial expressions) we may infer the existence of private stimuli. (iii) Overt verbal responses may be descriptions of (read: responses to) the speaker's covert behavior, which in turn (presumably) generates proprioceptive stimuli (another inference), with the proprioceptive feedback constituting the controlling S_D. How does this happen?

> There are two important possibilities. The surviving covert response may be regarded as an accompaniment of the overt (perhaps part of it), in which case the response to the private stimulus is imparted on the basis of the public stimulus supplied by the overt response…On the other hand, the covert response may be *similar to*, though probably less intense than, the overt and hence supply the *same* stimulus, albeit in a weakened form. (1945/1972, p. 375)

Finally, (iv) by stimulus generalization, an overt verbal response may be made to a private stimulus, which has "coinciding properties."

To the external observer all of this is an inference. Intuitively it seems to involve "some other level of observation" and certainly does not appear to be "directly observable," but if so, then why is it not "theoretical" in the to-be-rejected sense?

The Role of Instruments in Observation

Suppose we attempt to avoid this objection by allowing that instruments of the future may allow us to penetrate the skin of the observed organism and to detect these private stimuli, private responses, and private reinforcements. If we insist upon the criterion of 'direct observation,' won't we then be directly observing these private events? Skinner's answer here is unclear. Often he seems to imply that in such a case there would be direct observation, but at other times he concludes it would not be. For example, Skinner claims that although he is making inferences to private events, the future development of instruments will enable us to observe these events.

> The line between public and private is not fixed. The boundary shifts with every discovery of a technique for *making private events public*. Behavior which is of such small magnitude that it is not ordinarily observed may be amplified. Covert verbal behavior may be detected in slight movements of the speech apparatus. (1953, p. 282, my emphasis; cf. also 1945/1972, p. 374; 1957, pp. 130, 141, 434; 1969, pp. 242, 262)[11]

On the other hand, other passages in Skinner suggest that new instrumental technology will not enable us to make these private events publically observable. Skinner points out, for example, that "when privacy is invaded with scientific instruments, the form of stimulation is changed; the scores read by the scientist are not the private events themselves" (1969, p. 226). That is to say, an outside observer may observe what her instruments record, but these instrumental recordings will never *be* the very stimuli or responses occurring within the skin of the observed subject.

This is precisely what should be expected as a consequence of Skinner's theory of observation (1953, chapter 17, especially pp. 280–281). According to Skinner, when a subject perceives/

observes an internal stimulus (call it S_i), he reacts to it (R_i). This perceptual response R_i is an operant response under the control of S_i. Now suppose we have an instrumental recording of S_i. This recording, say, on an oscilloscope, constitutes a different stimulus (say S_o) partially caused by S_i. When we observe S_o we are making a response to it (R_o) which is under the control of S_o. Could R_o be said to be an observation of S_i on the grounds that S_i causes a response in our instrument, which in turn becomes a stimulus (S_o) for us? Only if S_i were controlling our perceptual response (R_o). But of course it need not be. Imagine, for example, a breakdown in the causal chain from S_i to S_o such that S_i changes but S_o does not (or such that S_o changes but S_i does not); S_o would continue to control our response, but S_i would not. In short we would be responding to S_o and not to S_i (i.e., we would be perceiving S_o but not S_i). In short, technological advances in our instrumentation will simply not "make private events public," nor will it make private events directly observable to us.

Of course, technical instrumentation may provide us with *independent evidence* for the inferred private event (1953, pp. 28, 280; 1957, pp. 6, 141; 1969, p. 262) and hence increase its warrant, but it does not eliminate the inference, nor does it abrogate the fact that such inferred entities occur "at some other level of observation."

Skinner's comments often confuse issues of justifying an inference to unobserved entity versus there being no need for such an inference. For example, Skinner sometimes defends his inferences to private events on the grounds that they have the *same properties* observable events have.

What [the behaviorist] refuses to accept are the dimensions traditionally assigned to what he observes. Some of the objects of introspection are private (covert) responses. Watson was particularly intrigued with this possibility. So far as we know, the responses are executed with the same organs as observable responses but on a smaller scale. The stimuli they generate are weak but nevertheless of the same kind as those generated by overt responses. It would be a mistake to refuse to consider them as data just because a second observer cannot feel or see them, at least without the help of instruments. (1969, p. 242)

But this is a point about the justification of inferring unobserved entities and processes; it is not a point about whether to employ them or not. If so, the issue becomes a question about what type of

inferences are justified and not over the stronger claim that hypothetical entities are not needed at all. This merges clearly, I think, if we compare Skinner's inferences regarding internal covert response with the very theoretical mechanism of fractional anticipatory goal responses (r_g) employed by Clark Hull (1930; see also Kitchener, 1977). Any point Skinner could marshal in defense of his account could also be used by Hull, viz., covert behavior can be reinforced and extinguished, it has the same dimensions as overt behavior, and so on. But the Hullian r_g–s_g mechanism surely counts as being theoretical in the sense of a hypothetical mechanism. But if so, then how does Skinner's account fail to be theoretical?

3.–4. *Described in different terms and measured in different dimensions.* Something is theoretical on the former criterion if it is described "in different terms." Presumably what Skinner wants to add is: "described in terms different from those employed in the description of behavior." As Skinner points out, such a criterion would make *all* of physiology theoretical, since physiology has its own terms and dimensions and psychology has its own.

The *physiological* inner man is, of course, no longer wholly inferential. New methods and instruments have brought the nervous system and other mechanisms under direct observation. The new data have their own dimensions and require their own formulations. The behavioral facts in the field of learning, for example, are dealt with in terms appropriate to behavior, while electrical and chemical activities occurring at the same time demand a different conceptual framework. Similarly, the effects of deprivation and satiation on behavior are not the same as the events seen through a gastric fistula. Nor is emotion, studied as behavioral predisposition, capable of being analyzed in terms appropriate to pneumographs and electrocardiographs. Both sets of facts, and their appropriate concepts, are important—but they are *equally* important, not dependent one upon the other. (1972, p. 325)

As these remarks seem to indicate, physiological concepts are theoretical; but if so, so are proprioception and autonomic responses. Insofar as Skinnerian inferences are inferences to these kinds of events they would, therefore, continue to be theoretical. Skinner cannot defend his inferences as harmless, therefore, on the grounds that they do not involve a different descriptive system. He could escape this charge only if the interoceptive, proprioceptive, and exteroceptive systems were not described in different terms, which they are, or if the inferred stimuli and responses were described *the same way* overt stimuli and responses were described, in which case his criterion for something being theoretical would be too broad, since it would include concepts such as expectancy, drive, r_g–s_g, and habit strength (Miller, 1959).

Many of these same points can also be made with regard to the fourth criterion. We measure behavioral responses in terms of, say, frequency, intensity and amplitude, and stimuli in terms of time, intensity, etc. If these are the dimensions appropriate for measuring behavior, what constitutes a different dimensional system?

Much of the trouble in answering this question stems from uncertainty concerning whether the "different dimensions" refer to quantitative properties of the theoretical entity or to the measurement of the property. For example, suppose we measure amount of attention (on a scale of 1 to 10) in terms of alpha blocking on an EEG recording. Is the "different dimension"—in terms of which attention is measured—to be taken as amount of attention (the most probable interpretation) or as the quantitative dimensions of our EEG? Skinner seems to maintain the first view. But if so, then presumably neural activity would be theoretical, because amount of neutral activity is a different dimension. But this simply reintroduces all the problems surrounding the other three criteria and does not help to decide the initial question of what counts as something being theoretical.

THE FOUNDATION OF SKINNER'S THEORY OF THEORIES

One of the things most often said of Skinner is that he has no theory and believes psychology should have none. By now this statement should seem to be overly simplistic, if not downright false. The issue depends on what meaning 'theory' has, but one can show that Skinner is strongly committed to a theory in several senses of that term. There is no doubt that he is opposed to theories involving hypothetical mechanisms. But even this point does not have the obviousness it appears initially to have, since Skinner's criteria are somewhat vague, and his own views seem to satisfy (some of) these criteria.

What seems unquestionable, however, is that Skinner is opposed to such hypothetical mechanisms, that he believes them to be both unnecessary and, in fact, positively harmful. But we have not

yet discussed why he believes this; we have not yet mentioned Skinner's arguments in support of these claims, nor have we discussed the underlying basis from which these arguments came and which provides the foundation for Skinner's general theory of theories.

I do not want to discuss in any detail Skinner's arguments against hypothetical mechanisms, nor do I want to assess their validity (this has been done by numerous authors). Instead, I want merely to point out that Skinner's arguments are based upon the positivistic assumption that the aim of science is to predict and control. This point is not new, but I hope to make it in a slightly different way by showing how Skinner's arguments derive their force—whatever they have—from such an assumption. Second, I want to point out that this positivism is not a pure, philosophical positivism, but contains, as its core, a psychological epistemology and that this psychological epistemology lies at the basis of Skinner's theory of theories.

One can find several arguments in Skinner against theories as hypothetical mechanisms. But three of these arguments occur so frequently as to warrant special mention: (1) the *surplus meaning* objection, (2) the *short-circuit* argument; and (3) the *vacuous* explanation claim.

Skinner sometimes faults hypothetical mechanisms (especially mentalistic ones such as 'expectancy') for having surplus meaning. These concepts, according to Skinner, are not identified with behavior, but are considered to be something more. Those who have followed the hypothetical construct versus intervening variable dispute in psychology (or those familiar with the empiricism of Hume or the positivism of Mach) will naturally be tempted to take this objection to be a philosophical or semantic one, based (one might suppose) upon a philosophical view about the nature of meaning and the foundations of knowledge. But although such an interpretation would not be (totally) incorrect, it would miss an important point. For Skinner cannot be objecting to surplus meaning on these philosophical grounds, since he has no place in his psychology for semantics, and in fact, like Quine (1951), Skinner claims (1957) that talk of 'meaning' is mentalistic (and presumably to be avoided). In keeping with Skinner's view that normative concepts should be replaced by empirical ones, his point could be put in a slightly different way—as a straightforward empirical claim that the use of theoretical terms in psychology has had (and will continue to have) overall bad effects on our behavior. The use of such terms distracts us from behavioral data, it reinforces the behavior of talking about mental terms, it encourages the use of certain methodological strategies, and so on. These psychological objections in turn reduce ultimately to saying that these behaviors do not allow us to deal effectively with the (behavioral) environment, i.e., they do not allow us to predict and to control behavior. The argument about surplus meaning, therefore, does not seem to be a *semantic* objection at all, but rather a psychological one, and this psychological objection, in turn, is rooted in Skinner's radical naturalism.

One of Skinner's most powerful arguments against hypothetical mechanisms is what I call his *short-circuit* argument. Suppose we have a mediating state, T, which is supposed to explain (cause) some behavior B. Assuming a tight causal chain, T must, in turn, be caused by some antecedent, environmental stimulus S. But if so, then by transitivity, we can eliminate T and treat B as a function of S (1953, pp. 34–35). "If we must always go back beyond the second link for prediction and control, we may avoid many tiresome and exhausting digressions by examining the third link as a function of the first" (1953, p. 35).

The key words here again are 'prediction' and 'control'. This point comes out clearly in the following passage:

> When a person says that he acted "because he felt like acting," we can put little faith in the "because" until we have *explained* why he had the feeling, but it has been objected that we must stop somewhere in following a causal chain into the past and may as well stop at the psychic level…It is true that we could trace human behavior not only to the physical conditions which shape and maintain it but also to the causes of those conditions and the causes of those causes, almost *ad infinitum*, but there is no point in going back beyond the point at which effective action can be taken. That point is not to be found in the psyche, and the explanatory force of mental life has steadily declined as the promise of the environment has come to be more clearly understood. (1974, p. 210)

Thus, by the short-circuit argument, intervening states can simply be bypassed. Skinner's assumption here is that these hypothetical mechanisms really do not explain behavior, that is, do not allow us to predict and control. How, we might ask, is explanation related to prediction and control? This

question can be answered, I think, by taking Skinner's argument that these explanations are really vacuous.

Hypothetical mechanisms are often vacuous explanations. They ascribe to the theoretical entity precisely those properties to be found in the explanandum and do no more. One cannot explain nest-building behavior, for example, by referring to a nest-building instinct, nor smoking behavior by reference to the habit of smoking because "A single set of facts is described by the two statements: 'He smokes a great deal' and 'He has the smoking habit' " (1953, p. 31). Here we have merely a redundant description and a spurious explanation.

How is it a spurious or vacuous explanation? Apparently because it is explaining itself. An explanation of behavior must apparently refer to something else besides that behavior. "An explanation is the demonstration of a functional relationship between behavior and manipulable or controllable variables" (1964, p. 102). We explain some item of behavior by asking, "What are the variables of which it is a function?" (1957, p. 10).

On this account, therefore, something T is an explanation of behavior B, only if T is a *manipulable* or *controllable variable*. T, in other words, must be a cause of B and, since T must be manipulable (directly or indirectly), it must be a cause in the sense of a "handle" or recipe for changing things (Collingwood, 1938; Gasking, 1955). This, in turn, necessitates the existence of an environmental variable S that is directly observable and which controls T. Explanation, therefore, is just the ability to predict and control!

How, on this account, would theoretical summarizing devices count as explanations of behavior? They could perform their role only if they mentioned or described a relation between behavior and some controllable antecedent variable. They seem to function, in other words, rather like recipes or rules to be employed in the manipulation and control of behavior (Kitchener, 1974, 1976), namely, they tell one what means to employ in order to produce a certain kind of behavior. On the other hand, hypothetical mechanisms lack such explanatory power, for since they are hidden, they cannot be "causal handles."

Furthermore, even if they are not faulted on this score, such hypothetical mechanisms can be shown to be unnecessary. Suppose, for example, we could (in some way) manipulate or control the hidden internal cause, thereby producing the desired external behavior. By Skinner's short-circuit argument, such hypothetical mechanisms would not be needed in a science of behavior at all. Thus, any hidden hypothetical mechanism is either vacuous or superfluous.

These same views seem to lie behind Skinner's often puzzling views concerning physiology. In several passages, for example, Skinner suggests that a future physiology will be able to "account for" behavior and our behavioral laws (1938, p. 428; 1969, pp. 282–283; 1974, p. 215), for it will be able to supply the missing gaps between a past event and current behavior.

> In a more advanced account of a behaving organism "historical" variables will be replaced by "causal" ones. When we observe the momentary state of an organism, we shall be able to use it instead of the history responsible for it in predicting behavior. When we can generate or change a state directly, we shall be able to use it to control behavior. (1969, p. 283)

In saying physiology will (one day) be able to explain behavior, this can only mean that a current, momentary internal state causes the behavior and this state is manipulable or controllable (either directly or indirectly). Because current causal variables will replace historical variables, a future physiology will be able to predict and control behavior in a way superior to that of current psychology. But if the physiological state meets Skinner's criteria for what constitutes an explanation, then it follows (by the short-circuit argument) that it is not needed. Thus physiological explanations may be real (and not vacuous) explanations, but even so they are otiose nonetheless.

CONCLUSION

Skinner's theoretical views rest upon classical positivism. I have suggested, however, that Skinner's version of positivism contains a psychological epistemology based upon a radical naturalism. We should not, therefore, misinterpret Skinner's claims as being philosophical in nature concerning what philosophical theory is correct. Skinner sometimes writes this way, but this only serves to obfuscate the issue.

Skinner's theory of theories contains, as a fundamental part, a naturalistic view about the nature of all normative claims. This is evident in some of his criticisms of the legitimacy of hypothetical mecha-

nism, but (as I have suggested) it is also the basis of his views about the theories as "interpretations of behavior" and "conceptual analyses." If this is so, and if Skinner's radical naturalism leads him to a psychological (as opposed to a normative) epistemology, then one can understand the sometimes peculiar and puzzling status of philosophical arguments in the writings of Skinner.

Philosophical objections to Skinner often seem to be beside the point simply because philosophical considerations have a paradoxical status in Skinner. For if epistemology is really psychology, then what is the point of raising nonpsychological objections to Skinner? The perplexity experienced by philosophers in reading Skinner is often due to the incommensurability of viewpoints: Philosophers expect Skinner to defend his views with philosophical arguments. But for someone who defends *psychologism* as staunchly as Skinner does, philosophical arguments are largely irrelevant, and when they are not irrelevant, they are no longer philosophical! If they are to be relevant, the requirement is that they cease to be normative (or logical) arguments and that they become psychological ones instead, viz., arguments that make some difference in the manipulation of behavior. In defending psychologism Skinner is making (some kind of) philosophical claim, but if psychologism is correct, then it really ceases to be an ordinary philosophical claim and becomes an empirical one. This is a paradox for anyone maintaining psychologism. It is perhaps equally difficult to see what a philosophical criticism can accomplish. For someone who does not hold logic qua logic in esteem, this will always be the case. Ultimately, therefore, à correct assessment of Skinner must include a systematic evaluation of his psychologism and his radical naturalism. (For a beginning see Ringen, 1993; Amundson, 1993; Smith, 1993). This, in turn, would involve a discussion of the philosophical status of logic in the natural sciences, especially psychology. At least this is the way a philosopher would put the point. Obviously a Skinnerian would phrase it differently.

ENDNOTES

1. I am not suggesting that these different senses are sharply distinct; on the contrary, several of them seem to overlap. All I am suggesting is that Skinner seems to recognize these various senses of 'theory.'

2. Certain comments of Skinner, e. g., those concerning misleading metaphors, suggest he is engaged in some

kind of philosophical analysis. As I will suggest below, however, these views are best seen not in the traditional philosophical way but in a more psychological way.

3. Skinner's unique version of operationalism—a version he sharply contrasts with that of the logical positivists—makes it difficult to put this point in a way that is not misleading. Skinner is surely offering analyses of concepts, but these analyses are behavioral analyses, not logical or semantic ones. Because he is not really giving definitions—operational or otherwise—it is somewhat misleading to describe them as operational definitions at all.

4. Skinner's views concerning logic and epistemology are often ambiguous and subject to two quite different interpretations. One interpretation (the stronger and more controversial one) reduces logic and epistemology to contingencies of reinforcement. This is what I call radical naturalism. The other interpretation is more modest and claims merely that logic and epistemology, in addition to their normative status, contain clear-cut behavioral implications. In a valid argument, for example, we are behaving in a certain way, since we are inferring; such behavior is subject to a psychological analysis. I (Kitchener, 1979b) have interpreted Skinner as maintaining the stronger view.

5. The similarity here between Skinner's naturalistic epistemology and Quine's (1969) leaps out and cries out for further discussion. As far as I know, no one has given a full analysis of the similarities and differences between Skinner and Quine.

6. It differs from most philosophical accounts in obviously being a psychological account. Skinner is not concerned to show, as philosophers are, that mental terms and behavioral terms are *logically related* to behavior whether in terms of explicit definition or in terms of public criteria (Fodor, 1965; for criticisms of this interpretation see Ringen, 1993; Smith, 1986). Skinner's version of behaviorism contains no corresponding logical thesis. Instead, mental terms are *replaced by* contingencies of reinforcement. Often, such a contingency will be expressed in a form indistinguishable from that of a disposition. For example, in a passage reminiscent of Gilbert Ryle, Skinner says: "I know that a man is angry, not because he is secreting adrenaline or because his blood pressure is increasing, but because he greets me dully, shakes hands slowly and weakly, responds to my remarks curtly, and avoids me if possible" (1938, p. 407). Skinner apparently did read Ryle and mentions him in one place (1957, p. 141). As the above passage shows, Skinnerian translations are not single if–then conditionals, but much more complex ones, involving several disjuncts reminiscent of Ryle's multiple-track dispositions. "I am angry," Skinner claims, "may be descriptive of the changes in glands and smooth muscles…; it may be a report of a facial expression or of a cry of anger… or of an inclination to emit such a cry; or it may be a description of the speaker's own inclination to act aggressively" (1957, p. 217).

7. In this paper a relatively sharp distinction is drawn between the "classical positivism" of Hume, Mill, Comte, Mach, Spencer, Pearson, Poincaré, Bernard and the Pragmatists (Kolakowski, 1968) and "logical positivism." In light of the program of the logical positivists, this seems justified, since they saw the difference between themselves and the earlier positivists to be one concerning the nature and role of logic in a positivistic epistemology. This same point (concerning logic) also arises in the case of Skinner (as I have already suggested).

8. Few individuals have sufficiently noted Mach's particular version of naturalistic epistemology. See, however, Campbell (1988).

9. The exact sense of 'criterion' here is unclear. Should we take the conjunction of these as constituting a sufficient condition for something being a theory or a disjunction? Since conjunction seems to be much too strong, I will assume the satisfaction of any one of them is a sufficient condition for something being a theory.

10. In private correspondence (January 5, 1977) Skinner has denied the necessity for direct observation. "I doubt very much whether there is ever pure observation or contemplation…", he says, and later he remarks: "I may have appeared to insist on public observation of behavior in the Behavior of Organisms, but I was certainly talking about private events seven years later in my Operationism paper, and I returned to that again in 1953 and 1957." However, if Skinner does not insist on direct observation, then several other claims (especially his distinctive claims about theories and his critique of mentalism) will have to be given up or radically modified, and Skinner's theory of theories would have to undergo fundamental revision.

11. Skinner has reiterated this same point in private conversation: "What is going on inside [the organism] short of the explicit response to be found in the tact is the kind of thing I must leave to the physiologist…" [January 5, 1977]. "I see no reason why an operant need be muscular movement. In fact, efferent nerve impulses have been taken off nerves and reinforcers made contingent upon them to increase the frequency of the impulses. I see no reason why operant behavior cannot become extremely minute, provided it is effective in producing consequences. The physiologist will have the instruments eventually to describe such behavior, I trust" (March 10, 1977]. I do not see, however, how these remarks are compatible with several other remarks by Skinner.

REFERENCES

Amundson, R. (1993). On the plurality of psycholgical naturalisms: A reply to Ringen. *New Ideas in Psychology*, *11*, 193–204.

Azrin, N. H., & Holz, W. C. (1966). Punishment. In W. K. Honig (Ed.), *Operant behavior: Areas of research and application*. New York: Appleton-Century-Crofts.

Campbell, D. (1988). *Methodology and epistemology for social sciences: Selected papers* (E. S. Overman, Ed., pp. 393–434). Chicago: University of Chicago Press.

Carnap, R. (1959). Psychology in physical language. (G. Schick, Trans.). In A. J. Ayer (Ed.), *Logical positivism* (pp. 165–198). (Original work published 1932)

Collingwood, R. G. (1938). On the so-called idea of causation. *Proceedings of the Aristotelian Society, 38*, 85–112.

Feyerabend, P. K. (1965). Problems of empiricism. In R. Colodny (Ed.) *Beyond the edge of certainty* (pp. 145–260). Englewood Cliffs, NJ: Prentice-Hall.

Fodor, J. (1965). *Psychological explanation*. New York: Random House.

Gasking, D. (1955). Causation and recipes. Mind, *64*, 479–87.

Hanson, N. R. (1959). *Patterns of discovery*. Cambridge: Cambridge University Press.

Hempel, C. (1949). The logical analysis of psychology (W. Sellars, Trans.) In H. Feigl & W. Sellars (Eds.), *Readings in philosopical analysis* (pp. 373–384). New York: Appleton-Century-Crofts. (Original work published 1935)

Hull, C. L. (1930). Knowledge and purpose as habit mechanisms. *Psychological Review, 37*, 511–526.

Kitchener, R. F. (1974). B. F. Skinner: The butcher, the baker, the behavior-shaper. In K. F. Schaffner & R. S. Cohen (Eds.),, *PSA 1972: Boston Studies in the Philosophy of Science* (pp. 87–98). Dordrecht, Holland: D. Reidel.

Kitchener, R. F. (1976). Are there molar psychological laws? *Philosophy of the Social Sciences, 6*, 143–154.

Kitchener, R. F. (1977). Behavior and behaviorism. *Behaviorism, 5*, 11–72.

Kitchener, R. F. (1979a). A critique of Skinnerian ethical principles. *Counseling and Values, 23*, 138–47.

Kitchener, R. F. (1979b). Radical naturalism and radical behaviorism. *Scienta, 114*, 107–116.

Kolakowski, L. (1968). *The alienation of reason*. New York: Doubleday.

Kuhn, T. (1970). *The structure of scientific revolutions* (2nd ed.). Chicago: University of Chicago Press.

MacCorquodale, K., & Meehl, P., (1948). On a distinction between hypothetical constructs and intervening variables. *Psychological Review, 55*, 95–107.

Mach, E. (1907). *The science of mechanics* (3rd ed., T. J. McCormach, Trans.) Chicago: Open Court. (Original work published 1883)

Mach, E. (1911). *History and root of the principle of the conservation of energy* (P. E. B. Jourdain, Trans). Chicago: Open Court. (Original work published 1872)

Mach, E. (1943). *Popular scientific lectures* (T. J. McCormach, Trans.). Chicago: Open Court. (Original work published 1896)

Mach, E. (1959). *The analysis of sensations* (C. M. Williams, Trans.). New York: Dover. (Original work published 1886)

Mill, J. S. (1872). *A system of logic: Ratiocinative and inductive* (8th ed.). London: Longman.

Miller, N. (1959). Liberalization of basic S-R concepts: Extensions to conflict behavior, motivation and social learning. In S. Koch (Ed.), *Psychology: A study of a science. Vol. 2: General systematic formulations, learning, and special processes* (pp. 196–292). New York: McGraw-Hill.

Pearson, K. (1892). *The grammar of science*. London: W. Scott.

Poincaré, H. (1952). *Science and hypothesis* ("W. J. G.", Trans.). New York: Dover. (Original work published 1902)

Quine, W. V. O. (1951). Two dogmas of empiricism. *Philosophical Review, 60*, 20–43.

Quine, W. V. O. (1969). Epistemology naturalized. In *Ontological relativity and other essays* (pp. 69–90). New York: Columbia University Press.

Ringen, J. (1993). Critical naturalism and the philosophy of psychology. *New Ideas in Psychology, 11*, 153–77.

Ryle, G. (1949). *The concept of mind*. New York: Barnes and Noble.

Scriven, M. (1956). A study of radical behaviorism. In H. Feigl & M. Scriven (Eds.), *Minnesota studies in the philosophy of science. Vol. 1: The foundations of science and the concepts of psychology and psychoanalysis* (pp. 88–130). Minneapolis: University of Minnesota Press.

Skinner, B. F. (1931) The concept of the reflex in the description of behavior. *Journal of General Psychology, 5*, 27–58. (Reprinted in *Cumulative record* [3rd ed., pp. 429–457]. New York: Appleton-Century-Crofts, 1972)

Skinner, B. F. (1935a). The generic nature of the concepts of stimulus and response. *Journal of General Psychology, 12*, 40–65. (Reprinted in *Cumulative record* [3rd ed., pp. 458–478]. New York: Appleton-Century-Crofts, 1972)

Skinner, B. F. (1935b). Two types of conditioned reflex and a pseudo-type. *Journal of General Psychology, 12*, 66–77. (Reprinted in *Cumulative record* [3rd ed., pp. 479–488]. New York: Appleton-Century-Crofts, 1972)

Skinner, B. F. (1937). Two types of conditioned reflex: A reply to Konorski and Miller. *Journal of General Psychology, 16*, 272–279. (Reprinted in *Cumulative record* [3rd ed., pp. 488–497]. New York: Appleton-Century-Crofts, 1972)

Skinner, B. F. (1938). *The behavior of organisms*. New York: Appleton-Century-Crofts.

Skinner, B. F. (1945). The operational analysis of psychological terms. *Psychological Review, 52*, 270–77, 291–94. (Reprinted in *Cumulative record* [3rd ed., pp. 370–384]. New York: Appleton-Century-Crofts, 1972)

Skinner, B. F. (1947). Current trends in experimental psychology. In W. Dennis (Ed.), *Current trends in experimental psychology* (pp. 16–49). Pittsburgh: University of Pittsburgh. (Reprinted in *Cumulative record* [3rd ed., pp. 295–313]. New York: Appleton-Century-Crofts, 1972)

Skinner, B. F. (1950). Are theories of learning necessary? *Psychological Review, 57*, 193–216. (Reprinted in *Cumulative Record* [3rd ed., pp. 69–100]. New York: Appleton-Century-Crofts, 1972)

Skinner, B. F. (1953). *Science and human behavior*. New York: Macmillan.

Skinner, B. F. (1954). A critique of psychoanalytic concepts and theories. *Scientific Monthly, 79*, 300–305. (Reprinted in *Cumulative record* [3rd ed., pp. 238–248]. New York: Appleton-Century-Crofts, 1972)

Skinner, B. F. (1956). A case history in scientific method. *American Psychologist, 22*, 332–333. (Reprinted in *Cumulative record*, [3rd ed., pp. 101–124]. New York: Appleton-Century- Crofts, 1972)

Skinner, B. F. (1957). *Verbal behavior*. New York: Appleton-Century-Crofts.

Skinner, B. F. (1964). Behaviorism at fifty. In B. F. Skinner (Ed.), *Behaviorism and phenomenology* (pp.79–97). Chicago: University of Chicago Press.

Skinner, B. F. (1969). *Contingencies of reinforcement*. New York: Appleton-Century-Crofts.

Skinner, B. F. (1971). *Beyond freedom and dignity*. New York: Alfred Knopf.

Skinner, B. F. (1972). The flight from the laboratory. In *Cumulative record* (3rd ed., pp. 314–32). New York: Appleton-Century-Crofts.

Skinner, B. F. (1974). *About behaviorism*. New York: Alfred Knopf.

Skinner, B. F. (1977). Why I am not a cognitive psychologist. *Behaviorism, 5*, 1–10.

Skinner, B. F. (1981). Selection by consequences. *Science, 213*, 501–4.

Skorupski, J. (1989). *John Stuart Mill*. London/New York: Routledge, Chapman & Hall.

Smith, L. D. (1986). *Behaviorism and logical positivism: A reassessment of the alliance*. Stanford: Stanford University Press.

Smith. L. D. (1993). Making sense of epistemological pluralism: A response to Ringen. *New Ideas in Psychology, 11*, 179–191.

Tolman, E. C. (1966). Operational behaviorism and current trends in psychology. In *Behavior and psychological man* (pp. 115–129). Berkeley: University of California Press. (Original work published 1936)

CHAPTER 9

LINGUISTIC BEHAVIORISM AS A PHILOSOPHY OF EMPIRICAL SCIENCE

Ullin T. Place

INTRODUCTION

B. F. Skinner (1969; 1974) used to maintain that his radical behaviorism is a philosophy of science. It is a philosophy of science, however, which is restricted in its application to the science of psychology conceived as the empirical and experimental study of the behavior of living organisms. I shall argue in this chapter that what I call 'linguistic behaviorism' is a philosophy of science that has application to every empirical science from physics to sociology. This claim rests on three premises:

1. *Philosophy* is the scientific study of the relation between language and the environmental reality it represents—the metaphilosophical thesis.
2. *Science* is the systematic attempt to increase the scope, generality, accuracy, and objectivity of linguistic representations of environmental reality—the metascientific thesis.
3. *Language* is a form of human social behavior which for scientific purposes needs to be studied and explained with the same methods and

principles as are used in studying and explaining the other aspects of the instrumental (operant) behavior of free-moving living organisms (animals)—the metalinguistic thesis.

Differences from Other Philosophies of Science

Linguistic behaviorism differs from other approaches to the philosophy of science in maintaining

- that the philosophy of science is a linguistic enquiry, an investigation of scientific language using the technique known as 'conceptual analysis', and
- that conceptual analysis and hence, the philosophy of science, considered as the application of conceptual analysis to scientific language, is an empirical sociolinguistic investigation of the norms or conventions governing the construction of intelligible sentences in natural language (Place, 1992b).

126

Differences from Other Behaviorist Approaches to Language

Linguistic behaviorism differs from other behaviorist approaches to language such as that of Skinner (1957) in that

- It treats the response of the listener/reader to verbal stimuli as of equal importance to, if not greater importance than, the verbal behavior of the speaker/writer.
- It identifies the sentence rather than the word as the functional unit of language, the unit that must be complete or whose completion must be predictable in order to be effective in controlling the behavior of the listener.
- It accepts and takes as axiomatic Chomsky's (1957) observation that sentences are seldom repeated word for word and are *constructed anew on each occasion of utterance.*[1]
- It accepts and takes as axiomatic Chomsky's claim that *linguistic competence* consists in the speaker's ability to construct and the listener's ability to construe indefinitely many sentences which are novel in the sense that the speaker has never previously constructed and the listener has never previously encountered that precise string of words before.
- It also accepts and takes as axiomatic Chomsky's further claim that novel sentences are made intelligible to the listener by their conformity to the *rules* (or 'conventions', as I prefer to say) governing the way words are combined together to form such sentences in the natural language in current use.

Differences from Other Approaches to Linguistic Theory

Linguistic behaviorism differs from other approaches within the science of linguistics, such as that of Chomsky,

- by its endorsement of the traditional *empiricist* thesis that linguistic competence is a skill that the child learns initially and fundamentally on the proverbial "mother's knee," but secondly and more significantly, as far as conformity to group norms are concerned, from interaction with the peer group,
- by its insistence that linguistic competence is acquired by the same process of *contingency-shaping* (error-correction) as is observed in the acquisition of motor skills by prelinguistic organisms (animals and prelinguistic human infants), and
- by the contention that the rules of syntax and semantics to which a speaker's sentence must conform if it is to be intelligible to the listener are embodied, not as a kind of computer program in the brains of each party, but as a set of *social conventions* that govern the *error-correcting practices of a linguistic community.*

SIGNS, CONTINGENCIES, AND NOVEL SENTENCES

The linguistic behaviorist account of the relation between sentences and the environmental reality they depict begins with the concept of a *sign*. A sign is a type of stimulus event which, when it impinges on the sensorium of a living organism (the sign recipient), *orients* the behavioral dispositions of that organism in a manner appropriate to an encounter with a particular type of *contingency*. A contingency is a relation, in most cases of causal dependence, in some cases of causal independence, whereby behaving in a certain way under certain antecedent conditions has or is liable to have a certain type of consequence. Most signs acquire the property of orienting the behavior of the organism toward an encounter with a particular contingency by virtue of having been associated with that sequence of events either, in the case of an innate behavioral disposition, in the history of the species or, in the case of an acquired disposition, in the course of the learning history of the individual concerned. It is the unique property of a *sentence* that it functions as a sign that can orient the behavior of a competent listener toward an encounter with a contingency the like of which neither speaker nor listener nor the ancestors from which they derive their genes need ever have encountered in their own case.

As a consequence of this ability to orient the behavior of the listener toward an encounter with contingencies the like of which he or she need have had no previous personal experience, the speaker is in a position to give instructions that will immediately induce the listener to do things she has never done before. As Goldiamond (1966) has pointed out, a prelinguistic organism, however intelligent, can be induced to perform such novel behavior only through a long process of progressive behavioral shaping. Not only does the ability to construct and construe novel sentences enhance the speaker's ability to control the behavior of the listener, it also enables the listener to receive from the speaker information about contingencies operating in the environment of which she (the listener) need have had no personal experience and of whose existence she would otherwise have been totally ignorant.

CONTINGENCY SEMANTICS: A PICTURE THEORY OF THE MEANING OF NOVEL SENTENCES

These remarkable properties of sentences are explained in linguistic behaviorism by invoking a version of Wittgenstein's (1921/1971) "picture theory" of sentence meaning which I have referred to in the past (Place, 1983; 1992a) as "behavioral contingency semantics," but which I am now inclined to call plain "contingency semantics." According to this theory a sentence acquires the property of orienting the behavior of the listener toward the impending presence of a contingency of a particular kind by virtue of an *isomorphism* between the structure and content of the sentence and the structure and content of one or more of the *situations* of which the contingency consists.

Sentences, like other signs, orient the behavior of the listener/reader toward a complete contingency—antecedent condition, behavior, and consequence. Some (compound) sentences, to use Skinner's (1957; 1966/1988) term, "specify" all three of the "terms" of which the contingency consists. An example of this is the sentence *If the baby cries* (antecedent), *give it a bottle* (behavior) *and it will go back to sleep* (consequence). This sentence is a compound of three *atomic sentences,* each of which specifies or depicts a different situation (event or state of affairs) corresponding to the three terms of the contingency (antecedent condition, behavior, and consequence). But you don't need to specify all three terms in order to orient the behavior of the listener/reader toward the contingency. In an appropriate context any one of these atomic sentences, the declarative *The baby is crying,* the imperative *Give the baby a bottle,* or the optative *I wish that baby would stop crying and go back to sleep,* can serve to alert the listener to that contingency. The same function can be performed by a compound conditional sen-

tence or "rule," in Skinner's (1966/1988) sense of that word, which combines two atomic sentences. Thus the 'prescriptive rule'—*If the baby cries, give it a bottle*—consists of two such sentences, one of which specifies the antecedent condition and the other the behavior to be performed under that condition; while the two sentences composing the 'descriptive rule'—*If you give it a bottle, it will go back to sleep*—specify the behavior and its consequence.

Such incomplete specifications of the contingency for which the sentence, nevertheless, acts as a sign have their effect either because the unspecified parts of the contingency have been specified so often in the past that no repetition is needed on this occasion or, as in the case of the social consequences of compliance and failure to comply with a request, because this part of the contingency is never mentioned outside the early years of the parent–child relationship *(Mummy will be cross if you do that again).* Needless to say, it is only in the case of those parts of the contingency that *are* specified that the novel sentence can act as a sign for novelty on the side of the contingency.

The smallest unit that a sentence can specify, the segment of environmental reality specified by an *atomic sentence,* is the contingency term (antecedent condition, behavior to be performed, or consequence to be expected). A contingency term is what Barwise and Perry (1983) call "a situation." A situation in this sense is either

• an *event* whereby a change occurs at or over time in the properties of something and/or in its relations to other things, or
• a *state of affairs* whereby the properties of something and/or its relations with other things remain unchanged over a period of time.

Substituting Barwise and Perry's term "situation" for Russell's (1918–1919/1956) term "fact" in this version of the picture theory has a number of advantages:

1. It avoids the systematic ambiguity of the term 'fact' as between
   • a true particular (existentially quantified) proposition,
   • the event or state of affairs (situation) which such a proposition describes and whose occurrence or existence makes the proposition true.

2. It avoids the implication that there is one and only one uniquely correct way of carving up reality into the facts of which it consists.
3. It allows us to recognize that events and states of affairs *qua* species of situation are segments of spatio-temporal reality, both of which involve the properties and relations between concrete particulars (Aristotle's "substances") and which differ only in that in the case of a state of affairs the properties and relations remain constant over a period of time, whereas in the case of an event they change either at (instantaneous event) or over time (process).
4. It allows us to draw a distinction between the situation that a sentence, any sentence, depicts and the *actual* situation to which, as I would say unlike Frege,[2] a true declarative sentence refers (*bedeutet*) and whose existence makes it true. What a sentence *depicts* is not an actual situation, but *a range of possible situations,* any one of which, if it exists, will constitute the referent and truthmaker of a declarative, or, if it is brought into existence by the listener, will constitute compliance with an imperative.

THE INTENSIONALITY OF THE DEPICTED SITUATION AND THE CORRESPONDENCE THEORY OF TRUTH

The advantage of defining the situation depicted by a sentence intensionally, as a range of possible situations one of which may or may not actually exist, rather than extensionally as one that actually does so, is that the theory of sentence semantics is no longer restricted, as is Tarski's (1930–1/1936/1956) truth conditional theory, to declarative sentences. On this view imperatives depict situations just as declaratives do. In both cases the situation depicted is a range of possible situations that may or may not correspond to one that actually exists now, has existed in the past, or will exist in the future. The difference is that, in the case of an imperative, a situation corresponding to that depicted comes into existence if and when the listener complies with it; whereas, in the case of a declarative, a situation corresponding to that depicted by the sentence exists at the time specified by the tense of the verb, if and only if the sentence is true.

Both the relation between the sentence and the range of possible situations it depicts and the rela-

tion between the range of possible situations depicted by the sentence and the actual situation that exists if an imperative is complied with or a declarative is true are relations of isomorphism or correspondence.[3] The term 'isomorphism' is more appropriate as a description of the former relation in that there is nothing in the situation depicted which is not contained in the sentence that depicts it. The term 'correspondence' is more appropriate as a description of the latter relation in that any actual situation will have many other properties and involve many other relations beside those mentioned in the sentence. In both cases, however, there is a parallel between the structure and content of the situation depicted by the sentence and, on the one hand, the structure and content of the sentence itself, and, on the other, the structure and content of those parts of the actual situation mentioned in the sentence.

THE FUNCTION AND ARGUMENT ANALYSIS OF SENTENCES AND ITS ONTOLOGICAL CONSEQUENCES

The idea that the structure of the sentence mirrors the structure of the segment of environmental reality it depicts is one that goes back to Aristotle's notion that his subject and predicate analysis of the sentence mirrors a reality composed of substances or property-bearing entities and the properties they bear.

In the light of Frege's (1879/1960) critique of the subject–predicate analysis of sentences that analysis is replaced within contingency semantics by his function and argument analysis. In a simple atomic sentence such as *The cat is on the mat* or *Ascitel de Bulmer purchased Marton of King Henry I* (Whellan, 1859) the functions *is on/is under* and *purchased/sold* generate respectively two and three[4] *argument places,* which in order to complete the sentence must be filled by singular terms designating a substance in Aristotle's sense of that term.

When incorporated into the picture theory of meaning, this more sophisticated analysis of the sentence allows the analysis of the situation that the sentence depicts to include changes in and persistence of complex *relations* between as many discrete substances as there are argument places in the sentence. It is no longer confined, as was the traditional analysis, to changes in and persistence of the properties of a single substance.

THE EPISTEMOLOGICAL PROBLEM AS A PROBLEM IN LINGUISTIC COMMUNICATION

The repudiation of truth conditional semantics in order to give imperatives an equal status to that of declaratives within the picture theory of meaning should not be taken to imply any inclination to undervalue the importance of truth as a property of declarative information-providing sentences. For the colossal advantages that accrue to an organism that is able both to convey and receive this kind of information about otherwise inaccessible aspects of its environment a price has to be paid. The ability to receive information from other speakers and writers about contingencies whose existence and precise nature she is in no position to check exposes the listener to the danger of being *misled* by deliberate lies and other more innocent forms of misinformation supplied by others.

Despite the central role played by the argument from sense-perceptual illusion in the induction of skeptical doubts about the truth of our common-sense beliefs, the fact of the matter is that our senses very seldom deceive us; and when they do, it is seldom, if ever, for very long. That this should be so is hardly surprising when you consider the millions of years that our sensory apparatus and the capacity to learn sensory discriminations have had to evolve and adapt to life on this planet, since our remote ancestors first acquired the ability to respond to sensory stimulation. The epistemological problem is not a problem for prelinguistic organisms. It arises only when the listener's ability to respond to novel sentences gives to the speaker the power to mislead, and thus presents the listener with the problem of discriminating between those items of information that are true, which accurately depict the way things really are out there, and those which do not, that are false and hence dangerously misleading.

PROPOSITIONS AS THE BEARERS OF TRUTH

Consonant with, if not a corollary of, the view that the problem of distinguishing between the true and the false arises only in the context of linguistic communication is the thesis that *propositions,* the bearers of truth and falsity, are purely linguistic entities closely related to, but not identical with the sentences which, as we say, 'express' them. As I put it in a recent article,

> The English sentence *All men are mortal* expresses the same proposition or thought as its equivalent in other natural languages, and as other equivalent English sentences, such as *Everybody dies sooner or later* or *In the long run we're all dead.* Moreover, there is no reason to prefer any one of these sentences as a more apt or accurate way of expressing the proposition than any of the others. (Place, 1991, p. 272)

In other words the concept of a proposition respects the principle to which, as we have seen, Chomsky has drawn attention, whereby sentences are seldom repeated word for word and are constructed anew on each occasion of utterance. Not only does the speaker invariably construct a new and slightly different sentence, when reporting what another speaker has said or written, she does the same when repeating what she herself has said on the same or on a previous occasion.

All these sentences constitute different ways of 'saying the same thing'. All of them, if they are declarative, have the same truth conditions. If one of them is true, they all are. If one of them is false, they all are. All of them, if they are declarative, 'express the same proposition'. A proposition is not a particular sentence. It is rather

> an 'intensional' or 'modal' class, that is to say, a class which includes possible instances as well as actual ones. This intensional or modal class comprises all possible sentence utterances in any natural language that now exists, may have existed in the past or may exist in the future whose common feature is that they are all indicative sentences, all have the same truth conditions and all identify the objects, states of affairs or events to which they refer in the same or corresponding ways. (Place, 1991, p. 273)

ANALYTIC AND SYNTHETIC TRUTH

To say that a proposition is true is to say that any proposition that contradicts it conflicts with the linguistic conventions governing the use of sentences expressing that proposition for descriptive purposes. In other words, given the semantic and syntactic conventions of the language only a declarative sentence expressing that proposition will do as a description of the situation the proposition describes. True propositions however, are of two different kinds. On the one hand there are true propositions that are

- *universal* in the sense that the description applies to *any* instance of a kind whether or not any such

instance exists (this would *exclude* empirical generalizations),[5]
- *analytic* in the sense that the application of the description is guaranteed by the relevant linguistic conventions regardless of whether or not a situation answering to the description actually exists,
- *a priori* in the sense that no observation is required in order to determine whether or not the proposition is true, and
- *necessary* in the sense that given the relevant linguistic conventions any denial of the proposition would be self-contradictory.

On the other hand, there are true propositions that are

- *particular* in the sense that they apply to a particular instance or a finite class of particulars (as in the case of an empirical generalization),
- *synthetic* in the sense that the proposition asserts the existence of something over and above what is implicit in the description given,
- *a posteriori* in the sense that some kind of observational evidence is required in order to determine whether or not the proposition is true, and
- *contingent* in the sense that the relevant linguistic conventions do not make it self-contradictory to deny that the proposition is true.

The view that the universal/particular, analytic/synthetic, a priori/a posteriori, and necessary/contingent distinctions are both co-extensive and intensionally equivalent runs counter to so much currently accepted wisdom in contemporary philosophy that some discussion is called for of two well-known counterexamples:

1. Quine's (1951/1980) example of a proposition that is universally quantified, yet arguably synthetic, true a posteriori and contingent: *Any creature with a heart has kidneys.*
2. The proposition *Two is the only even prime*, which is arguably analytic, true a priori and necessary, but nevertheless existentially quantified and particular.

In the case of the first of these examples two distinct interpretations of the sentence are possible depending on the criteria used to identify a heart and a kidney. Where the heart and kidneys are identified purely by their structural or anatomical characteristics, their external shape, their internal arrangement, and their relation to other organs such as the blood vessels and the gills or lungs, as the case may be, the sentence *Any creature with a heart has kidneys* is an empirical generalization recording the fact that no instance has been observed of an intact living creature that has a heart by these criteria, but lacks kidneys. This is no exception to our rule, since an empirical generalization summarizing the results of observation is not a universal proposition in the relevant sense. On the other hand, if the criteria for identifying hearts and kidneys are functional rather than structural, the meaning of those terms becomes inseparable from the function of the organs they stand for within the circulatory system as a whole. Using these criteria the proposition is genuinely universal; but it is also analytic, in that if what looked like a heart did not form part of a functioning system that includes a device for cleaning the blood of impurities (i.e., at least one kidney) it would not qualify as a heart. If that is correct, then it also follows that the truth of the proposition has been decided a priori in advance of observation and is necessary in that its denial would involve a theoretical contradiction.

The claim that *Two is the only even prime number* is a particular proposition rests on the assumption that numbers are abstract objects and that this proposition mentions only one of them, namely the number two. The alternative view sees numbers as universals which exist only insofar as instances of them exist. This interpretation makes *Two is the only even prime* a universal proposition in the relevant sense. That it is also analytic is clear from the fact that its truth can be deduced a priori from the definitions of an even number and a prime number, which also makes it necessary in that to deny it would contradict one or the other of those definitions.

As we shall see later, it is an implication of this view that the universal law statements of empirical science are analytic, true a priori and necessary. But it is also an implication that they only are so by virtue of current linguistic convention within the scientific community; and that may well change in the light of future empirical research. The fact that such laws have to fit the results of empirical research does not undermine either the claim that they are analytic, in the sense of being made true by the prevailing conventions for the use of the words involved, and true a priori, in the sense that, given

those conventions, they remain true however subsequent research turns out. If subsequent research
were to reveal cases of what by all other criteria is
water which do not have the chemical composition
H_2O, we would doubtless be compelled to give up
the convention whereby only samples with that
chemical composition are so classified. But given
that the convention *has* been adopted, as shown by
the fact that samples that do not have that composition are rejected as cases of water, such evidence
would not falsify the hypothesis that water has the
chemical composition H_2O, as it would have done
before the convention was incorporated into the
language and practice of science. Once the convention is in place, we either have to accept that what
is not H_2O is not water or, if exceptions are repeatedly encountered, devise a new convention.

THE RELATIVITY OF SYNTHETIC
TRUTH TO SEMANTIC AND
SYNTACTIC CONVENTION

An important feature of this version of the picture
theory of meaning is the claim that it is not only
analytic propositions whose truth depends on the
semantic and syntactic conventions governing the
context and structure of the sentences that express
them. A synthetic proposition only depicts the situation it does depict by virtue of the semantic and
syntactic conventions governing the content and
structure of the sentences that express it.

This has two consequences. In the first place it
means that there are no cases where we can
straightforwardly observe a correspondence
between a situation that exists and the situation
depicted by a sentence. It might be supposed that a
simple observation sentence like *There is a table
here in front of me* would be such a case. But the
correspondence between that sentence and the reality it purports to depict is uncertain, not because of
traditional skeptical doubts concerning the very
remote possibility that I might be suffering a hallucination, but because, in the absence of confirmation from other competent speakers of English,
there is no assurance that that is the correct description of the situation according to the semantic and
syntactic conventions of that language. Given that
confirmation, however, not only do we exclude the
already remote possibility that what we think we
are confronted with is some sort of hallucination,
we now have a declarative sentence that could only
fail to constitute an accurate linguistic depiction of

the situation confronting us in the extremely
unlikely case where our fellow observers are
engaged in a complex conspiracy to persuade us
either that we are suffering from a hallucination or
that the English sentence *There is a table here in
front of me* has a different meaning from that which
it actually has by virtue of the conventions of the
language, a contingency which, if it were realized,
would rapidly lead to a breakdown in the conditions necessary for interpersonal linguistic communication.[6]

OBJECTIVE OBSERVATION
SENTENCES AS THE ANCHORS OF
EMPIRICAL KNOWLEDGE

These objective observation sentences whose accuracy as a description of the state of affairs confronting them is agreed by a number of observers, all of
whom are competent speakers of the language or
code in use among them, are just the kind of incon-
trovertible empirical, synthetic and contingent
propositions which according to the intuitions of
the epistemic foundationalist are needed as an
anchor or foundation for empirical knowledge.
Without such an anchor, I contend, there is no way
that we can be assured that a system of propositions, however internally coherent it may be, actually corresponds to the extralinguistic reality it
purports to depict. Moreover this empirical anchor
is far superior to the private sensation protocols
that have been cast in that role by traditional empiricist epistemologies. For, however salient my
experience of what I call 'my pain' may be, how
can I be certain that this is really what they call
'pain' in English, when I can't feel what you call
'pain' and you can't feel what I call 'pain'? I can
only be satisfied on this point by observing that
what you call 'pain' in your case has the same kind
of publicly observable causes and the same kind of
publicly observable behavioral effects as what I
call 'pain' in my case.

PRIMITIVE SUGGESTIBILITY AND
THE DISCRIMINATION OF
MISINFORMATION

Objective observation sentences are at best only an
anchor attaching our linguistically formulated
beliefs to the reality they purport to depict. That
this is so becomes clear when we reflect that the
primary function of the ability to construct and

construe novel sentences is not to describe features of the current stimulus environment of a number of competent speakers and listeners. It is rather, as we have seen, to induce the listener to do things she has never done before and convey information to her about aspects of the environment to which she would otherwise have no access.

It is difficult to exaggerate the advantage which the ability to communicate this kind of novel information gives to the human species. Nevertheless, it is an advantage for which a price has to be paid, the danger of being deceived, either deliberately or involuntarily, by misinformation supplied by others.

The need to detect the lies and other false statements supplied by others is underlined by some evidence reviewed by Clark Hull in his book *Hypnosis and Suggestibility* (Hull, 1933, pp. 83-85). This evidence suggests that, in order to understand the novel sentences it encounters in the speech of others, a child must begin by acquiring

> a primitive habit tendency (of responding directly to verbal stimulations) which is useful in most situations but maladaptive...if a person responds positively and indiscriminately to all suggestions made by others, [in which case] he is likely to be taken advantage of by his associates in that the energies needed for his own welfare will be diverted to that of those giving the suggestions. (Hull, 1933, p. 85)

Holism and Cognitive Dissonance

Having acquired the initial propensity to accept as true everything that it is told by others, the child gradually learns to avoid these maladaptive consequences by discriminating between those statements made by others that demand further scrutiny and those that can be allowed to go through "on the nod," as the saying goes. After rising steadily up to the age of eight, as the child gradually acquires what Hull calls "a working knowledge of the language," suggestibility, as measured by the postural suggestibility test, begins to decline, and continues to do so into adolescence.

But what does the child have to go on in making this discrimination? Clearly it does not do it by tracing every statement back to its source in observation. To do that would take far too long, even in those cases where it could be done; would be impossible in the case of statements about the past and other unobservables; and defeats the object of the exercise, which is precisely to get information

from others to which one has no observational access oneself.

Since it is only in a minority of cases that its primitive tendency to accept everything it is told as true will let it down, what the child needs to do is to find some feature that will distinguish the odd piece of misinformation from the bulk of correct information, which it can accept without further question.

For this purpose the only principle on which we can ultimately rely is the principle of the *indivisibility of truth* or *holism,* as it is sometimes called. This is the principle according to which every true proposition must be consistent with every other true proposition. It is a straightforward consequence of the law of noncontradiction whereby, if p is true, *not p* must be false and vice versa. It follows from this law that if q entails *not p, p* and q cannot both be true. Either one is true and the other false or both are false. It follows from this that in building up a stock of beliefs about the world on which to base one's action, one should be made uncomfortable by any apparent contradiction or "cognitive dissonance," as Leon Festinger (1957) calls it, within one's existing belief system and endeavor to ensure that any such contradiction is ironed out, before the relevant beliefs are accepted as reliably true. The effect of this endeavor should be to ensure that by and large an individual's beliefs will constitute a coherent system and, provided most of the constituent beliefs are true, will thereby constitute a body of knowledge whose reliability will be confirmed by its overall utility as a guide to action (the pragmatic principle) and its conformity to the opinions of others (Wittgenstein's [1953] "agreement in judgments").

Given such a coherent body of beliefs whose overall correspondence with reality is guaranteed by its consistent reliability as a guide to action, the individual, whether child or adult, has a standard against which to evaluate any new piece of putative information presented to it by another speaker. If there is no obvious dissonance or contradiction between the new item and the existing stock, it can be allowed to go through on the nod. Only when a contradiction or dissonance is detected between the new item and the existing stock will alarm bells ring and all the armory of logical argument be brought to bear in order either to justify the new item's rejection or find some way of resolving the contradiction and incorporating the new item into the system.

Building a coherent body of propositions representing environmental contingencies, anchored to reality by objective observation and confirmed by its utility as a guide to action is not just a strategy designed to resolve the epistemological problem as it confronts the individual. It is a cooperative social process in which every member of the linguistic community is involved in the process of adding to, correcting and transmitting what Binswanger (1947) has called the *Mitwelt,* the body of coherent and validated knowledge and belief that is the shared property of that community. It is a process, however, which before the advent of what we now call 'science' proceeds by an unself-conscious process of progressive behavioral-shaping. This process ensures that where adequate evidence is available to the unaided human sensorium and contingencies are important for the survival and welfare of the individual and the social group, the linguistic specification of those contingencies within the system of commonsense practical belief will accurately represent the actual contingencies that obtain.

Commonsense Knowledge and Supernatural Belief

Where the ability to predict the contingencies is vital, but the evidence on which to base such prediction is lacking, beliefs and practices based on those beliefs develop within the linguistic community which, while they are not contradicted by the available evidence, postulate 'supernatural' contingencies whose formulation is not shaped by experience of the actual contingencies involved as are the beliefs that constitute the body of practical commonsense knowledge. Since they are not constrained by the actual contingencies involved, such supernatural belief systems tend to vary from one social group to another. Moreover, in a world in which law and morality does not extend to interactions between members of different social groups, sanctions based on the fear of supernatural retribution become an essential part of intertribal trade. In these circumstances differences between groups in their supernatural beliefs are a serious barrier to such trade.

THE ORIGINS OF PHILOSOPHY AND SCIENCE

Philosophy, in the Western tradition at least, began in ancient Greece as an attempt to resolve the problem of differences in supernatural belief as it pre-

sented itself in the circumstances of the Greek colonies in Asia Minor and elsewhere. Cities like Miletus, where Greek philosophy first appeared, lived by trading with peoples of other faiths among whom they had settled, but on whom, unlike a conqueror, they were unable to impose their own belief system by force. Instead, they sought to resolve the problem by the method of argument and debate, in a manner that did not prejudge the issue as to who was right and who was wrong. As time went on, part of philosophy developed into what we now call 'science' as it was gradually realized that such debates could sometimes be resolved by systematically subjecting the propositions in question to the kind of systematic shaping by the actual contingencies to which the practical belief of commonsense knowledge are subjected in the natural course of events. This is the experimental method.

Science and the Problem of Universals

Using the method of systematic observation and experiment allows the replacement of supernatural belief with the knowledge that results from shaping by rigorous exposure to the actual contingencies. Systematic observation and experiment, however, are not by themselves sufficient to yield the new ways of understanding the universe which are the characteristic products of scientific research. What is also needed is a restructuring of the concepts that are used to classify the particulars we encounter in the world around us as instances of the different universals or kinds of thing.

The dependence of knowledge on a preexisting ability on the part of the organism to classify features of its environment into instances of the same and different kinds is not confined to scientific knowledge, nor, indeed, to propositional knowledge generally. It is an implication of Darwin's theory of evolution by variation and natural selection that the survival and reproduction of complex free-moving living organisms, animals, in other words, depends on their ability to change the spatial relations between themselves and other objects, including other organisms of the same and of different species, and so bring about the conditions necessary for that survival and reproduction. In order to do that, the organism requires a system, its nervous system, whose function is to match output both to the current stimulus input and to the organism's current state of deprivation with respect to conditions required for its survival and successful reproduction.

Matching behavior to the conditions required for survival and reproduction is the function of the motivational/emotional part of the system. Matching behavior to current stimulus input is the function of the sensory/cognitive part of the system. The sensory/cognitive system cannot perform its function successfully without the ability to group inputs together in such a way that every actual and possible member of the class or category so formed is a reliable indicator of the presence of a particular contingency, an environmental situation in which a particular behavioral strategy or set of such strategies is going to succeed. In other words, the survival and reproduction of an organism of this kind depends crucially on its having a conceptual scheme, a conceptual scheme, moreover, that reliably predicts the actual behavior–consequence relations operating in the organism's environment.

Whether it is built into the organism's genetic constitution or acquired by some process of abstraction learning or, as seems most likely, develops through some combination of the two, this Darwinian perspective predicts that an organism's conceptual scheme will follow what Skinner (1938 p. 33) calls "the natural lines of fracture along which behavior and environment actually break."

Some recent evidence (Catania, Shimoff, & Matthews, 1989), however, suggests that once contingencies are specified by a linguistic formula or rule, the precise matching of expectations to the actual contingency, which is characteristic of the contingency-shaped behavior of prelinguistic organisms, disappears. There are three possible explanations of this phenomenon. One explanation proposes that where, as in these experiments, the contingency-specification is supplied by the experimenter, the contingencies controlling the subject's behavior are those involving the supply of social reinforcement by the experimenter, rather than those involved in the task itself. Another is that the expectation that is set up by a sentence is much more open and, consequently, less easily disconfirmed than one based only on previous encounters with the actual contingency. A third is that the consequences of failing to adapt behavior to minor changes in the contingency are not drastic enough for those changes to impress themselves on the behavior and prompt a reconsideration of how the contingency should be specified. Whatever the reason, there is evidently a connection between this insensitivity of a verbal specification to disconfirmation by subsequent experience of the actual con-

tingency and the ease with which supernatural explanations, reinforced by the verbal community, can survive what in other circumstances would be regarded as manifest disconfirmations.

But outside the domain of the supernatural, where the interest of the community is to ensure an *exact* correspondence between the linguistic specification and the actual contingency, we can be more satisfied that "the natural lines of fracture" are being followed, and that practical common-sense knowledge is what it purports to be: genuine knowledge of the contingencies it depicts. However, this accurate following of "the natural lines of fracture" extends only as far as the immediate concerns of human beings and the evidence available to the unaided human sensorium. The function of science is to extend the kind of verbally and mathematically formulated knowledge that can yield precise and accurate predictions of outcome into areas such as the causes of disease and natural disaster, where traditionally only supernatural explanations and ritual practices have been available. In order to do this, many of the time-honored conceptual boundaries of common sense are redrawn, with the result that sentences like *whales are fishes,* which once expressed propositions that were analytic, true a priori, and necessary cease to do so, while sentences like *water is H_2O,* which were once synthetic, true a posteriori, and contingent, become analytic, true a priori, and necessary.

From Contingencies to Causation

The concepts of common sense and those of science both group together things that have the same kinds of cause or same kinds of effect. They differ in that the causal relations that define the boundaries of the concepts of common sense are anthropocentric in the sense that they are viewed as contingencies confronting a human agent. By contrast, the causal relations that define the boundaries of the concepts of science are viewed, in Spinoza's phrase, *sub specie aeternitatis,* as they are in themselves, regardless of how they impinge on human affairs.[7] To take an obvious example, the common-sense concept of 'animal' excludes human beings. In science *homo sapiens* is just one among many species of free-moving living organisms. Needless to say, this scientific repudiation of anthropocentrism does not extend to the technological exploitation of the scientific discoveries that the adoption of the objective standpoint makes possible.

EMPIRICAL SCIENCE AS THE STUDY OF BEHAVIOR

It might be supposed that in moving away from anthropocentrism toward a more objective perspective the scientific attitude would require the abandonment of the concept of the three-term contingency with the behavior (of a living organism) as its middle term in favor of some less specifically biological and action-oriented conception of the causal relation. From the standpoint of linguistic behaviorism it is accepted that the concept of behavior in traditional behaviorism, in which its application is restricted to the molar aspects of the behavior of living organisms, is too narrowly parochial to satisfy the kind of universality and objectivity that the scientific attitude demands. The remedy, however, is not to abandon the concept of behavior, but to follow what is already a widespread linguistic practice in all branches of science and recognize that it is not just whole living organisms who behave. So do their constituent parts; and so does every entity in the universe that interacts causally with some other entity. Following that usage allows us to say that every empirical science uses the methods of systematic objective observation, measurement, recording and, wherever possible, experimental manipulation in order to study the behavior of some variety or kind of concrete particular or body extended in three dimensions of space and one of time.

THE CAUSAL RELATION

In studying behavior in this general sense, the scientist is studying causation, the causal action of one thing on another. Moreover, it is because and insofar as they behave in the same way, because and insofar as the same consequences follow when the same causes impinge, that we can be sure that our scientific conceptual scheme follows Skinner's "natural lines of fracture." It follows that without an understanding of the causal relation, we cannot hope to understand the scientific enterprise.

Viewed from the standpoint of linguistic behaviorism a proper understanding of the causal relation requires acceptance of the following (analytic) principles.

1. Causation is the relation between situations (events and/or states of affairs). It is not and should not be represented as a relation between propositions (such as the relation of material implication 'if p then q').

2. Causation is primarily a relation between particular actually existing situations.

3. Nevertheless all causal relations have two aspects:
   - a categorical aspect whereby two causally related situations are juxtaposed in space–time, and
   - a modal aspect that links the causally related situations to other possible situations that might have existed, if circumstances had been different.

4. Causes are always multiple. The belief in a single cause has more to do with the human urge to pin the blame for what has happened on a single scapegoat than it has with any reality.

5. The causes of a state of affairs are all themselves states of affairs, all of which exist so long as their effect exists.

6. All but one of the causes of an event are states of affairs (standing conditions), which are in position before the event occurs and persist at least until it begins to do so.

7. Every event has a single triggering event which, when combined with the standing conditions, completes the set conditions that are jointly *sufficient* for the coming about of the effect. The onset of the effect event coincides with occurrence or termination of the triggering event.

8. In its categorical aspect, every causal relation involves some kind of direct or indirect contact between at least two concrete particulars, the causal agent and the causal patient.

9. The *causal agent* is the concrete particular ('substance' in Aristotle's sense) whose continued direct or indirect contact with the causal patient maintains the effect, where the effect is a state of affairs, or whose coming into direct or indirect contact with the causal patient triggers the effect, where the effect is an event.

10. The *causal patient* is the concrete particular the persistence of or change in whose properties and relations with other things constitutes the effect.[8]

11. In its modal aspect, to say that the existence or occurrence of one situation is a *cause* or causally necessary condition for the occurrence or existence of another independently existing situation (its *effect*) is to say that, other things being as they were, if the cause had not existed or occurred, the effect would not exist or have occurred as and when it does or did (the *causal counterfactual*).

12. Since we can never observe what would exist or would have occurred if the situation had been different from that which actually existed or occurred, we can only establish the truth of this causal counterfactual by deducing it from some kind of law statement.

13. A law statement that "supports" a causal counterfactual is a statement to the effect that, *if at any time* during a period which includes the duration or moment of onset of the effect all other relevant conditions are as they were when the effect actually existed or occurred and a situation of the cause type existed or occurred, a situation of the effect type would exist or occur or would have a high probability of existing or occurring.

14. Law statements in this sense are of three kinds:
- individual law statements, which describe the dispositional properties of particular individuals (e.g., *this piece of glass is particularly brittle*)
- universal law statements, which describe the dispositional properties of things of a kind (e.g., *glass is brittle*)
- scientific law statements, which describe in quantitative terms the causal relation between the dispositional properties of things of a kind and the effect they produce (e.g., Ohm's Law)

15. Individual law statements, though universally quantified over (restricted periods of) time, are synthetic, determined as true or false by observation (a posteriori) and contingent. Universal law statements and scientific law statements, if true and generally accepted as such, are analytic, true a priori and necessary. If something proves not to have the dispositional properties that are conventionally and analytically ascribed to things of the kind of which it has hitherto been taken to be an instance, we conclude, not that the universal law statement is false, but that the individual in question has been misclassified.

16. The analyticity of scientific law statements, the fact that they are made true a priori by linguistic convention within the scientific community, explains the phenomenon of the scientific revolution as described by Kuhn (1962), whereby difficulties in describing observations in terms of the existing conventionally established conceptual scheme or "paradigm" leads eventually to its replacement by another set of conventions, which because of the change in conceptual boundaries are "incommensurable" with those of the previously dominant paradigm.

17. The linguistic conventions that make scientific law statements analytic survive only insofar as they facilitate the formulation of individual law statements describing the dispositional properties of concrete particulars which, despite their universal quantification over restricted periods of time, are synthetic, true, if they are true, a posteriori and contingent.

18. Since causes are always multiple, the individual law statements that support causal counterfactuals are true only insofar as they contain a *ceteris paribus* clause stipulating that a situation of the cause type will be effective, only if all other causes which together are jointly sufficient for the coming about or existence of a situation of the effect type are in place.

19. It follows from this that the only way to determine the truth of an individual law statement, and hence the truth of the causal counterfactuals it supports, is to use what Mill (1843) calls the method of "concomitant variation," in other words, the experimental method. This is the procedure whereby each 'variable' whose causal efficacy is suspected is systematically varied while all other factors whose causal efficacy in relation to the 'dependent variable' or effect in question is suspected are held as far as possible constant. Any change that occurs in the dependent variable under these conditions and fails to occur in its absence can then be attributed with some confidence to the only 'independent variable' whose value has been changed.

20. This method of concomitant variation relies, in order to validate the conclusions based upon it, on the assumption that like causes produce like effects. Though requiring some qualification to allow for those phenomena subject to restricted random variation, the principle that like causes invariably produce like effects is an analytic principle that differs from the laws of empirical science in that its analyticity, a priori truth determination and necessity is not simply a matter of existing linguistic conventions within the scientific community, conventions that are liable to change in the light of the results of future empirical research. *This* convention, like the arithmetical conventions that make *Two is the only even prime number* an analytic truth, is one that could not conceivably be other than it is. This is partly because if like causes did not produce like effects, no free-moving living

organism that relies on its brain to select an output appropriate to current input could survive and reproduce. Its brain could never anticipate what outcome is probable, given the current input. But it is also because, if like causes did not produce like effects, no ordered universe could have emerged from the primeval chaos.

The Ontological Independence of Dispositional Properties from Their Structural Basis

Based on this account of causation, linguistic behaviorism has a distinctive view on the issue of microreductive explanation. This takes as its starting point the view that a dispositional property depends for its existence on some feature or set of features of the structure of the entity whose property it is . This is to reject H. H. Price's claim that

> There is no *a priori* necessity for supposing that *all* dispositional properties must have a 'categorical basis'. In particular, there may be mental dispositions which are ultimate. (Price, 1953, p. 322; quoted by Armstrong, 1968, p. 86)

However, the present view differs from that of Armstrong (1968), who likewise rejects Price's claim, in that the principle that every dispositional property must have its "categorical basis" is seen as a special case of the (analytic) principle whereby there are no situations (events or states of affairs) for which some kind of causal story cannot be told. In other words, the relation between a dispositional state and its "categorical basis" is a causal relation. But if that is so, the dispositional state and its "categorical basis" must, in Hume's words, be "distinct existences," not one and the same thing, as proposed by Armstrong (1968, pp. 85–88).

Another consequence of the view that a disposition depends causally on its "categorical basis" is that the "categorical basis" cannot be purely categorical. For, as we have seen, every causal relation has both

> a categorical aspect whereby two causally related situations are juxtaposed in space and time, and…a modal aspect whereby the causally related situations…might have existed, if circumstances had been different. (Armstrong, p. 136)

In other words, the structural features that give an entity a dispositional property must include dispo-

sitional properties of the structure alongside its categorical spatio-temporal features.

These relationships can be illustrated by the example of the sharpness of a knife or needle. The adjective 'sharp' is systematically ambiguous as between the disposition to cut or pierce soft objects on which the property bearer impinges and those features of the property bearer, the fineness of its edge or point and the hardness/rigidity of the material of which it is composed, which give it that dispositional property. Once that ambiguity is recognized, however, it becomes apparent that the relation between the dispositional property and the features that give it that property is a causal relation, and that of the two causes of the disposition one, the fineness of the edge or point, is categorical, while the other, the hardness or rigidity of material, is modal or dispositional.

Considered as a dispositional property, the sharpness of something such as a knife or needle is remarkable in that the structural features on which its existence depends are features of the *macrostructure* of the property bearer, and are, consequently, accessible to our commonsense understanding of the matter. In most other cases, for example in the case of the dispositional property of hardness/rigidity on which the existence of the dispositional property of sharpness in part depends, the existence of the dispositional property depends on categorical and modal features of the *microstructure* which are accessible only to scientific scrutiny and understanding. Indeed, so successful has been the strategy of searching in the microstructure for a basis for the dispositional properties distinctive of natural kinds that it is often seen as the hallmark of the scientific enterprise—so much so that it has become very difficult to get a hearing for behaviorists such as B. F. Skinner, who have insisted that the scientific study of the environmental conditions governing the acquisition of the molar behavioral dispositions of living organisms should precede and be conducted independently of the study of the microstructural basis of those dispositions in the brain. Yet if, as is argued here, the relation between a dispositional property and its microstructural basis is a causal relation between "distinct existences," that is precisely the strategy demanded by the experimental method, the method of concomitant variation. For unless the environmental factors can be held constant or their effect on the resultant behavioral dispositions allowed for, there can be little hope of disentangling the complex microstructural changes in the brain by which those effects are mediated.

ENDNOTES

1. It should be emphasized that this construction is a matter of combining a ready-made and oft-repeated function or verb phrase with one or more equally ready-made and oft-repeated arguments or noun phrases, rather than a matter of assembling the sentence from its individual constituent words.

2. According to Frege, the referent (*Bedeutung*) of a sentence is its truth value. For an exposition and discussion of this aspect of Frege's thought, see Dummett (1973), pp. 180–186.

3. Since, as Brentano (1874/1911/1973, p. 272) points out, you cannot have a relation one of whose terms does not exist, it should be emphasized that the phrase "range of possible situations that a sentence depicts" refers to a dispositional orientation which is induced in a listener who understands the sentence and which is confirmed if it subsequently transpires that a situation falling within that range of possible situations either already exists, has come into existence, or has existed in the past within the range of times and places indicated in the sentence.

4. In discussing the *Ascitel de Bulmer* example in Place (1992a), I point out that there are another three argument places potentially generated by the function *purchase/sold* which specify the price paid, the place where, and the date on which the transaction took place, making a total of six argument places. But although they are filled by singular terms, those singular terms do not straightforwardly designate particular substances, as do those occupying the three 'substantive' argument places, those occupied in the example by *Ascitel de Bulmer, Marton* and *King Henry I*.

5. I first drew attention to the phenomenon whereby sentences that invariably turn out true become analytic because of a change in the conventions of the language whereby the situation depicted by the sentence becomes a criterion for the application of the terms it contains in my discussion of the *His table is an old packing case* example in Place (1956, p. 46). For a more recent exposition of this view, together with a defence of the analytic/synthetic distinction against well-known Quinean objections (Quine, 1951/1980), see Place (1991).

6. For a more extensive presentation of this argument and that of the following section see Place (1993).

7. I owe this Spinozistic conception of science to my old friend and former colleague, Professor J. J. C. Smart. See his *Our Place in the Universe* (Smart, 1989, p. 111.)

8. Since in every causal interaction both parties are changed as a consequence, the distinction between the causal agent and the causal patient is a matter of which of the two is changed most (the patient) and which comes off relatively unscathed (the agent). In a case where the changes are more or less equal, as when a cube of salt is dissolved in a bowl of water, it is a matter of which effect, the disappearance of the cube or the water's becoming salty, is of interest to the speaker. I am indebted to Professor C. B. Martin of the University of Calgary for this point.

REFERENCES

Armstrong, D. M. (1968). *A materialist theory of the mind*. London: Routledge and Kegan Paul.

Barwise, J., & Perry, J. (1983). *Situations and attitudes*. Cambridge, MA: M.I.T. Press.

Binswanger, L. (1947). *Ausgewälte Vorträge und Aufsätze*. Bern: Francke.

Brentano, F. (1874/1911/1973). *Psychologie vom empirischen Standpunkt*. Leipzig: Duncker u. Humblot. Second Edition, O. Kraus (Ed.). Leipzig: Felix Meinert. English trans., L. L. McAlister (Ed.), *Psychology from an empirical standpoint*. London: Routledge and Kegan Paul.

Catania, A. C., Shimoff, E., & Matthews, B. A. (1989). An experimental analysis of rule-governed behavior. In S. C. Hayes (Ed.), *Rule-governed behavior: Cognition, contingencies and instructional control* (pp. 119–150). New York: Plenum Press.

Chomsky, N. (1957). *Syntactic structures*. Gravenhage: Mouton.

Dummett, M. (1973). *Frege: Philosophy of language*. London: Duckworth.

Festinger, L. (1957). *Cognitive dissonance*. Stanford, CA: Stanford University Press.

Frege, G. (1879/1960). *Begriffschrift* (P. T. Geach, Trans.). In P. T. Geach & M. Black (Eds.), *Translations from the philosophical writings of Gottlob Frege* (2nd. Ed.). Oxford: Blackwell.

Goldiamond, I. (1966). Perception, language and conceptualization rules. In B. Kleinmuntz (Ed.), *Problem solving: Research, method and theory* (pp. 183–224). New York: Wiley.

Hull, C. L. (1933). *Hypnosis and suggestibility*. New York: Century.

Kuhn, T. S. (1962). *The structure of scientific revolutions*. Chicago: University of Chicago Press.

Mill, J. S. (1843). *A system of logic, ratiocinative and inductive, being a connected view of the principles of evidence and the methods of scientific investigation*. London: J. W. Parker.

Place, U. T. (1956). Is consciousness a brain process? *British Journal of Psychology*, 47, 44–50.

Place, U. T. (1983). Skinner's *Verbal Behavior* IV— How to improve Part IV, Skinner's account of syntax. *Behaviorism*, 11, 163–186.

Place, U. T. (1991). Some remarks on the social relativity of truth and the analytic/synthetic distinction. *Human Studies*, 14, 265–285.

Place, U. T. (1992a). Behavioral contingency semantics and the correspondence theory of truth. In L. J. & S. C.

Hayes (Eds.), *Understanding verbal relations.* (pp. 135–151). Reno, NV: Context Press.

Place, U. T. (1992b). The role of the ethnomethodological experiment in the empirical investigation of social norms, and its application to conceptual analysis. *Philosophy of the Social Sciences, 22,* 461–474.

Place, U. T. (1993). A radical behaviorist methodology for the empirical investigation of private events. *Behavior and Philosophy, 20,* 25–35.

Price, H. H. (1953) *Thinking and experience.* London: Hutchinson.

Quine, W. v. O. (1951/1980). Two dogmas of empiricism. *The Philosophical Review, LX,* 20–43. Reprinted in W. v. O. Quine, *From a logical point of view.* (pp. 20–46). Cambridge, MA: Harvard University Press.

Russell, B. (1918–1919/1956) The philosophy of logical atomism. *The Monist, xxviii,* 495, 1919, 527; *xxxix,* 32–63, 190–222, 345–380. In R.C. Marshall (Ed.), *Logic and knowledge, essays 1901–1950.* London: Allen and Unwin.

Skinner, B. F. (1938). *The behavior of organisms.* New York: Appleton-Century-Crofts.

Skinner, B. F. (1957). *Verbal behavior.* New York: Appleton-Century-Crofts.

Skinner, B. F. (1966/1988). An operant analysis of problem solving. In B. Kleinmuntz (Ed.), *Problem solving: Research, method and theory.* New York: Wiley. Reprinted with revisions and peer commentary in A. C. Catania and S. Harnad (Eds.), *The selection of behavior. The operant behaviorism of B. F. Skinner: Comments and consequences* (pp. 218–236). Cambridge: Cambridge University Press.

Skinner, B. F. (1969). *Contingencies of reinforcement.* New York: Appleton-Century-Crofts.

Skinner, B. F. (1974). *About behaviorism.* New York: Knopf.

Smart, J. J. C. (1989). *Our place in the universe.* Oxford: Blackwell.

Tarski, A. (1930–1/1936/1956).: O pojeciu prawdy w odniesieniu do sformalizowanych nauk dedukcyjnych (On the notion of truth in reference to formalized deductive sciences). *Ruch Filozoficzny, xii.* Revised version in German translation, Der Wahrheitsbegriff in den formalisierten Sprachen. *Studia Philosophica, 1,* 261–405. English translation by J. H. Woodger, The concept of truth in formalized languages. In *Logic, semantics, metamathematics: Papers from 1923 to 1938* (pp. 152–278). Oxford: Clarendon Press.

Whellan, T., & Co. (1859). *History and topography of the City of York and the North Riding of Yorkshire* (Vol. II). Beverley: John Green.

Wittgenstein, L. (1921/1971). Tractatus logico-philosophicus. Annalen der Naturphilosophie. *Tractatus Logico-Philosophicus* (with second English translation by D. F. Pears and B. F. McGuinness, 2nd ed.). London: Routledge and Kegan Paul.

Wittgenstein, L. (1953). *Philosophical Investigations* (G. E. M. Anscombe, Trans.). Oxford: Blackwell.

CHAPTER 10

SKINNER'S CASE FOR RADICAL BEHAVIORISM

Richard Garrett

Behaviorism comes in a variety of forms, including methodological behaviorism, logical behaviorism, Watsonian (S-R) behaviorism, and W. V. Quine's strange and unique version of behaviorism. But I am inclined to think that the most interesting and most promising case for behaviorism was B. F. Skinner's case on behalf of radical behaviorism. It is Skinner's version of behaviorism with which this chapter will be concerned.

Like behaviorism in all of its forms, Skinner's radical behaviorism reflects a deep aversion to the mentalistic language of folk psychology and other psychologies (e.g., Freudian psychology) that take over that language. The behaviorist's complaint is that such language is obscure; it refers to things that are hidden from public observation and control and so are difficult to deal with in a scientific or rigorous way. But mentalistic idioms are deeply embedded in folk psychology (and other psychologies as well) and so permeate our ordinary way of thinking and talking. In everyday life, we constantly say things like: "I went to the store in order to buy bread," "I ate because I was feeling hungry," or "I had a good reason not to admit the truth." In doing so we are ex-plaining our behavior in terms of private mental states or entities (the *purpose* of buying bread, the *feeling* of hunger, or a certain *reason* that is appre-hended only by the "mind," respectively). The problem for the behaviorist is to eliminate refer-ences to such things and this is no easy task, since such references are so natural and so pervasive in ordinary language. What distinguishes the different forms of behaviorism is the strategy used to bring about the proposed elimination. Ludwig Wittgen-stein, who was a logical behaviorist, for example, argued that reference to private states (feelings or qualia) is impossible. Methodological behaviorists, on the other hand, simply argued that private or mentalistic states (though real) could be safely ig-nored by psychology because they were causally ir-relevant. Skinner's radical behaviorist approach, in contrast, is derived from his analysis of the contin-gencies of reinforcement. As a rule Skinner's ap-proach entails two steps. The first step is to provide a behavioral analysis of the principles of reinforce-ment, i.e., to analyze and define these principles so that they only refer to behavior and to physical, pub-licly observable states or events that explain the behavior. The second step is to purge the language of psychology of mentalistic terms by showing either that mentalistic terms can be translated into the clearer language of reinforcement theory (behavioristically interpreted) or that the mentalistic terms must be discarded entirely because they are mythical and at odds with a truly scientific analysis of behavior, i.e., at odds with an analysis in terms of the contingencies of reinforcement.

In what follows, I will argue that Skinner's case for radical behaviorism fails, though his principles of reinforcement (nonbehavioristically interpreted) remain intact and may well be the most important contribution to psychology in the twentieth century. I shall also argue that the practical philosophy Skinner attempted to derive from his radical behaviorist principles also fails.

SKINNER'S PHILOSOPHY OF MIND

Skinner's psychology must be distinguished from his philosophy of mind. His psychology concerns the principles of reinforcement derived from his experimental work. His philosophy of mind, on the other hand, concerns the behavioristic analysis of the principles of reinforcement and the use he makes of those principles in an effort to eliminate all references to mental or private states in psychological explanations. The latter is what constitutes his radical behaviorism and is the proper target of this section.

Skinner took great pride in the fact that his principles of reinforcement could be interpreted behavioristically and this is understandable, since this was a crucial step for him in freeing psychology of all mentalism. Skinner's analysis of aversive stimulation is an example of his behavioral account of the principles of reinforcement. Pain is aversive, something a person or organism normally tries to escape. But pain (in the ordinary sense) is an inner feeling and so the sort of thing Skinner wanted to avoid in explaining behavior. Accordingly, Skinner defines aversive stimuli in terms of certain operations and their effect upon the organism's responses. In general, an aversive stimulus for Skinner is any event or condition whose removal (or reduction) reinforces (or, roughly, increases the likelihood of) any response that precedes it. This allows Skinner to talk about *painful stimulation* (such as the electrification of a cage floor) as an aversive stimulus (something physical and publicly observable) without considering pain as a private

feeling inside the organism. Skinner does not refuse to speak of feelings or sensations or "the world within the skin." His point is rather that such things are to be *explained* in an analysis of behavior, but not used to *explain* behavior. Pain, pleasure, and other feelings or sensations (what philosophers call qualia) have no causal teeth as far as Skinner is concerned, so they have no role to play in our explanations of behavior. This sounds like the methodological behaviorist. But it is not. For while the methodological behaviorist proposes to ignore such inner states entirely, Skinner is telling us to ignore them only as variables in light of which behavior is to be explained. On Skinner's view, inner states or qualia deserve serious attention, but only as something to be explained and analyzed — not as something to do the explaining.

Why does Skinner reject qualia and other inner states as variables of which behavior is a function? Why does he deny they are causally relevant? His argument is roughly this: The aim of a science of behavior is to predict and control behavior and reference to qualia or inner states is both an obstacle and unnecessary to this aim. It is an obstacle because feelings, sensations, and other inner states can't be publicly observed or directly manipulated and they only direct attention away from what can be publicly observed and directly manipulated (viz., physical states and events in the external environment).[1] Furthermore, inner-mental states are useless and unnecessary, according to Skinner. That is, Skinner believed that we could both predict and control behavior by simply observing and manipulating the publicly observable variables in the environment.[2] He concluded that inner-mental states are therefore not proper explanatory variables in a science of behavior.[3]

I believe that this argument of Skinner's fails on two counts: (1) First, it fails because it has too narrow a notion of the proper aim of a science of behavior. (2) And second, it fails because human behavior is not predictable or controllable in the way Skinner assumes it is. Let's consider each of these points in turn.

1. Skinner, sees prediction and control as the only end or goal of a science of behavior and as a result tends to think that an explanation of behavior should be judged according to its role in helping us predict and control behavior. But this is clearly too limited a way of looking at the role of explanations. To see that this is so, just imagine the following sit-

uation: You are sitting on a metal chair. Someone (unknown to you) heats up the chair, which causes you intense pain, to which you react by removing yourself from the chair. It seems entirely clear that had the person heated the chair *without causing you any feeling of pain, you would not have moved from the chair*. It follows that your moving from the chair was a function of (or caused by) the pain you *felt*. But this means that any explanation of your behavior that fails to make reference to your *feeling* of pain will thereby be inadequate (for it will fail to refer to the thing without which you would not have moved, namely, the *feeling* of pain). The person who heated up the chair can, of course, both predict and control your behavior without thinking about or even being aware of your pain. For heating up the chair normally causes the person on the chair pain and so gets her or him to move. But this does not mean that the person manipulating your behavior understands it nor that their explanation of your behavior (which makes no reference to your feeling of pain) is a good one. For the explanation leaves out the thing (viz., the feeling of pain) that is the immediate cause of your behavior, the thing without which the other causes (such as heating the chair) could not have resulted in your moving.

Consider the following story, which vividly dramatizes this point: Extraterrestrials (call them "Zebs") undertake the study of humans. Zebs, let us imagine, *never* feel pain. Moreover, Zebs are reinforcement theorists. We can well imagine Zebs being immensely successful by Skinner's standards in studying us humans, especially our pain behavior. Indeed, let us assume that they are even better at predicting and controlling our pain behavior than we are. In that case, granting Skinner's notion of explanation, we must say that they understand our pain behavior better than we do. Yet they have not the slightest clue of what the *feeling* of pain is, but we of course do. And, moreover, we know (but they can't know) that were it not for the *feeling* of pain, our behavior would be very different than it is. I submit, therefore, that precisely because the Zebs have not the slightest understanding of the crucial causal role played by pain in our behavior, they do not fully understand our behavior. Their explanation of our behavior, though a good one judged purely by Skinner's criteria of prediction and control, is really a very inadequate explanation at best.

What are the lessons to be learned from these reflections? For one thing, they show that an explanation can't be judged solely in terms of the goals of predicting and controlling behavior. For a good explanation may do little in the way of increasing our ability to predict and control someone's behavior, while an explanation that enables us to predict and control someone's behavior may be a very poor one, yielding no real understanding of that person at all. Second, good explanations of human behavior must include references to private mental states such as pain, pleasure, and other qualia. And third, because qualia are important causal antecedents of people's behavior, Skinner's *behavioral interpretation* of the principles of reinforcement should be rejected, e.g., we should not feel that we are being "unscientific" when we say people are positively reinforced by pleasure or that they are negatively reinforced by the removal of pain, and the like. Finally, we should reject Skinner's assumption that prediction and control are the only or ultimate goals of a science of behavior. We ought to consider *understanding* ourselves and others being at least as important as prediction and control, if not more so.

2. Before turning to the next section, I want to state the second problem with Skinner's defense of his philosophy of mind. I refer to Skinner's assumption that human behavior can be predicted and controlled in the same way the behavior of lower organisms can be predicted and controlled. I shall argue that this is not the case.

To be precise, the distinction I wish to call attention to is between *creatures who have a certain kind of language* versus *creatures who lack such a language*. To avoid confusion, let us note two different functions a language can have: on the one hand, languages can enable creatures to *communicate*. On the other hand, some languages, in addition to enabling creatures to communicate, also enable them to *think rationally* (a notion soon to be explained). The language of the bees, for example, enables bees to communicate with one another in apparently very complex ways. But I think it quite clear that bees cannot think rationally in the sense I shall shortly specify. So theirs is the first kind of language. In contrast, natural human languages (such as English or Chinese) enable humans both to communicate and to think rationally. So the natural languages of humans are examples of the second kind of language.

What do I mean by thinking rationally? One thing this means is an ability to think about things of a kind that one has never observed and that may or may not exist at all. Dogs can, perhaps, think about other dogs and about food and the like. I don't know. But I don't see how dogs can be said to think about things like atoms or black holes. I don't, for that matter, see how a human who had no language (such as English or Chinese) could be said to think about atoms or black holes. Atoms and black holes are things no one has observed or ever will observe and they may or may not exist. Still, humans who have human languages can and do think about such things and about even more abstract things such as Platonic forms, the number 2, spirits, and God. So being able to think about things of a kind that never have been observed and that may or may not exist is one characteristic of a rational thinker.

A second characteristic of a rational thinker is directly related to the first. Rational thinkers are not only able to think about things they have never seen and that may or may not exist, they quite often *act on behalf of such unseen things.* Humans run from ghosts, seek to smash atoms, pray to and obey God, labor to fly to new outreaches of space, produce works of art and literature unlike any that ever existed before, and struggle (as Skinner himself did) to understand and transform the world in entirely novel ways. What is unseen, what may or may not exist, and what is entirely novel can be conceived of by rational thinkers and often provide the most powerful goals or motives for what they do. A special case of action motivated by the unseen is action governed by rules, laws, and principles. Rules, laws, and principles (in the sense here meant) can only be expressed in words and can only be thought about by means of words. "A stitch in time saves nine," "Do unto others as you'd have them do unto you," "E = MC^2" and "Stop when the light is red" are all examples. Rules, laws, and principles are among the unseen things that play a major role in determining and shaping our daily lives, from the most lofty to the most mundane affairs.

A third characteristic of rational thinkers is that they can entertain, construct, and evaluate arguments (which are strings of logically related propositions or statements). This occurs in moral, legal, literary, philosophical, experimental, mathematical, religious, and everyday contexts and elsewhere. Arguments, moreover, provide reasons (or premises) for the things we do, say, and believe. Some arguments are good and some are bad;

humans can become quite expert at distinguishing which are which. Finally, it is in light of arguments that humans can determine what laws, rules, and principles we should act on and what goals or purposes it is best to pursue and value.

The point is that the things mentioned above are the defining characteristics of rationally thinking creatures (in the sense I intend that expression) and they are activities that only creatures having the right sort of language are capable of. A language such as the language of the bees is not the right sort, but the natural languages of humans are. Let's consider how all of this affects Skinner's radical behaviorism.

As we have noted, Skinner takes prediction and control to be the ultimate aim of a science of human behavior. The whole point of his radical analysis is to show that this aim can be achieved by merely attending to behavior and to the environment in which the behavior occurs without paying any attention to what is going on inside of the organism. The success of this approach in the case of lower organisms has been impressive, but its success with humans has not been impressive at all. Indeed, behavioral therapists have found it necessary to part company with Skinner on this matter, accepting his reinforcement principles, but rejecting his assumption that we can or should ignore what is going on in people's heads in attempting to deal with their behavior.[4] The central problem with Skinner's approach, I propose, is that when humans acquire a language, they can think about things unseen, reason about them, and be motivated by them and that makes all the difference. For when that happens, their behavior is now shaped by what goes on inside their heads (by what they think) and not simply by what goes on in the external environment. What people think is among the important variables determining what they do and say and what they think can and frequently does occur silently inside their heads, out of view and out of the direct control of others. So when therapists deal with people's behavior, for the most part they can only hope to succeed if they have access to what is going on in people's heads. They simply can't ignore the inside story as Skinner recommends.

It is not hard to see how Skinner was misled on this point. Skinner believed that rationality is made possible by language. And he also believed that his book *Verbal Behavior* entirely explains language in terms of the principles of reinforcement.[5] From this he concluded that the same radical behaviorist app-roach that succeeds with lower organisms would also succeed with humans, i.e., that just as the behavior of lower organisms can be predicted and controlled without paying attention to what is going on in their heads, the same must be true of humans.

Let us (for the sake of argument) concede Skin-ner's two premises: his assumption that language is the basis of rational thinking and his (more contro-versial) assumption that his book *Verbal Behavior* has explained the acquisition of language in terms of the same basic principles of reinforcement used to predict and control the behavior of lower organ-isms. Even granting these two assumptions, his conclusion does not follow. The reason this is so is quite simple: When people acquire a natural lan-guage, they are dramatically transformed by it—they undergo an intellectual metamorphosis com-parable to the physical metamorphosis a caterpillar undergoes when it becomes a butterfly. For just as a butterfly is no longer bound to the earth, the ratio-nal thinker is no longer strictly bound by the exter-nal, observable environment in the way lower organisms are. Humans can think about, reason about and be moved by worlds (real or imaginary) that lower organisms can't even dream of. Conse-quently, whether or not we can explain the acquisi-tion of this capacity by means of the principles of reinforcement or in some other way doesn't matter. Once humans have acquired the capacity to think rationally, we must tend to what is going on inside their heads (in a way we don't with lower organ-isms) if we are going to have even a hope of pre-dicting and controlling their behavior. Hence, Skinner's radical behaviorist claim that human behavior can be predicted and controlled by simply studying the physical, external environment must be rejected.

There is yet another consequence that follows from the fact that humans are rational thinkers. Not only must we pay attention to *what* people think, we must also pay attention to *how* they think as well. For you can't predict *what* someone will think (and so control him) unless you understand *how* he thinks, and this will be harder and harder to do (if not impossible) the more learned, intelligent, thoughtful, wise, resourceful, and creative he is (the very things education at its best strives to strengthen in the individual). If this is right, then we can never expect to predict and control people in the way nor to the extent Skinner wanted to (certainly not if they are educated in the way they should be).[6]

These reflections are supported by the experi-ments of Lowe and others.[7] In these experiments both linguistically incompetent children (LI) and linguistically competent children (LC) were ex-posed to the same contingencies of reinforcement. LI children responded in uniform ways to uniform contingencies of reinforcement *just as lower organ-isms do*. The behavior of LI children proved to be highly predictable and controllable; it was entirely a function of the external contingencies of reinforce-ment. LC children, in contrast, did not respond uni-formly to uniform contingencies of reinforcement. Their behavior was not simply a function of exter-nal contingencies and so was not predictable or con-trollable. And this is precisely what we should expect of creatures that can think about goals, rules, and values, reason about them, and be motivated by them, i.e., it is exactly what we should expect of rational thinking creatures. For such creatures, exposed to the same external contingencies of rein-forcement, may be expected to draw different con-clusions about their situation, hold different values, consider different options, and arrive at different decisions. We may conclude, therefore, that Skin-ner's radical behavioristic assumption (that adult human behavior is predictable and controllable) is unsound and needs to be rejected.

SKINNER'S PRACTICAL PHILOSOPHY

In this section I want to examine what conse-quences follow for Skinner's practical philosophy once we reject his philosophy of mind, i.e., once we reject his radical behaviorist thesis. I shall con-sider his ethics, his concept of the good life, and his social–political philosophy.

The entire edifice of Skinner's analysis of ethics rests upon the assumption that his psychological principles enable him to overcome the gap between the "is" of science and the "ought" of ethics. The impossibility of overcoming the is/ought gap is defended by Karl Popper as follows:

> In face of the sociological fact that most people adopt the norm "Thou shalt not steal," it is possi-ble to decide to adopt either this norm, or its oppo-site; and it is possible to encourage those who have adopted the norm to hold fast to it, or to dis-courage them, and to persuade them to adopt another norm. It is impossible to derive a sentence stating a norm or a decision from a sentence stat-ing a fact; this is only another way of saying that

it is impossible to derive norms or decisions from facts.[8]

In response to this passage Skinner makes the following comment:

> The conclusion is valid only if indeed it is 'possible to adopt a norm or its opposite.' Here is autonomous man playing his most awe-inspiring role, but whether or not a person obeys the norm 'Thou shalt not steal' depends upon supporting contingencies, which must not be overlooked.[9]

This counterargument of Skinner's may be restated as follows:

> Premise 1: The external contingencies of reinforcement determine all human behavior.
> Premise 2: If the external contingencies of reinforcement determine all human behavior, then we are not free to adopt a norm or its opposite.
> Premise 3: The validity or correctness of Popper's argument rests upon the assumption that we are free to adopt a norm or its opposite.
> Conclusion: Therefore, Popper's argument is invalid or incorrect.

Premise 1 of this argument is an assumption made by Skinner's radical behaviorist analysis, which we have just argued against. It was argued that qualia (feelings and sensations) as well as our thoughts and reasonings must be recognized among the variables responsible for our behavior. So premise 1 is false, if the analysis above is correct.

But suppose premise 1 and premise 2 are modified so that the word "external" is removed from them? In that case, premise 1 might be true, for it might be argued that inner states are to be counted among the contingencies of reinforcement that determine behavior and this might be right. At least, I don't wish to argue to the contrary. This move, however, will not save Skinner's argument, for now premise 2 will be false. Why is this so?

The reason this is so is because once you allow people's thinking and reasoning to be among the variables determining human behavior, people will have all the freedom that is needed in order to "adopt a norm or its opposite." For if you admit that people's thinking and reasoning can play such a determining role, it will follow that humans have the ability to construct and consider reasons for following norms or rules, to distinguish between good reasons and bad ones, and to act only upon those norms or rules that are supported by the better reasons or arguments. And if this is possible, then Pop-

per's argument has not been defeated. For this means that in the face of the sociological fact that most people adopt the norm "thou shalt not steal," people can still consider arguments pro and con adopting that norm, such that their choice will be determined by the best argument rather than by the sociological fact (just as Popper argues). Hence, Skinner's counterargument against Popper fails, which means that Popper's argument does indeed undermine Skinner's claim to have bridged the is/ought gap. Our conclusion, therefore, is that the entire edifice of Skinner's ethics falls to the ground.

There is a second, shorter way of seeing that Skinner is wrong in denying that we are free to adopt norms. If we are not free to adopt norms, which is to say to reason about them and act on the norm supported by the better argument, then the same holds for all of what we believe, say, and do. But if that is true, then science and mathematics and Skinner"s entire experimental analysis of behavior has really been determined by the external contingencies of reinforcement and not by *the better argument*. It follows that we can't really talk about good and bad arguments at all. To do so would be contrary to Skinner's assumptions. Hence, Skinner's position on the matter of adopting norms is self-stultifying, for to assume that the beliefs or norms we hold and that the actions we perform are never a function of our ability to determine which is the better of two arguments is to render the defense of Skinner's position itself impossible and entirely without any hope of rational support.

Skinner faces other problems of considerable importance to his practical philosophy. One of these concerns his notion of the good life.[10] In particular, there are two perspectives from which we can and do (if we are at all rational) consider the worth of our lives. Skinner's philosophy of mind (i.e., his radical behavioral assumption) can't make sense of either of these perspectives.

The first of these perspectives is what might be called the experiential or prudential perspective. When we assume this perspective, we evaluate our lives in terms of the quality of our consciously lived experiences or happiness, i.e., we consider to what extent our lives are full of pain and sorrow versus pleasure and joy. It is impossible to be indifferent to our happiness in this sense of the word and so impossible not to consider this perspective when evaluating the goodness or worth of our lives. But Skinner's radical behaviorism, as we saw, rejects qualia or feelings as explanatorily insignificant. Above, it was argued that this rejection of the explanatory importance of qualia is mistaken. For qualia such as pain and pleasure are not mere epiphenomena, but are frequently the immediate and crucial determinants of our behavior. We may add that from a practical point of view, it would be disastrous to ignore qualia in reasoning about our future actions and future lives. To do so would be to act as if the amount of pleasure and joy or pain and suffering that will befall us is utterly unimportant. And who would wish to do such a thing even if it were possible?

The second perspective that is relevant to the evaluation of our lives as a whole may be described as the judicial or, perhaps, tribunal perspective. As rational creatures we can and invariably do desire to be praiseworthy, to live praiseworthy lives. That is, we do not simply seek praise, but to be worthy of praise, which is a very different matter. A clever hypocrite may receive loads of praise without being worthy of any, while a person deserving the highest of praise may get none. Moreover, the highest form of being worthy of praises is to be worthy of *moral praise*. Universally, the world's heroes and heroines (the people most admired and respected in the world's literature and in the world at large) all share the quality of great moral courage and high moral character. But Skinner's radical behavioral analysis, we have seen, cannot make sense of morality or ethics and so can't make sense of being praiseworthy in the highest sense—the moral sense. Thus, it can't make sense of the judicial perspective or the prudential perspective and so fails on both counts to make sense of the good life.

Finally, we come to Skinner's social–political philosophy. In *Walden II* and in *Beyond Freedom and Dignity*, Skinner expresses antidemocratic themes. In *Walden II*, he envisions a community where democracy is entirely absent and in *Beyond Freedom and Dignity*, he argues that our cherishing of freedom and dignity is based upon false assumptions that have no place in the scientific analysis of behavior. Skinner argues that this attachment to freedom results in a misguided opposition to the experimental control of behavior and that this could prove lethal to the species.[11] Granted the correctness of Skinner's radical behavioral assumptions, his views on these matters make a certain sense. But if, as I have been arguing, his case in favor of radical behaviorism fails, Skinner's arguments against freedom and dignity also fail.

Let us begin with Skinner's attack on freedom. If, as I have argued, we are rational thinking creatures capable of assessing ethical rules or principles and of evaluating the goodness of our lives (from the prudential and judicial perspectives), then we have all of the freedom required to reasonably prefer democratic to nondemocratic forms of government. For the latter, assume that ordinary people should have no role in government. Such a presumption can only be defended if either no one is free (in the very strong sense of "not free," which entails being unable to think rationally) or if there is no is/ought gap (as Skinner also argues). But Skinner has failed to sustain either assumption. So his case against both freedom and democracy fails.

This brings us to dignity. The notion of dignity is a slippery one and is explained in various ways. However, I believe the most important aspect of dignity for moral theory is the notion of the equal and immeasurable worth of every human being conjoined with each person's right to work out their lives according to their own lights, so far as is compatible with the moral law. I see nothing in Skinner's analysis (once his radical behaviorist thesis has been dropped) that requires us to give up such a notion of human dignity.

Turning to Skinner's antidemocratic themes in *Walden II*, it must be admitted that he has identified some of the weakness of a democratic form of government, e.g., the tendency of people to vote their hearts and to vote for personalities, the ease with which they can sometimes be manipulated, and the difficulties in getting people to act for the longer-term collective good.[12] Nonetheless, his attempts to demonstrate that the community described in *Walden II* would be a *better* alternative fails, once we drop his radical behaviorist philosophy of mind and take into consideration all that flows from our rational nature. For in the first place (as seen in the Lowe experiments), it is naive to think rational creatures such as ourselves can really be controlled by the careful arrangement of the external contingencies of reinforcement. And second even if that were possible, it would not (given our freedom and dignity) be either desirable or morally acceptable.

In conclusion, then, Skinner's case for radical behaviorism fails, first as a viable philosophy of mind and second as a viable basis for a practical philosophy. This is not to say that we either must or should reject Skinner's weaker assumption that the principles of reinforcement truly apply to all voluntary human behavior. This notion is compatible with the idea that we are rational thinking creatures. Nor is this weaker assumption of Skinner's incompatible with the notion of an ethics based upon rational deliberation, our notion of the good life, or with our cherishing freedom or dignity or our democratic institutions and practices. My intention, therefore, has not been to argue against Skinner's principles of reinforcement (freed of their behavioristic trappings), but rather to argue against his radical behaviorist philosophy of mind and his practical philosophy, which he mistakenly took to follow from the principles of reinforcement.

ENDNOTES

1. See pp. 3–22 in Skinner's *Science and Human Behavior* (1953, Macmillan).

2. Ibid. and also pp.1–23 in Skinner's *Beyond Freedom and Dignity* (1972, Bantam/Vantage).

3. This conclusion lies at the core of Skinner's radical behaviorism.

4. See H. R. Beech's paper "Behavior Therapy" in *Behaviorism* (1974, Open University Press).

5. See Skinner's preliminary and refined definitions of verbal behavior in *Verbal Behavior*. It is evident from what he says there that he takes verbal behavior to encompass all of language and it is also evident that he takes his book *Verbal Behavior* as providing the basis for a complete account of the entire field of verbal behavior. For his preliminary definition, see pp. 2 and 14 and for his refined definition, see pp. 224–226 in *Verbal Behavior* (1957, Prentice Hall). Also see pp. 3–10 in *Verbal Behavior* for his comments on the traditional views of language.

6. Daniel Dennett takes a somewhat similar line to the one being developed in this chapter. See Dennett's papers "Skinner Skinned" and "Why the Law of Effect Will Not Go Away" in his book *Brainstorms* (1978, Bradford).

7. See C. Fergus Lowe's paper "Radical Behaviorism and Human Psychology," pp. 71–93, in *Animal Models of Human Behavior* (1983, John Wiley & Sons).

8. See p. 108 in Skinner's book *Beyond Freedom and Dignity* (1972, Bantam/Vantage).

9. Ibid.

10. The best glimpse of Skinner's conception of the good life may be caught by reading chaps. 6, 7 and 8 in his book *Beyond Freedom and Dignity* (1972, Bantam/Vantage). His book *Walden II* also gives an excellent and very concrete picture of Skinner's notion of the good life.

11. Chap. 2, *Beyond Freedom and Dignity* (1972, Bantam/Vantage).

12. See chaps. 3–8 in Skinner's *Walden II* (1976, Macmillan).

CHAPTER 11

MUST BEHAVIOR BE MECHANISTIC? MODELING NONMACHINES

Joseph F. Rychlak

I wonder if experimental psychologists ever ask themselves why they find it so plausible to speak of the "mechanisms" of human behavior? Sigmund Freud referred to the psychic "mechanisms of defense," which were in no way mechanistic, but I am now targeting my colleagues in the "basic science" wing of our profession. Why is it that virtually no experimental psychologist has dared construe human behavior/cognition as other than fundamentally mechanistic in nature? I think Searle (1992, chap. 1) has recently given us some general leads to an answer to this question, but I hope in the present paper to focus and elaborate certain of his arguments that I believe are paramount. I would like to begin with a discussion of what it means to say that some item under explanation is a mechanism, move to a consideration of explanatory grounds, and then give an overview of my efforts to model human beings in a nonmechanistic, teleological fashion.

WHAT IS A MECHANISM?

Colleagues who employ the machine concept almost never define it, much less clarify what it sig-nifies in relation to a nonmechanistic conception. In fact, I find them using the word "mechanism" as a synonym for "experimental effect" or "lawful regularity." Thus, a cognitive psychologist carries out an experiment, finds a statistically significant observed effect, and then elaborates on the sup-posed—but *unobserved*—mechanism underlying this effect. If there are two such statistically significant effects interacting in the experimental results, the psychologist speaks of "mechanisms." I have argued for some time that psychologists too readily confound their experimental *method* with their explanatory *theory* (Rychlak, 1968/1985, pp. 57–60). Empirical observation of an experimental effect which, if reliably occurring, tends to be called a law, is strictly on the side of *method*—the context of proof or "justification," as Reichenbach (1938) once called it. But the concept used to explain such an experimental effect is on the side of *theory*. Mechanism is therefore a theoretical conception introduced to make sense of the observed data array.

However, due to the fact that the scientific method is limited by the logical fallacy of *affirm-*

149

ing-the-consequent of the *if-then* line of reasoning, there is and always will be more than one (indeed, potentially *N*) theoretical explanation of any such observed data array (ibid., pp. 80–81). Such observed "facts" never speak for themselves! Those psychologists who believe that they are necessarily "seeing" mechanisms (theory) taking place in their empirical results (method) are succumbing to the affirming-the-consequent fallacy. To reason that "*If* my theory is correct, *then* the experimental data will array as I predict, in XYZ fashion" and then find that the data do indeed array "lawfully" in XYZ fashion (many times over!) *never* permits a psychologist to conclude that "My theory is *necessarily* correct." To conclude this would be comparable to reasoning: "*If* a human being, *then* a mortal being," affirming in turn that since the body standing before one "is mortal" it is *necessarily* human.

The irony here is that the scientific method is *not* mechanical; it is logical, although it frequently employs mechanical devices to achieve the controls required to test its hypotheses. Psychologists have reified the variable conception, speaking of the variables involved in any observable situation. Yet, the truth is, there is no such thing as a variable until some framing theory makes it so. Some psychologists hold theoretically that the world of experience is made up of such "real" variables, and their job as scientists is to learn how to track and thereby control and predict how these "lawful variables" array so that they can later be engineered in some way.

The reference to engineering is quite appropriate. I think the prime model for a "good," tough-minded, well-educated experimental psychologist has always been that of the engineer. I interpret the decline of molar theorizing in preference to molecular theorizing in psychology as one of the outcomes of this engineering bias. Psychologists are encouraged to avoid grand speculation in preference to studying the basic, instrumental *causes* of what brings about behavioral motions. But what do we mean by a cause?

I have been arguing for over 25 years that because of its subject matter (human beings) psychology must return to the use of all four of Aristotle's (1952, p. 128) causes—concepts that he identified in the writings of even earlier philosophers (i.e., he did not merely "think up" the causal meanings). Space does not permit elaboration on this point, but the reader should know that my use

of the causal meanings is not precisely as Aristotle employed them in all of his theorizing. However, I do think it is fair to say that basically, Aristotle teaches us that in accounting for any item or action in experience, we can rely upon one or more of the following: the "matter" that necessarily makes it up (*material cause*), the impetus that brought it about or shapes it (*efficient cause*), the essential pattern that it takes on (*formal cause*), and the reason why ("for the sake of which") it exists or is taking place (*final cause*).

As I have traced elsewhere (e.g., Rychlak, 1988, pp. 39–44; 1991, chap. 2), the rise of Newtonian science brought on the demise of final-cause analysis in science. Final causation enables teleological (purposive, intentional) description of the item in question. Formal causation is involved here as well, where it shows up as the patterned target "for the sake of which" an end (*telos*) is being intended. For example, the athletic coach frames a game plan or strategy to engage the opposition. This pattern per se would represent a formal cause, but the fact that the team members enact–or during the game decide spontaneously not to enact!–this strategy brings the final cause into the account as well. The formal cause pattern is the "that" (reason) and the enactment represents the "for the sake of which" team behavior is carried forward. Because of the teleological claims of the theologians during the Galilean debacle as well as other problems associated with the role of purpose in nature, the Newtonians eschewed all such description and turned instead to an exclusively material- and efficient-cause account of the universe (at least, in their formal writings they did so; many of these scientists, including Newton, employed final-cause meanings in their personal views, religious beliefs, etc.).

The Newtonians employed formal-cause conceptions in the mathematics that they believed traced this course of a presumably mechanical universe. Thus, when Laplace suggested "that a super-human intelligence acquainted with the position and motion of the atoms at any moment could predict the whole course of future events" (Burtt, 1955, p. 96) he was thinking of a mathematical estimation capturing the mechanical–that is, material- and efficent-cause—motions of atomic particles assembling and reassembling into ongoing events and products. Newton makes essentially the same point in his writings, as when he observes of his mathematical efforts:

By the propositions mathematically demonstrated...we then derive from the celestial phenomena the forces of gravity with which bodies tend to the sun and the several planets....I wish we could derive the rest of the phenomena of nature by the same kind of reasoning from mechanical principles; for I am induced by many reasons to suspect that they may all depend upon certain forces [*efficient causes*] by which the particles of bodies [*material causes*]...are either mutually impelled towards each other [*efficient causes*], and cohere in regular figures [*formal causes*], or are repelled and recede from each other. [italicized material in brackets added] (ibid., p. 209)

Nowhere in this analysis do we find a final-cause ascription (although Newton was not above speculating informally on a deity teleology; see ibid., pp. 287–290). Actually, the point of Newtonianism was to keep final causes out of formal accounts of the physical universe. Bacon (1952, p. 43) was among the first to elucidate this policy of restricting the description of physical nature to material and efficient causation. The danger here, Bacon believed, was that in employing final-cause description the natural scientist might forego consideration of the material and efficient causes that are fundamental to physical events. It adds little or nothing to the physical account to speak of "why" events occur; good scientists focus on "how" they take place. Also, the Newtonians did not wish to see a deity teleology return to physical science. One Inquisition was quite enough!

This brings us to a definition of "mechanism." One philosophical dictionary defines mechanism as a "total explanation by efficient, as opposed to final, cause" (Runes, 1960, p. 194). Another states that mechanical explanation is "any explanation which avoids teleology and final causation.... mechanical explanations stress efficient causation and are reducible to laws covering instances of matter in motion" (Reese, 1980, p. 345). As I am a teleological theorist, we can now appreciate why the immediate attribution of (unobserved) mechanisms to empirical research findings bothers me. I believe that human beings are agents—intentional, purposive organisms who work for ends and exert self-direction in the manner of what is popularly termed "free will." This means I require final-cause theoretical conceptions to convey my position. It must be possible for me to conduct a research experiment resulting in statistically significant findings that are due to something other than some underlying mechanism.

I can operationally define my hypothesized teleological conceptions as experimental variables and test them just as rigorously as my mechanistically inclined collegues define and test theirs (see Rychlak, 1988, chap. 9). But what difference does this make if every psychologist who conducts a successful experiment believes that the significant findings point—by definition—to unobserved mechanisms taking place somewhere in a postulated brain network, or whatever? In a shocking display of the fallacy of affirming-the-consequent, the sum total of all significant experimental findings conducted in psychology must then support only efficient-cause mechanisms. Teleologies "need not apply" as potential explanations of the data. No theory–method confound is admitted here, much less recognized. The mechanistic lingo keeps rolling along, for indeed it can never be put to falsification.

WHAT IS AN EXPLANATION?

There is more to consider in speaking of an explanation than simply the causal meanings that may be involved. The word *explanation* devolves from the Latin *ex* and *planare*, meaning "to make level or plain." When we explain something we therefore bring its description around to some common ground, a level basis on which everyone can agree that: "Yes, that description nicely clarifies (accounts for, captures, etc.) things." We need go no further because now everything makes sense. The causal meanings are not such grounds, because we can find the same form of causation being used across different groundings. I have recently argued that there are four main grounds (there could be more!) on which psychologists have based their explanations: *Physikos*, *Bios*, *Logos*, and *Socius* (Rychlak, 1993). Each ground has its own distinctive *process* that acts upon, moves, puts to shape, and so on, the *content* being processed. A process of the *Physikos* would be something like the gravitation that acts on inanimate contents like rocks, rain, planets, light, and so on, to influence their movements or hold them in place. The *Socius* ground employs a process like class-level identity to shape its contents (human beings) to behave in certain patterned ways.

The *Bios* is to be distinguished from the *Physikos* by the fact that the former concerns the animate in nature whereas the latter does not. Even so, these two grounds have frequently been combined in psychology, as when Hull (1937) suggested that the same (efficiently-caused) laws directing the actions of a raindrop directed the actions of a human being (p. 2). But more generally, *Bios* theories advance a process like genetics or a mediating organic "system" that moves its contents (i.e., behavioral acts) around entirely without agency. Thus, Hebb (1974) once stated flatly that "*Psychology is a biological science*" (p. 72; italics in original), from which it followed that "Free will has a physiological basis..." (p. 75). The final grounding for psychological explanation, which contrasts markedly with the *Bios*, is the *Logos*. These contrasting grounds delimit the historic "body–mind" debate that has plagued the description of human beings for centuries. A process of the *Logos* is, as I will enlarge upon in the next section, predication. The contents framed in predication—so-called thoughts, ideas, cognitions—are the meanings that people intend to understand and enact.

Unfortunately, problems arise when we presume that the process of one ground takes as its content another ground. For example, to theorize in the *Logos* realm is to propose a teleology relying upon final-cause conceptions. Meaning is fundamental here. To "mean" is intentionally to pattern or simply acknowledge extant organizations of experience that suggest a purpose. These organized patterns of meaning (formal-cause) are then affirmed or not, as the person intends (final-cause) to bring forward what will or will not be the case in ongoing experience. This view of human cognition, resting on a *Logos* ground, is teleological. It is irrelevant what the nature of the "body" is like—whether a reflection of the Hullian *Physikos* qua *Bios*, or a strictly *Bios* formulation like that of Hebb's. The logic of predication is not framable in the processes of the *Physikos*, *Bios*, or *Socius*.

Now, psychologists have been painfully aware of the difficulties involved in framing human beings either dualistically (body–mind) or monistically (materialism). Valiant efforts have been made to "unite" psychology in terms of a common grounding (see, e.g., Staats & Mos, 1987). Often, there is reliance on a "levels" interpretation of explanation—that grounds can be rank-ordered from the narrowest to the broadest formulations, on the analogy of moving from subatomic particles up through chemical unities to systemic organizations of one form or another. Simon (1992) recently argued this way as follows: "There is nothing mysterious about explaining phenomena at different

levels of resolution. It happens all the time in the physical and biological sciences. A theory of genetics need not (fortunately) rely on a knowledge of quarks" (p. 153). Since Simon construes an explanation as referring back to—the efficiently-causing!—antecedent events, thereby framing laws that produce new states in an ongoing system, he like so many in psychology today must admit that any "levels" approach to explanation must in principle admit that "the higher level mechanisms are reducible to those of the lower level" (ibid.). However, it is not his intention to defend such reductions, for as he spells things out:

> Complex phenomena can usually be segmented into levels from macroscopic to microscopic, separated by both the spatial and the temporal scales of the events they describe. Provided that the phenomena are roughly hierarchical in structure, as most natural phenomena are, we can build explanatory theories at each level, and then bridging theories that link the aggregated physiological behavior to the units of explanation at the symbolic level just above. (ibid., p. 158)

Unfortunately, the track record to date in psychology's "levels and linkings" theorizing is not encouraging to the teleologist. One finds that the "lower" level ground invariably "eats up" those above it, making them contents in its process. This is what Hebb does in suggesting that the *Logos* conception of "free will" is produced by the *Bios*. I have called for a complementarity principle in psychology, one that would place the four grounds under discussion on an *equal* footing (Rychlak, 1993). Any one theorist may wish to frame things in terms of levels, but this would not be a dictum to be obeyed by all psychologists. Further, I recommend that a psychologist, in any one theoretical effort, do his or her explaining solely within the aegis of a single ground, instead of mixing grounds together. This too is not a dictum. But it is my belief that psychologists muddle things when they borrow from different grounds in the same theoretical effort (for examples, see ibid.).

We often hear the "unity of science" being trumpeted, particularly as it applies to the physical sciences. What is overlooked here is that the so-called unity of *Physikos* and *Bios* conceptions stems from the fact that they both make exclusive use of material- and efficient-causation in their theoretical accounts (albeit measured and tracked by formal-cause mathematical conceptions). A difficult question such as the basis for animated action has not been "unified" to date, as no linking theory has welded the "living versus non-living" divisions existing across these grounds. The physical and biological sciences can rest with such non-telic, third-person ("It") explanations as occur when material- and efficient-causation is being used, but at least some of us in psychology are convinced that we require telic, first-person ("I") accounts to capture human cognition. My suggestion is that we select a given ground for any one theoretical task and then retain it exclusively throughout. We can then move in turn to a second, third, and fourth ground explaining the *same* item of interest. In other words, the aim of the proposed complementarity is not to close off alternative formulations. Rather, we hope to clarify alternatives, discern which of several theories is best suited to account for the item of interest, and in the long run develop better theories. I next turn to an effort of this sort grounded exclusively in the *Logos* .

LOGICAL LEARNING THEORY

I have proposed logical learning theory (LLT) in an effort to break away from the older mediational models of learning that have dominated psychology to date (Rychlak, 1994). Logical learning theory employs a predicational model, which can be pictured through use of typical Euler circles. When a person affirms "I am hungry" he/she has—in Euler-circle terms—essentially placed a little circle labeled "I" within a wider ranging (predicating) circle labeled "hungry" or some such. The circles represent realms of meaning, with one (the smaller) being targeted for meaning-extension by the other (the larger). The larger circle, representing in this example the meaning of "hungry," lends or extends this meaning to the targeted "I" within. There is a generic oppositionality involved here, for not only is the "inside" of the circle (i.e., hungry) lending meaning to "I," but the outside (i.e., nonhungry) is lending a contrasting meaning as well.

Unlike traditional mediational theorizing, which has antecedent, efficient-cause imprints and material-cause (drive) thrusts moving the person along over time as stimuli or inputs, the predication model functions logically, hence totally outside of time's flow. Indeed, "time" itself is a predicating meaning rather than an independent reality. According to LLT, people frame both understanding- and action-intentions in a predicational manner. To concretize

this process, LLT proposes that the following concept of "telosponse" be adopted in the *Logos* realm to replace the *Bios* conception of "response":

> A *telosponse* is the affirmation or taking of a position regarding a meaningful content (image[s], word[s], judgmental comparison[s], etc.) relating to a referent acting as a purpose for the sake of which behavior is then intended.

This is a final-cause conception, combining the Greek word for "end" (*telos*) with the Roman word (*spondere*) meaning "to make or do." Thus, to telospond is to make or do something for the sake of a reason or end. Note that I have violated proper etymological coinage to cross Greek and Roman roots in this fashion, but it was only after several imprecise efforts to capture what I wanted to say that I decided to forgo such scholarly propriety. Telosponse rhymes nicely with its opponent conception: response. I claim that we do not "respond" to the door stimulus as we begin leaving an unfamiliar room, but rather we "telospond," in framing this sensory pattern as "that" (formal cause qua reason) "for the sake of which" (final cause) we stroll toward the presumed exit—presumed, because we are always cognizant of the "outside the Euler circle" possibility that the door we are approaching might not be the way out after all. We might find a broom closet on the other side of the door. Even in familiar rooms, the process of behaving in relation to sensory patterns is not responsive but telosponsive.

Telosponsivity shifts the focus of meaning from behavior as occurring mechanically or reactively to a proactive formulation, from looking "at" the actor extraspectively to looking "with" the actor introspectively. According to LLT, when we affirm or take a position in ongoing behavior ("The door out is over there") the meaning so aligned serves as a precedent which then extends sequaciously into ongoing action. A *precedent* meaning is one that goes before others in logical order or arrangement and thereby sets the tone, frame of reference, or "context" of the meaning-extension to follow. A *sequacious* meaning-extension is one that is slavishly compliant (logical necessity) upon the meaning that has gone before it as a precedent (entirely outside of time). We are dealing here in the formal/final cause conceptions of the *Logos* and not in the material/efficient cause conceptions of the *Physikos* or the *Bios*.

Rather than efficient causation, the extensions of meaning in the *Logos* occur through the logic of tautology, on the order of *If A then A* (i.e., *If "A-like" precedents then "A-like" sequacious extensions*). If we view the world through rose-colored glasses (precedent), then the world is necessarily rosy (sequacious extension). If we have a prototypical schema (precedent) in a given life situation, then we enact the meaning being schematically framed (as a sequacious extension). Also, and this has been generally overlooked in traditional theories of learning, the fact that human beings always sense the opposite meanings "outside" a predicating Euler encirclement—the contrary, contradiction, negation, or contrast of what they are meaningfully aligning—it is possible for humans to reason analogically. There is in every analogy (metaphor, allegory, etc.) that which is tautologically identical (inside the predicating circle) and that which is disanalogous (outside the predicating circle). In fact, I claim that human cognition is always a question of "taking a position" within a sea of such oppositionality.

This capacity to know what is under implication beyond the delimiting lines of the larger Euler circle is what I mean by *generic oppositionality* (inside vs. outside the framing meaning). Generic oppositionality makes estimations of both "same/different" and "same/opposite" possible. The latter pairing includes what I call *delimiting oppositionality* in that it involves cases in which one meaning delimits, hence, enters into the definition of its opposite pole—as when "left" delimits "right" or "good" delimits "bad." It is important to appreciate that we are speaking of an intrinsic process here and not contending that—especially generic—oppositionality is being "mediated" by the words that are entered into this predicational process. A word can be designated the predicate of a sentence, of course, but it derives this descriptive label from the role that it plays in the predicational process. Indeed, it is possible to frame two predications in this process having different meanings by simply rotating the same words from the target or subject location of a sentence (smaller Euler circle) to the predicate location of this sentence (larger Euler circle)—as in saying "A person is like a tree" or "A tree is like a person." Either word, person or tree, can occupy the predicating location, extending thereby quite different meanings to the other word serving as target (or "subject").

We can now get some idea of how LLT approaches the explanation of human behavior as teleological. The "taking of a position" phrase in the definition of telosponsivity includes the possibility of "not" taking the position—of negating it preliminary to actually furthering an understanding–intention into an action–intention. In any stated belief, assumption, hope, desire, and so forth, there is always this possibility of declining what is indicated. Even as I affirm a major premise like "I will accomplish the task" I have the sense of "I will not accomplish the task" ("I will fail," etc.). Usually, I deny the latter implication and undertake the task with effort. But today the task seems daunting. "Can I do it? Do I really want to do it? Is it worth it?" These opposing points of view are but a short step across the delimiting affirmation line of the larger Euler circle (speaking figuratively, of course, in terms of our *Logos* model).

It is this intrinsic tie of oppositionality to predication that forces the person continually to "take a position"—inside or outside the framing circle—when a predicate meaning-affirmation is required by the circumstances of life. I have shown that whereas computers follow a Boolean form of *hard disjunction*, so that they never are cognizant of the negation, contradiction, contrary, or contrast of the so-called information that they process, human beings cognize according to a non-Boolean, *soft disjunction* in which they continually face such opposing possibilities to make their lives complex, doubt-laden, spontaneous, conflicted, exciting, and miserable (see Rychlak, 1991, pp. 54–59).

The obvious Kantian flavor of telosponsivity suggests a major problem: How does the human being begin this process of extending meaning in precedent-sequacious fashion at the very outset of cognition (or of life)? Is not the newborn a tabula rasa in the cognitive realm? How can predication as a process begin when there is no "encircling" predicate meaning to begin with? Am I proposing some initial list of predicates akin to the categories of the understanding or other forms of inborn ideas?

No, this is not my strategy. What is inborn is the process and not its idea contents. My suggestion is that initially the individual at the outset of cognitive life—whenever that may be said to occur—begins by predicating some target of itself. This is a tautological act in which, for example, the child might telospond "A nipple is a nipple." The resultant learning is that of an identity, an as yet unnamed sense of "nippleness," that can in turn serve as a predicate meaning in which the newborn begins to explore the world of nipplelike objects. Since everything is not nipplelike, or is only partially nipplelike (e.g., fingers), there is the oppositionality factor of such exploration to consider—which in turn broadens the range of learning all the more. In LLT we believe that people learn from what is *not* input or encountered by reasoning to the opposite of what *is* input or encountered. This sequence of telosponsive discrimination is carried forward, many times over, gradually extending "that" (predicate meanings) "for the sake of which" the person knows and behaves.

I would like to close by stressing that LLT is not simply a "thought experiment" or related philosophical speculation. Its tenets have been worked out for some 25 years to date, filled in by over 100 research experiments specifically designed to test the theory (Rychlak, 1994). For example, my colleagues and I have shown that a "predication effect" does indeed take place, having demonstrable effects on how learning is organized (Rychlak & Rychlak, 1991). We have found that cueing students with the predicate-words of sentences that they have forgotten leads to better recall of these sentences than cueing them with the subject-words (Rychlak, Stilson, & Rychlak, 1993). This finding is consistent with the precedent-sequacious direction of meaning-extension that LLT postulates. We have drawn what is probably the first learning curve for oppositionality in the literature, showing that people learn the opposite meaning to what they are asked to learn with a facility equal to a paraphrasing of this learning—and that this retention of opposite meanings increases with practice (Rychlak, Barnard, Williams, & Wollman, 1989).

My students have shown that affective oppositionality (like vs. dislike, etc.) plays a role in both initial learning and subsequent retrieval. Thus, a person knows the oppositely judged positive or negative affective quality of a word completing a sentence even before he learns (or has "encoded") the word per se (Ulasevich, 1991). At the other end of the learning cycle, retrieval of forgotten words can be facilitated if the learner shifts affective predications; for example, disliked words previously seen but not recalled can be pulled up from memory if the person's task-predication shifts from positive to negative (Hughes, 1993).

I have done broad surveys of the research literature other than verbal learning and memory, in which LLT has been shown to be entirely consistent with the findings on such varied topics as prototype, attribution, script, reactance, concept formation, depth of processing, encoding specificity, awareness in classical and operant conditioning, metacognition, recall versus recognition, figure-ground, *Einstellung*, impression formation, mood induction, split-brain, language development, modeling, and self-identity (Rychlak, 1994; 1988, chap. 9). The possible role of predication and oppositionality in the learning and general behavior of subhuman animals is also a topic of interest (see Rychlak, 1991, chap. 7). I relied on LLT to analyze a major longitudinal study of young men in business in order to demonstrate that we do not have to think of people as under the normative manipulation of "the system," or concepts of this ilk, in order to make sense of empirical ratings and test scores (Rychlak, 1982). I think that from all this work one point is clear: Human beings *can* be modeled as nonmachines, and scientific evidence is just as readily gathered in favor of this image as is now gathered under a predicating schematic of the person as a machine.

REFERENCES

Aristotle (1952). *Posterior analytics*. In R. M. Hutchins (Ed.), *Great books of the Western world* (Vol. 8, pp. 95–137). Chicago: Encyclopedia Britannica.

Bacon, F. (1952). *Advancement of learning*. In R. M. Hutchins (Ed.), *Great books of the Western world* (Vol. 30, pp. 1–101). Chicago: Encyclopedia Britannica.

Burtt, E. A. (1955). *The metaphysical foundations of modern physical science* (Rev. ed.). Garden City, NY: Doubleday.

Hebb, D. O. (1974). What psychology is about. *American Psychologist, 29*, 71–79.

Hughes, D. G. (1993). *Affective predication and the retrieval of personality-trait words*. Unpublished master's thesis, Loyola University of Chicago. Chicago, IL.

Hull, C. L. (1937). Mind, mechanism, and adaptive behavior. *Psychological Review, 44*, 1–32.

Reese, W. L. (1980). *Dictionary of philosophy and religion: Eastern and Western thought*. Atlantic Highland, NJ: Humanities Press.

Reichenbach, H. (1938). *Experience and prediction*. Chicago: University of Chicago Press.

Runes, D. D. (1960). *Dictionary of philosophy*. New York: Philosophical Library.

Rychlak, J. F. (1968/1985). *A philosophy of science for personality theory* (2nd ed.). Malabar, FL: Krieger.

Rychlak, J. F. (1982). *Personality and life-style of young male managers: A logical learning theory analysis.* New York: Academic Press.

Rychlak, J. F. (1988). *The psychology of rigorous humanism* (2nd ed.). New York: New York University Press.

Rychlak, J. F. (1991). *Artificial intelligence and human reason: A teleological critique.* New York: Columbia University Press.

Rychlak, J. F. (1993). A suggested principle of complementarity for psychology: In theory, not method. *American Psychologist.*

Rychlak, J. F. (1994). *Logical learning theory: A human teleology and its empirical support.* Lincoln: University of Nebraska Press.

Rychlak, J. F., Barnard, S., Williams, R. N., & Wollman, N. (1989). The recognition and cognitive utilization of oppositionality. *Journal of Psycholinguistic Research, 18,* 181–199.

Rychlak, J. F., & Rychlak, L. S. (1991). Evidence for a predication effect in deciding on the personal significance of abstract word meanings. *Journal of Psycholinguistic Research, 20,* 403–418.

Rychlak, J. F., Stilson, S. R., & Rychlak, L. S. (1993). Testing a predicational model of cognition: Cueing predicate meanings in sentences and word triplets. *Journal of Psycholinguistic Research, 22,* 479–503.

Searle, J. R. (1992). *The rediscovery of the mind.* Cambridge, MA: MIT Press.

Simon, H. A. (1992). What is an "explanation" of behavior? *Psychological Science, 3,* 150–161.

Staats, A. W., & Mos, L. P. (Eds.). (1987). *Annals of theoretical psychology (Vol. 5).* New York: Plenum Press.

Ulasevich, A. (1991). *Affective predication in memory for sentences: Anticipating meaningfulness before meaning.* Unpublished master's thesis, Loyola University of Chicago, Chicago, IL.

PART 3

COGNITIVE SCIENCE AND PSYCHOLOGY

The rise of cognitive science in the '60s produced a revolution not only in the kind of theories advanced by psychologists but also in philosophy of psychology and psychological metatheory. Hitherto, psychological metatheory was roughly conceived as being concerned with issues in the philosophy of science. As such it was fundamentally an applied epistemological enterprise driven largely by philosophical issues coming out of a liberalized logical empiricist tradition (see, e.g., Koch, 1959; Marx, 1963; Turner, 1967).

With the rise of cognitive science, however, the philosophy of psychology shifted somewhat and became more explicitly concerned with metaphysical issues of a certain sort, in particular, issues surrounding the philosophy of mind (together with correlative issues in the philosophy of language).[1]

The reason for this shift is not difficult to imagine. For a methodological behaviorist, the fundamental issue seems to be epistemological: How can we know there are other minds? What is the behavioral evidence for the existence of other minds? Once having answered these questions, their verification provided a answer to the correlative question: What is the conceptual relation between mind and behavior?

With the advent of cognitive science, the philosophy of psychology focused on more metaphysical issues, in particular, issues in the philosophy of mind, issues that concerned the very nature of cognition. The logical empiricists (e.g., Bergmann, Carnap, Feigl, Hempel) had, of course, spent considerable time on the philosophy of mind and the mind–body problem, but these activities were largely an application of more basic principles worked out in the context of general philosophy of science as applied to physics.

The cognitive revolution produced a more indigenous philosophy of mind modeled not upon physics but upon computer science; in fact very little of the earlier work of the logical empiricism on the philosophy of mind and the foundations of psychology is cited by the leading philosophers of cognitive science today. Indeed, what is striking is that most of these individuals are not considered to be philosophers of science at all (in the usual sense of that term) but rather philosophers of mind, with their primary philosophical interest centering on the nature of the knowing mind: How is it related to the brain? Is it possible to have a physicalistic account of the mind? What is an adequate account of the nature of representation? How can one define the uniqueness of the mental? and so on.

This shift from the epistemology of mind to the ontology of mind can be seen perhaps most clearly in the area that surely motivated the cognitive revolution, viz., the attempt to provide a mechanistic account of the mental that was at the same time a cognitive account—the *physical symbol system hypothesis* (Newell & Simon, 1976/1981). This hypothesis lies at the conceptual basis of cognitive science, in particular, that version of artificial intelligence known as Good Old-Fashioned Artificial Intelligence: GOFAI (Haugeland, 1985).

As individuals worked out the metatheory or philosophy of psychology underlying GOFAI, it became clear that GOFAI was committed to a set of correlated views: functionalism, computationalism, the representational theory of mind, the language of thought hypothesis, intentionalist psychology, methodological solipsism, and so forth. (For a brief summary of these views, see Sterelny, 1990). Chief among these views was *computationalism*, the view (roughly put) that *all mental processes are formal computations on formal symbols*. Herbert Simon, the leading spokesman for GOFAI and one of its chief designers, charts the basic features of computationalism in his contribution, "Computational Theories of Cognition."

As Simon points out, GOFAI is fundamentally committed to the notion that *all-mental processes are computational* and that such computations are linguistic-like computations across formal—typically syntactical—symbols. *Formalism* has thus been a key ingredient in GOFAI and this meant (roughly) a stress on the exclusively syntactical, propositional nature of the mind.

This basic assumption of GOFAI is critically examined and found wanting in the next two contributions by Bickhard and Hooker. Bickhard's "Troubles with Computationalism" is directed at the encodingist assumption of GOFAI, which he claims is incoherent on conceptual grounds. The encodingist assumption maintains that purely formal symbols need to be "coded" in a system of (linguistic) representations such that there is a correspondence between the symbol and that which the symbol is about. Bickhard argues that this assumption encounters innumerable concep-

tual and logical problems. In place of this, Bickhard suggests an alternative account of *interactivism*, which escapes these difficulties because it is committed to a naturalistic, organism–environment approach in which symbolic representation is an emergent phenomenon—emergent from the originally nonrepresentational realm of actions.

Hooker's approach ("Toward a Naturalized Cognitive Science") is also naturalistic and "interactivist." After criticizing the narrow syntactical approach of GOFAI (narrow AI), he discusses (but ultimately rejects) an improved semantic account (wide AI) and then suggests a more pragmatic approach, one stressing the key notions of problem solving, adaptation, control theory, cybernetics, self-organizing systems, and regulation, one wedded to a more connectionist architecture of the mind. Here again is a move toward the realm of praxis. Like Bickhard, Hooker claims what is needed is a more biological or evolutionary one— in fact, a naturalistic epistemology. (See the articles in Part 1, especially those by Siegel and Brown.)

Karl Pribram is also concerned with a more biological approach to the mind—not so much an evolutionary approach as a more neurological one— and with what current neurology, neuropsychology, and neurobehavioral science have to say about the nature of the mind and the mind–brain connection. In "Neurobehavioral Science, Neuropsychology, and the Philosophy of Mind" he summarizes the contribution of these areas toward an understanding of these traditional metaphysical issues. After discussing various solutions to the mind–brain issue, he argues for a modified dualism, in fact, a *neutral monism*.

Pribram approaches the traditional philosophical issue concerning the nature of the connection between mind and brain from a scientific perspective, that of neuroscience. His contribution illustrates how scientific evidence and empirical discoveries can shed light on what are often taken to be philosophical issues. The contribution of Ben-Ze'ev, on the other hand, adopts a different approach toward understanding the mind, in particular, emotion—a more traditional, philosophical account in which conceptual distinction and clarification predominate. Drawing upon recent work in cognitive psychology, viz., prototype theory, he illustrates some of the main features of "Typical Emotions," thus helping us understand their nature more clearly.

Emotions, like their family relatives, beliefs, desires, intentions, and so on, make up the furniture of the mind, at least according to the standard or commonsense theory of the mind: *folk-psychology*. Folk-psychology is the theory of mind of the ordinary, nontutored person on the street. In understanding his behavior and the behavior of others, the ordinary person employs a set of cognitive concepts (e.g., belief and desire) and a set of principles (e.g., if a person desires a certain end, then ceteris paribus, he will do whatever he believes necessary to reach that end). According to some cognitive scientists (e.g., Fodor, 1981), folk-psychology provides an initially adequate account of the basic features of the mind, e.g., beliefs and desires are propositional attitudes, which are ineliminable. Other cognitive scientists (e.g., Churchland, 1989) deny the reality of such entities and argue for the elimination and replacement of folk-psychology by a more respectable scientific approach. Still other cognitive scientists (e.g., Dennett, 1978) argue for an intermediate position, neither realism nor elimination, but "instrumentalism" in which it is useful for predictive and explanatory purposes to ascribe such states to others.

In the symposium on folk-psychology included here ("Folk Psychology and its Implications for Psychological Science"), several philosophers and psychologists examine the nature of folk-psychology and its implications for psychology. Since the introduction to the symposium by U. T. Place summarizes the respective contributions, which consists of several distinct conceptual interpretations of folk-psychology, the reader is referred to that discussion. The symposium closes with a discussion of the overall contributions and their significance for cognitive psychology. This interesting and informative symposium clearly illustrates the ineluctable and variegated connections between psychology and philosophy.

ENDNOTE

1. Although there was a revolution in the kinds of theories advanced by psychologists, it is less clear that there has been a fundamental shift in the methodology employed.

REFERENCES

Churchland, P. M. (1989). *A neurocomputational perspective: The nature of mind and the structure of science*. Cambridge, MA: M.I.T. Press.

Dennett, D. C. (1978). *Brainstorms: Philosophical essays on mind and psychology*. Cambridge, MA: M.I.T. Press.

Fodor, J. (1981). *Representations: Philosophical essays on the foundations of cognitive science*. Cambridge, MA: M.I.T. Press.

Haugeland, J. (1985). *Artificial intelligence: The very idea*. Cambridge, MA: M.I.T. Press.

Koch, S. (Ed.). (1959). *Psychology: A study of a science* (6 Vols.). New York: McGraw-Hill.

Marx, M. (Ed.). (1963). *Theories in contemporary psychology*. New York: Macmillan.

Newell, A., & Simon, H. A. (1981). Computer science as empirical inquiry: Symbols and search. In J. Haugeland (Ed.), *Mind design* (pp. 35–66). Cambridge, MA: M.I.T. Press. (Original work published 1976)

Sterelny, K. (1990). *The representational theory of mind*. Oxford: Blackwell's.

Turner, M. B. (1967). *Philosophy and the science of behavior*. New York: Appleton-Century-Crofts.

CHAPTER 12

COMPUTATIONAL THEORIES OF COGNITION*

Herbert A. Simon

In the late 1950s, the hypothesis was advanced that human thinking is information processing, alias symbol manipulation. Like most new ideas, this one had many harbingers, especially those collected under the general rubric of cybernetics. Allen Newell and I gave some account of these precursors in the historical addendum to our *Human Problem Solving* (1972). What was new, beginning about 1956, was the translation of these ideas into symbolic (nonnumerical) computer programs that simulated human mental activity at the symbolic level. The traces of these programs could be compared in some detail with data that tracked the actual paths of human thought (especially verbal protocols) in a variety of intellectual tasks, and the

programs' veracity as theories of human thinking could thereby be tested.

Thus the digital computer provided both a means (programs) for stating precise theories of cognition and a means (simulation, using these programs) for testing the degree of correspondence between the predictions of theory and actual human behavior. Prominent early examples of programs that were successful in matching substantial ranges of human behavior included EPAM, a program that simulates human perception and learning, and GPS, a program that simulates human problem solving. Over the years, EPAM has steadily expanded the range of tasks it handles, while GPS has been transmuted into Soar, a major step toward the unification of cognitive theories. Both are still very much alive.

Before the information-processing approach could play a substantial role in psychology, it had to overcome a number of deeply entrenched beliefs associated with behaviorism, on the one hand, and with Gestalt psychology, on the other. Behaviorists were suspicious of attempts to theorize about what went on inside the head (although hard-core behaviorism had already been somewhat softened on this

*This research was supported by the National Science Foundation, Grant No. DBS-9121027; and by the Defense Advanced Research Projects Agency, Department of Defense, ARPA Order 3597, monitored by the Air Force Avionics Laboratory under contract F33615-81-K-1539. Reproduction in whole or in part is permitted for any purpose of the United States Government. Approved for public release; distribution unlimited.

dimension by the theories of Tolman and Hull). Gestaltists were opposed to reductionism and to mechanistic accounts of the phenomena that they regarded as "intuitive" and "insightful." There was also a third view, which insisted that "real" explanations of psychological phenomena must be physiological and neural: that there was no room for a level of symbolic theories between behavior and the biological brain. All of these views had to be reconciled with the symbolic one for the latter to gain any great credence.

Finally, in the early years, few psychologists had opportunities for hands-on interaction with computers. For most of them, the computer was a "mechanistic" number-crunching device, a black box occupied by 0–1 bits. It hardly seemed a promising candidate for representing the flexibility, fallibility, and richness of human thought.

The idea was quite novel that *a program was analogous to a system of differential (or difference) equations, hence could express a dynamic theory.* Equally novel was the idea that *computers were not confined to the numerical, but could represent symbols (patterns with denotations) of all kinds.* Thinking aloud was confounded with introspection, hence not regarded as a legitimate source of empirical data. Standard statistical techniques were not of much use for judging the goodness of fit of computer traces to verbal protocols.

THE PHYSICAL SYMBOL SYSTEM HYPOTHESIS

Several decades passed before the foundational ideas of information processing permeated the psychological community and began to replace the established assumptions. In the 1970s the new approach had gained a dominant position in cognitive psychology. Even then, there were many more psychologists who, while accepting the greater freedom in experimentation and theorizing that accompanied the revolution, were less than enraptured by the "computer metaphor," as it was often called, or the validity of verbal protocols as data. Most research in cognition continued to use conventional experimental methods and designs and most theories continued to be expressed in loose verbal terms.

It was only after many psychologists began to interact with personal computers, thereby acquiring a more sophisticated picture of what a computer is, that appreciation grew for the idea of a computer program as a theory, or for the idea of testing theories by comparing computer outputs with human verbalizations. Nor has the view of information processing psychology that I have sketched above permeated the whole profession even today. Those of us who regard computer programs as "theories" rather than 'metaphors' are probably still in the minority. "*Weak* AI," as the metaphoric view is sometimes called, still probably has more advocates than "*strong* AI."

The basic assumption that underlies the strong view is the physical symbol system hypothesis, which Allen Newell and I set forth in our 1975 ACM Turing Award Lecture (Newell & Simon, 1976):

> A physical symbol system has the necessary and sufficient means for general intelligent action.

A *physical symbol system* (PSS) is a system that has the capacities of a modern digital computer: to input and output symbols, organize and reorganize them in symbol structures, store and erase them, compare them for identity or difference, and behave contingently on the outcome of such comparisons. *Symbols* in a PSS are simply patterns of any kind (and made of anything) that *point* to or *denote* something other than themselves. It should be emphasized that there is no assumption that the symbols in a PSS are in any sense verbal—they can be patterns of *any* kind: verbal, pictorial, abstract, neural. In the human brain, such patterns sometimes are and sometimes are not accessible to conscious awareness. They may denote other symbols in the brain or external objects or configurations.

The PSS hypothesis makes two empirical claims:

1. that a PSS can be programmed to behave intelligently;
2. that human beings are intelligent by virtue of being physical symbol systems; their intelligent behavior is to be explained in terms of symbols and symbol processes.

It is easy to see the connection between these claims and the "strong" version of information processing psychology: Because the symbolic processes that account for human intelligence are all available to computers, we can write computer programs that produce intelligent behavior using processes that track closely the processes of human intelligence. These programs, which predict each successive step in behavior as a function of the current state of the memories together with the current inputs, are theories, quite analogous to the differential equation systems of the physical sciences. To test these theories, we need moment-by-moment data on human thought processes; the finest-grained data of this sort currently available are verbal thinking-aloud protocols.

During the first several decades of information processing psychology, the thought processes hypothesized were predominately *serial*, one-at-a-time, processes. In recent years, there has been a growing interest in *parallel* systems as an alternative architecture. My personal view is that there is a large place for both in the working of the brain; but a final determination of the respective roles of serial and parallel processing in human thinking lies in the future, and I will not discuss the issue in this chapter.

Accompanying the interest in parallel architectures, the popularity has increased of systems that try to incorporate at least some of the neural organization of the human brain. These *connectionist* systems forego a purely symbolic level of theorizing in favor of representing cognitive activities directly by a network whose elements are somewhat nervelike in character. The "neurons" may be quite abstract, as in most connectionist systems (Rumelhart & McClelland, 1986), or they may attempt to capture more of the physico–chemical properties of actual neurons. In either case, these systems tend to return to an older tradition that sees no need for a symbolic level of theorizing above the neurological level. Until such time as the connectionist and other network models are able to handle a range of complex cognitive tasks comparable to those already explained by the symbol-level theories, there does not seem to be much point in trying to resolve this issue.

There is also some disagreement as to whether connectionist and neural-network systems are to be regarded as symbolic (as PSS's). Having discussed this question elsewhere (Vera & Simon, 1994), I will not take it up here.

The body of empirical evidence in support of the PSS as a theory of human cognition (in the first of the variant forms I have described) is by now very large. One can get a general picture of it from such sources as Newell and Simon (1972), Anderson (1983), Simon (1979, 1989), Langley et al. (1987), and Newell (1990). The successful applications of the theory range all the way from classical learning experiments, to problem solving, concept attainment, learning from examples, understanding written instructions, learning natural language (Siklossy, 1972), free recall, chess playing, visual perception, mental imagery, and scientific discovery. The references cited above are only a sample, and they exclude the numerous intelligent systems in AI that are not claimed to simulate human processes.

I sometimes find it surprising (and not a little frustrating) that this empirical literature is so seldom cited, and even less frequently examined in any detail, in discussions of the validity of the PSS hypothesis. There appears still to be a widespread belief that the nature of human thought processes can be determined from *first principles* without examining human behavior in painstaking detail and comparing that behavior with the claims of rigorous theories. I will try to avoid that mistake in the remainder of this paper; when I make empirical claims, I will refer to the relevant empirical research.

PHILOSOPHICAL IMPORT OF THE PSS

Before turning to more empirical matters, I should like to comment on the implications of the physical symbol system hypothesis for some classical topics in philosophy. The first of these is epistemology. The second is the mind–body problem.

Epistemology for Computers

Epistemology is concerned with the question of how, since we live, so to speak, inside our heads, we acquire knowledge of what there is outside our heads. Idealism ducks the question by locating everything of interest inside the head, thereby avoiding any problem of transport. Empiricism, in any of its forms, lacks this escape. Quine, in *Word and Object* (1960), abandoned the attempt to find out how *I* (Quine) know, and asked instead how *he* (a native informant) knows. Then everything was outside the head—at least Quine's head—and the difficulties of dealing with sensation and perception did not have to be faced. But they were replaced by the difficulty that the inside of the native informant's head was almost as inaccessible to Quine as the world outside his own (Quine's) head. The native informant's behavior, including his verbal behavior, was the only clue to what was going on inside his head.

As early as 1955, Rudolf Carnap (1956) had a suggestion for removing this problem. His idea was to employ an (intelligent) computer as the native informant. To determine what the computer knows and how it came to know it, one has access not only to its behavior (outputs) but also, in any desired detail, to its inner workings and the successive states of its memory. One can use these data to construct a wholly empirical theory of *how it comes to know*, and *what its knowledge consists in*—an epistemology for computers. Today, we can actually carry out this enterprise, and in a recent paper (Simon, 1992) 1 sketched out how the concept of *analyticity* might be explicated by this means.

But I can provide even more concrete evidence for the feasibility of this kind of exploration in epistemology. Humans progress from a state of innocence to a state in which they have some command of a natural language and the ability to use language to understand and communicate denotations relating to the world outside the user's head. The task of *acquiring a language* has appeared to some to be so difficult that they have postulated an innate "language capacity" to account for such acquisition. This avoids, at least in part, the necessity for solving the epistemological problem—in this view, it was solved before birth.

However, if we could build a computer program that, starting as a neonate, actually used its eyes, ears, and brain to acquire natural language, it would inform us about the preconditions for such an achievement—what a "language capacity" would consist of. If the program matched early language learning in humans, then it would provide an answer to that part, at least, of the epistemological question of how we know.

In the late 1960s, Laurent Siklossy built such a program (Siklossy, 1972), which consequently is at least a first approximation to an empirical theory of human language learning. The program is called ZBIE (which is not an acronym for anything). ZBIE demonstrably can learn at least the simpler parts of the vocabulary, syntax and semantics of whatever language it is exposed to, and has been tested with English, German, French, and Russian.

Siklossy assumes that the child is born with, or has acquired by the age when language learning begins, the ability to build symbol structures in memory ("mental pictures") of simple situations that appear before its eyes: the family dog chasing the family cat, say. This situation would be held in memory as a symbol structure consisting of two patterns corresponding to the objects (the cat and the dog) embedded in a larger pattern corresponding to the relation (chasing) that connects them. These structures are symbols, whose *denotation* is the external scene. They are built up in memory by sensory and perceptual processes that have no linguistic content, but are best regarded as "pictorial." They correspond to the ability that children have, before they begin to acquire language, of recognizing common objects and situations when they see them.

Now encoded situations are presented to Siklossy's system paired with sentences in the language to be learned. *The sentences are intended to denote the corresponding situations.* Thus, ZBIE would be given, with the symbol structure denoting that the dog is chasing the cat, the sentence: THE DOG CHASES THE CAT. After a series of such paired stimuli have been presented, ZBIE will have stored in memory (a) a net capable of recognizing the various objects it has encountered and the various situations (relations) in which they are found, (b) a similar net capable of recognizing the English words it has encountered, (c) structures that capture the rules for organizing words of various kinds into grammatical sentences, and (d) links that match words with the objects and relations that they denote.

Suppose, for example, that ZBIE has assimilated DOG, CAT, BOY, GIRL, PETS, CHASES, SEES, and so on, and also such scenes as the dog chasing the cat, the girl chasing the boy, and the boy petting the dog, together with sentences denoting those scenes. Now a new scene, never before encountered by ZBIE, is presented: the girl petting the cat. On request, ZBIE will produce the sentence, THE GIRL PETS THE CAT. Thus ZBIE satisfies Chomsky's first requirement for a learner or user of natural languages: that it be capable of understanding and generating sentences that it has never previously encountered.

For a more complete account of the capabilities and limits of ZBIE see Siklossy's account (1972). Our present interest is in the light that ZBIE throws on the symbolic processes that are involved in learning a language. In particular, even this simple example serves as a refutation of Searle's (1984) "Chinese Room" argument, that computers can't understand language. In-principle "impossibility" must yield to in-fact realization. Unlike the system of Searle's Chinese room, *ZBIE possesses links between its words and the outside-world things and relations that they denote.*

ZBIE also leaves some important epistemological questions unanswered. It indicates what kind of semantic information (mental images) would be needed to support language learning, but it does not indicate what sensory and perceptual processes would extract this information from the outside world. This is, of course, a question of great current research interest in artificial intelligence in general and robotics in particular. While it has not been answered in any comprehensive sense, there exist today a number of robotic systems that build internal symbol structures representing external situations: for example, the NAVLAB system that uses its own sensory, interpretive, and motor capabilities to navigate a vehicle at speeds up to about 50 miles per hour on a highway.

So we do possess the kind of in-principle answer that we require for purposes of epistemology. We only need look at NAVLAB to see how useful and veridical mental images of external situations can be acquired and used. This does not imply that NAVLAB's way of doing this resembles the human way in any close sense; what NAVLAB demonstrates is the existence of mechanisms that can build internal representations of the outside world that are usable for guiding action.

The Mind–Body Problem

With a large number of programs in existence capable of many kinds of performances that, in humans, we call thinking, and with detailed evidence that the processes some of these programs use parallel closely the observed human processes, we have in hand a clear-cut answer to the mind–body problem: How can matter think and how are brains related to thoughts?

The PSS hypothesis asserts that the prerequisites to thinking are patterns that can be stored and manipulated. Knowledge resides in the patterning of matter, in combination with processes that can create and operate upon such patterns. *A thought about a cat*, perhaps induced by looking at it or by remembering it, is a *symbol structure* in that part of the brain (probably the frontal lobe) where the "mind's eye" resides. The processes that operate on symbol structures at this site can extract, for example, information about substructures that might

reveal the color of the cat's fur, the length of its whiskers, or the presence or absence of a tail. There is nothing mysterious about all of this, for computers can and do accomplish such processes. If their present capabilities for doing so fall far short of human capabilities the discrepancy does not imply any gap in our knowledge of the fundamental principles involved.

We generally demonstrate our command of the laws of physics by performing very precise but simple laboratory experiments in which we allow only a few things to vary and lock out the rest of the world as best we can. The knowledge of the basic laws we gain by this strategy does not guarantee the predictability, much less constructibility, of more complex phenomena. Meteorologists may be (and frequently are) unable to predict the weather, and are even more frequently unable to do anything about it. This does not reduce our confidence that the atmosphere behaves in conformity with the laws of physics. Much confused discussion about artificial intelligence could be eliminated if we applied to it the same rules for evaluating our knowledge as we use in the older sciences.

THE LIMITS OF COMPUTATION

Our discussion of epistemology and the mind–body problem has not touched on one important issue that frequently arises in debates about the validity of the physical symbol system hypothesis. Even if it were granted that certain human activities usually regarded as entailing thought can be *simulated* by computer, perhaps there are other, qualitatively different, activities that cannot. Cognitive simulation is sometimes claimed to work only for "toy problems" (e.g., puzzles), or "laboratory problems" divorced from the everyday world, or "well-structured" problems that do not capture the vagueness of the situations that professionals must handle. Surely our examples drawn from language learning and robotic perception go well beyond these limits, but no matter: They do not guarantee that we have covered the full territory of human thinking. There may be forms of thinking qualitatively different from those that have been simulated.

There are at least two different lines of argument that claim to show that computer simulation cannot capture human thinking in all of its forms. The first objection is that the computer is too mechanistic and "rational." The computer cannot make mistakes ("creative" or otherwise) as people do and cannot think along the "nonlinear" paths that humans can follow, and which sometimes lead to their best ideas.

The second objection (really three related objections) is that computers are incapable of "intuitive," "insightful," or "creative" thinking. The two sets of objections are not wholly unrelated, but as they do raise somewhat different questions we will take them up in turn.

Is Computation Mechanistic and Logical?

By any reasonable definition of "mechanism," the computer is a mechanism. But most biologists and probably most cognitive psychologists would agree that the brain is also. If by a mechanism we mean a *system whose behavior at a point in time is determined by its current internal state combined with the influences that simultaneously impinge upon it from outside*, then any system that can be studied by the methods of science is a mechanism.

But the term "mechanism" is also used in a narrower sense to refer to *systems that have the relatively fixed, routine, repetitive behavior of most of the machines we see around us*. Any signs of spontaneity exhibited by our toaster, our washing machine, our automobile, or the factory's machine tools are to be attributed to our actions upon them (or, in more recent times, the actions of a computer that controls them).

Clearly the computer occupies an ambiguous position here. Its behavior is more complex, by orders of magnitude, than any machine we have known; and not infrequently it surprises us, even when it is executing a program that we wrote. Yet, as the saying goes, "it only does what you program it to do." But truism though that saying appears to be, it is misleading on two counts. It is misleading, first, because it is often interpreted to mean: "It only does what you believe you programmed it to do," which is distinctly not the case.

More serious, it is misleading because it begs the question of whether computers and people are different. They are different (on this dimension) only if people behave differently from the way they are programmed to behave. But if we include in "program" the whole state of human memory, then to assert that people "don't do only what they are programmed to do" is equivalent to asserting that peo-

ple's brains are not mechanisms, hence not explainable by the methods of science. It is not computer simulation that is at stake, but the possibility of explaining behavior at all.

It is best that we put aside the treacherous terms "machine" and "mechanical" and ask more directly in what sense a programmed system can exhibit spontaneity. By "spontaneity" we denote behavior that is unpredicted, perhaps even by the behaving system. Because we have very limited capacity to predict, for more than the shortest intervals, our responses to our thoughts, much less our responses to processes that are going on subconsciously in our minds, it is not surprising that we view our behavior as having large elements of spontaneity. Nor, considering the limited knowledge others have of our mental states, is it surprising that our behavior appears even more spontaneous to them.

But we can say the same of computers. If the computer is controlled by a program of any great complexity in a problem-solving task, we are unlikely to be able to predict much about what it will do next. Many of us have had the experience of playing against a chess program and addressing it in increasingly anthropomorphic terms as it surprises and threatens us by its responses to our moves. Computers only behave "mechanistically" when they are performing dull, number-crunching tasks like inverting matrices or solving partial differential equations. Then we may be able to detect the repetitive cycles in their work. In tasks of the kinds that are problematic for people, their behavior is much less simply patterned.

We must also take into account spontaneity in both the short and the long runs. In the long run, people can learn: They can change their programs. *But of course computers can also learn.* The EPAM program discriminates among objects by sorting them down through a net, testing them at each step to send them down different branches. EPAM has other processes that allow it to expand the net when it discovers that it has sorted something incorrectly (two different stimuli, say, to the same node). With the expanded net, it now discriminates differently (and presumably more finely) than it did before. It has learned.

Many learning mechanisms, some of them modeled on human learning processes as EPAM's is, have been incorporated in computer programs. Among the more interesting from a psychological standpoint are *chunking* (combining pieces of information or processes into larger familiar units), and *learning from examples* (modifying programs by examining the steps by which problems are solved and adding new processes to match the steps detected in the examples). Chunking mechanisms provide explanations for the gradual automation of highly practiced human skills, while learning from examples matches processes that have frequently been observed in school situations.

We conclude that computers are capable of the same kinds of spontaneity that people are capable of, and that how much spontaneity they exhibit depends on the task in which they are engaged (as is true of people) and the complexity of the program with which they address the task. To the extent that we succeed in modeling our simulation programs on the behavior of people, computers exhibit the same kinds and degrees of spontaneity as people do in the same tasks.

Similar comments can be made about the *rationality* of computers as compared with people. With care and luck, we can program a computer to add a column of figures or to multiply numbers without error. *If we want to simulate human behavior, we will not do this.* Instead (as has been done in the study of children's arithmetic "bugs"), *we will write programs that will reproduce the kinds of errors our human subjects make*, and thereby provide insight into the flaws (from a logical standpoint) of the human programs.

Let me provide a more subtle example. EPAM has recently been modified to simulate the behavior of a person who had learned (over a period of three years of daily practice!) to recall sequences of 100 numbers read to him at a rate of one digit per second. The human subject only succeeded on about half the lists; on the others he made one or two errors. To simulate the human expert, we had to construct and test a theory of the source of the human errors and match them in EPAM's performance. Furthermore, we had to incorporate the error sources in EPAM's program in such a way that EPAM would continue to match human behavior in the numerous other task environments in which it had previously been tested (Richman, Staszewski, and Simon, 1995). The goal was not to improve EPAM's performance but to understand and simulate the limits on the human performance.

Viewing the question of rationality more generally, *a system is rational to the extent that its behavior is well adapted to reaching its goals without excess time or effort.* Economics has attempted to explain human behavior in markets, with some degree of success, by assuming an impossibly high degree of human rationality (*maximization of expected utility*). The theory works, when it does, because in situations that are not too complex the behavior of an adaptive system will be closely molded by its goals and the shape of the environment it is in.

John Anderson (1990) has undertaken to show that the same process applies to some psychological phenomena. In this case, the learning mechanism is evolution, not thought. Over long periods of time, we would expect evolutionary mechanisms to mold both the behaviors and the structures of organisms so that they will be adaptive to their environments in the light of their goals and needs.

As complexity increases, departures from perfect rationality become more and more apparent, for the organism becomes less able to compute the optimal responses. In very simple environments, we can make good predictions of the behavior of adaptive organisms simply by asking what would be the most appropriate behavior to reach the goals of adaptation. In more complex environments, we need to take account of *the computational limitations of the organism*—the means, innate or learned, it has available for discovering appropriate courses of action. Cognitive psychology has identified limits in the capacity of short-term memory, along with limits on knowledge, as the two most important internal parameters that determine how, and how well, a person will adapt to a complex environment.

Human behavior is seldom perfectly rational. It is almost always *boundedly rational*, where the limits on its ability to find optimal paths are limits on the knowledge available to it and limits on human ability to compute the consequences of actions. In order to program computers to simulate human behavior in the face of cognitive complexity we must incorporate the same limitations in the computer simulation as we have found operative in humans. If the program is too "logical," if it is not boundedly rational, it will obviously not think as the human subjects do. That would be a failure in our programming, not an intrinsic limit on the capability of computers for simulating human thought.

To produce computer programs that are only boundedly rational is not very hard. If we propose a problem that is very large and that also lacks a simple and clean mathematical structure, it is generally not possible to produce a scheme, even for the most powerful computers, that will find an optimal solution. If we add the condition that the available information is radically incomplete and inaccurate, the boundedness of the rationality is guaranteed.

Deep Blue, the most powerful chess program today, is only boundedly rational; it does not have any way of guaranteeing that it has found the moves that are best in a game-theoretical sense, although its successes in competition with human players show that it generally finds very good moves (better moves than most human players can find). If we now limit Deep Blue's computing speed and capacity to a more human level, its rationality becomes even more severely bounded. To simulate human chess play, we try (with moderate success to date) to write programs that compensate for the computing power that is lacking in humans with selective heuristics that make the search more efficient.

The same comment applies to concerns about the "linear thinking" of computers. It is not clear whether the phrase "linear thinking" has any but a metaphoric meaning, but whether it does or not, there is nothing about computers that requires them to think either more or less "linearly" than people. All depends on the program.

Intuition, Insight, Creativity

Human thought, another argument goes, is not simply a matter of search, however selective, through a maze. There are more elegant forms of thought, and these are required in order to discover and formulate problems, to have intuitions about them and gain insights into them. These forms of thought, quite different from those that have been simulated, it is said, come into the picture when people are thinking creatively. A machine, the argument concludes, can only do mechanistic thought, and hence will fail when intuition, insight and creativity are called for.

To investigate these possibilities, we must have definitions of the key terms: terms like "intuition," "insight" and "creativity." If we can provide some criteria for judging when intuition has occurred, insight has been gained or thought has been creative, then we can inquire about the processes that produce such events.

Intuition

We usually recognize the presence of intuition when someone solves a problem quite rapidly ("instantaneously") upon presentation, and especially when he or she cannot give an account of how the solution came about. ("It just suddenly entered my mind.") You speak to your doctor, and after describing a few symptoms, she provides the Latin name of a disease (and perhaps some advice about treatment). You ask how she knows. "It's obvious; any competent doctor would recognize it immediately."

The word "recognize" is the clue. The process of solving problems intuitively is indistinguishable from the process of recognizing a familiar person or object. The recognition is sudden, and we are unable to describe exactly what features of the person or object led to it. Sometimes we make mistakes in recognition (read: "our intuitions are fallible"). It really isn't our friend but a stranger, who doesn't even look much like the friend as he comes closer. Or, the doctor responded with the wrong Latin word: The disease from which we are suffering has a different name, but the two diseases have some symptoms in common.

Our acts of recognition or intuition become more reliable as we become more knowledgeable, more *expert*. Evidence has accumulated over the past twenty years that possession of a large, richly indexed, "encyclopedia" of information about a domain is the key to expertise in that domain, and to having reliable intuitions (recognitions) about problems in the domain. (For some pointers to the extensive literature on this topic see Charness, 1989; and Ericsson & Staszewski, 1989). The index to the encyclopedia consists precisely of the cues that will be recognized when the problems present themselves to the expert. Recognition gives access to the information associated with the cue in memory.

Recognition processes are modeled in detail in the EPAM system, which provides a theory, supported by extensive empirical evidence, of expert behavior (Richman, Staszewski, & Simon, 1995). Recognition processes also play a central role in most expert systems, some of which imitate at least in part the processes of the human experts they were modeled on.

We conclude that no forms of thinking beyond those already modeled in recognition systems like

EPAM are required to account for human intuition, its general reliability in domains of expertise, and its frequent unreliability outside these domains.

Insight

The term "insight" is sometimes used almost synonymously with "intuition." But we also use it to refer to our depth of understanding of a situation, and especially to ways of representing the situation that yield the deeper understanding. Thus Einstein gained a new insight into the problem of relative motion when he realized (recognized?) that to synchronize clocks at different places, signals have to be sent from the one place to the other. This insight, together with his belief that the speed of light would be the same in every reference frame, led him to the Lorentz transformation and the theory of special relativity.

In a recent study, we helped students to understand special relativity by presenting the same word pictures that Einstein presented in his original 1905 paper (Qin & Simon, 1992). By drawing a simple diagram, they were able to compute the time it would take for a ray of light to go from one end of a rod to another and back, for different conditions of the rod's motion. Combining the equations for a moving and a stationary rod, they were able to set up the equation from which the Lorentz equations are derived. Einstein's word pictures (he published no diagrams in his paper!) led them to the insight that enabled them to understand the relation between the time and space coordinates in the two reference frames.

Let us consider a less esoteric example: the mutilated checkerboard, an AI problem first proposed, I believe, by John McCarthy (Kaplan & Simon, 1990). We have a checkerboard, and 32 dominoes, each capable of covering exactly two adjacent squares of the board. Obviously, we can cover the board completely with the dominoes. Now the northwest and southeast squares of the checkerboard are removed. Can we cover the remaining 62 squares with 31 dominoes?

Laboratory subjects given this problem work on it, with growing frustration, for a very long time. They try various coverings, always with no success. Sometimes they work on a simplified 4×4 board (also without success). Occasionally, and almost always after several hours of failure, a subject will notice that the squares left uncovered after

an unsuccessful attempt at covering the board are always the same color—the color opposite to the color of the two squares that were removed. Very frequently, subjects who notice this fact solve the problem within two or three minutes. In their verbal protocols they say: "Oh! The mutilated board has fewer red than black squares. But each domino covers one red and one black square, so it will be impossible to cover more of the one color than of the other. The problem has no solution."

The insight here consists of seeing that only the numbers of squares of each color is important, and not the arrangement of the dominoes on the board. If there are not the same number of each color, than there is no way to cover them with dominoes, which always cover a square of each color. Again, this insight appears to be closely associated with an act of recognition: recognition that each attempted covering leaves two squares of the same color uncovered.

This interpretation can be supported by repeating the experiment with some changes: providing a board with the squares uncolored; providing a board in which alternate squares are labeled "bread" and "butter." The former manipulation removes a cue that can lead to recognizing the lack of equality of colors on the mutilated board. The later manipulation calls attention to the parity of adjoining squares by labels that have no other meaning. As predicted, in the experiment the former manipulation reduces the probability of solving the problem in a given time; the latter increases it.

Kaplan (personal communication) has written a computer program that looks for properties that remain invariant when problem solutions are attempted. It adds such properties to the representations of the objects in the problem (adds color to the description of the dominoes and the squares). Previously, it could only compare total number of squares to be covered with the number of dominoes. Now it compares the number of each color covered by the dominoes with the number of each color on the board, and thereby discovers the impossibility.

An important source of insight in scientific discovery is surprise. Many examples can be cited of major discoveries that began with a surprise (e.g., Roentgen, X-rays; the Curies, radium; Tswett, chromatography; Fleming, penicillin; Krebs, the urea cycle; Faraday, induction of electric current by a moving magnet; and many others). In each case, surprise led to a major insight, but what are the mechanisms of surprise and insight?

Kulkarni built a program, called KEKADA, that plans experimental strategies for attacking scientific problems (Kulkarni & Simon, 1988). Starting with 2 statements (more or less precise) of the goal and the methods of experimentation available, it proposes an experiment. On the basis of the outcome of the experiment, it proposes another, and so on. It forms expectations, on the basis of previous knowledge and experience, about the outcomes of the experiments it proposes. If these expectations are violated, it experiences "surprise," and begins to plan new experiments to delineate the scope of the surprising phenomenon and the mechanisms that might produce it. Using this strategy, it succeeded in simulating Kreb's experimental program for discovering the synthesis path of urea, Faraday's for explaining the production of electric current by a moving magnet, and several others.

The mechanisms that underlie KEKADA's performance are familiar. To the extent that it possesses knowledge about a domain, KEKADA can form expectations about the outcome of experiments. Having formed expectations, it can be surprised if the expectations are disappointed. ("Accidents happen to the prepared mind"—Pasteur.) Using its expert knowledge, it can plan experiments to explicate the surprise. So the insights obtained by following up a surprise again depend on powerful capacities for recognizing familiar cues.

Programs like KEKADA teach an important methodological lesson about research on cognitive processes. Since we cannot put Krebs or Faraday in a laboratory, or even interview them at this date, how can we test whether the processes that the computer program is using resemble the processes they used to make their discoveries? There is certainly no way in which we can test such simulations with the time resolution that is available when we can take verbal protocols.

However, in the cases of Krebs and Faraday, we do have available their laboratory notebooks, which provide a complete listing of the experiments they performed—usually several each day. We can then compare the experiments they carried out with those proposed by KEKADA, matching them both with respect to content and temporal sequence. This gives us a substantial body of data (albeit with a time grain of days rather than min-

utes) for testing the theory. We can also examine the scientists' publications for their (retrospective) accounts of the reasoning they employed; and in the case of Krebs, we also have retrospective interviews that the historian of science, C. L. Holmes, conducted before Krebs's death.

When data of these kinds are available, we can test our models against discoveries of great historical interest and importance. We can have some confidence that if thinking at its most powerful and imaginative requires intuition and insight, then those qualities must be present in the psychological events that led up to such discoveries, and present also in computer programs that simulate these events, if only on a scale of days rather than minutes.

Creativity

Creativity is perhaps an even less precise term than intuition or insight. An action or its product is regarded as creative to the extent that the product has value along some dimension (aesthetic, scientific, economic, etc.) and to the extent that it is novel. Valuable novelty is the mark of creativity. Notice that the criterion refers to the outcome, not to the process. But perhaps there are special processes that are conducive to producing valuable novelty.

In our discussion of the theory of relativity and of the experimental strategies that KEKADA models we have already entered into the province of creativity. It would be rather eccentric to claim that Einstein, Krebs, and Faraday were not creative. But let us look a little farther to see whether other aspects of creativity may have been illuminated by attempts to simulate scientific discovery.

Formulating problems and providing them with effective representations is often mentioned as an important kind of creativity. We have already had at least a glimpse, in the example of the mutilated checkboard, of how new representations might be discovered that would make a difficult problem solvable. Closely related to new representations are *new concepts*. Concepts like momentum, energy, and mass were not simply "there" in nature. They emerge by dint of great human effort (in this instance, the effort of such figures as Descartes, Huygens, and Newton) in response to problems of characterizing real phenomena. What would be required to simulate the discovery of new concepts of these kinds?

We do not have to speculate about the answer to this question, because the BACON program, among others, already has the capability of constructing new theoretical concepts (concepts denoting things that are not directly observable) in the course of building theories to describe data (Langley, et al., 1987). BACON is a data-driven law discovery system. Given some data from experiment or observation, it seeks to find an algebraic law that will describe the data parsimoniously. Given data on the masses and temperatures of two vials of water and the equilibrium temperature when they are mixed together, it arrives at Black's law, which says that the equilibrium temperature is the average of the temperatures of the two component liquids, weighted by their respective masses.

But what if the liquids mixed are different, water and alcohol, say? With a little more trouble, BACON will discover that the equilibrium temperature is still a weighted average of the temperatures of the components, but the weights are now not simply the masses, but the masses multiplied by a characteristic constant for each liquid (say, w for water and a for alcohol). These constants, first discovered by Joseph Black and subsequently and independently by BACON, are known as the *specific heats* of the respective substances.

From this example, we see that the enrichment of a problem representation by the introduction of new concepts can also be simulated. We do not have any very good evidence, as yet, that the processes that BACON uses to accomplish this are close to the processes used by human discoverers, but BACON processes are built on to rather simple heuristics quite similar to the heuristics we have observed humans using in other situations.

IS NATURAL LANGUAGE DIFFERENT?

Almost all of the examples I have provided of the simulation of intuition, insight, and creativity have been drawn from scientific domains. People who are not scientists are sometimes reluctant to believe that these processes occur in such domains, for science is supposed to be orderly and "logical." Those of us who spend our lives in science know better, but perhaps it would be useful to allay doubts by turning to a quite different domain in which people can exhibit their intuition, insight, and creativity. Let me ask how we might go about simulating human thinking in reading a text.

The machinery we would require for this task would obviously include an indexed lexicon (i.e., an EPAM-like memory) and a parser. Parsers we know how to build, although perhaps not at the level of sophistication that some humans attain. In fact, ZBIE has already shown us how (simple) human language learning can be simulated. The more difficult problem would seem to be how we extract meanings from text that is made up of words in our lexicon and that we can parse.

How one extracts meanings from texts, or even whether texts *have* meanings, is a lively topic at the present time in the field of literary criticism. Jerry Hobbs has provided a very convincing answer to the question of what the meanings are. He says (Hobbs, 1990) that the meaning of a text is not a function of a single variable, the text, but of two variables, the text and the mind of the reader, $M = f(T, R)$. If we replace one text with another, we get a different meaning for the same reader; and if we replace one reader with another, we get a different meaning for the same text. I think we have known that for a long time. Texts become heavily laden with culture, not only because the author is embedded in a culture, but also because readers are embedded in the same or other cultures.

We can paint a very rough picture of what is going on in terms of mechanisms we have already considered, in particular, recognition mechanisms and inference mechanisms. Let me illustrate this briefly with the opening passage from one of Camus' short novels, *La Chute*:

> May I Sir, offer you my services without risking being importunate? I fear that you may not know how to make the estimable gorilla who presides over the destinies of this establishment understand you. Indeed, he speaks only Dutch. Unless you allow me to plead your cause, he will not guess that you want gin.

What might recognition evoke from this text? By the third sentence we become aware that we are in the Netherlands, perhaps in Amsterdam. Of course "Amsterdam" can now evoke the whole mass of information we have about that city, and associations with it. "Gin," in turn, cross-references to "bar," defining the milieu and identifying the "gorilla" as a bartender. Other possible connections are more subtle. "Plead your cause" suggests the law, and indeed foreshadows the profession of the speaker. And the word "importunate," applied to the relation of speaker to listener, can lead some readers to the Ancient Mariner.

Moreover, the tone of the passage may evoke in the reader whatever affect is associated in that reader's memory with a courtly (or pretentious?) manner.

We see here a whole series of recognitions evoking associations already stored in memory. Although one idea suggests another, there is very little here that a logician would recognize as "reasoning." That if gin is mentioned, we are in a bar? It would be more accurate to say that bar is *suggested* by gin than that bar is *inferred* from it.

What of the author? What can we say of his mental processes? Without more data than this short passage, only some conjectures. Presumably he began with a goal, perhaps of providing a setting and a mood for the tale he is about to tell. His memory provides him with a concrete description of a particular kind of establishment (very likely he draws from his own experience). He selects from his information store a series of words and phrases that will evoke from the reader the image of a bar, possibly in a lower-class neighborhood. He is counting on these words evoking somewhat the same associations in the reader's mind as are present in his own mind. Either he has some sense of what his readers know or he assumes that their knowledge stores resemble his.

I will not try to carry the analysis further. But perhaps it already suggests that the processes we are observing here, of both reader and writer, are not unlike the processes we have seen in other kinds of thinking, particularly those processes of recognition that we have associated with "intuition" and "insight." Just as we may "trick" a subject into solving the mutilated checkerboard problem by presenting a cue that draws attention to the alternating colors of squares on the board, so Camus "tricks" a reader into assigning personal traits to a speaker by his manner of describing him or reproducing his speech.

A brief, sketchily analyzed example is not a demonstration. But I hope my discussion of the passage from *La Chute* at least raises the possibility that mental activity, quite creative mental activity, outside the sciences may yield to the same analysis as the more thoroughly studied scientific domains that I have drawn upon for my other examples.

CONCLUSION

In this chapter I have explored some of the central characteristics of a computational theory of cognition, and particularly the kind of theory that has been associated with the physical symbol system hypothesis. I have sought to illustrate how a computational model can be used to address epistemological questions in philosophy and the mind–body problem.

My principal focus, however, has been on the claim that human thinking can be represented by such a computational theory. In particular, I have commented upon some of the main objections that have been raised to this claim, especially the concern that computationalism is "mechanistic," and consequently incapable of representing such important kinds of human thought processes as the non-numerical, intuitive, insightful, creative, error-prone and nonlogical. Mainly by pointing to examples of computer simulations of human processes that have actually been constructed and compared with human data, I have undertaken to show that all of these human characteristics can be, and have been, simulated.

It is a truism that the human mind is complex. So is physical and biological nature. Complexity has not prevented physical and biological scientists from identifying many of the main mechanisms that underlie physical and biological processes, even though they can seldom show in detail just how these mechanisms operate in complex real-world settings (e.g., they cannot predict accurately or in detail how the atmosphere produces the world's day-to-day weather, or how the laws of mechanics govern the stability or instability of soil subjected to the shocks of an earthquake).

In the same way, information processing psychology has identified many of the main mechanisms that human beings use to grope their way through a world whose complexity is orders of magnitude too great for their bounded rationality to handle with any exactitude. It cannot predict in any detail how a particular person will handle a particular complex business decision, or how a Cuban missile crisis will be resolved. This does not imply that different mechanisms govern such events than govern the simpler situations in the laboratory. The operation of the mechanisms I have discussed here has been demonstrated in a wide variety of tasks, most but not all of them relatively simple; and there is every reason to suppose that they operate in much the same way in the tasks that have not yet been simulated in detail.

REFERENCES

Anderson, J. R. (1983). *The architecture of complexity.* Cambridge, MA: Harvard University Press.

Anderson, J. R. (1990). *The adaptive character of thought.* Hillsdale, NJ: Erlbaum.

Carnap, R. (1956). *Meaning and necessity.* Chicago, IL: University of Chicago Press.

Charness, N. (1989). Expertise in chess and bridge. In D. Klahr & K. Kotovsky, (Eds.), *Complex information processing.* Hillsdale, NJ: Erlbaum.

Ericsson, K. A., & Staszewski, J. J. (1989). Skilled memory and expertise. In D. Klahr & K. Kotovsky (Eds.), *Complex information processing.* Hillsdale, NJ: Erlbaum.

Hobbs, J. R. (1990). *Literature and cognition.* Stanford, CA: Center for the Study of Language and Information, Stanford University.

Kaplan, C. A., & Simon, H. A. (1990). In search of insight. *Cognitive Psychology, 22,* 374–419.

Kulkarni, D., & Simon, H. A. (1988). The processes of scientific discovery: The strategy of experimentation. *Cognitive Science, 12,* 139–176.

Langley, P., Simon, H. A., Bradshaw, G. L., & Zytkow, J. M. (1987). *Scientific discovery.* Cambridge, MA: MIT Press.

Newell, A. (1990). *Unified theories of cognition.* Cambridge, MA: Harvard University Press.

Newell, A., & Simon, H. A. (1972). *Human problem solving.* Englewood Cliffs, NJ: Prentice-Hall.

Newell, A., & Simon, H. A. (1976). Computer science as empirical inquiry: Symbols and search. *Communications of the ACM, 19,* 113–126.

Qin, Y., & Simon, H. A. (1992). Imagery as process representation in problem solving. Proceedings of the 14th Annual Conference of the Cognitive Science Society, July 29–August 1, 1992.

Quine, W. V. (1960). *Word and object.* Cambridge, MA: Harvard University Press.

Richman, H. B., Staszewski, J. J., & Simon, H. A. (1995). Simulation of expert memory using EPAM IV. *Psychological Review, 102,* 305–330..

Rumelhart, D. E., & McClelland, J. L. (1986). *Parallel distributed processing.* Cambridge, MA: MIT Press.

Searle, J. R. (1984). *Minds, brains, and science.* Cambridge, MA: Harvard University Press.

Siklossy, L. (1972). Natural language learning by computers. In H. A. Simon & L. Siklosky (Eds.), *Representation and meaning.* Englewood Cliffs, NJ: Prentice-Hall.

Simon, H. A. (1979, 1989). *Models of thought* (Vol. 1 and 2). New Haven, CT: Yale University Press.

Simon, H. A. (1992). The computer as a laboratory for epistemology. In L. Burkholder (Ed.), *Philosophy and the computer.* Boulder, CO: Westview Press.

Vera, A., & Simon, H. A. (1994). Reply to Touretsky and Pomerleau: Reconstructing physical symbol systems. *Cognitive Science, 18,* 355–360.

CHAPTER 13

TROUBLES WITH COMPUTATIONALISM

Mark H. Bickhard

COMPUTATIONALISM

Computationalism is the dominant contemporary approach to cognitive phenomena: phenomena of perception, cognition, reasoning, language—any mental phenomena that involve representation. Computationalism permeates the intertwined fields of cognitive science, cognitive psychology, and artificial intelligence. It grew out of cybernetics and computer studies during the 1950s and '60s.

Computers were originally thought of as very fast and powerful calculators. It came to be realized, however, that there is nothing in the functioning of a computer that restricted its domain to calculations and other manipulations of numbers. The electrical patterns that corresponded to numbers in computers could just as easily be taken to represent characters—or tables, chairs, propositions, perceptual features, grammatical structures, and so on. During the 1960s, this move to a conception of computers as "symbol manipulators" rather than "number crunchers" became ascendant, and has remained so. The range of representation that has been thought to be capturable in such computer symbols has seemed limited only by the ingenuity of the designers.

The backbone of the computational approach to cognition is the presumption that symbolically encoded information flows from perception to cognition and from cognition to language. Perception is presumed to begin with the encoding of various sorts of limited and proximal information, such as light patterns and motions in the visual system. That initial limited information in proximal sensations is then enhanced in unconscious inferences about the organization of the layout of surfaces and edges—floors, walls, tables, etc.—and colors and so on (again in the visual system). Such perceptual encodings, in turn, serve as the foundation for the learning of symbolically encoded concepts and other more abstract representations, and help guide the cognitive manipulation of such symbols in reasoning. Further, such internal organizations and manipulations of symbols can themselves be re-encoded into linguistic form and uttered or written for the recipients to decode into their own internal symbols. Decoded, they constitute an understanding of the utterances or sentences. Sensations of color, form, and shape, for example, might generate the perception of a lion, which, in turn, guides reasoning to the conclusion that there is danger, and further initiates both the activity of running and vocalizations that, among other things, re-encode the mental symbol for "lion" into sound patterns to warn others of the danger. Connected to this cognitive backbone are many other phenomena, such as memory, motivation, emotions, and so on, all of which also involve representation, and all of which are assumed to therefore involve manipulations of encoded symbols.

Since the early '80s, a major rival has challenged computationalism in its classical form. This rival is known as connectionism, or parallel distributed processing (PDP). Connectionist systems consist of multiple nodes, usually in layers, and usually with the first layer directly connected to an environment. The nodes are connected, from each node in one layer to nodes in the next layer, by weighted lines. Activation is received from the environment and passed along the weighted connections to other nodes in accordance with the various weights. Each node, then, adjusts its own level of activation in accordance with the activations received along its incoming connections, adjusted by the weights on those connections, and in accordance with some internal function for collecting and combining those activations. Then each node, in the next step, transmits its own level of activation along its outgoing connections to the next layer of nodes, where the process repeats.

Connectionist nets can be trained by various alterations of the weights connecting node to node in response to feedback from sets of training instances. In particular, they can be trained to generate particular patterns of final layer activations in response to various categories of patterns of input activations. That is, connectionist nets can be trained to differentiate input patterns into categories. This capacity, and the ability to train this capacity, has generated enormous excitement in a large community of cognitive scientists. The final activation patterns are taken to be representations of the classes of input patterns that would generate them, and, on this interpretation, connectionist nets can learn new representations. There are many additional properties of these distributed patterns of activation that are proposed as advantages of the connectionist approach, and many variations on the

basic theme of input patterns classified into final layer patterns. Some net designs, for example, don't simply settle into some final layer activation pattern, but, instead, move into some classifying trajectory or cycle of changes in activation patterns, perhaps shifting among them in response to subsequent inputs. Heated arguments have been waged concerning the relative advantages and disadvantages of the two approaches.

The differences between standard computationalism and connectionism are many and important for a variety of reasons. But with respect to the basic critique that will be made of computationalism, there is no significant difference between the two—they both make the same basic assumptions, and they are both vulnerable to the same criticisms.

Between the two of them, computationalism and connectionism dominate contemporary cognitive science and related disciplines in the '90s. In spite of that, I wish to argue that both computationalism and connectionism are in serious trouble—fatal trouble, in fact. The problem lies in a ubiquitous presupposition about the nature of representation—the nature of those representational elements (or activation patterns)—a presupposition that is at root logically incoherent. I will present a central part of this critique and adumbrate an alternative approach to representation that avoids this incoherence. And I will point out how the basic argument against standard conceptions of representation holds just as strongly against connectionist and PDP approaches: For all their differences, the approaches hold precisely the same assumptions— incoherent assumptions—about the nature of representation.

ENCODINGIST APPROACHES TO REPRESENTATION

Throughout history, representation has been assumed to be some sort of correspondence between a representing element or structure and that which is to be represented, and, crucially, the representational relationship is assumed to be constituted in those correspondence relationships. It is universally recognized that not just any correspondence will do. There are myriads of factual correspondences in the universe, and most of them are not representational. The focus, then, is on what *sort* of correspondences are representational.

Various problems with this approach have been uncovered, and more are discovered periodically, but the assumption that "correspondences" is the correct genus within which to differentiate representation is still ubiquitous (Anderson, 1983; Fodor, 1990; Newell, 1980; Palmer, 1978; Smith, 1987). Each new problem generates new activity to find a fix—a further or a different constraint on correspondence that will capture all and only the real representations.

I hold that some of these problems are simply unsolvable from within this approach—they are among the multifold manifestations of the underlying logical incoherence. Others of these problems are simply red herrings—they appear to be problems *only* because representation is being approached as a kind of correspondence, and they cease to be problematic on the alternative that I offer (Bickhard, 1993).

Encodings and Encodingism

There *is*, in fact, a class of genuine representations that are constituted as correspondences: encodings. It is, in part, this genuine subclass that has produced so much confusion about representation and maintained the impression that all representation could be of the same sort—that all representation could be encoding correspondences. It is from this class of representations that I derive one of the general names for the approach that I wish to criticize. Approaches that presuppose that all representations are encodings, I call *encodingism*.

The arguments against encodingism form a rather large family, with some of them having ancient provenance and new ones being discovered even quite recently. I will outline only a few of these arguments. One convenient entree into this family is via the characterization of genuine encodings, and the demonstration that *that* kind of representation *cannot* be the general form. It is precisely the presupposition that it *can* be the general form that yields the logical incoherence.

So, I begin with a clear and obvious case of encodings: Morse code. Morse consists of a set of stand-in relationships between sequences of dots and dashes, on the one hand, and characters and numerals, on the other hand. For example, "..." stands in for the character "S". Such stand-ins are useful because, in this case, dots and dashes can be sent over telegraph wires, while characters and numerals cannot. The stand-ins of Morse code

serve to change the form and the medium of the representational contents of characters and numerals so that things can be done with them, such as telegraph transmission, that could not be done otherwise. Similarly, bit pattern encodings allow myriads of extremely fast manipulations in computers.

Encoding stand-ins carry representational content—they carry the same content as that which they stand in for. The stand-in relationship, in fact, is a relationship of "borrowing" the representational content of whatever is being stood in for. So, "..." represents the same thing as, performs the same representational functions as "S". Representational content is a functional notion; it is whatever serves the function of specifying what is supposed to be represented by some representation.

There are several essential aspects and prerequisites of such encodings that are relevant for this discussion. First, an encoding stand-in correspondence relationship must be defined. This requires that the element that is to be the stand-in and the element that is to be stood in for must be both specifiable—in this case, both "..." and "S". Second, in order for the stand-in to carry representational content, the stood-in-for must carry representational content: The encoding carries representational content only insofar as it borrows it from the stood-in-for.

It follows that such stand-in relationships cannot be defined with elements (properties, events, etc.) that are themselves unspecifiable, and that an encoding stand-in can only borrow representational content that is already available (from the stood-in-for). In particular, encodings cannot create *new* representational content. They can only borrow and combine representational content that is already extant.

These prerequisites are not a problem for genuine encodings, such as Morse code, precisely because genuine encodings are explicitly defined in terms of stand-in correspondence relationships with representational elements that are already available. The prerequisites are a problem, however, for any assumption that encodings could serve basic *epistemological* functions, such as in perception or cognition: the fundamental epistemological problem is to create new knowledge, new representation, and encodings can only borrow representational content that is already there.

It might seem that there could be some way in which encodings could generate or constitute new representational content. In fact, if it is assumed that representation *must* be some form of encodings—what else is there?—then it appears that there *has* to be some way in which encodings can generate new representational content, and the problem seems to be one of discovering a model that can account for that. This is the standard framework of assumptions in cognitive science, artificial intelligence, philosophy of mind and language, and so on. It is the assumption underlying computationalism and connectionism alike. And most of the work that concerns itself with this level of problem at all is devoted to attempts to discover such a model. I argue that this task is impossible, and that assumptions or presuppositions that it could ever be completed are incoherent (Bickhard, 1992b, 1993; Bickhard & Richie, 1983).

As outlined, an encoding can be defined in terms of already available representations with no particular logical difficulty. Furthermore, this can be iterated, yielding "X", say, defined in terms of "Y", which is defined in terms of "Z", and so on. But it can only be iterated a finite number of times: There must be some ground, some foundation, of representations in terms of which the combinatoric hierarchy of encoding definitions can begin. It is at the level of this ground that the incoherence emerges of assuming that all representation is encoding.

Incoherence

In particular, if it assumed that such foundational representations are themselves encodings, then there is no way for those encodings to have or to be given any representational content. There is no way, in other words, for those grounding encodings to be representations at all, and, therefore, certainly no way for them to be encodings. But, then, it is impossible for them to ground any hierarchy of encoding definitions, and the entire framework of encodingism collapses into incoherence.

If a purported foundational encoding is defined in terms of any other representation, then it is not foundational, contrary to assumption. But that leaves only that foundational element itself as a source of representational content, yielding something like "'X' stands in for 'X'" or "'X' represents the same thing as 'X'" for "X" that foundational element. This does not suffice to provide any representational content to "X", and, therefore, fails to render "X" an encoding. "X",

therefore, cannot ground any further definitions of encodings, and the framework collapses.

This problem of providing the basic representational contents has not gone unnoticed in the literature. It presents under such terms as "the empty symbol problem," "the symbol grounding problem," and so on (Bickhard & Richie, 1983; Block, 1980; Harnad, 1987). It underlies other positions and arguments, such as the "solution" that proposes that all such grounding representational contents are innate (Fodor, 1981). In that regard, note that the problem is logical, not practical—evolution cannot solve it either. Nativism is not a solution (Bickhard, 1991a; Campbell & Bickhard, 1987).

Note that, as a *logical* problem concerning the origin of representation, this makes representation, considered as encoding, impossible. There is no way for grounding encodings to emerge out of nonrepresentational phenomena. Encodings require prior representations in order to be defined. But presumably there were no representations at the moment of the Big Bang origin of the universe, and there are representations now. Representation has emerged out of nonrepresentation, and, since that is impossible for encodings, encodings cannot be the basic form of representation (Bickhard, 1991a, 1993).

The assumption, nevertheless, is that there *must* be a solution—after all, representation clearly does exist, and what else could there be but encodings?—and work continues. I am proposing that this programmatic approach to representation is logically impossible, and, therefore, that such work is ultimately fruitless.

Encodings are representations by virtue of *defined* correspondences with representations. The general approach assumes that representation can be understood in terms of correspondence (of some sort) with *that which is to be represented*. The problem, as with foundational encodings, is to model how any correspondence could yield representational content of what is to be represented—of what is on the other end of the presumed encoding correspondence.

What Kind of Correspondence?

There is no problem about the *existence* of correspondence. The universe contains myriads of them, of many different kinds: factual, causal, informational, nomological, and so on. All of these have been proposed as candidates for the *special* kind of correspondence that, unlike all the others, yields or constitutes representation at one end of the correspondence about whatever is on the other end of the correspondence. All have failed; some have been abandoned; some are still pursued. To assume that there is some special sort of correspondence with such unique representational power is to assume that there is some special sort of correspondence that carries representational information about its existence and about the other end of the correspondence.

There is, in fact, such a form of correspondence. Morse code is an example. But this form of encoding correspondence, the only genuine form, *presupposes all* of the epistemic issues that computationalism wishes to solve with encodings.

In-Principle Arguments

There is not space to rehearse the numerous attempts that have been made, and that are currently proposed, to find this special form of correspondence—and to recount all of the ways in which they have failed. Programmatic approaches to anything, including to representation, are capable of unbounded variation on the theme, with the continued hope and promise that the next attempt might do it. Only in-principle arguments can show a programmatic approach to be flawed, as in Chomsky's demonstration that *any* model constructed within the strictures of associationism will be necessarily inadequate to the facts of language. I have offered some in-principle arguments against encodingism above—the assumption that encodings can provide their own foundational representational contents is incoherent—and offer many more elsewhere (Bickhard, 1980, 1992b, 1993; Bickhard & Terveen, 1995; Campbell & Bickhard, 1986). Even in-principle arguments, however, are not persuasive if there is no known alternative— "What else could there be?" and maybe the in-principle arguments are wrong.

Tangles of Red-Herrings

Before turning to the conception of representation that I wish to offer as an alternative, however, I will illustrate with one example the sorts of logical and conceptual tangles that can be encountered in attempting to fulfill an encodingist approach to representation. Consider the disjunction problem

(Fodor, 1987, 1990; Loewer & Rey, 1991). This problem arises when it is assumed that the special representation-constituting form of correspondence might be one that arises from a causal connection from the "to be represented" to the "representation by correspondence." Such causal-connection correspondences are a natural possibility to pursue, since one paradigm for the investigation of representation is perception—perception construed as the processing of (and in) causally related chains of inputs from world through sensory transducers to the brain.

How Is Error Possible?

One problem that this approach gives rise to, however, is the problem of the possibility of error. In particular, if the causal relationships—the special form of correspondence relationship—*exist,* then the "to be represented" is *in fact* present and has in fact initiated the proper causal process, and the representational correspondence, therefore, is *necessarily* correct. On the other hand, if any part of this initiation, causal transmission, transduction, processing, or whatever else that is taken to be crucial to the representation-constituting special form of correspondence is absent or deficient, then the special correspondence does *not* exist, and, therefore, the representation doesn't exist. In particular, there is no representation in existence that could be *not correct.* The problem, then, is to explain how representation could even *possibly* be in error, in this view.

The Disjunction Problem

One version of this problem is the disjunction problem. This problem turns on the question of how it can be determined which correspondences are in fact the right correspondences to be constitutive of correct representation, and how they can be distinguished from those that constitute errorful representations. If a "cow" representation is normally evoked by cows, that is its correct and desired function. But if it is evoked by, say, a horse on some dark night, we would like to be able to say that that is an error. The disjunction problem poses the question: How can we avoid the conclusion that what had been taken as a "cow" representation is really a representation of the disjunction "either a cow or a horse on a dark night"?

Note that this is a problem from *within* the basic correspondence framework: *Assuming* that representation equals correspondence (of some sort), how can we distinguish the correspondences that constitute correct representations from those that constitute false representations?

Asymmetric Dependency

One proposed solution to this problem is "asymmetric dependency" (Fodor, 1987, 1990; Loewer & Rey, 1991). The idea of this "solution" is that there is an asymmetric relationship between the correct and the incorrect cases—between cows and horses on dark nights—and that that asymmetry suffices to distinguish them. The proposed asymmetry is one of counterfactual dependence of the *possibility* of the one kind of correspondence relative to the other. In particular, it is claimed that "horse on dark night" correspondences would never occur unless the "cow" correspondences occurred; conversely, "cow" correspondences could very well occur even if the "horse on a dark night" correspondences never did. The idea is that the correct correspondence—with "cow" in this case—is the critical one for the very existence of the (representation-constituting) correspondence relationship in the first place, so any instances of error must be in some sense parasitic on those correct versions.

A number of challenges can be made to this solution. I offer two here. They have the form of counterexamples. First, a transmitter molecule docking on a receptor in a cell surface, and thereby triggering appropriate activities internal to the cell, is an example of a causal chain correspondence (transmitter to internal activity), and, furthermore, a causal chain correspondence that is followed by appropriate functional and evolved functional activity (Bickhard, 1993). Yet, there is at best a functional story to be told here. There is no epistemic relationship between the internal cell activities and the transmitter molecule; the cell doesn't contain a representation of that molecule, nor of the activities of the previous cell that created that molecule, nor the activities that released it, and so on. The asymmetric dependency proposal, in other words, presupposes that *some* correspondence does in fact constitute representation. The transmitter molecule challenges that assumption: How can the genuine representation-constituting correspondence be distinguished from the transmitter correspondence?

One reply might be that representational correspondences are capable of asymmetric dependencies. So, only those that are capable of such asymmetries are representational at all. The asymmetries, in turn, distinguish within those representational correspondences between those that are correct and those that are false. Consider now my second counterexample: A poison molecule mimics that transmitter molecule, docks on the cell surface receptor, and inappropriately triggers those internal cell activities. Here is also a correspondence. Furthermore, it is a type of correspondence that is asymmetrically dependent on that of the transmitter molecule: The transmitter correspondences could exist quite nicely even if the poison correspondences never did, or never could, but the poison correspondences are *only* possible because of the transmitter correspondences. Yet, here again, we have only a functional story. Just as there is no representation in the cell that accepts that transmitter molecule, there is no *false* representation in the cell that accepts the poison molecule. The asymmetric dependency relationship captures at best a functional asymmetry, and it can be modeled at a strictly functional level. It suffices neither to characterize true representation from false representation, nor representational correspondence from nonrepresentational correspondence (Bickhard, 1993).

More Tangle

The disjunction problem and its asymmetric dependency proposal as a solution is but one of many problems about and within the encodingist framework. A sampling of others: How could we check our encodings for correctness, if we can only check them against themselves? We have no other access to what they are supposed to represent other than those encodings per se. How could we ever construct our encoding copies of the world without already knowing the world that we are attempting to copy? If we cannot encounter error in our checking of encodings, how can we ever control learning processes? Any element in correspondence with something in the world will necessarily also be in correspondence with thousands of other things in the world—not just the chair, but also the light patterns, activities in the retina, electron orbital activities in the surface of the chair, the motion that placed the chair at that position, the construction of the chair, etc.—which of these correspondences is the representational one? As mentioned above, how could representation come into being out of nonrepresentation in the history of the universe? And on and on (Bickhard, 1991a, 1992b, 1993; Bickhard & Terveen, 1995). None of these are solvable or resolvable from within the encodingist approach.

Part of the reason for rehearsing this problem and the purported solution and failure of that purported solution—and mentioning the host of additional problems—is to illustrate how tangled these investigations can be and to give some sense of how easy it can be to become lost in these tangles—looking for a way around this tiny barrier or looking for how to fill that small hole in the argument. A second reason for this overview of the disjunction problem and asymmetric dependency proposal is to illustrate that many, perhaps most, of the problems that occupy the efforts of work within the encodingist, representation as correspondence, approaches are simply red herrings (Bickhard, 1993). They are problematic *only* because of the approach taken, and do not offer fundamental problems for the alternative approach that I suggest. In particular, the possibility of "being in error" is trivially present for the model of representation that I urge. I turn to it now.

INTERACTIVISM

The alternative model of representation is called interactivism. Interactivism models representation, and representational content, as particular properties of systems that interact with their environments, rather than as particular kinds of correspondences. By beginning with a fundamentally different framework, interactivism simply never encounters most of the problems of encodingism.

Differentiation and Implicit Definition

Consider a system interacting with an environment. In part, the internal processes of the system that participate in that interaction will depend on the functional organization of the system that is engaged in the interaction. In part, however, the internal processes and the course of those internal processes will depend on the environment being interacted with. Similarly, the internal condition

that the system is in when that interaction has ended—when that subsystem ceases its processing, for example—will depend in part on the environment with which the interaction occurred. If there are two or more possible such internal conditions that the system could end up in—two or more possible final states of the interactive subsystem— then those states will serve to differentiate classes of possible environments, and the particular final state of a particular interaction will differentiate the particular environment that the interaction was with. So, if the subsystem ends up in final state "A", say, then it has encountered the type of environment that yields final state "A" when engaged in interaction, and similarly for final state "B". In effect, the possible final states implicitly define the classes of environments that would yield them, and actual interactions classify environments among those implicitly defined classes.

It is important to note that the differentiations involved here do not create nor constitute any representational content about the environments, or classes of environments, other than their property of yielding this final state rather than that final state. In particular, no such interactive differentiator could generate encodings, because there is no representational content about the environments differentiated.

Nevertheless, there will be some *factual* properties of environments that underlie their tendency to yield some final state, and a differentiation will, therefore, generate a *factual* correspondence with whatever those factual properties may be. That is, an interactive differentiator will create *precisely* the sort of correspondences that are classically taken to be constitutive of encoding representations. This is even more obvious in the case of an interactive differentiator that is simplified to the point of having no outputs—a differentiation based entirely on the processing of inputs, such as in sensory "transduction" (or connectionist "pattern recognition"). The same point holds: Such processing can be sufficient to differentiate categories of possible environments (or input patterns)—those that yield this internal outcome rather than that internal outcome—but they do not and cannot yield any representation about those (categories of) environments. The differentiations are open as to what is in fact being differentiated; the definitions of the categories are implicit, not explicit.

Interactive differentiators, then, model what is standardly construed as encodings. But the interactive model makes no claims that these correspondences somehow magically constitute representations of what has been differentiated. That, of course, raises the next question: How does the interactive model account for representational content?

Representational Content

Consider an interactive differentiator subsystem in the context of its broader system. It might be useful for that broader system to make use of the final states generated by the subsystem in determining the future course of overall system interactive activity. If, for example, the subsystem generated final state "A", that might indicate that, among other things, subsystem "S2" would, if engaged in interaction, yield final state "Q", and that subsystem "S22" would yield final state "R". Such final states can be constituted as functional or biological conditions in the system that could be sought in a goal-directed sense by that system, so the possible final states that could be indicated as possibilities by an initial final state "A"—upon appropriate intermediate further interaction, such as "S22"—potentially play an important role in the system satisfying its goals. Final state "A", for example, might be the outcome of a visual scan that internally indicates, among other possibilities, that, if a certain further interaction were engaged in, "S22", a further final state, "R", of raised blood sugar would be reached. If raising blood sugar is an active homeostatic goal, then that possibility might be selected as a next activity of the system.

The general point is that internal system indications of what further interactions would be *possible* for the system to engage in, and what further possibilities would follow if they *were* engaged in them, can be useful to the system. We should expect, in fact, potentially quite complex organizations of such indications of potentiality, which would yield further potentialities, which would yield still further potentialities, and so on, in complex interactive systems such as living systems.

The model to this point is strictly functional. No claims have yet been made concerning representation or representational content. In fact, a typical move of claiming representation for input processing correspondences has been explicitly eschewed. Nevertheless, the model does now contain a functional property that emergently constitutes representation. This is representation in a most minimal sense, but representation nevertheless.

The minimal property of representation is that of the possibility of being *false* from the perspective of the system itself and the possibility of being *falsified* by the system itself; more generally, the possibility of having some truth value for the system itself. The caveat concerning "the system itself" derives from the common practice of attempting such analyses from the perspective of some human observer or analyzer of the system, and smuggling the observer's perspectives and interpretations into the purported model of the system. If a human scientist, for example, were to be using some internal cell activity as a signal, an "encoding," of some prior activity that yielded the manufacture and release of a transmitter, then the poison molecule would generate a false representation *for the scientist*. At issue, however, are the sorts of representations in the *scientist-as-system* per se, not the representational usages that the scientist can derivatively make of aspects of other systems. That is, at issue is primary representationality, not derivative representationality.

The indication of the potentiality of further interaction in a system is an indication that has truth conditions *external to the system*. The indicated potentiality may in fact not be a potentiality, and it will be a potentiality only if the world in general supports the indicative relationships involved. Only if the world is in fact a place in which, whenever "this interaction yields this outcome," then "that interaction would yield that outcome," will an indication of that relationship hold. So, the indication, which is strictly functional and strictly internal to the system, depends on the world for its truth conditions. Note that such an indication *has* external truth conditions, but it does not *represent* those truth conditions.

Furthermore, if such an indication is false, there is a possibility for the system itself to discover that. If the system does in fact engage in an interaction, reaches a particular outcome, then engages in an indicated potential *further* interaction, and that further interaction fails to complete, or completes with a nonindicated final state, then the initial indication is false *for the system itself*. Indications of interactive potentiality are, on the one hand, functional indications, but, on the other hand, they have truth conditions testable by the system itself. Such indications are the primitive form of the emergence of interactive representation.

Indications of potential interactions constitute an emergence of minimal representationality in the sense of having truth values determinable by the system itself. They do not, however, look much like representations of our familiar world of objects in space and time, related causally, with other agents, language, and so on. They are a form of representation most readily found in primitive systems, such as paramecia.

From Action to Objects

Nevertheless, the claim is that this is the primitive form of representation out of which all others are constructed. That claim is a programmatic claim that can only be demonstrated progressively via presenting the models of such constructions (see below). Models of the nature of learning, emotions, consciousness, language, perception, memory, values, rationality, development, and others have, in fact, been offered (Bickhard, 1980, 1991b, 1992a, 1992b, 1992c, 1993; Bickhard & Campbell, 1992; Bickhard & Richie, 1983; Campbell & Bickhard, 1986, 1992). Obviously, much more work remains. The critical point for my current purposes, however, is that interactivism *does* constitute an alternative to the standard correspondence notions of representation—the notions of representation upon which computationalism is founded.

Pragmatism

Interactivism is a model of the emergence of representation out of action and interaction, rather than as a form of correspondence. As such, it participates in a tradition that has looked to action for representation—pragmatism. There are many differences of detail and some fundamental differences between interactivism and classical pragmatisms. The basic intuition, however, that representation is not a static correspondence, but instead is a functional emergent of action is in common.

Piaget and Objects

Furthermore, interactivism connects strongly with generally Piagetian ideas from within the pragmatist tradition (Peirce, James, Baldwin, Piaget) of how our world of objects, and so on, *can* be constructed out of action (Piaget, 1954). Roughly, for

example, objects, from a child's epistemological perspective, are complex patternings of interactive potentialities—visual scans, manipulations, translations, throwings, chewings, etc.—that remain *invariant as overall patterns* under large numbers of possible interactions. None of the visual scans, manipulations, etc., for example, change the overall pattern of interactive potentialities that *is* that object for the child. Burning or crushing, on the other hand, would change those potentialities: manipulable objects are generally not invariant in their interactive potentialities under burning or crushing.

Emergent Representation and False Representation

Interactive representation is emergent in relatively simply interactive system organizations. Most importantly, it is emergent in organizations of system organization that need not themselves be representational at all. Interactive representation is emergent *de novo*—it does not require that we already have representation in order to get representation, as does encodingism. Consequently, interactivism does not encounter the incoherence of encodingism in accounting for the representational content of its grounding elements—the interactive ground is not one of elements at all, and the representational content *is* the indicated potentiality of interaction. It does not have to be provided from anywhere else (Bickhard, 1991a, 1993).

Furthermore, interactive indications are trivially capable of being false and of being falsified. There is no problematic of the disjunction problem, and no necessity for gyrations such as the asymmetric dependencies. These are red herrings that simply do not arise from within the interactive framework. These are symptoms of the general approach to representation in terms of correspondence, not fundamental problems about representation per se (Bickhard, 1991a; Bickhard & Terveen, 1995).

THE DOMINANCE OF COMPUTATIONALISM

Computationalism is an approach to cognitive science that is deeply embedded in the encodingist perspective. Newell's symbol system hypothesis, for example, is a straightforward, even somewhat naive, statement of encodingism, yet it is proposed and accepted as the core foundation of cognitive science and artificial intelligence (Newell, 1980; Bickhard & Terveen, 1995), including of the major project of SOAR, for which has been claimed such wondrous properties as reflection, learning, intelligence, and other mental phenomena (Laird, Newell, & Rosenbloom, 1987; Laird, Rosenbloom, & Newell, 1986; Rosenbloom, Laird, & Newell, 1988; Rosenbloom, Laird, Newell, & McCarl, 1991; Bickhard & Terveen, 1995). Lenat's CYC project, attempting to construct a truly gigantic knowledge base of encodings—millions and millions of "facts" requiring tens of years and millions upon millions of dollars—on the assumption that the only problem with previous encodingist efforts is that they have been on too small a scale, is another testament to the power and ubiquity of the encodingist assumption (Lenat & Guha, 1988; Lenat, Guha, & Wallace, 1988; Lenat & Feigenbaum, 1991; Bickhard & Terveen, 1995). Encoded propositions, encoded features, encoded entities, encoded rules, completely dominate the efforts to understand the cognitive properties of the mind.

Connectionism

Connectionism offers, in some respects, a major alternative to standard symbol-crunching approaches to cognitive science. It offers, among other things, the possibility of training a system to generate internal categorizations of input patterns, instead of having to design a physical transducer or write a program. This has been construed as "learning" and has been part of the source of the excitement associated with connectionist approaches. There is much to analyze about connectionist approaches, both strengths and weaknesses, but, with respect to the basic issue of encodingism the issue is clear: Connectionism offers no alternative to standard encodingist assumptions concerning the nature of representation. The distributed patterns of activation that are taken as "representations" of input patterns in connectionist systems are simply passive differentiators, in the interactive sense, or noninferential transducers, in the symbol manipulation sense, that are supposed to represent by virtue of the *correspondences* they have with those input patterns. Connectionist "representations" are purported encodings (Bickhard & Terveen, 1995).

Computationalism Requires Encodingism

If encodingism fails, then computationalism necessarily fails. Without encodingism, computationalism has no claim to be able to address the fundamental problem of representation. Absent representation, computationalism has no claim to be able to address *any* intentional properties.

SUMMARY

I have argued that encodingism is incoherent and that computationalism does therefore fail. It is in serious trouble indeed. But a naturalism of mind—in which mind is addressed as constituted of natural phenomena in the world, rather than as some supernatural intrusion into the world—is not precluded by these arguments. Interactivism, in fact, offers an alternative naturalistic approach to understanding representational phenomena. Interactivism offers a naturalism of representation that is not subject to root incoherences, impossibilities of evolutionary and developmental emergence, impossibilities of error, and so on (Bickhard, 1992b, 1992c, 1993). Interactivism offers a *natural* approach to the naturalistic emergence of representation out of nonrepresentation.

REFERENCES

Anderson, J. R. (1983). *The architecture of cognition.* Cambridge: Harvard University Press.

Bickhard, M. H. (1980). *Cognition, convention, and communication.* New York: Praeger.

Bickhard, M. H. (1991a). The import of Fodor's anticonstructivist arguments. In L. Steffe (Ed.), *Epistemological foundations of mathematical experience* (pp. 14–25). New York: Springer-Verlag.

Bickhard, M. H. (1991b). A pre-logical model of rationality. In L. Steffe (Ed.), *Epistemological foundations of mathematical experience* (pp. 68–77). New York: Springer-Verlag.

Bickhard, M. H. (1992a). Commentary on the age 4 transition. *Human Development, 35,* 182–192.

Bickhard, M. H. (1992b). How does the environment affect the person? In L. T. Winegar & J. Valsiner (Eds.), *Children's development within social contexts: Metatheory and theory* (pp. 63–92). Hillsdale, NJ: Erlbaum.

Bickhard, M. H. (1992c). Levels of representationality. *Conference on The Science of Cognition.* Santa Fe, New Mexico, June 15–18.

Bickhard, M. H. (1993). Representational content in humans and machines. *Journal of Experimental and Theoretical Artificial Intelligence, 5,* 285–333.

Bickhard, M. H., & Campbell, R. L. (1992). Some foundational questions concerning language studies: With a focus on categorial grammars and model theoretic possible worlds semantics. *Journal of Pragmatics, 17*(5/6), 401–433.

Bickhard, M. H., & Richie, D. M. (1983). *On the nature of representation: A case study of James J. Gibson's theory of perception.* New York: Praeger.

Bickhard, M. H., & Terveen, L. (1995). *Foundational issues in artificial intelligence and cognitive science: Impasse and solution.* Amsterdam: Elsevier.

Block, N. (1980). Troubles with functionalism. In N. Block (Ed.), *Readings in philosophy and psychology* (Vol. I). Cambridge, MA: Harvard University Press.

Campbell, R. L., & Bickhard, M. H. (1986). *Knowing levels and developmental stages.* Basel: Karger.

Campbell, R. L., & Bickhard, M. H. (1987). A deconstruction of Fodor's anticonstructivism. *Human Development, 30*(1), 48–59.

Campbell, R. L., & Bickhard, M. H. (1992). Types of constraints on development: An interactivist approach. *Developmental Review, 12*(3), 311-338.

Fodor, J. A. (1981). The present status of the innateness controversy. In J. Fodor, *RePresentations* (pp. 257–316). Cambridge, MA: MIT Press.

Fodor, J. A. (1987). *Psychosemantics.* Cambridge, MA: MIT Press.

Fodor, J. A. (1990). *A theory of content and other essays.* Cambridge, MA: MIT Press.

Harnad, S. (1987). Category induction and representation. In S. Harnad (Ed.), *Categorical perception* (pp. 535-565). Cambridge: Cambridge University Press.

Laird, J. E., Newell, A., & Rosenbloom, P. S. (1987). SOAR: An architecture for general intelligence. *Artificial Intelligence, 33,* 1–64.

Laird, J. E., Rosenbloom, P. S., & Newell, A. (1986). Chunking in SOAR: The anatomy of a general learning mechanism. *Machine Learning, 1*(1), 11–46.

Lenat, D. B., & Feigenbaum, E. A. (1991). On the thresholds of knowledge. *Artificial Intelligence, 47*(1–3), 185–250.

Lenat, D., & Guha, R. (1988). The world according to CYC. MCC Technical Report No. ACA-AI-300-88.

Lenat, D., Guha, R., & Wallace, D. (1988). The CycL representation language. MCC Technical Report No. ACA-AI-302-88.

Loewer, B., & Rey, G. (1991). *Meaning in mind: Fodor and his critics.* Oxford: Blackwell.

Newell, A. (1980). Physical symbol systems. *Cognitive Science, 4,* 135–183.

Palmer, S. E. (1978). Fundamental aspects of cognitive representation. In E. Rosch & B. B. Lloyd (Eds.), *Cognition and categorization.* Hillsdale, NJ: Erlbaum.

Piaget, J. (1954). *The construction of reality in the child.* New York: Basic Books.

Rosenbloom, P., Laird, J., & Newell, A. (1988). Metalevels in SOAR. In P. Maes & D. Nardi (Eds.), *Metalevel architectures and reflection* (pp. 227–240). New York: Elsevier.

Rosenbloom, P. S., Laird, J. E., Newell, A., & McCarl, R. (1991). A preliminary analysis of the SOAR architecture as a basis for general intelligence. *Artificial Intelligence, 47*(1–3), 289–325.

Smith, B. C. (1987). *The correspondence continuum.* Stanford, CA: Center for the Study of Language and Information, CSLI-87-71.

CHAPTER 14

TOWARD A NATURALIZED COGNITIVE SCIENCE:

A Framework for Cooperation between Philosophy and the Natural Sciences of Intelligent Systems[1]

C. A. Hooker

We know, however, that the mind is capable of understanding these matters in all their complexity and in all their simplicity. A ball flying through the air is responding to the force and direction with which it was thrown, the action of gravity, the friction of the air which it must expend its energy on overcoming, the turbulence of the air around its surface, and the rate and direction of the ball's spin.

And yet, someone who might have difficulty working out what 3 × 4 × 5 comes to would have no trouble doing differential calculus and a whole host of related calculation so astonishingly fast that they can actually catch a flying ball.

People who call this "instinct" are merely giving the phenomenon a name, not explaining anything.

Douglas Adams, *Dirk Gently's Holistic Detective Agency*

INTRODUCTION: BETWEEN PHILOSOPHY AND PSYCHOLOGY

In this paper I aim to provide a certain perspective on the relations between philosophy and psychology in recent times and to advocate a naturalist conception of both as the most fruitful basis for future progress.

There are two basic conceptions of the relation between philosophy and psychology. The antinaturalist conception regards mind as a special object, set apart from the natural objects which may be studied by the natural sciences. In this case, typically, the mind itself is given a privileged, internal role in its self-understanding. Psychology becomes a discipline *sui generis* in systematic pursuit of that understanding. Philosophy, as the deepest reflective understanding that mind provides, gives a fundamental a priori framework for, and plays an intimate role in the structuring of, that understanding. The traditional position here is metaphysical idealism or dualism fed by epistemological rationalism. (Descartes and Leibniz will serve as models.) Later, there is the Kantian transcendental version with a corresponding transcendental psychology of mind and in the later part of the nineteenth century there was the intuitive version with the introspective psychology of Wundt and others as model. We shall shortly encounter a curious reflection of this position in late twentieth century cognitive psychology (viz., narrow artificial intelligence).

The alternative conception is to theorize mind as a natural object integrated with all other natural objects and arising naturally in the course of biological evolution. In that case the study of mind is to be integrated with the other natural sciences; we cannot expect psychology to be a discipline *sui generis* or set apart from others, except for pragmatic convenience. Nor can we expect philosophy to play any more special role vis-à-vis psychology than it does in relation to any of the other sciences. This view has its roots in the materialism of Democritus and the dynamics of Heraclitus, but it has largely run submerged beneath the dominant dualist–rationalist conception. More recently, one can find strands of it in realists like Thomas Case (1888–1906) and the U.S. Critical Realist and Australian Materialist movements, especially the doctrines of the unity of science and the primacy of metaphysics and science to epistemology, and the deliberate introduction of evolutionary considerations to philosophical analysis (see Hooker, 1987, chap. 1 for references).

The significance of shifts in late twentieth century cognitive science, as I shall present it, lies in the increasing possibility to break out from an essentially antinaturalist conception— whatever its scientific trappings (use of computer models, etc.)—to explore a thoroughgoing naturalist conception of both psychology and philosophy.

Philosophy vis-à-vis Psychology I: Substance Theory

Bridge-building between mind and matter theories has not been easy in the past. Newtonian atomism, encapsulating much of Cartesian mechanism and so successful in elementary physics and chemistry, evidently contains nothing to represent the central qualities of mind: intentionality, reason, feeling, and consciousness. The obvious move to dualism was reinforced both by religious commitment and by rationalist philosophical argument concerning the mind's grasp of abstract entities (numbers, meanings, etc.). Constructing a bridge meant either espousing an extreme materialism, in the form of a compositional reduction of mind to Newtonian matter, or forcing through a philosophical behaviorism on the basis of dogmatic adherence to an equally dubious empiricism. (For philosophical behaviorism's commitment to materialism see, e.g., Medlin 1967). For reasonable, open-minded people who found mind to be intimately involved

in this world, whatever its ultimate nature, neither the yawning gulf of dualism nor a simplistic mechanical materialism was acceptable.

Since that time the Newtonian conception of matter has given way to the relativistic and quantum conceptions, which are radically different in key respects from it. Not surprisingly, there has followed a flood of literature claiming that this shift provides the key to a new integrated understanding of matter and mind, typically by dematerializing matter rather than by materializing mind. I suggest caution in leaping to this conclusion. Much of the literature displays a willfully superficial understanding of the new theories of matter. The quantum transition probabilities for a given situation, for example, are fixed by the quantum mathematical formalism and, so far as that formalism goes, are irreducible. While this certainly marks a break of some kind with Newtonian causality, how are irreducibly random quantum events any better a model of purpose and reason than is a rigid Newtonian causal connection? As Popper, for example, recognized, to represent mental processes we really want something *plastic,* neither rigid nor random.[2] It is possible to claim, as the physicist Wigner does, that quantum theory requires the postulate of an independent mind in order to be given a coherent statement. But, first, this is by no means the only interpretation of quantum theory that has been put forward by competent people; second, there are current developments in quantum theory itself that would challenge even the relevance of an interpretation like Wigner's; and, third, beneath the froth of speculative inquiry we still do not understand the nature of quantum theory at all deeply.[3] In short, extreme caution is called for.

What relativistic and quantum theory no doubt leave us with is some different kind of connectedness from that of local Newtonian causal connectedness. Here two of the most thoughtful reinterpretive works are those of Bohm (1980) and Schumacher (1989), yet these move in significantly different directions. Likely our new conceptions of matter will ultimately make a substantial difference to our understanding of where mind fits in the scheme of things. Possibly a quantum physicalism will prove best supported, or possibly a Whiteheadian scheme in which we come to recognize within the strange new quantum properties essentially primitive mental components, components that only manifest themselves distinctively when a sufficiently complex, organized quantum object is assembled. Meanwhile much of the current search for a quantum foundation for mind seems to have been directed to a few exotic features, being dazzled, for example, by the prospect of a quantum underpinning for extrasensory perception. Whatever the future of this area, a quantum property theory is, I suggest, more likely to contribute to our understanding of the nature of mental qualia, both perceptual and feeling properties. Note that these considerations touch only indirectly those basic functions of mind that occupy the overwhelming proportion of normal experience: perceiving, learning, reasoning, deciding, and so on. To understand these we need to look at some suitable theory of process and organization, and among theories that will operate in the middle range of physical conditions where relativistic and quantum theories are largely powerless to assist understanding.

Philosophy vis-à-vis Psychology II: Process Theory

But it is just here that there has, in the last two decades, been a different scientific revolution in the making, with widespread ramifications: the shift from linear, reversible, and compositionally reducible mathematical models to nonlinear, irreversible, and functionally irreducible complex dynamic systems models, especially for complex adaptive (partially) self-organizing systems (which include all living systems). For general exposition see, e.g., Janstch (1981) and Prigogine and Stengers (1984), complemented by Churchland (1989) and Dyke (1988). Today there is a veritable explosion of new literature pursuing these ideas in every field from irreversible thermodynamics and chaos theory through engineering control theory, self-organization and hierarchy theory in biology, and dynamical neural net theory in neurophysiology and cognitive psychology, to evolutionary economics and mathematical models of international relations. The interested reader is directed to the starred items in the references for an introduction.

For all its value and conceptual importance, the ideas deriving from this revolution have as yet scarcely touched philosophy. For the most part, philosophers still model rational agents (explicitly or by tacit presumption) in terms of simple logical structure, and the whole of science likewise. In effect they are locked into the dominant artificial

intelligence (AI) model of cognition from the 1970s, the simple formal logical programming machine. There are various reasons why this is so, some of them evidential and scientific, some deriving from philosophical presumptions about the nature and status of normative principles (e.g., that reason reduces to formal logic), and no doubt others driven by domain ownership ambitions. Whatever the reasons, I hold that the formalist AI model is multiply defective when taken as *fundamental* and that a thorough scientific and philosophic rethink is called for based on a strategic (decision theoretic) conception of cognitive function married into an appropriate dynamic systems framework. (For work along these lines see "A Naturalist Philosophy of theNatural Sciences of Intelligent Systems" below and Hooker, 1987, 1995.) The story of this paper is the opening up of cognitive science to this wider conception of cognitive theory and its attendant naturalist philosophy.

For the past thirty years the logicist/AI model of mind has dominated scientific and philosophical imagination. This position also drives an unbridgeable gulf between mind and matter. Not, indeed, the same one that supported earlier dualism, for matter can clearly be organized so as to realise a computer mind. But even so, under this conception minds are to be wholly characterized by their formally structured symbolic programs, whereas matter remains characterized by cause. Fodor (1975) had already drawn the conclusion: Since whatever program a universal computer implements is independent of its specific material architecture, or even material composition, the study of AI programming is a science quite independent of any theory of its material implementation. Psychology again becomes a subject *sui generis,* without the need or possibility of basing its studies in neurophysiology or any other theory of matter. But the divorce runs still deeper. The power of a theoretical system depends on the formal structure it exploits. Churchland (1979) points out that while both folk/commonsense and cognitive psychologies exploit logical relations among propositions (generally: formal relations among semantically interpreted symbol structures), all other sciences exploit algebraic relations among algebraic objects (e.g., tensor algebra for mechanics and neural nets). This makes the basic structures of commonsense and cognitive psychologies distinct from their natural scientific counterparts and not merely independently accessible (cf. Hooker, 1988).

The new revolution in understanding complex adaptive self-organizing systems challenges this neat dualistic division of labor. Insofar as mind can be recognized as a species of organized activity, it offers the opportunity of a new and perhaps much more promising bridge that can be built between mind and matter. Taken in conjunction with whatever emerges from the quantum and relativistic conceptions of matter, the new understanding of complex adaptive systems provides perhaps the most promising opportunity for a unified understanding of ourselves and our world since the Renaissance birth of modern science.

In keeping with these remarks, in what follows narrow AI theory (NAIT) labels that doctrine of cognitive psychology which theorizes mind as a formal symbolic program. According to NAIT, mind is essentially a formal logical device in which its basic operations are structure-sensitive formal operations on semantically interpretable symbols to create new symbols. This conception of intelligence as a machine-implementable organization lies behind the bulk of work done in artificial intelligence and cognitive science over the period 1950–80.[4] By contrast, I define wide AI theory (WAIT) as the view that mind is a machine-implementable organization, that mental process is computation, but without the constraint to a formal logical programming realization. WAIT is designed to capture both NAIT and the recent explosion of work in connectionist models (see below). Despite the width of WAIT, we shall need a still more encompassing conception of theory of intelligence, which I shall label *general naturalized intelligence theory* (GNIT). GNIT is to encompass any systematic theory of the nature of intelligence, whether or not mental process is computational in either the NAIT or WAIT senses. In particular, GNIT includes cybernetic or control models and self-organizing nonlinear systems dynamics models of mind. GNIT is restricted to an account of intelligence as a natural feature of natural objects, to theories that are integrated with our natural scientific theories on the one side, so as to understand the evolutionary development of intelligence as a biological phenomenon, and integrated with our social sciences on the other side so as to understand intelligence as a natural expression of social interaction.[5]

The first part of this chapter briefly introduces some of the issues and lessons that emerge from the passage from NAIT to WAIT. The second part explores some theory fragments that lead from WAIT to GNIT. Finally, the third part is devoted to sketching a metatheory or philosophy for GNIT. The distinction between functional and causal descriptions of complex systems is crucial to clarity in these discussions.[6]

FROM NARROW AI THEORY TO WIDE AI THEORY

The story begins in the early part of this century with empiricist-inspired behaviorism. Here the mind is represented as a black box with an input, stimuli, and an output, response. A theory of mind is a function F such that $O = F(I)$ equivalently $R = F(S)$ where $I = S =$ input stimulus and $O = R =$ output response. There will be feedback from the environment E to the agent as a result of performing the response and this acts as a new input $I' = S'$. For fixed F this gives an iteration loop for evolving behavior or output, e.g., in successive movements to catch a ball. If F is modifiable according to some procedure L, then the iteration loop can result in a development of F to some stable F_L in a particular environment, which is called 'learning'. Reinforcement learning introduces an evaluation structure V to F called a 'reward system' and L is assumed either to incrementally modify F in the direction of greater reward (V) value of the fed back $I' = S'$ or a Darwinian-style random generation of output O was assumed with the highest reward or V value of the fed back stimuli being used to select the corresponding F variation that produced it. F needs some internal structure for these purposes, but empiricist scruples restrict it to a set of 'intervening variables' v_i that are ultimately explicitly definable in terms of stimulus and response patterns, $v_i = D(O,I) = D(R,S)$.

This simple black box model is actually a useful beginning on a characterization of mind for sufficiently simple creatures and/or simple problems, but it has many now well-recognized deficits, which stem from its simpleness and ultimately from the empiricist constraints that determined its construction. A prominent defect is that the structure of F is constrained to far too simple structures to accommodate the complexity of internal states, even of moderately elementary creatures (cf. Nelson, 1969). A second difficulty is that, at least for intentional agents, behavior is specified symbolically or semantically (the creature acts and perceives), not merely physically and causally. The net result is that it is difficult to obtain useful generalizations about behavior of any kind if constrained to describing input and output in strictly physical and physiological terms—there are too many different 'reasons' (combinations of stimulus + internal state) for performing any one physiological routine and conversely any one stimulus can lead to too many different physiological routines depending on the intervening internal state (see, e.g., Pylyshyn, 1984). There are, for example, infinitely many logically equivalent sentences, any one of which might be used as a response, depending on context.

The essential step that characterizes the newer cognitive psychology is to free F from the constraint to intervening variables. We then have $O = A = F(P,m)$, where P is an input perception, m is a mental state drawn from some collection of mental states M, and A is the action performed as output. Here all of the components are semantically interpreted. The distinctive feature of this stage in cognitive science is the restriction of F to the class of all machine-implementable formal computations, i.e., to the class of programs that could be run on a universal Turing machine, typically in von Neumann architecture form (cf., e.g., Smolensky, 1988, p. 4). The representations employed by NAIT are all language-like in the sense that they have an effective classical syntactic structure. Complex representations are formal complexes of simple representations and symbolic operations on complex representations are ultimately decomposable into basic operations on their constituents. Finally, the semantic content or meaning of a complex representation is a function of the semantic contents of its constituents and its syntactic structure. All this is meant to include not only beliefs but items in memory, perceptual items, including their spatial and temporal parts, and so on. (See, e.g., Fodor 1987; Fodor & McLaughlin, 1990.)

In this conception, cognitive science is a specification of F and AI is a theory of all possible Fs, ranked according to their capacity to carry out certain kinds of tasks efficiently. As noted, physiology specifies the neural implementation of these programs, the 'engineering specifications' of the machine on which the programs happen to run in humans. But the programs, F, can be specified and studied quite independently of implementation—any machine whatever that is equivalent to a universal Turing machine will do. This makes cognitive science and AI strongly self-contained; indeed, it makes these disciplines unique among the sciences.

But despite its initial successes, NAIT has proved to be exceedingly difficult to develop into a form where it captures any of the significant aspects of complex intelligence. Again there are several dimensions to the difficulties, e.g., the tendency to computational explosion because of NAIT's serial sequencing. Perhaps the most characteristic one is what Minsky has called "the frame problem." The programs that we execute (as this modeling has it) are complex and themselves typically sensitive functions of the contexts in which we are operating. The likely causes of smoke in a kitchen are different from those in the woods; maneuvering, counting, and so on in a world of solid blocks is quite different from swimming in a sea of constantly fluctuating waves that superpose and resolve again. How is one supposed to store all the millions of facts and generalizations that would be needed to represent these common capacities as formal programs, and sort through them and choose just the right ones in seconds? How is one supposed to have arrived at such a useful categorization in the first place (Minsky, 1981; cf. Churchland, 1989; Dennett, 1984; Ford & Pylyshyn, 1994)?

Ultimately, resolving the frame problem requires producing a theory of learning, i.e., again a procedure L for modifying F, such that we can understand how frames, or sufficiently detailed knowledge of contexts, come to be built up and specific programs chosen in their light. One problem is that, for consistency, L itself must be specified in programming terms and this evidently requires appeal to an innate fundamental set of concepts built into the design of the machine itself.[7] But the larger issue for NAIT concerns its restriction to formal resources for learning theory, in effect to formal induction, i.e., inductive logic and/or statistical inference. Formal induction faces many difficulties, including the evident inaccessibility of theoretical concepts, the difficulty of representing default reasoning, paradoxes, and computational intractability (see, e.g., Chater & Oaksford, 1990; Earman, 1992; Hooker, 1991; cf. Hooker, 1994, 1995).

In short, for all its increased richness, NAIT still turns out to be a constrained theory of rather austere resources in somewhat the same way as was its behaviorist predecessor. The significance of the introduction of WAIT is that these constraints can be relaxed still further. In particular, a wider range of procedures L for modifying F become available and it is precisely here that WAIT models have claimed some of their greatest advantages. Similarly, GNIT widens the characterization of both F and L yet again. The difficulties with understanding learning must be faced by any account, but the subconceptual, subformal approaches of WAIT and other GNIT models means that they are not restricted to formal inference and this may give them additional scope to tackle them.[8]

"Connectionism" is the broad term covering a class of cognitive models using parallel processing architecture and a wider conception of computation than NAIT provides (Feldman & Ballard, 1982); it now includes, for example, formal PDP programming models, cellular automata, and neural nnets. Rather than attempt to review here the vast field of connectionist theories, to meet length constraints the discussion will focus just on the nnet version and even here be extremely brief. For an introduction to the literature, see, e.g., Bechtel and Abrahamsen (1991), Churchland (1989), Rumelhart and McClelland (1986), Tienson (1987), Touretzky et al. (1990), and cf. Dennett (1986).

Nnets comprise an array of connected nodes, each node and connection carrying a numerical measure or strength, so that a set of values imposed externally on some input nodes is propagated iteratively through the net until a well-defined set of activation values appears on some output nodes. The simplest way to ensure a well-defined output is to employ purely feed-forward nets, but many other topologies and iteration procedures are possible. A given nnet with k input nodes and n output nodes defines a function F from the domain of all k-tuples to the range of all n-tuples. The simplest form for the node output function N is linear, $N(a) = ka$, where a is the activation value and k a constant, and then each F is a multilinear or tensor transform. Typically N is assumed nonlinear but continuously differentiable (Grossberg, 1988); this represents a large increase in the range of input–output functions that may be encompassed; indeed, with suitably weighted nets all computable functions may be captured, as in NAIT (Hornik et al., 1989; cf. Lindgren & Nordahl, 1990, for cellular automata). There are many different learning or training algorithms (systematic procedures L for modifying the nnets so that they come to instantiate desired functions F) in use in cognitive science and in engineering, where the use of nnets has an equally long history. (For introduction and review see, e.g., Hinton, 1989; Kohonen, 1984; Rumelhart et al., 1986; Rumelhart & McClelland, 1986; Widrow & Stearns, 1985; Yao, 1993.)

What has reexcited interest in nnets is their demonstrated capacity to learn (i.e., come to be modified so as to instantiate) complex and cognitively interesting functions using quite simple nets, and to do so with relatively brief training or other learning procedures. In particular, they have proven successful in precisely those areas where NAIT programming approaches have found most difficulty, e.g., in complex discrimination tasks (among object shapes using input surface shading, rocks from mines using input sonar signals, words from speech represented as input vocalized phonemes, and so on). Furthermore, they show several other distinctive and attractive features, e.g.: in general they "degrade gracefully," i.e., the functions they instantiate in general vary only incrementally under the random destruction of nodes or connections; and they accumulate incrementally, i.e., additional training on new but related data introduces only small, related strength changes; they show a capacity to generalize both across inputs beyond a training set—this might be called individual prototype capture since new instances are pulled into the range of a central prototype—and across related input–output patterns—pattern prototype capture—and conversely they show a capacity to specialize by localising the storage of unrelated inputs. All this makes them 'brainlike' and attractive for cognitive modelling (but not 'brain-identical'; see, e.g., Ballard, 1986; Churchland, 1989).

But what is most important here is the character of the representations involved in nnets and the available operations on them. From the functional or information-processing point of view, these representations are clearly not propositional. Pollack (1989, 1990; cf. discussion by Horgan & Tienson, 1992) has developed a way to internally represent inputs characterizing recursively organized data structures with all representations held in the same set of hidden layer nodes in a three-layer nnet, yet without sacrificing any discriminatory capacity. The storage cannot be in NAIT form, since different forms are stored on the same nodes. If not propositional, what kind of representation does an nnet generate? It is commonly noted that nnets are in effect feature cluster detectors, associators and discriminators. From this point of view they evidently work at something like the level of concepts rather than at the level of propositions. But these are concepts of a more basic kind than the formally, linguistically definable ones, for they can be represented by clusters of properties of varying numerical weight and they can be numerically associated to other concepts similarly: "...there will generally be no precisely valid, complete, computable formal principles at the conceptual level; such principles exist only at the level of individual units—the *subconceptual* level" (Smolensky, 1988, p. 6).[9]

This raises the philosophical issue of the nature and status of agency conceptions as a whole, including the commonsense and NAIT conceptions of mind, but these large issues cannot be pursued here.[10] It also undermines a common argument for a formal language of thought, and so for NAIT, from the occurrence of systematically structured outputs (e.g., Fodor, 1987, pp. 150–1). It suffices that, whatever the internal representations are, they have the causal effect of producing structured outputs. Thus the inference from structured output to similarly structured internal causes of that output breaks down. (See also Forster, 1992; Chalmers, 1990.) For the same reason it is a nonsequitur to argue, as Fodor and Pylyshyn (1988) and others do, that since its mode of computation is different nnet models cannot recapture NAIT functions that are central to psychology. Recently there have appeared an increasing stream of papers exploring doing just that re-capturing (see, e.g., Barndon & Srinivas, 1992; Chalmers, 1990; Hinton, 1990; Pollack, 1989, 1990; Smolensky, 1990). Thus it is not the case that nnet models are merely implementations, for a certain kind of engineered machine, of some parts of formal symbolic programs that provide the specification of cognitive function proper.[11]

Further, nnet competencies are rather more intimately connected to their internal causal structure than is the case for NAIT theories. Unlike NAIT, which confines itself to formally related representations, for nnets it is the quantitative causal interconnections among the causal constituents of representations which is crucial for explaining the overall functional capacities of the nnet.[12] Thus nnets exhibit a distinct concept of computation from NAIT; the latter is confined to structure-sensitive symbolic transformations while the former is confined to tensor transforms or some nonlinear generalization of these. Let us call these

NAIT computation and WAIT computation respectively. Given success in nnet modelling of NAIT processes, WAIT computation includes NAIT computation. Nnet theory then provides a genuinely explanatory account of cognition. (In principle at least; whether it can do so in practice is an empirical question currently being explored.)

From this perspective the key issue between the two accounts of cognition turns on the theory of learning. We have seen that nnets do have an intrinsic capacity for generalization and that they may well prove to have broader capacities in this respect than NAIT can easily produce. There remains the question of the generation of new concepts to permit higher order learning tasks. Forster (1990) provides an instructive example, exhibiting a simple nnet trained on two different sets of data concerned with weights, the one to do with the conditions for balancing a pivoted beam by weights placed on it at various distances from the pivot point and the other for relating the extensions of a spring to the weights hung from it. While a single nnet can be trained to generalize each set of data so as to capture the relevant principles, the compressed representation of these principles can be placed on the same collection of hidden nodes. The trained nnet then generalizes in all the usual ways but, Forster argues, when one examines these nodes their activations constitute a representation of the concept of mass. The nnet associates to each object, whether it appears with the beam balance or the spring, a set of activation values that are invariant and whose causal role corresponds to that of mass in the computation of balance or spring extension conditions. The nnet has created the basis for a new concept out of invariances in the data presented. Forster suggests that this is in fact a generalizable model for how scientific inference proceeds. How far an account of scientific nondemonstrative inference of this kind can be extended is an open and difficult question. Bickhard and Campbell (1992) and Churchland (1989) argue persuasively that some such preformal capacity must underly all formal development, since formal manipulation is capable only of symbolic rearrangement, not creation (see also Hooker, 1991). Churchland favors nnets for this task, linking them up with prototype–metaphor structure and generalization (see below). These are complex matters, still in their infancy; nonetheless, there is the beginning of a substantive account of concept generation in which a certain kind of structuring association natural to nnets plays an essential role. (See also, e.g., Bechtel & Abrahamsen, 1991; Touretzky et al., 1990). This suggests as much or more promise to nnet learning theory as any that NAIT displays.

For all their promise nnets are importantly incomplete as models for cognitive science in a basic way only touched on in passing so far: They need a control context. Nnet models in themselves say nothing about any of the following: (i) which input stimuli are to be selected and how they are to be processed, (ii) which processed items are to be stored in memory, (iii) how they are to be stored and how addressable, (iv) which goals the organism should choose to pursue and the hierarchical relations among those goals, (v) higher-order interactions between what has been learned and the goals pursued, between learning and learning how to learn, and so on. A system with these capacities is the functional equivalent of a sophisticated control system. Nnet training itself provides a further instance. Although Smolensky (1988), for example, speaks of connectionist networks as programming themselves, in effect the application of a training algorithm amounts to the construction of a control system which alters the net weights and activation values until the outputs of a desired reference system are achieved. While the application of the correction algorithm in laboratory practice may be carried out by the scientist modeling the nnet on some computer, when these networks are used in actual practice their correction must be brought about by a real process.

Models for these purposes have been devised by control system engineers for a long time (cf., e.g., Widrow and Stearns, 1985), including adaptive control networks retraining to perform a set of shifting tasks. At the present time hybrid models, which embed nnet processes within a NAIT control program, are now developing rapidly in many fields (see, e.g., Astrom & McAvoy, 1992; and *Expert Systems with Applications*, vol. 2, 1992). There are difficulties with standard control models and alternatives are available (see below). But, however realized, an account needs to be given of these control capacities and nnet models need to be embedded in the right kind of functional control structure before they are of real value to psychological theory. This directs our attention to the relation of control to intelligence. Following that relationship will lead us to a still wider conception of cognitive theory and more radical ideas for implementing control.

FROM WIDE AI THEORY TO GENERAL NATURALIZED INTELLIGENCE THEORY

Problem Solving: Fitting versus Computing

There are two very different ways to solve a problem. One way is to NAITcompute a solution and apply it. A problem is represented symbolically. Logicomathematical algorithms are then applied to NAITcompute a symbolic representation of the solution, which is then used to generate an appropriate output by the solver. This is the standard conception of problem solving. But it is not the only one. We can, for example, NAITcompute the size and shape of a hole and then use geometry to NAITcompute successive body configurations to squeeze through it or the size and shape of a piece of glass to fill it, but we can also wriggle through by feel, or place the glass sheet against the hole and trace it directly. In the latter case we have created a procedure that fits itself to a solution. No symbolic representation of the shape is used, no NAITcomputations are performed. Another example is guiding a lathe directly with a rod moving over a surface to be reproduced. Such problem-solving methods are time honored in many trades, but they have much more widespread application.[13] They are intuitively closer to how we think of learning to throw a ball, play music, or drive a car and perhaps become expert in wider domains (cf. Dreyfus & Dreyfus, 1986). Rather than NAITcompute a solution we can become a solution, i.e., become internally rearranged in such a way that appropriate solution outputs are generated. Let us refer to these two problem-solving modes as the NAITcomputational and fitting modes, respectively.

It is clear from these examples that the fitting mode can provide powerful and efficient methods for solving complex problems, including those not accessible to NAITcomputational methods. (The sun, moon, and earth, for example, constitute a model of a fitting solution of the gravitational 3-body problem and the planets as a whole of the gravitational *n*-body problem, and this is so whether or not an analytically representable, or even a digitally computable, solution exists for this problem.) And the possession of a fitting mode counts as knowledge, often expressed as knowing *how* rather than knowing *that*. Typically I know how to ride a bicycle and that the addition of 3 and

5 is 8. One normally cannot give a linguistic, or indeed any other symbolic, description of successful bike riding in the manner that one can give such a description of adding. On the other hand, the oculovisual to neuromuscular system that makes bike riding possible is now increasingly well understood and one can see in general terms how to construct a successful fitting mode control system to explain this capacity. So it is with our other practical capacities of this kind.

The fitting mode doesn't need linguistic concepts, or symbols in the NAIT sense, just sufficient functional control of processes.[14] Plausibly, most living activities are based on the fitting mode. Whatever its role in more complex neural processes, as we descend the scale of neural complexity of organisms the computational mode surely attenuates; eventually we reach a level below which all problem solving is in the fitting mode. (Conversely, on evolutionary grounds we might expect complex cognitive capacities to be constructed from more elementary fitting mode capacities, but of course this view awaits empirical support.)

Nnets are in general fitting systems, since they are mostly arranged to adjust their internal weights and activation levels until an appropriate input/output function is realized without symbolizing an error function. But once we have a problem-solving mode not confined to NAIT symbol manipulation, there is equally no reason to confine it to just the computations nnets can provide. As noted, the key is functional control, not computation. (Recall that nnets themselves require embedding in a control systems context.) As the examples cited make clear, the fitting mode is naturally modeled in terms of functional control. So we are led to consider generalized control models of intelligence, without restriction on computational mode. This is the distinctive domain of GNIT.

Control and Intelligence

The goal of developing an adequate cybernetic foundation for human psychology is many centuries old. It was given a major stimulus by the mid-century works of Ashby, von Bertalanffy, Wiener, and others in systems and control theory. The general nature of a *Homo cyberneticus* research program may be instructively explored through the contrasting work of two earlier pioneers, Cunningham (1972) and Powers (1973). Basically, Cun-

ningham's model employs a structure of nnet-like association networks which grow in complexity under stimulation according to simple rules. In essence they become a fitting solution to the problem of maximizing information extraction in their environment; in this process Cunningham claims they will (roughly) reproduce Piaget's main stages of cognitive development. By contrast Powers uses a fixed hierarchical classical control system of ten levels, each level utilizing signals from those below it and devoted to providing a distinctive cognitive capacity. First-order control is concerned with controlling the intensity of input stimuli, e.g., light (via physiological photoreceptor response to incident radiation), while second-order systems control relations among such stimuli. Powers believes that elementary notions of physical quantities originate at the first-order level while characteristic clustering of first-order signals is responsible for the creation of sensations, e.g., the complex of perceived qualities across the sensory modalities characterizing a particular prey. And so he slowly builds up the repertoire of cognitive capacities in something like the evolutionary sequence.

Though each author presents both psychological and neurophysiological findings in his favor, and each position captures important aspects of intelligence, they do it in very different ways. Cunningham gives a great deal of attention to the developing organization of the regulatory network and to its relationship to developmental psychology, while developmental notions are completely absent from Powers' model whose structures come genetically fixed at birth. Conversely, Powers emphasizes a distinctive control hierarchy as the essence of intelligence. Cunningham does not mention hierarchy until late in his book (p. 142ff), and only then to deny its significance. (A hierarchy is only a momentary coordination of element reverberation caused by input stimulation.) On the other hand, Cunningham's system certainly develops a precise order to the links among the elements, an order just as critical to its cognitive capacities as hierarchy is for Powers. But while Powers's notion of hierarchy is strict and explicit, Cunningham's order is partial, graded, often implicit, and dynamic. There is a corresponding divergence in the notion and role given to memory. For Cunningham, memory is distributed, every alteration of the regulatory network is a memory trace, and every memory trace is instantiated as such an alteration.

Powers never mentions memory until he reaches discussion of fifth-order systems and then it is considered basically as a programming notion and its physical connection to the control hierarchy remains distant. Correlatively, Cunningham has nothing to say about goals, values, etc.; the system is causally arranged to grow in a certain manner, which happens to have cognitive consequences. Powers's model, by contrast, provides a hierarchy of reference signals that supply the system goals. Some of the disparity has to do with the fact that both authors, Powers especially, work ambiguously between functional and causal specifications—Cunningham's model could provide a causal realisation for some of a Powers control hierarchy, read as functionally specified—but this cannot eliminate their basic differences.

It would be instructive to pursue this analysis further. Recently, Brooks has developed a Powers-like approach to intelligence, with stimulating initial success (Brooks, 1991). He emphasizes evolutionary-like sequence, but beginning with elementary motor operations as does Cunningham. And he is less reliant on rigid hierarchy of the Powers kind, allowing interaction among control processes to be environment context-dependent to some extent. This flexibility could perhaps be exploited to open up space for a Cunningham-style developmental capacity. On this kind of approach see also Beer (1990), Maes (1990), and Cherian and Troxell (1994). Conversely, Bickhard has been developing the consequences for cognitive theory of understanding representation as arising out of the operation of a structured collection of control (sub-)systems (see Bickhard, 1980; Bickhard & Terveen, 1995); this has led him to a fundamental critique of AI, e.g., over the frame problem, and formal linguistics, e.g., for its failure to understand context-dependence. Bickhard claims to resolve these problems through structures related to Piagetian learning. Space constraints prevent pursuing these issues here, but the problem of development is worth brief further comment.

Intelligence has to do with the depth of conditionalization of behavioral responses that are under regulatory control. If we think of a fixed behavior B as a first-order functional property, then a conditional response 'If $M(s, m)$ then B', where M is some internal condition comprised of a stimulus s and a mental state m, is a second-order property; a doubly nested conditional response 'If M', then if M then B' a third-order property; and so on. Holland's classifier systems, which employ only simple conditional structures, can nonetheless execute all programs (Holland, 1992). Animal behavior often displays behavioral processes of high order and, *ceteris paribus*, the capacity for higher order behavioral modification offers clear advantages. Organisms with this capacity can exploit freeing lower order behaviors to adapt to local environmental conditions so as to achieve an increased range of environmental inputs over which viability (i.e., relevant life parameters held invariant) can be maintained. It is then natural to introduce a distinction between adaptability and adaptation. Behavioral adaptation measures finesse (precision, efficiency, robustness) in fixed problem solving tasks. Behavioral adaptability is the capacity to behaviorally adapt, i.e., to modify behavioral repertoires in response to changing tasks. Shifting attention to the internal states that control behavior we introduce a corresponding distinction between cognitive adaptation (finesse) and cognitive adaptability, which is the regulatory control of cognitive adaptation so as to render it conditional on environmental information and internal state. Again increasing intelligence will show increasing accessible order of adaptability. Learning will in general consist in both increasing the adaptability order brought to bear on the task and increasing adaptation at various levels, the former being more fundamental. Contrast learning to bounce a particular ball more accurately (finesse) with learning to transfer that control to violin bowing and other periodic control processes (adaptability); in the latter specific control has been conditionalized on task context.

Powers's system is basically static; the hierarchical control system is specified at the outset and remains unaltered by learning. For Cunningham, by contrast, the whole emphasis is on the way the regulatory system changes as learning proceeds. This contrast raises the question of how a control system perspective can fit with and contribute to developmental psychology. But this is in turn an instance of a still more general question concerning the nature of improving control: How can a system be (self-)organizing so as to develop improved control capacity? It is not too hard to see how finesse in adaptation can be improved, e.g., by sampling at an increased rate or by sampling more finely discriminated features of the controlled system (e.g., by adding more elements to the nnet input and output vector fields), thereby reducing the error margin within which control is effected. And so on. It is less obvious, however, how to provide a plausible account of increase in adaptability. One requires a system capacity to learn about the environment and on that basis appropriately change the hierarchical level of control required.

We could postulate an internal master controller that carried out this task. This strategy tends to suppress the problem by assuming what needs to be understood; it is likely to throw only limited light on learning and development. Powers has such a unit (Powers, 1973, pp. 182–3, 195), which operates the general state of organization, but Powers's system is without any notion of which kinds of test signals it is to generate, which kinds of systems structural features act upon in response or how and why it arose and how it is integrated with more basic control. As with nnets, we wish to understand how these changes arise from within the nature of the basic control processes, not how they can be superimposed from without. Appealing to training algorithms applied by a human experimenter from outside the control system is an alternative covert form of this position.

By contrast, Cunningham's approach does not begin with any sophisticated control system at all; rather, this is built up in the course of experience according to a system of structural alteration rules, which are individually quite simple in application. While their operation needs to be causally explained, their functional result is (certain kinds of) learning. There is an obvious affinity between Cunningham's model and nnet modification, but now with nnet training extended to nnet construction and recognition of the need to understand the origins and nature of the control process for this. Cunningham simply assumes, for example, that an increasing number of neurons can be incorporated into a set of reverberating neurons as reinforcement proceeds and has little to say about the precise mechanism involved. The process through which higher order structure develops might be one of pure selection from among a plethora of undifferentiated connections (Edelman, 1989; Piatelli-Palmarini, 1989; Reeke et al., 1989), or random generation of new connections and selection among these (cf. Powers, above, and genetic algorithms; Holland, 1992), or a systematic growth of new connections (Cunningham). These processes are closely related. Farmer (1990) shows a functional equivalence between classifier systems using genetic algorithms to evolve their internal

rules and tuned nnets selected by running genetic algorithms on a suitable population of nnets (cf. Reeke et al., 1989); but their interrelations are subtle and still being explored. (In this connection it is a pity that models explicitly using the Cunningham connection dynamics approach currently seem to be largely ignored.)

These ideas are as yet only a gesture in the direction of an adequate explanation, for the details are largely lacking both in control theory and in mammalian neurophysiology. We do not yet clearly understand how structure implementing control is causally introduced nor how it issues functionally in fundamental development/learning. It seems clear that aspects of both Cunningham's and Powers's kinds of approaches need to be retained. And a rather rich notion of both developmental and mature cognitive capacities evidently may be obtained by combining them. But it is not obvious how to combine such disparate models. As noted, part (but only part) of the answer may be to understand Powers-style control models as functional models causally realized through Cunningham-style systems, including nnets (cf. Powers, 1973, p. 195). Another important part of the problem may stem from the standard or classical notion of control, which Powers uses and which, despite its sophisticated development in this century, has contributed surprisingly little to cognitive science. This is largely because it relies on manipulating a global model of the system to be controlled (in the form of a linearizable differential equation) somehow acquired prior to control—see Hooker et al. (1992a) where a definition or paradigm for control theory is constructed and the standard paradigm of control exhibited. The issue then is whether there is any alternative.

The answer is affirmative. Hooker et al. (1992a) also provides an alternative control paradigm, called local vector (LV) control. The new LV control systems work well across a wide range of engineering applications, including many that cannot be handled (or easily handled) by the standard approach (Penfold & Evans, 1989; Penfold et al., 1992). Moreover, LV control differs from standard control in important respects that are of cognitive relevance, such as the capacity to learn without significant prior assumptions and to do so without recourse to logico–symbolic manipulations. While there is no claim that LV control is a panacea for cognitive science, it may be able to illuminate some aspects of cognitive science.

The basic idea behind LV control is to control locally and only in terms of the immediate output of the controlled system S. An apt analogy is that of local managerial advice. There is a global ideal company policy but a well-trained local manager responds to particular circumstances with advice that (sufficiently) accurately reflects ideal company policy and is designed to bring the activities in some local department into line with that policy, beginning from their current position. That advice is "reset" for each new local circumstance. There is no attempt by head office to so control the company from the center that it is guaranteed to globally realize the overall policy (the standard approach). LV control has essentially this dual control structure. Two important consequences of this, which contrast it to the standard approach, are that required controller information is minimized and no explicit prior global model is needed.

The LV control algorithm has an intuitive mathematical interpretation. Consider the two global state–time vector fields, which represent all possible evolutions of the system states over time for the ideal system R and the system to be controlled S. Then the desired control input applicable during any time-slice is that signal which maximizes the mapping of the incremental state–time vector for the controlled system S onto that for the reference system R. Both of these vectors have the same origin in the state–time domain because the local controller is reset at each time-slice; the increment in the time–direction determines the rate at which control inputs are applied. The slogan is: Control is efficient local vector field deformation.[15] Hence the name LV control.

While it is not required that local control solutions be remembered, since only local (time-slice) S behavior is required, it is in fact possible to accumulate them and whether or not the system output departs from that of the ideal system. By remembering this information an LV controller can build up a global representation of the system it is controlling, time-slice by time-slice. This is equivalent to building up a representation of the global vector field describing the state–time behavior of the controlled system S point by point. In this way an LV controller may "back itself into" global information concerning S. It thus shows a basic capacity for concept learning and of the operational kind suited to evolutionary sequential development. Paradoxically, being freed from having to learn and remember any global information offers the opportunity of a much more powerful kind of learning than the standard approach is capable of representing.

Suppose, in Piagetian style, that every behavioral fitting solution represents some map from a sensory or proprioceptive input to a motor output. Now if the inputs and outputs are to be sufficiently coherent as to have allowed the intervening neural functions to be selected systematically to achieve their coordination, then each can be represented as a collection of stable factors. Then the collection of all possible inputs can plausibly be represented as a space with one dimension for each factor, and similarly for the collection of all possible outputs. The sensory inputs presented by some collection of systems, e.g., prey behavior, will be represented by a vector field on the input space and the appropriate motor behaviors can then be represented by a vector field on the output space (perhaps with suitable coarse graining). But the mapping between these vector fields, which represents the fitting solution, is precisely what LV control constructs. This notion of concept formation is explored in Hooker et al. (1992b), where possible extension to prototype structure with nonclassical conceptual relations determined by analogy, metaphor, and the like (see especially Lakoff, 1987) and related extensions are also considered.

Now for an LV controller to develop a global representation of a system S it needs an appropriate memory. This memory should be one that facilitates the representation of S in terms of a vector field, i.e., as a surface in some state–time space. Nnets provide just this memory facility, are capable of storing surface representations of nonlinear as well as linear systems, and they can learn the appropriate map through training. Conversely, an LV controller can exploit any stored system representation to extend prediction over longer times and to improve control accuracy. These features make nnets an appealing memory device for LV control implementation. Conversely, thus equipped, LV controllers augment their basic concept learning capacity with the learning capacities of nnets. Moreover, LV controllers may be implemented in a simple distributed form (one does not need physically separate causal implementation for the control components). This makes LV control equipped with a connectionist memory look like a potentially interesting candidate for biological and neurocognitive application. Thus LV control has some obvious connections to the models of Cunningham and Powers discussed earlier. If a similar approach to control development/learning could be provided it would offer the opportunity for a much more intimate integration of these processes into an overall systems control model. (Cf. also Bickhard, 1980; Bickhard & Campbell, 1992.) Certainly any and all of the processes for increasing adaptability (selection, quasi-evolution, and systematic growth) may be implemented in nnet-equipped LV control structures. It seems clear that aspects of both approaches need to be retained and the combination of flexibility and structure that LV control provides may open a way in which to integrate the strengths of the two models. However, there is no space to explore these ideas here.

Intelligence and Self-Organization

A system causally instantiating a trainable nnet will modify itself under stimulation in a systematic way that reflects the statistical regularities in its inputs. Similarly, a Cunningham network will grow internal connections in a systematic way under systematic input stimulation exhibiting characteristic information-processing stages. Both of these systems thus exhibit a basic self-organizing capacity. They have an internal causal capacity for systematic self-modification of a kind that succeeds in increasing the correlations among states of their internal components and in a way that is increasingly correlated with statistical regularities in their inputs. Self-organization of this kind is a powerful explanatory tool for understanding cognitive complex adaptive systems, and one of more general scope than any of those discussed so far.

Any learning system must be increasing some form of internal organization of this kind—otherwise learning would be a causeless miracle. The degree to which the system is *self*-organizing concerns only how far the learning process is under internal causal control. Thus all nnets, whatever their modification law, are organizing systems. But an nnet with back-propagation modification externally imposed is substantially less a self-organizing system than is, for example, an internally equipped nnet or an LV controller equipped with an nnet memory. Similarly, a classical NAIT system running some kind of systematic update program is a self-organizing system—though one exhibiting quite different self-organizing principles from any of the foregoing examples. (This is the fundamental reason for distinguishing nnets within connectionism at large; other connectionist

parallel distributed processing systems, to the degree that they exhibit self-organization at all, exhibit it in NAIT form.) Conversely, systems with very elementary response capacities, such as Brooks's robotic creatures (Brooks, 1991), may exhibit very complex behavior when placed in a complex environment but may instantiate only very modest self-organization if they learn very little from their behavior, or none at all (indeed, no increase in organization at all) if they cannot learn (as Brooks's creatures cannot).

The systems of particular interest here are the significantly self-organizing systems whose principle of organization derives from local interactions among the system's elementary components, interactions such that the system exhibits cognitive functional outcomes as the macro result of these micro modifications. A Cunningham system is one kind of example; another is an nnet where the connection strength between two nodes is updated by adding some function of the two node activity levels (generalized Hebb rule). Once this general idea is grasped, there is no need to confine attention to nnets as cognitive science currently utilizes them. The class of dynamical systems exhibiting this general kind of self-organization is very wide indeed and remains so even for the subclass showing significant functional control capacity. Such systems range from purely physical and chemical self-organization through biochemical self-organization, which likely lies at the foundations of all life forms (Eigen & Winkler, 1981; Peacocke, 1983). They appear throughout biology and are increasingly recognised as fundamental to understanding all economic and sociopolitical systems (see starred bibliography). There are deep connections between such irreversible nonlinear dynamical systems and generalized nnets (e.g., Green, 1992), but the specific causal diversity of self-organization is so great and so relevant to understanding that I shall set the matter of abstract representation to one side.

In particular, neurons are highly nonlinear dynamic devices and neuronal systems modify themselves under sufficiently regular stimulation in various ways similar to most of the learning processes discussed earlier. So we may expect brains to be examples of highly self-organizing systems. Recently models along these lines have emerged. Freeman and Skarda (1985), for example, have proposed a model of the olfactory bulb in which each discriminated odor of behavioral significance is associated with a spatially extended state of patterned activity modeled mathematically as a limit cycle attractor. At each smelling the relevant more ordered state repeatedly emerges from the background state, which itself is self-organized (Skarda, 1992; see also Skarda, 1986). For work on the visual cortex see, e.g., Bossomaier et al. (1992) and for other work see, e.g., Amit, (1989), Burkitt (1992), Churchland (1986), Freeman (1986), Hanson and Johnson (1990), and Malsburg (1987), and cf. Amari (1983). It has been suggested that these states themselves are self-organized into a critical condition where transition to any one of them can be initiated by small environmental stimuli, a condition described as "at the edge of chaos" (Kauffman, 1991; Kauffman & Johnson, 1991; Ito & Gunji, 1992, Skarda & Freeman, 1987; Winfree, 1987), and possibly new and subtly efficient forms of control exercised (see Schinbrot et al., 1993). We see in a model such as this a basis for elementary discrimination and learning which is quite different from both NAIT learning and from classical models of single-neuron modification and which generalizes nnet self-organization. And beyond these models lie a wider variety of approaches modeling the mind as a dynamical self-organizing system, e.g., Beer (1990); Brooks (1991), Cherian and Troxell (1994), Maes (1990), Port and van Gelder (1995). It is reasonable to expect an increasingly wide and internally sophisticated collection of these models in the future as we acquire facility with self-organizing models generally. With this general conception of self-organization, we have reached the widest class of models that may be used as a foundation for cognitive science.

Conclusion

These are preliminary and sketchy considerations, designed simply to open up the wider vista of GNIT theories of intelligent systems beyond what conventional approaches, especially NAIT, contain. They do not do more. Even so, along the way we have noted a number of issues that offer opportunity for fruitful interaction between philosophy and psychology, e.g., the nature of self-organization, computation, concepts, information, representation, problem solving, semantic content, reason, mental qualities and consciousness. More globally, they open up an approach to intelligence which is as much or more "bottom-up" rather than "top-down" based (macro or global pattern and

function emerge from interaction rather than being imposed); in which logic and language are derivative rather than central; in which concept-like association is quantitative and multidimensioned, prototype and analogy–metaphor governed, rather than all-or-nothing (1 or 0) and propositional; in which problem solving, indeed learning as a whole, is fundamentally self-organizing and fitting rather than computing—and thus in which there is a new basis for interaction and integration with neurophysiology and the other brain sciences, as opposed to the aloofness of an a priori separation of function from causal implementation. The contrasting alternatives can be accommodated to the (quantitative) degree required in hybrid models, and there may well be feedback from macro or global function to micro states and dynamics, but the contrast between the two approaches is clear. Allied with a suitable naturalist philosophy to support it, we have here the foundations of a new naturalist paradigm for cognitive science. So let us turn briefly to that latter issue.

A NATURALIST PHILOSOPHY OF THE NATURAL SCIENCES OF INTELLIGENT SYSTEMS

A Naturalist Perspective

Naturalists aim to build a unified account of the world. This means theorizing humans as a part of nature, and this in turn means theorizing mind as a natural phenomenon. Learning is to be conceived as a natural product of natural processes, a direct extension of the interrelated phylogenetic, ecological, and ontogenetic processes characterizing life at large. To a naturalist's eye there is something wrong with intruding into evolutionary history a nonnatural mind that inhabits a world of its own with laws of its own since there is nothing in the diverse evidence for the gradual development of increasing physiological and neurological complexity to suggest anything discontinuous of this sort.

Our currently best "picture" is something like this: Living creatures are dissipative structures; far-from-equilibrium structures stabilized by an energy flow, and all evolution (and ontogenesis) corresponds to the incorporation of order (negative entropy) available from the environment. The genotype/phenotype structure is the systemic device for the intergenerational transmission of basic biochemical order, and of increasing regulatory structure in the phenotype and ecology as complexity increases. Selection maps environmental features into an organism's structure. Causally, information is environmental order encoded in metastable structures whose states are a function of input; these appear functionally as conditional response structures. The point of regulatory organization is to realize a sufficiently rich structure of metastable states to control life processes. Thus the evolution of complexity is an information encoding.[16]

Similarly, in the central nervous system information is realized as its continually changing causally active structure. From this point of view the whole life-history of the brain is its ontogenesis and this includes all its cognitive history. The processes of (metastable) structural development and those of information encoding are one and the same. The connections drawn here between structure, metastability, encoded information, organization, and cognition, while yet rudimentary, form the basis for a naturalist retheorizing of mind–brain within a unified metaphysics of regulatory systems (see Hooker, 1995; cf. Hahlweg & Hooker, 1989; Bickhard & Campbell, 1992). Nature is theorized as a nested set of regulatory systems. These stretch down into the cell (mitochondria, for example, are already extremely complex biochemical systems), and they stretch upward to encompass successively organs, organisms, populations, ecologies, and the biosphere. Each systemic level has some degree of control over its functions and states, typically expressed as homeostatic conditions, and each is constrained by both the character of the subsystems it contains and the systems for which it is in turn a subsystem.

Paradoxically, the more general problem-solving capacity each individual has, the more immediate is the need for social coordination, i.e., for an "external nervous system." Human phenotypes are (relatively) complex, with longer lifespans and few progeny and (relatively) highly adaptable, the population relying for its survival on their socially coordinated abilities. Individuals have decidedly finite capacities, thus what must quickly become the focus of nervous system development are not individual strategies shaped to particular circumstances and inflexibly retained but general problem-solving capacities. General problem solvers have much greater adaptability, because of their higher order behavioral conditionalization and their greater collective distributed

processing and problem-solving capacities, but only if they can coordinate their individual learning, spread the collective result across the group, focus on it explicitly so as to adapt it, and transmit it from generation to generation. The social processes by which these four crucial cognitive processes occur are structured through social institutions. Institutions themselves may be modeled as complex adaptive systems. Economic and scientific autonomy and specialization achieves both a parallel distributed mode of operation across goods or disciplines even while specialization provides for "chains of command" or the equivalent, which permit multilevel organization.

Our epistemic institutions provide the framework for the scientific education necessary to our extending cognitive neoteny; they permit cognitive division of labor compatibly with coherence of cognitive strategy; and they organize the acquisition and storage of our collective information. Under many reinforcing feedback processes they have grown explosively over the past three centuries in scale, organization, effective operational intervention in the environment (adaptation), and adaptability, in like manner to any other biological system. This conception of science is studied in Hooker (1995; cf. Hahlweg & Hooker, 1989). It can perhaps throw useful light on individual cognitive processes and systems development generally.

Consider, for example, what can be said about the interrelations between increasing adaptation and increasing adaptability in science. Increases in scientific adaptation include increases in precision, scope of generalizations, technological applicability and diversity of laboratory procedure, and so on. In short, increasing adaptation corresponds roughly to what Kuhn refers to as normal science (Kuhn, 1962). Increasing adaptability involves introducing deeper levels of theory, which regulate the expression of erstwhile theory: from specific empirical generalizations (e.g., the behavior of this pendulum, this stone) to theories able to derive classes of generalizations through alteration of parameter values (e.g., the law of free fall, the pendulum law), to theories at successively higher levels (e.g., Newton's laws, Lagrangian and Hamiltonian theory, symplectic structure on differentiable manifolds, and so on "up"). Each ascent allows regulated response to be conditioned one nesting deeper. The widening range of data structures encompassed means a widening range of situations to which regulated adaptation becomes possible, i.e., an increasing adaptability. It corresponds roughly to Kuhn's notion of revolutionary science and to increasing invariance extraction (see Hooker, 1991, 1992).

The interrelationships between the development of adaptation and adaptability are complex, exhibiting both positive and negative feedback (see Hahlweg & Hooker, 1989, Part IV). No simple-minded relationship between them will capture the dynamics and certainly not the rigid formal rules of the kind one finds in conventional AI-style formalist philosophy of science. If we want to understand the history of science then we must begin by understanding it as a complex series of regulatory shifts rather than as some simple oscillation between normal science and revolutions or (at the other Popperian extreme) as permanent revolution.[17] This insight into the dynamics of scientific development may help to understand the corresponding developmental dynamics that need to be captured within cognitive science, and perhaps within genetic systems as well. The point of this brief excursus into philosophy of science is that science itself, and by extension other socioeconomic processes, are best understood as kinds of partially self-organizing complex adaptive systems, just as are neural and biological systems; the GNIT framework is itself part of a new naturalist paradigm for the development/evolutionary processes in these systems, in which the cross-fertilization should prove helpful and mutually supportive.

Criteria for an Adequate Philosophical Naturalism

Properly naturalizing our theory of mind requires as much philosophical as scientific work. There are, I believe, four basic and unavoidable steps to forming a naturalist theory of agency:

1. Disentangle the function/cause, normative/descriptive and mental/physical dichotomies.
2. Provide a naturalist account of the normative.
3. Provide a naturalist theory of function/structure relations, in particular a theory of ontological reduction for functional descriptions.
4. Provide a naturalist theory of agency across all of the relevant sciences.

Here it is only appropriate to make some very brief remarks about these steps.

Ad Step 1

The functional/causal distinction applies to all theories of mind, indeed to all systems, irrespective of their ontology. While functionalist theories of mind would (controversially) confine the mental to functional specification, presumably leaving only a physical ontology for causal specification, that thesis is independent of the distinction in specifications. And whether or not an assertion is considered normative, and in what normativeness consists, is quite clearly independent of the other two issues. Even if it be held that normative terms are all agency terms this entails nothing about their functionality or qualitative distinctness. Hence the distinctness of the three dichotomies. (Failure to distinguish them has often meant great pain for naturalists.)

Ad Step 2

Naturalizing the normative/descriptive dichotomy, as I understand it, consists in giving a naturalistic account of the nature of normativeness and of the properties appearing in (acceptable) normative assertions. My own tilt at (a) is simply stated: To use a theory T (functionally) normatively in pursuit of ideal I in some domain D is to accept that T is our best current guide to I in D (as measured by some function of I's proxies) and to apply T to distinguish what other acts of acceptance are also warranted. Thus a scientific theory may be used to distinguish what data in its domain ought to be accepted, and to what extent, in the pursuit of truth, and a theory of scientific method may be used to distinguish what procedures in its domain ought to be accepted, and to what extent, in the pursuit of rational assessment—and so also what theories ought then to be accepted. And so on. This account is set out in Hooker (1994) and elaborated in Hooker (1995); a naturalistic account of ideals, the truth ideal in particular, is set out in Hooker (1995, chaps. 5, 6). But each normative area (e.g., ethics, rationality, values) needs to be approached separately.[18]

Ad Step 3

Despite the fact that functional and causal descriptions cross-classify one another, I contend that it is possible to satisfy the requirements of step 3 above. In Part III of Hooker (1981) I have tried to provide both the theory of relations and of reductions that naturalism requires (cf. note 6). The theory turns out to throw some light on the requirements for naturalist accounts of engineering systems (e.g., computers), molecular vis-à-vis Mendelian genetics and body/mind (functional) relations. (But no reductive account of mind yet follows because there is still the nonfunctional qualitative character of consciousness, secondary qualities, feelings, etc. to be faced; see the remarks on quantum theory in the introduction.)

Ad Step 4

Naturalism requires integration of cognitive theory with theory of the natural world, not materialism *per se*. The foundations for an account of this kind have been laid in the preceding sections. Numerous tasks remain. Intentionality is presumably to be naturalized using the devices of representation and feedback. Some of the vast literature on the subject is promising (e.g., Christensen, forthcoming), but there remains a long string of difficulties compounded by the conceptual jungle where notions of order, entropy, information, content, and meaning meet. In Hooker (1978) I tried to develop a naturalist theory of the secondary qualities by defending a version of the adverbial theory of perception, again using a systems theoretic setting. Though I still consider the arguments powerful, the adverbial theory faces well-known difficulties. Moreover, as indicated in the introduction, one can at present only remain open about the nature and status of mental qualities as far as scientific evidence goes. (There is also personal experience to consider.) Naturalization is an immensely complex task and again to be completed in detail for each particular theoretical domain. One key area is epistemology, and complex adaptive systems foundations for a naturalist evolutionary epistemology are provided in Hooker (1995). Another key area is reason, which many have assumed nonnaturalizable. Hooker (1995, chap. 6) offers a naturalistic theory of reason in terms of functional (self-)organization. The remainder of the task awaits, each area distinctive; reviewing them is quite beyond the scope of this essay.

Despite the inevitable incompleteness of the program—precisely to be expected if naturalism is correct—I shall take it that a viable naturalism of the sort sketched above can be developed. It pro-

vides a framework for integrating the theories of mind discussed in this chapter into a general account of complex adaptive systems. This will then have provided a distinctive stage in the development of the natural sciences of intelligent systems and with that a particular integration of philosophy and psychology.

ENDNOTES

1. I gratefully acknowledge helpful criticisms of an earlier draft of this essay by Hal Brown, John Collier, Bill Herfel, and Bruce Penfold, though my response to their wisdom is my own folly.

2. Popper (1979); see Hooker (1995, chap. 3) for some discussion, including analysis of an argument by Popper which, contrary to his supposition, merely succeeds in labeling the problem without resolving it.

3. For Wigner's views see Wigner (1973) and for a review of interpretations of quantum theory, including comment on Wigner, see Hooker (1973). With respect to challenging traditional measurement theory, the basis of Wigner's interpretation, see, e.g., Hartle (1993). Arguments for our limited understanding of quantum ontology are given in Hooker (1992).

4. See, e.g., Glass et al. (1979), Minsky (1981), Stillings et al. (1987). It has been particularly championed by Fodor (1975) and Pylyshyn (1984); see recently Fodor and Pylyshyn (1988).

5. In principle one might challenge the assumption that mind is a form of organization, in any recognized sense of that term; we may, e.g., find special roles for the nonrelational properties of the neural substrate in reconstructing the qualities of mind and so will not have a purely organizational theory, or we might model mind as a single coherent quantum complex. Also, it might fundamentally be characterized by noncomputable functions; see, e.g., Geroch and Hartle (1986); cf. Penrose (1989). But these alternatives will not be explored here. GNIT excludes Cartesian dualism and other forms of dualism created by fiat or appeal to a priori argument, but is not committed to any narrow materialism. Following on the earlier discussion, a principled Whiteheadian property dualism, e.g., could be developed in a GNIT-acceptable manner.

6. This distinction has been discussed for genetic and cognitive systems in Hooker (1981, Part III) and presented for biology and psychology more widely in Hahlweg and Hooker (1989, Parts III and IV). The latter contains a summary analysis of Cummins (1983), which dissects psychological explanation, especially the explanation of complex information-processing properties and related functional capacities possessed by intelligent systems vis-à-vis their possible causal–dynamical realization. In effect, it must be possible to construct from the

dynamics of a system S a set of input–output nomic patterns which, modulo initial conditions, can model the functional capacities of S. This is precisely what functional reduction for systems requires, according to Hooker (1981). Only one system, one ontology, is involved but there is no simple way to identify the functional properties and states with S's structural–dynamical properties and states.

7. For programs are purely formal structures and are not themselves "creative"; they can only transform existing symbolic contents into other symbolic contents. Thus a program L for altering programs must itself rely on its own initial symbolic contents, or appeal to some further program L' for altering $L,$ which generates a vicious infinite regress of such programs or again terminates in some basic program whose symbolic contents are fixed beyond alteration. This is, e.g., the conclusion Fodor draws. See Fodor (1980) vis-à-vis Piaget (1980).

8. But of course we shall still require of theories of F and L that they capture the distinctive properties of intelligence, e.g., *systematicity*, expressing the systematic interrelations that symbolic structures have to one another, and its dual, *decomposition*, the capacity to add symbolic structures to the existing repertoire without automatically having to restructure the lot. Adding to or altering symbolic structures has systematic, but highly selective, effects on the remaining structures. Logical structure seems to capture this property nicely. These features are the bases for arguments by Fodor, Pylyshyn and others that cognitive theory must be of the NAIT type. They fail; see below. Nonetheless, any wider theory of mind than NAIT ought to have something to say about how such systematic selectivity is either reconstructed or explained away within its broader resources. But we should equally acknowledge the ubiquity of analogy, metaphor, and the like in human thinking and the centrality of vagueness, ambiguity, and partial conceptual variation, especially in creative learning processes. These features may be taken in turn as an argument for a more basic subconceptual, subformal mode of cognitive operation than the precise all-or-nothing character of NAIT's logic and formal programming. (Alternatives are restricted; the introduction of fuzzy logic, for example, still leaves the basic structure confined to boolean inference.) Here it is NAIT that must do a lot of explaining/ explaining away (whereas NAIT theorists have had a tendency to dismiss or suppress the issues) and WAIT that promises to do better. (It can also model fuzzy logic systems; see, e.g., Kasobov, 1993.)

9. For this reason, Smolensky locates the subsymbolic level "lower" than the symbolic level. Equally, because it abstracts away from many features of the brain that are "probably extremely important to understanding how the brain computes" (Smolensky 1988, p. 9), the subsymbolic level is located "higher" than the neuronal level which focuses around the specific geometries of neural interconnections and the electro–chemical dynamics of synaptic connection function (see Smolensky, 1988, table 1). Smolensky concludes that it therefore lies "between" the neuronal and symbolic levels. Such loose levels talk runs together a part–whole relation (a part is at a lower level than the whole, e.g. node to nnet), a causal relation (if parts so interact that a notion of dynamical state can be constructed for their whole obeying a dynamical law independently of fluctuations in the dynamical conditions of the parts, then the whole forms a distinct level; Collier, 1988), and the function–cause relation discussed in the introduction (the level of functional or information-processing specification of a system and that of the causal specification of the system). Symbolic descriptions belong to the class of functional specifications of a system while the numerical models of nets are not halfway houses but simply ambiguous as between functional (as purely formal models) and causal specifications (as physically realized propagating quantity, e.g., electrical charge).

10. Churchland (1979, 1989) and Stich (1983), for example, argue for the ultimate elimination of these conceptions. If substance or compositional reduction is clearly inappropriate, perhaps a function–cause analysis of reduction in systems (Hooker, 1981) allied to a related account of idealization (Hooker, 1994) will find room to accept both conceptual and subconceptual models (cf. Bickle, 1992). An important virtue of WAIT is that it allows what NAIT suppresses, namely the possibility that the basic categories of an empirically adequate cognitive science may be significantly different from those of commonsense agency conceptions and that, like the concepts of approximate macroscopic theories generally operating under (tacitly assumed) restricted conditions, the latter will be only approximately reconstructable.

11. Conversely, it does not matter that neural net models can be implemented on a traditional von Neumann architecture computer using formal symbolic programs, since the symbols here represent the strengths of connections and "do not have conceptual semantics" (Smolensky, 1988, p. 7). So the programs describing neural net function are not the same as those that would describe a cognitive psychology. Smolensky continues: "It is well known that von Neumann machines and connectionist networks can simulate each other. This fact leads some people to adopt the position that the connectionist approach cannot offer anything fundamentally new because we already have Turing machines and, following Church's Thesis, reason to believe that, when it comes to computation, Turing machines are everything. This position, however, mistakes the issue for cognitive science to be the purely syntactic question of whether mental programs are written for Turing/von Neumann machines or connectionist machines. This is a non-issue" (Smolensky, 1988, p. 7).

12. The formal characterization of these computations should not deceive; that belongs only to the formal model; in any actual realization they concern the propa-

gation of real physical signals (cf. neuronal operation). Technically, the characterization of computations will use the detailed functional specification of the nnet which mirrors, and holds only because of, the causal specification. This also does not alter the point made in the text.

13. Dreyfus (e.g., 1992) discusses the example of arriving at the shortest route between two of many cities. One obvious computational approach is to calculate the trip length of all the possible routes and then to choose the route with the smallest trip length in the set. Alternatively, one can construct a flexible net in which the intersection knots represent the actual cities. One then simply holds the net by the two relevant cities and pulls and the shortest route rises to the top as the tautest string. That is, one deforms the net into a suitable surface.

14. This is so however these capacities are causally organized. That a von Neumann digital computer, like any other physical device, has a causal specification that does not include any symbolic processing terms is irrelevant, since its causal realization will be distinctive of NAIT devices and be reflected in its functional specification.

15. The detailed computation of the control signal required to achieve local control of S is quite simple, but depends on the vector field curvatures and the accuracy and frequency of the measurement of S's output. If S is measured sufficiently frequently (sufficiently small sampling time) and with small uncertainty, then it is possible to show that the increment in control input over the existing value is simply calculated from the difference between the predicted flow deviation of the controlled and reference systems. For all practical applications it suffices to use linear extrapolation from their current settings. The details of the algorithm need not concern us here (see Penfold & Evans, 1989; Penfold et al., 1992).

16. The term "informational" is being used here in the sense of engineering information theory and not in the distinct sense of semantic information. The nature of the relation between these two senses is a difficult and unresolved question tied to the issue of the nature of the semantic (see above). Similarly, the relation of information to metastability and control is unresolved. Finally, the task of relating information to thermodynamic order is an equally complex and unresolved one. These difficult but important theoretical/philosophical issues cannot be pursued here.

Further, which particular subset of information encodings are the cognitive ones? The horse's hoof encodes features of the Russian steppe (Lorenz tells us), but it is not a cognitive system; our immune system encodes invading viruses—cognitively? This is a difficult question to which there is no good answer at the present time. Surely the encodings have to be systemically organized and at least partially hierarchical, but what else? How weak a connection to output is admissible? How weak an internal protological ordering? Fodor would go so far as

to demand that they constitute symbolic representations over which computations are made and that these latter be sufficiently rich (both internally and in connection to output) as to represent a structure for which a notion of mistaken belief makes sense, but this is likely excessive. Elementary controllers work off mismatch signals or errors; error signals will long precede anything like human belief in the evolutionary history of mind. (Of course human cognitive capacities must eventually be explained.)

17. Feyerabend is right. No specific transition in the history of science will be quite like any other, any more than any specific change in the evolutionary/developmental history of genetic or neural regulatory systems is quite like any other; but he is also wrong: This fact does not prevent our understanding them through theorizing them—to the contrary. See Hooker (1991) and Hahlweg and Hooker (1989, Part IV).

18. There are crass naturalist *cum* materialist positions, e.g., that values are merely causally induced prejudices and opaque to reason, that reason is mere optimization over such values, and ethics mere emoting, but these seem unacceptable and the real situation in each case is complex. Here cf. Hooker (1987, especially 7.11–13 and 8.4). But the text references supersede the precursor account of norms given in Hooker (1987).

REFERENCES

*Abraham, R., & Shaw, C. (1982). *Dynamics—The geometry of behaviour* (4 Vols.). *Vismath:* The Visual Mathematics Library. Santa Cruz: Ariel.

*Allen, Peter M. (1983). Self-organization and evolution in urban systems. In R. Crosby (Ed.), *Cities and regions as nonlinear decision systems.* AAAS Selected Symposia Series. Boulder: Westview.

Amari, S.-I. (1983). Field theory of self-organising neural nets. *IEEE Transactions on systems, man and cybernetics*, SMC-13, 741–9.

Amit, J. (1989). *Modelling brain function, the world of attractor neural networks.* Cambridge: Cambridge University.

*Anderson, P. W., Arrow, K. J., & Pines, D. (Eds.). (1988). *The economy as an evolving complex system.* Redwood City, CA: Addison-Wesley.

Astrom, K. J. & McAvoy, T. J. (1992). Intelligent control. *Journal of Process Control*, 2, 115–27.

Ballard, D. H. (1986). Cortical connections and parallel processing: Structure and function, *Behavioral and Brain Sciences*, 9, 67–120.

Barndon, J., & Srinivas, K. (1992). Overcoming rule-based rigidity and connectionist limitations through massively-parallel case-based reasoning. *International Journal of Man-Machine Studies*, 36, 221–46.

Bechtel, W., & Abrahamsen, A. (1991). *Connectionism and the mind.* Oxford: Blackwell.

*Beer, R. D. (1990). *Intelligence as adaptive behavior: An experiment in computational neuroethology.* New York: Academic.

Bickhard, M. H. (1980). *Cognition, convention and communication.* New York: Praeger.

Bickhard, M. H., & Campbell, R. L. (1992). Some foundational questions concerning language study: With a focus on categorial grammars and model-theoretic possible worlds semantics. *Journal of Pragmatics, 17,* 401–33, 557–602.

Bickhard, M.H., & Terveen, L. (1995). *Foundational issues in artificial intelligence and cognitive science: Impasse and solution.* Amsterdam: Elsevier.

Bickle, J. (1992). Revisionary physicalism. *Biology and Philosophy, 7,* 411–30.

Bohm, D. (1980). *Wholeness and the implicate order.* London: Routledge and Kegan Paul.

Bossomaier, T., Pipitone, J., & Stuart, G. (1992). Neural dynamics in biological information processing. In D. G. Green & T. Bossomaier (Eds.), *Complex systems: From biology to computation.* Amsterdam: IOS.

Brooks, R. A. (1991). Intelligence without representation, *Artificial Intelligence, 47,* 139–59.

Burkitt, A. N. (1992). External inputs to attractor neural networks. In D. G. Green & T. Bossomaier (Eds.), *Complex systems: From biology to computation.* Amsterdam: IOS.

Chalmers, D. J. (1990). Syntactic transformations on distributed representation. *Connection Science, 2,* 53–62.

Chater, N., & Oaksford, M. (1990). Autonomy, implementation and cognitive architecture: A reply to Fodor and Pylyshyn. *Cognition, 34,* 93–107.

*Cherian, S., & Troxell, W. O. (1994). Intelligent behavior in machines emerging from a collection of interactive control structures. *Computational Intelligence, 10,* 1–31.

Christensen, W. (forthcoming). A complex systems theory of teleology. *Biology and philosophy.*

Churchland, P. M. (1979). *Scientific realism and the plasticity of mind.* Cambridge, MA: Cambridge University.

Churchland, P. M. (1989). *A neurocomputational perspective: The nature of mind and the structure of science.* Cambridge, MA: Bradford/MIT.

Churchland, P. S. (1986). *Neuro-philosophy: Toward a unified understanding of the mind-brain.* Cambridge, MA: MIT.

*Collier, J. (1986). Entropy in evolution. *Biology and Philosophy, 1,* 5–24.

Collier, J. (1988). Supervenience and reduction in biological hierarchies. *Canadian Journal of Philosophy* (Suppl.: *Biology and Philosophy*). Calgary: University of Calgary.

*Collier, J. (1993). Out of equilibrium: New approaches to biological and social change. *Biology and Philosophy, 8,* 445–56.

Cummins, R. (1983). *The nature of psychological explanation.* Boston: Bradford/MIT.

Cunningham, M. (1972). *Intelligence: Its origin and development.* New York: Academic.

Dennett, D. C. (1984). Cognitive wheels: The frame problem of artificial intelligence. In C. Hookway (Ed.), *Minds, machines and evolution.* Cambridge: Cambridge University.

Dennett, D. C. (1986).The logical geography of computational approaches: A view from the East Pole. In M. Harnish & M. Brand (Eds.), *Problems in the representation of knowledge.* Tucson: University of Arizona.

*Diner, S., Fargue, D., & Lochak, G. (1986). *Dynamical systems: A renewal of mechanism.* Singapore: World Scientific.

Dreyfus, H. L. (1992). *What computers still can't do: A critique of artificial reason.* Cambridge, MA: MIT.

Dreyfus, H. L., & Dreyfus, S. E. (1986). *Mind over machine.* Oxford: Blackwell.

*Dyke, C. (1988). *The evolutionary dynamics of complex systems.* Oxford: Oxford University.

Earman, J. (1992). *Bayes or bust.* Cambridge, MA: MIT.

Edelman, G. M. (1989). *Neural Darwinism.* Oxford: Oxford University.

*Eigen, M., & Winkler, R. (1981). *The laws of the game: How the principles of nature govern chance* (Transl. R. Kimber and R. Kimber). New York: Knopf.

Farmer, J. D. (1990). A Rosetta stone for connectionism. In S. Forrest (Ed.), *Emergent computation.* Amsterdam: Elvsevier.

Feldman, J. A., & Ballard, D. H. (1982). Connectionist models and their properties. *Cognitive Science, 6,* 205–24; reprinted in D. Waltz & J. A. Feldman (Eds.) (1988). *Connectionist models and their implications: Readings from cognitive science.* Norwood, NJ: Ablex.

*Firrao, S. (1983). *The theory of self-organizing systems in physics, biology and psychology.* Milan: CENS.

Fodor J. A. (1975). *The language of thought.* New York: T. Y. Crowell.

Fodor, J. A. (1980). On the impossibility of acquiring "more powerful" structures. In M. Piatelli-Palmarini (Ed.), *Language and learning: The debate between Jean Piaget and Noam Chomsky.* Cambridge, MA: Harvard University.

Fodor, J. A. (Ed.). (1987). *Psychosemantics,* Cambridge, MA: MIT.

Fodor, J., & McLaughlin, B. (1990). Connectionism and the problem of systematicity: Why Smolensky's solution doesn't work. *Cognition, 35,* 183–204.

Fodor, J. A., & Pylyshyn, Z. W. (1988). Connectionism and cognitive architecture: A critical analysis. *Cognition, 28,* 3–71.

Ford, K. M., & Pylyshyn, Z. (Eds.). (1994). *The robot's dilemma revisited: The frame problem in artificial intelligence.* Norwood, NJ: Ablex.

*Forrest, S. (1990). *Emergent computation*. Amsterdam: Elsevier.

Forster, M. (1990). Learning, conceptual innovation and scientific discovery. Unpublished manuscript, University of Wisconsin, Madison.

Forster, M. (1992). The connectionist challenge to cognitve science. Unpublished manuscript, University of Wisconsin, Madison.

*Foster, J. (1987). *Evolutionary macroeconomics*. London: Allen and Unwin.

Freeman, W. (1986). *Mass action in the nervous system*. New York: Academic.

Freeman, W., & Skarda, C. (1985). Spatial EEG patterns, non-linear dynamics and perception: The neo-Sherringtonian view. *Brain Research Reviews, 10*, 147–75.

*Frehland, E. (Ed.). (1984). *Synergetics—From microscopic to macroscopic order*. New York: Springer-Verlag.

Geroch, R., & Hartle, J. B. (1986). Computability and physical theories. *Foundations of Physics, 16*, 533–50.

Glass, A. L., Holyoake, K. J. & Santa, J. L. (1979). *Cognition*. Reading, MA: Addison-Wesley.

Green, D. G. (1992). Emergent behaviour in biological systems. In D. G. Green & T. Bossomaier (Eds.), *Complex systems: From biology to computation*. Amsterdam: IOS.

*Grossberg, S. (1988). Non-linear neural networks: Principles, mechanisms, and architectures. *Neural Networks, 1*, 17–61.

Hahlweg, K., & Hooker C. A. (1989). Evolutionary epistemology and philosophy of science. In K. Hahlweg & C. A. Hooker (Eds.), *Issues in evolutionary epistemology*. Albany, NY: State University of New York.

Hanson, S. J., & Johnson, C. R. (Eds.). (1990). *Connectionist modelling of brain function*. Cambridge, MA: MIT/Bradford.

Hartle, J. B. (1993). The quantum mechanics of closed systems. In B. L. Hu, M. P. Ryan, & C. V. Vishveshwara (Eds.), *Festschrift for C. W. Misner*. Cambridge: Cambridge University.

Hinton, G. E. (1989). Connectionist learning procedures. *Artificial Intelligence, 40*, 185–234.

Hinton, G. E. (1990). Mapping part-whole hierarchy into connectionist networks. *Artificial Intelligence, 46*, 47–75.

*Holland, J. H. (1992). *Adaptation in natural and artificial systems*. Cambridge, MA: MIT/Bradford.

Hooker, C. A. (Ed.). (1973). *Contemporary research in the foundations and philosophy of quantum theory*. Dordrecht: Reidel.

Hooker, C. A. (1978). An evolutionary naturalist realist doctrine of perception and a nihilist doctrine of the secondary qualities. In C. W. Savage (Ed.), *Perception and cognition: Issues in the foundations of psychology*. Minneapolis: University of Minnesota.

Hooker, C. A. (1981).Towards a general theory of reduction. *Dialogue, XX*, Part I, Historical framework, 38–59; Part II, Identity and reduction, 201–36; Part III, Cross-categorial reduction, 496–529.

Hooker, C. A. (1987). *A realistic theory of science*. Albany, NY: State University of New York.

Hooker, C. A. (1988). Critical notice: Churchland, P.S., *Neurophilosophy. Australasian Journal of Philosophy, 66*, 240–8.

Hooker, C. A. (1991). Between formalism and anarchism: A reasonable middle way. In G. Munevar (Ed.), *Beyond reason: Essays on the philosophy of Paul Feyerabend*. Boston: Kluwer.

Hooker, C. A. (1992). Physical intelligibility, projection, objectivity and completeness: The divergent ideals of Bohr and Einstein. *British Journal for the Philosophy of Science, 42*, 491–511.

Hooker, C. A. (1994). Idealisation, naturalism, and rationality: Some lessons from minimal rationality. *Synthese, 99*, 181–231.

Hooker, C. A. (1995). *Reason, regulation and realism*. Albany, NY: State University of New York.

Hooker, C. A., Penfold, H. B., & Evans, R. J. (1992a). Cognition under a new control paradigm. *Topoi, 11*, 71–88.

Hooker, C. A., Penfold, H. B., and Evans, R. J. (1992b). Control, connectionism and cognition: Toward a new regulatory paradigm. *British Journal for the Philosophy of Science, 43*, 517–36.

Horgan, T., & Tienson, J. (1992). Cognitive systems as dynamical systems. *Topoi, 11*, 27–43.

Hornik, K., Stinchcombe, M., & White, H. (1989). Multilayer feed forward networks are universal approximators. *Neural Networks, 2* (5), 359–66.

Ito, K., & Gunji, Y.-P. (1992). Self-organisation toward criticality in the game of life. *Biosystems, 26*, 135–8.

*Jantsch, E. (Ed.). (1981). *The evolutionary vision: Toward a unifying paradigm of physical, biological and sociocultural evolution*. Boulder, CO: Westview.

*Jantsch, E., & Waddington, C. H. (1976). *Evolution and consciousness: Human systems in transition*. London: Addison-Wesley.

Kasobov, N. K. (1993). Towards connectionist realization of fuzzy production systems. In P. Leong & M. Jabri (Eds.), *Proceedings of the fourth Australian conference on neural nets*. Sydney: University of Sydney, Department of Electrical Engineering.

*Kauffman, S. A. (1991). Anti-chaos and adaptation. *Scientific American, 264*, 78–84.

*Kauffman, S. A. (1992). *Origins of order: Self-organisation and selection in evolution*. New York: Oxford University.

*Kauffman, S. A., & Johnson, S. (1991). Co-evolution to the edge of chaos, coupled fitness landscapes, poised states and co-evolutionary avalanches. *Journal of Theoretical Biology, 149*, 467–505.

Kohonen, T. (1984). *Self-organization and associative memory* (2nd ed.). New York: Springer-Verlag.

Kuhn, T. S. (1962). *The structure of scientific revolutions*. Chicago: University of Chicago.

Lakoff, G. (1987). *Women, fire and dangerous things: What categories reveal about the mind*. Chicago: University of Chicago Press.

*Langton, C. G. (Ed.). (1989). *Artificial life*. New York: Addison-Wesley.

*Langton, C. G., Taylor, G., Farmer, J. D., & Rasmussen, S. (Eds.). (1992). *Artificial life II*. Redwood City, CA: Addison-Wesley.

Lindgren, K., & Nordahl, M.G. (1990). Universal computation in a simple one-dimensional cellular automaton. *Complex Systems, 4*, 299–318.

*Maes, P. (1990). *Designing autonomous agents: Theory and practice from biology to engineering and back*. Amsterdam: Elsevier.

Malsburg, C. von der (1987). Ordered retinotectile projections and brain organisation. In F. E. Yates (Ed.), *Self-organising systems: The emergence of order*. New York: Plenum.

Medlin, B. (1967). Ryle and the mechanical hypothesis. In C. F. Presley, *The identity theory of mind*. St. Lucia: University of Queensland.

Minsky, M. (1981). A framework for representing knowledge. In J. Haugland. (Ed.), *Mind design*. Cambridge, MA: MIT.

*Nadel, L., & Stein, D. (Eds.). (1991). *1991 Lectures in complex systems*. Redwood City, CA: Addison-Wesley.

Nelson, R. J. (1969). Behaviourism is false. *Journal of Philosophy, LXVI*, 417–52.

*Nicolis, J. S. (1986). *Dynamics of hierarchical systems: An evolutionary approach*. Berlin: Springer-Verlag.

*Peacocke, A. R. (1983). *An introduction to the physical chemistry of biological organization*. Oxford: Clarendon.

Penfold, H. B., & Evans R. J. (1989). Control algorithm for unknown, time-varying systems. *International Journal of Control, 50*, 13–32.

Penfold, H. B., Mareels, I. M. Y., & Evans R. J. (1992). Adaptively controlling non-linear systems using trajectory approximations. *International Journal of Adaptive Control and Signal Processing, 6*, 395–411.

Penrose, R. (1989). *The emperor's new mind*. London: Vintage.

Piaget, J. (1980). The psychogenesis of knowledge and its epistemological significance. In M. Piatelli-Palmarino (Ed.), *Language and learning: The debate between Jean Piaget and Noam Chomsky*. Cambridge, MA: Harvard University.

Piatelli-Palmarini, M. (1989). Evolution, selection and cognition: From "learning" to parameter setting in biology and in the study of language. *Cognition, 31*, 1–44.

*Pines, David (1988). *Emerging synthesis in science*. Redwood City, CA: Addison-Wesley.

Pollack, J. B. (1989). Implications of recursive distributed representation. In D. S. Touretzky (Ed.), *Advances in neural information processing*. San Mateo: Morgan Kaufman.

Pollack, J. B. (1990). Recursive distributed representations. *Artificial Intelligence, 46*, 77–105.

Popper, K. (1979). *Objective knowledge*. Oxford: Oxford University.

*Port, R., & van Gelder, T. J. (1995). *Mind as motion: Explorations in the dynamics of cognition*. Cambridge, MA: MIT.

Powers, W.T. (1973). *Behaviour, the control of perception*. London: Wildwood House.

*Prigogine, I., & Stengers, I. (1984). *Order out of chaos*. Boulder, CO: Shambhala.

Pylyshyn, Z. (1984). *Computation and cognition: Toward a foundation for cognitive science*. Cambridge: Cambridge University.

Reeke, Jr., G. N., Sporns, O., & Edelman, G. M. (1989). Synthetic neural modelling, comparisons of population and connectionist approaches. In R. Pfeifer, Z. Shreter, F. Fogelman-Soulié, & L. Steels (Eds.). *Connectionism in perspective*. Amsterdam: Elsevier.

*Rosen, R. (1991). *Life itself: A comprehensive inquiry into the nature, origin and fabrication of life*. New York: Columbia University.

Rumelhart, D. E., Hinton, G. E., & Williams, R. J. (1986). Learning representations by back-propagating errors. *Nature, 323*, 533–36.

Rumelhart, D. E., & McClelland, J. L. (Eds.). (1986). *Parallel distributed processing* (Vol. 1). Cambridge, MA: MIT.

*Salthe, S. N. (1985). *Evolving hierarchical systems: Their structure and representation*. New York: Columbia University.

*Salthe, S. N. (1989). Self-organisation of/in hierarchically structured systems. *Systems Research, 6*, 199–208.

Schinbrot, T., Grebogi, C., Ott, E., & Yorke, J. A. (1993). Using small perturbations to control chaos. *Nature, 363*, 411–7.

Schumacher, J. A. (1989). *Human posture*, Albany, NY: State University of New York.

Skarda, C. (1986). Explaining behaviour: Bringing the brain back in. *Inquiry, 29*, 187–202.

Skarda, C. (1992). Perception, connectionism and cognitive science. In F. J. Varela, & J. -P. Dupuy (Eds.), *Understanding origins*. Dordrecht: Kluwer.

*Skarda, C., & Freeman, W. (1987). How brains make chaos in order to make sense of the world. *Behavioural and Brain Sciences, 10*, 161–73.

Smolensky, P. (1988). On the proper treatment of connectionism. *Behavioural and Brain Sciences, 11*, 1–74.

Smolensky, P. (1990). Tensor product variable binding and the representation of symbolic structures in connection with systems. *Artificial Intelligence, 46,* 159–216.

*Stear, E. B. (1987). Control paradigms and self-organisation in living systems. In F. E. Yates (Ed.), *Self-organising systems: The emergence of order.* New York: Plenum.

Stich, S. (1983). *From folk psychology to cognitive science: The case against belief.* Cambridge, MA: MIT.

Stillings, N., Weisler, S., Chase, C., Feinstein, M., Garfield, J., & Risland, E. (1987). *Cognitive science: An introduction.* Cambridge, MA: MIT.

Tienson, J. L. (1987). Introduction to connectionism. *Southern Journal of Philosophy, 26* (Suppl.), 1–16.

Touretzky, D. S., Elman, J. L., Sejnowski, T. J., & Hinton, G. E. (Eds.). (1990). *Proceedings of the 1990 connectionist models summer school.* San Mateo, CA: Morgan Kaufmann.

*Weber, B., Depew, D., & Smith, J. (Eds.). (1988). *Entropy, information, and evolution.* Cambridge, MA: MIT.

Widrow. B., & Stearns, S. D. (1985). *Adaptive signal processing.* Englewood Cliffs, NJ: Prentice-Hall.

Wigner, E. (1973). Epistemological perspective on quantum theory. In C. A. Hooker (Ed.), *Contemporary research in the foundations and philosophy of quantum theory.* Dordrecht: Reidel.

*Winfree, A. (1987). *When time breaks down.* Princeton: Princeton University.

Yao, X. (1993). A review of evolutionary artificial neurone networks. *International Journal of Intelligent Systems, 8,* 539–68.

*Yates, F. E. (Ed.). (1987). *Self-organising systems: The emergence of order.* New York: Plenum.

*Zurek, W. H. (Ed.). (1990). *Complexity, entropy and the physics of information.* Redwood City, CA: Addison-Wesley.

CHAPTER 15

NEUROBEHAVIORAL SCIENCE, NEUROPSYCHOLOGY, AND THE PHILOSOPHY OF MIND

Karl H. Pribram

INTRODUCTION

The advent of the cognitive revolution in psychology ushered in a resurgent interest in the mind/brain connection. In this essay I discuss three forms this interest has taken. Neurobehavioral science, based to a large extent on animal brain–behavioral research, has made strides in determining the nature of memory storage, and the brain systems involved in attention and in different sorts of learning. Currently the neurochemical basis of emotion and motivation is being clarified. Clinical neuropsychology has added to the neurobehavioral base, and has been supplemented by it: An examination of memory retrieval processes and the exploration of brain function in the organization of human consciousness needs a human population to study. The yield has been rewarding and has given rise to a reexamination by philosophers and others of the nature of mind and spirit as these relate to the material world.

NEUROBEHAVIORAL SCIENCE

Parts and Wholes

Three closely related issues concerning the organization of brain function have been the subject of controversy for two centuries. The first of these concerns localization versus distribution of functions within the brain. The second issue stems from the first: Does processing proceed among different localizable systems or modules in a hierarchical fashion, or is processing global and heterarchical? Finally, is processing within and between systems serial or parallel?

Toward the end of the eighteenth century, Gall brought these issues to the fore by correlating different local brain pathologies to the histories of the cadavers he autopsied. Though often wrong in detail, Gall was correct in the methods he carefully detailed (see Gall & Spurtzheim, 1809/1969). He was naive in delineating the faculties of mind for which he sought localization. But systematic classification of mental functions still eludes us despite a half-century of operational behaviorism. Today, it is popular to discuss the modularity of mind (Fodor, 1980) and component systems of the brain (Thatcher & John, 1977) and relate them both in the clinic (McCarthy & Warrington, 1990) and in the laboratory (Pribram, 1971, 1991) by crafting experimental designs and behavioral and verbal testing procedures. The use of these techniques traces its heritage directly to Gall's enterprise.

The excesses of phrenology brought reaction. First, the question was raised as to which brain system brought together the various faculties into a conscious self. The unity of being, the soul of mankind, was challenged by breaking his mentation into a mere collection of faculties (see Pribram & Robinson, 1985, for the full impact on inquiry this view had). Furthermore, experimental evidence accrued to demonstrate a relation between impairments in complex behaviors and verbally reported experiences and the amount of brain tissue destroyed irrespective of location. In the recent past, Lashley (1929) became the exponent of this mass action view.

The distributed aspect of brain function becomes most evident in memory storage. Even with large deletions of brain tissue such as those resulting from strokes or resections for tumor, specific memories, engrams, are seldom lost. When amnesias do occur they are apt to be spotty and difficult to classify. This suggests that memory is stored in a distributed and statistically more or less random fashion. The storage process dismembers the input, which is then remembered on the occasions necessitating recognition and recall. The retrieval processes, in contrast to storage, are localized, at least within systems such as those that are sensory specific. When such systems are damaged, sensory-specific (see Pribram, 1954/1969, 1960, 1969, 1974, 1991) and even category-specific agnosias (see, e.g., McCarthy & Warrington, 1990) result.

Thus with regard to memory, both distributed and localized processes can be identified depending on which property of the process is being considered. This principle of analyzing a mental process to identify specific aspects will stand us in good stead throughout this chapter as we shall see.

If one reads Lashley carefully, one finds the seeds of conciliation between the "localist" and the "distributed" approaches to brain function. In a letter to Mettler, Lashley once stated his exasperation

with being misinterpreted: "Of course I know the front of the brain does something different from the back end. The visual sensory input terminates in the occipital lobes. Electrical stimulations of the pre-Rolandic areas elicit movements and the front parts are more enigmatic in their functions. But this is not the issue." Elsewhere he states the issue clearly: "...certain coordinated activities, known to be dependent upon definite cortical areas, can be carried out by any part (within undefined limits) of the whole area" (Lashley, 1960, pp. 237–240).

What Lashley emphasized was that certain psychological processes appear to be related to brain processes that are nonlocal. For instance, he pointed out that sensory and motor equivalences could not be accounted for even by a duplication of brain pathways: "Once an associated reaction has been established (e.g., a positive reaction to a visual pattern), the same reaction will be elicited by the excitation of sensory cells which were never stimulated in that way during training. Similarly, motor acts (e.g., opening a latch box) once acquired, may be executed immediately with motor organs which were not associated with the act during training" (ibid.).

An example of motor equivalence was reported by Ukhtomski (1926). A dog was conditioned to raise his right hind leg to the sound of a tone. After this conditional response was well established, his right motor cortex (which controls the left side of the body) was exposed. Then during the performance of the conditioned reaction a patty of strychninized filter paper (which chemically excited the cortical tissue) was placed on the area that controls the left forepaw. Immediately the dog switched the responding leg: He now raised his left forepaw to the conditional signal. A temporary dominant focus of excitation had been established in the cortex by the chemical stimulation. A totally different set of neural and muscular systems carries out an action "equivalent" to the one the animal has been trained to perform.

The fact that a temporary dominant focus in the cerebral cortex can take control of the expression of a learned behavior indicates that, without a doubt, hierarchical control operates in the central nervous system. Equally persuasive is the evidence for control over spinal cord activity by the brain stem and forebrain. Neuronal activity in the spinal cord displays an extremely high rate of spontaneous impulse generation. These generators are modulated by inhibitory local circuit neurons in such a way that the resultant activity can be modeled in terms of "coupled ensembles of limit cycle oscillatory processes" (Kelso & Saltzman, 1982; see also extensive reviews by Grillner, 1974, 1981, & 1985).

In turn, these ensembles of oscillators become organized by brain stem systems that consist of cholinergic and adrenergic neurons. The cholinergic set regulates the frequency of a wide range of tonic rhythmic activities such as those involved in locomotion, respiration, cardiovascular responses, and sleep. This cholinergic system is coupled to an adrenergic set of neurons that segment the rhythmic activities into episodes (Garcia-Rill & Skinner, 1988). Both systems are subject to further hierarchical control by the dopaminergic system of the basal ganglia.

Clinically, loss of this hierarchical control becomes manifest in an exaggeration of the normally present, almost subliminal tremors which under extreme conditions lead to spastic paralysis, hyperreflexia, and uncontrollable fits of oscillatory muscular spasm.

But the evidence from the experiments that demonstrated temporary dominant foci can be viewed from another perspective: The flexibility demonstrated by the shift from one controlling locus to another shows the organization of the cortical system to be heterarchical. Any locus within the system can become dominant if sufficiently excited.

Ordinarily hierarchical control is conceived to be accomplished by way of a serial process. This is because when control is direct, there is a causal connection between the controller and the controlled. Causality implies that the origination of the control signal precedes its effect on the system being controlled. Seriality remains when there are feedback loops. Heterarchical organization, by definition, involves the potentiality for parallel processing. At the same time, however, when control is exerted over other systems, a serial process becomes implemented. In general, the brain is composed of hierarchies of heterarchical systems.

Processing in the cerebral cortex is massively parallel. Simulations of these parallel cortical processes have, during the past decade, become implemented on personal computers to such an extent that the endeavors have been dubbed a cottage industry. These simulations of neural networks are capable of pattern recognition, language learning, and decision making which are remarkably true to life. Single-layered simulations have given way to three-layered computations that involve an input

layer, an output layer, and a hidden layer. All the elements of the network are interconnected, each element with all the others. In several such simulations the input is fed forward through the net and the output compared with one that is desired, and the difference between the actual and the desired is fed back to the net. The process is repeated until the desired output is achieved. Variations on this theme abound, each variation being better adapted than its alternates for a particular purpose. (Several excellent texts detailing the various types of neural networks are available; see, e.g., Dayhoff, 1990; Levine, 1991. For an exposition of the utility of such networks, see, e.g., Hinton & Anderson, 1981; Rumelhart & McClelland, 1986.)

One of the most fascinating attributes of these neural networks is the fact that the information contained in the input becomes fragmented and distributed in the elements of the layers. The simulations are therefore said to be parallel distributed processes (PDP). This makes them akin to optical information processing systems such as holography and tomography, from which they were in fact derived (Bracewell, 1989; Pribram, 1971, 1991; Willshaw, 1981).

Basal Forebrain Systems, Emotion, and Motivation

Beginning with Walter Cannon's (1927) experimentally based critique of James, followed by Lashley's (1960) critique of Cannon (1929), to the anatomically based suggestions of Papez (1937) and their more current versions by MacLean (1949), brain scientists have been deeply concerned with the processes that organize emotional and motivational experience and expression. Two major discoveries have accelerated our ability to cope with the issues and placed the earlier, more speculative accounts into better perspective. One of the discoveries has been the role of the reticular formation of the brain stem (Magoun, 1950) and its chemical systems of brain amines (see, e.g., the review by Barchas, Ciaranello, Stolk, & Hamburg, 1982; and Pribram & McGuinness, 1992) that regulate states of alertness and mood. Lindsley (1951) proposed an activation mechanism of emotion and motivation on the basis of the initial discovery and has more recently (Lindsley & Wilson, 1976) detailed the pathways by which such activation can exert control over the brain processes. The other discovery is the system of brain tracts, which when electrically excited results in reinforcement (i.e., increase in probability of recurrence of the behavior that has produced the electrical brain stimulation) or deterrence (i.e., decrease in probability that such behavior will recur), by Olds and Milner (1954).

In my attempts to organize the results of these discoveries it was necessary to distinguish clearly between those data that referred to experience (feelings) and those that referred to expression (see Darwin, 1872), and further to distinguish emotion from motivation (reviewed by Pribram, 1971). Thus feelings were found to encompass both emotional and motivational experience, emotional as affective and motivation as centered on readiness processes. Not surprisingly the affective processes of emotion were found to be based on the process of arousal, the ability to make phasic responses to input that "stop" the motivational processes of activation that maintain selective readiness. Thus, feelings were found to be based on neurochemical states (dispositions or moods), which become organized by neural systems involved in appetitive (motivation, "go") and affective (emotional, "stop") processes.

The wealth of new data and these insights obtained from them made it fruitful to reexamine the Jamesian position (Pribram, 1981). James overemphasized the visceral determination of emotional experience (attitudinal factors depending on sensory feedback from the somatic musculature were included by James but not emphasized) and, more important, he failed to take into consideration the role of expectations (the representational role of the organization of familiarity and novelty) in the organization of emotional expression. On the other hand, James rightly emphasized that emotional processes take place primarily within the organism while motivations reach beyond into the organism's environment. Further, James is almost universally misinterpreted as holding a peripheral theory of emotion and mind. Throughout his writings he emphasizes the effect that peripheral stimuli (including those of visceral origin) exert on brain processes. The confusion comes about because of James's insistence that emotions concern bodily processes, that they stop short at the skin. Nowhere, however, does he identify emotions with bodily processes. Emotions are always the result of the effect of bodily processes on the brain. James is in fact explicit on this point when he discusses the nature of the input to the brain from the viscera. He points out two possibilities: Emotions are processed by a separate brain system or they are processed by the same systems as are perceptions. Today we know that both possibilities are realized: Parts of the frontolimbic forebrain (especially the amygdala and related systems) process visceroautonomic bodily inputs, and the results of processing become distributed via brain stem systems that diffusely influence the perceptual systems (Pribram, 1961, 1991).

NEUROPSYCHOLOGY

Attentive Consciousness and Unconscious Processes

Additionally, William James (1901/1950) noted that the delineation of minding, that is, consciousness, devolves on processes we usually refer to as attention and intention (volition). I would add, thought. Controls on attention determine the span of sensory processing; those on intention determine the span over which action becomes effective; and those controlling thought, the span of memories that become considered.

For over a decade and a half my laboratory investigated the neural processes involved in the control of attention. A comprehensive review of these data and those gathered elsewhere (Pribram & McGuinness, 1975, 1992) discerned three classes of such mechanisms: One deals with short phasic response to an input (arousal); a second relates to prolonged tonic readiness of the organism to respond selectively (activation); and a third (effort) acts to coordinate the phasic (arousal) and tonic (activation) processes. Separate neural and neurochemical systems (Pribram, 1977; Pribram & McGuinness, 1992) are involved in the phasic (arousal) and tonic (activation) processes: The phasic centers on the amygdala; the tonic, on the basal ganglia of the forebrain. The coordinating system (effort) critically involves the hippocampus, a phylogenetically ancient part of the neural apparatus.

Evidence (reviewed by Pribram & McGuinness, 1992) from the analysis of changes in the electrical activity of the brain evoked by brief sensory stimulation has shown that the arousal and activation systems operate on a more basic process centered on the dorsal thalamus, the way station of sensory input to the cerebral cortex. Brain electrical activity evoked by sensory stimulation can be analyzed into components. Early components reflect processing via systems that directly (via the thalamus) connect sensory surfaces with cortical surfaces. Later components reflect processes initiated in cortical and related basal ganglia systems that operate downward onto the brain stem (tectal region) which, in turn, influence a thalamic "gate" that modulates activity in the direct sensory pathways. It is the activity reflected in these later components of the brain electrical activity that constitutes "activation."

The thalamic "gate" is, however, also regulated by input from the system centered on the amygdala—the arousal system. This system, when stimulated, produces an effect on the "gate" opposite to that of the activation system.

The evidence also indicates that the coordination of phasic (arousal) and tonic (activation) attentional processes often demands "effort." When attention must be "paid," the hippocampal system becomes involved and influences the arousal system rostrally through frontal connections with the amygdala system and influences the activation system caudally via connections in the brain stem. At this juncture the relation of attention to intention, i.e., to volition (will), comes into focus. Again, William James had already pointed out that a good deal of what we call voluntary effort is the maintaining of attention or the repeated returning of attention to a problem until it yields a solution.

The distinction between the brain mechanisms of motivation and will (volition) is treated by James, but clarity did not come until the late 1960s when several theorists (e.g., MacKay, 1966; Mittlestaedt, 1968; Waddington, 1957; W. R. Ashby, personal communication, 1960; McFarland, 1971; Pribram, 1971) began to point out the difference between feedback, homeostatic processes on the one hand and programs, which are feedforward, homeorhetic processes, on the other. Feedback mechanisms depend on error processing and are therefore sensitive to perturbations. Programs, unless completely stopped, run themselves off to completion irrespective of obstacles placed in their way.

Clinical neurology had classically distinguished the mechanisms involved in voluntary from those involved in involuntary behavior. The distinction rests on the observation that lesions of the cerebellar hemispheres impair intentional (voluntary) behavior, while basal ganglia lesions result in disturbances of involuntary movements. Damage to the cerebellar circuits are involved in a feedforward rather than a feedback mechanism (as already described by Ruch in the 1951 Stevens *Handbook of Experimental Psychology,* although Ruch did

not have the term feedforward available to him). I have extended this conclusion (Pribram, 1971) on the basis of more recent microelectrode analyses by Eccles, Ito, and Szentagothai (1967) to suggest that the cerebellar hemispheres perform calculations in fast-time, i.e., extrapolate where a particular movement would end were it to be continued, and send the results of such a calculation to the cerebral motor cortex where they can be compared with the target to which the movement is directed. Experimental analysis of the functions of the motor cortex had shown that such targets are composed of "images of achievement" constructed in part on the basis of past experience (Pribram, 1971, chaps. 13, 14, & 16; 1991, Lecture 6; Pribram, Kruger, Robinson, & Berman, 1955–56; Pribram, Sharafat, & Beekman, 1984).

Just as the cerebellar circuit has been shown to serve intentional behavior, the basal ganglia have been shown to be important to involuntary processes. We have already noted the involvement of these structures in the control of activation, the readiness of organisms to respond. Lesions in the basal ganglia grossly amplify tremors at rest and markedly restrict expressions of motivational feelings. Neurological theory has long held (see, e.g., Bucy, 1944) that these disturbances are due to interference by the lesion of the normal feedback relationships between basal ganglia and cerebral cortex. In fact, surgical removals of motor cortex have been performed on patients with basal ganglia lesions in order to redress the imbalance produced by the initial lesions. Such resections have proved remarkably successful in alleviating the often distressing continuing disturbances of involuntary movement that characterize these basal ganglia diseases.

The distinction between the systems that control intentional and those that control involuntary behavior extends to the control of sensory input (see Pribram, 1977, for review) and the processing of memory. With regard to sensory input, the distinction between the contents of awareness and the person who is aware was delineated by Brentano (1973) and called intentional inexistence. This dualism of a minding self and the objective material contents of perception was also present in the writings of Ernst Mach (1914) and of course, René Descartes (1927). Although Cartesian dualism is perhaps the first overt nontrivial expression of the issue, the duality between subject and object and some causal connection between them is inherent in language once it emerges from simple naming to predication. Neumann (1954) and Jaynes (1977) have suggested that a change in consciousness (i.e., in distinguishing an aware self from what the self is aware of) occurs somewhere between the time of the Iliad and the Odyssey. My interpretation of this occurrence links it to the invention and promulgation of phonemically based writing. Prehistory was transmitted orally/aurally. Written history is visual/verbal. In an oral/aural culture a greater share of reality is carried in memory and is thus personal; once writing becomes a ready means of recording events they become a part of extrapersonal objective reality. The shift described is especially manifest in a clearer externalization of the sources of conscience—the Gods no longer speak personally to guide individual man.

This process of ever clearer distinctions between personal and extrapersonal objective realities culminates in Cartesian dualism and Brentano's intentional inexistence, which was shortened by Husserl (1901/1975) to "intentionality." It is this reading of the subject–object distinction that philosophers ordinarily mean when they speak of the difference between conscious and unconscious processes.

Freud had training both in medical practice and in philosophy. When he emphasized the importance of unconscious processes, was he implying the medical definition or the philosophical? Most interpretations of Freud suggest that unconscious processes operate without awareness in the sense that they operate automatically much as do respiratory and gastrointestinal processes in someone who is stuporous or comatose. Freud himself seems to have promulgated this view by suggesting a "horizontal" split between conscious, preconscious, and unconscious processes with "repression" operating to push memory-motive structures into deeper layers where they no longer access awareness. Still, in the *Project* (Freud, 1895/1966) memory-motive structures are neural programs—located in the core portions of the brain, which access awareness by their connections to cortex that determine whether a memory-motivated wish comes to consciousness. When the neural program becomes a secondary process, it comes under voluntary control, which involves reality testing and thus consciousness. To use language as an example, one might well know two languages but at any one time "connect only one to cortex" and thus the other remains "unconscious" and voluntarily unexpressed. (See Pribram & Gill, 1976, chaps. 2 and 5 for details.)

The linking of reflective consciousness to cortex is not as naive as it first appears. As the recently reported cases of Weiskrantz et al. (1974; Weiskrantz, 1986) have shown, "blindsight" results when patients are subjected to unilateral removal of the visual cortex. As noted, these patients insist they cannot see anything in the field contralateral to their lesion but when tested they can locate and identify large objects in their blind hemifield with remarkable accuracy. Furthermore, there are patients with unilateral neglect following parietal lobe legions (see Heilman & Valenstein, 1972, for review). Neglect patients often can get around using their neglected limbs appropriately. H. M., a patient who sustained an amygdala-hippocampal resection, has been trained in operant tasks and the effects of training have persisted without decrement for years, despite protestations from the patient that he doesn't recognize the situation and that he remembers nothing of the training (Sidman et al., 1968). In monkeys with such lesions we have shown almost perfect retention of training after a two-year period, retention that is better than that shown by unoperated control subjects (Pribram, unpublished observations). These monkeys and H. M. and the blindsight patients are clearly conscious in the medical instrumental sense. What has gone wrong is their ability to reflect on their behavior and experience, an inability within the impaired sphere of clearly distinguishing personal from extrapersonal reality. This leaves them with impaired consciousness in the philosopher's sense: Behavior and experience are no longer intentional.

The thrust of most recent psychoanalytical thinking as well as that of experimentalists such as Hilgard (1977) is in the direction of interpreting the conscious–unconscious distinction in the philosophical sense. For instance, Matte Blanco (1975) proposes that consciousness be defined by the ability to make clear distinctions, to identify alternatives. Making clear distinctions would include being able to tell personal from extrapersonal reality. By contrast unconscious processes would, according to Matte Blanco, be composed of infinite sets "where paradox reigns and opposites merge into sameness." When infinities are being computed the ordinary rules of logic do not hold. Thus, dividing a line of infinite length results in two lines of infinite length, i.e., one = two. Being deeply involved allows love and ecstasy but also suffering and anger to occur. In keeping with this, Carl Jung

(1960) defined unconscious processes as those involving feelings.

My interpretation of this conscious–unconscious distinction as it relates to human behavior and experience is in line with Matte Blanco's and others which are closely related to the philosophical distinction, and not to the medical. Thus, bringing the wellsprings of behavior and experience to consciousness means the making of distinctions, to provide alternatives, to make choices, to become informed in the Shannon (Shannon & Weaver, 1949) sense of reduction of uncertainty. One of these distinctions distinguishes episodes of *feeling* states and related them to one another.

An important change in views becomes necessary when these interpretations are considered seriously: Unconscious processes as defined by psychoanalysis are not completely "submerged" and unavailable to experience. Rather, unconscious processes produce feelings that are difficult to localize in time or in space and difficult to identify correctly. The unconscious processes construct the emotional dispositions and motivational context within which extrapersonal and personal realities are constructed. As the classical experiments of Schachter and Singer (1962) have shown, feelings are to a large extent undifferentiated, and we tend to cognize and label them according to the circumstances in which the feelings become manifested. (For a recent review of other experiments that have led to such a view see Hermans, Kempen, & van Loon, 1992.)

It is in this sense that behavior comes under the control of the unconscious processes. When I have burst out in anger, I am certainly aware that I have done so and of the effects of the anger on others. I may or may not have attended the build-up of feeling prior to the blow-up. And I may have projected the build-up onto others or introjected it from them. But I could have been aware of all this (with the guidance of a friend or therapist) and still found myself in uncontrolled anger. Only when the events leading to the anger become clearly separated into alternative or harmoniously related distinctions is unconscious control converted into conscious control. It is ridiculous to think that a person with an obsession or compulsion is unaware of his experience or behavior. The patient is very aware and feels awful. But he cannot, without aid, differentiate controls on the behavior generated by his feelings.

Objective Consciousness and the Posterior Cerebral Convexity

Surrounding the major fissures of the primate cerebral cortex lie the terminations of the sensory and motor projection systems. Rose and Woolsey (1949) and Pribram (1960) have labeled these systems extrinsic because of their close ties (by way of a few synapses) with peripheral structures. The sensory surface and muscle arrangements are mapped more or less isomorphically onto the perifissural cortical surface by way of discrete, practically parallel lines of connecting fiber tracts. When a local injury occurs within these systems a sensory scotoma, or a scotoma of action, ensues. A scotoma is a spatially circumscribed hole in the "field" of interaction of organism and environment: A blind spot, a hearing defect limited to a frequency range, a location of the skin where tactile stimuli fail to be responded to. These are the systems where what Henry Head (1920) called epicritic processing takes place. These extrinsic sensory-motor projection systems are so organized that movement allows the organism to project the results of processing away from the sensory (and muscular) surfaces where the interactions take place, out into the world external to the organism (Bekesy, 1967). Thus processing within these extrinsic systems constructs an objective reality for the organism.

In between the perifissural extrinsic regions of cortex lie other regions of cortex variously named association cortex (Fleschig, 1900), uncommitted cortex (Penfield, 1969), or intrinsic cortex (Pribram, 1960). These names reflect the fact that there is no apparent direct connection between peripheral structures and these regions of cortex that make up most of the convexity of the cerebrum.

Lesions of the intrinsic cortex of the posterior cerebral convexity result in sensory-specific agnosias in both monkey and man. Research on monkeys has shown that these agnosias are not due to failure to distinguish cues from one another, but due to *making use* of those distinctions in making choices among alternatives (Pribram & Mishkin, 1955; Pribram, 1969). This ability is the essence of information processing in the sense of uncertainty reduction (Shannon & Weaver, 1949), and the posterior intrinsic cortex determines the range of alternatives, the sample size of which a particular informative element must address. A patient with agnosia can tell the difference between two objects but does not know what the difference means. As Charles Peirce (1934) once noted, what we mean by something and what we mean to do with it are synonymous. In short, alternatives, sample size, choice, cognition, information in the Shannon sense, and meaning are closely interwoven concepts. Finally, when agnosia is severe it is often accompanied by what is termed "neglect." The patient appears not only not to know that he doesn't know but to actively deny the agnosia. Typical is a patient I once had who repeatedly had difficulty in sitting up in bed. I pointed out to her that her arm had become entangled in the bedclothes — she would acknowledge this momentarily, only to "lose" that arm once more in a tangled environment. Part of the perception of her body, her corporeal consciousness, seemed to have become extinguished.

These results can be readily conceptualized in terms of extracorporeal and corporeal objective reality. For a time it was thought that corporeal (egocentric) reality ("personal body space") depended on the integrity of the frontal intrinsic cortex and that the posterior convexal cortex was critical to the construction of extracorporeal (allocentric) reality (see, e.g., Pohl, 1973). This scheme was tested in my laboratory in experiments with monkeys (Brody & Pribram, 1978) and patients (Hersh, 1980; Ruff, Hersh, & Pribram, 1981) and found wanting. In fact, the corporeal/extracorporeal distinction involves the parietal cortex. Perhaps the most clear-cut example of this comes from studies by Mountcastle and his group (Mountcastle, Lynch, Georgopoulos, Sakata, & Acuna, 1975) which show that cells in the convexal intrinsic cortex respond when an object is within view, but only when it is also within reach. In short, our studies on patients and those of others have been unable to clearly separate the brain locations that produce agnosia from those that produce neglect. Furthermore, the studies on monkeys as well as those on humans (McCarthy & Warrington, 1990, chap. 2) indicate that agnosia is related to meaning as defined by corporeal use.

In monkeys the disturbances produced by restricted lesions of the convexal intrinsic cortex are also produced by lesions of the parts of the basal ganglia (implicated in activation, selective readiness) to which those parts of the cortex project (Heilman & Valenstein, 1972). This finding takes on special meaning from the fact that lesions of the thalamus (which controls the relaying of sensory

input to cortex) fail to produce such effects. Further, recent experiments have shown that the neglect syndrome can be produced in monkeys by lesions of the dopaminergic nigrostriatal system (Wright, 1980). This special connection between intrinsic (recall that this is also called association) cortex and the basal ganglia further clarifies the intentional process that these systems make possible: The distinction between an objective egocentric corporeal self (the "me") and an extracorporeal allocentric reality (the "other"). (See Pribram, 1991, Lecture 6 for detailed exposition of how this process operates.) An excellent review of the history of differentiating this corporeal objective "me" from a subjective "I" can be found in Hermans, Kempen, and van Loon (1992). The next section develops the relation between brain processing and the "I".

Narrative Consciousness and the Frontolimbic Forebrain

As is well known, frontal lesions were produced for a period of time in order to relieve intractable suffering, compulsions, obsessions and endogenous depressions. When effective in pain and depression, these psychosurgical procedures portrayed in humans the now well-established functional relationship between frontal intrinsic cortex and the limbic forebrain in nonhuman primates (Pribram, 1950, 1954/1969, 1958). Further, frontal lesions can lead either to perseverative, compulsive behavior or to distractibility in monkeys, and this is also true of humans (Pribram, Ahumada, Hartog, & Roos, 1964; Oscar-Berman, 1975). A failure to be guided by the outcomes, the consequences of their behavior can account for this effect— as well as its opposite: The alleviation of obsessive–compulsive behavior. Extreme forms of distractibility and obsession are due to a lack of "sensitivity" of the activation (readiness) process to feedback from consequences. Both the results of experiments with monkeys (Pribram, 1961) and clinical observations attest to the fact that subjects with frontal lesions, whether surgical, traumatic or neoplastic, fail to be guided by consequences (Luria, Pribram, & Homskaya, 1964; Knonow & Pribram, 1970).

Consequences are the outcomes of behavior. In the tradition of the experimental analysis of behavior, consequences are reinforcers that influence the recurrence of the behavior. Con-sequences are thus a series of events (Latin ex-venire, out-come), outcomes that guide action and thereby attain predictive value (as determined by confidence estimates). Such con-sequences, i.e., sequence of events form their own confidence levels to provide contexts which, in humans, become envisioned eventualities (Pribram, 1963, 1971, 1991, Lecture 10 and Appendix G).

Confidence implies familiarity. Experiments with monkeys (Pribram, Reitz, McNeil, & Spevack, 1979) and humans (Luria, Pribram, & Homskaya, 1964) have shown that repeated arousal to an orienting stimulus habituates, i.e., the orienting reaction gives way to familiarization. Familiarization is disrupted by limbic (amygdala) and frontal lesions (Pribram, Reitz, McNeil & Spevack, 1979; Luria, Pribram and Homskaya, 1964). Ordinarily familiarization allows continued activation of readiness; disruption of familiarization (orienting) leads to repeated distraction and thus a failure to allow con-sequences to form. When the process of familiarization is disrupted, the outcomes-of-behaviors, events, become inconsequential. When intact, the familiarization process is segmented by orienting reactions into episodes within which confidence values can become established.

In such an episodic process the development of confidence is a function of coherences and correlations among the events being processed. When coherence and correlation spans multiple episodes, the organism becomes *committed* to a course of action (a prior intention, a strategy), which then guides further action and is resistant to perturbation by particular orienting reactions (arousals). The organism is now *competent* to carry out the action (intention-in-action; tactic). Particular outcomes now guide competent performance, they no longer produce orienting reactions (Brooks, 1986; Pribram, 1980).

This cascade which characterizes episodic processing leads ultimately to considerable autonomy of the committed competence. Envisioned events are woven into coherent subjectivity, a story, a narrative, the myth by which "I" live. This narrative composes and is composed of an intention, a strategy that works for the individual in practice, a practical guide to action in achieving (temporary) stability in the face of a staggering range of variations of events.

Consciousness is manifest (by verbal report) when familiarization is perturbed—an episode is updated and incorporated into a larger contextual scheme (the narrative), which includes both the

familiar and novel episodes (Pribram, 1991, Appendices C & D). Consciousness becomes attenuated when actions and their guides cohere —the actions become skilled, graceful, and automatic (Miller, Galanter, & Pribram, 1960; Pribram, 1971, chap. 6).

THE PHILOSOPHY OF MIND

Extremists

As in every human endeavor various shades of opinion emerge when an issue becomes "hot," fashionable and of general concern. Pronouncements regarding the nature of mind and especially of its conscious aspects are no exception. Daniel Dennett (1991) has humbly contributed a volume entitled, *Consciousness Explained*. In it he replaces the Cartesian theater (Shakespeare's "stage"?) with a tentative pluralistic set of narratives recounting our experience. Those of us who are visually and kinesthetically as well as verbally inclined might prefer to stick with Descartes and Shakespeare. Marvin Minsky (1986) has also emphasized the plurality of mental processes in his *Society of Mind*. My question is: Have these volumes made any significant change in the basic proposition forwarded by Francis Gall at the end of the eighteenth century that a variety of "faculties of mind" can be correlated with a corresponding variety of cerebral systems? The details of correspondence have, of course, been immensely enriched during the ensuing two centuries of research and observation. But, as to philosophy, what is new?

At the other extreme are those who espouse an "eliminative materialism." Folk psychology, the wisdom and folly enfolded in language and in cultural expression over the ages, is to be eliminated as scientific explanation in favor of a neural explanation. One is reminded of psychology's era of behaviorism. Stephen Stich (1986) has contributed to this endeavor a book entitled *From Folk Psychology to Cognitive Science*. Its subtitle is *The Case Against Belief*. The arguments presented in support of this extreme materialism are convoluted but seem to me to ignore the issue of scale or level. How can anyone currently ignore the fact that those who, in the former Yugoslavia, as proponents of ethnic cleansing are operating on any basis other than belief? Only differences between Orthodox, Roman Catholic, and Islamic beliefs separate the protagonists. The origins and consequences of these differences in belief can be ascertained and many of them shown to be material in nature. But, just as in the word processing performed by my computer in the writing of this essay, the material instantiations of the cultural history would be as cumbersome to communicate as would the contents of this essay in machine language. Each level of description has value determined by the use to which the description is to be put.

Scientific Dualisms: Mental and Material

Attention to the levels at which analysis is pursued helps resolve many of the hitherto untractable issues surrounding the mind/brain interface. In the ordinary world of appearances there is no question but that human mental experiencing can be distinguished sharply from the contents of the experience. As noted earlier, the issue has been labeled "intentionality" (or intentional inexistence) by Franz Clemens Brentano and has given rise to inferences about the nature of reality (Brentano, 1973; Chisholm, 1960). The question is often phrased: Are my perceptions (my phenomenal experiences) the "real," or do the contents of those perceptions make up the "real" world? My phenomenal experiences are mental; the world as it appears to me is material. I can give primacy to my experience and become a phenomenologist, or I can give primacy to the contents of the experience and become a materialist. But I can also give primacy to neither and attest to the dual nature of the reality.

Materialism and phenomenology run into difficulty only when each attempts to deny the other. As long as only primacy is at stake, either view can be made consistent. After all, our experiences are primary, and empiricism is not inimical to a real material world. And we do appear to be experiencing something(s), so our experiences may well become organized by those real (material) somethings (see Bunge, 1980, for a persuasive development of this position).

However, by accepting such a moderate position with regard to mind and matter we immediately come up against a set of dualist problems. Are the contents of perception "really" organized by the experience of the perceiver? Is that experience in turn organized by brain function, sensory input, and the energies impinging on the senses? Would a complete description of brain function of an organism also be a description of the experience of that organism? If so, are not the material descriptions of

brain, senses and energies sufficient? Or at least do the descriptions of experience add anything to the material descriptions? Cannot the inverse be equally true? What do the descriptions of brain, senses, and energies materially add to what we so richly experience?

I believe that today there are answers to those questions where only a few years ago there were none. These answers come from "unpacking" conceptual confusions and demonstrating where each conceptualization captures a part of the truthful whole.

A semantic analysis shows that descriptors of brain, senses, and energy sources are derived from an analysis of experience into components. The components are organismic and environmental (biological and physical or social), and each component can be subdivided further into subcomponents until the quantum and nuclear levels of analysis are reached. This procedure of analysis downward in a hierarchy of systems is the ordinary way of descriptive science. Within systems, causes and effects are traced. When discrepancies are found, statistical principles are adduced and probabilities invoked. Scientists have become adept and comfortable with such procedures.

Mental language stems from different considerations. As in the case of descriptive science, mental terms take their origin in experience. Now, however, experience is validated consensually. Experience in one sensory mode is compared with that obtained in another. Then validation proceeds by comparison of one's experience with that of another. A little girl points to a horse. Up to now, her mother has allowed her to say "cow" whenever any animal is pointed to. But the time has come to be more precise, and the experience of horse becomes validly different from that of a cow. Mental language is derived from such upward validations in a hierarchy of systems.

Elsewhere I detail the differences in scientific approach that this upward—or outward—look entails (Pribram, 1965). It is certainly not limited to psychology. When Albert Einstein enunciated his special and general theories of relativity, he was looking upward in the set of hierarchically arranged physical systems. The resultant relativistic views are as applicable to mental conceptualizations, as they are to physical ones. It is these relativisms that existentialists and phenomenologists constantly struggle to formulate into some coherent principles. My own belief is that they will be successful only to the extent that they develop the techniques of structural analysis (deconstruction). But structured analyses often depend on enactment to clarify the complexities involved. Abhorrent as the computer and other engineering devices may be to philosophers and psychologists of the existential–phenomenal persuasion, these tools may turn out to be of great service to their mode of inquiry.

If the above analysis is correct, then a dualism of sorts can be entertained as valid. First, however, let me provide a cautionary note. This form of dualism is concerned with the everyday domain of appearances—of ordinary experiences. Commencing with such ordinary experiences, two modes of conceptualization have developed. One mode operated downward in a hierarchy of systems, analyzing experience into components and establishing hierarchical and cause-effect relationships between these components. The other operated upward toward other organisms to attain consensual validation of experiences by comparing and sharing them.

Thus two mirror images—two optical isomers, as it were—are constructed from experience. One we call material and the other mental. Just as optical isomers in chemistry have differing biological properties, although they have identical components and arrangements, so the mental and material conceptualizations have different properties even though they initially arise from the selfsame experiences.

I suggest that this is the origin of dualism and accounts for it. The duality expressed is of conceptual procedures, not of any basic duality in nature. As we will see, there are other dualities that are more basic, but these are not the ones that have become the staple of those arguing for dualism.

Thus, strictly speaking mentalism and materialism imply each other, because there would be no need for mentalism if there were no materialism. There is no up without a down. Further, Sperry (1980) and Searle (1984) attempted to limit their mentalism to those structures that are organized by and in turn organize the brain. But it is not clear whether they would be willing to go to an epistemological limit that holds that mind interacts with the elementary components making up the brain. Intuition regarding biological roots of mentality is certainly accurate. To confuse the analogy of the computer with the historically based homologies that have given rise to psychological processes is akin to calling a whale a fish. By the same token,

however, Sperry and Searle are adamantly opposed to an "independent existence of conscious mind apart from the functioning brain" (Sperry, 1980, p. 195); their mentalism does not stretch to cover the very essence of what motivates mentalism in the hands of those who oppose it to materialism; that is, the *primacy and independence* of mental structures.

What Computers Can Tell Us

Within the above caveat, let us look at the usefulness for an analysis of the mind/brain connection of computers, programs, and the processing of information in some detail because in many respects these artifacts so clearly portray some of the problems involved in the mind/brain issue. As noted (see e.g., Searle, 1984), the computer is not a brain, but its programs are constructed by people who do have brains. Nonetheless, computers and their programs provide a useful metaphor in the analysis of the mind/brain issue in which the distinction between brain, mind, and spirit can be seen as similar to the distinction between machine (hardware), low-level programs (e.g., operating systems), and high-level programs (e.g., word processing packages). Low-level programs such as machine languages and assemblers are not only idiosyncratic to particular types of computer hardware, but there is also considerable similarity between the logic of these languages and the logic operations of the machines in which they operate. In a similar vein, to some extent, perceptual processes can be expected to share some similarity to brain processes. On the other hand, high-level languages such as Fortran, Algol, and Pascal are more universal in their application, and there is less obvious similarity between their implicit logic and the logic of machines. At the highest level, in languages such as English, with which I address my computer in order to use it as a word processor, the relation between the logos of English (word, concept, logic) and that of the machine is still more remote. However, English relates me to a sizable chunk of the human social order. To complete the analogy, humanity's spiritual nature strives to make contact with more encompassing orders whether they be social, physical, cosmological, or symbolic.

Understanding how computer programs are composed also helps to tease apart some of the issues involved in the "identity" approach in dealing with the mind/brain relationship.

Because our introspections provide no apparent connection to the functions of the neural tissues that comprise the brain, it has not been easy to understand what theorists are talking about when they claim that mental and brain processes are identical. Now, because of the computer/program analogy, we can suggest that what is common to a mental operation and the brain "wetware" in which the operation is realized is some order that remains invariant across transformations. The terms *information* (in the brain and cognitive sciences) and *structure* (in linguistics and in music) are most commonly used to describe such identities across transformations. Order invariance across transformations is not limited to computers and computer programming. In music we recognize a Beethoven sonata or a Berlioz symphony irrespective of whether it is presented to us as a score on sheets of paper, in a live concert, over our high fidelity music system, or even in our automobiles when distorted and muffled by noise and poor reproduction. The information (form within) and the structure (arrangement) is recognizable in many embodiments. The materials that make the embodiments possible differ considerably from each other, but these differences are not part of the essential property of the musical form. In this sense, the identity approach to the mind/brain relationship, despite the realism of its embodiments, partakes of Platonic universals, that is, ideal orderings that are liable to becoming flawed in their realization.

In the construction of computer languages (by humans) we gain insight into how information or structure is realized in a machine. The essence of biological as well as of computational hierarchies is that higher levels of organization take control over, as well as being controlled by, lower levels. Such reciprocal causation is ubiquitous in living systems: Thus, the level of tissue carbon dioxide not only controls the neural respiratory mechanism but is controlled by it. Discovered originally as a regulatory principle that maintains a constant environment, reciprocal causation is termed *homeostasis*. Research over the past few decades has established that such (negative) *feedback* mechanisms are ubiquitous, involving sensory, motor, and all sorts of central processes. When feedback organizations are hooked up into parallel arrays, they become feedforward control mechanisms that operate much as do the words (of bit and byte length) in computer languages (Miller et al., 1960; Pribram, 1971).

Equally important, programming allows an analysis to be made of the evolution of linguistic tools that relate the various levels of programming languages. Digital computers with binary logic require a low-level language (coded in the numerals 0 or 1) that sets a series of binary switches. At the next level, switch settings can be grouped so that binary digits (bits) are converted into a more complex code consisting of bytes, each of which is given an alphanumerical label. Thus, for example, the switch setting 001 becomes 1, the setting 010 becomes 2, and the setting 100 becomes 4. Given that 000 is 0, there are now eight possible combinations, each of which is an octal byte.

This process is repeated at the next level by grouping bytes into recognizable words. Thus 1734 becomes ADD; 2051 becomes SKIP, and so forth. In high-level languages, *groups* of words are integrated into whole routines that can be executed by one command.

It is likely that some type of hierarchical integration is involved in relating mental processes to the brain. Sensory mechanisms transduce patterns of physical energy into patterns of neural energy. Because sensory receptors such as the retina and the cochlea operate in an analog rather than a digital mode, the transduction is considerably more complex than the coding operations described above. Nonetheless, much of neurophysiological investigation is concerned with discovering the correspondence between the pattern of physical input and the pattern of neural response. As more complex inputs are considered, the issue becomes one of comparing the physically determined patterns with subjective experience (psychophysics) and recording the patterns of response of sensory stations in the brain.

These comparisons have shown that a number of transformations occur between sensory receptor surfaces and the brain cortex. The transformations are expressed mathematically as transfer functions. When the transfer functions reflect identical patterns at the input and output of a sensory station, the patterns are considered to be geometrically isomorphic (*iso* means same; *morph* means form), that is, of the same form. When the transfer functions are linear (i.e., superposable and invertible, reversible), the patterns are considered to be secondarily or algebraically isomorphic (Shepard & Chipman, 1970). Thus, as in the case of computer programming, levels are due to transformations that progressively alter the form of the pattern while they maintain intact some basic order, an informational structure.

What I propose, therefore, is a "monism," which states that the truly basic components of the universe are neither material nor mental, but neutral to this dichotomy. The dematerialization of energy in modern physics (which I will review in the next section), thus supports a "neutral monism" (James, 1909; Russell, 1948). Critical philosophers (e.g., Herbert Feigl, 1960), who were steeped in linguistic analysis, developed this monistic view by suggesting that the "mental" and "material" are simply different ways of talking about the same processes. Thus "mind" and "brain" come to stand for separate linguistic systems, covering different aspects of a basic commonality. The problem has been to find a neutral language to describe the commonality without being either mental or material in its connotations.

I have taken this "dual aspects" view a step further by proposing that each aspect not only is characterized linguistically but in fact is a separate "realization" or "embodiment" (Pribram, 1971). As noted, I have further proposed that what becomes embodied is informational "structure." Thus, in essence I have stood the critical philosopher's approach on its head: The enduring "neutral" component of the universe is informational structure, the negentropic organization of energy. In a sense, this structure can be characterized as linguistic—or mathematical, musical, cultural, and so on. Dual aspects become dual realizations—which in fact may be multiple—of the fundamental informational structure. Thus, a symphony can be realized in the playing at a concert, in the musical score, on a record or on a tape, and thence through a high-fidelity audio system at home.

Mind and brain stand for two such classes of realization, each achieved, as described earlier, by proceeding in a different direction in the hierarchy of conceptual and realized systems. Both mental phenomena and material objects are realizations and therefore realities. Both classes of reality are constructions from underlying "structures," which it is the task of science to specify in as neutral a language as possible (neutral, i.e., with respect to connotations that would suggest that the "structures" belong in one or the other class). I note elsewhere the relationship of such a constructional realism to critical realism, pragmatism, and neo-Kantian rationalism (Pribram, 1971).

There is thus an important difference between a constructional realism such as I propose and materialist, mentalist, dualist, and triadic interactionisms. In a constructional scheme the precise place of brain mechanisms can be specified. There is no global "mind" that has to make mysterious contact with global "brain." Many mysteries are still there—to name only one, for example, how emergents come about and why they are so utterly different from their substrate. But issues become scientific and manageable within the broader context of philosophic enquiry.

The World of Appearance and the World of Potentiality

Holding the identity "position" with regard to the mind/brain issue involves specifying what it is that remains identical. Unless something remains constant across all the coding operations that convert English to binary machine code and back to English, my word processing procedures would not work. Identity implies reciprocal stepwise causation among structural levels. Contrary to the usually held philosophical position, identity does not necessarily mean geometrical or even algebraic isomorphism. Transformations, coding operations, occur that hierarchically relate levels of complexity with one another. A level is defined by the fact that its description, that is, its code, is in some nontrivial sense more efficient (i.e., requires less work, less expenditure of energy) than use of the code of the components that compose it. In the case of the word processor, the coding is arbitrary, and the arbitrariness is stored on a diskette and copyrighted. In the case of the mind/brain relationship, the nature of the coding operations is more universal and the efforts of two centuries of psychophysical, neuropsychological, and cognitive research have provided knowledge concerning at least some of the coding operations involved.

I am belaboring these findings of scientific research to indicate that, contrary to what some philosophers hold (see, e.g., Dewan et al., 1976), they have relevance to philosophical issues. *If the mind/brain problem arises from a distinction between the mental and the material and we find that at a certain level of analysis we no longer can clearly make such a separation, then the very assumptions upon which the issue is joined may be found wanting.*

Levels of analysis thus concern the fundamental assumption that has given rise to the mind/brain problem: Mental phenomena and the material universe must in some essential fashion differ from each other. As we have seen, in the ordinary domain of appearances, at the Euclidean-Newtonian level of analysis, this view is certainly tenable. But at the levels of the macro- and microphysical universes dualism becomes awkward. Niels Bohr's complementarity and Werner Heisenberg's uncertainty principle emphasize the importance of the observer in any understanding of what presumably is observed (Bohr, 1966; Heisenberg, 1959). Eugene P. Wigner (1969) stated the issue succinctly: Modern microphysics and macrophysics no longer deal with relations among observables but only with relations among observations.

An objection can be entered that such difficulties of distinguishing observables from observations encountered today by physicists are temporary, superficial, and of no concern to philosophers interested in the eternal verities. But that is not the message these thoughtful pioneers in physics are attempting to convey. They have been exploring universes where the everyday distinction between material and mental becomes disturbingly untenable at a very fundamental level. As I proceed, I shall tender some explanations that may help account for their views.

The dematerialization of energy can be traced in some sense to earlier formulations. For instance, physics was conceptually understandable in James Clerk Maxwell's day when light waves were propagated in the "ether." But then physicists did away with the "ether." Still, they did not rid themselves of Maxwell's wave equations or the more recent ones of Erwin Schroedinger (1928) or Louis Victor Prince de Broglie (1964). One readily can conceptualize waves traveling in a medium, such as when sound waves travel in air, but what can be the meaning of light or other electromagnetic waves "traveling" in a vacuum? Currently physicists are beginning to fill that vacuum with dense concentrations of energy, potentials for doing work when interfaced with matter. It is this potential that, I propose, is neutral to the mental–material duality.

In science, such potentials are defined in terms of the actual or possible work that is necessary for realization to occur and are measured as change in terms of *energy*. Thus, multiple realization imply a neutral monism in which the neutral essence, the potential for realization, is energy. And, as stated in

the second law of thermodynamics, energy is entropic, that is, it can have structure.

Energy is not material, only transformable into matter. It is measured by the amount of work that can be accomplished by using it and the efficiency of its use depends on its organization as measured by its entropy. The invention of the vacuum tube and subsequent devices have shown that properly configured minute amounts of energy can control large expenditures and that these minute organizations provide "information," that is, they inform and organize energy. Measures of information and entropy thus were seen as related (see, e.g., Brillouin, 1962; von Weizsacker, 1974). Computers were constructed to process information, and programs were written to organize the operations of computers. Is the information contained in a program "material" or "mental"? If it is either, what then of the information in a book? Or the entropy that describes the behavior of a heat engine or of a warm-blooded mammal? Clearly, we have come to the limit of usefulness of a distinction between the material and the mental.

Heisenberg (1959) developed a matrix approach to understanding the organization of energy (and momentum, i.e., inertia). Currently, this approach is used in s-matrix, bootstrap theories of quantum and nuclear physics by Henry Stapp (1965) and Geoffry Chew (1966). These investigators (among others, Dirac, 1951) have pointed out that measures of energy and momentum are related to measures of location in space-time by way of a Fourier transform. The Fourier theorem states that any pattern of organization can be analyzed into, and represented by, a series of regular waveforms of different amplitudes, frequencies, and phase relations. These regular waveforms can in turn be superimposed, convolved, with one another and, by way of the inverse Fourier procedure, can be retransformed to obtain correlations in the original space-time configuration. Thus, the Fourier transform of a set of patterns displays a spectral organization that is, of course, different from that which is displayed after the inverse Fourier transform has again converted the pattern into the space-time order.

In terms of the proposition put forward by Dirac, Stapp, and Chew, this means that the organization of energy and momentum is considerably different from the space-time organization of our ordinary perceptions that can be expressed in Euclidean, Cartesian, and Newtonian terms. David Bohm (1971, 1973, 1976) has identified these nonclassical organizations of energy potentials as "implicate," that is, enfolded, and has used the hologram as an example of such enfolded orders. Dennis Gabor (1946, 1948), the inventor of the hologram, based his discovery on the fact that one can store on a photographic film interference patterns of waveforms produced by the reflection or refraction of light from an object and reconstruct from such a film the image of the object. It is probably no accident that holograms were a mathematical invention (by Dennis Gabor) that used a form of mathematics, the integral calculus, invented by Gottfried Wilhelm Leibniz, who also came to a vision of the implicate order. Leibniz's monadology (1951) is holographic; his monads are distributed, windowless forms each of which is representative of the whole. Substitute the term *lensless* for windowless, and the description of a monad and a hologram is identical. Today the description of the enfolded organization of the stored potential for reconstruction is related to the unfolded space-time description of the object by a Fourier transform.

The Fourier theorem has also played an important role in the recent discoveries in the brain sciences. In the late 1960s, several groups of investigators found that they could explain their findings in visual research when they realized that their results indicated that encoding of spatial patterns in the visual system involved what they called *spatial frequency*. This term describes the spectral domain that results when a Fourier transform is performed on space-time. Fergus Campbell and John Robson (1968) of Cambridge University discovered unexpected regularities in their data: Responses to gratings of different widths and spacings adapted not only to the particular grating shown but also at other data points. These additional adaptations could be understood by describing the gratings as composed of regular waveforms, with a given frequency and the regularities in terms of harmonics. The spectral frequency was determined by the spacings of the grating, and thus the term spatial frequency. Spatial and temporal frequencies are related, of course: Scanning by a steadily moving beam would describe the grating's temporal frequency. Physicists therefore use the term *wave number* to denote the purely frequency, spectral form of description of patterns.

What this means is that the optical image is decomposed into its Fourier components: Regular waveforms of different frequencies and amplitudes. Cells in the visual system respond to one or another of these components and thus, in aggregate, comprise an image processing filter or resonator that has characteristics similar to the photographic filter comprising a hologram, from which images can be reconstructed by implementing the inverse transform.

There are, however, important differences between ordinary photographic holograms and the visual nervous system. Ordinary holograms are composed by a global Fourier transform that distributes the information contained in a space-time image throughout the transform domain. In the visual nervous system, distribution is limited anatomically to the input channeled to a particular cortical cell. Nonetheless, there are holographic techniques that use similar "patch" or multiplex constructions. Bracewell (1965) at Stanford University pioneered these techniques in radioastronomy by stripping together the holographic transformations of limited sectors of the heavens as viewed by radiotelescope. When the inverse transform is applied, space-time images of the whole composite can be viewed in three dimensions.

Furthermore, the transform that best describes the process in the visual system is a Gabor, not a Fourier. The Gabor transform (Gabor 1946, 1948; Daugman, 1985; Marcelja, 1980; Pribram & Carlton, 1987) is formed by placing a Gaussian envelope on the otherwise unlimited Fourier transform. This is another way of stating that the transformation is patchlike and not global, and gives mathematical precision to the limits involved.

Finally, the arrangement of the visual channels and the cortical cells is not haphazard with regard to one another. A clear retinotopic to cortical spatial arrangement is maintained. Thus the gross grain of the visual filter determines space-time coordinates, whereas its fine grain describes the Fourier components.

What advantage is gained by this fine-grain holographic-like organization? Recall that in the transform domain correlations among patterns are readily performed. This is why the fast Fourier transform (FFT) as performed by computer is such a powerful tool in statistical analysis and in computerized tomography (CT scans). The brain is an excellent correlator by virtue of its fine-grain processing potential.

The dual properties of an enfolded fine-grain (technically, the synaptodendritic receptive field organization) and a gross-grain space-time organization applies to other sense modalities as well, although the experimental evidence is not as complete. Georg von Bekesy (1967) performed critical studies in the auditory and somasthetic modalities, Walter Freeman (1960) conducted studies in the olfactory, and Pribram, Sharafat, and Beekman (1984) have shown that cells in the sensorimotor cortex are tuned to specific frequencies of movement. At the same time, in all these sensory systems the spatial organization of the receptor surface is topographically represented in the gross-grain arrangement of the cortical cells that receive the sensory input.

In summary, there is good evidence that another class of orders lies behind the ordinary classical level of organization we ordinarily perceive and which can be described in Euclidean and Newtonian terms and mapped in Cartesian space-time coordinates. The other class of orders is constituted of fine-grain distributed organizations described as potential because of the radical changes that occur in the transformational process of realization. When a potential is realized, information (the form within) becomes unfolded into its ordinary space-time appearance; in the other direction, the transformation enfolds and distributes the information as this is done by the holographic process. Because work is involved in transforming, descriptions in terms of energy are suitable, and as the structure of information is what is transformed, descriptions in terms of entropy (and negentropy) are also suitable. Thus, on the one hand, there are enfolded potential orders; on the other, there are unfolded orders manifested in space-time.

The point was made earlier in this chapter that the dualism of mental versus material holds only for the ordinary world of appearances—the world described in Euclidean geometry and Newtonian mechanics. An explanation of dualism was given in terms of procedural difference in approaching the hierarchy of systems that can be discerned in this world of appearances. This explanation was developed into a theory, a constructional realism. But it was also stated that certain questions raised by a more classical dualistic position were left unanswered by the explanations given in terms of an identity position.

Two issues can be discerned: (1) What is it that remains identical in the various levels of the hierarchy of programs or compositions? and (2) Is the correspondence between machine language (program or musical notation) and the machine or instrument's operation an identity or a duality? I believe the answer to both the questions hinges on whether one concentrates on the order (form, organization) or the embodiments in which these orders become instantiated (Pribram, 1986, 1993).

There is a difference between surface structures of different grains that become *trans*-formed and the deeper identity that *in*-forms the transformations. Transformations are necessary to material and mental "instantiations"—Plato's particular appearances—of the ideal in-forms: The instantiation of Beethoven's Ninth Symphony is transformed from composition (a mental operation) to score (a material embodiment) to performance (more mental than material) to recording on compact disc (more material than mental) to the sensory and brain processes (material) that make for appreciative listening (mental). But the symphony as symphony remains recognizably "identical" to Beethoven's creative composition over the centuries of performances, recordings, and listenings.

Instantiations depend on transformations among orders. What remains invariant across all instantiations is "in-formation," the form within. Surprisingly, according to this analysis, it is a Platonic "idealism" that motivates the information revolution ("information processing" approaches in cognitive science) and distinguishes it from the materialism of the industrial revolution. Further, as in-formation is neither material nor mental, a scientific pragmatism akin to that practised by Pythagoreans displaces mentalism and dualism as well as materialism. At least the tension between idealism (the potential) and realism (the appearance), which characterized the dialogue between Plato and Aristotle, will replace that between mentalism and materialism.

REFERENCES

Ashby, W. R. (1960). *Design for a brain: The origin of adaptive behavior* (2nd ed.). New York: John Wiley.

Barchas, J. E., Ciaranello, R. D., Stolk, J. M., & Hamburg, D. A. (1982). *Biogenic amines* and behavior. In S. Levine (Ed.), *Hormones and behavior* (pp. 235–329). New York: Academic Press.

Bekesy, G. von (1967). *Sensory inhibition.* Princeton, NJ: Princeton University Press.

Blanco, M. I. (1975). *The unconscious as infinite sets.* London: Gerald Duckworth.

Bohm, D. (1971). Quantum theory as an indication of a new order in physics. Part A. The development of new orders as shown through the history of physics. *Foundation of Physics*, *1*, 359–381.

Bohm, D. (1973). Quantum theory as an indication of a new order in physics. Part B. Implicate and explicate order in physical law. *Foundations of Physics*, *3*, 139–168.

Bohm, D. (1976). *Fragmentation and wholeness*. Jerusalem: VanLeer Jerusalem Foundation.

Bohr, N. (1966). *Atomic physics and human knowledge*. New York: Vintage.

Bracewell, R. N. (1965). *The Fourier transform and its application*. New York: McGraw-Hill.

Bracewell, R. N. (1989). The Fourier transform. *Scientific American*, 86–95.

Brentano, F. (1973). *Psychology from an empirical standpoint* (A, C. Rancmello, D. B. Terrell, & L. L. McAlister, Trans.). London: Routledge & Kegan Paul.

Brillouin, L. (1962). *Science and information theory* (2nd ed.). New York: Academic Press.

Brody, B. A., & Pribram, K. H. (1978). The role of frontal and parietal cortex in cognitive processing: Tests of spatial and sequence function. *Brain*, *101*, pp. 607–633.

Brooks, C. V. (1986). How does the limbic system assist motor learning? A limbic comparator hypothesis. *Brain and Behavioral Evolution*, *29*, 29–53.

Bucy, P. C. (1944). The *precentral motor cortex*. Chicago, IL: University of Illinois Press.

Bunge, M. (1980). *The mind-body problem*. Oxford: Pergamon Press.

Campbell, F. W., & Robson, J. G. (1968). Application of Fourier analysis to the visibility of gratings. *Journal of Physiology*, *197*, 551–566.

Cannon, W. B. (1927). The James-Lange theory of emotions: A critical examination and an alternative theory. *American Journal of Psychology*, *XXXIX*, 106–124.

Cannon, W. B. (1929). *Bodily changes in pain, horror, fear and rage: An account of recent researches into the function of emotional excitement*. New York: Appleton-Century-Crofts.

Chew, G. S. (1966). The *analytic s-matrix. A basis for nuclear democracy*. New York: Benjamin.

Chisholm, R. M. (1960). *Realism and the background of phenomenology*. New York: Free Press.

Darwin, C. (1872). *The expression of the emotions in man and animals*. London: John Murray.

Daugman, J. G. (1985). Uncertainty relation for resolution in space, spatial frequency, and orientation optimized by two-dimensional visual cortical filters. *Journal of the Optical Society of America, 2*(7), 1160–1169.

Dayhoff, J. (1990). *Neural network architectures*. New York: Van Nostrand Reinhold.

Dennett, Daniel C. (1991). *Consciousness explained*. Boston: Little, Brown .

Descartes, R. (1927). *Selections*. New York: Scribner.

Dewan, E. M., Eccles, J. C., Globus, G. G., Gunderson, K., Knapp, P. H., Maxwell, G., Pribram, K. H., Savage, C. W., Savodnik, I., Scriven, M., Sperry, R. W., Weimer, W. B., & Wimsatt, W. C. (1976). The role of scientific results in theories of mind and brain: A conversation among philosophers and scientists. In G. G. Globus & G. Maxwell (Eds.), *Consciousness and the brain* (pp. 317–328). New York: Plenum Press.

Dirac, P. A. M. (1951). Is there an aether? *Nature, 168*, 906.

Eccles, J. C., Ito, M., & Szentagothai, J. (1967). *The cerebellum as a neuronal machine*. New York: Springer-Verlag.

Feigl, H. (1960). Mind-body, not a pseudoproblem. In S. Hook (Ed.), *Dimensions of mind* (pp. 33–44). New York: Collier.

Fleschig, P. (1900). *Les centres de projection et d'association de cerveau humain*. XIII Congress International de Medecine (Sect. Neurologie): 115–121. Paris.

Fodor, J. A. (1980). Methodological solipsism as a research strategy for cognitive psychology. *Behavioral and Brain Sciences*, *3*, 63–110.

Freeman, W. J. (1960). Correlation of electrical activity of prepyriform cortex and behavior in cat. *Journal of Neurophysiology*, *23*, 111–131.

Freud, S. (1895/1966). *Project for a scientific psychology*. Standard Edition, Vol. 1. London: Hogarth Press.

Gabor, D. (1946). Theory of communication. *Journal of the Institute of Electrical Engineers*, *93*, 429–441.

Gabor, D. (1948). A new microscopic principle. *Nature, 161*, 777–778.

Gall, F. J., & Spurtzheim, G. (1809/1969). Research on the nervous system in general and on that of the brain in particular. In K. H. Pribram (Ed.), *Brain and behavior* (pp. 20–26). Middlesex, England: Penguin.

Garcia-Rill, E., & Skinner, R. D. (1988). Modulation of rhythmic function in the posterior midbrain. *Neurosciences*, *27*, 639–654.

Grillner, S. (1974). Locomotions in vertebrates: Central mechanisms and reflex interactions. *Physiology Review*, *55*, 274–304.

Grillner, S. (1981). Control of locomotion in bipeds, tetrapods, and fish. In V. B. Brooks (Ed.), *Handbook of physiology—the nervous system II* (pp. 1199–1236). Baltimore: Waverly Press.

Grillner, S. (1985). Neurobiological bases of rhythmic motor acts in vertebrates. *Science*, *228*, 143–144.

Head, H. (1920). *Studies in neurology*. London: Oxford University Press.

Heilman, K. M., & Valenstein, E. (1972). Frontal lobe neglect. *Neurology*, *28*, 229–232.

Heisenberg, W. (1959). *Physics and philosophy*. London: Allen & Unwin.

Hermans, H. J. M., Kempen, H. J. G., & van Loon, R. J. P. (1992). The dialogical self: Beyond individualism and rationalism. *American Psychologist*, *47*(l), 23–33.

Hersh, N. A. (1980). *Spatial disorientation in brain injured patients*. Unpublished dissertation, Department of Psychology, Stanford University.

Hilgard, E. R. (1977). *Divided consciousness. Multiple controls in human thought and action.* New York: Wiley.

Hinton, G. E., & Anderson, J. A. (1981). *Parallel models of associative memory.* Hillsdale, NJ: Lawrence Erlbaum.

Husserl, E. (1901/1975). *Fifth logical investigation* (in German). Hamburg, Germany: Meiner.

James, W. (1901/1950). *Principles of psychology* (Vols. 1 and 2). New York: Dover.

James, W. (1909). *A pluralistic universe.* London: Longman's, Green.

Jaynes, J. (1977). The *origin of consciousness in the breakdown of the bicameral mind.* Boston, MA: Houghton-Mifflin.

Jung, C. G. (1960). *Collected works* (2nd ed.) Bollingen Series #20. Princeton: Princeton University Press.

Kelso, J. A. S., & Saltzman, E. L. (1982). Motor control: Which themes do we orchestrate? *The Behavioral and Brain Sciences, 5*(4), 554–557.

Knonow, A., & Pribram, K. H. (1970). Error recognition and utilization produced by injury to the frontal cortex in man. *Neuropsychologia, 8,* 489–491.

Lashley, K. S. (1929). *Brain mechanisms and intelligence.* Chicago, IL: University of Chicago Press.

Lashley, K. S. (1960). The thalamus and emotion. In F. A. Beach, D. O. Hebb, C. T. Morgan, & H. W. Nissen (Eds.), *The neuropsychology of Lashley* (pp. 237–240). New York: McGraw-Hill.

Leibniz, G. W. (1951). *The Monadology and other philosophical writings.* London: Oxford University Press. (Original work published 1714)

Levine, D. S. (1991). *Introduction to neural & cognitive modeling.* Hillsdale, NJ: Lawrence Erlbaum.

Lindsley, D. B. (1951). Emotion. In S. S. Stevens (Ed.), *Handbook of experimental psychology* (pp. 473–516). New York: Wiley.

Lindsley, D. B., & Wilson, C. L. (1976). Brainstem-hypothalamic systems influencing hippocampal activity and behavior. In R. L. Isaacson & K. H. Pribram (Eds.), *The Hippocampus (Part IV)* (pp. 247–274). New York: Plenum.

Luria, A. R., Pribram, K. H., & Homskaya, E. D. (1964). An experimental analysis of the behavioral disturbance produced by a left frontal arachnoidal endothelioma *(meningioma). Neuropsychologia, 2,* 257–280.

Mach, E. (1914). *The analysis of sensations and the relation of the physical to the psychical.* Chicago: Open Court.

MacKay, D. M. (1966). Cerebral organization and the conscious control of action. In J. C. Eccles (Ed.), *Brain and conscious experience* (pp. 422–445). New York: Springer-Verlag.

MacLean, P. D. (1949). Psychosomatic disease and the "visceral brain": recent developments bearing on the Papez theory of emotion. *Psychosomatic Medicine, 11,* 338–353.

Magoun, H. W. (1950). Caudal and cephalic influences of the brain reticular formation. *Physiological Review, 30,* 459–474.

Marcelja, S. (1980). Mathematical description of the responses of simple cortical cells. *Journal of the Optical Society of America, 70,* 1297–1300.

McCarthy, R. A., & Warrington, E. K. (1990). *Cognitive neuropsychology: A clinical introduction.* New York: Academic Press.

McFarland, D. J. (1971). *Feedback mechanisms in animal behavior.* London: Academic Press.

Miller, G. A., Galanter, A., & Pribram, K. H. (1960). *Plans and the structure of behavior.* New York: Henry Holt.

Minsky, M. (1986). *Society of mind.* New York: Simon & Schuster.

Mittelstaedt, H. (1968). Discussion. In D. P. Kimble (Ed.), *Experience and capacity,* (pp. 46–49). New York: The New York Academy of Sciences, Interdisciplinary Communications Program.

Mountcastle, V. B., Lynch, J. C., Georgopoulos, A., Sakata, H., & Acuna, C. (1975). Posterior parietal association cortex of the monkey: Command functions for operations within extrapersonal space. *Journal of Neurophysiology, 38,* 871–908.

Neumann, E. (1954). *The origins and history of consciousness.* Princeton: Princeton University Press.

Olds, J., & Milner, P. (1954). Positive reinforcement produced by electrical stimulation of septal area and other regions of rat brain. *Journal of Comparative and Physiological Psychology, 47,* 419–427.

Oscar-Berman, M. (1975). The effects of dorso-lateral-frontal and ventrolateral-orbito-frontal lesions on spatial discrimination learning and delayed response in two modalities. *Neuropsychologia, 13,* 237–246.

Papez, J. W. (1937). A proposed mechanism of emotion. *Archives of Neurological Psychiatry, 38,* 725–743.

Peirce, C. S. (1934). *Pragmatism and pragmaticism.* Collected papers, Vol. 5, Lectures VI & VII (pp. 94–131). Cambridge, MA: Harvard University Press.

Penfield, W. (1969). Consciousness, memory and man's conditioned reflexes. In K. H. Pribram (Ed.), *On the biology of learning* (pp. 127–168). New York: Harcourt, Brace & World.

Pohl, W. G. (1973). Dissociation of spatial and discrimination deficits following frontal and parietal lesions in monkeys. *Journal of Comparative Physiological Psychology, 82,* 227–239.

Pribram, K. H. (1950). Psychosurgery in midcentury. *Surgery, Gynecology and Obstetrics, 91,* 364–367.

Pribram, K. H. (1954/1969). Toward a science of neuropsychology (method and data). In R. A. Patton (Ed.), *Current trends in psychology and the behavior sciences* (pp. 115–142). Pittsburg, PA: University of Pittsburg Press. Excerpt in K. H. Pribram (Ed.), *Brain and behavior (*Vol. 1) (pp. 54–66). London: Penguin.

Pribram, K. H. (1958). Comparative neurology and the evolution of behavior. In G. G. Simpson (Ed.), *Evolution and behavior* (pp. 140–164). New Haven, CT: Yale University Press.

Pribram, K. H. (1960). The intrinsic systems of the forebrain. In J. Field, H. W. Mogoan, & V. E. Hall (Eds.), *Handbook of physiology, neurophysiology, II* (pp. 1323–1344). Washington, DC: American Psychological Society.

Pribram, K. H. (1961). Limbic system. In D. E. Sheer (Ed.), *Electrical stimulation of the brain* (pp. 563–574). Austin, TX: University of Texas Press.

Pribram, K. H. (1963). Reinforcement revisited: A structural view. In M. Jones (Ed.), *Experimental foundation of clinical psychology* (pp. 442–468). New York: Basic Books.

Pribram, K. H. (1965). Proposal for a structural pragmatism: Some neuropsychological considerations of problems in philosophy. In B. Wolman & E. Nagel (Eds.), *Scientific psychology: Principles and approaches* (pp. 426–459). New York: Basic Books.

Pribram, K. H. (1969). On the neurology of thinking. *Behavioral Science, 4,* 265–287

Pribram, K. H. (1971). *Languages of the brain: Experimental paradoxes and principles in neuropsychology.* Englewood Cliffs, NJ: Prentice-Hall.

Pribram, K. H. (1974). How is it that sensing so much we can do so little? In K. H. Pribram (Contrib. Ed.), *Central processing of sensory input* (pp. 249–261). F. O. Schmitt & F. G. Worden (Eds.), *The Neurosciences Third Study Program.* Cambridge, MA: MIT Press.

Pribram, K. H. (1977). New dimensions in the functions of the basal ganglia. In C. Shagass, S. Gershon, & A. J. Friedhoff (Eds.), *Psychopathology and brain dysfunction* (pp. 77–95). New York: Raven Press.

Pribram, K. H. (1980). The orienting reaction: Key to brain representational mechanisms. In H. D. Kimmel (Ed.), *The orienting reflex in humans* (pp. 3–20). Hillsdale, NJ: Lawrence Erlbaum.

Pribram, K. H. (1981). Emotions. In S. B. Filskov & T. J. Boll (Eds.), *Handbook of clinical neuropsychology* (pp. 201–234). New York: Wiley.

Pribram, K. H. (1986). The cognitive revolution and mind/brain issues. *American Psychologist, 41,* 507–520.

Pribram, K. H. (1991). *Brain and perception: Holonomy and structure in figural processing.* New York: Lawrence Erlbaum.

Pribram, K. H. (1993). Afterword. In K. H. Pribram (Ed.), *Rethinking neural networks: Quantum fields and biological data* (pp. 531–536). Hillsdale, NJ: Lawrence Erlbaum.

Pribram, K. H., Ahumada, A., Hartog, J., & Roos, L. (1964). A progress report on the neurological process disturbed by frontal lesions in primates. In S. M. Warren & K. Akart (Eds.), *The frontal granular cortex and behavior* (pp. 28–55). New York: McGraw Hill.

Pribram, K. H. & Carlton, E. H. (1987). Holonomic brain theory in imagining and object perception. *Acta Psychologica, 63,* 175–210

Pribram, K. H., & Gill, M. (1976). *Freud's "Project" reassessed.* New York: Basic Books.

Pribram, K. H., Kruger, L., Robinson, F., & Berman, A. J. (1955–1956). The effects of precentral lesions on the behavior of monkeys. *Yale Journal of Biology & Medicine, 28,* 428–443.

Pribram, K. H., & McGuinness, D. (1975). Arousal, activation and effort in the control of attention. *Psychological Review, 82*(2), 116–149.

Pribram, K. H. & McGuinness, D. (1992). Attention and para-attentional processing: Event-related brain potentials as tests of a model. *Annals of the New York Academy of Sciences,* 65–92.

Pribram, K. H. & Mishkin, M. (1955). Simultaneous and successive visual discrimination by monkeys with inferotemporal lesions. *Journal of Comparative Physiology and Psychology, 48,* 198–202.

Pribram, K. H., Nuwer, M., & Baron, R. (1974). The holographic hypothesis of memory structure in brain function and perception. In R. C. Atkinson, D. H. Krantz, R. C. Luce, & P. Suppes (Eds.), *Contemporary developments in mathematical psychology* (pp. 416–467). San Francisco: W. H. Freeman.

Pribram, K. H., Reitz, S., McNeil, M., & Spevack, A. A. (1979). The effect of amygdalectomy on orienting and classical conditioning in monkeys. *Pavlovian Journal, 14*(4), 203–217.

Pribram, K. H. & Robinson, D. (1985). Biological contributions to the development of psychology. In C. Buxton (Ed.), *A history of modern psychology: Concepts, methods, viewpoint* (pp 345–377). New York: Academic Press.

Pribram, K. H., Sharafat, A., & Beekman, G. J. (1984). Frequency encoding in motor systems. In H. T. A. Whiting (Ed.), *Human motor actions: Bernstein reassessed* (pp. 121–156). Amsterdam: North-Holland/Elsevier.

Prince de Broglie, L. V. (1964). *The current of wave mechanisms: A critical study* (Express Transaction Service, Trans.). Amsterdam: Elsevier.

Rose, J. E., & Woolsey, C. N. (1949). Organization of the mammalian thalamus and its relationship to the cerebral cortex. *EEG Clinical Neurophysiology, 1,* 391–404.

Ruch, T. C. (1951). Motor systems. In S. S. Stevens (Ed.), *Handbook of experimental psychology* (pp. 154–208). New York: Wiley.

Ruff, R. M., Hersh, N. A., & Pribram, K. H. (1981). Auditory spatial deficits in the personal and extrapersonal frames of reference due to cortical lesions. *Neuropsychologia, 19*(3), 435–443.

Rumelhart, D. E., McClelland, J. L., & the PDP Research Group. (1986). *Parallel distributed processing,* (Vols. 1 and II). Cambridge, MA: MIT Press.

Russell, B. (1948). *Human knowledge, its scope and limits.* New York: Simon & Schuster.

Schachter, S., & Singer, T. E. (1962). Cognitive, social and physiological determinants of emotional state. *Psychological Review, 69,* 379–397.

Schroedinger, E. (1928). Quantization as a problem of proper values. In J. F. Shearer & W. M. Deans (Eds.), *Collected papers on wave mechanics.* London: Blackie.

Searle, J. R. (1984). *Minds, brains and science.* Cambridge, MA: Harvard University Press.

Shannon, C. E. & Weaver, W. (1949). *The mathematical theory of communications.* Urbana, IL: University of Illinois Press.

Shepard, R. N., & Chipman, S. (1970). Second-order isomorphism of internal representations: Shapes of states. *Cognitive Psychology, I,* 1–17.

Sidman, M., Stoddard, L. T., & Mohr, J. P. (1968). Some additional quantitative observations of immediate memory in a patient with bilateral hippocampal lesions. *Neuropsychologia, 6,* 245–254.

Sperry, R. W. (1980). Mind/brain interaction—Mentalism, yes—Dualism, no. *Neuroscience, 2,* 195–206.

Stapp, H. P. (1965). Space and time in s-matrix theory. *Physiological Review, 135B,* 257–270.

Stich, S. P. (1986). *From folk psychology to cognitive science—The case against belief.* Cambridge, MA: MIT Press.

Thatcher, R. W., & John, E. R. (1977). *Functional neuroscience* (Vol. 1). Hillsdale, NJ: Lawrence Erlbaum.

Ukhtomski, A. A. (1926). Concerning the condition of excitation in dominance. *Novoe y refteksologie i fiziologii nervoisystemry, 2,* 3–15.

Waddington, C. H. (1957). *The strategy of genes.* London: Allen & Unwin.

Weiskrantz, L. (1986). *Blindsight. A case study and implications.* Oxford: Clarendon Press.

Weiskrantz, L., Warrington, E. K., Sanders, M. D., & Marshall, J. (1974). Visual capacity in the hemianopic field following a restricted occipital ablation. *Brain, 97*(4), 709–728.

Weizsacker, E. von. (1974). *Offene systems I.* Stuttgart, Germany: Verlag.

Wigner, E. P. (1969). Epistemology of quantum mechanics: Its appraisals and demands. In M. Grene (Ed.), *The anatomy of knowledge* (pp. 31–45). London: Routledge & Kegan Paul.

Willshaw, D. (1981). Holography, associative memory and inductive generalization. In G. E. Hinton & J. A. Anderson (Eds.), *Parallel models of associative memory* (pp. 83–102). Hillsdale, NJ: Lawrence Erlbaum.

Wright, J. J. (1980). Visual evoked response in lateral hypothalamic neglect. *Experimental Neurology.*

CHAPTER 16

TYPICAL EMOTIONS

Aaron Ben-Ze'ev

Emotions are of interest to everyone. Indeed, they play a central role in our lives. Talking to lay people about emotions is instructive: Ordinary people are highly curious and knowledgeable about emotional phenomena. Common sense, poems, novels, movies, historical accounts, psychological studies, and philosophical discussions supply us with a host of information about emotions. Despite their apparent simplicity and the great deal of available information, emotions are an extremely crucial and complex topic. The problem in understanding emotions is the formulation of a comprehensive framework to adequately explain the various emotional phenomena. Owing to the enormous complexity and diversity of emotions, the presentation of such a framework is difficult and rare.

One aim of this chapter is to offer an outline for such a framework by providing an initial characterization of typical emotions. Because of space limitations I will concentrate on the presentation of the framework itself rather than on critical discussions of possible objections to its various contentions.

The typical emotional cause is suggested to be a perceived significant change in our situation; the typical emotional concern is a comparative concern; and the typical emotional object is a human being. Typical emotions are considered to have four basic characteristics: instability, great intensity, relative brevity, and a partial perspective; and to consist of four basic components: cognition, evaluation, motivation, and feeling. I will try to show that this is not an arbitrary characterization, but one that is helpful in understanding emotions and is compatible with commonsense as well as scientific usages.

THE PROTOTYPE ANALYSIS

In light of the great complexity of emotions, and in particular their great sensitivity to contextual and personal factors, we should adopt a conceptual tool that can describe the basic characteristics of emotions while preserving their complexity and sensitivity. A prototype analysis of emotions is a suitable tool for this task.

Emotions in general and each particular emotion separately constitute prototypical categories. Inclusion is determined by the degree of similarity to the best example. Hence, there is no single essence that is a necessary and sufficient condition for all emotions, and no simple definition of emotions or even one type of emotion exists: "Everyone knows what an emotion is, until asked to give a definition. Then, it seems, no one knows" (Fehr & Russell, 1984, p. 464). Membership in the category of emotions, as well as membership in the category of a particular emotion, is a matter of degree rather than an all-or-nothing affair; accordingly, the category has a certain internal structure and no sharp boundary separates members from nonmembers. Thus, the boundaries between romantic love, liking, and friendship are fuzzy, as are those between envy and jealousy. Different phenomena can be reliably ordered from better to poorer examples of the general category of emotions or of categories of particular emotions. The typical basic characteristics of emotions are fully manifest in paradigmatic, or prototypical examples; in less typical examples these characteristics occur in a less developed form and some may even be absent (see also Alston, 1967; Fehr, 1988; Kovecses, 1990; Lakoff, 1987; Rosch, 1978; Russell, 1991; Shaver et al., 1992; Smith & Lazarus, 1990).

In the prototype framework emotions are analyzed *as if* they were context-free. For example, the characterization of typical envy is supposed to be valid for all instances of envy. Indeed, in psychological experiments when subjects are asked to describe prototypical categories of emotions, they are left to imagine whatever contexts they like (Fitness & Fletcher, 1993). The sensitivity of emotions to a particular context is not to be found in different characterizations of typical envy, each suitable for a different context, but rather in the flexibility of a single characterization of typical envy. Not all instances of envy have all features of typical envy; nor do they possess these features in the same intensity. Each person may have a somewhat different version of typical envy; the membership of the particular instance in the category of envy is determined by its similarity to the typical case. This manner of analysis can provide general characteristics common to the diverse instances of emotions while preserving their contextual sensitivity.

The use of prototypical categories may draw the criticism that there can be no counterexamples to the prototypical characterization, since any such example may be regarded as atypical. It is true that confirmation and falsification of a prototypical cat-

egory are more complex than those of the ordinary binary (all-or-nothing) category, but so is their characterization. Working with categories that have clear-cut and definite boundaries is easier, but they do not represent reality adequately. Since in reality there are usually no clear and definite boundaries between things, working with prototypical categories is often more to the point. In light of the prototypical nature of emotions, we should frequently use terms such as "usually," "typically," and "often" while characterizing emotions. Although employing such terms will make it harder to refute the suggested claims, it is implied by the use of a prototypical category. It is no one's fault that various instances of emotions are not nicely divided and clearly arranged as we want them to be. The refutation of the suggested characterization is still possible, but it could not consist of describing one isolated case that seems to be an exception; it would have to show that most phenomena are different from the suggested characterization or that the conceptual analysis is inconsistent.

THE TYPICAL EMOTIONAL CAUSE: A PERCEIVED SIGNIFICANT CHANGE

Emotions typically occur when we perceive highly significant changes in our situation. A significant change may be characterized as that which significantly interrupts or improves a smoothly flowing situation of us. It is not the presence or absence of favorable or unfavorable circumstances that generates emotions, but our evaluation of these circumstances as involving a significant change. Like burglar alarms going off when an intruder appears, emotions signal that something needs attention. When no attention is needed, the signaling system can be switched off (Oatley, 1992, p. 46). We respond to the unusual by paying attention to it. The extraordinary does not permit us to shrug it off and walk away. In contrast, the usual is taken for granted, safe, almost invisible. A change, emotional or otherwise, is always related to a certain framework of reference against which it is evaluated and its significance is attained. The role of changes in emotions has been indicated by various philosophers (see, e. g., Aristotle, *Rhetoric,* 1984, 1378a2l; Spinoza, 1677/1985, V, p. 39, s; III, Def. aff. ; Lyons, 1980) and psychologists (see, e. g., Frijda, 1988; Lazarus, 1991; Oatley, 1992).

The importance of changes in the generation of our emotions is evident from many everyday phenomena and scientific findings. People are very excited when facing changes in their life: birth of a first child; first marriage; entering school for the first time; going to an interview that can significantly change their life, and so on. When walking in a crowd of people, our attention and excitement will be directed at those who are unusual; for instance, a nun passionately kissing a young man; a very young man and an old woman making love; a white couple in a crowd consisting of black people. Likewise, almost all young children react with an acute emotion of mild fear for several minutes upon encountering a large group of unfamiliar children. A certain kind of change is also required for our happiness. This may explain boredom in marriage and the excitement of love affairs. It may also explain why rich people who seem to have everything are not necessarily happy. After a while rich people get used to having everything, and only changes make them happy (Freedman, 1978, p. 228; Kagan, 1992, p. 99).

It is not the change itself, but its significance in our mind which is crucial in determining emotional intensity. When, for example, a certain team wins the championship for the first time, this change generates intense emotions among the team's fans, but leaves other people completely indifferent. Highly emotional individuals perceive their daily events as being more significant than lower emotional people do. The world of the highly emotional people is a place where many events are highly significant (Larsen & Diener, 1987).

The view presented here may also be formulated in terms of "adaptation level," namely, the type and level of stimulation an organism experiences for long enough to become accustomed to it. An emotional state is generated when we deviate from this level. The change, rather than the general level, is of emotional significance. Accordingly, continued pleasures wear off; continued hardships lose their poignancy. The importance of changes for the generation of emotions indicates the dynamic and complex nature of our emotional life (Frijda, 1988).

A significant emotional change may involve perception of changes that have actually taken place or imagined, counterfactual changes. Both types of change are present in typical emotional states: When we perceive an actual change we also perceive some of its alternatives. The first kind of change refers to actual modifications in our situation. The greater this change, the more intense the emotion. The imaginary kind of change encompasses the mental construction of a counterfactual alternative, to be compared with actual reality. Because of the significance of the change, we are keenly aware of an alternative to the current situation. The more available the alternative, namely, the closer the imagined alternative is to reality, the more intense the emotion. A crucial element in emotions is, indeed, the imagined condition of "it could have been otherwise."

The contribution of each type of change to the overall emotional significance differs in different emotional situations. The imagined element is present in all emotions, but its importance varies. In some emotions, such as regret, grief, guilt, relief, envy, jealousy, and pity, it is strongly dominant; in others, such as love and happy-for, it matters less. This element is usually more dominant in negative emotions where the preferred reality is counterfactual. Emotions in animals involve mainly (though not merely) the first kind of change, whereas the complex forms of the second kind, requiring developed intentional capacities, are more typical of human beings. Human beings do not live exclusively in the immediate present. Through our intentional capacities we imagine what is likely to happen, what happened or might happen.

Although the first kind of change may be considered as more objective than the second, it is also essentially a subjective change. It is the subject who perceives the change and accordingly considers it more or less significant. Moreover, changes associated with emotions may not merely refer to the subject but also to those constituting the subject's environment. Again, it is the subject who determines which people belong to this environment. The subject not only determines the significance of the change but also its scope. The same change may give rise to different emotions or to a different emotional intensity if we evaluate its significance differently. A distinction can be made between the ("objective") size of the change and its ("subjective") significance. We construct a psychological reality in which despite the apparent great "objective" weight of some changes they are not emotionally significant and hence are perceived as smaller.

Not only emotions, but consciousness in general is strongly activated when the organism is confronted with changes. Perceptual awareness, for example, is also connected with changes. Thus, under normal conditions we are unaware of air pressure although it affects us constantly. We only perceive it when the level of air pressure changes, as when we take off or land in an airplane. The same applies to the visual system. The lack of relational properties such as motion and change results in the disappearance of perception. For instance, when a uniform color fills our field of vision, the color vanishes, to be replaced by a dark gray. Higher systems of consciousness, too, such as focusing one's attention, come into play when a sudden change takes place in our circumstances. One can drive a car without paying particular attention to the sidewalk; however, if a child playing with a ball on the sidewalk should suddenly come into view, the driver will take notice. The pleasure system also tends to satiate without enough variety. Thus, we become bored when doing the same thing over and over, even if that activity was pleasant at first (Ben-Ze'ev, 1993a).

Responding primarily to changes is a highly economical and efficient way of using limited resources. From an evolutionary point of view it is advantageous for an organism to focus its attention on changes in the environment rather than on stationary stimuli. Such changes indicate to an organism that its conditions have altered, and awareness of this is important for survival. When we are accustomed to the change, mental activity decreases since there is no sense in wasting time and energy on something when we have already developed ways to deal with it.

THE TYPICAL EMOTIONAL CONCERN: A COMPARATIVE CONCERN

The importance of changes in the generation of emotions is connected with the importance of the comparative concern. An event can be perceived as a significant change only when compared to a certain background framework. Like other types of meaning, emotional meaning is relational, and as such it involves a certain comparison. Two major types of emotional comparison may be discerned: (a) a comparison of the whole emotional situation to an alternative situation, and (b) a comparison, within the given situation, of our standing to that of others. The first comparison refers to the alternative-availability and the second is a social comparison. Consider, for instance, envy of a colleague

who wins a prestigious prize. One comparison underlying this envy is that of the present situation with an imaginary alternative situation in which I, rather than my colleague, win the prize. The second comparison is within the given situation: It compares my inferior social standing to that of my colleague. Similarly, in gratitude we compare the reception of a certain gift to an alternative in which we receive another gift or no gift at all, and we also compare our own standing to that of the giver.

Spinoza emphasizes the importance for the generation of emotions of conceiving an alternative to the present situation. He argues that the better the wise man grasps the fully deterministic nature of events around him, the less likely he is to experience passions. That is, the better a person realizes the lack of an available alternative, the less likely it is for this person to be affected by emotions. Generally, "Insofar as the mind understands all things as necessary, it has a greater power over the affects, or is less acted on by them" (1677/1985, V, p. 6).

The importance of the alternative-availability is illustrated in the fact that we envy people when we can easily imagine ourselves in their place; hence, we envy more those who are like us or equal to us. Likewise, sexual arousal often depends on imagining the availability of an alternative. (A recent survey reveals, for example, that many British men think about the singer Madonna while making love with their mate.) Similarly, gratitude and pride involve the realization of the superior nature of the current situation over its alternative. In light of the importance of alternative-availability, "almost situations" have additional emotional nuances (Ben-Ze'ev, 1992b; Heider, 1958, pp. 141–4; Kahneman & Miller, 1986; Ortony et al., 1988, pp. 74–5).

Some alternatives are closer to reality than others, since they are more likely to occur. Availability, or feasibility, is determined by how remote from actual reality the relevant event is considered to be. This comparison of actual reality with the counterfactual alternative is accompanied by evaluation of the comparison. The notion of an alternative-availability is connected with that of abnormality: An abnormal event is one that has highly available alternatives. Indeed, a significant change responsible for the generation of emotions is a change departing significantly from our normal situation. Accordingly, abnormal events are surprising and often associated with intense emotions. The more available the alternative, or the more abnormal the situation, the more the subject of negative emotions considers the current situation to be unfair and the more the subject of positive emotions considers it to be good luck. In such situations emotional intensity is greater (Kahneman & Miller, 1986).

The second major type of emotional comparison is a social comparison referring to relationships within the given emotional situation. Social comparison is important in determining our happiness and values, reducing uncertainty about ourselves, and maintaining or enhancing self-esteem. However, we neither compare ourselves with everyone nor do we compare everything. Social comparison is not exercised indiscriminately; it refers to people and domains relevant to our well-being.

A comparative significance of something is derived from an explicit or implicit reference to a certain background framework. In the first type of emotional comparison our current situation is the background against which the alternative's significance is determined. In social comparison the background framework is a certain personal baseline. We envy most those whose standing is evaluated to be a bit higher than our baseline (we may also envy those who are significantly above the baseline, but the intensity of this envy will be less since the availability of overcoming the gap is small). We pity or have contempt for those who are significantly below our baseline. We are ashamed when our behavior is well below the standards included in our personal baseline, and are proud when it is well above these standards. We feel gratitude when the gift received exceeds our expected baseline, and we feel anger when others' behavior deviates from what is considered in our personal baseline as decent behavior.

Describing one's personal baseline is complex because it depends on many biological, social, personal, and contextual features. The baseline reflects features such as our current stand, norms, beliefs, desires, and expectations. The baseline is not a rigid entity but it has certain flexibility enabling it to match our experiences. However, this flexibility is limited since our ability to change our personality and current situation is limited. The possibility of differing baselines is one reason why the same event occurring at different times may be associated with different emotions.

Social comparison may be expressed in a few basic relationships: rivalry, cooperation, and conformity (Dakin & Arrowood, 1981). Rivalry prevails in emotions such as envy and pleasure in others' misfortune where our satisfaction or dissatisfaction depends on our position in relation to others. Social comparison is cooperative in nature in emotions such as compassion and love where our satisfaction or dissatisfaction depends on whether both we and others do well. Conformity prevails when we are concerned with whether our behavior and that of others are the same or different. It is found in emotions toward the whole personality of others or oneself, for example, pride, shame, hate, and some cases of love.

A common form of rivalry is direct competition. However, rivalry may be more subtle. Keith can be pleased over the misfortune of the Conservative ministers of Great Britain, who have been caught in sex scandals just after preaching about the importance of keeping family values, without competing with them over public positions. However, Keith probably opposed the views of the Conservative party in the first place; hence, his attitude toward them may be described as a kind of rivalry. If sex scandals were prevailing among the leaders of the party he favors, he may be frustrated or sad, but probably would not be pleased with their misfortunes. The competitive form of rivalry makes emotions more frequent and intense than in a distant rivalry. Emotions are more frequent in this form of rivalry since in most competitions there are many losers for every winner. They are also more intense since a competitive rivalry is more personal and relevant for our self-esteem: Another person's gain is interpreted as our loss since it changes our comparative stands. Accordingly, we often identify worse situations with bad situations.

In cooperative situations rewards are allocated on the basis of joint excellence. Where rivalry is absent, the other's comparative gain need not necessarily lead to an actual change in our situation. Similarly, improvement in our comparative stand need not necessarily lead to improvement in our situation. An endless competition for a better comparative stand often does not lead to a greater level of satisfaction: Competitive comparison is not the sole source of satisfaction. Cooperation may prove to be satisfying in many situations.

Conformity is similar to rivalry and cooperation in presupposing diversity; hence, the comparative concern. In cooperation the diversity is viewed favorably and the participants equally. In rivalry the diversity is viewed favorably and the participants are considered to be unequal. In conformity, the diversity is not viewed favorably and the participants are not considered to be equal. The unity desired is not that achieved by cooperation of different parties, but by the abolishment of all other parties except the one considered to be positive.

In light of the importance of social comparison in emotions, emotions are typically directed at human beings. The typical (but in no way the only) emotional object is a certain agent who may be another person (or another living creature in general), or the subject experiencing the emotion.

The social nature of most emotions is also explained by referring to the major cause for the generation of emotions: significant change in our situation. Such a change usually depends on the activity of other people who are crucial for evaluating our situation. Reid characterizes emotions as "principles of actions in man, which have persons for their immediate object, and imply, in their very nature, our being well or ill affected to some person, or, at least, to some animated being." He explains, "When we speak of affection to a house, or to any inanimate thing, the word has a different meaning; for that which has no capacity of enjoyment or of suffering, may be an object of liking or disgust, but cannot possibly be an object either of benevolent or malevolent affection" (Reid, 1768, pp. 558–9; see also Oatley, 1992, p. 179). Strong positive or negative evaluations with a strong tendency to act accordingly is typically directed toward agents who can enjoy or suffer. Hence these agents are the focus of concern in typical emotions: "The nature and development of the human relationships has been shaped largely by the fascination the human race holds for itself—people are more interesting to people than anything else" (Izard, 1991, p. 128).

The two major types of emotional comparison, that is, the alternative-availability and social comparison, are related: The significance of our social comparison is determined, among other things, by the alternative-availability, and in assessing the availability of an alternative, its social significance is an important factor. Both types of comparison are crucial for emotional intensity.

BASIC CHARACTERISTICS: INSTABILITY, INTENSITY, BREVITY, AND PARTIALITY

I suggest considering instability, great intensity, relative brevity, and a partial perspective as the basic characteristics of typical emotions.

Instability

In light of the crucial role changes play in generating emotions, instability of the mental (as well as the physiological) system is a basic characteristic of emotions. Emotions indicate a transition in which the preceding context has changed, but no new context has yet stabilized. Emotions are like a storm at sea or a tempest in the air: Unstable states that signify some agitation (Reid, 1768, p. 571). Like a storm or a tempest they are intense, occasional, and of limited duration. The opposite of being emotional is being indifferent, namely, being apathetic. Contrary to the emotional person, the indifferent person is unresponsive to and detached from the emotional change; this person remains stable in the face of such a change. The instability associated with emotions is vividly expressed in the following song by Carole King: "I feel the earth move under my feet, I feel the sky tumbling down, I feel my heart start to trembling, whenever you're around."

The instability associated with intense emotions is revealed by their interference with activities requiring a high degree of coordination or control. One cannot easily thread a needle while trembling with fear or seething with anger. When we are in the grip of a strong emotion our rational faculties no longer function normally, with the result that we "lose our heads" and act in ways different from usual. An emotional change significantly improves and not only interrupts a smoothly flowing situation. Thus, it makes life more exciting. As Richard Taylor remarks: If one's days are all alike he has little need to live more than one of them.

Individuals low and high on the scale of emotional intensity typically experience happiness and unhappiness in very different ways. The life of a person low in emotional intensity is characterized by "enduringness, evenness, and lack of fluctuation." The life of a person high on emotional intensity is characterized by "abruptness, changeableness, and volatility" (Larsen & Diener, 1987, p. 27).

It is plausible that the instability associated with the generation of emotions is also typical of the sociological domain. That is, most emotions are probably less prevalent in a stable than in an unstable society. Thus, when society is stable in the sense that people cannot easily change their status, envy is less intense and less frequent. In stable societies the availability of an alternative, an essential element in generating emotions, is hardly present. The greater availability of an alternative in unstable societies also expresses the greater insecurity of the individual in this society, thereby intensifying most emotions. Some emotions may be stronger in stable societies. For example, people who consider the stable social order as humiliating and unjust may experience emotions such as hate and despair more intensely.

Great Intensity

One of the typical characteristics of emotions is their relative great intensity. In emotions the mental system has not yet adapted to the given change, and therefore many resources must be focused on the change. Owing to its significance, the change requires the system's attention; it must mobilize its various resources and hence the great intensity. Indeed, one basic evolutionary function of emotions is physiological and psychological mobilization. This function enables us to regulate the timing and locus of investment in the sense of allocating resources away from situations where they would be wasted and toward those where investment will yield a significant payoff (Lazarus, 1991; Oatley & Jenkins, 1992, p. 78).

Low intensity of the feeling dimension, as well as of other mental components, usually express neutral or indifferent states of the mental system. Emotions are the opposite of such states. Accordingly, it is preferable to consider low intensity states as nonemotional. Typical emotions characterized as possessing relatively great intensity should be distinguished from extreme manifestations of very intense emotions which are the focus of interest in a great deal of psychological research. Very intense emotions are rare and have limited impact on long-term well-being (Diener & Larsen, 1993; Diener et al., 1991).

If indeed perceiving significant changes determines emotional intensity, we should indicate what makes us perceive (or rather evaluate) one change as significant and another as insignificant. It is beyond of the scope of this article to have a detailed discussion of this important issue; accordingly, I will merely list what I believe to be the basic factors (see also Ben-Ze'ev, 1992b, 1996).

Perceiving a change to be significant depends on (a) our personal make-up, and (b) the circumstances associated with the specific event. Our personal make-up can be divided into two: (a)

personality, and (b) current personal situation. Variables of the first group are relatively stable and include, for example, personality type (e. g., nervous or calm), sensitivity to other people, fundamental beliefs (e. g., moral and religious beliefs), gender, and age. Variables constituting our current situation are more transient and include, for instance, our moods, attitudes, and resources. The circumstances associated with the specific event may also be divided into two: (a) impact on well-being, and (b) background circumstances. The first group of variables refers to the nature of the eliciting event and its current implications for our well-being. Its major variables are the strength, reality, and relevancy of the event. The second group refers to characteristics of the agency credited with or blamed for the change. Its major variables are controllability, readiness, and deservingness. The first group of variables involves primary appraisals in the sense that they are directly relevant to our current situation. The second group addresses secondary appraisals in the sense that they refer to background circumstances not directly relevant to our current situation. Primary appraisals focus on actual changes, whereas in secondary appraisals the availability of an alternative is predominant.

Brief Duration

Typical emotions are essentially transient states. The mobilization of all resources explains the relatively brief duration of emotions: A system cannot be unstable and mobilized for a long period and still function normally. A change cannot persist for a very long time; after a while, the system construes the change as a normal and stable condition. Accordingly, typical emotions are transient states. An emotional event may be compared to a large rock being thrown into a pool of still water: "for a short time chaos, in the shape of the emotions, reigns before calm gradually returns" (Horder, 1992, p. 75). The transient nature of emotions prevents the mental system from exploding due to continuous increase in emotional intensity. The association of emotional intensity with significant changes causes the intensity constantly to decrease owing to the transient nature of changes. This association is then a natural mechanism enabling the system to return within a relatively short period to normal functioning (which may be somewhat different from the previous normal functioning). If emotions endured for hours regardless of what was occurring in the external world, they would not have an adaptive value.

The exact duration of emotions is a matter for dispute. Thus, Ekman (1992) believes that emotions usually last only for seconds. Among other things his view is based on the duration of both expressive and physiological changes; thus, most adult facial expressions last from approximately half a second to four seconds. Other scholars, as well as common sense, indicate that emotions last longer. Thus, a cross-cultural study found that fear rarely lasted longer than an hour, and in many cases less than five minutes. Anger usually lasted for more than a few minutes, but rarely more than a few hours. Sadness and joy lasted over one hour in most cases. In more than half of the cases sadness lasted even more than a day. Emotions such as love and jealousy can last longer. Some emotions have concrete (usually negative) specifications with respect to their duration. An attitude cannot be regarded as grief or love if it lasts only five seconds; nor can anything lasting for years count as relief. Other emotions, however, do not have such temporal specifications and can last for different periods of time (Frijda, 1986, p. 101; Frijda et al., 1991; Oatley & Jenkins, 1996; Scherer et al., 1986).

The transient nature of emotions does not imply that emotions must last no more than a few seconds: Sometimes the transition from one stabilized state to another is longer. Such transition "is not just a switch from one state to another"; it involves profound changes in our plans and concerns and as such it may occupy us for some time (Oatley, 1992, p. 23). It seems that all typical and diagnostic features of emotions are present for a very short time. The longer an emotion lasts, the more such features drop out. When we speak about an emotion that lasts for a long period of time, we refer to a state that is sometimes dispositional but has frequent momentary peaks during the period we consider it to exist continuously.

Although typical emotions are occurrent, transient states, enduring emotions exist as well. For one, emotions are ongoing states and not isolated entities. An emotion can be enduring if all major components are present for a certain period. In this straightforward sense all emotions are enduring states; they differ, however, in length of period. In order to express this difference we may distinguish between emotions and sentiments. Sentiments are enduring emotions that last longer than typical emotional states. A man's long-standing love or jealousy of his wife, a parent's long-standing grief for his son, or children's long-standing hostility to their parents may be termed a sentiment. (The persistence of grief and love suggests that time neither heals all wounds nor suppresses all types of excitement.)

Understanding the difference between transient emotional states and long-term sentiments requires clarification of the different senses of emotional disposition. The different senses can be illustrated by considering the difference between: (a) "I am easily disposed to feel embarrassed"; (b) "I have been embarrassed about it several times during the past week"; and (c) "I have been embarrassed about it for weeks." The first sense, which expresses an emotional trait, is a general sense of disposition common to all emotions. When particular circumstances activate the given trait, a transient emotional state is generated. The second sense describes a situation in which an emotion toward a particular object recurs quite often. All emotions can be dispositional in this sense, which may be described as a form of memory related to the intensity of the original emotion. The third sense of emotional disposition describes sentiments. A person may be described as having a sentiment if all intentional components (namely, cognition, evaluation, and motivation), but not the feeling component, are present. Anti-Semitic people can be characterized as hating Jews in this sense even while they do not think about Jews. They may experience no actual emotion of hate, but their persisting attitude involves intentional components of cognition, evaluation, and motivation that are typical of hate. Moreover, asked if they hate Jews, they will answer in the affirmative. Similarly, love and grief may persist for a long time, but the feelings typical of these emotions are not present every moment of that time span.

In describing sentiments we assume their continuous existence, not merely their frequent occurrence. The assumed continuous existence is sometimes dispositional. Being dispositional in this sense does not mean merely repeating the emotion in the future, but also shaping (or "coloring") our present behavior. The disposition is not pure potentiality: It affects actual states and behavior. A man's long-standing love of his wife does not involve continuous feelings but it influences his attitudes and behavior toward her and other people. For example, it influences his interest in what she does, the things he does in her company, his desires toward her and other women, and so on. Similarly, a mother can grieve years for a lost child. In that period she often feels intense sadness, she cannot concentrate on any complex activity, her attention is focused on the lost child, and her evaluative architecture has been considerably changed.

Emotions differ in their tendency to become sentiments. Emotions involving a more general attitude toward the object, for instance, love, hate, pride, shame, and grief, often turn into sentiments. More specific emotions, such as sexual attraction, anger, and embarrassment, are not likely to become sentiments. Their very limited focus and the dominant place of their feeling component make it hard to conceive them as expanding over a long period of time.

Although the distinction between emotional states and sentiments is not clear-cut, it is valuable in understanding emotional phenomena.

Partiality

Emotions are partial in two basic senses: (a) they focus on a narrow area, e. g., one or very few objects; (b) they express a personal and interested perspective. Emotions are partial states that involve evaluations made by an interested agent from a specific and partial perspective. Emotions direct and color our attention: They limit what can attract and hold our attention; they make us preoccupied with some things and oblivious to others. Emotions draw on a very personal and interested perspective. They are not detached theoretical states; they address a practical concern, often personal, associated with readiness to act.

Not everyone and not everything is of emotional significance to us. We usually cannot assume an emotional state toward someone utterly unrelated to us. Thus, when we hear of the death of thousands of people in an earthquake occurring in a remote (that is, from our vantage point) part of the world, our emotional response comes nowhere near the intensity of our grief at the death of someone close to us, nor does it approach the level of feeling we experience in watching the death throes of a single victim of that same earthquake on television (thereby establishing some affinity with this particular victim). As Stalin argued: "One death is a tragedy; a million is a statistic." Emotions require many resources such as time and attention. Since these resources are finite, emotions must be

partial and discriminative. Spinoza argues that "the affects are excessive, and occupy the mind in the consideration of only one object so much that it cannot think of others." For example, "a greedy man thinks of nothing else but profit, or money, and an ambitious man of esteem" (1677/1985, IV, p. 44, s).

The partial nature is compatible with the great subject–object proximity typical of emotions. This proximity frequently requires a partial and momentary perspective, which contradicts the impartial and broad perspective required for reliable cognition. When we look at someone from a short distance our vision is often distorted. In the extreme case where there is no distance at all, namely, when we place the object upon the eye itself, we do not see it at all. We need some distance in order to achieve a perspective that encompasses multiple aspects of the object and thereby makes the perspective less fragmentary. But keeping a distance is contrary to the involved and intimate perspective typical of emotions. Poets, who are usually overwhelmed by emotions, sometimes testify to the partiality of emotions. The poet Rachel writes: "Only about myself I could speak, my world is as narrow as the ant's world." The partiality of emotions may also have some advantages, for example, cognitive advantages relating to our ability to know better others included in our partial perspective. Thus, people who want something become increasingly aware of others who have this thing. Likewise, one who hates people from a certain ethnic group is often better than most other people in identifying these people. Similarly, partisans on both sides of a rough football game will tend disproportionately to notice penalties committed by the opposing team (Hastorf & Cantril, 1954; see also Smith & Lazarus, 1990).

The partiality of emotions is clearly demonstrated by their intentional components, namely, cognition, evaluation, and motivation. The cognitive field of emotions does not engage varied and broad perspectives of our surroundings but a narrow and fragmentary perspective focused upon the emotional object and its relation to us. Thus, love limits our range of interest, focusing almost exclusively on the beloved and his or her relationship with us. As the popular song has it, "Millions of people go by, but they all disappear from view— 'cause I only have eyes for you" (Rubin, 1970). Similarly, the cognitive field of the envious person is limited to some (often petty) aspects of the envied person and to the subject's own inferiority. Because of the partiality of the cognitive field in emotions, it is often distorted. Aristotle compares emotions (or more specifically, anger) to hasty servants "who run out before they have heard the whole of what one says, and then muddle the order" and to dogs who "bark if there is but a knock at the door, before looking to see if it is a friend" *(Nicomachean Ethics*, 1149a26–29). The evaluative field of emotions is narrow owing to its highly polarized nature. In comparison with other people, the emotional object is often characterized as either highly positive or highly negative. Emotional evaluations are clearly more partial (in both senses) than moral evaluations (Ben-Ze'ev, 1992a). The motivational field is narrow in the sense that the desired activity is often clearly preferred to any alternative. Even in emotions, such as love, where the range of activities concerning the emotional object is wide, these are clearly preferred to other activities unrelated to the object; the latter are hardly considered at all. The partiality of the intentional field is typical of all emotions, though varying in degree. It is more evident in negative emotions, where the immediate situation is of great concern to us.

The importance of changes for emotions is bound up with their partiality. It is more likely that changes in our situation will have a significant impact when our perspective is partial rather than broad. The emotional perspective is usually restricted to specific types of circumstances occurring for a short time. A broader perspective takes into account broader types of circumstances and is less likely to change significantly with any change in the subject's surrounding. Partiality is also correlated with emotions' transient nature as well as with their great intensity. A partial and intense state cannot last for a long time. An intense state, focusing our entire resources on a single object, must be transient; the neglect of other objects may be quite harmful.

Reducing emotional intensity may be done, then, by broadening our perspective. Consider the following popular advice: Remember that whatever misfortune may be your lot, it could only be worse in Cleveland. Similarly, flight attendants are taught to avoid anger at an obnoxious passenger by focusing on what he might be thinking and feeling; to imagine a reason that excuses his or her behavior (Hochschild, 1983, p. 113). In the same vein, a perspective that does not merely focus on the object's superior position but also on that person's character may reduce envy. If the object is kind and modest, envy may decrease since it can be assumed that the object respects the subject. Envy may also decrease if the object is mean since the negative evaluation of the object's character will outbalance his or her superiority (accordingly, it has been claimed that "only the shameless envy the wicked"). What matters in reducing envy in these cases is not so much how we evaluate the object, but that we do so from a broader perspective referring to many aspects of the object. The broader the perspective, the lesser the weight of the particular inferiority that generates envy. Similar considerations hold for other emotions. We say that company in distress makes sorrow less. Likewise, counting ten before venting our anger enables us to take a broader perspective that could reduce anger. A broader perspective is typical for people who can calmly consider multiple aspects of a situation; it is obviously not typical for people who experience an intense emotion. Broadening our perspective creates a certain detachment, which is not typical of emotions.

Partiality is an important, not an incidental feature of emotions. In intense emotional states we are somewhat similar to children. Like children our perspective is highly partial and involved. Our very partial situation is the only thing that interests us; no rational explanations concerning broader perspectives are relevant.

BASIC COMPONENTS: COGNITION, EVALUATION, MOTIVATION, AND FEELING

I consider intentionality and feeling (or sensation) to be the two basic mental dimensions (Ben-Ze'ev, 1993a). Intentionality refers to a subject–object relation, whereas feeling expresses the subject's own state of mind. When Dean is in love with Ruth, the feeling dimension surfaces in a particular feeling, say a thrill, that he experiences while being in love with her; the intentional dimension is expressed in the way Dean knows Ruth, evaluates her personality and his desires toward her. The feeling dimension is a mode of consciousness associated with our own state; unlike higher types of awareness, such as those found in perception, memory, and thinking, it has no meaningful cognitive content. It expresses our own state, but is not in itself directed at this state. Since this dimension is a mode of consciousness, one cannot be unconscious of it; there are no unfelt feelings. The homogeneous and basic nature of feelings makes it difficult, though perhaps not impossible, to describe them. Indeed there are few words for feelings and we often have to resort to metaphors and other figures of speech in referring to them. It is not easy to identify the varying characteristics of the feeling dimension. No doubt feelings have intensity and duration and some have location as well, but what about other qualities? The qualities of being painful or pleasurable are obvious. Can we analyze these qualities further? Do pain and enjoyment constitute the only continuum of the feeling dimension? An additional continuum is that of calm and arousal. There is indeed evidence for the independence of the pleasure–displeasure continuum (the hedonic level) and the degree of arousal (Larsen & Diener, 1985). The intentional dimension includes several references to objects such as those involved in perception, memory, thought, dreams, imagination, desires, and emotions. Typical mental states in human beings have both dimensions; these vary in type and degree for different mental states.

The intentional dimension in emotions can be divided into three basic components: cognitive, evaluative, and motivational. The cognitive component includes the information about the given circumstances; the evaluative component assesses the personal significance of this information; the motivational component addresses our desires, or readiness to act, in these circumstances. When John envies Adam for having better grades, John has some information about Adam's grades, evaluates his inferior position negatively, and wishes to abolish this inferiority. Neither these three intentional components nor the feeling dimension are separate entities or states. Emotions do not entail the separate performance of four varieties of activity: knowing, evaluating, desiring, and feeling. All four are distinct aspects of a single state.

The descriptive element is the cognitive component; it supplies the required information about a given situation. No attitude toward something can emerge without some information about it (whether veridical or distorted); intentionality presupposes a cognitive system. Whereas the cognitive component describes the object, the evaluative component expresses a certain assessment of the same. Owing to the partial nature of emotions, the cognitive component is often distorted (see, e. g., Ellsworth, 1991, pp. 150–2; Lazarus, 1991, chap. 10; Wilson & Klaaren, 1992). The intense feeling dimension in emotions tends to set aside our ability to make sound cognitive claims. When we are in the grip of intense feelings our rational faculties no longer function normally. The more intense the emotional state, the easier it is for cognitive distortions to occur. Proper understanding requires many and divergent types of cognitive perspectives. Employing such perspectives implies a certain detachment from the object: When something is very close to us, it is often hard to apprehend it adequately. The required cognitive detachment and variety clashes with the partial and personal nature of emotions. Thus, the emotional perspective is frequently in conflict with the scientific perspective. The cognitive component in emotions is not always distorted; sometimes the closer you are to the object, the better you know it. Thus, a person living in a ghetto may see its deprivations more accurately through indignation and anger than a person who does not live in a ghetto and looks at it from a detached and "objective" perspective. However, it is clear that a too intimate perspective may often lead to distortion (De Sousa, 1987; Hochschild, 1983, p. 30).

The evaluative component is highly important in emotions. Every emotion entails a certain evaluation. Hate implies the negative evaluation of a certain person, whereas pride implies a positive evaluation of oneself. In a state devoid of an evaluative component, or in which its weight is marginal, the subject is indifferent. In emotions the subject is neither neutral nor indifferent, but has a significant personal stake. The evaluative component in isolation cannot always generate emotions. Evaluating the death of someone as bad is far from experiencing the emotion of grief. The two states may share an identical cognitive and a similar evaluative component, but they often differ in their feeling and motivational components.

The motivational component refers to the desire or readiness to maintain or change present, past, or future circumstances. In the case of "passionate" emotions, such as anger, the desire is typically manifested in overt behavior; in "dispassionate" emotions, such as envy or hope, the behavioral element is less in evidence and often appears merely as a desire. The importance of the motivational component is suggested by the etymological link between "emotion," "motion," and "motives." Every typical emotion incorporates readiness to act (Frijda, 1986; Oatley, 1992). Since emotions are essentially evaluative states, representing a positive or negative stance toward the object, they also require taking action, or being disposed to act, in a manner compatible with the evaluation. For example, a positive emotional evaluation is often correlated with readiness to be with the object and improve the object's situation.

In emotions both mental dimensions of intentionality and feeling are dominant. In most other mental states one of these is the dominant dimension. For example, the feeling dimension is dominant in painful experiences, in thirst or hunger, and in moods such as anxiety, apathy, depression, and euphoria. The intentional dimension dominates the cognitive capacities of perception, memory, and thinking. To a greater extent than other mental states emotions include divergent components within their scope, ranging from intense and primitive feelings to complex and rational evaluations. It is therefore better to treat emotions as unique combinations of the entire range of mental components, rather than to account for them by referring merely to a single basic component.

The intentional and feeling dimensions in emotions are, to a certain extent, dependent upon each other. When one of these dimensions is predominant, the other often recedes to be hardly noticeable. It is known, for example, that seriously wounded soldiers frequently feel almost no pain while on the battlefield; they only begin to experience severe pain from their wounds when they are evacuated (Melzack, 1973, pp. 29–31). While in combat they were absorbed by their intentional object (the enemy); the feeling dimension was pushed into the background. Feelings of pain or hunger may also diminish when one is deeply immersed in an intellectual activity. The inverse relation between the complexity of the intentional dimension and the intensity of the feeling dimension is typical of cases in which the activity level of the mental system remains constant. When the level changes, as is the case in old age or situations of intense agitation, both dimensions often change in the same direction. An intense feeling dimension does not have to marginalize the intentional dimension, but it often limits its scope or changes it in other respects. The intense feeling dimension in emotions is usually associated with a partial intentional dimension.

COMPARING THE DIFFERENT COMPONENTS

The following relationships can be traced between intentional components. Cognition, namely, descriptive information about the object, is logically prior to its evaluation, namely, to a normative claim concerning its value. Hence, there can be cognition without evaluation. Evaluation presupposes a certain degree of cognition; we cannot evaluate something without having some information about it. Evaluation is typically prior to motivation; motivation usually implies evaluation. In having desires one makes certain evaluations, but (as Aristotle contends) one can evaluate something as good without being thereby motivated to pursue it. The latter involves practical considerations, which may result in different types of desires. However, when the evaluation is highly positive or negative, it is likely to be expressed by a certain motivation. The feeling dimension has no logical connection with the intentional components, but is associated with them in typical emotions.

Which component is the distinguishing, or individualizing, component of emotions? It is clearly not the cognitive component since a similar cognitive content can generate multiple, even opposing, emotions. For example, information about the appearance of someone may result in love, sexual attraction, admiration, or envy. Emotions are not generated in the presence of every event; they emerge in the presence of significant change. Determining the significance of a change is basically an evaluative rather than cognitive task. Accordingly, reference to the cognitive content is not sufficient for the distinction between different emotions (see also Descartes, 1649/1984 art. 52).

The motivational and feeling components show a higher degree of correlation with the nature of the emotion in the sense that they can indicate its positive or negative character. Essentially, positive emotions incorporate a positive evaluation, pleasant feelings, and the desire to maintain the situation; negative emotions incorporate a negative evaluation, unpleasant feelings, and the desire to change the situation. This global correlation is due to the centrality of the evaluative component. Distinctions in the motivational domain typically mirror distinctions in the evaluative domain. Distinctions in the feeling domain can be more arbitrary, but some general correlation with the evaluative domain can be found.

Motivational and feeling components may serve to distinguish between some emotions. For example, the motivational component is crucial in distinguishing between pity and compassion: Readiness to assist the object is much more evident in compassion. This component is also instrumental in distinguishing fear from courage. In both cases, however, the difference in the motivational component also surfaces in the evaluative component. Thus, pity involves evaluating the object to be inferior to the subject whereas compassion requires a more egalitarian evaluation. Similarly, in the case of fear and courage the choice of fleeing from the emotional object or confronting it usually derives from different assessments of our ability to overcome the threat. In this case the feeling dimension may differ as well: Fear is always associated with a disagreeable feeling, whereas a courageous attitude may not be. Not all emotions can be distinguished on the basis of their motivational or feeling component. Thus, shame and embarrassment may often have a similar motivational component. Likewise, different emotions (and perhaps also nonemotional states) have a similar feeling component.

Distinguishing one emotion from another is best done by referring to the evaluative component. Although there are some elements of similarity in different emotional evaluations (for example, concerning their positive or negative nature), the uniqueness of each emotion is determined by a specific evaluative pattern (or core evaluative theme). Consider the following thought experiment: Take any emotion you like, change one of its basic components, and see whether the nature of the emotion changes. In most cases the cognitive component allows for the greatest and the evaluative component for the least variation. The motivational and feeling components can specify the positive or negative nature of a given emotion better than the cognitive component, but frequently they cannot further specify the unique nature of the given emotion. The evaluative component, allowing for the least variation, is therefore the most reliable means to distinguish between different types of emotion. Regarding the other three components, even their most detailed specification will not preclude the possibility of two different emotion types possessing this specific component. It may be the case that finer distinctions between certain types of emotion require a reference to some other components besides evaluation. Still, this component remains

by far the best means to differentiate between emotions. A basic change in our emotional state should require a change in our evaluative stand (see also Lyons, 1980).

Each emotion is characterized by an evaluative core theme conveying our essential concern (see also Lazarus, 1991; Lazarus & Smith, 1988). The following are the core evaluative themes of a few emotions:

Envy: A negative evaluation of our undeserved inferiority.

Jealousy: A negative evaluation of the possibility of losing something (typically, a favorable human relationship) to someone else.

Pity: A negative evaluation of the substantial misfortune of someone considered to be basically inferior to us.

Compassion: A negative evaluation of the substantial misfortune of someone considered to be basically similar to us.

Happy-for: A positive evaluation of someone's good fortune.

Pleasure-in-others'-misfortune: A negative evaluation of someone's deserved and usually minor misfortune.

Anger: A specific negative evaluation of someone considered to have inflicted unjustified harm upon us.

Hate: A global negative evaluation of someone considered to possess fundamentally negative traits.

Gratitude: A positive evaluation of someone considered to have performed some praiseworthy, desirable action benefiting us.

Love: A global positive evaluation of someone considered to have fundamentally attractive and praiseworthy traits.

Sexual attraction: A specific positive evaluation of someone considered to have attractive traits.

Since the core evaluative theme expresses the essence of our attitude, it is fruitful to classify the various emotions in relation to these themes (Ben-Ze'ev, 1990; Ortony et al., 1988).

The distinguishing nature of the evaluative component does not mean that it constitutes a sufficient condition for the generation of emotions, namely, it is not the sole criterion distinguishing emotion from nonemotion. I may harbor a negative evaluation of the good fortunes of others, but if this evaluation is not part of a more complex state including motivational features and a certain type of feeling, my state is not that of envy or jealousy. I may negatively evaluate King Solomon's good fortune in having 1000 women, and may even wish to be in his position, but my attitude toward King Solomon need not be envy. Emotions are complex states drawing upon a subtle equilibrium of diverse components; the presence of the evaluative component (or for that matter, any other component) alone is not sufficient for the generation of emotions. However, when the presence of an emotional state is not in question but rather the identification of its nature, reference to the evaluative component is in order.

We should, then, delineate two questions: (a) What is the criterion for distinguishing one emotion from another? (b) What is the criterion for distinguishing emotion from nonemotion? Concerning (a), the evaluative component, or more precisely the core evaluative theme, is the major distinguishing criterion. Answering (b) is more complex; it requires description of a subtle equilibrium of all four basic components. I do not intend to describe this equilibrium here, and I doubt whether such a description is altogether possible; but I would like to make two general remarks. First, each emotional component may be described as having a certain weight. A significant increase in the weight of one component may reduce the weight of other components and thus disturb the subtle emotional equilibrium. Thus, too much weight on the feeling dimension may reduce the role of the intentional dimension in a way which is not typical of emotions. The difference between anger and a negative nonemotional evaluation of a particular act may be expressed by the fact that the latter lacks the minimal intensity of the feeling and motivational components, which is typical of emotions. Second, there is no clear-cut borderline between emotional and nonemotional states. There is an obvious difference between typical emotional and nonemotional states, but there is also a large gray area whose classification is arbitrary to a certain degree. Because of the prototypical nature of emotions, precise distinction between these and other states is not feasible, nor has it significant implications.

The presence of a global correlation between evaluation, motivation, and feelings is not always obvious. One reason is the compound and diverse nature of emotions. Thus, since emotional objects are complex, we may evaluate some of their aspects positively and others negatively; hence, our emotions may have both positive and negative components. Pity, for example, which involves sorrow stemming from the object's misfortune, also involves pleasant feelings associated with the subject's superior position. Similarly, we may enjoy a current sexual relationship but worry about its negative consequences. Likewise, hate is not always painful—it may provide us with opportunity to unload negative feeling—and love is not always pleasant—it may involve the fear of losing the beloved (Ben-Ze'ev, 1993b; Neu, forthcoming).

The complex nature of emotions makes it harder to identify the nature of a given emotion, but it does not cancel global correlation between evaluation, motivation, and feeling. A positive evaluation is basically connected with a favorable motivational component and pleasant feelings. If we positively evaluate the beloved, this evaluation is connected with pleasant feelings and the wish to be with this person. We may also negatively evaluate the possibility of losing the beloved; this evaluation is connected with unpleasant feelings and a different type of motivational attitude. Both types of evaluation are part of the complex emotion of love and in both the general correlation (at least that between positive/negative evaluation and pleasant/unpleasant feeling) is kept. When we say that love is basically a positive emotion, we mean that the positive evaluation and its correlated positive motivation and pleasant feeling are more essential in love than are the negative elements. The essential nature of the emotion is expressed in its core evaluative theme. For example, such a theme in love is a global positive evaluation of someone considered to have fundamentally attractive and praiseworthy traits. Despite the frequent presence of conflicting elements in complex emotions, we can nevertheless characterize their typical cases as either positive or negative.

SUMMARY

The classical question of "what is an emotion?" has been answered by describing typical emotions. It has been suggested that the typical emotional cause is the perception of a significant change in our situation; the change may be either actual or imaginary. The typical emotional concern is a comparative one. Such a concern consists of two related types: (a) comparison of the current situation with its alternatives; (b) social comparison within the given situation of our standing with that of others. Social comparison is made with those who are most related to us, namely, human beings. Accordingly, the typical emotional object is a human being. The basic characteristics of typical emotions are instability, great intensity, relatively brief duration, and a partial perspective. Another helpful division of emotions is into their basic components: cognition, evaluation, motivation, and feeling. The evaluative component constitutes the main criterion for distinguishing one emotion from another, but not for distinguishing emotions from nonemotions.

REFERENCES

Alston, W. P. (1967). Emotion and feeling. In P. Edwards (Ed.), *Encyclopedia of philosophy* (Vol. 11, pp. 479 – 486). New York: Macmillan.

Aristotle. (1984). *The complete works of Aristotle: The revised Oxford translations* (J. Barnes, Ed.). Princeton: Princeton University Press.

Ben-Ze'ev, A. (1990). Describing the emotions. *Philosophical Psychology, 3*, 305–317.

Ben-Ze'ev, A. (1992a). Emotional and moral evaluations. *Metaphilosophy, 23*, 214–229.

Ben-Ze'ev, A. (1992b). Envy and inequality. *Journal of Philosophy, 89*, 551–581.

Ben-Ze'ev, A. (1993a). *The perceptual system: A philosophical and psychological perspective.* New York: Peter Lang.

Ben-Ze'ev, A. (1993b). You always hurt the one you love. *Journal of Value Inquiry, 27*, 487–495.

Ben-Ze'ev, A. (1996). Emotional intensity. *Theory & Psychology, 6*, 509–532.

Dakin, S., & Arrowood, A. J. (1981). The social comparison of ability. *Human Relations, 34*, 89–109.

Descartes, R. (1649/1984). *The passions of the soul.* In J. Cottingham, R. Stoothoff, & D. Murdoch (Trans.), *The philosophical writings of Descartes.* Cambridge: Cambridge University Press.

De Sousa, R. (1987). *The rationality of emotions.* Cambridge: MIT Press.

Diener, E., & Larsen, R. J. (1993). The experience of emotional well-being. In M. Lewis & J. M. Haviland (Eds.), *Handbook of emotions.* New York: Guilford Press.

Diener, E., Sandvik, E., & Pavot, W. (1991). Happiness is the frequency, not the intensity of positive versus negative affect. In F. Strack, M. Argyle, & N. Schwarz (Eds.), *Subjective well-being.* New York: Pergamon.

Ekman, P. (1992). An argument for basic emotions. *Cognition and Emotion, 6*, 169–200.

Ellsworth, P. C. (1991). Some implications of cognitive appraisal theories of emotions. *International Review of Studies on Emotion, 1*, 143–161.

Fehr, B. (1988). Prototype analysis of the concepts of love and commitment. *Journal of Personality and Social Psychology, 55*, 557–579.

Fehr, B., & Russell, J. A. (1984). Concept of emotion viewed from a prototype perspective. *Journal of Experimental Psychology: General, 113*, 464–486.

Fitness, J., & Fletcher, G. J. O. (1993). Love, hate, anger and jealousy in close relationships: A prototype and cognitive appraisal analysis. *Journal of Personality and Social Psychology, 65*, 942–958.

Freedman, J. L. (1978). *Happy people.* New York: Harcourt Brace Jovanovich.

Frijda, N. H. (1986). *The emotions.* Cambridge: Cambridge University Press.

Frijda, N. H. (1988). The laws of emotion. *American Psychologist, 43*, 349–358.

Frijda, N. H., Mesquita, B., Sonnemans, J., & Van Goozen, S. (1991). The duration of affective phenomena or emotions, sentiments and passions. *International Review of Studies on Emotion, 1*, 187–225.

Hastorf, A. H., & Cantril, H. (1954). They saw a game: A case study. *Journal of Abnormal and Social Psychology, 49*, 129–134.

Heider, F. (1958). *The psychology of interpersonal relations.* New York: Wiley.

Hochschild, A. R. (1983). *The managed heart: Commercialization of human feeling.* Berkeley: University of California Press.

Horder, J. (1992). *Provocation and responsibility.* Oxford: Clarendon Press.

Izard, C. E. (1991). *The psychology of emotions.* New York: Plenum Press.

Kagan, J. (1992). Temperamental contributions to emotion and social behavior. *Review of Personality and Social Psychology, 14*, 99–118.

Kahneman, D., & Miller, D. T. (1986). Norm theory: Comparing reality to its alternatives. *Psychological Review, 93*, 136–153.

Kovecses, Z. (1990). *Emotion concepts.* New York: Springer-Verlag.

Lakoff, G. (1987), *Women, fire, and dangerous things.* Chicago: The University of Chicago Press.

Larsen, R. J., & Diener, E. (1985). A multitrait-multimethod examination of affect structure: Hedonic level and emotional intensity. *Personality and Individual Differences, 6*, 631–636.

Larsen, R. J., & Diener, E. (1987). Affect intensity as an individual difference characteristic: A review. *Journal of Research in Personality, 21*, 1–39.

Lazarus, R. S. (1991). *Emotion and adaptation.* New York: Oxford University Press.

Lazarus, R. S., & Smith, C. A. (1988). Knowledge and appraisal in the cognition-emotion relationship. *Cognition and Emotion, 2*, 281–300.

Lyons, W. (1980). *Emotion.* Cambridge: Cambridge University Press.

Melzack, R. (1973). *The puzzle of pain*. New York: Basic Books.

Neu, J. (forthcoming). Odi et Amo: On hating the ones we love. In J. O'Neill (Ed.), *Freud and the passions*.

Oatley, K. (1992). *Best laid schemes: The psychology of emotions*. Cambridge: Cambridge University Press.

Oatley, K., & Jenkins, J. M. (1992). Human emotions: Function and dysfunction. *Annual Review of Psychology, 43*, 55–85.

Oatley, K., & Jenkins, J. M. (1996). *Understanding emotions*. Cambridge: Blackwell.

Ortony, A., Clore, G. L., & Collings, A. (1988). *The cognitive structure of emotions*. Cambridge: Cambridge University Press.

Reid, T. (1768). *Essays on the active powers of man*. In *Philosophical works* (Ed. W. Hamilton). Hildesheim: Georg Olms.

Rosch, E. (1978). Principles of categorization. In E. Rosch and B. B. Lloyd (Eds.), *Cognition and categorization*. Hillsdale: Erlbaum.

Rubin, Z. (1970). Measurement of romantic love. *Journal of Personality and Social Psychology, 16*, 265–273.

Russell, J. A. (1991). In defense of a prototype approach to emotion concepts. *Journal of Personality and Social Psychology, 60*, 37–47.

Scherer, K. R., Walbott, H. G., & Summerfield, A. B. (1986). *Experiencing emotions: A cross-cultural study*. Cambridge: Cambridge University Press.

Shaver, P., Wu, S., & Schwartz, J. C. (1992). Cross-cultural similarities and differences in emotion and its representation. *Review of Personality and Social Psychology, 13*, 175–212.

Smith, C. A., & Lazarus, R. S. (1990). Emotion and adaptation. In L. A. Pervin (Ed.), *Handbook of personality: Theory and research*. New York: Guilford.

Spinoza, B. (1677/1985). Ethics. In E. Curley (Ed.), *The collected works of Spinoza*. Princeton: Princeton University Press.

Wilson, T. D., & Klaaren, K. J. (1992). "Expectation whirls me round": The role of affective expectation in affective experience. *Review of Personality and Social Psychology, 14*, 1–31.

CHAPTER 17

"FOLK PSYCHOLOGY" AND ITS IMPLICATIONS FOR PSYCHOLOGICAL SCIENCE

INTRODUCTION

A major impediment to the development of a science of psychology is the existence in ordinary nontechnical discourse of a prescientific language/ theory, which is in constant use by the man-and-woman in the street when they describe their own and other people's psychological states and explain their own and other people's behavior. This is what is known in contemporary philosophical parlance as "folk psychology." The psychologist cannot afford to ignore folk psychology in the way a physicist can ignore folk physics. For folk psychological descriptions and explanations given by subjects and clients are part of the data of psychology, in a way that folk physical descriptions and explanations are not part of the data of physics.

Recent discussions of folk psychology within the overlapping fields of the philosophy of mind and cognitive science have focused on two issues:

1. Is folk psychology a naturally occurring theory which, like other scientific theories, must either be accepted or rejected in the light of the best available empirical evidence?
2. Whether or not it is properly described as a theory, can we and, if so, should we avoid using the language and concepts of folk psychology for the purposes of psychological science?

Four different positions can be distinguished, depending on the answer that is given to these two questions. Of the five articles in this section each of the first four defends a different one of these four possible positions:

1. Nick Chater and Mike Oaksford defend a version of the so-called 'eliminative materialist' position, advocated by philosophers such as Stephen Stich and Paul and Patricia Churchland, who think that folk psychology is a genuine theory, but one that has been discredited by contemporary scientific evidence.
2. Barry Smith expounds and defends the view advocated by Jerry Fodor, who claims not only that folk psychology is a genuine theory, but

that it is one that science can only refine, not replace.

3. Ullin Place invokes conceptual analysis in defense of the behaviorist position, which holds that folk psychology is a language rather than a theory, but one that, for a variety of reasons, is unsuitable for scientific purposes.

4. Graham Richards defends what may be thought of as the Wittgensteinian position, which denies that folk psychology is a theory, but differs from the behaviorist in thinking that no alternative scientific language is possible that could act as a substitute.

The section concludes with a discussion by Elizabeth Valentine of the issues raised in the four preceding papers.

Ullin T. Place

The Falsity of Folk Theories:
Implications for Psychology and Philosophy

Nick Chater
Mike Oaksford

We assume that commonsense knowledge, including our commonsense understanding of human behavior, is organized into theories. After considering certain difficulties in finding out about these theories, we argue that folk theories are analogous to bad scientific theories, and that the ontology of common sense is on a par with epicycles or the *yin* and *yang*. That is, folk theories are false, and their entities that they postulate do not exist. We consider various possible replies to our arguments, and suggest that the underlying reason that folk theories are bad science is that common sense must deal with matters that do not yield to scientific analysis. We draw out some philosophical and psychological implications of our position.

INTRODUCTION

It has become increasingly popular to assume that everyday, commonsense knowledge is organized into theories. In philosophy, it has become standard to conceive of our commonsense beliefs about the mind as a theory: folk psychology (e.g., Fodor, 1987; Stich, 1983). In developmental psychology there has also been much discussion of the child's theory of mind (e.g., Leslie, 1987; Perner, 1991; Wellman, 1990), and more generally there has been an emphasis on children as theorizers (e.g.,

Carey, 1988; Karmiloff-Smith, 1988). In social psychology, there has been much study of "lay theories" of a wide variety of domains (e.g., Furnham, 1987), and everyday thought has been compared extensively to scientific theorizing (Nisbett & Ross, 1980). The psychology of concepts has increasingly stressed that concepts are theoretically embedded (e.g., Medin & Wattenmaker, 1987; Murphy & Medin, 1985). In artificial intelligence, commonsense ideas concerning the everyday world have been formalized as axiomatic theories, where inference is supported by formal logical methods, or some variant (Charniak & McDermott, 1985; McCarthy & Hayes, 1969).

Most researchers who view knowledge as organized into folk theories shy away from trying to give a precise account of exactly what a theory is. Viewing theories as made of knowledge does not amount to a precise and specific doctrine, it seems, but rather to an emphasis on an analogy between the structure of everyday knowledge in individual cognitive agents, and the structure of knowledge in science, from which talk of theories is borrowed. We believe that this analogy is a valuable one, and that when taken seriously it yields significant conclusions for folk psychology and cognitive science.

The structure of the paper is as follows. We first consider the problem of how folk theories can be known, stressing that natural language does not give direct access to them. Nonetheless, we suggest that it is possible to judge folk theories in broad terms by looking at the explanations to which they give rise, and we present a range of arguments to show that these explanations fair poorly when judged by the standards applied to explanation in science. We conclude that folk theories are false. We then consider the status of the ontologies of our putative folk theories and argue that from the point of view of scientific enquiry, they should naturally be viewed as on a par with terms of other false theories, such as phlogiston or epicycles. We conclude that the entities described by folk ontologies do not exist. Until this point, the discussion appears to take rather a dim view of folk theories, when compared to science; we attempt to correct this impression by stressing the differing roles of scientific and folk theorizing. Finally, we briefly draw out some philosophical and psychological implications of our position.

WHAT DO WE KNOW ABOUT FOLK THEORIES?

One of the most pressing and problematic points of difference between folk and scientific theories is that folk theories are not explicitly articulated for public consumption, but appear to be buried in the individual's cognitive innards. This means that the folk theories that guide thought and action must somehow be inferred from what agents do or say.

Naively, we might hope that speakers can simply tell us what their underlying theories are, so that if, for example, people tell us that they believe that people usually act in their own best interests, then this is likely to be part of their underlying folk theory of human behavior.

A first difficulty with this naive picture is that social psychologists have persistently found that people's reports of their underlying beliefs do not readily cohere into a single picture of the world, but often reflect a wide variety of conflicting points of view (e.g., Potter & Wetherall, 1987). This has led to the view that the ideas expressed in linguistic behavior are better thought of as constructed for a specific purpose, dependent on the particular occasion, rather than as direct reflections of an underlying fund of knowledge.

A second difficulty is that it is not clear to what extent we are able to verbalize commonsense knowledge at all. This point has been stressed

across a range of disciplines. For example, the psychology of memory has stressed the importance of implicit information, which cannot be verbalized (Schacter, 1987). Coming from a very different point of view, ethnomethodologists have stressed that shared commonsense assumptions tend to be inaccessible to individuals; ethnomethodological investigation attempts to discover such assumptions by trying to violate them, rather than relying on introspective reports (Garfinkel, 1964; see Place, 1992, for discussion). A final example is given by philosophical enquiry, in which (among other things) intuitions concerning meaning, good and evil, or beauty are taken as starting points for constructing theories in the philosophy of language, ethics, or aesthetics. The very fact that developing philosophical theories that capture such intuitions is so extraordinarily difficult is a testament to the fact that any folk theories underlying these intuitions are not readily available to the investigator.

These problems in articulating our folk theories of the world have been an important stumbling block for artificial intelligence. It has proved to be extremely difficult to specify the knowledge underlying the most mundane aspects of everyday thought. Specifying such knowledge is, of course, a prerequisite for putting such knowledge into a machine, according to standard artificial intelligence methodology. Attempts to formalize apparently constrained aspects of common sense, such as the naive physics of the behavior of fluids, have been instructive. First, it is not possible simply to take verbal descriptions of what people say is the relevant knowledge and embody this in logical axioms, which can be used as the basis for inference. Instead, it has been necessary to attempt to formulate extremely complex underlying theories of the ontology that people are implicitly using and to devise very complex and subtle principles concerning what people know about this ontology and how this knowledge can be used to reason successfully. Such sophistication is required to even begin to build systems that reason about such everyday matters as the spread of spilt coffee and the results of leaving a tap running (e.g., Hayes, 1978, 1984a, 1984b). Needless to say, the formalization of folk psychology and other more complex domains has scarcely even been attempted.

This work suggests that, in general, the terms of folk theories may not always have correlates in everyday natural language. But terms of folk theories will be little, if any, easier to understand even if they do happen to be expressed by the words of natural language. For the mere existence of a natural language label goes no way at all toward explaining the meaning of the term and its relation to the rest of the folk theory. After all, it took enormous theoretical effort to make sense of intuitive notions of "weight" or "set" (in the sense of collection), which do have natural language labels. Whether this effort should be thought of as making coherent previously incoherent ideas, or simply as making explicit what was really being talked about all along is a controversial question, to which we shall return briefly below. In any event, it is clear that even if we are able to identify people's concepts with words of natural language, this does not solve the problem of specifying what these concepts are. Thus, even though we have a natural language label for "chair," "elbow," and "jazz," and have an intuitive sense of what these labels are supposed to signify, it is notoriously difficult to define (Fodor, 1981) or characterize in any way what these terms mean. If knowledge is organized into theories, then explicating such terms involves specifying the particular folk theories in which they figure; and, as we have seen, this is extremely difficult to do.

The upshot of these considerations is that, if common sense consists of folk theories, then the nature of these theories is unknown and likely to be subtle, complex, and only indirectly related to explicit verbal behavior. The problem of discovering the theories underlying commonsense thought seems, therefore, to be analogous to, for example, the problem of discovering the underlying knowledge of language that governs linguistic behavior. Linguistics uses verbal behavior (and grammaticality judgments, and the like) as the starting point for constructing theories of the underlying knowledge involved in language processing. The resulting linguistic theories are highly elaborate and sophisticated and are, of course, entirely inarticulable from the point of view of everyday speakers. It seems likely to be an equally difficult task to tease out the theories underlying commonsense thought; and the nature of such underlying theories is likely to be no more apparent to naive intuition. In particular, the ontology of folk theories cannot be assumed to be limited to the vocabulary of natural language—indeed, restriction to the ontology of natural language appears to be entirely inadequate to formalize commonsense thought, which is what drives

Hayes (1984a) to define notions such as "portal," "enclosure," "directed surface" in attempting to formalize the naive physics of fluids. It seems likely, then, that much of the ontology of folk theories may be no more captured by everyday language than are phonemes, island constraints, or traces.

ARE FOLK THEORIES GOOD SCIENCE?

We have argued that folk theories must be inferred from verbal and other behavior and are not directly accessible by, for example, verbal report. Although the details of such theories are hidden, however, it is nonetheless possible to use the verbal and other behavior to which they give rise to assess how such theories fare when considered as scientific theories. We shall concentrate on assessing the quality of commonsense explanations and assume that the scientific respectability of these explanations is a reasonable reflection of the scientific status of the underlying folk theories. We outline two arguments why folk explanations are very poor by scientific lights. The first argument compares folk and scientific ideas in domains that are well understood by science; the second, more general argument declares that the ineliminably defeasible character of folk explanation is a hallmark of bad science. Given that the underlying folk theories giving rise to these explanations are hidden, it is just possible, of course, that these theories are actually consistent, coherent, well-confirmed and scientifically respectable accounts but that, for some reason, they give rise to verbal explanations that are confused, *ad hoc*, and readily succumb to counterexamples. This possibility is sufficiently bizarre, and lacking in any evidential support, that we shall not consider it further, and shall simply judge folk theories by folk explanations.

Let us turn to our two lines of argument.

Where Common Sense and Science Compete

An obvious way to assess how folk theories compare with science is to consider domains that can be described in both folk and scientific terms. In such domains, it may be possible to assess the quality of commonsense thought by directly comparing it against the corresponding scientific account. We shall concentrate on the physical sciences in the examples below, leaving aside, for the present, the more controversial case of folk psychological explanation.

The development of physics, chemistry, biology, medicine, and so on no doubt originate in folk intuitions. However, in modern accounts of the phenomena of these areas, little or no vestige of this heritage remains. Rather than supplementing and regimenting folk intuitions about dynamics, reactions, the basis of life, and the cure of disease, modern theories have totally discredited and supplanted these accounts.

There are numerous illustrative examples of folk accounts, which even had a measure of scientific respectability but which now appear completely unfounded. In physics, the motion of an artillery shell was commonly conceived of as consisting of a straight line motion along the line of sight of the gun barrel followed by a vertical descent. In chemistry, it was commonly believed that there are few constraints on the ability of substances to transmute from one form to another, which motivated the search for the "philosopher's stone," which would turn base metals into gold. Even after the development of scientific chemistry, our folk taxonomy of substances has little or nothing to do with the periodic table and molecular composition. In biology, the spontaneous generation of life from decaying substances was a prevalent view as recently as the seventeenth and eighteenth centuries. It was thought that flies arose spontaneously from feces and even that signets emerged from rotting logs. Equally, folk accounts of medicine, some of which go under the banner of "alternative" medicine, do not provide a foundation for, but appear completely at variance with, modern Western medicine. For example, the effectiveness of acupuncture is usually justified as bringing the life forces of *yin* and *yang* into balance.

These examples show that commonsense conceptions of the world, while they may provide a historically important starting point for scientific investigation, are typically superseded and, crucially, dismissed as false. In particular, the intuitive notions of "impulse" and "natural place" that underwrote naive understandings of ballistics are no longer considered to make sense. Similarly, the philosopher's stone and the alchemical conception of transmutation are not thought to refer to any aspect of the real world. Equally, modern biology does not countenance the possibility of spontaneous generation. Modern Western medicine claims

that the postulates of "alternative" accounts, such as "life force," "yin," and "yang" do not exist. Notice that modern science does not simply contend that the categories of folk science happen to have no members. Since the entire standpoint of folk theory is rejected, it becomes difficult or impossible to conceive of what it would be to encounter an example of such putative categories—the categories are simply rejected wholesale as completely nonsensical. (Of course, some of the vocabulary of false naive theories may survive, for example, "impulse" above, but be construed very differently.)

Backing up such historical considerations are experimental studies of folk beliefs about scientific matters. Modern students of physics are prone to reveal a bizarre conception of basic physical principles (McCloskey, 1983). For example, when asked to describe the trajectory along which a ball will travel after being released from constrained spiral motion, a common response is that it continues in a spiral motion, rather than traveling in a straight line (Kaiser, McCloskey, & Proffitt, 1986). Furthermore, such misconceptions are remarkably difficult to change by instruction (Carey, 1985, 1986; Gentner & Stevens, 1983; West & Pines, 1985; see Kuhn, 1989, for discussion). It is remarkable that we are able to navigate our way through a complex world so successfully, when our explicitly held beliefs about its structure seem to be consistently and dramatically off-target.

Now, if folk theories appear to be bad science in domains that are scientifically well understood, there seems little reason to suppose they will fare better in domains that are scientifically poorly understood. It seems reasonable to assume that domains that have resisted scientific analysis are likely to be especially complex; hence, in these domains, folk theories are even less likely to provide a scientifically respectable analysis. In particular, folk psychology, along with folk economics, folk sociology, and folk theories concerned with tables, cars, music, and shopping, are all likely to prove to be scientifically ill-founded.

The Defeasibility of Commonsense Generalizations

In the previous section, we did not consider folk psychology directly, but drew morals from the firmer ground of explanation of physical phenomena. In this section, by contrast, we start by considering folk psychological explanation and extend our conclusions to folk theories in general. Consider this schematic folk psychological generalization:

1. If you desire D and have the belief B that action A will lead to D, then you will perform action A.

This can be filled out as, for example, a useful rule for parents: "If a child desires ice cream and has the belief that tidying her room will lead to her being given ice cream, then she will tidy her room." However, bitter experience indicates that this, like other specific instances of the schema, admits of many counterexamples. For example, the generalization will not hold if the child believes that ice cream will be forthcoming in any case, because her parents are weak-willed. Equally, she may believe that the room is so untidy that it is not worth the effort, that there is a fierce dog in the room, that her big sister will take the ice cream anyway, or that there is an alternative, more desirable, action available, such as watching a favorite television program, going swimming, and so on. For this specific instantiation of the generalization, it is clear that there will be no way of ruling out all these possibilities one by one. There cannot be a clause ruling out the possibility of swimming, one for watching television, one for each of the possible dangers that might be encountered in the bedroom, and so on. The only hope of ruling out such possibilities without specifying an exhaustive and presumably indefinitely long list of exceptions is to attempt to save the folk psychological generalization at the schematic level (Chater & Oaksford, 1990; Oaksford & Chater, 1991).

However, at the schematic level, too, it is hard to imagine how the appropriate modification can be achieved. One possibility, which takes account of the counterexamples above, might be that the generalization should read:

2. If you desire D and you have no other more pressing desire D' and have the belief B that action A will lead to D, and that it will not lead to any unwelcome consequences, and that D will not be satisfied if A is not performed, and that you are able to exploit D if it occurs, then you will perform action A.

But this, of course, succumbs to further counterexamples. There may well be a less pressing desire

D', which can be achieved by action A', which is less arduous than action A. In this case, it may be judged not worth going to the extra trouble of performing A, even though the desire D is the most pressing. Further, it must be *possible* to perform A, and the agent must believe that A can be performed (the child will not attempt to tidy the room if she believes that the door is locked and that she cannot get a key). Clearly, further elaboration of this generalization by adding extra clauses of the same kind will not help because further counterexamples can always be generated.

The fact that folk psychological generalizations succumb so readily to counterexamples is recognized in that they are usually stated as holding *ceteris paribus* or "everything else being equal." That is, the situations in the counterexamples described above are viewed as situations in which all other things are not equal. Of course, the use of such a locution does not remove the problem of counterexamples, but simply changes the problem from that of adding conditions to refine the original generalization so that it is always true to specifying the conditions under which all other things are equal. This is, of course, simply the original problem in a different guise.

If it is impossible to reconstruct folk psychological generalizations so that they are true, then surely folk psychology must be rejected as a false account of human behavior. In consequence, the postulates of the theory—beliefs, desires, and their kin—should be treated as incoherent. Beliefs and desires will not figure in a scientific account of mind any more than the *yin* and *yang* figure in modern Western medicine. Putting the point bluntly, folk psychology is false and beliefs and desires do not exist.

While this kind of argument is reasonably familiar with regard to folk psychology (see Fodor, 1991; Schiffer, 1987, 1991), which has been the center of intense debate (e.g., Churchland, 1986; Fodor, 1987; Kitcher, 1984), parallel arguments appear to be equally persuasive with regard to other folk theories, to which much less philosophical attention has been devoted.

Consider the falsity of the following commonsense generalizations: "All chairs have legs," "All birds can fly," "If you turn the key, the car starts." Armchairs do not have legs, swivel chairs have a central column; ostriches, penguins, and injured birds cannot fly; if the battery is dead the car will not start. Perhaps these generalizations are false because they are formulated with insufficient precision—perhaps not *all* birds can fly, but all uninjured garden birds can fly. But what about very young birds, very old birds, birds tangled up in nets, birds in extremely cold weather or high winds, birds with clipped wings, and so on. Refining further, we may say that "all birds can fly" means that every bird will have or has had the ability to fly at some time in its life—according to this reading, very young, very old, and entangled birds count as flyers; and transient meteorological conditions may be ignored; and perhaps having clipped wings counts as an injury. What, then, of very young abandoned birds, destined to starve before they learn to fly; genetically abnormal birds; caged birds, and so on. The terms used in these attempts to refine the generalization themselves equally require refinement in order to save the original generalization from counterexamples. What counts as a garden bird—a turkey in a run at the end of the garden? an ostrich in an African garden? There seems to be no end to this refinement—every term adduced in refining the original generalization itself requires refinement.

This phenomenon has been given many different labels in different areas of cognitive theory, from cognitive psychology and philosophy to artificial intelligence. Folk theories are said to: be context-sensitive (Barsalou, 1987); hold only relative to some background conditions (Barwise & Perry, 1983), be defeasible (Minsky, 1975), admit exceptions (Holland, Holyoak, Nisbett, & Thagard, 1986), lack generality (Goodman, 1983), have intention-relative categories (Winograd & Flores, 1986). These are many ways of saying that every commonsense generalization, just like the generalizations of folk psychology, succumb to endless counterexamples.

We have focused above on the fact that folk generalizations have counterexamples. On the reasonably standard assumption that every good scientific law is without exceptions, this immediately implies that folk theories are bad science. But it has been argued that scientific laws are quite generally defeasible but not thereby false. An extreme version of this view has been advocated by Cartwright (1983), who argues that the "phenomenological" laws of science, which are defeasible, are the only candidates for truth and that "deep" putatively exceptionless laws should be rejected as false.

Even independently of the inference from counterexamples to falsehood, however, folk theories,

when judged as scientific theories, are woefully inadequate—they correspond to bad science rather than good science. This inadequacy has a number of aspects, including the inchoate poorly articulated nature of such theories, internal inconsistency, the *ad hoc* character of explanation, lack of predictive power, and so on. These properties are evident in the commonsense explanations considered above.

So our reaction of folk theories does not presuppose that the laws of a good scientific theory do not admit some exceptions. We merely require that there be some distinction between good and bad science and that common sense falls into the latter category. In view of this, the discussion could stop here. However, while our arguments do not hinge on the issue of defeasibility, we actually believe that it is central to a proper understanding of the distinction between good theory and bad theory. In particular, we view the abundance of exceptions to the laws of common sense as the diagnosis for its other ailments. An abundance of exceptions goes hand in hand with an abundance of predictive and explanatory failures, the invocation of *ad hoc* rules to account for these exceptions, and an inability to retain theoretical consistency in the face of endless counterexamples. Hence, although for the purposes of our argument we need not be committed to drawing a distinction between the defeasibility of commonsense generalizations and good scientific laws, we actually believe maintaining such a distinction to be very important.

In any case, the defeasibility of scientific laws does not offer a means of maintaining the truth of folk theories. Whether or not defeasibility can ever be entirely eliminated within scientific theories, it is uncontroversial that defeasibility should be *minimized*. The degree of defeasibility (in conjunction with other factors such as breadth of coverage and simplicity) is a crucial measure of theoretical adequacy. As we have already argued, the generalizations of folk theories are defeasible through and through. So on this score, folk theories will always be ranked at the bottom.

In this section, we have argued that folk theories are false. We now argue that this means that the entities of folk theories do not exist.

FOLK ENTITIES DO NOT EXIST

If common sense is organized into theories, then commonsense categories correspond to the meaning of theoretical terms. If folk theories are bad science, then, *prima facie* at least, it seems that their ontologies should also be rejected.

After all, because we assume that modern chemistry is true, we assume that oxygen is ontologically respectable—what it refers to is determined by chemistry. On the other hand, since we reject alchemy, we assume that "phlogiston" does not apply to anything; it is a term without reference. That is, terms of the internal theories underlying commonsense knowledge are analogous to phlogiston rather than to oxygen. In plain terms, the upshot may be stated: The referents of the terms of folk theories do not exist.

If this formulation seems shocking (and we have found in presentations that it certainly does!), we recommend an alternative: that folk ontologies cannot be used as the basis for scientific explanation. This leaves open the possibility of making sense of some notion of existence in some extrascientific sense. Given the problems involved in making sense of just one kind of existence, the postulation that there are two or even more kinds does not strike us as attractive. We shall continue to use the shocking formulation below.

The conclusion that folk entities do not exist (or its milder variant) appears to be too rapid, however. It may be objected that surely the adoption of a new scientific theory cannot automatically mean the wholesale rejection of the ontology of the previous theory. After all, the vocabulary of one theory is typically largely preserved in subsequent theories. During a scientific revolution, when one theory replaces another, many of the terms in the discredited theory will be preserved in the new theory. For example, modern relativistic physics retains mass, momentum, and so on from Newtonian mechanics, although rejecting such constructs as the luminiferous aether (the medium through which light waves were supposed to travel). Or consider the stability of the term "electron" over the vagaries of the development of twentieth-century physics (Hacking, 1983). Such examples suggest that some terms of false theories may refer after all. It might be argued that "table" and "chair" may be more like "mass" and "momentum" than "epicycle" and "phlogiston." Therefore, it may seem entirely plausible that a significant fragment of folk ontology may exist despite the falsity of the folk theories in which they are embedded.

One version of this position is that a term may refer not because the theory in which it currently plays a role is true, but because some future theory in which it will one day figure is true. This line appears to be advocated by Putnam (1975), who argues that "gold" was a referential term even before the chemical composition of gold was known, and that this coherence is underwritten by the truth of modern chemistry. This suggestion presupposes that a theoretical term may continue to have the same reference when the theory in which it is embedded changes; this is a controversial thesis. Moreover, adversion to a future true theory is of no avail in attempting to maintain the coherence of folk categories, since it seems, to put it mildly, unlikely that "table," "chair," and "eating ice cream" will feature in any future scientific theory.

There is, however, a more radical way of retaining ontology and rejecting theory: by denying that the coherence of terms is dependent on the truth of a theory in which they may be embedded. This position, entity realism, views entities as prior to theories about them. If it is denied that ontology is determined by an embedding theory, some other account of how ontologies are fixed is required. Two possibilities have been advanced, one that applies specifically to *biological* categories and can offer a defense of folk ontologies if they can be treated in the same way; and one that applies more generally. Very roughly, the first approach individuates entities *historically* and the second individuates entities by their *effects*. We now consider these in turn and argue that they do not change our conclusion that, like phlogiston and epicycles, the entities of folk theories do not exist.

Individuation by History

Millikan (1986) aims to explain what makes biological categories coherent, without assuming that coherence must be guaranteed by embedding in a true theory, for the now familiar reason that biological generalizations, like folk generalizations, typically have counterexamples. She notes that generalizations about, for example, hearts, like the generalizations about birds, tables, and so on that we considered earlier, seem to admit of countless exceptions: "A heart...may be large or small (elephant or mouse), three-chambered or four-chambered etc., and it may *also* be diseased or malformed or excised from the body that once contained it, hence liable to pump blood" (Millikan, 1986).

For Millikan, counterexamples to biological generalizations pose no threat to the coherence of biological categories, since coherence is judged by other historical–functional standards to which we shall turn presently. If an appropriate alternative basis for ontological coherence can be found for biology, this might be applied to folk theories—indeed, Millikan suggests that folk psychological terms should be construed as biological categories.

Millikan's approach is complex, but can be illustrated by example:

> A heart…falls in the category *heart*, first, because it was produced by mechanisms that have proliferated during their evolutionary history in part because they were producing items which managed to circulate blood efficiently in the species that contained them, thus aiding the proliferation of that species. It is a *heart,* second, because it was produced by such mechanisms in accordance with an explanation that approximated, to some undefined degree, a Normal explanation for production of the majority of Normal hearts of that species. By a "Normal explanation" I mean the sort of explanation that historically accounted for production of the majority of Normal hearts of that species. And by a "Normal heart," I mean a heart that matches in the relevant respects the majority of hearts that, during the history of that species, managed to pump blood efficiently enough to aid survival and reproduction. (Millikan, 1986, p. 51)

This approach turns out, however, to be extremely liberal. Suppose, for example, you are skeptical about the laws of Freudian psychoanalytic theory and doubt the relationship between the failure to resolve certain conflicts that arise at specific psychosexual stages and consequent specific forms of neurosis. On the orthodox view, this would entail a similar skepticism with respect to the Freudian categories of, for example, the Oedipus complex, the id, the ego and the superego. However, according to Millikan's account, these categories can be maintained in the face of skepticism concerning the laws in which they figure. Consider how the term *superego* may be grounded in the same way as Millikan grounds heart:

> A superego…falls in the category *superego*, first, because it was produced by mechanisms that have proliferated during their evolutionary history in part because they were producing items which managed successfully to resolve psychosexual conflicts in the species that contained them, thus aiding the proliferation of that species. It is a *superego,* second, because it was produced by such mechanisms in accordance with an explana-

tion that approximated, to some undefined degree, a Normal explanation for production of the majority of Normal superegos of that species. By a "Normal explanation" I mean the sort of explanation that historically accounted for production of the majority of Normal superegos of that species. And by a "Normal superego," I mean a superego that matches in the relevant respects the majority of superegos that, during the history of that species, managed to successfully resolve sufficient psychosexual conflicts to aid survival and reproduction.

For the Freudian theorist such a line of argument might seem to be extremely appealing. For it appears to establish the coherence of the fundamental categories of Freudian theory, even though the laws of Freudian theory may not hold; similar arguments appear to establish the *yin* and *yang* as respectable entities, whose purpose is setting life forces in balance. This liberalization of the criterion for ontological commitment appears to allow the grounding of the terms of false theories of all sorts, folk psychology and other folk theories perhaps included. But if the categories of folk theories exist only in the sense that the *yin* and the *yang* exist, this sense of existence is surely too weak to be of any interest.

It might seem that there is a crucial difference between Millikan's grounding of *heart* and the apparently analogous grounding for *superego* or the *yin* and *yang*, however: that the first explanation seems to be intuitively plausible and the second does not. For example, it seems entirely plausible that the heart has proliferated because of the survival-related benefits of pumping blood; it may seem far less plausible that the superego has proliferated because of the survival-related benefits of resolving psychosexual conflicts; and it seems entirely implausible that the *yin* and *yang* have proliferated because of the survival-related benefits of balancing the life forces.

In what, however, does the intuition that these cases are different consist? Why shouldn't the superego, the *yin* and the *yang* proliferate because of their survival-related benefits? The most obvious reply is that this is because, unlike hearts, they don't exist. Yet existence is the very issue which the historical account is supposed to decide, so this appeal is illegitimate. A further suggestion may be that while 'heart' is a biologically respectable category, the superego, the *yin* and the *yang* are not. But the historical account is intended to distinguish genuine biological categories from bogus biological categories, so this appeal too begs the question. Finally it could be suggested that 'heart' plays a role in some true biological theory, whereas the superego plays a role in an at best highly controversial theory, and the yin and the yang are parts of a radically false folk theory of medicine. Yet the historical account is intended to provide an alternative to this appeal to the truth of the embedding theory and thus cannot rely upon it. In sum, it seems that the historical account is entirely neutral between purportedly genuine and presumably bogus categories. Hence it cannot be used to demonstrate that folk ontologies have a legitimate basis, despite the falsity of folk theories.

Individuation by Effects

While Millikan's approach to individuating entities theory-independently seems too liberal, an alternative approach, developed in the philosophy of science, is motivated by the stability of theoretical terms, such as electron, in the context of dramatically changing scientific theories. As mentioned above, in the last hundred years there have been a wide variety of very different scientific accounts of the electron. Nonetheless, it seems natural to view all of these accounts as theories *of the electron*. That is, while theories have come and gone, entities seem to have remained the same.

Hacking (1983) suggests that what is common between the same entity in different theories is its effects. For example, in theories as different as the plum pudding model of the atom and contemporary particle physics, the electron is held to propel a vane in a vacuum (the "electron wind"); be sensitive to both electrical and magnetic fields (as evidenced, for example, in the Maltese cross experiment); produce, on average, a three-centimeter track in a cloud chamber, and so on. That is, although theories about electrons have changed considerably, the set of effects that electrons have been taken to explain has remained relatively stable.

However, while in some cases the set of effects that a theoretical account attempts to explain has a real basis, in other cases more than one entity or property explains what was erroneously supposed to be a set of phenomena with a coherent basis. For example, the putative negative weight of phlogiston could be used to explain both the gain in mass of materials after burning (since phlogiston was released) and the fact that hot air balloons rise (by

trapping phlogiston released from burning). However, these phenomena have very different origins. The first is explained by oxidization during burning and the second is explained by the expansion of air when heated. Because the set of phenomena that phlogiston was postulated to explain turned out to *fractionate* in just this way the preservation of the term "phlogiston" would have been rather confusing from the point of view of Priestley's account of bleaching and burning. Thus, a new term "oxygen" was used to refer to the postulated entity, which explained the gain in mass of materials after burning.

The criterion of individuation by effects appears to apply equally well to entities that are dismissed by modern science as to entities that have been accepted. That is, it could explain the stability of the term "phlogiston" over hundreds of years of chemical theorizing just as well as it explains the preservation of the term "electron" over the last hundred years. It is, therefore, entirely neutral with regard to the existence of the entities postulated. In particular, it will apply to folk terms whether they refer or not, and hence provides no defense of the coherence of folk entities.

In the previous section, we argued that folk theories are bad science; in this section, we have argued that the ontologies of folk theories are not scientifically respectable. These conclusions appear to cast common sense in a very poor light; the next section aims to correct this impression. Folk theories, while poor science, are remarkably successful at helping us make sense of and act in a world that is far too complex for scientific analysis to be tractable.

DIFFERING GOALS: THE ART OF THE SOLVABLE VERSUS COPING WITH COMPLEXITY

Despite the notional goal of explaining all aspects of the natural world, in practice, science is, to use Medawar's famous dictum, the art of the solvable. That is, scientists seek out and explore just those areas where theories can be built, tested, and applied; they shy away from areas that presently appear to be intractable to scientific methods. The ability to choose to focus on tractable matters and ignore the intractable marks an important difference between science and common sense. Folk theories must allow us to make the best possible sense of our everyday world and guide our actions as successfully as possible; to do this they must face up to the full complexity of the everyday world, which, we suggest, science rightly prefers to avoid.

Most aspects of our everyday world are simply too complex, and too downright messy, to be the basis of science; there simply is no clear-cut theory of the behavior of everyday objects, of the changing patterns of food supply, of the nature and degree of various types of danger, or, most challenging of all, of human nature itself. From the point of view of science, each of the domains is criss-crossed by a myriad of different causal paths, most of which are little understood by science; furthermore, the complexity of these causes, and their interactions, makes such matters inherently resistent to scientific analysis. Consider, for example, the problem of predicting the likely effects of falling down the stairs: the range of relevant biological and physical factors—exact layout of the stairs, shape of body, clothing worn, etc.—make scientific study quite impossible. The scientist may choose to pick apart these multiple causes, studying gravitation, blood flow, bone strength, and so on, independently, without ever having to put all these factors back together to deal with a specific case of falling.

The agent faced with the problem of successfully coping with the baffling complexity of the everyday world has no such luxury. Folk theories must provide rough and ready advice—that here falling is dangerous and extreme care must be taken; that there, it is not so dangerous and it is safe to hurry, and so on. Our folk understanding of mind provides another good example. Human behavior appears to be generated by an extraordinarily complex mix of factors, both psychological and biological, upon which scientific psychology and biology have made only partial inroads. Yet folk theories allow us to make rough and ready assessments of how and why people behave; and when it comes to guiding action appropriately, such theories, for all their faults, are much better than nothing.

In general, then, folk theories must deal with aspects of the world that science avoids as intractable, i.e., it must deal with domains in which good science is more or less impossible, and rough and ready generalization must suffice. Thus, the fact that folk explanations do not stand up to scientific scrutiny should not be viewed as a criticism of folk theories; it is an inevitable consequence of the fact that folk theories must venture where science cannot. If we are right, then the very domains that folk theories must cover, where scientific analysis is impossible, means that folk theories will inevitably be bad science; and that the ontology of common sense will not be scientifically respectable.

We now turn to briefly consider some of the implications of this perspective for the study of mind.

CONSEQUENCES AND CONCLUSIONS

We have argued that folk theories are false and that the entities they postulate do not exist. If we are right in equating the objects and relations of common sense with the ontology of false scientific theories, then folk ontologies do not carve nature at the joints any more than Ptolemaic astronomy. Just as the theory of epicycles was a remarkable *product* of human attempts to make sense of the astronomical world, so our everyday categories "chair," "home," and "friend" represent remarkable *products* of human attempts to understand the everyday world of artifacts, dwellings, and human relationships. The character of common sense is perhaps obscured because we are so close to its objects; but just because we make friends, build homes, and manufacture chairs does not lessen the individual and social achievement of creating the folk theories in which these terms are embedded. This is the heart of the thesis of this chapter—common sense is an *explanandum*, not an *explanans*. A science of cognition must explain the basis of our folk theories and cannot use folk theories as its foundation.

This view has significant consequences for the theory of meaning, whether for natural language or for mental states: It undercuts the project of devising a theory of reference for the terms of natural language, as this project is traditionally conceived. Typically, the problem is viewed as that of specifying some naturalistic relation between, for example, the symbol "chair" or "ice cream" and actual chairs and ice cream. There are a number of suggestions about how this "naturalization" problem can be solved. The crudest suggestion is that the appropriate relation is that the tokening of symbols is caused by encounters with their referents, or that symbol-tokenings *correlate* with such encounters. Causal theories of reference (e.g., Kripke, 1972; Plantinga, 1974; Putnam, 1975) and informational semantics (Dretske, 1981; Fodor, 1987, 1990; Stampe, 1977) have devised extremely sophisticated versions of these views. But if commonsense categories are incoherent, then there are no chairs or ice cream. *A fortiori*, the tokening of the symbols "chair" and "ice cream" cannot be caused or correlated with instances of chairs and ice cream, since there are none. A causal/correlational story is no more appropriate for commonsense categories than it would be for explaining the meaning of "phlogiston" and "epicycle." Quite generally, any view that attempts to explain the meaning of commonsense terms as a relation to the corresponding category in the environment is simply not applicable—the naturalization problem for everyday folk terms cannot, in principle, be solved.

Since this argument applies just as much to mental states as to natural language, this view also poses problems for any representational theory of mind that specifies the content of mental representations in terms of commonsense, folk categories. For example, any theory that assumes that mental representations correspond to the contents of propositional attitudes is ruled out immediately, since there is no coherent folk ontology to which the contents of the attitudes can map. In particular, this constitutes a rather nonstandard attack on folk psychology as a basis for scientific psychology. Typically, folk psychology is attacked directly that it postulates entities, beliefs and desires that do not exist. According to our more general arguments to the falsity of folk theories the contents of propositional attitudes are equally in doubt. Hence folk psychology is doubly vulnerable, if folk theories are put into doubt: It is vulnerable first because the integrity of the contents of folk psychology presuppose the truth of other folk theories; and it is vulnerable because folk psychology is itself a folk theory.

A practical consequence of this additional line of attack on folk psychology is that a putative scientific psychology cannot merely reject the attitudes while retaining their contents to act as the interpretations of the representations it postulates. So practical work in knowledge representation in cognitive science and artificial intelligence, which is typically neutral with respect to the nature of the attitudes, nevertheless must be rejected, since they retain the folk ontology of tables, chairs, and so on. Such considerations apply just as much to most connectionist approaches to knowledge representation, where states of networks are interpreted in terms of folk ontologies (e.g., see papers in McClelland & Rumelhart, 1986; Rumelhart & McClelland, 1986). Notice that this applies to "dis-

tributed" as well as "localist" connectionist representation. A distributed representation of an object in a connectionist network modeling commonsense inference still relies on a featural decomposition such that the feature nodes of the network correspond to the types of which the object represented is a token. The types that provide the interpretation of the feature nodes are typically the categories of our folk ontologies. Hence on the current position interpreting features is as pressing a problem for connectionism as interpreting the predicate symbols of the knowledge representation language is for traditional AI (Christiansen & Chater, 1992, 1993).

In the light of these considerations it is perhaps not surprising that the areas of cognitive science and cognitive psychology in which most progress has been made are those that do not involve knowledge-rich inferential processes. That is, progress is only really apparent in those areas which, from a philosophical standpoint, as Davies (1992) has pointed out, are not really *cognitive* domains at all. Fodor (1983) captures the distinction very neatly. He divides the cognitive system into informationally encapsulated input (and output) "modules," on the one hand, and informationally unencapsulated central processes on the other. Central processes are explicitly identified as those involving knowledge-rich inferential processes of belief fixation and revision, i.e., precisely the processes for which our theories postulate inference over representations whose content is given in terms of our folk ontology. Fodor argues that progress in the cognitive sciences has only been and is only likely to be forthcoming for the informationally encapsulated input and output modules.

One way of viewing this diagnosis of lack of progress is that cognitive science has failed to resolve the problems that beset behaviorism. Behaviorists eschewed an introspectionist methodology and imposed rigorous strictures on psychological practice and theory. In particular, they demanded that stimulus and response be physicalistically rather than intentionally characterized. However, as Fodor (1968), Chomsky (1959), and other pioneers of cognitive science observed, in behaviorist theorizing (e.g., Skinner, 1957), such physicalistic characterizations were in practice supplanted by inadvertent use of intentional terminology—in particular, the stimulus and response were not described in the terms of physical (or other) science, but rather in terms of the experimenter's commonsense understanding of the task. Description of the conditioned stimulus as a pencil and the conditioned response as, say, the act of writing is description in terms of folk theories rather than physics. The cognitivist response was to attempt to legitimize this nonphysicalistic, intentional vocabulary. This presupposed that such everyday vocabulary can be naturalistically grounded as a relation between mental representations and the world. Since the domain of this intentional vocabulary is folk ontology, and since the entities of folk ontology do not exist, naturalization is impossible. "The assumption that scientific psychology can be based on the principal *product* of psychological processes—commonsense theories and commonsense ontologies—whether implicit, as in behaviorism, or explicit, as in contemporary cognitive science, is unsustainable.

REFERENCES

Barsalou, L. W. (1987). The instability of graded structures: Implications for the nature of concepts. In U. Neisser (Ed.), *Concepts and conceptual development* (pp. 101–140). Cambridge: Cambridge University Press.

Barwise, J., & Perry, J. (1983). *Situations and attitudes*. Cambridge, MA: MIT Press.

Carey, S. (1985). *Conceptual change in childhood*. Cambridge, MA: MIT Press.

Carey, S. (1986). Cognitive science and science education. *American Psychologist, 41*, 1123–1130.

Carey, S. (1988). Conceptual differences between children and adults. *Mind & Language, 3*, 167–181.

Cartwright, N. (1983). *How the laws of physics lie*. Oxford: Oxford University Press.

Charniak, E., & McDermott, D. (1985). *An introduction to artificial intelligence*. Reading, MA: Addison-Wesley.

Chater, N., & Oaksford, M. (1990). Autonomy, implementation and cognitive architecture: A reply to Fodor and Pylyshyn. *Cognition, 4*, 93–107.

Chomsky, N. (1959). A review of B. F. Skinner's *Verbal Behavior*. *Language, 35*, 26–58.

Christiansen, M., & Chater, N. (1992). Connectionism, learning and meaning. *Connection Science, 4*, 227–252.

Christiansen, M., & Chater, N. (1993). Symbol grounding—the emperor's new theory of meaning? *Proceedings of the Fifteenth Annual Conference of the Cognitive Science Society* (pp. 155–160). Hillsdale, NJ: Lawrence Erlbaum.

Churchland, P. S. (1986). *Neurophilosophy*. Cambridge, MA: MIT Press.

Davies, M. (1992). Thinking persons and cognitive science. In A. Clark & R. Lutz (Eds.), *Connectionism in context* (pp. 111–122). Berlin: Springer-Verlag.

Dretske, F. (1981). *Knowledge and the flow of information*. Cambridge, MA: MIT Press.

Fodor, J. A. (1968). *Psychological explanation*. New York: Random House.

Fodor, J. A. (1981). The present status of the innateness controversy. In J. A. Fodor (Ed.), *Representations* (chap. 10, pp. 257–316). Cambridge, MA: MIT Press.

Fodor, J. A. (1983). *The modularity of mind*. Cambridge, MA: MIT Press.

Fodor, J. A. (1987). *Psychosemantics: The problem of meaning in the philosophy of mind*. Cambridge, MA: MIT Press.

Fodor, J. A. (1990). *A theory of content and other essays*. Cambridge, MA: MIT Press.

Fodor, J. A. (1991). You can fool some of the people all of the time, everything else being equal: Hedged laws and psychological explanations. *Mind, 100*, 18–34.

Furnham, A. (1987). *Lay theories: Everyday understanding of problems in the social sciences*. Oxford: Pergamon Press.

Garfinkel, H. (1964). Studies in the routine grounds of everyday activities. *Social Problems, 11*, 225–250.

Gentner, D., & Stevens, A. (Eds.). (1983). *Mental models*. Hillsdale, NJ: Erlbaum.

Goodman, N. (1983). *Fact, fiction and forecast* (4th ed.). Cambridge, MA: Harvard University Press. (Originally published 1954)

Hacking, I. (1983). *Representing and intervening*. Cambridge: Cambridge University Press.

Hayes, P. (1978). The naive physics manifesto. In D. Michie (Ed.), *Expert systems in the microelectronic age*. Edinburgh: Edinburgh University Press.

Hayes, P. (1984a). Liquids. In J. Hobbs (Ed.), *Formal theories of the commonsense world*. Hillsdale, NJ: Ablex.

Hayes, P. (1984b). The second naive physics manifesto. In J. Hobbs (Ed.), *Formal theories of the commonsense world*. Hillsdale, NJ: Ablex.

Holland, J. H., Holyoak, K. J., Nisbett, R. E., & Thagard, P. (1986). *Induction: Processes of inference, learning and discovery*. Cambridge, MA: MIT Press.

Kaiser, M. K., McCloskey, M., & Proffitt, D. R. (1986). Development of intuitive theories of motion: Curvilinear motion in the absence of external forces. *Developmental Psychology, 22*, 67–71.

Karmiloff-Smith, A. (1988). The child is a theoretician, not an inductivist. *Mind & Language, 1*, 183–196.

Kitcher, P. (1984). In defense of intentional psychology. *Journal of Philosophy, 81*, 89–106.

Kripke, S. (1972). *Naming and necessity*. Oxford: Basil Blackwell.

Kuhn, D. (1989). Children and adults as intuitive scientists. *Psychological Review, 96*, 674–689.

Leslie, A. M. (1987). Pretense and representation in infancy: The origins of 'theory of mind'. *Psychological Review, 94*, 412–426.

McCarthy, J., & Hayes, P. (1969). Some philosophical problems from the standpoint of artificial intelligence. In B. Meltzer & D. Michie (Eds.), *Machine intelligence 4*. Edinburgh: Edinburgh University Press.

McClelland, J. L., & Rumelhart, D. E. (1986). *Parallel distributed processing: Explorations in the microstructures of cognition. Vol. 2: Psychological & biological models*. Cambridge, MA: MIT Press.

McCloskey, M. (1983). Intuitive physics. *Scientific American, 24*, 122–130.

Medin, D. L., & Wattenmaker, W. D. (1987). Category cohesiveness, theories and cognitive archeology. In U. Neisser (Ed.), *Concepts and conceptual development: Ecological and intellectual factors in categorization* (pp. 25–62). Cambridge: Cambridge University Press.

Millikan, R. G. (1986). Thought without laws: Cognitive science without content. *Philosophical Review, 95*, 47–80.

Minsky, M. (1975). Frame-system theory. In R. Schank & B. L. Nash-Webber (Eds.), *Theoretical issues in natural language processing*. Cambridge, MA: B. B. N.

Murphy, G. L., & Medin, D. L. (1985). The role of theories in conceptual coherence. *Psychological Review, 92*, 289–316.

Nisbett, R. C., & Ross, L. (1980). *Human inference: Strategies and shortcomings of social judgement*. Englewood Cliffs, NJ: Prentice-Hall.

Oaksford, M., & Chater, N. (1991). Against logicist cognitive science. *Mind & Language, 6*, 1–38,

Perner, J. (1991). *Understanding the representational mind*. Cambridge, MA: MIT Press.

Place, U. T. (1992). The role of the ethnomethodological experiment in the empirical investigation of social norms and its application to conceptual analysis. *Philosophy of the Social Sciences, 22*, 461–474.

Plantinga, A. (1974). *The nature of necessity*. Oxford: Oxford University Press.

Potter, J., & Wetherall, M. (1987). *Discourse and social psychology: Beyond attitudes and behaviour*. London: Sage.

Putnam, H. (1975). The meaning of 'meaning'. In *Mind, language & reality: Philosophical papers, Vol. II* (pp. 215–271). Cambridge: Cambridge University Press.

Rumelhart, D. E., & McClelland, J. L. (1986). *Parallel distributed processing: Explorations in the microstructures of cognition. Vol. 1: Foundations*. Cambridge, MA: MIT Press.

Schacter, D. L. (1987). Implicit memory: History and current status. *Journal of Experimental Psychology: Learning, Memory and Cognition, 13*, 501–518.

Schiffer, S. (1987). *Remnants of meaning*. Cambridge, MA: MIT Press.

Schiffer, S. (1991). Ceteris paribus laws. *Mind, 100*, 1–17.

Skinner, B. F. (1957). *Verbal behavior*. New York: Appleton-Century-Crofts.

Stampe, D. (1977). Toward a causal theory of linguistic representation. In P. French, T. Euling, & H. Wettstein (Eds.), *Midwest studies in philosophy* (Vol. 2). Minneapolis: University of Minnesota Press.

Stich, S. (1983). *From folk psychology to cognitive science*. Cambridge, MA: MIT Press.

Wellman, H. M. (1990). *The child's theory of mind*. Cambridge, MA: MIT Press.

West, L., & Pines, A. (Eds.). (1985). *Cognitive structure and conceptual change*. Orlando, FL: Academic Press.

Winograd, T., & Flores, F. (1986). *Understanding computers and cognition*. Reading, MA: Addison-Wesley.

Does Science Underwrite Our Folk Psychology?

Barry C. Smith

Folk psychology is part of common sense. It is that part we use to make sense of our own and other people's words and deeds. We rely on it to predict what people will do and say on particular occasions, and to make them intelligible even when what they do and say surprises us.[1] It comprises a complex body of knowledge about the workings of the mind and its effects on behavior, which in the loosest sense may be called a theory. Viewed in this way it is akin to our commonsense understanding of the physical world and the naive physics we use to predict and explain the behavior of objects and the forces affecting them. The claim to be a theory is not what matters here; it is the status of claims made in the commonsense idiom that we are interested in. For whether or not folk psychology is a theory, it does seem to afford us broad generalizations about the workings of the mind and its likely effects on behavior.

But what are we committed to when we make folk psychological attributions and generalizations; what makes these statements true, if they are true; and more importantly, do they pick out real properties in nature? A range of possible answers has been suggested in the literature, including at one end of the spectrum the claim that folk psychological descriptions are relatively a priori, belonging to a self-standing practice that is immune to empirical challenge; and at the other end, the claim that they are contestable empirical hypotheses that may well turn out to be just as misguided and false as the judgments we make in accordance with naive physics.

To assess these claims we first have to ask whether commonsense psychological explanation needs to be vindicated by scientific explanation; and if so, whether it can be. Let us begin at the a priori end of the spectrum.

The practice of commonsense psychological explanation might be justified without help from science by defending the usefulness of giving explanations of one another in rational terms. We make others intelligible by supplying interpretations of what they say and do against a background of beliefs and desires that lends a certain narrative coherence to the course of their mental lives. Attributions of particular beliefs and desires will count as the reasons for someone's action only if they preserve the rational pattern in this continuous narrative of an individual's mental history.

According to this (narrative) defense of commonsense practice, each individual will have a distinct cast of mind; and insofar as we can generalize across individuals we will pick out broad similarities that fall far short of anything like psychological laws. People's behavior, like the weather, cannot be predicated but can be explained, although the explanations we can give will be, at best, *post hoc* and partial.

The absence of laws offers one reason why commonsense psychology may be remote from science, but there are others. Things outside the

individual's body may be relevant to determining which intentional states he is in since the objects of someone's attention or desire may play an integral role in fixing just what he is thinking about, and thus in fixing the identity of his intentional states. This makes it problematical, to say the least, to identify those states with neural structures whose identity is determined solely by their role within the organism. And finally, exponents of the 'narrative' defense will insist that the seams of mental life answer to divisions that pick out no corresponding shapes at the neural or physical level; nor should they. It is inappropriate, defenders will say, to judge our everyday psychological categories by the standards of the cognitive or brain sciences. And yet it is this failure of fit with scientific taxonomies that seems to impugn the truth of belief–desire psychology and the reality of its constructs.

As an early example of these eliminativist worries, consider the following passage from Brian Loar's *Mind and Meaning* (1981):

> ...if it were to turn out that the physical mechanisms that completely explain human behaviour at no level exhibited the structure of beliefs and desires, then something we had all along believed, viz. that beliefs and desires were among the causes of behaviour, would turn out to be false. Naturally, we would continue to use the belief-desire framework to systematise behaviour, but that should then at the theoretical level have the air of fictionalising and contrivance. (pp. 14–15)

A realist about belief–desire psychology who clings to the 'narrative' defense may simply refuse the challenge to substantiate his constructs at any lower level. The claims of commonsense psychology, he will say, are answerable to no other criteria than their own. As an exponent of this line of reasoning Donald Davidson claims that beliefs, desires, hopes and fears are:

> ...just those states whose contents can be discovered in well-known ways. If other people or creatures are in states not discoverable by these methods, it can be, not because the methods fail us, but because these states are not correctly called states of mind—they are not beliefs, desires, wishes or intentions. (1989, p. 160)

Davidson is claiming both that it is *necessary* for intentional states to answer to our ordinary criteria, and that when individuals do meet those criteria that is *sufficient* to establish truths about them as rational agents acting on particular beliefs and desires. To say no more than this leaves open the possibility that states of mind picked out in these (ordinary) ways might have real natures, which can be further investigated by scientific research. Davidson would deny this: What makes any particular folk psychological explanation we give of someone true is a matter of whether we have applied those criteria correctly, not an "objective internal matter" about what states they are in. When we have assured ourselves that we have applied the criteria correctly there is nothing more to say about what it is for someone to be in a particular intentional state; thus beliefs and desires are exhausted by the criteria we have for awarding them to one another. To have a particular belief is to be apt to be ascribed that belief in the course of giving an interpretation of the person that makes the best overall narrative sense of his total life and conduct (Davidson, 1980).

So on this view the mind is an attributed property: a level of description of otherwise physical things. As Michael Root aptly puts it:

...we owe our idea of the mental to our interest in explaining the behaviour of others, and...our idea of the mental is constituted by the way we pursue that interest: we offer a rational explanation of the behaviour...Other minds, on Davidson's view, are what we get when we interpret the behaviour of others. Bodies are what we have before we interpret their behaviour. (1986, p. 294)

This may seem to relieve Davidson of any obligation to seek a closer fit between commonsense psychology and science, but one obligation remains to be discharged. This is the task of explaining how these mentalistic notions are to be located in the world of causes, and this requires a closer fit between the intentional and physical levels of description. For whether or not our interpretative practices pick out any real category in nature, our intended behavior has its home in the realm of physical effects and common sense seems committed to treating beliefs and desires as causes of our actions. So now we need some account of the features of states like belief and desire that enable them to play this causal role in producing behavior.

It is commonly assumed that physical effects have physical causes and need no help from outside agencies, so we shall most likely have to locate those features in the domain of the natural sciences where causal notions get their explanatory pur-

chase. Thus even on this strategy we have to face up to the question of how the facts of mental life can be fitted into the world of facts as described by the natural sciences. Some may object here by denying that commonsense psychological explanation incurs causal commitments, but we can assure ourselves of this just by examining the form of such explanations.[2] Thus when we say: "She did it because she wanted to hurt him," "He went to the house because he believed she'd be there," "She stood up because she wanted to leave," the use of "because" is the causal use, as we can see when we contrast it with the use of "because" in statements like: "She broke the law because she was parked on a double yellow line."[3] Hence reflection on our ordinary practice shows that in stating reasons for action we are also stating causes. It is this requirement that highlights the need to relate our ordinary mental talk to the underlying physical conditions. Davidson's attempt to knit the two levels together is based on the notion of action. Actions are episodes in a person's physical history, which are also episodes in her mental history. Therefore, events in mental life can be identified with particular events in the world, and the mind can be given an observable foundation. It is this move that retrospectively licenses the identification of the beliefs and desires that explain behavior with the neural events that cause it. Mentalistic descriptions become a way of labeling inner, neural causes of events in intentional terms. However, Davidson despairs of finding any more precise means of identifying the particular neural states or structures that bear these psychological ascriptions. The best we can do by way of correlating behaviors, caused in a law-like way by a set of neural events, with the intentional descriptions that give reasons for acting, is to say that parts of the mentalistic description the creature as a whole can sustain will mention the beliefs and desires that on occasion give it reason to act in the way it is caused to by some parts of its total physical state. Whatever reasons can be given will serve as an intentional gloss on the actual physical causes, whatever they are, of the various behaviors. This is the only sense in which reasons are causes of our actions.

For Davidson and other defenders of the autonomy of the mental, little or nothing can be said about the relation between this high level of intentional description and the cognitive and neural levels of organization brought to light by empirical research. The only relation is one of imposition of intentional concepts on the levels below; so nothing discovered at lower levels can have anything to contribute to our understanding of the mental. Our ordinary psychological explanations bring to light only particular causes of particular behavioral effects, producing a catalogue of single events in the course of an individual mental life. Generalizations across individuals will be at best fortuitous, and scientific psychology will in the end prove fruitless.

There is no room here to respond in full to this position; so I shall confine my remarks to the mention (though not the defense) of three criticisms, which point up fundamental inadequacies in the attributionist's view of the mind.

First, there is no room for an account of why interpretation seems to work in some cases but not in others. What is it about some creatures that enables us to explain their behavior in rational terms? We are denied any nontrivial explanation—they simply succumb to intentional redescriptions, or fail to—but surely some account of this is needed. Second, the absence of general psychophysical laws still leaves us with the task of explaining how the psychological and physical qualities of *particular* events can be related. But no explanation of this is even likely. And third, nothing is said about what equips an interpreter to engage in the practices that introduce mental notions into the world. In summary, then, the three worries can be expressed as follows:

1. Our interpretative practices tell us *which* physical events are mental events, but not *why* they are.
2. There is no explanation of how the mental and physical characteristics of particular events are related.
3. There is no account of what equips us to engage in the practice of interpreting one another.

Let us now contrast this position with that of Daniel Dennett, who like Davidson is an attributionist about intentional psychology, but who unlike Davidson believes in the explanatory merits of scientific psychology. What relation does he see between folk psychology and scientific psychology?

First of all, Dennett accepts that there are laws of folk psychology, though at best they should be seen as approximations that help us to predict and interact with others. Hence:

> ...folk psychology is best seen not as a sketch of internal processes, but as an idealised, abstract, instrumentalistic calculus of prediction. (1987, p. 48)

Beliefs and desires are "calculus bound entities, or logical constructions." So although we find it useful to attribute such intentional properties to thinkers they correspond to no real joints in nature. At best they are patterns in the behavior of creatures perceived by creatures like us: creatures who engage in interpretative practices, ascribing beliefs and desires to one another. [4] This may lead us to think that there really are no such things as beliefs according to Dennett. But this is too quick. For he stresses that:

> ...any object—whatever its innards—that is reliably and voluminously predictable from the [intentional] stance is in the fullest sense of the word a believer. (1987, p. 15)

But if this is the fullest sense of the word Dennett allows for, we can easily see why there is no science of intentional psychology: There is no scientifically respectable property that all thinkers who are ascribed a given intentional property must share. There will still be room, however, for scientific psychology to explain the cognitive subsystems of creatures that give rise to the behavior we characterize, instrumentally and heuristically, in those intentional terms. But the very disparate nature of the actual inner causes of behavior in different creatures undermines the explanatory pretensions of folk psychology, and so Dennett's moral is that:

> ...folk-psychology is idealised in that it produces its predictions by calculating in a normative system. It is abstract in that the beliefs and desires it attributes need not be presumed to be intervening states of an internal behaviour-causing system. (1987, p. 52)

Bizarrely, this diagnosis is not offered as a reason to replace or dispense with the categories of intentional psychology: It is just a warning to the friends of folk psychology not to project details from the intentional level onto the levels of organization below. But we are still allowed to ask the question:

> Exactly what feature must we share for [a given belief ascription] to be true of us? More generally, ...what must be in common between things truly ascribed an *intentional* predicate—such as "wants

to visit China" or "expects noodles for supper"?
(1987, p. 43, brackets and underlining mine)

What is Dennett's answer? It must be:

> a shared property that is visible, as it were, from
> one very limited point of view—the point of view
> of folk psychology. Ordinary folk psychologists
> have no difficulty imputing such useful but elu-
> sive commonalities to people. If they then insist
> that in doing so they are postulating a similarly
> structured object in the head, this is a gratuitous
> bit of misplaced concreteness, a regrettable lapse
> in ideology. (ibid., p. 55)

The point of view of folk psychology is what
Dennet (1987) calls *the intentional stance*: a perspective from which we make use of a predictive
strategy, ascribing creatures (and computers)
beliefs and desires under the idealizing assumption
that they are rational agents. The assumption of
rationality, however, is only an ideal: "the myth of
our rational agenthood structures and organizes our
attributions of belief and desire" (Dennett, 1987).

The fatal weakness in this approach is there in
Dennett's phrase "useful but elusive commonality"; for either these intentional ascriptions pick out
real properties of thinkers or we must succumb to
what Loar calls an "air of fictionalising and con-
trivance." Just like Davidson, Dennett is unable to
offer any satisfying account of why the intentional
strategy works. But unlike Davidson he cannot
establish the reality of these phenomena by their
roles in genuine explanations, for Dennett, unlike
Davidson, is committed to the explanatory impo-
tence of folk psychology (cf. its predictive utility)
and the explanatory importance of scientific psychology. The absence of a connection between the
theories of the cognitive underpinnings and the
commonsense psychology of ordinary folk make
his difficulties all the more acute. For there are just
two kinds of answers to the original question of
what thinkers who are truly ascribed the same
intentional property (like believing or desiring
something) must have in common. The first answer
says they are disposed to do and say this, and to
judge that, an answer that requires further attributions. The second kind of answer cites some underlying microproperty, or functional property, they
all share. The first type of answer belongs to common sense, the second to scientific theorizing.
Dennett's mistake is to have stranded himself
between both, denying the strict literalness of commonsense talk and failing to revise or vindicate it in

scientific terms. This leaves an embarrassing gap
when it comes to explaining why many predications from the intentional stance are so reliable. But
this is the very heart of the matter.

What do all thinkers who share a given thought
have in common? We know they don't need to be
neurophysiologically identical. So just:

> how much (and what kinds of similarity) between
> thinkers does the intentional identity of their
> thoughts require?

asks Jerry Fodor, taking up Dennett's challenge
where Dennett peters out. Fodor goes on:

> This is, notice, a question one had better be able to
> answer if there is going to be a scientifically inter-
> esting propositional attitude psychology. (Fodor,
> 1986, p. 426)

Now Fodor has long been an advocate of the view
that scientific psychology will vindicate commonsense psychology. But the problem all along has
been to understand how a science of the mental can
explain what we do without replacing or reducing
our commonsense concepts. If we stress the role of
belief–desire psychology as part of common sense,
it is obvious that it won't be replaced, any more
than talk of cold water cooling my bath, or the sun
sinking low in the sky, has been replaced by what
we know to be the true explanations of these matters. So we must separate how the folk understand
their claims from the issue of what makes certain
generalizations of intentional psychology true or
predictive. It is on the latter level that the concern
about replacement has force. For if it turns out that
the intentional categories that the folk use do no
useful scientific work will explanations in scientific psychology simply dispense with them? Or, if
it preserves them, will they have to be reduced to
the more scientifically respectable categories of,
say, computational psychology?

Notice that the reductive option need not lead to
us dispensing with *our* use of folk psychological
terms. It may be that our folk conceptions help to
pick out, or fix the reference of, the very states we
are interested in, and that a more advanced science
will tell us about the nature of these states: what
beliefs and desires *really are*. And so the threat of
reduction does not present an insuperable difficulty
since the friends of folk psychology can insist that
law-like reduction need not amount to meaning-

reduction. That one set of claims is *made true* by the *truth* of claims of a somewhat different kind does not show that the *meanings* of one set of statements can be reduced to the *meanings* of the other. Moreover, reduction guarantees what we want: a close connection between the different levels. Far from eliminating the folk psychological descriptions, these reducing statements would show us how to accommodate our intentional notions in our descriptions of the physical world. [5]

The more pertinent objection to reductionism is just that so far no such reduction of the intentional to the physical strikes one as remotely plausible. The replacement worry is then the more pressing problem in that it might lead to wide-scale revision of our intentional theorizing.

Fodor aims to steer between these two dangers (e.g., reduction—not likely, and replacement—not palatable) by insisting that the causal laws of intentional psychology that capture generalizations about individuals have to be explained by the computational and syntactic laws that *implement* them. However, the computational laws governing the mechanisms that mediate the connections between intentional causes and their behavioral effects are many and varied, so no strict reduction of the intentional laws is possible. The lack of reduction doesn't loosen all connection between the levels, for although there are intentional causal laws that explain why we think and act as we do, we are always entitled to ask, for any such law, why do *those* causes bring about *those* effects *in that individual*? The reasons will be given in terms of computational laws, though we can expect different laws to be provided for different thinkers. All that is required is that there be *some* computational account of the mediating mechanisms that explain why those intentional states engender those behavioral effects. But the computational mechanisms involved may be a heterogeneous lot.

This strategy is a general feature of the special sciences, according to Fodor.[6] For any special science law *L* which says that *F*s cause *G*s we can always ask why they do; and so long as the law in question is not a basic law of physics, there will always be some further explanation of it in terms of the properties of *F*-instantiations that render them sufficient to bring about something with the properties of *G*-instantiations. In the case of intentional psychology, the mediating mechanisms that ensure that states with certain intentional contents bring about effects of a certain kind are the mental representations and the computational operations defined over them.

It is a consequence of Fodor's story that "semantics doesn't cross implementation boundaries" (in Brian Cantwell Smith's useful phrase). This is because the computational laws of mental processing that implement the higher level intentional laws are purely syntactic. Therefore, to preserve what needs to be explained and to secure the widest application to cases we have to frame our generalizations in content-using terms at the intentional level.

But where does this leave us with respect to Dennett's question: What do thinkers who share a particular belief have to have in common? Remember, Fodor claimed that unless there is some commonality we can point to, there will be no "scientifically interesting propositional attitude psychology." So when two or more people share a belief what do they have in common? They are not required to be functionally identical: to make just the same inferences and to have just the same accompanying states. This is extremely unlikely in all but molecule for molecule duplicates ("twins"). So what else do they share? Pretty much they will be subsumed by the same intentional psychological laws: i.e., satisfy the same causal regularities picked out by an intentional covering law. But what makes this true? Fodor's answer will be different for different thinkers since the vast disjunction of intervening states of mind and cognitive computational mechanisms are "typically quite heterogeneous" according to Fodor. So, surprisingly, he can agree with Dennett that there is no reason to suppose possessors of particular beliefs must be "ultimately in some structurally similar internal condition" (Dennett, 1987, p. 55) narrowly construed; though Fodor has independent reasons for thinking they must each be in *some* structured condition. This is the Fodorian commitment to mental representations whose syntactic structure follows the contours of conceptual content of mental states. But the defense of the language of thought doesn't require thinkers to share type-identical mental representations, i.e., to have the same mental syntax: It is enough that they each have some structured state to play this role. So now we can see that the only commonalities among thinkers are not to be found *at the level of computational psychology* at all, but rather they belong *at the highest intentional level*.

All that such thinkers share is the property of sat-isfying the same laws of intentional psychology. But what it is to satisfy this property has different explanations for different thinkers. So Fodor's argument for a content-using psychology rests on the claim that the intentional level psychology remains indispensable in securing generalizations across individuals who may have no physical or computational properties in common. Many differ-ent internal mechanisms will serve to implement the higher level laws. And all that unifies these diverse creatures are the intentional generaliza-tions—the intentional causal laws—they fall under. So the scientifically interesting level of description for psychology—the level at which thinkers of the same thoughts have something in common—is not computational psychology, but the highest and relatively observational "level of description at which mental states are represented as having intentional content": the level at which we predict *behavior* by finding generalizations across individuals; generalizations to the effect that when thinkers have particular beliefs and particular desires they will do such and such, *ceteris paribus*. Folk psychology is to be vindicated by science, it seems, simply by treating its laws—the laws of intentional psychology—as scientific laws. As Fodor has always maintained: It is only insofar as there are intentional causal laws that there can be a science of psychology at all. But then if vindication is not achieved by recourse to the levels below, in what sense is vindication really explanatory?

Fodor will say that there has to be some ground-ing of the higher level in the levels below. For the laws of intentional psychology, treated as scientific laws (albeit *ceteris paribus* laws), have to be implemented computationally. This is what explains how content-bearing states can have their causal effects on behavior. But to stress the rele-vant point once more: Scientific vindication comes at the highest level, not the level of computational psychology with its Fodorian commitment to com-putational operations defined over sentences in the language of thought. This is a distinct level of sci-entific theorizing, thinks Fodor, with its own moti-vations.

But we are left with an unexplained mystery: Why should creatures with such different innards all satisfy the same intentional laws? On Fodor's official story, our intentional generalizations quan-tify over a variety of computational mechanisms that can sustain this law-like behavior. So although

any belief of a given type *will have to be a compu-tational state of an agent*, it is a mistake to think for any such belief there is some *one* computational state it has to be. Thinkers with different internal organizations will still be answerable to the same higher level psychological laws, which means that those laws capture generalizations that cannot be formulated at the computational level.[7] On the other hand, Fodor does think that creatures with very different patterns of belief and desire can still be subject to the same intentional generalizations and hence the same psychological laws. So com-monalities preserve the claim that one is thereby picking out genuine properties of individuals that generalize across cases. Moreover, what they must have in common to fall under the same intentional taxonomy is a matter for science to decide, not a priori philosophy.

The urge to secure the scientific status of propo-sitional attitude psychology may lead to some revi-sions in what Fodor calls Granny psychology: the everyday use of belief and desire psychology that is pragmatic, context-sensitive, and vague.[8] These features will not affect the causally explanatory laws of intentional psychology, whose terms have been adapted to fit the generalizations we *can* see as implemented in computational terms. Of course this may lead to some minor revisions in our every-day intentional idiom. But Fodor will claim that it cannot lead to massive revision or else the laws of intentional psychology would not work as well as they do, nor would the computational mechanisms operating in us really be implementations of them. In other words, Fodor is holding out for the claim—a hostage to empirical fortune—that there is a class of computational syntactic processes that makes up a natural domain for psychological explanation. This will be the domain of creatures like us who satisfy the same intentional generaliza-tions we do, and the relation between the computa-tional underpinnings and the level of intentional states, though contingent, will be reliable and explicable.[9] Certainly, all believers and desirers have this much in common: They must all have mental representations that are syntactic vehicles for the contents of those states. This is an independ-ently motivated claim (see Fodor's arguments for LOT in the Appendix to Fodor, 1987), which does generalize across thinkers, however different their beliefs and desires. So regardless of their specific mental states and the particular psychological explanations we give of their behavior, they will satisfy the same *general* explanatory patterns of acting in such a way as to do what they believe will secure for them their fondest wish. And the claim that the internal mediating mechanisms of thinkers can differ from individual to individual will still have to leave room for the claim that they have enough overlap to ensure that the syntax of their mental representations, whatever form it takes, mediates the same broad behavioral similarities among thinkers:

> ...the syntax of the mental representations which have the facts that P in their causal histories [and so are about P] tends to overlap in ways that support robust *behavioural similarities* among P-believers. (Fodor, 1994, p. 53, italics and brackets mine)

The trick is to find in each of us mentalese sentences that are the causes "of the sorts of behavioural proclivities that the laws of psychology say that P-believers share" (ibid., p. 54). For if no such overlapping set of causes exists it is hard to see what relation of constraint between the levels Fodor's view imposes. And if it turned out to be none at all, we should have left Fodor no better off for a story about the relationship between folk psychology and scientific psychology than Dennett. On the other hand, a Fodorian view that found commonalities, that is to say overlap, among the heterogeneous syntactic vehicles of thought would challenge Dennett's picture by foisting on him a language of thought among the otherwise diverse subsystems of thinkers; a language of thought story which, Fodor argues, is essential to have conceptually organized thoughts—the contents of intentional attitudes. Claims to intentional realism rest on a detailed working out of this issue.

Finally where does empirical psychology stand in all this? It seems that *pace* Fodor and Dennett, contemporary cognitive psychology goes in for generalizations that do not respect these divisions between the personal and subpersonal levels, the subsystems and the central systems. For the laws of cognitive psychology make cross-level claims about the effects on conscious awareness of certain unconscious intermediate levels of processing, or the effects on our judgments of grammaticality of the presence or absence of certain syntactic features of structures remote from the surface form of sentences and from conscious reflection. Similarities in these processes and effects would not point to the diversity of computational or mediating

mechanisms that Fodor talks about. At the same time they would give far more substance to the personal level of experiential content and judgment than Dennett seems prepared to grant. Perhaps neither has yet provided sufficient grounds for denying a priorism while claiming that an indispensable folk psychology can coexist in some explicable relation to scientific psychology. [10]

ENDNOTES

1. Some philosophers favor the view that although people's actions may not be predictable, they should at least be explicable in the folk psychological idiom.
2. Note that all I am claiming is that it incurs these commitments, not that it honors them. I leave this question open here.
3. The use of this example was suggested by Jessica Brown.
4. Dennett favors the Hofstatder remark that minds are patterns perceived by other minds.
5. In much the same way I can introduce abstract objects like directions into descriptions of the world by pointing out that *the direction of line A* equals *the direction of line B*, whenever line A is parallel to line B. Thus, just as Frege thought, we have criteria for the sameness or difference of these abstract entities grounded in claims about observable features of the empirical world.
6. See Fodor's "Special Sciences" in his *RePresentations* (1981).
7. Fodor tells us that Mentalese sentences "...with similar broad contents...overlap enough in their syntax to sustain robust psychological generalisations. But not enough to make the minds that these generalisations subsume homogeneous under *syntactic* description" (Fodor, 1994, pp. 52–3).
8. Fodor concedes that "...even Intentional Realists can take an instrumental view of beliefs and desires which, by assumption (Dennett's) aren't occurrent causes. It's only mental states that are episodes in mental processes that Realism requires Realists to be Realistic about" (1991, p. 317).
9. See Fodor (1994) and note 7 above.
10. Thanks are due to Jessica Brown for valuable comments on an earlier draft of this paper. The remaining weaknesses are my responsibility.

REFERENCES

Dennett, D. (1987). *The intentional stance*. Cambridge: Bradford MIT.
Davidson, D. (1980). *Essays on actions and events*. London: Blackwell.
Davidson, D. (1989). The myth of the subjective. In M. Krausz (Ed.), *Relativism: Interpretation and confrontation*. South Bend, IN: Notre Dame.

Fodor, J. (1981). *RePresentations*. Cambridge: MIT Press.

Fodor, J. (1986). Banish DisContent. In H. Butterfield (Ed.), *Logic, mind and languages*. London: CUP.

Fodor, J. (1987). *Psychosemantics: The problem of meaning in the philosophy of mind*. Cambridge: MIT Press.

Fodor, J. (1991). Replies. In B. Loewer & G. Rey (Eds.), *Meaning in mind: Fodor and his critics*. London: Blackwell.

Fodor, J. (1994). *The elm and the expert*. Cambridge: MIT Press.

Loar, B. (1981). *Mind and meaning*. London: CUP.

Root, M. (1986). Davidson and social science. In E. Lepore (Ed.), *Truth and interpretation*. London: Blackwell.

Folk Psychology from the Standpoint of Conceptual Analysis

Ullin T. Place

Before deciding what status should be given to folk psychology within scientific psychology, we must understand its linguistic peculiarities. To do that, we need to attend to research on the topic within the philosophical tradition known as "conceptual analysis." This research enables us to identify six respects in which folk psychological language can lead us astray when used in a scientific context:

1. The creation of bogus abstract entities by the process of "nominalizing" predicates and other nonsubstantival parts of speech.
2. The persistent use of adjectives with evaluative (good/bad) connotations.
3. The systematic evaluation of the content of other people's cognitive attitudes and judgments from the standpoint of the speaker.
4. The distortion of causal accounts of human action by the demand for a single scapegoat on whom to pin the blame when things go wrong.
5. The use of the metaphor of linguistic control when explaining behavior that is not subject to that type of control.
6. The unavoidable use of simile when describing private experience.

FOLK PSYCHOLOGY AS A LINGUISTIC UNIVERSAL

I begin with a large claim. Folk psychology, I maintain, is a linguistic universal. In every natural language currently spoken, in every ancient language and culture of which we have decipherable records, the same basic concepts, the same explanatory scheme, are deployed in the accounts that are given of the actions both of the speaker/writer and of other human beings. I take this fact, if it is a fact, to be a serious difficulty for, if not a decisive refutation of the "eliminative materialist" position, as defended by Nick Chater and Mike Oaksford.

In his classical exposition of eliminative materialism in his paper "Mind-Brain Identity, Privacy, and Categories," Richard Rorty (1965) compares what we are here calling "folk psychology" to the beliefs in witches and witchcraft that were widespread in Christian Europe and in European colonies in America and elsewhere to the end of the seventeenth century. Just as witchcraft beliefs became discredited as a consequence of the scientific revolution of the seventeenth century, so, Rorty argues, we may confidently expect folk psychology to be likewise discredited and abandoned in the light of contemporary discoveries in the neurosciences.

The weakness of this analogy is that it represents folk psychology as a system of supernatural beliefs. Examination of such belief systems shows, I believe, that their function is to fill significant gaps in the body of practical commonsense knowledge that is required in order to communicate and deploy the technologies on which even a society of hunters and gatherers depends for its survival. Such significant gaps arise in areas of major human concern such as the causes of rainfall or the lack of it, natural disasters, the fortunes of war, and disease, both in the case of human beings and in the case of the plants and animals on which they depend. They arise because the causes of such events are not accessible to observation at the level of common sense, with the result that common sense lacks the resources with which to effectively predict and control them.

Unlike the practical commonsense knowledge whose gaps they fill, supernatural beliefs are not tightly constrained by the contingencies that actually govern the phenomena they purport to predict and over which they purport to provide a measure of control. They are constrained only by (a) the need to give a spurious sense of comprehension and control over phenomena which, at the level of common sense, are beyond the reach of such comprehension and control; (b) the need to avoid obvious disconfirmation by the way things actually turn out; and (c) the need for "agreement in judgments" within the social group constituted by those who subscribe to the belief system in question. The effect of these constraints is that supernatural belief systems, though they tend toward uniformity of belief within a given culture, vary widely from culture to culture, partly as result of differences between cultures in what are the significant gaps in the technology and associated practical knowledge for the particular culture, and partly for idiosyncratic reasons of history and geography. Practical commonsense knowledge, by contrast, varies from culture to culture only to the extent that different cultures rely on different technologies to wrest a living from similar or different environments. There is no such variation from culture to culture in the technology used to predict and manage interpersonal human relations, the domain for which folk psychology supplies the appropriate conceptual framework. Hence the universality of that branch of practical commonsense knowledge we are here calling "folk psychology".

Viewed from this perspective, the project of empirical science is to use the method of systematic observation and experiment to generate a well-grounded alternative to supernatural belief. Having been exposed artificially to the same kind of rigorous shaping by the contingencies they specify as is commonsense practical knowledge by generations of practical experience in the natural course of events, the belief systems generated by the application of the scientific method enjoy the same kind of universal acceptance and the same right to be regarded as established knowledge. In addition to the practice of systematically submitting hypotheses to practical/experimental test, science succeeds where common sense is forced to give way to supernatural gap-filling by (a) using devices such as the telescope and microscope, which extend observation beyond the limits of the observation available to common sense; (b) using precise and standardized measurement techniques; and (c) using mathematical formulas to describe and predict the results of exact measurement and the relation between one measure and another.

But besides these technical innovations, there is another respect in which scientific method improves on common sense which is of particular importance in relation to the present topic. This is the substitution of a more objective perspective for the anthropocentrism characteristic of common sense, a perspective from which things are viewed, in Spinoza's words, *sub specie aeternitatis*.

We have seen that practical commonsense knowledge is shaped by the actual behavior–consequence relations that obtain in the environment and which it specifies. These behavior–consequence relations or "contingencies," to use B. F. Skinner's term, are causal relations. But they are causal relations viewed from a particular perspective, from the perspective of a human agent trying to master a hostile environment. It is this anthropocentric perspective that is rejected and replaced by the more objective perspective of science. Two well-known examples of the scientific repudiation of anthropocentrism are

1. The rejection of commonsense talk about the "rising" and "setting" of the sun, the moon, and those planets visible to the naked eye in favor of an interpretation of those events in terms of the rotation of the earth on its axis, the rotation of the moon around the earth and the rotation of the planets around the sun.
2. The abandonment of the commonsense contrast between human beings and animals in favor of the conception of *homo sapiens* as one among many species of mammal.

FOLK PSYCHOLOGY AND CONCEPTUAL ANALYSIS

If, as I have argued, folk psychology is a form of practical commonsense knowledge, rather than supernatural infilling, it follows that it has been shaped over thousands of years of intimate contact with the contingencies involved in the prediction and management of human interpersonal relations. This means that, on the one hand, it contains a unique reservoir of knowledge concerning the causal relations governing human behavior, which no scientific psychology can afford to ignore. Viewed from the perspective of science, on the other hand, its perspective on those causal relations is severely distorted by its exclusively anthropocentric and, when applied to the behavior of animals, anthropomorphic assumptions. It is distorted not only by parochial human assumptions, such as the assumption that behavior is controlled by self-directed talk on the part of the agent, but also by the role played by this conceptual scheme in the way language is used in the management of human affairs.

If this is correct, in order to make use of the insights into the mechanisms controlling behavior that folk psychology contains, we need some way of separating the scientifically important wheat from the anthropocentric chaff. In order to do this, I maintain, we need to call on the resources of a technique for elucidating the meaning of words and expressions in natural language known as conceptual analysis.

Conceptual analysis is a way of making explicit the intuitive understanding a fluent speaker/listener of a human natural language has of the words she uses and hears. It does this by studying the kinds of sentence in which such words can and cannot meaningfully occur and the kinds of context in which the resulting sentences can and cannot be meaningfully uttered. Its ultimate source is Frege's (1884/1950) contention that the meaning of a word is the contribution it makes to the meaning of those sentences in which it occurs that are sufficiently well formed to be intelligible to the average listener. It first appeared in Wittgenstein's (1953, 1958) later writings where it is referred to as "a grammatical investigation." Properly so-called conceptual analysis was a product of the "ordinary language" school of analytic philosophy which flourished at Oxford in the years immediately following the end of World War II. Its most important exponents were Gilbert Ryle, John Austin, my own philosophy tutor, Paul Grice, and the only leading member of the group who is still alive, Sir Peter Strawson.

For reasons that have more to do with the philosopher's reluctance to be drawn into what was becoming an empirical investigation of matters of linguistic fact than with any demonstration that its

conclusions are unsound, ordinary language philosophy and with it conceptual analysis have fallen out of favor among philosophers in recent years. For the psychologist the idea that conceptual analysis is a branch of empirical linguistics should be a recommendation. In a recent paper (Place, 1992) I have argued that conceptual analysis is an empirical sociolinguistic investigation of the norms and conventions governing the construction and use of intelligible sentences in any natural language or technical code in which the investigator is fluent. It relies on what I regard as the only satisfactory methodology for demonstrating the existence of a social norm, the ethnomethodological experiment (Garfinkel, 1964/1967). As I construe it, the ethnomethodological experiment is a way of getting around the difficulty that statistical studies of the incidence of a particular variety of social behavior fail to distinguish between behavior that has a low natural frequency of occurrence whose incidence is enhanced by sanctions favoring it, and behavior that has a high natural frequency of occurrence whose incidence is reduced by sanctions designed to discourage it. It demonstrates the existence of a social convention by flouting the convention and observing the consternation that results. As applied by the conceptual analyst to the linguistic conventions involved in the construction of intelligible sentences, it takes the form of a thought experiment in which the analyst invites the reader, *qua* fluent speaker of the language, to share the consternation provoked by a sentence in which a particular convention is flouted, showing in other words that the resulting sentence is nonsensical, absurd, unintelligible.

SORTING THE SCIENTIFICALLY IMPORTANT WHEAT FROM THE SCIENTIFICALLY IRRELEVANT CHAFF

I have already suggested that the importance of conceptual analysis for the purposes of scientific psychology is that it provides a way of distinguishing between those aspects of folk psychology that reflect the nature of the actual psychological processes and capacities involved in the control of human behavior and those that are mere artifacts of the linguistic devices used to depict those processes and capacities or that reflect the anthropocentric preoccupations of the human agent. A full treatment of this topic would require

1. a detailed description of how the methodology of conceptual analysis is applied to the language of folk psychology,
2. an analysis of those features of such language that are artifacts of the method of linguistic representation or the anthropocentric perspective, and
3. an analysis of those features that reflect and provide us with information about the nature of the underlying psychological processes and capacities.

In this paper I attempt only the second of these projects. In the case of the first project, for an appreciation of what conceptual analysis looks like when applied to the language of folk psychology, I cannot do better than refer the reader to Ryle's classical study in his book *The Concept of Mind* (Ryle, 1949). Although almost half a century has elapsed since its publication, many of its lessons have either never been learned or, if they have, have long been forgotten. It is true that, as Medlin (1967) has argued, Ryle's work suffers from a deplorable lack of understanding of and sympathy for the scientific enterprise, both in general and in the fields of psychology and neuroscience in particular. What is needed, therefore, is a reworking of Ryle's linguistic data in a way that both reflects more recent developments in conceptual analysis (e.g., those associated with the problem of intentionality) and linguistics (e.g., transformational grammar) and, at the same time, adopts a more positive attitude to science and scientific psychology.

As to the positive contribution which, in my view, conceptual analysis can make to our understanding of psychological processes and capacities, that is for the future, something that will emerge only when the artifacts of linguistic representation and the anthropocentric perspective have been cleared away or suitably discounted.[1] However, once these impediments have been cleared away, it is my belief that important insights into the way behavior is in fact organized and controlled can be derived from a study of (a) mental activity verbs, particularly those which Ryle (1949) refers to as "heed concepts" (cf. Place, 1954/1964); (b) locutions in which a mental state or mental event verb, such as 'expect,' 'remember,' 'imagine,' 'learn,' 'see,' 'hear,' 'recognize' or 'notice,' takes as its grammatical object a noun phrase describing an object or event, thereby escaping the metaphor of the linguistic control of behavior which is intro-

duced whenever the grammatical object is an embedded sentence in indirect reported speech; and (c) the complex and subtle language of feeling and emotion.

In what follows I shall describe six features, revealed by the application to it of conceptual analysis and other empirical approaches to the study of meaning, such as Osgood's (Osgood, Suci, & Tannenbaum, 1957) "semantic differential," all of which obscure the important contribution the study of folk psychology can make to psychological science and render it, at least in its unreformed state, unsuitable as the language of psychological theory. In each case I shall try to indicate how the feature in question arises either from the peculiarities of our ordinary linguistic representations of psychological reality or from the anthropocentric concerns of human speakers/agents, and why and to what extent this feature disqualifies folk psychological language for use in a scientific context.

Nominalization and the Generation of Abstract Objects

A feature of folk psychology that has generated conceptual confusion since the time of Plato is the invariable use of predicate expressions in the form of a verb or a copula-plus-adjective combination to characterize the mental processes, events, and states of an individual identified by the subject term. When they are incorporated into a scientific theory, the syntax of natural language sentences drives these predicates into argument places, such as the subject and direct object positions, which are normally reserved for what Aristotle calls "substances," things like material objects and living organisms. In order to occupy these positions in the sentence these predicates have to be 'nominalized,' i.e., converted into a noun, which is then taken to stand for an abstract object, as in the case of the 'faculties' of perception, imagination, memory, motivation, etc. Since it is a feature of natural language in general, rather than of folk psychology in particular, and since it is often a convenient shorthand that saves a great deal of circumlocution, the nominalization of predicate expressions is not something a scientific psychology could hope to eliminate altogether. The most that can be hoped for is that psychologists be aware of what they are doing when they use these noun phrases and check back every now and then to the sentences in which the expression occurs as a verb phrase, so as to make sure that what we say in the nominalized form is not an absurdity when expressed as a predicate.

The Evaluative Factor

Folk psychology is deeply infected with terms whose meaning is distinguished only by the evaluation of the characteristic as desirable or undesirable, as in the case of 'intelligent' (good), 'cunning' (bad), 'young' (good), 'immature,' 'childish' (bad), 'outstanding' (good), 'abnormal' (bad), and so on. This phenomenon was drawn to the attention of psychologists, not through conceptual analysis, but through the work of Osgood et al. (1957) on the semantic differential. From their factor analysis of subjects' ratings of a list of stimulus nouns on a series of bipolar scales constructed by pairing a list of adjectives with their opposites the first factor to emerge was "clearly identifiable as *evaluative* by listing the scales which have high loadings on it" (p. 36). It is hardly surprising that common sense should be preoccupied with classifying contingencies according to whether they are advantageous or disadvantageous, friendly or hostile, relative to the interests of the individual concerned. Nor is it surprising that such evaluations should be thought incompatible with scientific objectivity. The fact that value judgments are part of the data and explanatory resources of both psychology and the social sciences generally has sometimes been advanced as grounds for exempting these disciplines from the demands of scientific objectivity in this respect; but there seems to be no rational justification for that view. Though it is not restricted to folk psychology, evaluation is a feature of common sense, not of language in general as is nominalization. There is, therefore, no reason why it should not be eliminated in order to achieve an entirely objective descriptive account for the purposes of science; and if it can be eliminated for these purposes, then it should be. That, of course, is a value judgment; but it is a metascientific value judgment, not a scientific description.

Assigning a Truth Value to the Content of Other People's Cognitive Attitudes

A similarly anthropocentric feature peculiar to folk psychology is the systematic evaluation of the content of other people's cognitive attitudes and judgments from the standpoint of the speaker. This is illustrated by the fact, well known to conceptual analysts[2] and only now being painfully rediscovered by other philosophers, that the difference between saying *Joe knows it is going to rain* and *Joe thinks it is going to rain* does not entail any difference in Joe's state of mind in the two cases. In saying *Joe knows it is going to rain*, the speaker endorses Joe's opinion as the correct view. In saying *Joe thinks it is going to rain*, she allows that Joe may be mistaken. Once this point is appreciated, we are compelled to confront what to many psychologists is the uncomfortable conclusion that there is, to say the least, a very big question mark over the propriety of using the verb 'know,' its derivatives, and other verbs of cognitive achievement drawn from folk psychology in a scientific context.

The Need for a Scapegoat: The Myth of the Single Cause and the Freedom of the Will

The theory of the causation of behavior embedded within folk psychology is distorted by the need (intelligible in terms of the psychology of the anger response to frustration and aversive stimulation) to pin the blame on a particular individual when anything goes wrong. This results in a reluctance to allow that causes in general and the causes of behavior in particular are multiple, and an insistence on the freedom of the human will and human responsibility, the doctrine that the individual is the sole cause of his or her actions. This is one part of the critique of folk psychology from the scientific standpoint that psychologists of all persuasions have been most ready to take on board. Unfortunately, they have not always appreciated the strength of the scientific case against right-wing libertarianism.

The Myth of Universal Linguistic Control

Folk psychology is deeply infected with the often counterfactual assumption or, as it sometimes is, the blatant fiction that behavior is controlled by the agent's self-directed talk. This fiction of the linguistic control of behavior is manifested in the widespread practice whereby the 'content' of a psychological state is characterized by means of an embedded *oratio obliqua* sentence (i.e., a quotation of what the agent might be expected to say) in the direct object position after a psychological verb. Sentences that are said by philosophers to ascribe a 'propositional attitude' to an agent are of this kind. Unless you believe with Fodor (1975) that both animal and human behavior are controlled by what he calls "the language of thought," explaining the behavior of an animal by quoting what it might say, if only it could talk, must be regarded as a gross anthropomorphism, wholly unacceptable in a scientific theory. Even in the case of the behavior of adult humans, this way of talking greatly exaggerates the extent to which behavior is subject to linguistic control, while creating a biologically unacceptable gulf between human and animal behavior. It is these considerations, I suggest, that justify the behaviorists' repudiation of what they describe as the 'mentalism' of folk psychology. The alternatives they have proposed thus far may leave something to be desired; but that an alternative is needed is difficult to gainsay. The eliminative materialist's proposal that we should rely on neuroscience to provide us with an alternative language is not satisfactory, in my view. Folk psychology operates at a much more molar level of analysis than that of the neuron and its synapses where neuroscience is at home. If both folk psychology and behaviorism are dismissed, there are no conceptual resources with which to describe the properties of a simple neural network, let alone a system as complex as the avian or mammalian brain.

The Use of Simile in Phenomenological Descriptions of Private Experience

Descriptions of the so-called 'phenomenological properties' of private experiences, i.e., those properties that the subject ascribes to her experiences which are over and above the thoughts and emotional reactions they provoke take the form of a simile: "It was as if _____ were the case." Though unavoidable, similes such as this are deeply alien to standard scientific conceptions of how descriptions of events should be constructed. This, however, I regard as the least damaging of the criticisms of folk psychology we have considered. This is because phenomenological descriptions of private experience do not, contrary to popular belief, provide either the data or the concepts on the basis of which folk psychological explanations of behavior are constructed. Their only apparent function in every-

day life, apart from that of soliciting sympathy for the speaker's predicament and making an application for the exemption from normal obligations provided by admission to what Parsons (1951/1953) calls the "sick role," is to allow the listener to imagine to some extent what it must have been like to have had the experience the speaker is describing. From the standpoint of scientific psychology they would seem to provide a kind of "inside view" of some as yet unidentified part of the process in the brain that is controlling the behavior of the speaker. But because they remain unidentified, we can only speculate as to what part they play in the control of behavior. From the standpoint of the neuropsychologist, the fact that all descriptions of private experience take the form of a simile is only a small part of the wider problem of how to integrate evidence from the verbal utterances of the self-reporting subject with the expanding body of anatomical, physiological, biochemical, and objective behavioral evidence. Indeed, as I argued in my paper "Is Consciousness a Brain Process?" (Place, 1956), once we recognize that phenomenological descriptions invariably take the form of a simile,

> we realize that there is nothing that the introspecting subject says about his conscious experiences which is inconsistent with anything the physiologist might want to say about the brain processes which cause him to describe the environment and his consciousness of that environment in the way he does. (p. 50)

ENDNOTES

1. The writer has made two hitherto unpublished attempts (Place, 1988; 1991) to construct a link between conclusions derived from the conceptual analysis of folk psychological language and Broadbent's "information-flow diagram for the organism" (Broadbent, 1958, Figure 7, p. 299), as revised in his *Decision and Stress* (Broadbent, 1971, pp. 7–16). Though these links are, I believe, still valid, their diagrammatic representation has been overtaken by more recent developments in the rapidly evolving fields of neuropsychology, artificial intelligence, and cognitive science.

2. That you cannot say that someone knows something if what they claim to know is false has been known to philosophers since it was first pointed out by Plato in the *Theaitetos*. But the full significance of this discovery was not appreciated until Ryle (1949) pointed out that the primary function of what we are here calling 'folk psychology' is to enable us to talk about *other people* rather than to talk about ourselves. For in the first person case, the difference between *I know* and *I believe* is indeed a

psychological distinction, a matter of the strength of the speaker's conviction of the truth and defensibility of the statement the phrase introduces.

REFERENCES

Broadbent, D. E. (1958). *Perception and communication*. Oxford: Pergamon.

Broadbent, D. E. (1971). *Decision and stress*. London: Academic Press.

Fodor, J. A. (1975). *The language of thought*. New York: Crowell.

Frege, G. (1884/1950). *Die Grundlagen der Arithmetik: eine logische-mathematische Untersuchung über den Begriff der Zahl*. Breslau. English trans. J. L. Austin, *The foundations of arithmetic: A logico-mathematical enquiry into the concept of number*. New York: Philosophical Library.

Garfinkel, H. (1964/1967). Studies in the routine grounds of everyday activities. *Social Problems, 11*, 225–250. Reprinted with revisions in H. Garfinkel, *Studies in ethnomethodology* (chap. 2). Englewood Cliffs, N. J. : Prentice-Hall.

Medlin, B. (1967). Ryle and the mechanical hypothesis. In C. F. Presley (Ed.), *The mind-brain identity theory* (VI, pp. 94–150). St. Lucia, Queensland: University of Queensland Press.

Osgood, C. E., Suci, G. J., & Tannenbaum, P. H. (1957). *The measurement of meaning*. Urbana: University of Illinois Press.

Parsons, T. (1951/1953). Illness and the role of the physician: A sociological perspective. *American Journal of Orthopsychiatry, 21*, 452–460. Reprinted in C.

Kluckhohn and H. A. Murray (Eds.), *Personality in nature, society and culture* (2nd ed., pp. 609–617). New York: Knopf.

Place, U. T. (1954/1964). The concept of heed. *British Journal of Psychology, 45*, 234–255. Reprinted in D. F. Gustafson (Ed.), *Essays in philosophical psychology* (pp. 206–226). New York: Doubleday.

Place, U. T. (1956). Is consciousness a brain process? *British Journal of Psychology, 47*, 44–50.

Place, U. T. (1988). Consciousness as an information processing system. Paper presented to the Inaugural Symposium of the Mind-Body Group, Second Annual Conference of the History and Philosophy of Psychology Section of the British Psychological Society, University of Leeds, April.

Place, U. T. (1991). From syntax to reality: The picture theory of meaning. Paper presented to conference on "Footprints of the Brain in the Syntax of Natural Language," Neurosciences Institute, New York, February.

Place, U. T. (1992). The role of the ethnomethodological experiment in the empirical investigation of social norms, and its application to conceptual analysis. *Philosophy of the Social Sciences, 22*, 461–474.

Rorty, R. (1965). Mind-brain identity, privacy, and categories. *The Review of Metaphysics, xix*, 24–54.

Ryle, G. (1949). *The concept of mind*. London: Hutchinson.

Wittgenstein, L. (1953). *Philosophical investigations* (Trans. G. E. M. Anscombe). Oxford: Blackwell.

Wittgenstein, L. (1958). *The blue and brown books*. Oxford: Blackwell.

On the Necessary Survival of Folk Psychology

Graham Richards

Paul Churchland (1988) and others have recently claimed that Folk Psychology will, or could, be replaced by a new psychological language drawn directly from the scientific findings of cognitive neuroscience. The thesis of the present paper is that this argument is unsound. First, Folk Psychology is not, as the Churchland case assumes, a crude "theory" at all, in fact "theorizing" is one of the things it enables us to do—"theorizing" itself being a folk psychological term. Second, the truth of propositions about phenomenological experience is established in a different way from that of propositions about physical facts, even though they share much of the same vocabulary. Third, the use in everyday life of a language such as Churchland envisages is quite unclear.

CHURCHLAND'S THESIS

The primary target of this chapter is Paul Churchland's *Matter and Consciousness* (revised edition of 1988). In this (most clearly in the final three pages) Paul Churchland makes quite explicit an ambition to replace something he calls "Folk Psychology" by a novel cognitive neuroscientific "Psychology." Cognitive neuroscience is cast in a Copernican or Newtonian role as marking the point where science at last transcends prescientific conceptual frameworks in construing the psychological. A truly scientific psychological understanding has at last made its debut, which will involve the rejection of such primitive folk psychological concepts as 'belief,' 'desire,' 'knowledge,' 'memory,' 'wish,' 'idea,' etc., and their replacement by terms that accurately denote neurological realities. As Churchland paints the prospects before us, cognitive neuroscience will, in the foreseeable future, enhance our introspective perceptual skills to a point where we will be able to refer directly to the neurological events really taking place (a skill akin, in his account, to the skills of a musical connoisseur in identifying the technical features of a musical performance).

No more, it seems, will we say things like "It is my belief that you are profoundly mistaken," "I have a vivid memory of my fifth birthday party," or even "You have some strange ideas"—no, and I quote,

> glucose consumption in the forebrain, dopamine levels in the thalamus, the coding vectors in specific neural pathways, resonances in the *n*th layer of the peristratial cortex, and countless other neurophysiological and neurofunctional niceties, could be moved into the objective focus of our introspective discrimination and conceptual recognition. (Churchland, 1988, p. 180)

which would, presumably, yield such locutions as, respectively, "There is a major lack of congruence between our neural coding vectors on this one," "A strong resonance in my 8th peristratial cortex level is reactivating an earlier biostate with a cognitive temporal verbal coding of 'fifth birthday party,'" and "You've got some abnormal levels of glucose consumption in your forebrain."

FOUR THINGS TO BE DISTINGUISHED AND HOW THEY ARE CONFLATED[1]

In order to analyze what I think is going on here I wish to differentiate the following:

a. Folk psychology in the subject matter sense, that which our discipline is in fact largely concerned with understanding. The term "folk" is actually fairly redundant here.
b. Folk psychological language ("fpl" henceforth). This is the entire corpus of terms and expressions we use when discoursing about (a) (and indeed animal psychology too) in everyday life.
c. Folk Psychology with a capital P. Theories about psychological matters deploying (b). One should note that "theorizing" is itself an fpl term (and indeed one peculiar to Western culture). I use this to differentiate the analysis and explanation of psychological matters from other activities such as expression, evaluation, and description (plus illocutionary performances that may relate to them such as insulting or seducing) in which fpl is also used.
d. Psychology. The discipline, developed over the last 150 years, which seeks a scientific theoretical understanding of (a). It arose for several reasons, the two most relevant here, leaving aside the social contextual factors, being, first, the perceived limitations of engaging in (c)-type activities within fpl terms (on such grounds as Ullin Place has identified), and second the advent of exciting new concepts and theories in areas as varied as evolutionary thought, statistics, and computing.

The difficulties generated by the Churchland project arise in large part from a failure to clarify the relationships between these. Specifically:

1. (a) and (b) have been too readily differentiated. It has been generally assumed that there is an enduring subject matter, "the psychological" existing in itself, as it were, behind the language; fpl is thus construed as itself consisting of attempts at theorizing about this subject matter. As I argue in my book *On Psychological Language* (Richards, 1989), this is mistaken. Insofar as we can have any

communicable access at all to the psychological it is in terms of psychological language. To a large, perhaps even total extent, therefore, (a) and (b) are operationally synonymous. At the very least (b) is the level at which (a) is most patently accessible. Culturally, it is fpl itself that defines and even creates the psychological phenomena our discipline purports to study, which evaluates them, governs their roles in both our private and collective lives, and so on. Thus, (b) is, at a minimum, part of (a). Talking and thinking about the psychological is a psychological process in its own right and even if this is ostensibly about phenomena other than thinking and talking, these phenomena are only knowable insofar as they are thought and talked about—and this thought and talk can only be conducted in terms of psychological language.

2. (b) and (c) have been conflated. Churchland and others write as if (c) activities are the primary function of fpl. This is clearly not the case. As just indicated, (c) activities are something fpl provides us with the resources for engaging in. It is not in itself an instance of (c). That is demonstrated by the fact that within fpl terms a variety of folk Psychological theories can and have been produced (e.g., the majority of the Psychological accounts to be found in eighteenth-century philosophy). To call (b) a theory is like calling algebra a theorem. This point must be stressed—fpl concepts do not *per se* constitute a theory identifiable as "Folk Psychology"—a supposedly crude rival to "Cognitive Psychology." It is people, not concepts, who create theories. One might concede the Whorfian point that fpl constrains the kinds of theories formulable within it, but the latitude of variation available remains vast. My immediate point, though, is that fpl is not used only, or even primarily, for (c) purposes. Critics of (c) should therefore focus on specific instances of (c) rather than on fpl itself, except insofar as it figures in such specific instances.

3. (c) and (d) have been overdifferentiated. Churchland, oddly, believes folk Psychology has been static for 2000 years, even though Plato spoke Greek and he speaks American English. In fact, fpl changes continually, and (c) along with it, more obviously by expansion due to addition than by obsolescence (a point I will return to). Neologisms from (d) are readily deployed in (c) and thence enter (b), e.g., 'unconscious,' 'repressed,' 'neurotic,' 'I. Q.,' 'conditioned,' 'programmed,' 'super-ego,' 'extravert,' 'compulsive,' etc. Note here

- that fpl terms can persist as useable for all kinds of purposes other than (c), thus becoming obsolete for (c) purposes will not eliminate them
- that (d) terms incorporated into (c) are then available for non-(c) purposes (this is a major difference from the situation in the sciences—e.g., 'phlogiston' had no role outside of chemical theory)

4. Insofar as (b) changes, including changes derived from (d) via (c), so too, for all intents and purposes, does (a), creating an intrinsically reflexive situation that Psychologists, including Churchland, fail to confront. This has peculiarly disturbing implications because, coupled with the previous points, it implies that under the guise of scientifically explaining the psychological the Churchland program is actually to dismantle it. He is in the odd position of construing his subject matter as a rival to be defeated. To see science as "conquering Nature" was a common cliché, of course, but Psychology conquering psychology is something else. This is not to say that our discipline can or should not engage in generating new (d)-type systems, rather that it should acknowledge the reflexivity of what it is doing—that it is actively and creatively engaging in psychological change, not approaching some final truth about a hitherto less well-comprehended objective subject matter—"the psychological." Now this dilemma is deep-rooted—whether there is an objectively existing fixed subject matter, "the psychological," scientifically studiable by Psychology, or whether the discipline's goal is to change its subject matter. But new psychological ideas, whatever their source, actually *are* instances of change in the subject matter, since verbally encoded psychological concepts must themselves be included under the heading of 'psychological phenomena.' Psychology has always striven to have it both ways, since the former position is necessary for scientific status and the latter necessary for giving the discipline a marketable social role. Rarely, however, is the bind quite so patent as in this case.

WHAT IS WRONG WITH THE CHURCHLAND STORY?

How have the Churchlands (Paul and Patricia being of one mind on the issue) got themselves into this fix? Partly from overreliance on the dramatic rhetorical gambit of casting opponents as neo-Luddites, fearfully clinging to obsolete modes of thinking, blind to the life-enhancing possibilities of that "expansion of introspective consciousness" awaiting them if they will but throw in their lot with cognitive neuroscience (which, curiously, thereby acquires a kind of psychedelic character). I believe Paul Churchland's account is seriously, even fatally, flawed in several ways. The primary misapprehension, one shared with Stephen Stich (1983), is that folk Psychology is a theory. This I have already questioned. I do not deny that there are folk Psychological theories of various kinds, nor even that they generally lack scientific rigor (if they were not so lacking, Psychology would have been unnecessary); but that is not what fpl, as such, is primarily concerned with. Thus to aspire to a wholesale conversion of fpl into neuroscientific terms is to indulge in pure fantasy. It is nonetheless worthwhile elaborating this somewhat further. Neither the Churchlands nor Stich have actually grasped, apparently, the sheer scope of fpl, ranging as it does from basic sensory property and behavioral terms ('bright,' 'hard,' 'warm,' 'hold,' 'grasp,' 'point out,' 'touch,' 'handle') via natural objects and phenomena to modern technical expressions ('let off steam,' 'in top gear,' 'high-flier,' 'on autopilot,' etc.). Hankering after fulfilling William James's hope for a Psychological Newton, they seem to overlook the fact that fpl has already had its Sophocles, Kalidasa, Shakespeare, Dostoevski, and George Eliot. The analogy with the physical sciences simply will not hold. Pliny, Lucretius, Galen, and Roger Bacon simply have not remained live influences in modern science to whom all modern scientists respond with awe. The great fpl users, by contrast, retain their power despite the obsolescence of their psychological vocabulary. The Churchlands and Stich focus almost exclusively on a handful of basic terms such as 'belief,' 'idea,' 'memory,' 'thought,' and 'wish,' which figure commonly in folk Psychological explanations. If you actually study, as a variety of psychologists have occasionally done (including Dennis Bromley in a book called *Personality Description in Everyday Language*, 1977), the psychological language people actually use, a picture emerges of us ranging across every nook and cranny of the cosmos in quest of expressions that will satisfactorily encode the nuances of our phenomenological experience. The idea that all this is potentially superfluous and replaceable by a restricted technical vocabulary

devised for handling brain functioning would be difficult, in all honesty, to take seriously were Churchland not so unapologetically unambiguous on the matter, and had not American Psychology been here before in the person of J. B. Watson, whose alternative vocabulary would have consisted exclusively of learning theory jargon.

THE REAL LESSON OF HISTORY

This easy historical analogy between modern cognitive science's position and those of Astronomy in Copernicus's time or Physics in Newton's cannot stand. If we wish to invoke history, let us look at cases nearer to home. One closely resembling the present situation is the influx of physiological terms into fpl during the late seventeenth and eighteenth centuries as a result of advances in physiology which, in their day, were no less momentous than those of the present century. This augmented existing notions of 'high' and 'low spirits' and 'the humors' with new terms, such as 'irritable,' 'liverish,' 'the vapors,' 'sensitive,' 'sensible,' and 'nervous,' and generally led people to account for and express their psychological states in terms of clogged pores, taut nerves, the viscosity of their blood, and so forth. Indeed, they became quite expert at introspectively diagnosing such, to us, mythical physiological conditions.

The lesson of this closer historical analogy is rather different from that which Churchland would have us draw from the Copernicus and Newton analogies. Indeed, it suggests that we may well expect cognitive neuroscientific terms to similarly enter fpl, and folk already talk of people 'being programmed' and of 'imbalances between left and right hemispheres.' The things to note, though, are first that we *still* use 'irritable,' 'nervous,' and 'sensitive,' even though the physiological framework is defunct (we also use 'low-spirited,' 'sanguine,' 'splenetic,' and 'melancholic' from even earlier physiological models). Second, such terms did not permanently oust others, far less monopolize the fpl vocabulary. True, some have a distinct period flavor, but this is no drawback, for it is precisely such nuancing that can provide us with the resources for subtle fpl discourse.

CHURCHLAND'S TREATMENT OF MEANING

This Copernican rhetorical pose is not, however, the only misleading factor in play. Another is

Churchland's curious treatment of the issue of meaning. He spends some time explaining why he favors a network theory of meaning, and most of this I am quite happy with. But while espousing a network theory of meaning, Churchland fails to notice the special considerations applying to the meaning of psychological terms (notably those, related to the private language argument, requiring that it be physiomorphically generated). It is difficult in general to reconcile his insights into the nature of meaning and the theory-ladenness of perception with the rumbustious positivist temper of his conclusions. On the one hand he agrees that meanings are governed by networks, socially maintained by users, *and* agrees that perception and observation statements are theory-laden, while on the other hand he claims that the language of cognitive neuroscience provides a univalent, unambiguous means of directly referring to psychological reality, replacing prescientific speech by speech that states objectively what is really happening. This has echoes of nothing so much as Bishop Wilkins's 1668 *Essay Towards a Real Character and a Philosophical Language*, which sought a somewhat similar end, a language and indeed script, which would unambiguously and directly picture reality. Another historical echo is his view of self-consciousness as quite literally a mode of perception in which we may train ourselves up to high levels of expertise—this surely has some serious affinities with Wundtian introspection. Ironically, the same modern linguistic philosophy that has exposed the fallacious nature of both of these also underpins Churchland's own network account of meaning.

AN EPISTEMOLOGICAL OBJECTION TO CHURCHLAND'S POSITION

This raises a further central and, for Churchland, problematic feature of psychological language. Even when couched in physiological terms, the truth of psychological propositions is determined by different criteria from those governing physical-world propositions, even though the vocabulary may be the same. While it is conceivable that "I love you" will be replaced by propositions such as "the stimulus configuration you have established in my LTM has acquired strong hippocampal connections," the criteria determining their truth as psychological propositions will continue to differ from those determining their truth as physiological propositions. The former are determined by interpersonal social processes, including meaning negotiation itself (which a network theory of meaning is committed to), the latter are in principle determined by physiological enquiry within a scientific theoretical framework of meaning on which the users are likely to have a provisional consensus. As I explain in *On Psychological Language*, negotiating whether a statement is to be interpreted as one or the other is often precisely what is going on, e.g., does "It's very hot in here" more appropriately elicit "Turn off the radiator" or "You're just looking for an excuse to leave" (or, leaving it open for one more move, "Why not take that sweater off?" holding out the possibility that the statement was a seduction ploy)? Furthermore, the meanings of many psychological utterances cannot conceivably be reduced to events within the brain, since they are about managing, expressing, and indeed theorizing on social and interpersonal relations. It is pertinent to note here that one obvious respect in which fpl often differs in its function from scientific Psychology, at any rate overtly, is in its pervasive concern with evaluation, including moral evaluation. This is closely bound up with its role as a framework for managing interpersonal relations, which includes expression of attitudes, and defining, identifying, and evaluating the kinds of interpersonal relationships that are possible. It is within such "games" that fpl usage is perhaps most often employed.

But what Churchland promises in the final pages of his book is something quite the opposite to this, namely that psychological language could indeed conceivably consist of univalent physiological propositions, referring "objectively" to what we introspectively *and correctly* perceive (quite literally) to be the neurological, neurochemical, or whatever events happening in our brain. This, incidently, would presumably include being able to physiologically specify the events that constituted this enhanced introspective ability itself; but I will leave this infinitely regressive argument to one side. One puzzle about this, of course, is what on earth the point of such a mode of discourse would actually be. What functions currently served by fpl would be better served by talking in this fashion? If, however, it is argued that it serves new functions, then it might augment, but would not replace, existing fpl.

CONCLUSION

In conclusion then, folk Psychological language, and pragmatic folk Psychological theorizing, do not represent some primitive precursor to a scientific account of the psychological. Rather, they are both source and subject matter of such scientific accounts as we produce and the final repository of any widely valuable insights such accounts achieve. Fpl is not unchanging. It is very much a living medium in which we conduct our lives. It positively feeds on novelty, unsurprisingly since much of its job is, after all, to enable us to manage environmental and social novelty. As brain-language acquires a wider circulation, so its vocabulary may partially enter fpl, and I doubt not that neuroscience will discover much about the brain of sufficient general import to do likewise. But let us get things the right way around. It is not fpl's appropriateness for scientific purposes that will seal the cultural fate of the language of folk Psychology, but its appropriateness for folk Psychological purposes that will seal that of scientific Psychology. Fpl—a rich heterogeneous language drawn from all areas of human experience over many millennia—will necessarily continue its Protean career for as long as we wish to talk to one another about ourselves.

ENDNOTE

1. I have, throughout, followed my usual policy of capitalizing "Psychology" (and cognate terms) to denote its usage in a disciplinary sense and using the lowercase to denote its usage in a subject matter sense. Thus "child Psychology" might refer to the work of Piaget, while "child psychology" would refer to the way children thought and behaved.

REFERENCES

Bromley, D. B. (1977). *Personality description in everyday language*. Chichester: Wiley.
Churchland, P. M. (1988). *Matter and consciousness* (rev. ed.). Cambridge, MA: MIT Press.
Richards, G. D. (1989). *On psychological language*. London: Routledge and Kegan Paul.
Stich, S. (1983). *From folk psychology to cognitive science: The case against belief*. Cambridge, MA: MIT Press.
Wilkins, J. (1668). *An essay towards a real character and a philosophical language*. London: S. Gellibrand & J. Martyn.

Folk Psychology and Its Implications for Cognitive Science: Discussion

Elizabeth R. Valentine

If inclined to Rorty's (1965) view that folk psychology is little better than witchcraft, one may be tempted to suggest that time devoted to its discussion might more profitably be spent debating the language appropriate to scientific psychology or cognitive science, a point to which I shall return. In fact, I suspect that the label 'cognitive science' licenses, or at least encourages, discussion of folk psychology. Rather than present detailed comments on the excellent set of papers presented here, I shall raise some general issues and in so doing attempt to draw threads together. There seem to me to be at least three important issues:

1. What *is* folk psychology?
2. What are its strengths and weaknesses from the point of view of scientific psychology?
3. What is the relation of folk psychology to scientific psychology, and in particular what differences are there between them?

WHAT IS FOLK PSYCHOLOGY?

It can be quite difficult to find out. Most of the authors assume it is already known and concrete examples are fairly thin on the ground. Smith's paper (this chapter, p. 256) has the merit of providing a definition:

> Folk psychology is part of common sense. It is that part we use to make sense of our own and other people's words and deeds. We rely on it to predict what people will do and say on particular occasions, and to make them intelligible even when what they do and say surprises us.

In addition, he gives the following concrete examples:

> 'she did it because she wanted to hurt him'; 'he went to the house because he believed she'd be there'; 'she stood up because she wanted to leave.'

And in a quotation from Dennett (1987):

> 'wants to visit China' or 'expects noodles for supper.'

Richards (this chapter, p. 271) offers us:

> 'It is my belief that you are profoundly mistaken'; 'I have a vivid memory of my fifth birthday party'…'You have some strange ideas.'

The main point I wish to make with respect to these is that they include very different types of statements, so that answers to questions one may wish to raise about folk psychology will vary accordingly. Thus, we may have descriptions of mental states or sensory contents (though Place, this chapter, p. 269, claims that phenomenological descriptions of private experiences do not provide either the data or the concepts on the basis of which folk psychological explanations of behavior are constructed); descriptions of the process of behavior (e.g., how one sets about carrying out a task); or *par excellence* explanations or reasons for behavior. In accord with my analysis of introspection (Valentine, 1978), the validity of these may decrease from the first to the last. Philosophers have tended to focus attention on beliefs and desires, a Fodorian "language of thought," based on the computational model of mind because they have tended to gloss folk psychology as propositional attitudes (Greenwood, 1992). Social psychology is largely ignored, whereas the primary explanatory constructs in folk psychology are generally emotions, motives, and opinions (Dennett's "linguistically infected" beliefs). I agree with Patricia Churchland (1986) that not all mental life is a

matter of sentence crunching (except perhaps for philosophers) and that the linguistic control of behavior is often a fiction. Neither am I convinced, contrary to the claims of utility theory, that people generally do what they believe will achieve their fondest wish. But, as Greenwood (1992) argues, the inaccuracy or inadequacy of explanations advanced by folk psychology does not entail the rejection of the ontology of contentful psychological states; likewise, the inadequacy of sentential theories of cognitive processing does not entail the inadequacy of scientifically developed forms of folk psychological explanations of behavior, e.g., as advanced by contemporary social psychology. Similarly, McGinn (1989) has distinguished the ontology of persons, attitudes, and propositional contents as independent aspects of folk psychology with respect to its theoretical viability.

STRENGTHS AND WEAKNESSES OF FOLK PSYCHOLOGY FROM THE POINT OF VIEW OF SCIENTIFIC PSYCHOLOGY

In everyday life the main function of folk psychology is to give an account of others' behavior. This is reminiscent of Humphrey's (1983) view that the function of self-consciousness is to enable social animals empathically to make sense of the behavior of other members of the group. For science, folk psychology could provide preliminary hypotheses, as in the method of *Verstehen*, by means of empathic understanding, which then need to be tested by more objective empirical or experimental methods. Folk psychology helps to pick out or fix the reference of the states in which we are interested (Smith, this chapter, p. 260). Conceptual analysis may provide important insights, as in the analysis of mental activity verbs, e.g., Ryle's 'heed' concepts (Place, 1954); intensional statements such as those containing the words 'imagine' or 'see'; and the subtle language of emotion and feeling (Place, this chapter, p. 267). Some scientific psychology is refined folk psychology: Greenwood (1992) cites Latané and Darley's (1970) explanation of bystander apathy as an example of the replacement of one folk psychological explanation by another.

On the other hand, folk psychology can be misleading. Place (this chapter, pp. 267–269) carefully details six respects in which this may be so. Why are we misled? Chater and Oaksford (1990) suggest that folk psychology is a paradigm in which we are indoctrinated from birth. Greenwood (1992) cites data from Leslie (1988) suggesting that children engage in folk psychology from about 3 to 4 years of age, although this claim has been disputed (Wellman, 1988).

Is the fact that we think we have a ready-made language just the respect in which psychology differs from other sciences? Is it different from other sciences? Should it be? A technical language has never really been established: For reasons which we need not discuss here, the behaviorist language didn't catch on. It seems to me that we should be considering the sort of language(s) that scientific psychology requires. This issue was not really addressed by the participants; Chater and Oaksford (this chapter, pp. 246–252)) were plentiful in their criticisms of folk psychology without offering any positive suggestions as to alternatives. Some might be inferred by contrast with the dangers exposed by Place (this chapter, pp. 267–269). For example, the warning about reification ("nominalization") suggests that the focus should be on processes rather than entities (though capacities and competences might be allowed). Should we aim for the expression of generalities by means of mathematical formulas rather than verbal propositions? Perhaps the fault has been to be too atomistic and insufficiently relational and holistic:

> A theoretically adequate social psychology will only be developed when it embraces a relational conception of the psychological states, one that recognizes the social embeddedness of human emotions, motives and opinions. (Greenwood, 1992)

Or the complaint may be that what is missing from theories of personality is the person (Paranjpe, 1993). Or, more fundamentally, that a dialectical rather than a causal model should be pursued.

RELATION OF FOLK PSYCHOLOGY TO SCIENTIFIC PSYCHOLOGY

This issue was ably addressed by Smith (1993). As we have already noted, in some areas there may be a partial overlap between folk psychology and scientific psychology. There is also an important sense in which folk psychology is part of the subject matter of scientific psychology (Chater & Oaksford, this chapter, p. 253; Goldman, 1993): Scientific psychology has to give an account of folk psychology, among other things. I consider work on attribution and locus of control, and in particular the differences in attributions given for one's own behavior compared with that of others, to be cases in point. It is part of the task of scientific psychology to give an account of the determinants and consequences of engaging in folk psychology. Both folk psychology and scientific psychology primarily aim to give an account of others' behavior (a point that Place (this chapter, p. 269) reminds us was originally made by Ryle, 1949), though by extension it applies also to one's own. The question thus arises as to whether folk psychology just does what scientific psychology does, but badly. Would people be better off using scientific psychology? Fontana (1992) makes the point that, since we are so often mistaken in our attributions of other people's behavior, we would be better off using folk psychology a lot less than we do, simply observing rather than interpreting.

However, it appears that there are a number of important differences between folk psychology and scientific psychology, first, with respect to functions. Folk psychology is a framework for managing interpersonal relationships, and thus often has moral, theological, or epistemological overtones and purposes (Richards, this chapter, p. 274). Wilkes (1981) and Gergen (1989) have argued that it serves sociolinguistic functions such as excusing and entreating. The fact that folk psychological terms continue in use after any scientific backing has ceased (Richards, this chapter, p. 273) also confirms the hypothesis that it serves a different function or functions from scientific psychology. It has often been argued that they have different criteria: pragmatic utility in the case of folk psychology, whereas scientific psychology claims to be true in some sense. This view of folk psychology is reminiscent of Rycroft's (1966) suggestion with regard to psychoanalysis, that it is simply a language for making symptoms intelligible rather than a scientific theory that is empirically testable.

Folk psychology and scientific psychology also differ with respect to their scope. The former is primarily concerned with social and personality psychology, whereas the latter deals with the whole range of behavior, including cognitive and physiological aspects.

> The sorts of linguistically informed psychological states that are posited by explanatory folk psychology are complex states of *persons*: complex states of organisms with a certain developmental history, linguistic competence and social position. (Greenwood, 1992)

This is in contrast to the sorts of basic representational states that are the subject matter of competing theories of cognitive processing—states of the brain with representational properties (Greenwood, 1992).

Another important difference is that folk psychology is generally concerned with the explanation of particular actions of individuals and is hence idiographic, context-sensitive, and normative (McGinn, 1979), whereas scientific psychology is concerned with general competence in the species. It is for this important reason that Russell (1984) argues that folk psychological explanations can never form part of scientific psychology.

Folk psychological statements are subjective ('egocentric'), value-laden (Place, this chapter, p. 268), and vague (Fodor's "granny psychology"); whereas those of scientific psychology purport to be objective, value-free, and precise. I suspect that, *contra* Place (this chapter, p. 264), folk psychology is subject to both individual and cultural differences (consider, for example, cross-cultural differences in the relative importance attached to individual and group processes, or the aboriginal Australian language in which everything is expressed in the passive voice; Dixon, 1980).

Finally, folk psychology is based on a much more limited perspective, what one is conscious of; thus, belief in free will, for example, may be the result of being aware of the consequences, but not the determinants, of behavior. I believe that Nisbett and Wilson (1977) have convincingly shown that we are frequently unaware of the causes of our behavior. Scientific psychology, on the other hand, is much more broadly based, on the results of behavioral experiments aimed at elucidating the causal network; it is empirically tested and supported, and replicated by peers. It includes more levels of description: Dennett's (1971) physical and design as well as intentional stances.

I conclude, therefore, that folk psychology differs from scientific psychology in its functions, scope, criteria, and evidential base.

REFERENCES

Chater, N., & Oaksford, M. (1990). Logicist cognitive science and the falsity of common-sense theories. Technical report no. UWB-CNU-TR-90-4, Cognitive Neurocomputation Unit, Department of Psychology, University of Wales, Bangor.

Churchland, P. S. (1986). *Neurophilosophy*. Cambridge, MA: MIT Press.

Dennett, D. C. (1971). Intentional systems. *Journal of Philosophy*, 68, 87–106.

Dennett, D. (1987). *The intentional stance*. Cambridge, MA: Bradford/MIT Press.

Dixon, R. M. W. (1980). *The languages of Australia*. Cambridge: Cambridge University Press.

Fontana, D. (1992). *Know who you are, Be what you want*. London: Fontana.

Gergen, K. J. (1989). Warranting voice and the elaboration of the self. In J. Shotter and K. J. Gergen (Eds.), *Texts of identity*. Newbury Park, CA: Sage.

Goldman, A. I. (1993). The psychology of folk psychology. *Behavioral and Brain Sciences*, 16, 15–28.

Greenwood, J. D. (1992). Against eliminative materialism: From folk psychology to *Völkerpsychologie*. *Philosophical Psychology*, 5, 349–367.

Humphrey, N. (1983). *Consciousness regained: Chapters in the development of mind*. Oxford: Oxford University Press.

Latané, B., & Darley, J. M. (1970). *The unresponsive bystander*. New York: Appleton-Century-Crofts.

Leslie, A. M. (1988). Some implications of pretense for mechanisms underlying the child's theory of mind. In J. W. Astington, P. L. Harris, & D. R. Olton (Eds.), *Developing theories of mind*. Cambridge: Cambridge University Press.

McGinn, C. (1979). Action and its explanation. In N. Bolton (Ed.), *Philosophical problems in psychology*. London: Methuen.

McGinn, C. (1989). *Mental content*. Oxford: Blackwell.

Nisbett, R. E., & Wilson, T. de C. (1977). Telling more than we can know: Verbal reports on mental processes. *Psychological Review*, 84, 231–259.

Paranjpe, A. (1993). Is the person missing from theories of personality? In I. Lubek, R. van Hezewijk, G. Pheterson, & C. Tolman (Eds.), *Recent trends in theoretical psychology*, vol. 8. New York: Springer-Verlag.

Place, U. T. (1954). The concept of heed. *British Journal of Psychology*, 45, 234–255.

Rorty, R. (1965). Mind-brain identity theory, privacy, and categories. *Review of Metaphysics, xix*, 24–54.

Russell, J. (1984). *Explaining mental life*. London: Macmillan.

Rycroft, C. (1966). Causes and meaning. In C. Rycroft (Ed.), *Psychoanalysis observed*. London: Constable.

Ryle, G. (1949). *The concept of mind*. London: Hutchinson.

Valentine, E. R. (1978). Perchings and flights: Introspection. In J. Radford and A. Burton (Eds.), *Thinking in perspective*. London: Methuen.

Wellman, H.M. (1988). First steps in the child's theorizing about the mind. In J. W. Astington, P. L. Harris, & D. L. Olton (Eds.), *Developing theories of mind*. Cambridge: Cambridge University Press.

Wilkes, K. V. (1981) Functionalism, psychology and the philosophy of mind. *Philosophical Topics, 12*, 147–167.

PART 4

CLINICAL PSYCHOLOGY AND PHILOSOPHY

In recent years applied psychology has drawn an increased amount of philosophers' attention. Some of this attention might be due to the increased complexities that arise in applied pursuits. For example, epistemological issues can become more of a concern in applied psychology because: (1) typically there are severe limits to the psychologist's ability to view applied phenomena under controlled conditions; and (2) the applied psychologist typically deals with phenomena that are more idiographic. As another example, it is also fair to say that ethical questions are more likely to arise in applied areas than in basic, nonapplied psychology. However, beyond these considerations, metascientific discourse probably takes place concerning applied psychology because of the slow progress of what Meehl (1978) has called "soft psychology." This discourse attempts to understand and remediate the problems impeding satisfactory scientific progress.

However, it has not always been the case that philosophers have concerned themselves with applied psychology. The logical positivists were largely interested in the physical sciences and

when they paid attention to psychology they focused on experimental psychology to help bolster their phenomalist epistemology. One of the first philosophers of science to be concerned about applied psychology was Karl Popper. (This was probably somewhat natural for Popper since he received his doctorate in psychology.) However, Popper's remarks about applied psychology were largely negative—he claimed that Freudian (as well as Adlerian) psychoanalysis was a pseudoscience because it was unfalsifiable:

> Psychoanalysis is a very different case [from Marxism]. It is an interesting psychological metaphysics (and no doubt there is some truth in it, as there is so often in metaphysical ideas), but it never was a science. There may be lots of people who are Freudian or Adlerian cases: Freud himself was clearly a Freudian case, and Adler an Adlerian case. But what prevents their theories from being scientific in the sense here described is, very simply, that they do not exclude any physically possible human behaviour. Whatever anybody may do is, in principle, explicable in Freudian or Adlerian terms...Neither Freud nor Adler excludes any particular person's acting in

any particular way, whatever the outward circumstances. Whether a man sacrificed his life to rescue a drowning child (a case of sublimation) or whether he murdered the child by drowning him (a case of repression) could not possibly be predicted or excluded by Freud's theory; *the theory was compatible with everything that could happen—even without any special immunizing treatment.* (Popper, 1974, p. 985)

This was a serious challenge that was mounted on philosophical grounds. For if psychoanalysis could not be refuted "come what may," then any attempt by a psychologist to test psychoanalysis empirically was misconceived.

More recently, Adolf Grünbaum addressed the evidential credentials of psychoanalysis in his classic, *The Foundations of Psychoanalysis* (1984). *Contra* Popper he claimed that psychoanalysis was falsifiable—e.g., Freud's claim that paranoia is always caused by repressed homosexuality was viewed by Freud himself as having been falsified. However, in his book Grünbaum criticizes the quality of evidence gathered by analysts during therapy sessions, the ability of psychoanalysts to support the causal assertions of the theory by their method of clinical investigation, and the evidence of the effectiveness of its therapy. In "Is Psychoanalysis Viable?" Grünbaum elaborates on these issues and provides a critical response to Gellner's sociopolitical account of the influence of psychoanalysis.

Applied psychology seeks to produce some end. In the next chapter Erwin examines the question of reasonable ways of choosing the goals for psychotherapy. What standards can be used to evaluate these goals? Are goals relative to the particular therapy paradigm and does this relativism result in an incommensurability between schools of psychotherapy? These questions are critical because given the large number of competing psychotherapies (one recent source lists over 400; Beitman, Goldfried, & Norcross, 1989) and given what economists call opportunity costs (doing one thing precludes the opportunity to do another), clients and psychotherapists must ask which therapy has the greatest likelihood of producing positive outcomes. To answer this one must address the question of how we judge the value of a therapeutic outcome for a client and how we judge the likelihood that a certain therapy will produce that outcome. Erwin argues that psychoanalytic outcomes may have severe problems in meeting his proposal for valued therapeutic outcomes and that there is no experimental evidence that psychoanalysis cost-effectively causes these outcomes to occur.

It seems fair to say that psychoanalysis has received the majority of philosophers' attention, particularly when one considers the attention given to it by continental philosophers. However, in the final chapter, O'Donohue and Vass critically examine the epistemology of a more contemporary form of psychotherapy—rational emotive therapy (Ellis, 1977). Rational emotive therapy seeks to remediate certain forms of psychotherapy by teaching clients to think more rationally. Thus, rational emotive therapy is predicated upon an account of what good thinking or rationality actually is—matters that have also been of concern to philosophers. In their paper O'Donohue and Vass question whether Ellis provides a coherent, consistent, and accurate account of rationality. They suggest that if Ellis wants to follow Bartley's pan-critical rationalism then he needs to make changes in his therapeutic methods and his metatherapy claims.

REFERENCES

Beitman, B. D., Goldfried, M. R., & Norcross, J. C. (1989). The movement toward integrating the psychotherapies: An overview. *American Journal of Psychiatry, 146,* 138–147.

Ellis, A. (1977). The basic clinical theory of rational-emotive therapy. In A. Ellis & J. M. Whitely (Eds.), *Theoretical and empirical foundations of rational-emotive therapy* (pp. 33–60). Monterey, CA: Brooks/Cole.

Grünbaum, A. (1984). *The foundations of psychoanalysis.* Berkeley: University of California Press.

Meehl, P. E. (1978). Theoretical risks & tabular asterisks: Sir Karl, Sir Ronald, and the slow progress of soft psychology. *Journal of Consulting and Clinical Psychology, 1,* 806–834

Popper, K. R. (1974). Replies to my critics. In P. A. Schilpp (Ed.), *The philosophy of Karl Popper.* LaSalle, IL: Open Court.

CHAPTER 18

IS PSYCHOANALYSIS VIABLE?

Adolf Grünbaum

The noteworthy "Spécial Freud" issue of *Le Nouvel Observateur* (Numéro 1401, 3–9 Octobre, 1991) featured an article by Catherine David entitled "Pourquoi Freud Est Toujours Vivant." Its thesis is: "Aujourd'hui encore, Sigmund Freud fait mentir allègrement ceux qui annonçaient la mort de sa théorie." Moreover, on the cover page of this issue, this viability is contrasted with the dire fate of Marxism: "Le marxisme s'effondre, la psychoanalyse résiste."

Clearly, a theory may well be viewed with great skepticism in the pertinent professional community while enjoying a great vogue in the culture at large, and conversely. Thus, at least in the United States, we are now witnessing a clear decline of psychoanalysis in several respects: (1) a sharp decrease in the influence of psychoanalytic theory and therapy in departments of psychiatry at universities, (2) a precipitous drop in the number of young candidates applying for training in psychoanalytic institutes, and (3) a likely reduction in the reimbursement of patients undergoing psychoanalysis by health insurance companies and other third-party agencies.[1]

This crisis of professional survival is occurring even as Freudian theory has gained widespread uncritical acceptance in literature and other humanities departments in American universities.[2] Indeed, although psychoanalysis was greeted with unabashed hostility in Roman Catholic circles in the immediate aftermath of World War II,[3] it has since found warm sponsorship even among some prominent members of the Catholic clergy in universities.[4]

My critical work on psychoanalysis has been addressed to its *evidential* merits as a theory and therapy, as well as to the explanatory fruitfulness of its hypotheses.[5] But I have *not* been concerned with the sociopsychological or political causes of its widespread cultural influence.

Such a sociocultural explanation has been offered by the English philosopher and social anthropologist Ernest Gellner.[6] As he tells us (p. 5) his aim "is to offer an account of how, within the span of less than half a century, this [psychoanalytic] system of ideas could conquer so much of the world, at any rate to the extent of becoming the dominant idiom for the discussion of the human personality and of human relations." By contrast, Freud was concerned to explain the *rejection*, sometimes hostile, of psychoanalytic theory and therapy.

Speaking of such opposition, Freud told us in his 1914 "History of the Psychoanalytic Movement":

> ...psychoanalytic theory enabled me to understand this [hostile] attitude in my contemporaries and to see it as a necessary consequence of fundamental analytic premises. If it was true that the set of facts I had discovered were kept from the knowledge of patients themselves by internal resistances of an affective kind, then these resistances would be bound to appear in healthy people too, as soon as some external source confronted them with what was repressed. It was not surprising that they should be able to justify this rejection of my ideas on intellectual grounds though it was actually affective in origin. The same thing happened equally often with patients; the arguments they advanced were the same and were not precisely brilliant. In Falstaff's words, reasons are "as plenty as blackberries." The only difference was that with patients one was in a position to bring pressure to bear on them so as to induce them to get insight into their resistances and overcome them, whereas one had to do without this advantage in dealing with people who were ostensibly healthy. How to compel these healthy people to examine the matter in a cool and scientifically objective spirit was an unsolved problem which was best left to time to clear up. (S. E. 1914, 14:23–24)[7]

In two articles specifically devoted to explaining opposition to psychoanalysis, Freud elaborates on that facet of his 1914 paper. As he sees it, Copernicus's heliocentric theory of the solar system, Darwin's theory of evolution, and his own theory of the unconscious each delivered a great blow to man's narcissism. Of these, he deems the third of these blows "probably the most wounding" (S. E. 1917, 17:141), because it showed that *"the ego is not master in its own house...*No wonder, then, that the ego does not look favourably upon psychoanalysis and obstinately refuses to believe in it" (S. E. 1917, 17:143).

But, in a 1925 follow-up paper, Freud is careful *not* to attribute all dissent from his doctrines to their psychologically threatening content (S. E. 1925, 19:221):

> Thus the strongest resistances to psycho-analysis were not of an intellectual kind but arose from emotional sources. This explained their passionate character as well as their poverty in logic. The situation obeyed a simple formula: men in the mass behaved to psycho-analysis in precisely the same way as individual neurotics under treatment for their disorders. It is possible, however, by patient work to convince these latter individuals that everything happened as we maintained it did:...
>
> If we cast our eyes once again over the various resistances to psycho-analysis that have been enumerated, it is evident that only a minority of them are of the kind which habitually arise against most scientific innovations of any considerable importance. The majority of them are due to the fact that powerful human feelings are hurt by the subject-matter of the theory.

The explanations offered by Gellner for the prevalence of psychoanalytic doctrines pose an interesting question: Does Freud's motivational account of their rejection leave sufficient scope for their triumph in much of our culture, as depicted by Gellner? Gellner himself claims that it does, but I disagree.

As he would have it (p. 2),

> Not only does the [presumed] truth of the [psychoanalytic] ideas themselves exercise a positive attraction, but also, as is well known, the system of ideas also contains, as an integral part of itself, an explanation of the occasional failure of those ideas to secure conviction. The idea of resistance, which leads people in some circumstances to reject the ideas in question, explains the occasional failure or delay of conversion as cogently as the [presumption of the] truth of ideas can explain their eventual success.
>
> In fact, it may even seem to do it a little more cogently: the unconscious forces which, according to the theory, have such a strong hold over us, but which apparently can recognize and fear (even in anticipation and at a distance) the doctrine which understands and may eventually tame them—these forces clearly have every incentive to resist, by all the formidable and elusive hidden means at their disposal, the acceptance of those doctrines. So perhaps the problem facing the historian of psychoanalytic ideas may even be the inverse of that which faced...any historian of a [supposedly] true belief: is he not redundant precisely when attempting to single out the social factors obstructing the recognition of [presumed] truth? Has he not been anticipated by the theory itself? Does not the [purportedly] convincing evidence of the doctrine itself explain, better than anyone else can, its occasional failures? Be that as it may...

Gellner's book is an "endeavor to cope with the interaction of social and psychological causes and of [supposedly] valid reasons" for the theory.

Yet Gellner has overlooked the import of Freud's own aforecited concession (S. E. 1914, 14:24): "How to compel…healthy people to examine the matter [of the validity of psychoanalytic theory] in a cool and scientifically objective spirit was an unsolved problem which was best left to time to clear up." After all, if the resistances to the acceptance of psychoanalysis, among analytic patients and healthy people alike, are so strong that it takes the "pressure" of Freudian treatment to overcome them among the former, how can they have been overcome unaidedly by those who never undergo psychoanalysis and who vastly outnumber the former?

Besides, how does Gellner know that a majority of the numerous adherents of the theory were induced to accept it, because they actually examined the evidence for it and found it cogent, despite their unconscious resistance? And if evidential reasons are as motivationally powerful as Gellner thinks, why do just such reasons—rather than neurotic resistance—not explain the greater part of the opposition to the theory from those who claim that the evidence for it is wanting? It would appear that Gellner's attempt to explain the rejection of psychoanalysis by nonrational, if not irrational factors, while attributing its acceptance to presumedly cogent evidential considerations, envisions a rather utopian scenario. For example, he offers no statistics at all to rule out a quite plausible rival explanation: The theory appealed just emotionally and morally, because it was seen as a liberating gospel, undercutting deeply resented sexual prohibitions, oppressive prudery, and widespread, frustrating hypocrisy.

Therefore, I deny Gellner's contention that his own account of the presumably large-scale acceptance of psychoanalytic theory on the basis of evidence is compatibly complementary to Freud's explanation of the failure of psychoanalysis to command assent.[8]

Indeed, as I have noted elsewhere,[9] Freud adduces neurotic resistance to his hypotheses not only to explain the conscious rejection of his theory, but also the production of many of the so-called counterwish dreams. Such dreams feature "the frustration of a wish or the occurrence of something clearly unwished for" (S. E. 1900, 4:157). For example, a trial attorney dreamed that he had lost all of his court cases (S. E. 1900, 4:152). Since the distressing manifest contents of these dreams pose a prima facie challenge to his wish-fulfillment theory of dreaming, Freud tells us: "One of the two motive forces leading to such [counterwish] dreams is the wish that I [Freud] may be wrong." As he would have it (S. E. 1900, 4:158), this wish is harbored not only by resisting patients in analysis, but also by readers of his *The Interpretation of Dreams*, and by those who heard his lectures on that book.

But as I argued (see note 9), Freud's attempt to reconcile counterwish dreams with his wish-fulfillment theory fails multiply. In fact, it does turn out there that this failure creates a strong presumption of the falsity of that dream theory. But this result also impugns Karl Popper's charge that the Freudian corpus is unfalsifiable by contrary evidence.[10]

Concerning the psychoanalytic enterprise, Popper has repeatedly made two claims, one of which pertains to the alleged deductive content of Freudian theory, while the other is sociological and attributes methodological dishonesty to its advocates: (1) Logically, psychoanalytic theory is irrefutable by any human behavior whatever, and (2) in the face of seemingly adverse evidence, Freud and his followers always dodged refutation by resorting to immunizing maneuvers. According to (1), *none* of the deductive consequences of Freud's hypotheses are refutable by potentially contrary empirical findings. As Popper puts it: "Freud's theory…simply does not have potential falsifiers."[11]

But clearly, this charge of unfalsifiability against psychoanalytic theory itself does not follow from the sociological objection that Freudians evade or discount all evidential criticism of their hypotheses. After all, a theory may well be invalidated by known evidence, even as its true believers offer sham defenses to escape such refutation. Besides, if Popper were right that "Freud's theory…simply does not have potential [empirical] falsifiers," why would it have been necessary at all for Freudians to dodge refutations by means of immunizing gambits? Popper's (1) and (2) seem incoherent. Note that Popper speaks interchangeably of falsifiability and genuine "testability."

Ironically, it emerges clearly from some of his other doctrines that the recalcitrance of many Freudians in the face of falsifying evidence, however scandalous, is not at all tantamount to the empirical irrefutability of their theory. As Popper tells us, theories on the one hand and the intellectual conduct of their protagonists on the other "belong to *two entirely different 'worlds'*."[12] Yet because Popper sometimes discusses them in the same breath, my response to his views on psychoanalysis takes both into account. My principal objection to him pertains to his logical thesis of empirical irrefutability, although I have argued elsewhere that he also used straw men and misleading oversimplifications to make his case for his sociological objection that Freud always engaged in evasive methodological behavior.[13]

In a volume on his philosophy, Popper had claimed—once again—that psychoanalysis is an empirically untestable psychological metaphysics, which does "not exclude any physically possible human behaviour."[14] And from this allegation of empirical unfalsifiability, he immediately drew the fallacious inference that psychoanalysis indeed can, in principle, *explain* any actual behavior. Thus, on the heels of saying that Freud's and Adler's theories do not exclude any possible human behavior, Popper tells us that "whatever anybody may do is, in principle, explicable in Freudian or Adlerian terms."

But if a theory, in conjunction with particular initial conditions, *does not exclude* any behavior at all, how can it deductively *explain* any *particular* behavior? To explain deductively is to exclude: As Spinoza emphasized, to assert (entail) *p* is to deny every proposition incompatible with it. Note that in psychoanalytic theory, just as in Newton's physics, for example, law-like or other general statements cannot explain particular behavior without initial conditions: Without suitable initial velocity specifications, Newton's laws of motion and gravitation do not yield an elliptical orbit for the earth under the gravitational action of the sun. Hence, if no potential behavior could falsify psychoanalysis under given initial conditions *I*, then this theory, *cum I*, could not explain any actual behavior deductively. A fortiori, if the theory *T* were unfalsifiable, it could not explain *all* such behavior, as Popper claims. Furthermore, if the conjunction *T* and *I* fails to explain some particular behavior *b* deductively, then *I* and *b* cannot confirm (support) *T* hypothetico-deductively. Thus, if psychoanalysis were unfalsifiable, how could any actual behavior—let alone *all* physically possible behavior—be explained by it so as to confirm it inductively, as Popper claims?[15] On the contrary, the alleged unfalsifiability would preclude such hypothetico-deductive confirmability.

These considerations are illustrations drawn from my reasons for maintaining that Popper's

indictment of the Freudian corpus as inherently unfalsifiable has fundamentally misdiagnosed the failure of psychoanalysis as a scientific theory. More often than not, the intellectual defects of psychoanalysis are too subtle to be detected by Popper's falsifiability criterion of demarcation. For example, there is no systematic published critique by him of Freud's method of free association, *qua* purported method of causal validation. And yet just that method is *the* method of clinical investigation in psychoanalysis. Alas, Popper's myth of nonfalsifiability has entrenched itself in current philosophic folklore.

Indeed, it is ironic that Popper should have pointed to psychoanalytic theory as a prime illustration of his thesis that inductively countenanced confirmations can easily be found for nearly every theory, if we look for them. *It is precisely Freud's theory that furnishes poignant evidence that Popper has caricatured the inductivist tradition by his thesis of easy inductive confirmability of nearly every theory!* I have joined the issue with Popper directly as part of a 1986 review-symposium on my *Foundations* book.[16]

Speaking of my disagreement with Popper on the epistemic demerits of psychoanalysis, Gellner[17] writes: "Grünbaum's work [on psychoanalysis] offers little solace to apologists of psychoanalysis, but it does claim to rebut Popper's view that psychoanalysis is untestable. Grünbaum's argument [against Popper] is rich, complex and important, and requires and deserves much fuller treatment than can be given here. Nevertheless, its main point can be summarized and dealt with briefly." But Gellner's purported summary is entirely incorrect: "The Grünbaum testability-of-Freudianism thesis hinges on the so-called double-conditional theory of therapy,"[18] i.e., my case allegedly rests on just my critique of what I have called "Freud's Tally Argument" (*Foundations*, chap. 2, Section B), which Gellner renamed Freud's "double-conditional theory of therapy."

Yet a mere glance at Chapter 1 of *Foundations*, which I directed against Popper's charge that psychoanalysis is unfalsifiable, shows that my scrutiny of the Tally Argument played no role at all in my *plaidoyer* that psychoanalysis is falsifiable, let alone was it my centerpiece. A fortiori it was surely not my only counterexample to Popper's view of psychoanalysis. Indeed, in my cumulative rebuttals to him,[19] which include the *Foundations* Chapter 1 previously available to Gellner, I met precisely the desideratum enunciated by Gellner as part of his altogether incorrect claim (p. 186) that "Grün-baum's philosophical point against Popper," i.e., my evidence for the bona fide testability of psycho-analysis, hinges "on a single instance." As Gellner states his red herring: "In practice, most of us would be loath to put such a burden [of demonstrat-ing falsifiability] on a single instance, however well authenticated, and would prefer to be pre-sented with a whole class of such cases, large enough to be convincing."[20] I had actually given just such a set of examples.

As will be recalled, I have emphasized that Pop-per's charge of logical unfalsifiability against psy-choanalytic theory itself does not follow from the sociological objection, however well documented, that many Freudians are methodologically unre-sponsive to evidential criticism of their hypotheses, as manifested by their resort to even wildly ad hoc immunizing maneuvers in order to neutralize falsi-fying evidence.

In the case of psychoanalytic theory, Gellner, in effect, disregards this distinction between the semantics and the pragmatics of a theory as artifi-cial, if not misleading. Oddly enough, he himself does appeal to the distinction between the syntac-tics of a theory and its pragmatics without any mention of its semantics: The syntactics is "con-cerned with the formal structure of proposition, seen in isolation, whereas pragmatics are con-cerned with what the users concretely *do* with the proposition."[21]

Nonetheless, to prepare for his diagnosis of the untestability of psychoanalysis, Gellner first denies (against Cioffi) that "the pragmatics were arbi-trarily added to the content of the doctrine when the doctrine is in trouble." Instead, we are told,[22] "the pragmatic strategies [of theory-immunization by psychoanalysts] are direct and manifest corollaries of the central ideas of the doctrine! The pragmatics protect the doctrine, but the doctrine also engen-ders, produces, protects, guarantees the pragmatic practices."

Alas, Gellner gives no evidence for this grandi-ose assertion *from the actual core hypotheses of the Freudian corpus*. Nor does he address two highly pertinent fundamental issues: (1) Do the central ideas of such theories as Newton's or Einstein's not likewise license the pragmatics of physicists? and, (2) Is it demonstrable that the very content of these physical theories do *not* likewise provide scope for immunization maneuvers in the face of contrary

evidence, if physicists were minded to resort to them?

The latter questions derive enormous poignancy from the fact that Gellner's indictment of psycho-analysis overlooks a great insight developed by Pierre Duhem in his book *La Théorie Physique: Son Objet, Sa Structure*: Even in physics, major hypotheses can be saved from refutation by suit-able modifications of the auxiliary hypotheses that are used in deriving observational predictions from them. As Duhem had explained, when a hypothesis H is at issue in a given inquiry, then observational predictions p made by means of H are typically deduced not from H and some initial condition I alone, but only from their *conjunction* with some of the auxiliary hypotheses A of the larger theoretical system of which H is a part. What, then, can the physicist infer deductively from the failure of the predictions p under experimental test? Duhem replies:

> when the experiment is in disagreement with his predictions, what he learns is that at least one of the hypotheses constituting this group [H, I, and A] is unacceptable and ought to be modified; but the experiment does not designate which one should be changed.[23]

Imre Lakatos[24] deployed this Duhemian insight against Popper, although he gives it an inappropri-ate sociological twist by asking rhetorically: "If psychoanalysts are to be condemned as dishonest by Popper's standards, must not Newtonians be similarly condemned?" In his reply to Lakatos, Popper himself employs the logical rather than sociological mode to summarize Lakatos's objec-tion as the charge that "Newton's theory of gravi-tation is no more open to refutation than is Freud's theory of psychoanalysis."[25] Yet Gellner takes no account at all of this Duhemian state of affairs.

Relying on his altogether gratuitous contention that the immunizing strategies employed by (most?) psychoanalysts are intrinsic to the (seman-tic?) content of their theory, Gellner offers a con-cluding judgment on my divergence from Popper on psychoanalysis: "this issue [of its unfalsifiabil-ity] is so pertinent to its [i.e., Gellner's book's] main argument that certain observations are appro-priate. The untestability, or rather, the test-evasion charge does indeed remain the main and, in the end, valid charge against psychoanalysis."[26] Yet I deem this conclusion to be misleading, if only because Gellner has unwarrantedly asserted the empirical unfalsifiability of psychoanalytic theory, offering nothing better than a wholesale sociological charge of evasive behavior of psychoanalysts. An examination of the literature shows, however, that such improper conduct by analysts is by no means universal.[27]

As I argue elsewhere, the so-called "hermeneutic" reconstruction of Freud's psychoanalytic enterprise has misappropriated psychoanalysis in the service of an ideology philosophically alien to it.[28] Indeed, the sterility of the hermeneutic approach for the constructive utilization of the Freudian legacy in psychology and psychiatry is becoming increasingly apparent.[29] Yet hermeneutic psychoanalysis has genuine appeal in some quarters: It is a citadel of apologetics for those believers who are in search of a rationale for obviating the imperative to validate the Freudian enterprise scientifically. Understandably, clinicians who have a lifetime professional investment in psychoanalytic practice wish to safeguard that investment. To them it is naturally quite tempting to succumb to the hermeneutic gospel, since it affords both methodological *and* ethical absolution from stringent probative demands. But these are rear-guard actions, not advances or theory improvements in the theory of human nature or in psychiatry: What new hypotheses or extensions of psychoanalysis do we owe to the hermeneuticists? Their reconstruction is a cul-de-sac.

By contrast, my arguments (see note 28 above) for the poverty of the hermeneuticist construal of psychoanalysis yield an important, yet sour fruit for classical psychoanalysis: They fundamentally undermine the cardinal Freudian theory of transference *qua* etiologic hypothesis. Yet my doubts strike the psychoanalytic biographer and historian Peter Gay as themselves being an obsessional symptom: "The most formidable among the skeptics, who has made the credibility of Freudian science (or lack of it) an obsessive concern for a decade, is the philosopher Adolf Grünbaum."[30] But Gay seems to have overlooked that if my single decade of skepticism qualifies as obsessive, then a fortiori the same psychological verdict applies to his own insouciantly credulous espousal of psychoanalysis for much longer than that.

In my *Foundations*, I addressed two main questions: (1) Are the psychoanalyst's observations in the clinical setting reliable as "data"? and (2) if so, can they actually support the major hypotheses of the theory of psychic conflict or repression, which

is Freud's avowed cornerstone of his psychoanalytic edifice (S. E. 1914, 14:16)? In that book, I argued for giving a negative answer to both of these questions. Clearly, if the evidence from the couch is unreliable from the outset, then this defect alone suffices to jeopardize the very foundations of the clinical theory. But, as I strongly emphasized (p. 172), even if clinical data were *not* contaminated by the analyst's influence, the inability of the psychoanalytic method of clinical investigation by free association to warrant the required sort of *causal* inferences leaves the major pillars of the theory of psychic conflict ill-supported. Thus, I see a twofold threat to the psychoanalytic case-study method as a means of scientific inquiry.

It is an immediate corollary of my challenge that it applies not only to Freud's own original hypotheses, but also to any and all post-Freudian revisionist versions of psychoanalysis that rely on his clinical methods of validating causal inferences, though the specific content of their theories of psychic conflict is different. After all, the alteration in the content of the hypotheses hardly makes their validation more secure.

The well-known American academic psychoanalyst Marshall Edelson has given poignant rebuttals to ill-conceived objections that my critique of psychoanalysis has elicited from some segments of the psychoanalytic community.[31] For example, he rejects the charge of anachronism against me:[32]

> Referring to post-Freud developments in psychoanalysis *as a way of neutralizing Grünbaum* is apposite only if these developments make a difference with respect to the problems he has raised. Grünbaum could surely ask whether those who respond in this way to his critique make much of a case that these developments make that kind of a difference.

More generally, in his introduction (pp. XIII–XIV), Edelson sets the stage for our dialogue by saying:

> The most telling outside challenge to psychoanalysis [from *non*-analysts] has been the questions raised by Adolf Grünbaum about its empirical foundations and mode of inquiry. The most telling manifestations of the difficulties in which psychoanalysis now finds itself are both the lack, for the most part, of a cogent response to these questions (I except my own work, of course), and the various kinds of responses these questions have received instead.

Edelson and I are also of one mind in claiming that the hermeneutic reconstruction of psychoanalysis is a veritable kiss of death for the Freudian enterprise.[33]

But he offers arguments against my strong doubts concerning the epistemological capabilities of the psychoanalytic treatment-setting for validating the *major causal hypotheses* of Freud's clinical theories of psychopathology, dreaming and slips.[34] Just these doubts of mine have been endorsed by the widely recognized American academic psychoanalyst Philip Holzman in his Fiftieth Anniversary Address to the Boston Psychoanalytic Society.[35] And I have given my pessimistic critical reply to Edelson's hopes for the clinical testing designs envisioned by him.[36] Yet the summary he gives of his appraisal of my views is truly generous.[37]

> My own view of Grünbaum's critique is that, because of the explicitness and utter lucidity of his argument, and the thorough scholarship with which he has documented his depiction of psychoanalysis, the critique can function as a powerful stimulus to hard thinking about the issues he has raised. I do not know for what more one could ask from a philosopher of science [footnote omitted].

From the very extensive further critical literature evoked by my writings on psychoanalysis, Edward Erwin has selected some of the most recent publications for rebuttal.[38] For example, he defends my views against David Sachs's 1989 critique.[39] But I shall also publish a detailed reply to Sachs of my own.

My psychoanalytic studies have had two kinds of spin-off:

1. Although the placebo concept originated largely within pharmacology, as I have shown elsewhere the distinction between placebo therapies (and the infelicitously labeled) "specific" therapies is just as applicable to psychotherapies as to treatments for various sorts of somatic disorders.[40] Indeed, as is shown in my *Foundations*, it matters importantly to the credentials of the clinical theory of psychoanalysis whether treatment gains from psychoanalysis are placebogenic. Thus, the issues posed by Breuer and Freud in their 1893 Preliminary Communication to their *Studies in Hysteria* (S. E. 1983, 2:1–17) prompted me to give a careful articulation of the multifaceted notions of placebo therapy and placebo control that is applicable across all of medicine and psychiatry.[41]

Incidentally, in my view, one need only combine the conceptualizations in Freud's excellent typology of causes (S. E. 1895, 3:135–139; reply to Löwenfeld) with the stated demonstrated neutrality of the placebo concept as between somatic medicine and psychiatry to discredit Thomas Szasz's reductive physicalization of the concept of disease.[42]

2. Freud saw his psychological critique of belief in theism as an extension of psychoanalysis, coupled with a utilization of Ludwig Feuerbach's critique of religion. Therefore, I was able to examine Freud's treatment of religion in the light of my prior scrutiny of psychoanalytic explanations.[43]

Yet I fully share his atheism. And elsewhere I have argued at length against the theological misinterpretations of recent physical cosmologies that are now enjoying an ill-deserved vogue in France[44] and elsewhere. I claim that none of them lend any support at all to theological creationism, so that atheism has nothing to fear at all from any of them.[45]

ENDNOTES

1. As shown by several sessions at the 1987 international congress of psychoanalysis held in Montréal, my 1984 book *The Foundations of Psychoanalysis: A Philosophical Critique* (Berkeley: Univ. of California Press) [hereafter cited as *Foundations*] was seen in the psychoanalytic community as jeopardizing such third-party reimbursements. And just that consternation about the therapeutic import of my book prompted a lengthy article concerning my challenge to psychoanalysis in the popular Italian magazine *L'Espresso* (G. Forti, "Freud Sotto Accusa: Panico Sul Lettino" ["Freud under Fire: Panic on the Couch"], *L'Espresso*, N. 41, 18 October, 1987, pp. 118–125). Yet in an interview I gave to the *New York Times* for an article about my book (Daniel Goleman, "Pressure Mounts for Analysts to Prove Theory Scientific," January 15, 1985, pp. 15 and 18), I was correctly reported as *not* advising people against undergoing psychoanalytic treatment. Nonetheless, I consider it imperative that its practitioners meet the challenge to the cost-effectiveness of psychoanalytic therapy, and similarly for other therapies.

More recently, a group of psychoanalysts have claimed on the basis of an "inquiry conducted from a psychoanalytic perspective," that "patients suitable for psychoanalysis derive substantial therapeutic benefit" [Harry M. Bachrach et al., "On the Efficacy of Psychoanalysis," *Journal of the American Psychoanalytic Assn.* 39 (1991), pp. 871–916]. In their 45-page report on the results of psychoanalytic therapy, these psychoanalysts tell us (p. 873): "we shall maintain a specially *psychoan-*

alytic perspective, rather than perspectives derived from related disciplines. For too long psychoanalytic [therapeutic] research has been defensively toned, and analysts have failed to fully appreciate that it is both a common and legitimate strategy for scientists to work within their own disciplinary matrix (Kuhn, 1977)....This, we believe, is a more productive approach to scientific inquiry than reactive efforts to respond to critics from other fields." Having emboldened themselves "to conduct our inquiry from a point of view native to psychoanalysis," they admit that their outcome study does "not enable meaningful comparisons of the effectiveness of psychoanalysis with that of other forms of treatment for specific kinds of patients experiencing specific kinds of illnesses" (p. 911). Thus, this self-validating study admittedly begs the key questions of therapeutic efficacy summarized in my *Foundations* (p. 161): What are the verdicts of comparisons of treatment-outcome from psychoanalysis with the results from rival therapies and from spontaneous remission, such that specified desiderata of improvement serve as a common denominator?

Indeed, this therapeutic *petitio principii* crudely misinvokes Thomas Kuhn's notion of normal vs. revolutionary science in an unsuccessful attempt to *exempt* psychoanalysis from the criteria of comparative validation widely recognized for decades as applicable to claims of therapeutic efficacy *for all rival psychotherapies alike* (cf. Julian Meltzoff and Melvin Kornreich, *Research in Psychotherapy* [New York: Atherton Press, 1970]; Irene Elkin et al., "Conceptual and Methodological Issues in Comparative Studies of Psychotherapy and Pharmacotherapy," *American J. Psychiatry 145* [1988], Part I: 8 August, pp. 909–917; Part II: 9 Sept., pp. 1070–1076). Clearly, the legitimacy of the practices of Kuhnian "normal science" would not vindicate coronary bypass surgery, if the surgeons were to reject comparisons with outcome from angioplasty, beta-blockers, and other drugs. How then could psychoanalysis be correspondingly exempt in, say, its treatment of depression? For an excellent statement of the required kind of research design, see Michael Scriven, "The Experimental Investigation of Psychoanalysis," *Psychoanalysis, Scientific Method and Philosophy*, ed. S. Hook (New York: New York Univ. Press, 1959), pp. 226–251.

A reductio ad absurdum from physics will convey the unsoundness of the spuriously Kuhnian justification offered by Bachrach et al. for their self-validating therapeutic *petitio principii*: Though Newtonian physics and Einstein's general theory of relativity represent different theoretical "paradigms" in Kuhn's sense, no astronomer engaged in testing the predictions of Einstein's theory would dream of declaring its observational validation *sui generis*, and disqualify telescopes and other instruments previously employed to test Newtonian theory.

2. For a strong antidote to that acceptance by a quondam Freudian literary critic, see Frederick Crews, *Skeptical Engagements* (New York: Oxford Univ. Press, 1986).

3. See Fulton J. Sheen, *Peace of Soul* (New York: Whittlesey House, 1949). Sheen, a Roman Catholic bishop, was a nationally well-known TV personality in the U.S.

4. See, for example, Hans Küng, *Freud and the Problem of God* (New Haven, CT: Yale Univ. Press, 1979); and William W. Meissner, S.J., *Psychoanalysis and Religious Experience* (New Haven, CT: Yale Univ. Press, 1984).

5. See Barbara von Eckardt's chapter "Adolf Grünbaum and Psychoanalytic Epistemology" [in J. Reppen (Ed.), *Beyond Freud: A Study of Modern Psychoanalytic Theorists* (Hillsdale, NJ: The Analytic Press, 1985), pp. 353–403] for a detailed survey of my relevant writings up to the appearance of my *Foundations*.

Foundations appeared in Italian, German, and French translations as follows: (1) *I Fondamenti della Psicoanalisi* (Milan: II Saggiatore, Arnoldo Mondadori, 1988), (2) *Die Grundlagen der Psychoanalyse* (Stuttgart: Phillipp Reclam jun., 1988); *Les fondements de la psychanalyse* (Paris: Presses Universitaires de France, 1996). For a *pro*-Freudian critique of it, see Paul Robinson, *Freud and his critics* (Berkeley, 1993, chap. 3).

6. *The Psychoanalytic Movement, The Cunning of Unreason* (London: Paladin Books, Granada Publishing, 1985).

7. Unless otherwise indicated, citations of Freud's writings in English translation will be from the *Standard Edition of the Complete Psychological Works of Sigmund Freud*, Trans. J. Strachey et al. (London: Hogarth Press, 1953–1974, 24 vols.). Each reference will use the abbreviation "S.E.," followed by the year of first appearance, volume number and page(s).

8. For a discussion of relevant issues other than those raised by Gellner in particular, see Adolf Grünbaum, "The Role of Psychological Explanations of the Rejection or Acceptance of Scientific Theories," M. P. Hanen et al. (eds.), *Science, Pseudo-Science and Society* (Waterloo, Ontario, Canada: Wilfrid Laurier University Press, 1980, pp. 29–53).

9. A. Grünbaum, *Validation in the Clinical Theory of Psychoanalysis* (Madison, CT: International Universities Press, 1993), chap. 10.

10. See K. R. Popper, *Conjectures and Refutations* (New York: Basic Books, 1962), chap. 1, pp. 33–38; 255–258; "Replies to My Critics," in P. S. Schilpp (ed.), *The Philosophy of Karl Popper* (LaSalle: Open Court, 1974), Book II, pp. 984–985; and *Realism and the Aim of Science*, W. W. Bartley III (ed.), (Totowa: Rowman and Littlefield, 1983), chap. 2.

11. K. R. Popper, "Replies to My Critics," in P. S. Schilpp (ed.), *The Philosophy of Karl Popper* (LaSalle: Open Court, 1974), Book II, p. 1004.

12. K. R. Popper, "Replies to My Critics," in P. S. Schilpp (ed.), *The Philosophy of Karl Popper* (LaSalle: Open Court, 1974), Book I, p. 144.

13. A. Grünbaum, *Foundations*, chap. 1; *Validation in the Clinical Theory of Psychoanalysis* (Madison, CT:

International Universities Press, 1993), chap. 2. The latter chapter is drawn from my larger essay, "The Degeneration of Popper's Theory of Demarcation," in I. C. Jarvie & F. D'Agostino (eds.), *Freedom and Rationality*, Festschrift for John Watkins, Boston Studies in the Philosophy of Science (Boston & Dordrecht: Reidel, 1989, pp. 141–161). It also appeared in the Italian *Epistemologia XII*, no. 2 (1989), pp. 235–260.

14. K. R. Popper, "Replies to My Critics," in P. S. Schilpp (ed.), *The Philosophy of Karl Popper* (LaSalle: Open Court, 1974), Book II, p. 985.

15. See K. R. Popper, *Conjectures and Refutations* (New York: Basis Books, 1962), chap. 1, p. 35.

16. This symposium consists of my "Précis" of my *Foundations* book, nearly 40 commentaries by as many authors, and my "Author's Response," in *Behavioral and Brain Sciences 9*, no. 2 (1986), pp. 217–284. Hereafter this symposium will be cited as *BBS*. A German translation is published in Adolf Grünbaum (ed.), *Kritische Betrachtungen zur Psychoanalyse* (Heidelberg: Springer-Verlag, 1991). An Italian translation, with an Introduction by Marcello Pera, entitled *Psicoanalisi: Obiezioni e Risposte*, was published in 1988 as a paperback by Armando Editore, Rome, Italy.

For Popper's criticism of what he *conjectured* to be my view without having read my work on the topic, see his "Predicting Overt Behavior versus Predicting Hidden States," *BBS*, pp. 254–255. My response to him is given in my "The Falsifiability of Psychoanalytic Theory," *BBS*, pp. 266–269. My most recent response to Popper is given in A. Grünbaum, *Validation in the Clinical Theory of Psychoanalysis* (Madison, CT: International Universities Press, 1993), chap. 2.

17. Gellner, op. cit., p. 185. Gellner's 1985 book appeared before the publication of my 1986 *BBS* debate with Popper.

18. Gellner, op.cit., p. 182.

19. See note 16 above.

20. Gellner, op. cit., p. 186.

21. Gellner, op. cit., p. 187.

22. Gellner, op. cit., p. 187.

23. P. Duhem, *The Aim and Structure of Physical Theory*, trans. P. P. Wiener (Princeton: Princeton University Press, 1954, p. 187).

24. I. Lakatos, "Popper on Demarcation and Induction," in P. A. Schilpp (ed.), *The Philosophy of Karl Popper* (LaSalle, IL: Open Court, 1974), Book I, p. 247.

25. K. R. Popper, "Replies to My Critics," in P. S. Schilpp (ed.), *The Philosophy of Karl Popper* (LaSalle: Open Court, 1974), Book II, p. 999. For an account of Popper's own failure to take account of the difficulties raised by Duhem for Popper's avowed epistemological asymmetry between verification and falsification, see Adolf Grünbaum, "Is Falsifiability the Touchstone of Scientific Rationality? Karl Popper vs. Inductivism," in R. S. Cohen, P. K. Feyerabend, and M. W. Wartofsky

(eds.), *Essays in Memory of Imre Lakatos* (1976); Section V: "Duhem vs. Popper: Epistemological Comparison of Refutations and Corroborations," pp. 247–250.

26. Gellner, op. cit., p. 179.

27. Though methodological dishonesty is demonstrably not universal among psychoanalytic writers, Freud himself (inexcusably) was not above resorting to it in several important instances. See F. Sulloway, "Reassessing Freud's Case Histories," *Isis 82* (1991), pp. 245–275.

Moreover, as Morris Eagle has documented, theory-change in the psychoanalytic community is considerably more affected by sociopolitical considerations, as distinct from evidential ones, than in the scientific community at large. Indeed, the ability of Kohut's self-psychology and so-called object-relations theory to be accepted as psychoanalysis, while earlier theoretical departures from Freud were decried as heretically dissident, is more a matter of the former post-Freudians *not* having set up their own separate institutes. See Morris Eagle, "The Dynamics of Theory-Change in Psychoanalysis," in John Earman et al. (eds.), *Philosophical Problems of the Internal and External Worlds: Essays on the Philosophy of Adolf Grünbaum* (Pittsburgh, PA: University of Pittsburgh and University of Konstanz Presses, 1993). As for the evidential merits of these post-Freudian developments, Eagle concludes (p. 404): "There is no evidence that contemporary psychoanalytic theories have remedied the epistemological and methodological difficulties that are associated with Freudian theory."

28. A. Grünbaum, *Validation in the Clinical Theory of Psychoanalysis* (Madison, CT: International Universities Press, 1993), chap. 4. Earlier, in my *Foundations*, I devoted nearly 100 pages to the critical scrutiny of the hermeneutic construal of psychoanalytic theory and therapy (see pp. 1–95 there).

29. In his new essay on the epistemology of psychoanalysis entitled *Between Hermeneutics and Science*, (Madison, CT: International Universities Press, 1991), Carlo Strenger makes "an attempt to present versions of claims of the hermeneuticist conception of psychoanalysis, which stand up to the sharp critique it has been subjected to by Grünbaum" (p. 5). But unfortunately, Strenger could not take account of two of my directly relevant papers: (1) "The Role of the Case Study Method in the Foundations of Psychoanalysis," *Canadian Journal of Philosophy 18* (1988), pp. 623–658; this paper is also available in H. Vetter and L. Nagl (eds.), *Die Philosophen und Freud* (Vienna: Oldenbourg Verlag, 1988), pp. 134–174, and it is reprinted as chap. 4 in my 1992 book *Validation in the Clinical Theory of Psychoanalysis, op. cit.*; and (2) "Meaning Connections and Causal Connections in the Human Sciences: The Poverty of Hermeneutic Philosophy," *Journal of the American Psychoanalytic Association 38* (1990), pp. 559–577.

30. Peter Gay, *Freud* (New York: W.W. Norton, 1988), p. 745.

31. Marshall Edelson, *Psychoanalysis: A Theory in Crisis* (Chicago: University of Chicago Press, 1988), chap. 14, section "Responses to Grünbaum's Critique."

32. Marshall Edelson, *Psychoanalysis: A Theory in Crisis,* op. cit., p. 318.

33. Marshal Edelson, *Psychoanalysis: A Theory in Crisis,* op. cit., chap. 11, "The Hermeneutic Turn and the Single Case Study in Psychoanalysis," especially the section on "Meaning," pp. 246-251. Also, see pp. xii–xiii. A. Grünbaum, *Validation in the Clinical Theory of Psychoanalysis* (Madison, CT: International Universities Press, 1993), chap. 4.

34. Marshal Edelson, *Hypothesis and Evidence in Psychoanalysis* (Chicago: University of Chicago Press, 1984), Part 3: chaps. 8–11; *Psychoanalysis: A Theory in Crisis,* op. cit., chaps. 12,13, and 15.

35. Philip Holzman, "Psychoanalysis: Is the Therapy Destroying the Science?" *Journal of the American Psychoanalytic Association 33* (1985), pp. 725–770.

36. Adolf Grünbaum, *BBS,* "Author's Response," Section "What Would Unbiased Clinical Data Prove?" pp. 277–279; *Validation in the Clinical Theory of Psychoanalysis,* op. cit., chap. 6: "Reply to Marshall Edelson."

37. Marshall Edelson, *Psychoanalysis: A Theory in Crisis,* op. cit., p. 313.

38. Edward Erwin, "Philosophers on Freudianism: Replies to Grünbaum's *Foundations,*" in John Earman et al. (eds.), *Philosophical Problems of the Internal and External Worlds: Essays on the Philosophy of Adolf Grünbaum,* op. cit.; cf. also Eagle's essay therein.

39. David Sachs, "In Fairness to Freud: A Critical Notice of *The Foundations of Psychoanalysis by Adolf Grünbaum.*" *Philosophical Review 98,* no. 3 (July 1989), pp. 349–378. For appraisals of *Foundations* diametrically opposite to Sachs's, see the review-essays by Morris Eagle, *Philosophy of Science 53* (1986), pp. 65–88; Frederick Crews, *The New Republic,* Issue 3653, January 21, 1985, pp. 28–33 (reprinted in Crews's *Skeptical Engagements,* op. cit. chap. 4); Carlo Strenger, *International Journal of Psychoanalysis 67,* Part II, 1986, pp. 255–260; Paolo Parrini and Giordano Fossi (in Italian), *L'Indice 5,* no. 10, June 1988, pp. 4–5.

40. A. Grünbaum, *Validation in the Clinical Theory of Psychoanalysis* (Madison, CT: International Universities Press, 1993), chap. 3.

41. Adolf Grünbaum, "The Placebo Concept in Medicine and Psychiatry," *Psychological Medicine 16* (1986), pp. 19–38; reprinted in a World Health Organization volume: M. Shepherd & N. Sartorius (eds.), *Non-Specific Aspects of Treatment* (Bern & Toronto: Hans Huber Verlag, 1989), pp. 7–38; also reprinted in D. Cicchetti and W. Grove (eds.), *Thinking Clearly about Psychology* (Minneapolis: University of Minnesota Press,

1992); and in George Graham & G. Lynn Stephens (eds.), *Philosophical Psychopathology: A Book of Readings* (Cambridge, MA: MIT Press, 1992). A German translation is included as an appendix chapter in Adolf Grünbaum (ed.), *Kritische Betrachtungen zur Psychoanalyse,* op. cit.

42. For literature on the antipsychiatry issue, see "Philosophie, Psychiatrie et Antipsychiatrie," *Revue Internationale de Philosophie 32,* no. 123 (1978), pp. 3–90; Thomas Szasz, *The Myth of Mental Illness* (New York: Harper and Row, 1974); L. Reznek, *The Philosophical Defense of Psychiatry* (New York: Routledge, 1991), chap. 5: "Thomas Szasz and the Physicalizing of Disease," pp. 71–95.

43. Adolf Grünbaum, "Psychoanalysis and Theism," *The Monist 70,* April 1987, pp. 152–192. Reprinted in my *Validation in the Clinical Theory of Psychoanalysis,* op. cit., chap. 7. An Italian translation, *Freud e il Teismo,* with an introduction by Alessandro Pagnini, was published as a small book by Ediziono Scientifiche Italiane (Rome, 1992).

44. cf. Jean Guitton, *Dieu et la Science* (Paris, Grosset, 1991).

45. See Adolf Grünbaum, "The Pseudo-Problem of Creation in Physical Cosmology," *Philosophy of Science 56,* pp. 373–394. Reprinted in *Epistemologia XII,* No. 1, pp. 3–32. A version of it appeared in *Free Inquiry 9,* no. 4, pp. 48–57, and in J. Leslie (ed.), *Physical Cosmology and Philosophy* (New York: Macmillan, 1990) pp. 92-112. A German translation entitled "Die Schöpfung als Scheinproblem der physikalischen Kosmologie" appeared in A. Bohnen (ed.), *Wege der Vernunft, Festschrift für Hans Albert,* pp. 164–191; Tübingen: J.C.B. Mohr (Paul Siebeck). Furthermore, see Adolf Grünbaum, "Pseudo-creation of the Big Bang," *Nature 344* (No. 6269), April 1990, pp. 821-822; "Creation in Physical Cosmology: Pseudo-Problem or Superior Truth?" *Nuova Civiltà delle Macchine,* vol. VIII, no. 4, 1990, pp. 114–123. An Italian translation of this paper, "La creazione nella cosmologia fisica: Uno Pseudo-problema o una verità superiore?" appeared in the same issue on pp. 13–23. See also Adolf Grünbaum, "Creation as a Pseudo-Explanation in Current Physical Cosmology," *Erkenntnis,* Vol. 35, July 1991, pp. 233–254, which is reprinted in Wolfgang Spohn (ed.), *Erkenntnis Orientated,* a centennial volume for Rudolf Carnap & Hans Reichenbach (Boston: Kluwer). Finally, Adolf Grünbaum, "Creation as a Pseudo-Explanation in Current Physical Cosmology," is to appear in the *Boston Studies in the Philosophy of Science,* a volume of the proceedings of the April 1991 Boston celebration of the centenary of Reichenbach and Carnap.

CHAPTER 19

THE VALUE OF PSYCHOANALYTIC THERAPY: A QUESTION OF STANDARDS

Edward Erwin

Freudians and non-Freudians have long disagreed about the value of psychoanalytic therapy, but even some supporters of Freud's theory have doubts about the therapy. For example, Paul Kline, the author of a book (1981) generally supportive of Freudian theory, says of psychoanalytic therapy that no good evidence exists that it is effective (Kline, 1988, p. 225). Gene Glass, one of the authors of an influential book (Smith, Glass, & Miller, 1980) supporting the efficacy of psychotherapy, points out that he is sympathetic to psychoanalytic theory, but then adds that in the Smith, Glass, and Miller database there is not a single experimental study that qualifies by even "the shoddiest standards" as an outcome evaluation of orthodox psychoanalysis (Glass & Kliegl, 1983, p. 40). In contrast to these pessimistic views, a recent review of the psychoanalytic outcome literature by a subcommittee of the American Psychoanalytic Association (Bachrach et al., 1991) concludes that patients suitable for psychoanalysis derive substantial therapeutic benefits from the therapy. Fisher and Greenberg (1985, p. 334) are more cautious, but still reach a partially favorable conclusion

based on six studies: "While we cannot conclude that the studies offer unequivocal evidence that analysis is more effective than no treatment, they do indicate with consistency that this seems probable with regard to a number of analysts and their non-psychotic, chronic patients."

Such disagreement about the value of psychoanalysis has persisted for more than four decades (see Eysenck, 1952, and replies by psychoanalysts). Why? One possible factor is psychological. Perhaps opponents feel threatened by both psychoanalytic theory and therapy, whereas proponents do not. This explanation, however, is not even prima facie plausible when extended to disagreement within the class of supporters of Freudian theory (or some psychoanalytic variant of it). Another possibility is that those who disagree may be looking at different evidence. In some cases that is probably correct, but in others, it is demonstrably not true. A third factor, which I will discuss here, both because I believe it to be an important causal factor and because of its philosophic interest, is that some and perhaps a great deal of the disagreement is due to the employment of different stan-

dards. Some of these standards are epistemological; others are "evaluative" in a nonepiste-
mological sense. I will begin with the latter.

SKEPTICISM, RELATIVISM, AND THERAPEUTIC OUTCOMES

Once we fix the goals for analysis, the question of
whether it typically contributes to their being realized appears to be straightforwardly empirical.
What, however, about the goals themselves: Can
their "correctness" be established empirically? A
common response is that this cannot be done. For
example, Woolfolk (1992, p. 220) replies as follows
to Hawkins's contention that the scientific question
underlying every clinical assessment is what opti-
mizes adjustment, adaption, competence, or habilitation: "What Hawkins seems not to realize is that
no experiment can establish the legitimacy or desirability of a *fundamental* goal, such as adjustment,
adaption, competence, habilitation, or even happiness, for that matter." Woolfolk concludes that
some aspect of psychotherapy must always be non-
empirical. One could agree and still argue that ultimate choices about therapeutic goals can be
defended in an a priori fashion, but many commentators appear to rule out that possibility as well. As
Garfield and Bergin (1986, p. 16) put it: "Recent
progress in developing new and more effective
techniques of psychotherapy has obscured the fact
that subjective value decisions underlie the choice
of techniques, the goals of change, and the assessment of what is a 'good' outcome."

One reason for concluding that decisions about
therapeutic goals and outcomes are subjective is
the lack of agreement about standards for assessing
outcome. For example, cognitive behavior therapists often use symptom remission without relapse
as the main criterion of success. Psychoanalytic
therapists, however, often conceptualize clinical
problems, such as depression or anxiety, as symptoms of unconscious emotional conflicts. If the
conflicts are not resolved, it is often held, then the
patient may have not improved very much as a consequence of symptom remission and, in fact, may
have become worse. The patient is likely to be
worse off if, as Freudians theorize, symptoms are
the most economical resolution of unconscious
conflicts. For, if we take away the best available
way to resolve an unconscious conflict that is left
intact, then an even worse symptom is likely to
appear (if the theory is true).

Even those who agree that symptom remission is
generally good do not necessarily agree that it provides a proper standard for measuring effectiveness. Some hold that the proper goal of therapy is
the achievement of some deeper result. For example, Anthony Ryle writes (1982, p. 3): "The central
aim and value of psychotherapy, as I see it (and this
will become clearer in the course of the book) is
that of enlarging people's ability to live their lives
by choice." A similar goal is stressed by Carl Rogers in his (1956) symposium with B. F. Skinner,
although he also recommends other goals, such as
helping the client to be more self-directing, less
rigid, more open to the evidence of his senses, and
better organized and integrated. Many other therapists, especially those in the psychoanalytic tradition, advocate as the main goal of therapy the
achievement of etiological insight, or the lifting of
repressions, or character change (or some combination of these). Other therapists stress the need to
"get in touch with one's feelings."

Given the wide variety of opinions about criteria
for judging outcomes, disagreements about therapeutic effectiveness are likely to persist even if
clarity and consensus are achieved concerning
empirical questions about the effects of psychotherapy.

One reaction to the diversity of standards for
judging outcomes is to retreat to what may be
termed "paradigm relativism." For example, in
their recent review of the psychoanalytic outcome
evidence, Bachrach et al. (1991) conclude that
patients suitable for psychoanalysis derive substantial therapeutic benefits from their therapy, but
stress (p. 873) that they (the reviewers of the evidence) maintain a specifically *psychoanalytic* perspective. Thus, the authors accept without comment
psychoanalytically based outcome criteria (such as
change in ego strength or transference resolution)
that would not be acceptable to most behavior therapists. If questioned, the authors would probably
respond that nonacceptance by behavior therapists
is irrelevant: They are recommending that each
therapy be judged by the criteria appropriate to its
respective paradigm (see p. 873). Other therapists
(Kazdin, 1986; Malan, 1976) have also recommended such a relativization of outcome criteria.

One problem with paradigm relativism is that
even within a single paradigm, criteria of outcome
evaluations can vary considerably. So the problem
that the appeal to relativism was designed to
solve—the problem of diverse and conflicting cri-

teria—can reappear even after relativism (at least of this type) is accepted. Thus, in the outcome studies assessed by Bachrach et al. (1991), a wide variety of psychoanalytic criteria are used to judge outcomes. These include insight into core conflicts (p. 883), global improvement (p. 883), transference resolution (p. 883), change in ego strength (p. 883), circumstances of termination of therapy (p. 887), change in test scores (p. 887), changes in reality testing, object relations and affect availability (p. 896), and many other criteria as well.

Even if there were not conflicting evaluative criteria within a single paradigm, there would be a second problem: Guaranteeing that a paradigm-generated outcome criterion is appropriate. For any outcome criterion internal to a paradigm, we can always ask: Why is satisfaction of that criterion guarantee of a *successful* outcome? For example, in one case reported by Bachrach et al. (p. 880), a client who came to treatment because of insecurity and difficulties in maintaining relations with women was judged "moderately improved" despite no indication in the report that either of his two problems had diminished. The basis for the verdict of improvement was that he had acquired "helpful intellectual insights." One could question, however, whether that is a satisfactory basis for saying he had improved even if the alleged insights were veridical. Legitimate doubts can also be raised about the other psychoanalytic criteria mentioned earlier, such as change in ego strength or transference resolution. One problem is empirical: How do we know that the criterion has been met in any given case? A second problem is a deeper one. Even if a client's ego strength has definitely increased, has his or her therapy been successful to any degree? A relativist might reply that "therapeutic success" simply means *therapeutic success relative* to one or more criteria of a particular paradigm. However, we can then ask why a "therapeutic success" in this sense is valuable. The relativist might, of course, also claim that "therapeutic benefit" is also to be defined relativistically, but there is no way to demonstrate this. Some relativists are likely to reply that if outcome criteria are not relativized to a paradigm, then there is no way to determine whether there has been a successful outcome. Even if this were true, it would be no justification for relativism; rather, it would provide grounds for skepticism about the evaluation of therapies. Before being forced toward a skeptical conclusion, however, I want to examine some other approaches.

Another standard approach is to judge a therapy in terms of how well it meets the goals of individual therapists. This, too, constitutes a kind of relativism: A single outcome can be both good and bad relative to conflicting therapeutic aims. However, this sort of relativism has two advantages over paradigm relativism. First, it does not matter that within the same paradigm different outcome criteria are used, as long as therapists in the paradigm have different goals. Second, for many therapies, there is nothing that is recognizable as a full-blown paradigm; so, paradigm relativism is not easily applied to them. Nevertheless, goal-related relativism encounters the second problem mentioned earlier: Even if a therapist does exactly what he or she aims to do, we can still ask if the outcome was valuable. Suppose that the client entered therapy to eliminate his problem drinking, but now drinks just as much as before. Perhaps the therapist's goal was to increase his ego strength, or to help him get in touch with his feelings, and the goal was achieved. Still, there *may* have been no therapeutic benefit or, at best, a rather minor one. So appealing to the aims of the therapist does not by itself resolve the problem of how one decides if a therapy has been successful.

Perhaps we should look to the client's goals rather than those of the therapist. After all, if a client enters therapy with a particular aim in mind, and the aim is met as a consequence of the therapy, has not a result occurred that is good to some degree? Not necessarily, although the point may be too obvious to pursue very far. A client may undergo therapy so he can drink with less anxiety, but if his problem is alcoholism the result may not be good at all. If a client is depressed about her extramarital affair, and rational emotive therapy facilitates her continuing in the affair without depression, she may achieve her therapeutic aim but be worse off than before, even from her point of view.

Another problem with appealing to client aims in assessing therapy is that clients often are confused about the nature of their problems when they enter therapy. Even if the outcome they hope to achieve is a good one, it may be peripheral to their real problem and provide, at best, a superficial test for judging the therapeutic outcome. Furthermore, there is research suggesting that clients often adopt the values of their therapists (Tjeltveit, 1986; Jensen & Bergin, 1988). So, even if they value the outcome (the test shows that ego strength has increased), they may simply be mirroring the theory-determined values of the therapists, and the outcome may not be beneficial.

There are other standard views about the proper way to judge therapeutic outcomes, but they all encounter problems. For that reason, I want to argue for a somewhat different approach.

We can begin by distinguishing a normative and metaethical question. The first question, the one that mainly concerns me here, is: By what criterion (or criteria) should we judge that a therapeutic outcome has been beneficial to the client? Suppose we find a criterion that is intuitively plausible. We can still ask the metaethical question: How do we prove that the criterion is correct? Can intuition itself serve as a kind of proof, at least under certain conditions? Philosophers disagree about the evidential value of intuitions, and indeed about whether any type of value judgment, even of a nonmoral kind, can be justified. I will say nothing about these metaethical issues except this: If a total skepticism about value judgments is correct, then the psychoanalyst is no worse off than his or her counterpart in physical medicine. Yes, the operation saved the client's life or eliminated unspeakable pain, but, the skeptic will ask, how does one prove that either outcome is good for the client? I will put to one side such a general skepticism, making no judgment about whether it is true or not, and ask: *If* we can sometimes know whether an outcome in psychotherapy is good, by what criterion can we determine this?

A commonsensical approach is to appeal to the preferences and goals of the client, but for reasons given earlier, there are problems with this idea. The client may prefer a certain outcome, but be unduly influenced by the underlying clinical theory and mistakenly judge a neutral outcome to be good. The alcoholic may want to learn to drink with less anxiety, but if he succeeds, he may be worse off. So we need to ask if there is any objective way to distinguish between cases in which the client's preferences are a suitable criterion and those in which they are not.

There is a long philosophic tradition according to which that distinction cannot be drawn. I have my own goals, desires, likes and dislikes, so the argument goes, and they determine what is good or bad for me. I like opera and philosophy; you like neither. You enjoy reading romantic poetry, gambling, and drinking alcohol in large quantities. I like none of these things. That is all there is to say; there is no objective, rational way to criticize our

respective preferences, aversions, and goals. If we rely on client preferences, we introduce an ineliminable subjective element in the determination of therapeutic effectiveness. Whatever result *seems* good to the client will be good.

There is something correct embedded in the aforementioned view, but it goes too far. Suppose my client is six years old or psychotic. Cannot his evaluation of his own welfare be simply mistaken? Even the nonpsychotic adult may value a therapeutic outcome because of a false belief. The client agrees with the therapist, say, that the therapy has been partly successful given his increase in ego strength, but he may value this only because he mistakenly believes it to correlate with something else that is valuable. Some clients determine that they are now improved because they are in better touch with their feelings, but they may simply, and temporarily, have embraced a therapeutic value of the therapist. If they were to discover that the outcome in no way makes them happier or improves the quality of their lives, they might soon decide that it was of no value.

Brandt's Theory of the Good

Is there, then, a way to use client preferences as a criterion but sift out those that are rationally unacceptable? The philosopher Richard Brandt, in his theory of the good (1979), provides an answer. His theory is attractive for several reasons. First, it has an initial plausibility. Second, it provides an *empirical* way to criticize even ultimate preferences and goals. We do not have to appeal to our own values, on his view, to object to the value preferences of others. Third, because of its therapeutic elements Brandt's theory seems particularly relevant to clinical issues. Even if it turns out to be unsatisfactory as a general theory of the good, it might serve the more limited function of aiding in the evaluation of therapeutic outcomes.

Brandt's key idea is that a "good" thing is one that it is *rational* to desire in the sense that one would desire it after undergoing "cognitive psychotherapy." This therapy— which is not identical to any standard form of cognitive therapy— involves the use of logic, the science of today, and propositions supported by publicly accessible evidence in examining one's desires. Roughly, those desires that would survive such critical examination are rational. There need be no circularity in employing Brandt's definition of the "good" and talking of cognitive therapy results. That is, we need not first judge whether "cognitive therapy" (in his sense) generally produces *good* outcomes and then appeal to such outcomes in order to determine whether they are good. Rather, we merely try to figure out which desires would be likely to survive such therapy: These are rational and their objects are good. So, if people generally desire to be free from depression, phobias, and anxieties, then being free from these conditions is generally good provided that people would retain their desires even after sustained cognitive therapy.

To see how Brandt's theory may be used, consider its application to some controversial cases. Suppose that a client is satisfied with his therapy because of his improvement on a Rorschach test. If the evidence, unknown to him, indicates that the test fails to measure anything of value, then his liking the outcome presumably would not survive cognitive therapy and can be criticized. Or consider a client of a behavior therapist who reduces his problem drinking, but does not like the result because his reading of Freud convinces him that symptom substitution is inevitable. If the evidence tells against this conviction, then the dislike is not likely to survive cognitive therapy. These sorts of cases do not involve judgments of intrinsic value and raise primarily empirical issues. However, consider an actual case of a heterosexual accused of having sex with children. With his consent, his therapist trained him to enjoy homosexual sex. Commentators on the case disagreed strongly as to whether this was a good outcome (Davison, 1976). A similar question can be raised by efforts to "cure" gays of their homosexuality (see the work of Feldman & MacCulloch, 1971). In questioning such outcomes, one might be raising a moral issue of what ought to be done rather than one about the value of the result. The moral question is: Whether or not the outcome is beneficial to the client, should the therapist try to produce it? That is not the question of interest here. I am asking only about the value of the outcome, not about the morality of pursuing that outcome. Once again, on Brandt's theory, if the client desires the outcome and that desire would not be extinguished by cognitive therapy (in Brandt's sense) if the client were to undergo it, then the outcome is good for that client.

Consider one other type of case. Alan Bergin (1991) and others have argued for the use of religious criteria in the evaluation of outcomes. If we use Brandt's theory, that can be done, but the evidence for the related religious belief would also have to be assessed. For example, suppose that a marriage counselor encourages a client to get a divorce but the client finds that unsatisfactory because he believes he will be condemned to hell if he follows the therapist's advice. On Brandt's criterion, his aversion to divorce can be criticized if there is reason to believe that cognitive therapy would extinguish it. Of course, even if the client's verdict is criticizable, it might still be wrong for the therapist to urge divorce upon him.

Problems and Possible Modifications

I turn now to some problems with Brandt's approach. Some that have been raised in the philosophic literature (Harman, 1982; Gibbard, 1990) concern his attempt to construct a *general* theory of either the good or the rational; they need not concern us here unless they also bear on the more limited issue of adapting his account to the study of psychotherapy outcomes. However, I will make one exception and make brief mention of the issue of the cognitive status of Brandt's criterion. How do we know that a desire that would survive cognitive therapy is either rational or good? Brandt's answer, roughly, is this (1979, chap. 8): He is stipulating that such a desire is "rational," but whether it is also "good" in any ordinary sense is unclear, he argues, because the ordinary sense is unclear. Despite this unclarity about the ordinary sense of "good," there are some facts, Brandt argues, that will recommend rational desires to virtually everyone. I will not discuss here what these facts are or the adequacy of Brandt's defense, but if his argument does not work, we might settle for something more modest than a proof of what the good is. We can at least ask the following two questions. First, is Brandt's criterion potentially useful in therapeutic contexts? Second, will its use square with our intuitions about what is or is not a good outcome? I am not assuming that even a perfect fit with our intuitions (where our intuitions agree) is a guarantee of correctness, but I will assume, without argument, that if an evaluative criterion is fundamental, then a lack of fit counts against it— unless there is some reasonable explanation consistent with its correctness for the discrepancy.

On the first issue, that of potential usefulness, there is much in favor of Brandt's criterion. As noted earlier, its use requires no appeal to other evaluative criteria, and, subject to certain qualifications, it can be applied empirically. To evaluate a client's preference, we need not actually provide cognitive therapy; we need only appeal to our background evidence to decide whether the preference is likely to be extinguishable by cognitive therapy. Given all we know, it is likely, for example, that for most clients the desire to be free from a crippling anxiety or depression is likely to survive cognitive therapy. However, one limitation is that in some cases we may not have enough information about a client to reach a reasonable decision about certain fundamental preferences. Another problem concerns the specification of what "cognitive therapy" is. The therapy is said to involve the confrontation of desires with relevant information by repeatedly representing it in an ideally vivid way and at an appropriate time (Brandt, 1979, p. 113). This is obviously rather vague. What counts as *relevant* information, an *ideally* vivid way, and an *appropriate* time? Without a more precise description of the therapy, we are likely to have a wide range of cases in which there will be no way to tell how to apply Brandt's criterion *even if* we know a great deal about the client.

I turn next to some questions about the intuitive plausibility of Brandt's criterion.

One problem that analysts are likely to raise concerns the role of repressed wishes. Suppose that a client has what looks like an irrational desire to persist in a very troubling sexual relationship. Even if the desire truly is "irrational" in an ordinary sense, it might not be extinguishable by cognitive therapy if it is the product of a repressed wish. Even if there are no such things as repressed wishes, there are nonpsychoanalytic types of cases that also pose a challenge to Brandt's criterion. Suppose that someone has a phobic reaction to riding on elevators. If the aversion is long-standing and deeply rooted, even if it is not due to a repressed wish, Brandt's cognitive therapy might not extinguish it. In this latter sort of case, perhaps we could draw a distinction between phobias due to conditioning and those due to cognitive factors (see Wolpe, 1977). We might then modify Brandt's criterion and say that an aversion is rational if and only if: a) it is not due to conditioning, and b) it would survive cognitive therapy.

However, a more general problem than that is posed by phobias or repressed wishes. There may be various classes of irrational desires, aversions, and preferences that are so woven into someone's personality that cognitive therapy will not extin-

guish them. We may try to handle these by further complicating Brandt's criterion, but another way out is to treat his conditions for being rational as necessary but not sufficient. A desire is rational, it might be said, *only if* it would survive cognitive therapy. Of those that would survive, some may be rational and some not. So a conscious desire resulting from a repressed wish or a phobic aversion may be irrational, on Brandt's modified theory, even if cognitive therapy cannot eliminate them.

An opposite sort of problem is the possible extinguishability of desires that seem to be rational and good. As Gil Harman (1982, p. 128) argues, benevolence (i.e., the desire to be benevolent toward others) might prove to be a casualty of cognitive therapy. Suppose, for example, that our cognitive therapy involves the following: We repeatedly show the subject pictures of people around the world who are starving. It is possible that the individual will infer that helping people is a hopeless task and, as a consequence, he or she may lose the desire to help. The general worry here is that some preferences in some people may be rational but fragile: Subjecting them repeatedly to certain types of information might extinguish them even if the desires are rational.

Perhaps some of the problems associated with Brandt's theory can be solved in the following way. First, delete the idea that preferences capable of surviving cognitive therapy are necessarily rational. Some preferences may be neither rational nor irrational; they just "are," so to speak. My colleague Ramon Lemos suggests the following example. A client is envious of certain people and prefers that they suffer and fail in their endeavors. Assuming that his having this preference has no bad consequences that we can bring to the client's attention, it might survive cognitive therapy and, thus, not be irrational, but not be rational either (unless we stipulate that we will use "rational" in a technical sense to cover all such preferences). However, we need not take a stand on the rationality of the preference. It is enough, for my purposes, that a client's preference not be irrational. If it is not, we can leave open the question of whether it is rational. My second suggestion is that we adopt a proposal that Harman (1982) makes in passing but does not develop. Keep some of Brandt's ideas, but eliminate the appeal to cognitive therapy. Instead of trying to figure out if a desire would survive if confronted with information *repeatedly* represented in an *ideally* vivid fashion, develop various criteria for criticizing desires, preferences, and aversions.

One way to criticize a client's preference for a certain outcome is to demonstrate that it is causally linked to a false belief. Someone might value a result not for its own sake but because of a mistaken belief that it will lead to something else of value. The client, say, values an increase in ego strength because he or she believes it to be a reliable indicator of improved mental health, and this might be a mistake. Even if something is valued for its own sake, say chastity or self-sacrifice, it may be valued because of a religious, moral, or political belief that is false, or at least unwarranted. A second line of criticism concerns final ends: A client may value something for its own sake, but it may be unobtainable and its pursuit may have deleterious effects. Thus, some clients reportedly want "everyone to love them" or they wish to live a life of total perfection. These ends may be good from the client's point of view, but it may be unreasonable to prefer them to more modest goals if their pursuit is bound to be futile and harmful. A third form of criticism involves the comparison of competing final ends. For example, a client may value fame for its own sake, but pursuing that end may conflict with an end valued even more, such as contentment. (Strictly speaking, these second two types of criticism may be applicable not to the client's preference for certain ends, but to his or her desire to pursue them.)

I conclude that it may be possible to adapt Brandt's theory to the evaluation of therapeutic outcomes, provided that the problems I mentioned can be worked out. Even in the absence of a general philosophical theory, however, we can and should appeal to client preferences, purified by rational criticism, to question the widespread practice of accepting at face value the satisfaction of a paradigm's aim or the aims of an individual therapist as a criterion of therapeutic success. If a therapy's effectiveness is determined by its capacity to help a client, then the satisfaction of his or her preferences, filtering out those that are irrational, is the proper criterion for judging therapeutic success. It then becomes an empirical question as to which of the many theory-driven criteria, such as a certain score on a Rorschach test, an increase in ego strength, or getting in touch with one's feelings, are reliable indicators of satisfying this more basic criterion. In many outcome studies and reviews, including that of Bachrach et al. (1991), the needed empirical evidence is missing. Consequently, there is no way to tell whether the therapy was effective in helping the clients *even if* we have established a causal relationship between therapy and outcome.

EXPERIMENTAL ISSUES

Let us waive any further discussion about the evaluation of outcomes that follow psychoanalysis and assume that a certain percentage of them are beneficial to the client. There remain, of course, disputed issues about the confirmation of alleged causal connections between analysis and the beneficial outcomes. One basic issue concerns the need to meet an experimental standard to confirm such causal connections. In their review of psychoanalytic outcome studies, Bachrach et al. (1991, pp. 873–4) list five criteria for evaluating research on treatment outcomes, such as the need to demonstrate that the treatment being evaluated is taking place, the requirement that the patient be suitable for treatment, and so on. The criteria do not require, however, that a study be *experimental* (with random assignment to treatment and comparison groups, and the inclusion of at least a no treatment or wait-list control group). Furthermore, although the authors make a number of criticisms of the studies they review, they nowhere fault a study for being nonexperimental. Finally, despite their criticisms, Bachrach et al. conclude (p. 911) that the studies, *none of which is experimental*, "... confirm that patients suitable for analysis derive therapeutic benefit." I infer from the foregoing that the authors do not agree that it is generally necessary to meet an experimental standard to confirm the efficacy of psychoanalysis.

A likely explanation for Bachrach et al.'s adoption of a nonexperimental standard is that they are consciously employing criteria they believe acceptable to the psychoanalytic community. Thus, they write: "For too long psychoanalytic research has been defensively toned, and analysts have failed to fully appreciate that it is both a common and legitimate strategy for scientists to work within their own disciplinary matrix.... For this reason it is important to conduct our inquiry from a point of view native to psychoanalysis" (p. 873). The major difficulty with this sort of relativization of epistemological standards to a psychoanalytic paradigm is the same as that raised earlier about outcome criteria. Yes, most psychoanalysts (let us assume) will agree with the Bachrach et al. criteria, but are they the *right* criteria? That is, if outcome studies satisfy all such criteria (and any others that the authors employ), will that suffice for the production of credible evidence that psychoanalysis generally causes beneficial outcomes? Merely pointing out that analysts generally accept such criteria and, more pointedly, generally do *not* insist on the introduction of experimental controls, does nothing to answer the question. Some reply must be given to those who argue (e.g., Erwin, 1994; Grünbaum, 1984, 1993) that experimental controls are generally necessary in assessing claims of psychoanalytic effectiveness.

The Case for Experimentation

The first step in an argument for an experimental standard is the assumption that a psychoanalytic outcome hypothesis H is not confirmed by data D if a competing hypothesis is at least as credible as H, all things considered (i.e., given D and our background evidence and the appeal to any nonobservational criteria that are epistemically relevant). If this initial assumption were challenged, as it apparently is by Fine and Forbes (1986), I would appeal to philosophical arguments designed to show that all confirmation must be "differential" (see Erwin & Siegel, 1989). If the initial step is conceded, the next one is well known: It is the claim that for the types of nonpsychotic problems typically treated by analysts, generally at least two credible hypotheses need to be defeated. First, factors external to the therapeutic situation or, second, placebo factors (or a combination of both) caused most or all of the therapeutic gains. Most psychotherapy researchers agree about the need to discount the first rival, but not everyone agrees about the placebo hypothesis. However, the case for rejecting this hypothesis, too, is argued in Erwin (1994).

One could reply to the above argument that even if experimentation is *generally* required in evaluating therapeutic claims, there are exceptions, such as cases where the therapeutic changes are so sudden and dramatic that spontaneous remission and placebo hypotheses can be ruled out even in the absence of experimental controls. Paul Meehl (1983) describes two such psychoanalytic cases that he finds convincing. I disagree about the interpretation of these cases, as interesting as they are (see Erwin, 1988, pp. 206–209), but here I wish to stress a different point. There is an extraordinary case in the placebo literature (see Kazdin, 1980, pp. 21–22) of a patient with large cancerous tumors who was treated with Kreboizen, a fake cancer

cure. Given the pattern of subsequent dramatic changes in the patient, it looks as if his confidence in Kreboizen caused a remission of his cancer and a temporary elimination of his tumors. Yet no one should infer from this one case that a placebo treatment is generally effective for the treatment of any type of cancer. The lesson here is clear. If our question is not "Has the use of analysis ever produced a significant therapeutic benefit?" but rather "Is analysis, when employed by a trained therapist, *generally* effective in treating a certain type of patient with a certain type of problem in a certain type of clinical setting," then a *body* of evidence, not a few scattered cases, will be needed to answer the question with assurance (see Erwin, 1988, for further discussion of the evidential value of case studies).

Another reply to the insistence on experimental controls is to argue for the relativization of standards not to a paradigm but to a science. For example, Paul Robinson (1993, p. 62) criticizes Grünbaum (1984) for (allegedly) complaining that psychoanalysis does not meet the evidential standards routinely used in physics. The proper standards for psychoanalysis, Robinson claims, are those employed in historical biology. He notes: "In historical biology the demands for laboratory comparisons and group control studies to justify causal assertions is, if anything, even more a counsel of perfection than it is in psychoanalysis" (p. 262).

I agree with Robinson's contention that psychoanalysis should not be held to higher standards than historical biology, but I question whether the relevant biological standards are different from those applicable in physics. In both physics and biology, it is *not* a necessary condition for confirmation of a causal hypothesis that a controlled study be done. Grünbaum (1984, p. 259) gives examples from physics where the probative equivalent of a control group is provided by other means, rendering experimentation unnecessary in such cases. In contrast, it *is* necessary for any causal hypothesis, no matter what the science, that it meet a "differential" standard in order for confirmation to occur. That is, as noted earlier, H is confirmed by data D only if D provides some reason for believing H, but does not provide an equal or better reason for believing some incompatible rival at least as plausible as H given our total evidence (for the argument that this standard must be met, see Erwin & Siegel, 1989). Whether experimentation is needed to meet this differential standard for any particular causal hypothesis depends on the empirical details concerning that hypothesis. As argued earlier, for psychoanalytic outcome hypotheses, the empirical details are such that experimentation is generally needed for confirmation.

The Equal Effectiveness Thesis

One could concede that experimental evidence is needed to confirm outcome claims, but then argue that psychoanalysis can, so to speak, "piggyback" on the experimental data collected for other treatments. That is, a widely accepted thesis, based largely on the Luborsky et al. (1975) review and the metaanalysis of Smith, Glass, and Miller (1980), is that *all* forms of psychotherapy are effective and are equally effective. Thus, Jerome Frank (1984, p. 18) writes: "The relative superiority of psychotherapy of whatever form over no-treatment control groups has also been conclusively demonstrated by massive meta-analyses of controlled studies of psychotherapy by Smith, Glass and Miller (1980) and Shapiro and Shapiro (1982)."

Frank does not uphold a strict form of what may be termed the "Equal Effectiveness Thesis." His view might be expressed as follows (Frank, 1984, p. 18): With some possible exceptions (such as the use of cognitive therapy with depressed patients),

1. all psychotherapies are effective, and
2. all psychotherapies are equally effective.

There are reasons to doubt (2) (see Rachman & Wilson, 1980, chap. 12; Wilson, 1985), but thesis (1) is all that the psychoanalyst need appeal to, to invoke the "piggyback" argument. If psychoanalysis is a form of psychotherapy, then (1) entails that it too is effective. Thus, if we know (1) to be true, we can know that psychoanalysis is effective without studying it experimentally.

Is (1) true? Notice that Frank in the above quotation does not claim that psychotherapy has been found to be more effective than a placebo; indeed, he claims elsewhere (1984, p. 22) that symptom relief generated by psychotherapy is the same on average as that produced by a placebo. If, however, the proper standard for judging effectiveness is its capacity to outperform a credible placebo, as I argue in Erwin (1994), then Frank's grounds for thesis (1) are questionable. Clients of psychotherapy may do better than those in a no-treatment control group, but unless placebo factors have been

adequately discounted, that may yield no evidence that the therapy caused the beneficial outcome. Even apart from doubts about the failure to include a placebo comparison, there is reason to question the metaanalytic evidence cited by Frank as well as the review by Luborsky et al. (1975; see Erwin, 1994; Rachman & Wilson, 1980).

Suppose, contrary to the doubts just expressed, that the Equal Effectiveness Thesis were true. That would create another problem for psychoanalysts. If all psychotherapies are equally effective, then it is hard to justify employing psychoanalysis when rival therapies will produce the same benefits in a much shorter time and at a cheaper cost. Some psychoanalysts, however, have their own reasons for doubting that all psychotherapies are equally effective: They claim that some benefits, such as profound character change, can be produced only by psychoanalysis. But how can they know this in the absence of experimental evidence to support their claim? Even if thesis (1) were supported by solid evidence, it does not entail that all psychotherapies are effective for any and every clinical problem; it entails only that all psychotherapies are effective in treating certain types of problems, namely those successfully traced by psychotherapy in experimental outcome studies. The problem of how to produce deep character change is not among the problems studied (if it were, the claim of superiority of psychoanalysis for this problem would be undercut).

I have been arguing that controlled studies are generally needed to confirm psychoanalytic outcome hypotheses. However, would such studies be sufficient to establish effectiveness (if psychoanalysis is effective)? Many psychoanalysts are skeptical. For example, Goldberg (1990, p. 9) disputes the reasonableness of Grünbaum's (1984) thesis that one must go outside of the clinical situation to verify psychoanalytic propositions; he does so on the grounds that the quest for extraclinical validation is likely to prove futile. His particular reason for being skeptical is that he insists on an extremely high evidential standard, one that requires that psychoanalytic propositions be proved with certainty (see p. 9). If we were to use that standard, however, the quest for experimental validation in medicine, chemistry, and physics would also prove futile. This fact does nothing to show that experimentation cannot yield evidence that is solid even if it falls short of certitude. Nevertheless, even if we do not insist on certitude, many analysts will still be skeptical about the value of experimentation in their field. I do not agree about the futility of experiments, but suppose that their skepticism is warranted. That still does not answer the arguments of Grünbaum (1984, 1993) or myself. What we are arguing is that experimentation is generally *necessary* to confirm psychoanalytic propositions (although in this chapter, I am talking only about outcome hypotheses). Whether experimentation will prove *sufficient* to confirm (or disconfirm) such propositions is a different issue.

The above point about necessity is also relevant to questions about the feasibility and morality of doing a controlled study of long-term psychoanalysis, especially if a placebo control is insisted on. Whether or not the ethical and practical issues can be resolved, experimentation is generally necessary if psychoanalytic outcome claims are to be confirmed. There may (or may not be) good reasons not to do the required experiments, but without them the value of psychoanalysis will remain unestablished.

Single-Subject Designs

Some analysts may agree with the use of an experimental standard for judging the worth of psychoanalysis, but argue that we can still rely on clinical data. Behavior therapists, after all, have successfully used single-subject experimental designs in testing outcomes hypotheses within a clinical setting. In a basic ABAB design, a baseline is taken; in the next phase, therapy is given; in the third phase, therapy is withheld and a new baseline is taken; and finally therapy is restored (for a discussion of this design and more complicated single-subject designs, see Barlow & Hersen, 1984).

It might be argued, then, that the distinction between clinical and experimental evidence is potentially misleading. In using single-subject designs, analysts can obtain clinical evidence that is also experimental evidence. Furthermore, by using such designs some of the practical and ethical problems associated with group designs with a placebo control might be avoided.

Can analysts, then, successfully adapt for their purposes the single-subject experimental strategies used by behavior therapists? The analyst Marshall Edelson argues that they can. He begins his case (1984) by noting certain epistemic difficulties in using group designs. For example, it is often difficult to obtain truly random samples in clinical prac-

tice. Without such randomization, there is a serious problem if one wishes to generalize the results of a group experiment to other populations. Another problem, which seems inherent in any group design, concerns the need for averaging the results. In a large-scale study, not everyone in the treatment group will improve, at least not to the same extent. So the investigator compares the mean treatment outcome to that of the mean outcome for the control groups. However, as Edelson points out, taking an average may obscure important individual differences. Some people in the treatment group might not have been helped and some might have been made worse, even if the average treatment effect is positive. Edelson makes other useful criticisms of group designs and concludes (p. 63), following Chassan (1979), that there is a convincing argument for favoring single-subject designs over large group studies (Edelson, 1984, p. 63).

To date, single-subject experimental designs have been used rarely, if at all, in evaluating psychoanalytic outcome hypotheses. However, the issues that Edelson raises are important for future investigations and deserve comment. I have several.

First, I would agree that in much psychotherapy research, one can find the defects that Edelson lists. However, in many cases, such problems as lack of random allocation of subjects are marks of poor research; the problems are not inherent in group designs as such. There are, in addition, effective strategies for overcoming some of the typical problems with group designs (Kazdin, 1980).

Second, some of the problems with group designs also arise for single-subject designs. For example, if we do a number of single-subject studies, which we must if we wish to confirm that a therapy is generally effective, problems about random selection can also arise. Or consider the averaging problem. Suppose that one investigator uses a group design with 50 subjects and another does 50 separate single-subject experiments. If it is likely that not all of the 50 subjects in the group experiment will improve even if the treatment is effective, that is also true of the 50 subjects in the series of single experiments, provided that the relevant conditions are comparable. So, if one wants to extrapolate to other populations, the averaging problem will also arise for the single-subject designs.

Third, single-subject designs have special liabilities of their own. It is more difficult with them than with a group design with a placebo control to rule out a placebo hypothesis. Another problem is the difficulty of supporting a general hypothesis about effectiveness unless a lot of experiments are done. In short, a more balanced conclusion would be this: Under certain conditions and given certain research purposes, single-subject designs are superior to group designs; for other conditions and purposes, they are not.

Finally, whether they are generally superior or not, can single-subject designs be adapted to the study of psychoanalysis? Consider the basic ABAB design used in certain behavior therapy outcome studies. What would correspond in psychoanalysis, for example, to a behavior therapist providing electric shock and later withholding it? Would the analyst see the patient only every other week, or every other month? As usually conceived, analysis is supposed to achieve its lasting therapeutic gains relatively late in the course of treatment, generally not before transference occurs. It is unclear, then, what would be shown by providing analysis in, say, alternate weeks or months. Perhaps one could turn on the transference and then turn it off, and then on again and off again, and so on. We could then gauge the effects. But how does one turn the transference on and off? Unless one spells out in detail exactly how a particular single-subject design can be applied to the study of psychoanalytic outcomes, a proposal to use single-subject designs is difficult to evaluate.

Edelson does discuss a case that might be taken as a model for single-subject research by psychoanalysts. The case is that of Breuer's treatment of Anna O. Edelson (1984, p. 124) and argues that because Breuer attacked his client's symptoms separately or independently, one is justified in eliminating a general placebo effect as an alternative explanation. As Grünbaum has noted (1993), however, a placebo explanation was not ruled out by Breuer. The patient's confidence in Breuer may have caused each separate remission. Breuer himself conceded this possibility. In addition, although Breuer's "talking cure" was an antecedent of Freudian therapy, it was not full-blown psychoanalysis. Even if a placebo explanation had been ruled out in the Anna O. case, there would remain the problem of explaining exactly how single-subject designs are to be transferred to the analytic setting in the study of outcomes. I am not arguing that this cannot be done, only that there are obstacles; without a detailed and concrete proposal to examine, it is difficult to judge in advance whether the obstacles are likely to be overcome. (For other problems in adapting single-subject designs to the study of psychoanalysis, see Grünbaum, 1993, pp. 233–255.) Edelson, incidentally, also appears to have reservations. He concludes (1984, p. 124) that single-subject designs can be used to test psychoanalytic hypotheses, but not necessarily those focused on etiology or therapeutic efficacy. Still, regardless of how confident Edelson is or is not about testing analytic outcome hypotheses, the issues he has raised about the subject warrant further discussion.

CONCLUSION

This paper has been concerned not with the empirical data concerning the effectiveness of psychoanalysis but with philosophical issues about the proper standards for interpreting the data. However, if I am right about these standards, then the alleged benefits of long-term psychoanalysis, contrary to Bachrach et al. (1991), have not yet been demonstrated. Although there is a body of experimental evidence concerning psychoanalytic theory (Kline, 1981; Fisher & Greenberg, 1985), there is no similar body of experimental evidence concerning the therapy (although the absence of such evidence, of course, is not by itself evidence of ineffectiveness).

If we were to change the subject and talk not about orthodox psychoanalysis but about short-term psychoanalytically oriented psychotherapy, matters would become much more complex. There *are* experimental studies of this "type" of therapy but the evidence is conflicting. Although the Smith, Glass, and Miller (1980) review did not cover orthodox psychoanalysis, it did analyze studies of short-term psychodynamic therapies and claims to have found evidence of effectiveness. In contrast, Prioleau, Murdock, and Brody (1983) used a more demanding standard (which I believe to be correct; see Erwin, 1994)—the capacity to outperform a credible placebo—and, after examining the same data, found no evidence of effectiveness for any short-term psychodynamic therapy. More recently, Swartberg and Stiles (1991) reviewed 19 studies of this type of therapy and found (p. 710) a small but significant superiority to wait-list patients at post-treatment. However, the studies did not control for placebo effects. Furthermore, as research quality increased, superiority to no treatment decreased. The psychodynamic treatments also showed a small but significant inferiority to alternative therapies (such as cognitive behavior therapy) at posttreatment and close to a large-sized inferiority at one year follow-up. Finally, a number of different types of psychotherapy are generally classified as "psychodynamic" or "psychoanalytically oriented." Some borrow heavily from Freud's work; some do not. If we group these therapies together, we could ask the further question: Of those, if any, that are generally effective in producing a certain type of benefit for a certain type of client, do the specifically psychoanalytic ingredients mainly account for the beneficial outcomes? Because the studies done so far have generally lacked a placebo control, the evidence we now have does not warrant a positive answer.

REFERENCES

Bachrach, H., Galatzer-Levy, R., Skolnikoff, A., & Waldron, S. (1991). On the efficacy of psychoanalysis. *Journal of the American Psychoanalytic Association*, *39*, 871–916.

Barlow, D., & Hersen, M. (1984). *Single case experimental designs: Strategies for studying behavioral change*. New York: Pergamon.

Bergin, A. (1991). Values and religious issues in psychotherapy and mental health. *American Psychologist*, *46*, 394–403.

Brandt, R. (1979). *A theory of the good and right*. New York: Oxford University Press.

Chassan, J. (1979). *Research design in clinical psychology and psychiatry*. New York: Irvington.

Davison, G. (1976). Homosexuality: The ethical challenge. *Journal of Consulting and Clinical Psychology*, *44*, 157–162.

Edelson, M. (1984). *Hypothesis and evidence in psychoanalysis*. Chicago: University of Chicago Press.

Erwin, E. (1988). Psychoanalysis: Clinical versus experimental evidence. In P. Clark & C. Wright (Eds.), *Mind, psychoanalysis and science*. New York: Basil Blackwell.

Erwin, E. (1994). The effectiveness of psychotherapy: Epistemological issues. In G. Graham & L. Stephens (Eds.), *Philosophical psychopathology: A book of readings*. Cambridge, MA: MIT Press.

Erwin, E., & Siegel, H. (1989). Is confirmation differential? *British Journal for the Philosophy of Science*, *40*, 105–119.

Eysenck, H. J. (1952). The effects of psychotherapy: An evaluation. *Journal of Consulting Psychology*, *16*, 319–324.

Feldman, M., & MacCulloch, M. (1971). *Homosexual behavior: Therapy and assessment*. Oxford: Pergamon Press.

Fine, A., & Forbes, M. (1986). Grünbaum on Freud: Three grounds for dissent. *Behavioral and Brain Sciences*, *9*, 237–238.

Fisher, S., & Greenberg, R. (1985). *The scientific credibility of Freud's theories and therapy*. New York: Columbia University Press.

Frank, J. (1984). Therapeutic components of all psychotherapies. In J. Myers (Ed.), *Cures by psychotherapy: What effects change?* New York: Praeger.

Garfield, S., & Bergin, A. (1986). Introduction and historical overview. In S. Garfield & A. Bergin (Eds.), *Handbook of psychotherapy and behavior change*, (3rd ed.). New York: John Wiley and Sons.

Gibbard, A. (1990). *Wise choices, apt feelings: A theory of normative judgement*. Cambridge, MA: Harvard University Press.

Glass, G., & Kliegl, R. (1983). An apology for research integration in the study of psychotherapy. *Journal of Consulting and Clinical Psychology*, *51*, 28–41.

Goldberg, A. (1990). *The prisonhouse of psychoanalysis*. Hillsdale, NJ: Analytic Press.

Grünbaum, A. (1984). *The foundations of psychoanalysis: A philosophical critique*. Berkeley, CA: University of California Press.

Grünbaum, A. (1993). *Validation in the clinical theory of psychoanalysis: A study in the philosophy of psychoanalysis*. Madison, CT: International Universities Press.

Harman, G. (1982). Critical review: Richard Brandt, *A theory of the good and right*. *Philosophical Studies*, *42*, 119–139.

Jensen, J., & Bergin, A. (1988). Mental health values of professional therapists: A national interdisciplinary survey. *Professional Psychology Research and Practice*, *19*, 290–297.

Kazdin, A. (1980). *Research design in clinical psychology*. New York: Harper and Row.

Kazdin, A. (1986). The evaluation of psychotherapy: Research design and methodology. In S. Garfield & A. Bergin (Eds.), *Handbook of psychotherapy and behavior change*, (3rd ed.). New York: John Wiley and Sons.

Kline, P. (1981). *Fact and fantasy in Freudian theory*, (2nd ed.). London: Methuen.

Kline, P. (1988). Freudian theory and experimental evidence: A reply to Erwin. In P. Clark & C. Wright (Eds.), *Mind, psychoanalysis and science*. New York: Basil Blackwell.

Luborsky, L., Singer, B., & Luborsky, L. (1975). Comparative studies of psychotherapy: Is it true that "Everyone has won and all must have prizes"? *Archives of General Psychiatry*, *32*, 995–1008.

Malan, D. (1976). *Toward the validation of dynamic psychotherapy: A replication*. New York: Plenum.

Meehl, P. (1983). Subjectivity in psychoanalytic inference: The nagging persistence of Wilhelm Fliess's Achensee Question. In J. Earman (Ed.), *Testing scientific theories. Minnesota Studies in the Philosophy of*

Science, vol. X. Minneapolis: University of Minnesota Press.

Prioleau, L., Murdock, M., & Brody, N. (1983). An analysis of psychotherapy versus placebo studies. *The Behavioral and Brain Sciences, 6,* 275–310.

Rachman, S., & Wilson, G. T. (1980). *The effects of psychological therapy.* New York: Pergamon Press.

Robinson, P. (1993). *Freud and his critics.* Berkeley, CA: University of California Press.

Rogers, C., & Skinner, B. F. (1956). Some issues concerning the control of human behavior: A symposium. *Science, 124,* 1057–1065.

Ryle, A. (1982). *Psychotherapy: A cognitive integration of theory and practice.* London: Academic Press.

Shapiro, D., & Shapiro, D. (1982). Meta-analysis of comparative outcome studies: A replication and refinement. *Psychological Bulletin, 92,* 581–604.

Smith, M., Glass, G., & Miller, T. (1980). *The benefits of psychotherapy.* Baltimore: Johns Hopkins University Press.

Swartberg, M., & Stiles, T. (1991). Comparative effects of short-term psychodynamic psychotherapy: A meta-analysis. *Journal of Consulting and Clinical Psychology, 59,* 704–714.

Tjeltveit, A. (1986). The ethics of value conversion in psychotherapy: Appropriate and inappropriate therapist influence on client values. *Clinical Psychology Review, 6,* 515–537.

Wilson, G. T. (1985). Limitations of meta-analysis in the evaluation of psychological therapy. *Clinical Psychology Review, 5,* 35–47.

Wolpe, J. (1977). Inadequate behavior analysis: The Achilles heel of outcome research in behavior therapy. *Journal of Behavior Therapy and Experimental Psychiatry, 8,* 1–3.

Woolfolk, R. (1992). Hermeneutics, social constructionism and other items of intellectual fashion: Intimations for clinical science. *Behavior Therapy, 23,* 213–224.

CHAPTER 20

WHAT IS AN IRRATIONAL BELIEF?

Rational-Emotive Therapy and Accounts of Rationality*

William O'Donohue

Jason S. Vass

Rational-emotive therapy (RET), which was originated by Albert Ellis over 30 years ago (Ellis, 1958, 1962, 1987a, 1987b), is one of the most widely practiced models of psychotherapy and counseling (Heesacker, Heppner, & Rogers, 1982; Smith, 1982). RET's popularity may be partly due to its commitment to the scientist–practitioner model and its emphasis upon empirical evaluation (Ellis, 1989a). Its popularity with practitioners is also likely to be the result of RET's directness, economy, and apparent efficacy for a wide variety of psychological problems. A recent metaanalysis of 70 RET outcome studies suggests that RET leads to significant improvement in clients relative to initial assessments and control groups (Lyons & Woods, 1991). Moreover, recent articles have suggested a strong and perhaps causal link between irrational beliefs and emotional distress (Hart, Turner, Hittner, Cardozo, & Paras, 1991; Woods, Silverman, Gentilimi, Cunningham, & Grieger, 1991).

* The authors would like to thank Raymond DiGuiseppi and Lizette Peterson for their comments on earlier drafts of this chapter.

The concept of "rational" and its correlative, "irrational," are central to RET's conceptualization of psychopathology and psychotherapy (Ellis, 1958, 1976, 1984, 1985, 1987a). In fact, Ellis and Dryden (1987) suggest that one of the key contributions of RET is "its distinction between rational and irrational beliefs" (p. 5). Mahoney, Lyddon, and Alford (1989) also have pointed to the centrality of this distinction: "A reliance on the therapist's abilities to recognize irrational thinking processes and to actively intervene and persuade clients to change their thoughts from irrational to rational is an essential feature of RET" (p. 78). However, these abilities would appear dependent upon the quality of the account of rationality contained in RET.

We will critically examine the concepts of irrational and rational beliefs utilized in RET. An accurate understanding of rationality is useful not only because this concept is central to RET. Other cognitive therapies rely on concepts such as "cognitive errors" (Beck, 1984) and "dysfunctional thinking" (Mahoney, 1974), which are related to rationality in that rationality is a normative account of reasoning. These constructs have an epistemological dimension in that they imply erroneous beliefs or reasoning. Thus these accounts of psychopathology and cognitive therapy rely upon a (often implicit) regulative account of correct reasoning and as such can be evaluated on the grounds of the adequacy of these accounts. Ellis should be commended in that he has explicitly recognized this philosophical dimension of this theory and has tried to tie his cognitive account of psychopathology and psychotherapy to the views of the prominent philosopher of science Sir Karl Popper (1957) as well as to the more recent work of the neo-Popperians (Bartley, 1984). The Popperian pan-critical account of rationality is based on a fallibilistic, evolutionary epistemology. In this view, certitude is never reached and all beliefs are perennially open to criticism. Criticism is extremely valuable because, if used properly, it can allow error to be eliminated, and thus an approximation to truth can occur (Popper, 1965). Important questions in the pan-critical approach are, What possible evidence counts against my belief? How can I expose my belief to criticism? What are alternative beliefs and what is their evidentiary status?

In this chapter we evaluate the account of rationality utilized in RET on four criteria: clarity, consistency, applicability, and accuracy. Part of the goal of these sections is to assess the degree to which the conventional RET account is problematic and therefore in need of revision. Ellis (1989b) himself has recently suggested that he has revised his account of rationality:

I abandoned even more elements of logical positivism when I later read Bartley (1962), Mahoney (1976), and Popper (1963), all of whom hold that to be scientific a hypothesis had better be falsifiable. In recent years I adopted Bartley's (sic) more open ended position, which states that no hypothesis can be completely proven (or disproven) by empirical "evidence." (p. 200)

Because we agree with Ellis that this view represents a more accurate account of rationality, pan-critical rationalism will be discussed in more detail in the section on accuracy. However because it is unclear to what extent the practitioners of RET have understood this key reformulation and its implications (see also Jacobs, 1989; Rorer, 1991), we will also attempt to outline some

of the major implications of a pan-critical account of rationality for the practice of RET.

First, let us briefly summarize the role of rationality in Ellis's account of human behavior and its problems to set this review in its proper context. Ellis (1987a) suggests that individuals have a basic desire "to remain alive and to be reasonably happy" (p. 366). However, the world is not ideal and hence these desires are frequently blocked. When individuals experience barriers in their pursuit of survival and happiness, they may respond in "two basic and exceptionally different ways" (Ellis, 1987a, p. 366). They may react with a set of "rational beliefs" and experience "appropriate feelings" such as "sorrow, regret, disappointment, frustration, and annoyance" (Ellis, 1987a, p. 366). Rational beliefs allow people to cope with the difficulties of life and, presumably, to function more adequately in the future. According to Ellis, if people consistently respond with rational beliefs they are unlikely to experience psychopathology. On the other hand, if people resort to irrational beliefs, they are likely to "make and keep themselves emotionally disturbed" (Ellis, 1987a, p. 366). RET consists of identifying a client's relevant irrational beliefs, challenging them, and helping the client replace them with rational beliefs (Ellis, 1958, 1962, 1977, 1987a).

WHAT ARE RET'S CRITERIA OF "RATIONALITY" AND "IRRATIONALITY"?

Figure 1 contains a list of quotations in which Ellis attempts to define or elucidate "rationality" and "irrationality," as well as the concepts of "rational" and "irrational beliefs." These are organized chronologically and listed by citation.

This list is by no means exhaustive as other prominent RET researchers and practitioners provide still other definitions of rationality and irrationality. Dryden and DiGiuseppe (1990), for example, suggest that an irrational belief may involve: (1) low frustration tolerance (a belief that the person is unable to function, persist, or exist in the presence of some stressor); (2) demandingness (a belief that the world or some other entity must be as the person desires it to be); or (3) human worth (a belief that denotes a global, permanent devaluation of a person based on some trait or behavior).

Irrational

"By irrationality I mean any thought, emotion, or behavior that leads to self-defeating or self-destructive consequences that significantly interfere with the survival and happiness of the organism" (Ellis, 1977, p. 15).

"…'self-defeating' …" (Ellis, 1990, p. 176).

Rational

"It can be assumed that almost all humans have the basic goals of wanting to survive, to be relatively happy, to get along with members of their social group, and to relate intimately to a few selected members of this group. Once these basic values are assumed, anything that aids them is rational or appropriate and anything that sabotages them is irrational and inappropriate" (Ellis, 1974, p. 195).

"The term 'rational,' as used in RET, refers to people's (a) setting up or choosing for themselves certain basic values, purposes, goals, or ideals and then (b) using efficient, flexible, scientific, logico–empirical ways of attempting to achieve such values and goals and to avoid contradictory and self-defeating results" (Ellis & Whitely, 1979, p. 40).

" …scientifically, clearly, flexibly…" (Ellis & Bernard, 1985, p. 5).

"…as used in psychotherapy, rational not only means based in or derived from reason but also means efficiently aiding human happiness" (Ellis, 1989a, p. 1161).

"…'self-helping'…" (Ellis, 1990, p. 176).

Rational Beliefs

"…a reasonable or a realistic belief…" (Ellis, 1973, p. 57).

"…can be supported by empirical data and is appropriate to the reality that is occurring, or may occur, at Point A" (Ellis, 1973, p. 57).

"Rational Beliefs (rBs) in RET mean those cognitions, ideas, and philosophies that aid and abet people's fulfilling their basic, or most important, Goals" (Ellis, 1984, p. 20).

"Rational thoughts (or rational ideas or beliefs) are defined in RET as those thoughts that help people live longer and happier, particularly by (1) setting up or choosing for themselves certain (presumably) happiness-producing values, purposes, goals, or ideals; and (2) using efficient, flexible, scientific, logico–empirical ways of (presumably) achieving these values and goals and of

avoiding contradictory or self-defeating results" (Ellis & Bernard, 1985, pp. 5–6).

Irrational Beliefs

"…cannot be supported by any empirical evidence and is inappropriate to the reality that is occurring, or may occur, at Point A" (Ellis, 1973, p. 57).

"…unprovable premises…" (Ellis, 1973, p. 153).

"Not all irrational Beliefs include should or must; some of them merely consist of unempirical or unrealistic statements" (Ellis, 1977, p. 8).

"Irrational Beliefs (iBs) are those cognitions, ideas, and philosophies that sabotage and block people's fulfilling their basic, or most important, Goals" (Ellis, 1984, p. 20).

"…almost invariably consist of absolutistic, dogmatic, illogical, unrealistic Beliefs. Instead of being expressions of flexible desire and preference (as Rbs seem to be), they are inflexible, rigid oughts, musts, and necessities" (Ellis, 1985, p. 136).

"…beliefs are judged to be irrational when they express unconditional and absolutistic demands that do not help the individual remain happy and goal achieving" (Ellis & Bernard, 1985, p. 11).

"…are self-defeating and seriously interfere with your basic goals and desires—especially your goals of surviving and being happy" (Crawford & Ellis, 1989, p. 4).

"…are antisocial and sabotage the well-being of the social group in which you choose to live" (Crawford & Ellis, 1989, p. 4).

"…are absolutistic, highly exaggerated, rigid, and dogmatic. They consist of unconditional shoulds, oughts, musts, commands, demands, and insistences that you lay upon yourself, on other people, and on the conditions under which you live" (Crawford & Ellis, 1989, pp. 4–5).

"…are unrealistic and contradict the facts of life" (Crawford & Ellis, 1989, p. 5).

"…are illogical and contradictory. They are inconsistent with each other. Or they do not follow from normal premises. Or they logically follow from false premises" (Crawford & Ellis, 1989, p. 5.)

"…thoughts, feeling, and actions that people create or construct that frequently defeat or sabotage their own personal goals, values, and interests" (Ellis, 1990, p. 176).

Figure 20–1 Ellis's Characterizations of Irrationality, Rationality, Rational Beliefs, and Irrational Beliefs.

An Evaluation of these Criteria

Clarity

By clarity we mean freedom from ambiguity. The first problem regarding clarity is that each of these criteria taken singly raises a number of questions. The terms used in the definitions are themselves

sufficiently vague and subjective that they do not provide a clear definition of rationality. For example, in stating that irrational beliefs are "antisocial and sabotage the well-being of the social group in which you choose to live" (Crawford & Ellis, 1989, p. 4), several questions arise: Are a white supremist's racist beliefs rational because his or her choice of "social group" is like-minded and like-skinned individuals? What exactly is meant by the vague term "social group"? As various social groups (family, neighborhood, community, city, state, nation, ethnic group, social class, religious group) can have competing interests, which of these should be considered in applying this criterion? Finally, how much cost constitutes "sabotage"?

A further problem regarding clarity is that when listing multiple criteria (as in Crawford & Ellis, 1989, pp. 4–5), it is not clear how these are related. How many of these criteria does a belief have to meet before it is properly regarded as irrational— all, one, or the majority? Are these (or some combination of these) sufficient or necessary criteria? If criteria conflict, are some superordinate?

The ambiguity in these attempts at defining rational and irrational beliefs may have important clinical implications. There is no direct research that bears on this question. Part of the purpose of this chapter is to point to the need for further research regarding the extent to which clients can accurately and fully understand and apply the model of rationality. This is an important but neglected process question. However, the vagueness noted above may render both the identification of rational and irrational beliefs and the defense of these judgments a difficult, nebulous process. It would appear countertherapeutic in RET to rely upon appeals to authority or to the therapist's strength of personality to decide these matters. Thus to allow clients to fully and usefully understand why some particular belief is irrational, and to allow clients to continue to make these decisions on their own in the future, a much clearer explication of rationality and irrationality would seem critical.

Thus, at present, RET's theory (or theories) of rationality is vague at best. This ambiguity, although problematic in itself, leads to greater concerns in regard to the consistency of RET's definitions of rationality. Next, we will evaluate the consistency of Ellis's statements about irrationality by considering the extent to which Ellis's account is coherent in that it renders consistent judgments regarding the rationality or irrationality of a particular belief.

Consistency

Evans (1984–85) has noted problems with the variability of Ellis's definitions. Evans suggests that one of Ellis's theories is "evolutionary" in that it appears to rely heavily on the Darwinian concept of "survival value." For example, Ellis states that irrational beliefs "interfere with the survival...of the organism" (Ellis, 1977, p. 15). Evans suggests that the second theory of rationality, which he terms the "empirical or scientific," is "...implicit in Ellis' clinical practice" (p. 131) of attempting to dispute beliefs that are inconsistent with "facts." Evans suggests that there is some inherent inconsistency in these theories; it seems plausible that beliefs that may be justified by the scientific method may not also lead to survival (e.g., beliefs associated with making weapons of mass destruction).

Although not mentioned by Evans, experimental evidence suggests that empirical accuracy might not be "goal consistent" with increased happiness, as Ellis argues. Taylor and her colleagues (e.g., Taylor, 1988) have a program of research which they interpret as indicating that unrealistically positive self-evaluations, exaggerated perceptions of control, and unrealistic optimism contribute to an individual's ability to functional well and to be happy. Moreover, Nelson and Craighead (1977) found evidence to suggest that depressed individuals are more veridically "empirical" in some ways than nondepressed persons. Nelson and Craighead found that depressed individuals were accurate in assessing the amount of negative feedback that they received during a laboratory task while nondepressed individuals tended to underestimate negative feedback. If this finding may be generalized, it suggests that, contrary to Ellis, "happiness" may require an individual to be somewhat "unempirical" and ignore some negative elements of the environment.

Although there is considerable variation in Ellis's definitions of rational beliefs there are some possible trends. Ellis's criteria for rational beliefs appear to be of four general types. Rational beliefs are (a) goal consistent (Crawford & Ellis, 1989; Ellis, 1974, 1977, 1989a, 1990; Ellis & Bernard, 1985; Ellis & Whitely, 1979), that is, they help individuals achieve their basic goals. Rational beliefs may also be (b) logical (Crawford & Ellis, 1989; Ellis, 1985, 1989a; Ellis & Harper, 1961), that is, they inductively or deductively follow from other beliefs, which function as premises. Rational beliefs are also (c) empirical/scientific (Crawford & Ellis, 1989; Ellis, 1973, 1985; Ellis & Bernard, 1985; Ellis & Whitely, 1979), that is, they are based in reality and are consistent with observable facts. Finally, rational beliefs may be (d) flexible/

nonabsolutistic (Crawford & Ellis, 1989; Ellis, 1977, 1985; Ellis & Bernard, 1985), that is, they involve the absence of unconditional musts and shoulds.

In most of his works, Ellis apparently uses the "goal consistent" criterion of rationality either most prominently or exclusively in defining rationality/irrationality or rational/irrational beliefs (Ellis, 1974, 1977, 1979, 1984, 1989a, 1990; Ellis & Harper, 1961). Ellis (1984–85), himself, states that RET "mainly uses survival and happiness as criteria of rationality" (p. 138).

An example illustrates further difficulties. Many individuals hold the belief, "I should honor my parents." According to two of the criteria offered by Crawford and Ellis (1989) this belief may be irrational because it is "absolutistic" and contains a "should." However on other criteria of rationality offered by Ellis it is certainly not "antisocial" and it is not clear that it is "self-defeating," "unrealistic," or "illogical." Therefore on these criteria the belief appears to be rational. This ambiguity may present real difficulties to clients with interpersonal problems with their parents. Thus the various criteria that Crawford and Ellis (1989) list for defining rationality can lead to inconsistent classifications of beliefs. Admittedly it might be the case that in practice, this potential for inconsistency is not realized. Thus, the interrater reliability of judgments regarding the rationality/irrationality of beliefs is an important empirical question that has not been evaluated to date.

The problems with consistency would seem, again, to have clinical as well as theoretical implications. Contradictory judgments from the various criteria would likely cause considerable confusion for clients. An unfortunate paradox might arise: The better clients understand RET (and its multiple criteria), the more confused they become in making judgments about rational and irrational beliefs. It would also be unfortunate and countertherapeutic for clients to believe that they must consult an RET therapist to resolve these contradictions.

Applicability

The next issue to be addressed is the applicability of these criteria of rationality. That is, are there explicit procedures for applying these criteria so that it is possible to categorize in a systematic and decidable manner whether a given belief or act is rational or irrational?

Crawford and Ellis (1989) list "You should treat me fairly and properly" (p. 7) as an irrational belief. How can a spouse actually apply this criterion to determine if the behavior of his or her partner meets it? What becomes clear is that Ellis offers no decision procedure for applying his criteria to this belief and rendering a decision about the rationality of the belief. Furthermore, no heuristics or other hints on how this might be done are offered. Apparently, this decision process is viewed as unproblematically straightforward.

Again, this problem can have important negative implications for clinical practice. If a goal of RET is to help clients to become independently rational, then it would seem countertherapeutic for clients to be unable to accurately apply criteria to evaluate particular beliefs. To the extent that this procedure is a quasi-mysterious or a seemingly arbitrary process, then it is likely clients would have difficulty and be frustrated in making judgments regarding the rationality of a belief. Thus, it would appear to be most useful if a systematic method for the decision procedure that takes criteria of rationality and beliefs and renders reliable judgments about the rationality of these beliefs could be developed and explicated.

Accuracy

In this section we will examine the question, Does the conceptualization of rationality and irrationality utilized in RET actually capture the phenomenon of interest, i.e., rationality and irrationality? We will do this by examining the consistency of his depiction with the influential account of rationality of W. W. Bartley (1962, 1984, 1988), who extended and developed Popper's (1957) critical rationalism. This appears reasonable within Ellis's (1990) own account in that he has explicitly stated that he now follows the view of Bartley (1962) and Popper (1965) (Ellis, 1990, p. 169).

It is also important to note that such a philosophical analysis is a reasonable method of criticism because Ellis himself regards RET as having an important philosophical dimension. For example, he has stated, "From the beginning, RET was highly philosophic…" (Ellis & Bernard, 1985, p. 2). He has stated that RET "…had its roots in philosophic writings of ancient Greek and Roman stoics" (Ellis, 1977, p. 4).

Finally, these philosophical roots appear to have actual implications in the process of therapy: "One of its goals, therefore, is to help clients make a profound philosophical change that will affect their future as well as their present emotions and behaviors" (Ellis, 1990, p. 326).

GOAL CONSISTENCY AS A MARK OF RATIONALITY

Ellis suggests that beliefs and acts are rational if they are consistent with the individual's goals. Of course individuals may have a number of goals and due to opportunity costs alone pursuing one goal can be inconsistent with pursuing another. However, beyond the possible inconsistencies of multiple goals, it is simply not rational to have certain goals. Examples of irrational goals include: Wanting to be blue all over and red all over at the same time (criticizable on the grounds of logical impossibility); a male wanting to give birth to Dan Quayle's baby (criticizable on the grounds of physical impossibility); seeking to have sex with children (criticizable on the grounds of immorality); or seeking to have frequent unprotected sex (criticizable on the grounds of imprudence). Because of the irrationality of these goals, behavior that is consistent or that attempts to lead to the realization of these goals also is not rational. Thus, being consistent with a goal is not a sufficient condition for rationality since the goals themselves may be problematic and irrational.

NECESSITY AND THE LACK OF QUALIFICATION AS MARKERS OF RATIONALITY

Ellis also takes "rigid oughts, musts and necessities" (Ellis, 1985, p. 19) as usually constituting irrational beliefs. This would be a syntactic criterion that may be expressed, "If a sentence contains an 'ought,' 'must,' or statement of necessity and it is insufficiently qualified or if it is 'rigidly' held then this statement is irrational." Of course, this sort of rule has problems with clarity in that a good deal of judgment is needed to decide whether a statement is sufficiently qualified and how much flexibility is warranted. More importantly, it is also not clear that the rationality/irrationality distinction can be captured in this manner. For example, for Plato (1973) one of the characteristics distinguishing knowledge (episteme) from opinion (doxa) was that opinion changes while knowledge is constant. Thus, one should rigidly persist in a belief one

knows to be true ("The snake won't hurt me" or "My hands aren't dirty so I don't need to wash them again"). Therefore, the inflexibility and rigid criteria appear to be problematic: Inflexibility is desirable provided that a belief has been exposed to and withstood severe criticism and that there is no overriding good reason to abandon the belief for one of its competitors. Thus, this criterion appears to be begging the question. Although beliefs should always be exposed to relevant criticism, they should be held until such criticism exposes a better competitor. Thus, it is not rigidity alone that is a marker of irrationality. It is rigidity in the face of a balance of good reasons to adopt an alternative belief.

More importantly, in certain important cases statements of necessity and impossibility may not only be poor indicants of irrationality but may in fact be essential constituents of rational statements. Both logical arguments and scientific laws—that is, what we and Ellis would take to be paradigmatic cases of rationality—contain claims of necessity and impossibility. First, let us take the case of logic. For example, Kalish, Montague, and Mar (1980) state:

> Logic is concerned with arguments, good and bad. With the docile and the reasonable, arguments are sometimes useful in settling disputes. With the reasonable, this utility attaches only to good arguments. It is the logician's business to serve the reasonable. Therefore, in the realm of arguments it is the logician who distinguishes good from bad. Virtue among arguments is known as validity. An argument is valid if it is *impossible* for its premises to be true and its conclusion false. (p. 1, italics added)

Valid deduction involves a statement about impossibility or necessity—a valid argument is truth preserving because in a valid deductive argument if the premises are true then it is *impossible* for the conclusion to be false. In the well-known syllogism, "All men are mortal. Socrates is a man. Therefore (it is necessarily the case) that Socrates is mortal" (and in all deductive argumentation), the concepts of necessity and impossibility play an essential role. Therefore, statements involving the construct of necessity play an essential role in logical deduction and hence at a minimum represent an important exception to Ellis's connection of necessity with irrationality.

Second, scientific laws state necessities of a different kind. Newton's second law of motion, for example, states that when the mass of an object is *x* and its acceleration is *y*, then necessarily its force is *xy*. In fact, scientific laws often state empirical impossibilities. In the previous example, Newton's law would state that it is impossible for the force to be anything other than *xy*.

Finally, it is not at all clear in the realm of morality that necessity is the mark of the irrational. Ellis does not refute Kantian (1977) ethics and Kant proposed that morality is embodied in the categorical imperative (i.e., in unqualified oughts or musts). Thus, according to Kant, all individuals have moral duties which are unqualified imperatives. That is, we have a moral duty that we must treat no one solely as a means but always as an end in themselves. This duty is unqualified and cannot be abrogated on the grounds that it may not aid us in seeking some end, including our "happiness." According to Kant a moral act is executed for its own sake, not for the purpose of some end beyond the moral act. Qualified imperatives for Kant were markers not of moral laws but of what he somewhat derisively called "counsels of prudence." These have only hypothetical force. That is, if one wants such and such (being well liked or being happy), then one ought to do *x*. Although it is beyond the scope of this chapter to present a balanced view of all the diverse theories of morality, the point is that since Ellis does not present a refutation of the influential moral theory of Kant (and in fact seems to simply ignore him) and because Kant has argued that morality must have the character of absolute musts, it is at least unfortunate that Ellis should simply ignore this influential account of morality and take the characteristic of being unqualified as indicative of irrationality.

These problems with the validity of Ellis's criteria of rationality may have serious clinical implications. Given the rest of the theoretical structure of RET, it is of paramount importance to correctly distinguish rational from irrational beliefs. For example, if irrational thoughts do tend to lead to unhappiness, then if a mistake is made due to the inaccuracies noted above, a therapist would be promoting an irrational belief, which would expose the client to an increased rather than a decreased risk of unhappiness. However, we must hasten to add that no data bear on either side of this question. Informal reports of some prominent RET adherents suggest that the difficulties outlined above are problems for only a small number of clients (around 10 percent; R. DiGuiseppi, 1993, personal

communication) or that these present little problem but that improvements could result in an improved efficacy of RET (P. Woods, 1993, personal communication).

BARTLEY'S PAN-CRITICAL RATIONALISM

Finally, we turn to a discussion of what some contemporary philosophers take to constitute rationality. Here we concentrate on the views of Karl Popper (1957) and W. W. Bartley (1962, 1984, 1988), not only because Ellis seems to react favorably to these accounts of rationality but also because we agree with Ellis and view the neo-Popperian account as having considerable merit.

Bartley (1962, 1984, 1988) and others (e.g., Brown, 1988) have criticized what may be called *justificational* or *foundational* accounts of rationality. A justificational or foundational account attempts to demarcate rational beliefs or actions from irrational beliefs or actions by the degree to which the former are supported, warranted, verified, confirmed, probabilified, or justified by appeals to some reasons or evidence. Thus, according to this view, it is rational for me to believe that "All copper conducts electricity" because this claim is verified (or "supported," "confirmed," etc.) by numerous empirical observations.

There are a number of problems with this account of rationality. First, there are numerous disagreements regarding what constitutes an authority that can bestow justification. Some have claimed it is the reason or the intellect that can justify beliefs. Here Descartes's (1955) "clear and distinct ideas" are probably the paradigmatic examples. Others have claimed that it is sense experience, although, again, there has been wide disagreement concerning whether the evidence is first-person phenomenalist sense experience, or rather expressed in third-person thing language. The second problem is that the evidence of pure reason or sense experience is not authoritative. Individuals can disagree on what is clear and distinct, and sense observations are subject to error, illusion, and biases due to theoretical commitments.

Moreover, sense evidence is inadequate to justify some important beliefs, e.g., beliefs in scientific laws, causality, and the existence of other minds. For example, the appropriate set of observations has not been conducted to actually confirm the statement, "All copper conducts electricity." It is possible that some as yet to be conducted test on some as yet to be examined piece of copper would reveal that this statement is false. A further problem still is these requirements for justification need to be iterated so that one is providing (a higher order) justification for one's previous justification. Thus one becomes involved in an infinite regress. This problem can be avoided by attempting to anchor these series of justifications in "foundational" beliefs that are self-justifying. However, there is no consensus that such beliefs have been found. Also, it is important to note that the justificatory rationalism is inconsistent in that it itself (i.e., "All beliefs if they are rational must be justified by sense experience") is not justified by sense experience and hence it renders itself irrational.

Finally, propositions need to be derived from other (justifying) propositions through the use of certain rules. However, there are further problems regarding what rules to use (e.g., conventional deductive logic, relevance logic, or by one of the various confirmationist logics). Moreover, Brown (1988) points out that justified beliefs should all be logically consistent with one another. He suggests that at times uncovering inconsistency is an extremely subtle process, as when Bertrand Russell uncovered the inconsistency of Frege's set theory, which had been accepted by mathematicians for years.

Given the number and magnitude of problems with justificatory rationalism, Bartley (1962, 1984, 1988) proposes an approach to rationalism which he calls pan-critical rationality or comprehensive critical rationality. This account explicitly denies that justification must be given for some belief or act to be considered rational. According to Bartley there is no such thing as a "well-founded" belief or act. Pan-critical rationalism states that everything is open to criticism including this proposition itself (thus escaping the self-referential inconsistency problem of justificationism). The questions become, What would count against my belief or my act? Are there alternative relevant beliefs or acts that better survive this criticism? How can I maximize criticism of my beliefs? That is, how can we "...arrange our lives and institutions to expose our positions, actions, opinions, beliefs, aims, conjectures, decisions, standards, frameworks, ways of life, policies, traditional practices, etc. to optimum examination, in order to counteract and eliminate as much error as possible?" (Bartley, 1988, p. 213).

A belief is rational to the extent that it has been subjected to and survived criticism, especially the best criticism. Criticism is admittedly infinite in that one can criticize indefinitely. But this is not a regress since one is not seeking a final, definitive proof or foundation. No final position is sought: Inquiry and criticism are open-ended processes. The Einstein revolution shows how Newton's theory, which was once an accepted set of beliefs that had survived much criticism (i.e., experimentation), eventually succumbed to criticism.

It is important to note that not only do we learn where our errors are, we also learn how to learn, i.e., we learn how to better criticize and eliminate error more efficiently. This is why glib comments about "the scientific method" are so problematic. Method in science is not ossified. As Brown (1988) has stated, "Modern studies of the history of science indicate that science is not just a process of learning about the world, it is also a process of learning how to learn about the world" (p. 7).

Critical rationality is fallibilistic in that it rejects (because of the problems of justificationism noted above) the possibility of infallibly determining certitude. As Radnitzky has stated, "Fallibilism entails the perennial willingness to re-examine any position when, and if (but *only* if) there are good reasons for problematizing it" (1988, p. 292).

Radnitzky (1988) also nicely contrasts the justificational and critical accounts of rationality:

> The justificationist asks: When is it rational to accept a particular theory [or belief]?; and he suggests and answer on the lines: When it has been verified or probabilified to a sufficient degree. In the critical context the key question is: When is it *rational* (fallibly) to prefer a particular position (statement, view, standard, etc.) over its rival(s)? The answer suggested is along the lines: 'It is *rational* (fallibly) to prefer a position over its rivals if and only if it has so far withstood criticism—the criticism relevant for the sort of position at stake—better than did its rivals.' (p. 288)

Thus, an important part of fallibilism is that alternatives receive a fair hearing and all competitors are considered on their own merits without consideration of factors such as previous psychological attachment to the position.

The critical fallibilist is especially critical of moves that attempt to immunize a position against criticism. Thus, statements such as "There is an undetectable God whose existence shall not be questioned" can be seen as an attempt to minimize criticism and therefore is problematic as it has little opportunity for error correction. Similar problems are encountered in any attempt to dogmatize any belief or practice.

Pan-Critical Rationality and Evolution

Bartley (1988) sees pan-critical rationalism as part of a larger evolutionary epistemology. In evolutionary epistemology Darwinian biology is used to explain both the ability of organisms to know and the process of knowing itself. According to this account, evolution is a knowledge process (i.e., a process of the elimination of error in attempts to survive and reproduce) that occurs through random variation and selective retention, and, conversely, knowing is an evolutionary process (i.e., a process of variation and selective retention aimed at error elimination). As Popper (1979) has pointed out,

> Animals and even plants are problem-solvers. And they solve their problems by the method of competitive tentative solutions and the elimination of error. The tentative solutions which animals and plants incorporate into their anatomy and their behavior are biological analogues of theories; and vice versa: theories correspond (as do many exosomatic products such as honeycombs, and specially exosomatic tools, such as spiders' webs) to endosomatic organs and their ways of functioning. Just like theories, organs and their functions are tentative adaptations to the world we live in. (p. 145)

For example, the characteristics of things that contain nutrients necessary for an organism's survival pose problems that the human species knows how to solve. This knowledge is embodied in the structure, variety, and placement of teeth, by the glands that secrete special chemicals that lead to catabolic processes, by a critical length of intestinal tract, and by other physiological structures and mechanisms. In the history of the species, past environments have criticized (i.e., selected against) certain other competing problem-solving attempts. Relatively good attempts have survived, but their survival does not indicate that there are not better possible solutions or that these solutions are absolutely justified. They may in fact contain a great deal of error (as undigested nutrients, dental cavities, and ulcers indicate).

Random variation and selective retention have not only produced embodied knowledge (which is fallible, unjustified, and continually responsive to further criticism), but these mechanisms also produce knowledge in the lifetime of the organism (knowledge which, again, is fallible, unjustified, and continually responsive to further criticism). According to Popper (1979) the major difference between the problem solving of subhuman animals and humans is that for animals, death and suffering constitute the major feedback in error elimination, but humans can advance theories and arrange experiments (error-eliminating attempts) so that our (to some degree) mistaken theories and beliefs can die in our stead. Again, this selection/criticism process is never final. Under ideal circumstances what remains is what has best survived this criticism, not a belief that is justified or infallibly true.

This evolutionary epistemological context for pan-critical rationalism has a number of implications for RET. First, evolutionary epistemology provides a larger context for an account of rationality and therefore can provide answers to metaquestions of rationality (e.g., Why is rationality good? How did rationality come to exist?). Moreover, evolutionary epistemology may be seen as using the best source of knowledge—science—to answer an important question. Thus, this account of rationality is seen as consistent with, and in fact an implication of, biology.

Furthermore, other influential psychologists are evolutionary epistemologists (e.g., Donald Campbell, 1960; B. F. Skinner, 1984) and therefore hitherto unexplored agreements between RET and the views of these psychologists can be explored. Given that RET is usually thought of as a cognitive–behavioral psychotherapy, it is especially significant that evolutionary epistemology provides a common, coherent account for RET and other behavior therapies (O'Donohue & Smith, 1992). Finally, evolutionary epistemology explicates the relationship between three of Ellis's proffered criteria for rationality: the evolutionary, scientific, and empirical criteria.

Pan-Critical Rationality and RET

Ellis, in his account of his empirical/scientific criterion of rationality, holds an explicitly justificational account. For example, he states rational beliefs "...can be supported by empirical data..." (Ellis, 1973, p. 57). This again is puzzling given that he has stated that he follows the views of Bartley and may be indicative of erroneous exegesis on the part of Ellis. However he has recently appeared to notice this and has begun to revise his account (Ellis, 1989b).

Many of these strategies and methods implied by a pan-critical account of rationality would be similar to those of existing rational–emotive therapy. For example, in both conventionally practiced RET and in a pan-critical approach the A-B-C-D-E (*A*ctivating Event-*B*elief-*C*onsequences-*D*isputation-*E*ffects) paradigm would be stressed. Both would emphasize the importance of identifying relevant irrational beliefs and increasing the client's awareness of relevant beliefs. Thus, both would highlight associated therapeutic techniques such as the therapist probing and encouraging the explication of these beliefs. Both would stress the *B-C* connection as an important point of intervention and would emphasize rationality as the relevant valuative dimension. Moreover, both would believe that it is important for clients to understand the psychological sequelae of certain kinds of irrationality. Finally, both would have a generally didactic orientation and accentuate the importance of putting learning into practice through exercises and homework.

However, the pan-critical account of rationality would also have implications for modifying the practice of RET. In a pan-critical-based therapy, the purpose of therapy would be to teach clients how to be appropriately critical of their beliefs and acts. Thus, a major goal of therapy would be to teach criticism skills. In this view, currently practiced RET does some of this (through modeling effects and other implicit mechanisms) and teaches this for circumscribed beliefs and situations, but may not do this with optimum generality or with the explicitness that would tend to increase the transfer of such skills to other beliefs and acts.

The pan-critical rational–emotive therapist would be more systematic and specific about the criticism process. Promoting a particular attitude toward error would be of primary importance. Popper (1965, p. 281) has stated, "The wrong view of science betrays itself in the craving to be right." The same holds for rationality and thus an attempt would be made in therapy to understand that an uncritical attitude is problematic because we are often wrong and an uncritical outlook does not produce error-eliminating attempts. Thus the value of good criticism is that it can help us to eliminate error and successively improve our attempts at avoiding the negative consequences of our mis-

takes. The "craving to be right" of a justificational account is transformed to "craving to learn our errors and to learn from our errors."

Of critical importance is teaching how to accurately identify what set of beliefs should be problematized. Ellis sometimes provides a list of what he takes to be frequent and particularly troublesome irrational beliefs (e.g., Ellis, 1977, p. 10). Generally, these would also appear to be irrational in the pan-critical approach (e.g., "The idea that life proves awful, terrible, horrible, or catastrophic when things do not go the way you would like them to go"). However, some new irrational beliefs would be added to these lists, beliefs such as, "I must not ever be wrong or admit that I might be wrong, as this would be a terrible, embarrassing thing"; "It is important to prove that I am right by finding evidence that supports my position"; and "I must avoid or deflect criticism at all costs. Because if some criticism of me, my behavior, or my beliefs turns out to have some merit, this is a terrible thing and means I am a worthless person." However, an important and unanswered empirical question is whether a broader focus on criticism skills and an increased ability to criticize and revise these as well as more subtle irrational beliefs is superior to a more focused concentration on the irrational beliefs already identified by Ellis.

The pan-critical approach would emphasize new sets of techniques and therapy goals. For example, the pan-critical approach would emphasize the importance of judging when and which beliefs should be problematized. This may not be a straightforward matter but would require a fair amount of judgment and discrimination. For example, although there are certainly clear cases, there are also ambiguous cases, such as whether it is reasonable or unreasonable to question your belief that your spouse loves you. The pan-critical approach would also stress teaching how to explicate alternative competing beliefs and acts and how to fairly assess their merits and demerits, especially how to bracket biases that are associated with prior commitments to one of these.

Finally, of utmost importance, the pan-critical approach would stress imparting skills regarding how to construct new and telling (i.e., potentially falsifying) tests of relevant beliefs. In this approach the therapist should not ask clients to support their beliefs and practices, but rather to invent and conduct tests that would criticize these. As Popper (1965) has argued, astrology (like psychoanalytic therapy and Marxism) has many empirical "confirmations"; its problem is that it excludes no observable possibilities and therefore cannot be falsified. The question is not, Is my belief confirmed? but rather, Is there evidence that can be gathered which falsifies this belief? (e.g., what observable states of affairs does this belief exclude?).

EVALUATING A PAN-CRITICAL-BASED RATIONAL–EMOTIVE THERAPY

Criticism is encouraged in the pan-critical approach, including criticism of the approach itself. Thus, it is reasonable to ask, Does a pan-critical rational–emotive therapy provide a clear, consistent, straightforward, applicable, and accurate account of rationality? Reasons suggestive of its improved accuracy have already been discussed and will not be dealt with further. The pan-critical approach avoids problems of inconsistency because it does not provide multiple criteria of rationality.

In regard to the first criterion, there is admittedly some lack of clarity in the hallmark of rationality in the pan-critical approach, i.e: Expose beliefs, particularly those relevant to psychological problems, to good criticism, and learn to be persuaded by the results of this criticism. Questions can be legitimately raised concerning what is meant by "good criticism" in regard to determining what beliefs are relevant to psychological problems, and concerning ascertaining how and when clients accept and are persuaded by flaws discovered in their beliefs. However, it is important to note that the last two problems are also shared by conventionally practiced RET. Defining good criticism and implementing the criticism process is admittedly somewhat of an art. Some guidelines can be given—i.e., find out what observable states of affairs are inconsistent with your beliefs and see if these observable states of affairs actually exist. If criticism is partly an art, then an explicit algorithm or "cookbook" for exposing beliefs to the best criticism would not be forthcoming. An advantage of the pan-critical approach is that this is a general account of the role of criticism in the growth of knowledge, which was developed as an account of the rationality of science. Most philosophers of science agree that there are no algorithms for scientific discovery and justification, and therefore it might be wrong to expect such exactness in the criticism process. However, this does suggest lines

of future research into the identification of heuristics that can aid clients in the criticism process.

If the above considerations are correct, the pan-critical account does better on these evaluative criteria than does the conventional account of rationality contained in RET. However, an important source of criticism of the pan-critical approach is obviously missing from this conceptual review. That is, outcome and process research needs to be conducted in order to provide criticism concerning the extent to which these differing accounts of rationality actually produce change for different types of clients and problems.

CONCLUSION

Albert Ellis has made a significant contribution in focusing on helping individuals with their psychological problems by assisting them to think and act in a more rational manner. He also has correctly realized the philosophical dimensions of any form of psychotherapy that attempts to correct thinking. However, the conventional conceptualization of rationality contained in RET has a number of problems. This is understandable in that an attempt to develop an adequate account of epistemology and rationality is a very difficult task. It is hoped that a more adequate account of rationality can further aid the development of this valuable approach to therapy.

REFERENCES

Bartley, W. W. (1962). *The retreat to commitment.* New York: Alfred A. Knopf.
Bartley, W. W. (1984). *The retreat to commitment* (2nd ed.). LaSalle, IL: Open Court.
Bartley, W. W. (1988). Theories of rationality. In G. Radnitzky & W. W. Bartley (Eds.), *Evolutionary epistemology, rationality, and the sociology of knowledge* (pp. 205–216). LaSalle, IL: Open Court.
Beck, A. T. (1984). Cognition and therapy. *Archives of General Psychiatry, 41,* 1112–1114.
Brown, H. I. (1988). *Rationality.* London: Routledge.
Campbell, D. T. (1960). Blind variation and selective retention in creative thought as in other knowledge processes. *Psychological Review, 67,* 380–400.
Crawford, T., & Ellis, A. (1989). A dictionary of rational-emotive feelings and behaviors. *Journal of Rational-Emotive & Cognitive-Behavior Therapy, 7,* 3–28.
Descartes, R. (1955). *The philosophical works of Descartes* (E. Haldane & G. Ross, Eds.). Cambridge: Cambridge University.

Dryden, W., & DiGiuseppe, R. (1990). *A primer on rational-emotive therapy*. Champaign, IL: Research Press.

Ellis, A. (1958). Rational psychotherapy. *Journal of General Psychology, 59*, 35–49.

Ellis, A. (1962). *Reason and emotion in psychotherapy*. Princeton, NJ: Lyle Stuart.

Ellis, A. (1973). *Humanistic psychotherapy: The rational-emotive approach*. New York: Crown and McGraw-Hill.

Ellis, A. (1974). Experience and rationality: The making of a rational-emotive therapist. *Psychotherapy: Research and Practice, 11*, 194–198.

Ellis, A. (1976). The biological basis of human irrationality. *Journal of Individual Psychology, 32*, 145–168.

Ellis, A. (1977). The basic clinical theory of rational-emotive therapy. In A. Ellis & R. Grieger (Eds.), *Handbook of rational-emotive therapy* (pp. 3–34). New York: Springer.

Ellis, A. (1979). The theory of rational-emotive therapy. In A. Ellis & J. M. Whitely (Eds.), *Theoretical and empirical foundations of rational-emotive therapy* (pp. 33–60). Monterey, CA: Brooks/Cole.

Ellis, A. (1984). Expanding the ABCs of RET. *Journal of Rational-Emotive Therapy, 2*, 20–24.

Ellis, A. (1984–85). Yes, how reasonable is rational-emotive therapy? *Review of Existential Psychology and Psychiatry, 19*, 135–139.

Ellis, A. (1985). *Overcoming resistance: Rational-emotive therapy with difficult clients*. New York: Springer.

Ellis, A. (1987a). The impossibility of achieving consistently good mental health. *American Psychologist, 42*, 364–375.

Ellis, A. (1987b). Note on Ian Gilmore's distinction between quantitative and qualitative inappropriate or irrational beliefs. *Journal of Rational-Emotive Therapy, 5*, 194–196.

Ellis, A. (1989a). Comments on Debra Hull's concept of rationality. *American Psychologist, 44*, 1160–1161.

Ellis, A. (1989b). Comments to my critics. In M. Bernard & R. A. DiGiuseppe (Eds.), *Inside RET: A critical appraisal of the theory and therapy of Albert Ellis* (pp. 220–233). San Diego: Academic.

Ellis, A. (1990). Is rational emotive therapy (RET) "rationalist" or "constructivist"? *Journal of Rational-Emotive Therapy & Cognitive-Behavior Therapy, 8*, 169–193.

Ellis, A., & Bernard, M. E. (1985). What is rational-emotive therapy (RET)? In A. Ellis & M. E. Bernard (Eds.), *Clinical applications of rational-emotive therapy* (pp. 1–30). New York: Plenum.

Ellis, A., & Dryden, W. (1987). *The practice of rational-emotive therapy* (RET). New York: Springer.

Ellis, A., & Harper, R. A. (1961). *A guide to rational living*. Englewood Cliffs, NJ: Prentice-Hall.

Ellis, A., & Whitely, J. M. (1979). *Theoretical and empirical foundations of rational-emotive therapy*. Monterey, CA: Brooks/Cole.

Evans, C. S. (1984–85). Albert Ellis' conception of rationality: How reasonable is rational-emotive therapy? *Review of Existential Psychology and Psychiatry, 19*, 129–134.

Hart, K. E., Turner, S. H., Hittner, J. B., Cardozo, S. R., & Paras, K. C. (1991). Life stress and anger: Moderating effects of type A irrational beliefs. *Personality and Individual Differences, 12*, 557–560.

Heesacker, M., Heppner, P. P., & Rogers, M. E. (1982). Classics and emerging classics in counseling psychology. *Journal of Counseling Psychology, 29*, 400–405.

Jacobs, S. (1989). Karl Popper and Albert Ellis: Their ideas on psychology and rationality compared. *Journal of Rational-Emotive & Cognitive-Behavior Therapy, 7*, 173–185.

Kalish, D., Montague, R., & Mar, G. (1980). *Logic: Techniques of formal reasoning*. New York: Harcourt Brace Jovanovich.

Kant, I. (1977). Metaphysical foundations of morals. In C. J. Friedrich (Ed. and Trans.), *The philosophy of Kant*. New York: Modern Library.

Lyons, L. C., & Woods, P. J. (1991). The efficacy of rational-emotive therapy: A quantitative review of the outcome research. *Clinical Psychology Review, 11*, 357–369.

Mahoney, M. J. (1974). *Cognition and behavior modification*. Cambridge, MA: Ballinger.

Mahoney, M. J., Lyddon, W. F., & Alford, D. J. (1989). An evaluation of rational-emotive theory of psychotherapy. In M. Bernard & R. DiGiuseppe (Eds.), *Inside rational-emotive therapy* (pp. 69–94). San Diego: Academic Press.

Nelson, R. E., & Craighead, W. E. (1977). Selective recall of positive and negative feedback, self-control behaviors, and depression. *Journal of Abnormal Psychology, 86*, 379–388.

O'Donohue, W., & Smith, L. D. (1992). Philosophical and psychological epistemologies in behaviorism and behavior therapy. *Behavior Therapy, 23*, 173–194.

Plato. (1973). *Theaetetus* (J. McDowell, Trans.). Oxford: Clarendon Press.

Popper, K. (1957). *The poverty of historicism*. London: Ark.

Popper, K. (1963). *Conjectures and refutations*. New York: Harper.

Popper, K. (1965). *The logic of scientific discovery*. (2nd ed.). New York: Harper & Row.

Radnitzky, G. (1988). In defense of self-applicable critical rationalism. In G. Radnitzky & W. W. Bartley (Eds.), *Evolutionary epistemology, rationality, and the sociology of knowledge* (pp. 279–312). LaSalle, IL: Open Court.

Rorer, L. G. (1991). A modern epistemological basis for
    rational-emotive theory. *Psychotherapy in Private
    Practice, 8*, 153–157.

Skinner, B. F. (1984). Selection by consequences. *Brain
    and Behavioral Sciences, 7*, 477–510.

Smith, D. (1982). Trends in counseling and psychother-
    apy. *American Psychologist, 37*, 802–809.

Taylor, S. E. (1988). Illusion and well-being: A social
    psychological perspective on mental health. *Psycho-
    logical Bulletin, 103*, 193–210.

Woods, P. J., Silverman, E. S., Gentilimi, J. M., Cun-
    ningham, D. K., & Grieger, R. M. (1991). Cognitive
    variables related to suicidal contemplation in adoles-
    cents with implications for long-range prevention.
    *Journal of Rational-Emotive & Cognitive-Behavior
    Therapy, 9*, 215–245.

PART 5

ETHICS AND PSYCHOLOGY

Discourse about ethics and values, as opposed to empirical "facts", has a long and respectable history in philosophy. In psychology there has been a more complex history. Some of the early psychologists were explicitly interested in weaving Christian ethics into empirical psychology. This movement was later replaced by psychologists who had concerns similar to the logical positivists regarding ethics and values: That value and ethical statements were nonscientific and ought to be avoided or minimized because they were meaningless or disguised statements about emotions. Those following this set of belief often derided any attempt to address normative problems. Other psychologists were tempted to reduce ethics to psychological, empirical entities. Skinner's attempt to define the predicate "is good" with "is reinforcing" is a case in point. In addition, there were other prominent psychologists such as Piaget and Kohlberg who attempted to empirically study moral matters such as moral development. Finally, beginning in the 1950s the American Psychological Association adopted a professional ethical code that regulates the behavior of psychologists—and

it seems reasonable to take this as indicating that ethical discourse is meaningful and is relevant to psychologists.

In recent years psychologists have become less dismissive of the normative aspects of their pursuits. This might be due in part to the work of influential philosophers of science (e.g., Laudan, 1977) who have explicated the role of normative matters in the practice of science (e.g., the role of epistemic values in research methods). Hempel's (1965) classic statement about the role of ethical considerations in science clearly illustrates some of the roles of the normative in science:

> Let us assume, then, that faced with a moral decision, we are able to call upon the Laplacean demon as a consultant. What help might we get from him? Suppose that we have to choose one of several alternative courses of action open to us and that we want to know which of these we ought to follow. The demon would then be able to tell us, for any contemplated choice, what its consequences would be for the future course of the universe, down to the most minute detail, however remote in space and time. But, having done this for each of the alternative courses of action under

consideration, the demon would have completed his task; he would have given us all the information that an ideal science might provide under the circumstances. And yet he would not have resolved our moral problem, for this requires a decision as to which of the several alternative sets of consequences mapped out by the demon as attainable to use is the best; which of them we ought to bring about. And the burden of the decision would still fall upon our shoulders; it's we who would have to commit ourselves to an unconditional (absolute) judgment of value by singling out one of the sets of consequences as superior to the alternatives. (pp. 88–89)

The next collection of papers examines several major issues relating to ethics and psychology. In the first paper, Lacey and Schwartz examine the manifold meanings of the construct of "values" and the ways in which this construct relates to behavior and psychology, particularly with regard to research attempting to understand why individuals hold certain values. Next, Professor Agassi criticizes the institutional leadership of psychiatry. He suggests that the criticisms of psychiatry leveled by the radical psychiatrists such as Szasz are misdirected. He sees psychiatry as burdened by a leadership that is unduly defensive instead of open and willing to see and address criticisms. He views this as an ethical matter concerning responsibility and suggests that openness to criticism is related to psychiatry's status as a scientific enterprise.

The next three chapters explicitly deal with matters of professional ethics. In the first, Ringen describes the behavior therapist's dilemma: If individuals are autonomous, then how do we find laws of behavior? And if humans are not autonomous, then how do we make sense of informed consent

procedures that are used in research and in psychotherapy? He states that behavior therapists, at least those influenced by Skinner, because of their objections to mentalism cannot resolve this dilemma by following the compatibilist move of stating that intentional acts are law-like and autonomous. The last two chapters examine the recent revision of the American Psychological Association's ethical code. The first, by K. Kitchener, takes a largely positive view of the current code and the other, by O'Donohue and Mangold, a largely negative one. Kitchener, after describing the major changes in the recent revision of the code, describes the philosophical issues involved in the revisions in the ethics of confidentiality, multiple relationships, and deception in research. O'Donohue and Mangold address the following four questions: (1) What is this ethical code attempting to do and is it doing this? (2) What are the ethical presuppositions that are embedded in the code and what is the quality of these? (3) To what degree are the ethical principles mere authoritarian pronouncements as opposed to well-argued claims? (4) To what degree is the code consistent with a science of human behavior? This is related to the issue that Ringen has discussed: How are science and ethics compatible?

REFERENCES

Hempel, C. G. (1965). Science and human values. In C. G. Hempel (Ed.), *Aspects of scientific explanation*. New York: Free Press.

Laudan, L. (1977). *Progress and its problems*. Berkeley: University of California Press.

CHAPTER 21

THE FORMATION AND TRANSFORMATION OF VALUES*

Hugh Lacey
Barry Schwartz

VALUE

The word "value" has varied and complex uses. This variety and complexity reflect the wide range of tasks carried out by "values" in our communicative practices, and also that the depth of our grasp of the meaning of "value" depends partly on the values that we hold. In ordinary discourse, when we refer to a personal value, we may be pointing to some or all of the following:

1. A fundamental good that a person pursues consistently over an extended period of his or her life; one of the person's ultimate reasons for action.

2. A quality (or a practice) that gives worth, goodness, meaning, or a fulfilling character to the life a person is leading, or aspiring to lead.

3. A quality (or a practice) that is partially constitutive of a person's identity as a self-evaluating, a self-interpreting, a self-making being.

4. A fundamental criterion for a person to choose what is good (or better) among possible courses of action.

5. A fundamental standard to which one holds the behavior of self and others.

6. An "object of value," an appropriate relationship with which is partially constitutive both of a worthwhile life and of one's personal identity. Objects of value can include works of art, scientific theories, technological devices, sacred objects, cultures, traditions, institutions, other people, and nature itself. Appropriate relations with objects of value, depending on the particular object, include the following: production, reproduction, respect, nurturance, maintenance, preservation, worship, love, public recognition, and personal possession.

This list outlines only the surface usages of "value." Its items remain open to various interpretations. For example, item 2, value as a quality that gives worth or meaning to a person's life, is open to at least three interpretations: (a) a quality that one holds as giving worth to one's *own* life or aspirations; (b) a quality that one holds as giving worth

* Preparation of the article was supported by the Brand Blanshard Faculty Fellowship (to both authors), and grants from the Swarthmore College Research Fund and N.S.F., SE8308604 (to Hugh Lacey).

to *any* human life; (c) a quality that *actually* gives worth to any human life. Interpretation (a) represents a subjective (personal) stance toward a subjective phenomenon; (b) a subjective stance toward an objective phenomenon; (c) an objective claim about an objective phenomenon. In leaving open the interpretation, indeed in leaving open whether in the long run any interpretation other than (a) can be sustained, we impart no philosophical theory of value into the surface usages of the word.

Discourse about values is often highly divisive, suggesting that values may be a source of permanent and ineliminable conflict. In the hope of avoiding this conflict, many have tried to relativize value to the person by insisting that only interpretations of type (a) are possible, and by diagnosing the appearance of conflict as due to the compounding of two errors: one that the object of one's personal stance is an objective phenomenon (interpretation b), and the other that one's personal stance can itself be considered to accord with an objective position (interpretation c). With interpretation (a), what appears as disagreement is revealed as mere difference. Many expect that recognition of the fact of mere difference will ground a universal tolerance. However, modernity also tells us that facts do not entail values; so this expectation has a precarious logical grounding.

There is a distinction to be made between facts (what is the case) and values (what is good, what has worth). If there were not, evaluation would be unintelligible. But in practical life facts and values cannot be separated, to the point that it is commonplace and appropriate that a single sentence simultaneously serves descriptive and evaluative roles. Consider, for example, "chaotic, lawless violence followed in the aftermath of the Rodney King verdict," or "the disadvantaged of the inner city of Los Angeles, the limits of their tolerance of injustice having been reached, rose up in rebellion." Given this inevitable intermingling of the factual and the evaluative, if values must always be relativized to the person, can we avoid the conclusion that facts also are relativized to the person? Let us look more closely at the view that values are always relativized to the person.

In the United States, discourse about values tends to cause discomfort. Values, for many, are deeply personal, even private; they are part of one's self-definition, of who one is; one is not responsible to others for one's values, and one's values need not be responsive to the standards of others. One might

clarify one's values, but one's values need no defense when they are different from those of others, even from those of the bulk of one's culture. One's values are one's own. For some, it is slightly unseemly to talk about one's values. For others, values are to be unapologetically affirmed, and public respect demanded for them (see Taylor, 1992). (Public respect can only be demanded. That it is owed cannot be soundly argued, unless one acknowledges commitment to some values beyond the merely subjective.) Whether one keeps quiet about one's values or affirms them publicly is itself a reflection of one's personal values. Either way, the critical scrutiny by others of one's values, or of the choices that flow from them, is seen as a kind of violence against one's self.

People for whom privacy and subjectivity are defining characteristics of values tend to prefer the language of rights (negative rights) to the language of values. They claim the right to choose as they will, subject only to the restriction that their chosen actions not harm others, where harm includes preventing others from acting according to their personal values. It is unintelligible to claim a right for oneself and not acknowledge that it is owed to everybody. Thus, universality is built into the discourse of rights, so long as rights are understood negatively: It is owed to everyone not to be interfered with in the course of acting on one's values. And this universality does not depend upon agreement about values.

Nevertheless, invoking rights does imply that there are some nonsubjective limits to acceptable values. It is not right, for example, to value harming others. Thus, personal values are moved at least a bit away from the realm of the purely subjective, for personal values are commonly manifested in contexts where there is impact on others. Moreover, personal commitment to rights is itself a value, and it is linked with commitment to such social values as tolerance and the primacy of individual (negative) freedom. Given the conception of values as private and subjective, it is easy to explain why many people hold (in word, if not always in practice) such social values. But that explanation does not generate a parallel rational justification. It is equally easy to explain why many others reject such social values, for they may be incompatible with their more deeply held personal values. Thus, while the discourse of (negative) rights is important, it neither substitutes for nor is independent of the discourse of values.

This analysis suggests that the conception of values as private and subjective, when taken to apply to all values, may ultimately be incoherent. It *does* matter to one what the values of others are, and one *does* expect others to account for at least some of their values. Whether or not one can act on one's own values, whether or not one can express the kind of person one aspires to be, depends socially, and even logically, upon others holding certain personal and social values. Most action is also interaction. For example, we cannot teach unless we have a class of students to teach. In numerous ways, one's actions presuppose social conditions, and that others are acting in accordance with certain values. The expression of one's values presupposes that relevant others are expressing certain (often different) values, so that it becomes difficult to abstract the desirability and the legitimacy of one's own values from that of the values of others. Perhaps, then, there are at least some values appropriate to human beings as such. That one shares a significant subset of one's values with others, and that one can count on others to act in accordance with certain values, are not matters of personal indifference, but prerequisites for being able to express one's own values.

A public and (to some extent) shared discourse of values cannot, if this suggestion is correct, be avoided. However, the insistence on the subjectivity of values dampens our capacity to discern the rationality required for this discourse, and tends to leave it to happenstance or socialization processes to form groups with shared values, and to develop the resources to deal with conflicts of values. If values are fully private and subjective, there is no sound argument that generally prioritizes tolerance over authoritarian imposition of one's group's values.

AN ANALYSIS OF VALUES

In practical life, beliefs and desires constitute an essential part of the explanation of human action: One performs an action because one desires a certain outcome, and believes that the action will contribute toward bringing about the outcome. Desires are thus among the causes of action, and as such, they may be objects of psychological and social inquiry. But in addition, desires are objects of evaluation. They can be judged by the people who hold them, and others, concerning the possibility of their realization and their worth in one's own life or in a human life in general. In particular, where desires

can be represented as the having of goals, agents aim, as an ideal, to have the desires that play a causal role in their behavior included among the positively evaluated desires, those that are consonant with their values.

That desires are subject to evaluation is not meant to imply a process that is cold and dispassionate. Especially when one's values are at the root of one's desires, we would expect that passion would also be in play, for values are part of the expression of our deepest being. Love might drive our interactions with those with whom we share the most valued moments of our lives, indignation our response to injustice, gratitude our acceptance of a service, compassion our tending to the sufferings of another, anger our retort to a threat of violence, irritation our carrying out an institutionally imposed task, and so on. Evaluation ought not suppress (as distinct from channel) passion, profound desire or feelings, and reduce itself to calculation. Moreover, when we speak of desires being consonant with values, we don't suggest that it is necessary to evaluate desires antecedent to acting (though sometimes it may be); indeed a strong case can be made that a measure of spontaneity is itself a value.

Explaining actions in terms of an agent's beliefs and desires always presupposes a broader context in which the action in question is related to other actions (including acts of evaluation) through developing networks of beliefs and desires, which eventually make contact with the agent's fundamental goals and desires, i.e., the agent's values. Through such developed explanations, the causal role of values in behavior becomes apparent. Ordinary intentional explanations of action thus presuppose that values play a causal role in behavior.

Personal Values

We may think of personal values as dialectically both the products and the points of reference of the processes with which we reflect upon and evaluate our desires (see Nerlich, 1989, and especially Taylor, 1981; the analysis of this section owes much to these works). Holding values, then, involves second-order desires, desires about the first-order desires that play and will play a causal role in our lives. Values are desires that only first-order desires with certain features will mark our lives, as lives that are experienced as fulfilling and worthy of a human being (see Sen, 1976). Holding a value involves the second-order desire, which represents one of a person's fundamental goals, that one's (acted upon, as distinct from merely felt) first-order desires are or become of the kinds that lead to actions that shape or produce a life marked by a certain quality (by participation in a certain practice, or by appropriate relationship with a certain object of value) that makes for a fulfilling (good, meaningful, well-lived) life, and that is partially constitutive of one's identity. The role of values as criteria of choice and standards of behavior are derived from this core meaning. Desires are personal. The desire component of holding values points to the personal character of values, that one's values are tied to one's most fundamental desires, and to one's deepest feelings. Holding a value also involves a belief component, the belief that the quality referred to is indeed linked with the experience of a fulfilled life, and perhaps also the belief that a life marked by this quality does not cause or rest upon conditions that cause diminished lives for others.

Understood in this way, values are *manifested* in *behavior* whenever they (and their associated feelings and emotions) figure in the explanatory schemes that are formed to frame the behavior of an agent. Values are *woven into a life* to the extent (always a greater or lesser extent) that the trajectory of an agent's life displays behavior constantly, consistently, and recurrently manifesting the values. A value is *expressed in a practice* where conduct within the practice is furthered by and requires behavior that manifests the value (see Hodges & Baron, 1992, for examples of the way in which values can be expressed in practices). Values can also be *present* (both felt and reflected upon) in *consciousness,* and *articulated in words,* representing a partial account of who one is (or would like to be or would like others to think one is), one's aspirations for the future, and what one believes about human well-being and its condition. There will always be some measure of a gap between values-as-manifested and values-as-articulated. One comes to hold values reasonably in the light of the desire and the commitment to narrow that gap (see "Understanding the Sources of Personal Values" below). The gap has various sources. On the one hand, one's aspirations can, and often should, properly go beyond current realities. On the other hand, the gap can be a consequence of inadequate self-understanding, limited or underdeveloped capacity for self-interpretation, the desire to appear to conform to the norms of some group, and even willful self-deception.

There are a number of types of deformation of evaluative discourse. Discourse is deformed when what one calls "values" become separated from one's desires, one's aspirations, one's sense of what is genuinely possible, and one's attempts to define the trajectory of one's life. Then evaluative discourse becomes simply a discourse of commendation and condemnation, a voluntaristic discourse that treats of the will in abstraction from the conditions of its operation. The recent rhetoric of "family values" is an instance. Whether or not these values are woven into the lives of their proponents, the rhetoric functions as a kind of moral club to batter one's opponents in order to demean them. And evaluative discourse is deformed when the articulation of values becomes identified with "values clarification." Since critique of values is excluded, the possibility of a gap between values-as-articulated and values-as-manifested is effectively denied and the belief component of values is ignored. Values clarification in effect reduces values to values-as-articulated, to an accounting of one's conscious (usually idealized) aspirations, in abstraction from the material, psychological and social conditions of their realization. Thus it is likely to hide the values manifested in one's behavior and embodied in society. Critical discussion of values cannot abstract from any of the modes (manifestation in behavior, woven into a life, expression in a practice, presence in consciousness, articulation in words) that we have attributed to values. Limiting values to the articulation mode is bound to lead to subjectivist accounts of values, for it is true that there are no sound arguments supporting some rather than other values, if the arguments deal only with values-as-articulated.

But while values-as-articulated, abstracted from the other modes of values, lose their distinctive character, the articulation of values is critically important. The articulation of values is not just talk *about* values, as if values had a kind of being separable from their articulations, making the articulation a verbal representation of a separate, perhaps mental, reality (as a sentence describing a material object is separate from the material object). It is part of the nature of values that they be articulated; articulation is itself an essential mode of values—part of their formation, maintenance, transformation, deepening, clarification, recognition, and definition. And the very act of articulation of values may also manifest our values, since to whom we articulate our values, how and with what depth, will vary according to whether the immediate audience is composed of loved one, friends, colleagues in a movement, and so on. Such articulation is part of the practice of self-interpretation, a practice necessary for a life without self-deception. It helps to define one's aspirations; it implies not only an anticipation or prediction about the future trajectory of one's life, but also implies promises concerning that trajectory—that the values-as-articulated will become the values-as-woven-into one's life. To be credible as aspirations, values-as-articulated must go beyond values-as-manifested currently. To be credible as predictions and promises, the gap must not be too great, for one's future possibilities are constrained by the present realities of one's life, and the values that are manifested in one's current behavior do involve real desires. The credibility is enhanced when one is consciously engaged in practices that offer a well-founded possibility of realizing the aspirations. There can be tension here and ample space for self-deception. Finally, the articulation of values enables values to become objects of investigation (psychological, epistemic, and evaluative), of reflection, of discussion, and of critical argument, and when one discovers—as a consequence of articulation—that one shares one's values with others, they can become the basis of participation in shared practices and in the construction of community, the ground for living together without violence. This articulation makes it possible to reason about values; and if one does not reason about values, one will not value reason.

Embodiment of Personal Values in Social Institutions

Personal values can also be *embodied* (to a greater or lesser degree) *in social institutions,* and *in society* as a whole. An institution embodies a value to a high degree when its normal functioning offers roles into which the value is woven, encouraging behavior that manifests it and practices that express it, reinforcing its articulation and providing the conditions for its being further woven into its members' lives. In this sense, elite liberal arts colleges embody to a high degree the value of intellectual cultivation and distinctiveness, but not that of solidarity with the poor; and capitalist economic institutions embody to a high degree various egoist values, but not cooperation and sharing. An entire social order embodies a value to a high degree if it provides conditions that support institutions that embody the value, and

especially if its maintenance and normal functioning depend on such institutions.

The values that can be woven into a person's life are constrained significantly by the values that are embodied to a high degree in the society in which the person lives. That is partly because articulation is an essential mode of values, and what can be articulated is a function of the linguistic resources available in one's society. The language available for the articulation of values will reflect to some degree the conceptions of well-being that are dominant and reinforced in the society. This language may not readily permit the expression that one's own experience of well-being (or diminishment) does not fit well with the reigning accounts of what constitutes well-being. For example, in a society that highly embodies egoist values, in which persons are respected and recognized in virtue of their possessions, the language is not readily available for one to articulate the experience (if one has it) that manifesting such values does not produce a sense of well-being. And so the pull is to submit one's experience to the reigning accounts of well-being, if only for the sake of being recognized and respected. In this way, values are partially constituted by the available discourse of value, and part of the reality of holding values is essentially linking one's life to the community (and its traditions), which is the source of the language of one's values.

The constraint due to the social embodiment of values exists also because people live their lives in interaction with others. Most actions are also interactions, as mentioned earlier, so that one's values will include the fundamental relations one desires to establish with others. Typically our interactions with others are mediated by social institutions: family, school, church, political and economic institutions, clubs, and so on—so that we interact in accordance with our institutional roles, and with relations structured by institutions. To a considerable extent, one cannot manifest one's personal values without participating in institutions that permit their manifestation. Not every institution encourages or even permits the manifestation of one's personal values, so that whether a personal value can be woven into a life depends considerably upon the availability of institutions in which it is embodied to some degree.

To illustrate this point, we have argued elsewhere (Schwartz, 1986; Schwartz & Lacey, 1982; Schwartz, Schuldenfrei, & Lacey, 1978) that the modern, industrial workplace is an institution that has evolved over the centuries (with guidance, at various points along the way, by people whose interests were served by this particular evolutionary direction) to make the manifestation of values like excellence, social solidarity, and meaning in work almost impossible. The modern workplace is well suited to those who view work merely as a means to the ends of wealth accumulation and consumption. It is well suited to those who value individualism and egoism. It is poorly suited to those for whom work is at least partly expressive of the self, and expressive of a self that is enmeshed in a communal project (see Marglin, 1976; Polanyi, 1944). Attending to the role played by social institutions in constraining the kinds of values that people can reasonably be expected to hold becomes especially important when efforts are made by social or psychological or economic theorists to characterize a particular set of values that happens to be dominant at a particular place and time as reflective of an essential feature of human nature (Schwartz, 1990; see "Implications for Psychological Investigation" below).

We have discussed personal values as articulated in words, as present in consciousness, as manifested in action, as expressed in practices, as woven into lives, and as embodied by social institutions. It is our view that values do not have being separated from these modes. In particular, personal values cannot be reduced to mental representations or simple conscious phenomena. Ontologically, values reside in the interplay of these six modes, all of which are constitutive of values, and so necessarily values are developing and not simply given. They may be shared, in virtue of their being expressed in practices, articulated, and embodied in institutions—and to a considerable extent they must be. At the same time, in virtue of their manifestation in action and their weaving into individual lives, their character retains a personal element.

Social Values

A social order is marked by the personal values that are predominantly embodied by it, and also by the social values that are woven into it. As in the case with personal values, social values involve the interplay of several modes. Social values are *manifested* in the programs, laws, and policies of a society, and *expressed* in the practices whose conditions it provides and reinforces. These are the

values that become *articulated* in histories of the society's tradition in explaining the kinds of institutions it has fostered, and in the rhetoric of its leadership. Again, there is always some gap between manifestation and articulation, the handling of which partially defines positions on the political spectrum. Social values are *woven into* a society to the extent that they are manifested constantly and consistently, and the gap is quite narrow. For example, liberty, the primacy of property rights and, to a much lesser extent, equality are social values highly woven into U.S. society.

Articulation of values has a special significance in the case of social values, since typically social values are contested among various members and groups in the society. Different groups within society perceive and interpret the gap between values-as-articulated and values-as-manifested quite differently, and much of modern political discourse centers on the various competing assessments of the significance of this gap.

There is a close link between the social values woven into a society and the personal values a society embodies, and also between the values that are articulated by the dominant institutions of a society (ideology) and the personal values that become articulated throughout the society. This link need not be formal, and may only become apparent as the social order unfolds concretely over time. Thus, for example, liberty (negative liberty) and the primacy of property rights, as woven into the concrete economic and legal institutions of the U.S., foster the embodiment of individualistic, egoistic, and competitive personal values. Indeed, the embodiment of such personal values may itself be construed as a social value highly woven into the society. Under conditions in which the link between social and personal values is especially tight, the personal values people hold may come to seem natural and inevitable. Indeed, if society is sufficiently univocal in the way in which its institutions embody certain personal values, they may not appear to members of society as values at all, but rather as mere desires—unreflected upon because no reflection is necessary, or perhaps even possible.

A social value can also be *personalized*, when a person's acts directed toward the maintenance, modification, or transformation of the social order are guided by the personal desire for a society into which this social value is woven. For example, where individualist personal values predominate, the social values of tolerance, of relations mediated by contract, and of justice as fairness under the law tend to be widely personalized. This is presumably because it is believed that, given the concrete economic and legal institutions into which they are woven, these social values are among the conditions that shape a society that embodies the desired personal values. The stability of a society depends on the widespread personalizing of its predominant social values.

Furthermore, if a person's aspirations are impeded because of the prevailing predominant social values, then it makes sense to personalize other social values and to engage in political action in order to produce social forms in which they are manifested. Thus, for example, if one aspires to express the value of solidarity with the poor, one will seek social change that would produce a social order into which positive freedom (the availability of conditions in which all have the possibility to live significant lives of their own choosing) and the primacy of economic and social rights are woven, and so personalize these social values. In this way, social values—either those predominantly manifested, or those aspired to—are included among personal values.

There are, of course, differences and disagreements in the realm of values, and we cannot cut through their complexities here. Their existence, however, highlights the question of which values one is to hold, and what is the relevance of public discussion to settling the matter. Public discussion cannot be expected to result in a consensus about what values one is to hold. Indeed, we subscribe to the view that a certain difference in the values people hold is essential within the texture of an environment that can sustain human freedom. Without some diversity and tension among values, people could easily come to view the values they currently hold as the only possible values—a result that would seriously erode the scope of human aspiration and the possibilities for human development. But what public discussion can lead to is well grounded knowledge about the social conditions needed for holding particular values. And this is significant, for it provides a causal understanding of the formation and holding of values that enables arguments to be made for the modification of existing social institutions and structures in some directions rather than others. In the light of this, we will explore a number of issues relevant to explaining the values that people do come to hold.

UNDERSTANDING THE SOURCES OF PERSONAL VALUES

Human discourse is not merely "factual"; it is not limited to providing descriptions and explanations of the way things are or have been. It is also future oriented, and so contains evaluative aspects. While explanation relates present states of affairs to past ones (according to causal laws, or within an explanatory narrative), evaluation relates the present to desired future possibilities. Evaluation serves, in part, to set the course of our lives, in the light of the constraints of actual realities. The future is neither determined by the present, nor is it the product of voluntarist action unconstrained by the present. Rather, it takes shape in part as present realities are modified, and sometimes transformed, through intentional action. Our beliefs and desires play a causal role in shaping the future, but under powerful constraints that are not themselves subject to modification simply in the light of our present beliefs and desires. Values, we maintain, are intelligible only within this context of constraint.

This focus on constraint also enables us to define with reasonable precision a number of phenomena of frequent and repeated salience in everyone's lived experience. We propose the hypothesis that, to a large degree, people come to hold the values they hold in the course of responding to these phenomena, and that there are a limited range of possible responses, each providing coherence to a complex of values that are woven into a person's life. These phenomena, of which we will list four, concern various gaps between aspiration and realization.

1. The first phenomenon is related to the gap, already referred to, between the manifestation and articulation of values. It is what we will call the gap between intention and effective action, between desire and the outcomes of action. Frequently our actions do not lead to what we intend, and our desires are not fulfilled through the actions they engender. This gap reveals limits to our expressive capacity, our power to shape our own lives, our self-understanding, our grasp of what we can expect from others, and our understanding of the social and material conditions of our lives. Those who propose that a life consisting of a sequence of actions on spontaneous desires will bring a source of happiness and contentment often find that it brings instead a sense of degradation, emptiness, self-contempt, and shame. Those who wish to do

just "what they feel like" are often bewildered by their ineffectualness, and they often discover that they fail to develop the capacities they need later on to realize desires that then take on importance for them. While first-order desires may, and often do, predate second-order desires (values) in a person's life, the continual coherence of first-order desires depends upon one's developing (more or less articulately) second-order ones. There may be social or psychological conditions in which some people are unable to develop constant second-order desires, and so are unable to hold values (even to hold one's self to be an object of value). Under such conditions, we might expect to find profound psychological pathology, and even little appreciation of the value of life, with consequent recourse to indifference to others or to gratuitous violence.

2. The second phenomenon is another gap, between what we experience to be the case and what we sense *can* be. We experience and observe suffering of various kinds, and we sense that some of it can be mitigated, that there need not be so much suffering, that things can be "better," that the salience of suffering can be reduced, and that more fulfilling possibilities can be realized. The experience of suffering, as it were, provides impetus to rank, in some sort of moral order, the possibilities that may be realized in the future. It attunes us to a sense of what well-being might be, and that sense might be heightened by the observation of lives (and interaction with them) that seem to realize more fulfilling possibilities.

3. The third phenomenon is that each of us is placed (early in life largely as a consequence of one's family's position in society; later to some degree by choice) in a variety of institutions, each embodying a different collection of values. Some of these embodied values can be seen as complementary, mutually contributing toward a fulfilled life. Others "contradict" one another, setting up conflicting tendencies in the person. In the extreme case, one might be living the greater part of one's life in institutions that embody values in conflict with the most central personal values that one holds, and the values articulated in those institutions may deny credibility to the values that one is personally inclined to articulate.

4. Finally, within each of the institutions referred to above there is often a gap between values-as-articulated and values-as-manifested. Although institutions exist for the sake of the values they embody and hold, in order to maintain them-

selves, they are often pushed to pursue extraneous (though important) values. For example, the core values of the university (e.g., the pursuit of the truth) may find themselves compromised or overridden by the values of producing professionals to serve the current predominant order, which the university finds itself emphasizing in the service of the ends of funding and recruitment, without which it could not continue to pursue its primary values. Institutions thus simultaneously create the conditions for the manifestation of certain values and also establish limits to their manifestation. (See MacIntyre, 1981, for an illuminating account of tensions that can exist between practices and the institutions whose fundamental value is to foster the practices.) The magnitude and severity of the tension between the values that justify the existence of an institution and the values that enable it actually to function can be expected to vary from institution to institution and from society to society. But the tension will always be present in some degree, and as such will underlie the gap between aspiration and manifestation of institutional values.

These four phenomena are among those that engulf our lives. We cannot avoid them, though they can impinge on our consciousness and conscience more or less sharply. They cause disequilibrium in our lives—so much so that we propose that, to a considerable degree, we can conceive the unfolding of a life (which manifests values as distinct from simply desires) as the narrative of one's attempts to strive toward a satisfying, or at least a tolerable, equilibrium. (We are aware that this is a controversial proposal, specifically rejected in a number of postmodernist writings which regard the quest for an integrated life as the reflection of a particular—and unrealizable—value, rather than as a condition for there being any value at all. We will not address this point here.) In modern times, the gap between desire and outcome of action is especially disconcerting, for it reflects limits on our personal freedom. In a free life there is no significant gap of this kind. In order to reduce the gap, one can attempt either to change the shape of one's own life, or the social conditions of one's life, or both.

Paths toward Equilibrium

We propose that the paths toward equilibrium can, to a first approximation, be classified into the following five kinds, and that the ordered complex of values that a person comes to adopt reflects the path followed. We expect that the classification will be refined in the light of criticism and further study.

1. *Adjustment.* One adjusts one's goals to the way things are, the path of "realism" that accepts (more or less consciously) that there will be no fundamental change in the predominant institutions that shape one's life, that there are no possibilities for the immediate future outside of the current predominant institutions, that the future is framed by those institutions. Accordingly, one chooses to participate—taking into account, where one can, one's opportunities, one's education, one's family, one's talents and interests, and one's assessment of the viability of various institutions and the further opportunities they might open up—in those current institutions to which one has access so as to bring about the least tension and the greatest equilibrium. And one adjusts one's goals largely to what is realizable within these institutions, leading a life into which are woven values that are embodied in one's society. Various ways of life fall under the path of adjustment, reflecting the variety of institutions present, class differences, and even the existence of "fringe" niches in a society. While the path of adjustment admits of variety, within it the range of acceptable values is limited by those embodied in current dominant institutions—and the fact that they are socially embodied becomes de facto a reason for holding them, or at least the ground that makes them immune to criticism.

Adopting the path of adjustment can be more or less conscious. Because the values manifested within this stance are embodied in society, normally the question of their legitimation does not arise, and if it does, the reigning societal articulations of value (ideology) quickly provide answers that prima facie are compelling. Adopting this stance, therefore, needs little personal reflection, and indeed critical reflection is not a highly rated value within it, at least not critical reflection upon social structures, or the kind of reflection that leads to self-consciousness within dominant practices. Critical reflection may make one become aware of the disvalue (e.g., oppression, discrimination, domination) that may also be embodied in the structures, and thus intensify the sense that there are fuller possibilities waiting to be realized, and create the perception of an even larger gap between the value socially manifested and that articulated.

The path of adjustment enables, for some, the experience of a measure of fulfillment, reinforced by institutional articulation (ideology) that the values woven into adjusted lives are those that define a fulfilled life. The stabler and more highly developed the structures are, the more they provide space for large numbers of people to live adjusted lives, and to have their "realistically" limited desires satisfied. The stability of such structures reflects the fact that within them, the actual desires of many are being satisfied, and may have the consequence that these desires appear to be fundamental and universal—reflective of human nature (see Schwartz, 1986, 1990, 1993).

The predominant economic and political institutions of any society reinforce the path of adjustment for a significant number of people—and "privilege" those who adopt it. Even so, this path requires a little luck, since it is vulnerable to collapse should extreme suffering or institutional collapse occur. Rarely, however, can it be adopted by everyone, for in most if not all societies, such privileged lives depend upon relations of domination, where the possibilities for the dominated to gain fulfillment are severely limited.

2. *Resignation.* One comes to resign oneself to the inevitability of the social and personal conditions of one's life, that one's desires are inefficacious, that one's aspirations are empty, that where there is change it happens outside of the operation of one's will. Then desire becomes reduced to the desire to survive, or perhaps to make life barely tolerable, and life becomes a reaction to outside forces. Here we find the phenomena of fatalism, lack of self-value, internalized oppression, diminished intelligence, suppressed consciousness and conscience, and nihilism (see West, 1993). The path does admit of variety: Among other possibilities, it can generate gratuitous (voluntaristic) violence, the deep involvement in religious practices that transfer one's aspirations beyond the world of history, dependence on alcohol and drugs, as well as countless lives following the daily grind of survival (see Martín-Baró, 1991b).

There is, of course, no sharp dividing line between the paths of adjustment and resignation. Interpretive methods are needed to assign a life to one or the other type, methods that need to recognize the remarkable human capacity to find or create niches in which a meaningful life is possible. Nevertheless, resignation is a dialectical counterpart of adjustment in societies structured by dominative relations (whether they be economic, patriarchal, racial, or other). In such societies, stability requires that both paths be followed; indeed, since dominant ideology serves to disguise the structuring relations or to make them immune to critique, for most people only these two paths will be available concretely for adoption. Since the path of resignation is not conceived as having structural sources, ideology explains adopting of it in terms of personal "defects" (laziness, lack of intelligence, etc.) woven into one's life—hence the ready willingness of the "privileged" to accept that the lives of the resigned (and, no doubt, others when it cannot distinguish them from the resigned) be "managed," and even subjected to institutional violence. Such violence is not seen as reflecting structural domination, but as protecting the value that the society should be embodying and manifesting. This conception is reinforced by the perception of various (though few) individuals moving from places where the resigned abound into the ranks of the adjusted. Unaware of structural limits, it supposes that what is available to some is available to all.

3. *Creative marginality.* The resigned are also marginalized, and they make little contribution even to defining the shape of the margins. The adjusted adopt for the most part the value embodied in the current predominant institutions, and so they, too, do not push the limits of the margins, but live within them. Another path accepts that the fundamental structures of society will (can, ought) not be changed in the near future, so that they will continue to frame viable lives, but rejects many of the values they embody, regarding them as unworthy of human aspiration. For example, it may reject the consumerist, possessivist values common in our society as degenerate versions of the aspiration of freedom; it may also be aware of the dialectic between adjustment and resignation, and react with indignation and outrage to the suffering and misery that it maintains are grounded in the prevailing structures. The response of this path is to push beyond the margins, to create spaces for the (greater) manifestation of worthier values, and for lives into which these values are woven. A number of distinct versions of this path can be distinguished.

a. *Individual creativity.* One recognizes that, within the prevailing structures, there are possibil-

ities for creative expression (in art, music, science, etc.). One then pursues a talent and works on it, gaining relevant skills, in order to generate something new—an object of value that is recognized in one's culture as such—that is distinctive, expressive of the self, and that expands the realm of value that can be embodied within the culture. While the link between individuality and novelty makes this path compelling, it is not a solitary affair; it involves participation in shared practices, which often are institutionalized. At times the path of adjustment shades into this path. At least in some domains, the value of producing and respecting objects of value is highly embodied in most societies. Indeed, it is quite common for dominant ideology to "justify" current social structures with reference to the objects of value generated within the structures, implying that the generation of such value is sufficient to legitimize the material and social conditions necessary for its generation. One may include in this path certain feats of entrepreneurship or creative administration. And certain corrupt practices, unusual forms of the accumulation of property and conspicuous consumption, may be considered as degenerate versions. Its defining mark is that of individual creativity in pushing out the margins, and it is not uncommon for one who follows it to find it necessary to contest the values embodied in particular institutions (e.g., universities, foundations, government departments, publication houses, art museums).

b. *Communal service.* One participates in or attempts to create communities manifesting values that run counter to those of the mainstream such as service to the needy and marginalized, and, through such communities, one seeks out ways to be less dependent on the material and social conditions that sustain the marginalization of some people. It is difficult to find space for this path. Sometimes it is found within parts of religious institutions. It is also an important factor in the women's and civil rights movements. Reforms in predominant structures may be instigated from this path, as its proponents act to make the values manifest in the dominant institutions more closely approximate their authoritative articulations, opening the path of adjustment (at least) to more of the resigned. This path also, at times, generates remarkable lives that display the creative power of radical love—the "saints," whose lives exhibit rarely realized potentials of human nature, whom we all admire even when we do not aspire to emulate them. This path may be open more to those from the marginalized sectors of society than to those from elsewhere.

c. *Preservation of an alternative tradition.* One participates in an institution or movement for the sake of preserving an alternative tradition (religious, cultural, ethnic). This can involve creating new spaces (and sometimes eventually new structures) in governmental, economic, educational and other institutions. Much of the current activity subsumed by the label "multiculturalism" in educational institutions falls into this category.

The emphasis in the first three paths is on individual change or adaptation in the light of structures that are perceived effectively as given conditions of one's life. Each of them can recognize the possibility of structural reforms, and viable structures may even need to include a place for adjusted paths committed to the administration of reforms. The remaining two paths put the emphasis on fundamental structural change.

4. *The quest for power.* This path reflects the desire to gain power (political or economic) in order to adjust social structures to one's (and, no doubt, to those one thinks that others "ought" to hold) intentions, interests and values, to use power to transform institutional structures so that one's interests or perceived obligations can be satisfied. There can be both military and electoral varieties of this path.

Within prevailing structures there are roles for the exercise of power. These roles fall under the category of adjustment. The present category, in contrast, involves the use of power for fundamental structural change. Power may be used to conserve what is, to produce reform or to produce revolution. The lines between conservation and reform, and reform and revolution are not always easy to define or to identify—and one who gains an office of power may, when confronted with the realities of exercising it, move away from an intended use of power in another direction.

5. *Transformation from below.* One may hold that existing structures, even under reform, cannot provide conditions in which everyone can live lives into which are woven values that are plausibly considered their own, expressive of their human selves. One may also hold that the quest for power, at best, will only bring about changes in who occu-

pies the privileged places in dominative structures (or perhaps replace old structures of domination with new but no less dominating kinds). Holding these views, one might enter into organizations, practices and communities whose objectives are: (1) to enable their members, composed largely from the marginalized groups, to manifest values that are their own, and to practice service and cooperation to this end; (2) to expand the compass of these organizations by creating new ones and cooperating with others, so that more and more people become included in the process; (3) to work with sectors from the more mainstream institutions, in a spirit of reciprocity, so as together to open up more space for fulfilling options for increasing numbers of people; (4) and in so doing, to form the institutions in which values like cooperation, participation, and openness to difference can be embodied, (5) eventually to constitute the institutional base of new social structures in which relations of domination would be diminished.

In Latin America groups with objectives like these are said to belong to the "popular movement." They include grassroots communities of the poor engaging in self-reliance, educational and health projects, movements for housing and land tenure, institutes for human rights, food and agricultural cooperatives, women's organizations, black and native people's consciousness movements and refugee organizations (Martín-Baró, 1991a). They seek out collaboration with sectors of universities, churches, the professions (law, engineering, medicine), business, unions and government. Their critiques of the status quo and of reliance on power are reciprocally related to their participation in the groups. The critique need not precede the participation, and characteristically does not. Reflection on the participation and the obstacles it faces may lead to the critique.

This path of transformation from below has similarities to the path of communal service; it begins with addressing the needs of the marginalized but, rather than service and charity, it emphasizes personal empowerment, solidarity, and cooperation. Because it emphasizes the dialectic of personal and social change, it does not rest upon the agency of power. It is argued that power cannot bring about the desired changes, for power cannot make people live lives into which are woven their own values. This does not imply, however, that those adopting this path may not in actual fact sometimes become allied with groups that are using violent means to gain state power. The gaining of power by such groups is not the desired change. But, where oppression and repression are intense, expedient alliances may be judged necessary to remove crucial obstacles to progress along this path of transformation from below. Ambiguity will always be present when the followers of this path, attempting to bring about the fuller embodiment of the values it represents, interact with institutions of power. Sometimes (perhaps most of the time), the conditions of the expedient alliance will bring about a lapse into path 4, where the values associated with power supplant the initially motivating community values. Nevertheless, where the path of transformation from below is followed authentically, only the growth of the movements, in dialectical interaction with the formation of personal values, can produce the desired transformation. It rests upon a step-by-step process of change, testing each step for viability as it proceeds, a process in which there is organic unity between means and ends. It does not evaluate each step in terms of whether or not it is a means to a systematically articulated social objective, for such evaluation is unresponsive to the personal/social dialectic and open to having key roles being granted to power and violence. On the contrary, each step is evaluated in terms of its bringing about a fuller embodiment of the values articulated by the movements, and what the limits of that embodiment are; thus, of whether it represents, embryonically or in anticipation, a society that thoroughly embodies the desired values, and provides a ground for proceeding with fuller exploratory steps, out of which the concrete structures of a transformed society can emerge.

We suggest that these five paths are the ones that are open to people when they experience the kind of disequilibrium that we described at the beginning of this section. We do not want to suggest that these are pure paths. To a point, everyone shares some aspects of all the paths, but for each person, a particular path eventually comes to the fore, reflecting who the person is and his or her most fundamental values—the complex of values that is largely constitutive of his or her identity. We propose the further hypothesis that paths 1 and 2 are the most common in the contemporary world, and that to adopt any of the other paths one must have substantial motivation, because pursuing these paths often introduces new forms of disequilibrium and disorientation. However, it is these latter paths that permit

interesting lives and, in the last analysis, meaningful lives. They represent attempts to discover and realize some of the human possibilities that have not yet been realized, and to develop critical and creative consciousness in all of its dimensions.

REASONS FOR ADOPTING A PARTICULAR PATH TOWARD EQUILIBRIUM

According to our analysis the path that a person adopts provides a unity to the complex of values that the person holds. People have various reasons, which may be more or less articulated, for adopting and persisting in their respective paths. We do not want to suggest that one chooses one's path as a consequence of an isolatable deliberative process, as if one deliberates considering the reasons for and against each path and then adopts one. Rather one makes choices about such matters as educational objectives, friendships to cultivate, skills to obtain, jobs or careers to pursue, places to live, commitments to family (as well as choices about countless matters of consumption and possessions), and so on—choices that are made possible, enhanced and constrained by such matters as family, class, and religious background. From this multiplicity and complexity of choices emerge the contours of one's adopted path and the complex of values that largely constitute a person's identity. The reasons for adopting one's path become apparent not antecedently, but as one attempts to create or articulate or discern unity in the values that are manifested in the various choices and commitments that one has made, and as one looks forward to a life that displays coherence, a life into which a complex of values is increasingly woven. Such a complex of values, we propose, is itself subject to evaluation in the light of a number of criteria, which often become explicit when one attempts to articulate the legitimacy of one's adopted path in the face of challenges. These criteria also play an explanatory role, at least to the extent that recognizing that one's complex of values fails to meet one or other of them can occasion a life change.

We will discuss at length two criteria, which are particularly pertinent in the context of psychological investigation.

1. *The possibility criterion.* The genuine possibility—given the actual constraints of prevailing material and social conditions—of the complex of

values being woven consistently, constantly, and coherently into a concrete personal life, and so of being embodied in society.

2. *The human nature criterion.* The availability of an articulated view of human nature, with some empirical support, that renders intelligible the claim that holding the complex of values shapes a life that is fulfilling.

In practice, these two criteria are deployed in conjunction with a number of other criteria. We list without elaboration, categorization, and defense several of these other criteria that we think important.

3. The formal consistency of the complex of values.

4. The continuity of the complex of values, perhaps under considerable reinterpretation, (1) with some of the values that one has "inherited," that one shares with some others, and that appear "obvious" (e.g., rejection of murder) and also (2) with values that are actually woven into concrete lives (or compelling literary characters) that one recognizes as fulfilled. Psychological research can inform (2) by exploring which complexes of values, when woven into lives, generate a sense of well-being. Such research can also contribute by identifying the characteristic pathologies of each of the five paths of response to the gaps between aspiration and realization, and the conditions under which these pathologies can be avoided.

5. The inclusion in the complex of values of those values that are constitutive of the intelligibility of evaluative discourse in general (e.g., respect for the participants in the discourse, elevation of dialogue over power, truthfulness).

6. The universalizability of the core values of the complex—that the material and social conditions of their embodiment are compatible with all participants in the discourse being able to conduct lives into which these values (or, more generally, those expressive of their own individual identities) are woven.

We have left it open whom one considers the participants in evaluative discourse to be, for that—perhaps—reflects one's own values, rather than a general criterion. If everyone (in principle) is included among the participants then, as (5) and (6) are met, one gains a greater capacity to understand well the actions of other persons and social

movements, even those that manifest values quite different from one's own. Gaining such a capacity is a core value of our fifth path, the path of "transformation from below." So too is gaining a clear consciousness of the conditions necessary for one's values to be woven into one's life.

Whatever one may think of the proposed criteria 3–6, the possibility and human nature criteria are of utmost importance for evaluating the complex of values that a person holds, although they do not function independently of attempts to gain "reflective equilibrium" with other criteria. The view of human nature underlies the coherence and intelligibility of the complex; the genuine possibility of its being held is necessary for its social salience. Frequently these two criteria lie at the heart of evaluative disputes, often functioning in concert. For example, arguments about the possibility or impossibility of social transformation often appeal to a view of human nature, and the possibilities encapsulated in its articulation. Moreover, if one articulates values not embodied in the current social order, and it is not possible to generate social transformation of the desired kind, then that is a reason to reconsider one's aspirations. And if social transformation is possible, then that a rival value complex is embodied in the current order ceases to be a compelling argument for one's aspirations being limited by it. If arguments can be mounted simultaneously that social transformation is possible, and that there is a supported view of human nature that suggests more fulfilling possibilities in the proposed new order, then the value complex embodied in the current order may come into crisis and, for want of coherence and salience, the extent of their embodiment may decline.

If evaluation is to guide lives and not become reduced to mere idealistic criticism, considerations of what is possible are always very important. Formal consistency of a value complex is not sufficient for such possibility. For example, community values like cooperation and sharing are formally consistent with the primacy of property rights, but arguably the material and social conditions required for the steadfast manifestation of one preclude that of the other. More than consistency is involved in assessing the possibility of coherently holding a value complex. When a value complex is already highly embodied in a society, there is no further question about its possibility. What is actual is possible. A particularly difficult question confronts us when our fifth path, the path of social transformation, is under consideration. Unless the kind of social transformation proposed is possible, the path of social transformation reduces to the path of communal service. In our society, this kind of social transformation is widely believed to be impossible—hence most lives can be charted on the first three paths. It is widely believed that any viable social possibilities (for the foreseeable future) will be framed by the institutions of private property, the free market, and formal, electoral democracy (see Lacey, 1991). Why? There are various answers: (a) because those institutions are arguably better (more fulfilling, more encouraging of human freedom, more conducive to social justice), and recognized as such, than any available and most imaginable alternatives; (b) because of the inertia and ever growing momentum of those institutions; (c) because of the virtual hegemony of power associated with those institutions and the expectancy that this power will be used to maintain their hegemony; (d) because of the belief that these institutions effectively embody human nature, which is understood to underlie individualist and egoist values (see Schwartz, 1986, 1993). If (a) and (d) are soundly grounded, then the use of power, referred to in (c), will often be legitimate—but not otherwise. Much hinges, then, on an assessment of what human nature is, and an assessment of what makes it that way.

IMPLICATIONS FOR PSYCHOLOGICAL INVESTIGATION

It accords with the two criteria under discussion that beliefs about what is possible and about human nature may properly influence the personal values that one holds and desires to be embodied in society, and the social values that one attempts to personalize. Indeed, the applicability of the criteria depends upon such beliefs. As already indicated, beliefs about what is possible and about human nature are deeply intertwined. Our beliefs about the values that can be woven into lives and articulated authentically depend (in part) on our beliefs about human nature; and our beliefs about human nature draw heavily upon the values that we observe to be actually woven into lives. Broadly speaking, these beliefs are open to empirical scrutiny. What kind of empirical inquiry could throw light on them?

Answering this question is made exceptionally difficult by the fact that the possibility of genuinely holding values depends not only upon what human nature is, but also upon the values that are embodied in actual societal institutions and upon the power (authority) relations that structure these institutions. Prevailing power relations may actually prevent certain possibilities allowed by human nature from being realized, especially in those cases where their being realized rests upon social conditions that are incompatible with the prevailing conditions. Moreover, the human desires that are actually present at a given time might reflect not the full potential of human nature, but the possibilities reinforced in actual institutions. If this is so, then an empirical charting of what is actually manifested cannot result in a comprehensive account of human potential, for there may be hitherto unrealized possibilities. The actual informs, but cannot settle definitively matters of the possible; at the same time, empirical investigation is tied to the actual—the playing out of the resulting tension is at the heart of all experimental science.

What kind of empirical, psychological inquiry can properly inform beliefs about the possibility (not necessarily high probability) or impossibility of value complexes, such as those implicit in our fifth path, that have not hitherto been realized to any significant extent? What is the appropriate methodology? What are the appropriate theoretical constraints? What are the appropriate empirical phenomena to select to investigate? Answers to these questions are usually intertwined, and reflect the practices (and the values they express) that the research informs (Lacey, 1990). If most research informs practices within our first three paths, then the question about alternative possibilities is not likely to arise (except at the margins). If today these paths are framed by the institutions of private property, the free market, and so on, and those institutions tend to embody egoist values, made coherent and intelligible by an individualist view of human nature, then we would expect to find psychological theory today constrained by the individualist view of human nature, and its evidential base would draw principally from the characteristic phenomena of these institutions, where one observes the predominance of egoist values. And indeed, methodological individualism, an approach to research that draws upon an individualist view of human nature, has been throughout this century the dominant methodological approach in psychology (see Wallach & Wallach, 1983). However, methodological individualism does not provide an adequate context for answering the question we have posed.

Where it is just taken for granted, it begs the question. How can we not beg the question? What are the alternatives to methodological individualism?

Individualist Conception of Human Nature

An individualist conception of human nature proposes that human beings (persons) are in the first instance individuals—conscious, active, expressive, bodily beings—whose relatedness with others is contingent and subsidiary to the well-being of the individual. Each individual has its own being separate from and even opposed to that of others for there can be competition and conflicts among the interests (preferences, desires for well-being) of individuals. So understood, a person is not primarily a potential contributor to the common good, someone who belongs to a group, a role-player in institutions, a participant in practices with others, or a being whose well-being is essentially linked with that of others. The fundamental desires of persons represent subjective preferences, which are understood as self-defined and self-determined. The self, if free to do so, does what it likes to do, and—provided one remembers the proper role of second-order desires in shaping and directing first-order desires—it serves its own interests, which typically are defined in terms of the achievements, pleasures, or possessions of the self, so that its fundamental personal values typically are egoistic, and its primary social value is autonomy. That, according to the individualist view, is the way human nature is.

Communal Conception of Human Nature

Another view, which we will call the communal conception of human nature, conceives of persons as essentially connected with (some) others. Persons, *in addition to* the conscious, active, expressive and bodily dimensions highlighted in the individualist conception, also essentially have a social dimension, such that human well-being is expressed in (as well as being a consequence of) the appropriate interaction of all the dimensions, and this includes establishing such relations as love, friendship, and respect for and recognition by others. Selves are construed as interdependent beings; some others form a part of the self; their values, interests, and needs become essentially

linked to one's own and so the self is not opposed to (all) others (e.g., Markus & Kitayama, 1991). This is not to devalue individuality (self-reliance, agency, or personal achievement), but rather to open up the possibility that the uniqueness of the self can (must) be tied to generating a unique set of fulfilling relations with others.

On this view, then, persons are—by nature—participants in practices, communities, and institutions with others, and their well-being is implicated dialectically with that of members of the groups with which they are, or conceive themselves to be, connected. It still makes sense to say that persons desire fundamentally their own well-being, but now that well-being is inclusive of that of (some) others, so that responsibility for others cannot be separated from concern for the self, and the desires to belong, to participate, and to be recognized by others are as basic as the desires to have and to accomplish. Primary personal values include those of cooperation and service to the community; the social value of autonomy remains important, but now it is interpreted as in dialectical interaction with that of solidarity.

Selfishness and Altruism

The concepts of selfishness and altruism, and the phenomena held to reflect them, provide useful touchstones for bringing out the different implications of the two conceptions of human nature. Selfishness refers to putting one's self ahead of others, even at their expense; altruism to serving others ahead of seeking one's individual gain, even at the expense of one's self.

Individualist View

On the individualist view, if altruism is among a person's fundamental values, it is simply a subjective, individualist preference. Some people prefer wealth, others fame, others pleasure, and a few to serve other people; individuals are just different. [One may seek to explain personal differences—in sociobiology (e.g., Alexander, 1987; Dawkins, 1976), social psychology, psychoanalysis, etc.—but such explanations carry no evaluative implications.] As such, altruism is neither representative of higher value than the values usually associated with selfishness, nor indicative of objective possibilities for human well-being. All acts, in the final analysis, are the outcome of individual subjective preferences, including both altruistic and selfish acts (see, e.g., Margolis, 1982, for a discussion of this view). Thus, one cannot criticize selfishness in the name of the primacy of altruism without, in so doing, holding others accountable to one's own preferences, which do not have a nonsubjective grounding. The individualist view provides no nonsubjective grounds (other than formal and causal consistency) for ranking subjective preferences in order of value, and hence for sustaining a morally significant distinction between altruistic and selfish acts.

Interpreted in this way, the individualist view recognizes the possibility of altruism but denies its moral significance. It is a feature of this interpretation that, although altruism and egoism are distinguished, the grounding of each of them lies in facts about their respective individual bearers, what their likes and preferences are. One person's fundamental value may be to gain wealth, another person's to serve others; one acts for the sake of gaining wealth, the other for the sake of serving others; one acts for the sake of gaining wealth *because he likes* to gain wealth, the other acts for the sake of serving others *because he likes* to serve others.

Another interpretation of the individualist view, perhaps a more common one and the one we will discuss for the remainder of the chapter, maintains that the phrase, "because he likes" disguises the deeper meaning "for the sake of his gaining a certain kind of satisfaction (pleasure, happiness, feeling good, lessening of feelings of guilt and shame)." Thus all (free) acts are performed for the sake of the self's gain, gain of satisfaction; all acts manifest egoist values. In particular, one serves others for the sake of the self's gain, i.e., serving others represents not a fundamental value for a person, but a value adopted because it is instrumentally related (perhaps in the long term) to the person's fundamental egoist values. Of course, if "altruistic" acts derive instrumentally from egoist values, they are not genuinely altruistic.

Given this common interpretation of the individualist view, genuine altruism is not possible, and so neither is its opposite, genuine selfishness, the sort of selfishness that inherently morally demeans a person. If, by nature, our fundamental values are egoist, it cannot be morally blameworthy to act out of "selfishness." All acts are "selfish"; "altruistic" acts are a subset of "selfish" acts and not opposed to them, so that one cannot properly criticize "selfish" acts in the name of the alleged primacy of altruism (see Dawkins, 1976; Ghiselin, 1976). When it is said, "Human beings are by nature selfish," the concept "selfish" has been naturalized and displaced from its integral role in moral discourse. This saying also leads to the prescription that one reduce moral arguments to those that show how "doing good" actually serves (or it is believed that it will likely serve) one's own "selfish" interests.

Communal View

The communal conception of human nature provides a different way to understand selfishness and altruism. Since one's self is essentially connected with other selves, one's well-being implies, fosters, depends upon, and is partially constituted by that of others, and it is manifest largely through participation in relationships, practices, and communities. The experience of well-being is internal to such participation, and so it cannot be construed as an individual feeling *caused* by the participation but also in principle caused in other ways; that is, it cannot be seen as an "effect" that is logically or empirically distinct from its social "cause." Thus, personal well-being is not simply an individual possession, experience, or attribute, something an individual gains (nor is it reducible to a person maintaining certain sets of social relations). Personal well-being does involve a variety of conscious states, e.g., feelings of contentedness, memories of love and friendship, a sense of value of other people and of justice, recognition of achievements—"pleasures"—but these pleasures are the internal accompaniments of participation in practices that express such values as collaboration, creativity, service, friendship, and solidarity. These various pleasures that accompany social relations, and others that may be the causal consequences of certain behaviors or external stimuli, are mutually incommensurable. That is, pleasure, as such, is not a value; it may not even be a meaningful ontological type. Persons—by nature—desire their own well-being. While this well-being includes essentially the experience of various pleasures, it is a misleading abstraction to affirm that pleasure is a fundamental desire.

In actual lives, one's desire for one's own well-being is shaped by one's beliefs about what constitutes well-being. On the communal view, such beliefs may be true or false, one false belief being that personal well-being can be identified with individual gain, and that a life into which are woven egoist values characteristically experiences well-being. It is possible to live such a life, a life into which are woven fundamentally egoist values, and to legitimize that life by reference to the false view that the being of self is separate from that of others. That legitimation draws upon a degenerate sense of the self, since such separation is possible only in conception but not in nature. Holding egoist values as fundamental is what defines selfishness. Selfishness is a real phenomenon. It follows, on the communal view, that identifying someone as selfish has a moral sting, for selfishness is opposed to the well-being of others *and* of the self. It also reflects a lack of adequate self-understanding. Not only is selfishness a real phenomenon, it may also be a universal tendency. But it is not the only possibility allowed by nature. Among our fundamental desires are those for friendship, participation, belongingness, and recognition. It is these desires that render intelligible such emotions as grief at the loss or misfortune of a loved one, and compassion for those suffering from injustice. Selfishness weakens these desires and these emotions. Its manifestations are open to psychological and sociological explanation, whereas, on the individualist view, only individual differences with respect to the particular egoist values manifested—not the manifestation of egoist values as such (selfishness)—are open to such explanation.

On the communal view, actions—unless informed by false beliefs about the self and personal well-being—are simultaneously for the sake of the self and of (some) others; there is no separation. Thus, there is no threat of paradox when a person puts service to others (and other nonegoist values) ahead of individual gain. Normally, the manifestation of nonegoist values will go hand in hand with personal enhancement. It is *not*: self *or* others; but rather: self *and* others. The bodily separation of self and others does not imply that relations with others are not partially constitutive of the self. Nevertheless, certain special conditions may cause there to be a disjunction between self and others. Then, even bodily survival may become subsidiary to the value of others. Altruism is possible. Like that of selfishness, the manifestation of altruism requires explanation.

Auxiliary Interpretive Strategies

The two conceptions of human nature that we have sketched, the individualist and the communal,

underlie conflicting beliefs about what is possible. According to the former, in contrast to the latter, altruism and our paths of "communal service" (3b) and "transformation from below" (5) are impossible. However, simple appeal to which of the possibilities are or are not realized does not enable one to provide clear empirical support to either of the views. Neither view of human nature, like any other metaphysical view, can be directly validated or invalidated empirically. The research methodologies associated with each of them carry sufficient auxiliary interpretive strategies to recast into their own frameworks any apparently refuting phenomena. As we have seen, the individualist view recasts the holding of nonegoist values as instrumental for manifesting egoist values, and thus as not fundamental for a person. And the communal view interprets the widespread (even near universal) dominance of egoist values to reflect not human nature as such but the hegemony of social structures in which egoist values are highly embodied.

The plausibility of the individualist interpretive strategy derives in part from reducing personal well-being to a species of individual gain. The communal view recognizes that I may experience well-being *because* I serve others. It does not follow that I serve others *in order to* experience my own well-being. The individualist view, not recognizing this distinction, interprets personal testimony that service is accompanied by a sense of well-being as evidence that service is for the sake of individual gain. Then the articulation of nonegoist values as fundamental becomes interpreted as a sign (not necessarily a conscious disguise) of lack of sound self-understanding. The plausibility of this strategy is further reinforced by the fact that there is probably no one who would deny the pull ("temptations") of selfishness in his or her life. Selfishness may indeed be a universal tendency. But that is compatible both with it being a source of human diminishment, and with there being universal countertendencies (e.g., to belong, to communicate, to take responsibility for certain others).

The plausibility of the communal interpretive strategy is rooted in the dialectical linkage that we have suggested to exist between the values that are most manifested and those highly embodied socially. Selfishness is possible anywhere, but its predominance would reflect the hegemony of social structures that highly embody egoist values. It has often been suggested that the empirical record shows that people desire possessions, pleasures, consumption, and so forth and no doubt, a sociological survey of Western, advanced industrial societies would largely confirm this. (One should not push this too far. At the present moment we are witnessing a striking resurgence of affirmations of group identity and of the value of community affiliations.) However, the results of such a survey would be equally compatible with the interpretation that high social structural embodiment explains the predominance of egoist values. Then articulating egoist values as universal becomes interpreted as a sign that the social relations that make possible one's life are being hidden. One may conjecture that this is most likely to happen where the relations include dominative and oppressive ones. This conjecture is open to empirical investigation.

Relevant Kinds of Psychological Research

Enough has been said to indicate the resourcefulness of the interpretive strategies of each of the two viewpoints. Thus neither viewpoint derives authority simply from the empirical record (see Kohn, 1990; Schwartz, 1993 for illustrative reviews). It does not follow, however, that they have equivalent explanatory and predictive adequacy, and thus equal degrees of confirmation.

The individualist view posits that everyone's fundamental values are egoist, and that the wide variety of values actually held is bounded by the limits (no doubt expanding with the course of history) of egoism. In contrast, the communal view admits of variety that crosses these bounds. It predicts variability that will correlate with such variables as social structure, culture, institutional affiliations, and class position. (Such variability, as elaborated above, is not inconsistent with the individualist view. However, this view interprets the variability differently, as one really of egoist values, and it does not *predict* the variability.) The communal view also predicts that people's basic desires are not limited to selfish ones, but also include the desires to belong, to participate in loving relationships, to be just and compassionate, and so on. Genuine tension among sometimes competing desires is a mark of all human life. However, the communal view can also explain that—where the prevailing dominant social structures embody egoist values, and where the predominant articulations of social values lend legitimacy to these structures—selfishness comes to the forefront and that

institutions that embody nonegoist values become undermined or recreated, so that the hegemony of egoist values extends ever deeper into the social fabric (Schwartz, 1993, 1994).

For the communal view to have any credibility, its predictions must have some empirical vindication. Clearly the absence of relevant variation within powerful social structures that highly embody egoist values does not constitute counter evidence; nor does it constitute positive evidence.

One place to look for relevant evidence is in cross-cultural studies of values, and here we suggest there is considerable evidence to support some version or other of the communal view. We cite three studies. In the first place, Markus and Kitayama (1991) have shown that how the self is conceived, and how it is conceived in relation to others, is culture-specific, and that even in an advanced industrial society like Japan the self is generally conceived as an interdependent being (without this diminishing the importance of agency and achievement). In the second place, if connectedness is an essential part of human well-being, we would expect the breaking of it to manifest itself in psychological pathology. Seligman (1991) interprets a tenfold increase in the incidence of depression in the U.S. over the past two generations as being due in part to the disconnection of individuals from social groups that give meaning and significance to their lives. This interpretation remains consistent with his earlier theory that the undermining of agency is the principal cause of depression; now effective agency becomes tied essentially to the social dimension of human nature. In the third place, Fiske (1991) has presented an argument that all forms of social interaction in all cultures can be represented in terms of four fundamentally different rule systems: Communal sharing, authority ranking, equality matching, and market pricing. Fiske suggests that in every culture there are social domains in which each system operates, so that an individual person's life can manifest different values as fundamental as one moves from domain to domain (from family to corporation to religious institution, for example). What distinguishes different cultures from one another are the domains in which each of the rule systems operates. Where a particular rule system operates, a particular set of social values is articulated and a particular set of personal values highly embodied.

A second place to look for relevant evidence is in studies that investigate values across classes. Few such studies exist. Martín-Baró (1991a), however, reports among certain groups of poor workers, who can be interpreted as attempting to follow the path of transformation from below, the presence of such values as "solidarity and cooperation, sobriety and persistence, sensitivity and capacity to sacrifice."

These studies provide some confirmation for the communal view of human nature, and some support that path 3b (communal service) and perhaps path 5 (transformation from below) represent possibilities allowed by human nature. While they do not suffice to falsify the individualist view, they challenge it to deploy its auxiliary interpretive strategies. These strategies involve positing egoist desires that people in the groups studied do not recognize as present in themselves, and deny the reality of the coherence that these people recognize between their articulations of value and the lives they lead. The strategies thus imply that there is a vast gap between the desires manifested in their behavior (egoist) and the values articulated (nonegoist), but a gap that these people fail to recognize (indeed, they reject it) when it is brought to their attention. The otherwise self-conscious and coherent behavior of these people casts doubt on the empirical credentials of such an interpretive strategy. Insisting on it suggests that its roots are self-interested rather than empirical; it may even suggest the intention to use (or—more benignly—the cognitive acceptance that the prevailing socioeconomic and political powers will) force to prevent the embodiment of nonegoist values in domains that impinge on one's self-interest. Or perhaps the major currents of modernity have, to a significant extent, swept away the sensibility, the consciousness, and the discourse needed to treat fundamental nonegoist values as real options both for our lives and for framing research in the human sciences.

We pointed out that research conducted within the frame of methodological individualism effectively begs the question concerning the possibility of nonegoist values being fundamental in a person's life. Research framed by a communal conception of human nature does not. That conception predicts the variation of fundamental values across a range of variables. If that variation is not found or found only in marginal ways, then that would provide powerful confirmation of the individualist view. Individualism, therefore, as well as versions of communalism, are possible outcomes of research framed by a communal view, which thus involves an empirically richer approach. This does not render methodological individualist research irrelevant, especially if it is true that egoist values are virtually hegemonic today. Rather, it means that the products of methodological individualist research need to be compared, with respect to their explanatory and predictive power and the empirical adequacy of their auxiliary interpretive strategies, with research framed by communal viewpoints. In this way, psychological research can cast light on the values human nature permits to be held fundamentally.

But psychological research can only inform, not settle, matters of the possibility of holding certain values. Prevailing social structures also constrain possibilities. Psychological research may also help to identify the contribution of the social structures—the more successfully it does so, the more there is enabled a discussion about the desirability of such structures not cut short by the trump of appealing to impossibility. Of course, possibilities are more or less distant from being realized. Path 5, the path of transformation from below, no doubt represents at best a distant possibility. Whether recognition of this dim possibility can support one adopting path 5 (with its attendant risks and uncertainties) or not will largely depend on one's assessment of the possibility of living a life into which are woven values that one can plausibly claim authentically as one's own; thus, path 5 would appeal more to the resigned than to the adjusted. Similarly, interest in engaging in psychological research to explore the sources of motivation (hope, necessary desires) that lead people into such a path would reflect an assessment that currently available human possibilities are problematically limited. So research into values cannot help being itself value laden.

CONCLUSION

We have offered a multimodal analysis of values. Our account purports to put order into the variety of linguistic usages of "value," and also to reflect the phenomenology of values, particularly the relationship between values and behavior. The account also has implications for psychological research aimed at understanding why people hold the values they hold, what the sources are both of the commonalties and the variations among the values people hold, and how the set of viable values is to be identified. It provides a conceptual framework in which a "perspicuous contrast" (see Taylor, 1981) can be made between two competing viewpoints—the individualist and the communal—regarding what is possible concerning the fundamental values that human beings hold. In the long run, the cognitive value of the account will rest on its role in generating adequate understanding on these issues.

REFERENCES

Alexander, R. D. (1987). *The biology of moral systems.* Hawthorne, NY: Aldine de Gruyter.

Dawkins, R. (1976). *The selfish gene.* Oxford: Oxford University Press.

Fiske, A. P. (1991*). Structures of social life: The four elementary forms of human relations.* New York: Free Press.

Ghiselin, M. (1976). *The economy of nature and the evolution of sex.* Berkeley: University of California Press.

Hodges, B. T., & Baron, R. M. (1992). Values as constraints on affordances: Perceiving and acting properly. *Journal for the Theory of Social Behavior, 22,* 263–294.

Kohn, R. (1990). *The brighter side of human nature.* New York: Basic Books.

Lacey, H. (1990). Interpretation and theory in the natural and human sciences: A note on Kuhn and Taylor. *Journal for the Theory of Social Behavior, 20,* 197–212.

Lacey, H. (1991). Understanding conflicts between North and South. In M. Dascal (Ed.), *Culture, relativism and philosophy* (pp. 243–262). Leiden: E. J. Brill.

MacIntyre, A. (1981*). After virtue.* South Bend: Notre Dame University Press.

Marglin, S. (1976). What do bosses do? In A. Gorz (Ed.), *The division of labour* (pp. 13–54). London: Harvester Press.

Margolis, H. (1982). *Selfishness, altruism, and rationality.* Cambridge: Cambridge University Press.

Markus, H. R., & Kitayama, S. (1991). Culture and the self: Implications for cognition, emotion and motivation. *Psychological Review, 98,* 224–253.

Martín-Baró, I. (1991a). Towards a liberation psychology. In J. Hassett & H. Lacey (Eds.), *Towards a society that serves its people: The intellectual contribution of El Salvador's murdered Jesuits* (pp. 319–332). Washington: Georgetown University Press.

Martín-Baró, I. (1991b). Violence in Central America: A social psychological perspective. In J. Hassett & H. Lacey (Eds.), *Towards a society that serves its people: The intellectual contribution of El Salvador's murdered Jesuits* (pp. 333–346). Washington: Georgetown University Press.

Nerlich, G. (1989). *Values and valuing: Speculations on the ethical life of persons.* Oxford: Clarendon Press.

Polanyi, K. (1944). *The great transformation.* New York: Rinehart.

Schwartz, B. (1986). *The battle for human nature: Science, morality, and modern life.* New York: W. W. Norton.

Schwartz, B. (1990). The creation and destruction of values. *American Psychologist, 45,* 7–15.

Schwartz, B. (1993). Why altruism is impossible . . . and ubiquitous. *Social Service Review, 67,* 314–343.

Schwartz, B. (1994), *The costs of living: How market freedom erodes the best things in life.* New York: W. W. Norton.

Schwartz, B., & Lacey, H. (1982). *Behaviorism, science and human nature.* New York: W. W. Norton.

Schwartz, B., Schuldenfrei, R., & Lacey, H. (1978). Operant psychology as factory psychology. *Behaviorism, 6,* 29–54.

Seligman, M. E. P. (1991). *Learned optimism.* New York: Alfred A. Knopf.

Sen, A. (1976). Rational fools. *Philosophy and Public Affairs, 6,* 317–344.

Taylor, C. (1981). Understanding in the *Geisteswissenschaften.* In S. H. Holtzmann & C. M. Leich (Eds.), *Wittgenstein: To follow a rule* (pp. 191–210). Cambridge: Cambridge University Press.

Taylor, C. (1992). *The ethics of authenticity.* Cambridge: Cambridge University Press.

Wallach, M. A., & Wallach, L. (1983). *Psychology's sanction for selfishness: The error of egoism in theory and therapy.* San Francisco: W. H. Freeman.

West, C. (1993). *Race matters.* Boston: Beacon Press.

CHAPTER 22

PRESCRIPTIONS FOR RESPONSIBLE PSYCHIATRY

Joseph Agassi

The ills of psychiatry are currently diagnosed with the aid of deficient etiologies. The currently proposed prescriptions for psychiatry are practically impossible. The defective part of the profession is its leadership, which in its very defensiveness sticks to the status quo, thereby owning the worst defects and impeding all possible cure. The current discussions of the matter are pretentious and thus woolly. The minimal requirement from the profession as a whole and from each of its individual members is that they be not defensive and clear. In this vein I offer here preliminary discussions of propriety, of responsibility, and of science.

INTRODUCTION

The claim that psychiatrists are irresponsible is repeatedly made, usually linked with prescriptions for improvement. Irresponsibility is diagnosed as a social ill, and variation in diagnosis is linked to variation in prescription. The common diagnoses are these:

1. Mental disorder is no illness.

2. Psychiatry is unscientific (perhaps because mental disorder is no illness).
3. The dignity of the mentally troubled is regularly violated (perhaps because psychiatry is unscientific, perhaps because mental disorder is no illness).

The common prescriptions are these:

1. Abolish psychiatry.
2. Render psychiatry scientific.
3. Increase psychiatrists' responsibility to their patients.

A suggested variant of (1) is the proposal to convert the status of psychiatry from that of medicine to that of counseling, which is neither here nor there, since no objection to psychological counseling was ever raised. The variants of (2) rest on the diverse characterizations of science tagged to it. The variants of (3) rest on the diverse characterizations of responsibility tagged to it.

The ideas behind the three diagnoses are questionable: In order to implement them, more knowledge is required of mental ailments, of science, and even of responsibility. The diagnoses are shaky because of the absence of background knowledge, because they rest on shaky etiologies. Consequently, no one knows how to implement any of these prescriptions. Unfortunately, public debates nowadays center on the prescriptions, at times on the diagnosis, but we need more background knowledge, more etiology. Thus far, in the absence of firm etiology, there is no scientific basis to support any of the diagnoses mentioned. Moreover, each of the prescriptions mentioned is impracticable and so they are all of little value. Should we, then, suspend the discussion until more background knowledge is gathered, until more is known about science and about mental illness? Or is there an alternative approach that circumvents this defect?

Fortunately there is a way to circumvent the defect: What can and should be done, and more or less at once, and with no problem as to missing background knowledge, is to institute safeguards against the defensive attitude prevalent in the leadership of the profession, because this attitude prevents an open and critical debate of the extant criticism of the profession. Public discussion may dispel criticism that is unjust or misdirected. Public discussion may lead to the discussion of the possible ways to reduce the level of such criticism. As to valid criticism, public discussion of it will help in meeting it. The defensive attitude of the current professional leadership of the profession betrays a terrible, unjust, tacit admission that the current criticism of the profession is just and that the complaint is not removable. (If the current professional leadership renders the fault irremovable, then it should be replaced.) The defensiveness of the current professional leadership, then, is the target of the severest criticism of the profession possible, yet this fact is missing from the three diagnoses mentioned above.

Nevertheless, it is valuable to examine the background knowledge concerning responsibility, concerning science, and concerning mental illness; it is particularly valuable to center on responsibility, because the severest ill of psychiatry is that it is saddled with an irresponsible professional leadership that seemingly takes care of the membership of the profession, but in truth harms it by tacitly admitting that their interest conflicts with the quest for the truth. Of course, the question of responsibility here is therefore inevitably linked with the other

problems raised here regarding background knowledge, but then at least the discussion will be confined to the limits of what is required to be known in order to be responsible: It stands to reason that the responsible must be knowledgeable to some extent, but not more than the expert. It so happens that the experts on science, the philosophers of science, are particularly ignorant, confusing, and downright irresponsible; this inevitably lowers the standard of responsibility required of psychiatrists, of course.

PROPRIETY

What all diagnoses of the ills of psychiatry share is that they present it as somehow improper—on social grounds, not on personal ones, of course. This alters the status of psychiatry: It is no more a patient, it is an accused; subsequently even its practitioners are appraised as culprits; this is so even when the appraisal is offered quite impersonally. It is akin to the old appraisal of intrigues and of hired guns and of bribes to foreign politicians—at the time when intrigues were practiced by Jesuits and when respected citizens were employed as assassins and when, only yesterday, international corporations almost openly engaged in briberies of foreign political leaders. Even as these activities were still permitted, they were already frowned upon and even if their practitioners were not brought to trial, they were censured.[1]

One ought to note here some subtlety. When an immoral activity is legal, there are strong incentives to partake in it: In such situations the executive who refuses to bribe foreign dignitaries is ousted by a less restrained competitor. When an immoral activity is also illegal, the transgressors are worse off, but defensible suspects are better off: The court can exonerate them. Criticisms of this kind at times are unjust and at times they herald improvements of current public attitudes, improvements of standards of propriety—moral or political or legal or any other. To be able to distinguish between the just and the unjust criticism of current standards of propriety, then, we should examine the idea of propriety in the first place.

The currently received notion of propriety is a confusion of three different notions. The civic tradition suggests that proper individual conduct is in accord with the best standards of their community. The scientific tradition suggests that proper individual conduct is speaking and acting knowledgeably and not otherwise. The Romantic tradition suggests that proper individual conduct is action in accord with the actors' best sense of mission and with their innermost convictions. Each of these standards is deficient; they contradict each other and they are put into use in different situations. Each has a recognized if not easily well-characterized domain of applicability, where the other two clearly break down. The broadest domain of applicability belongs to the civic tradition, according to which propriety is secured by the compliance with current received standards. Yet it cannot be taken as all-embracing, or else all reform of the current standards will be a priori precluded. It is the received opinion that the currently received civic standards are incomplete, and invite precedents and legislations whenever new circumstances invite improvement—usually in the form of new rulings. Applying current civic standards thoughtlessly to unusual circumstances, even if not new, is at times unacceptable, and even to the point of culpability: Such conduct may, and at times is, deemed negligent. To take a very simple example, medical services by the ignorant are forbidden by custom and by law, yet this is no excuse for neglect in cases of emergency in which expert services are unavailable. Even in cases in which such neglect is not deemed culpable, it is always deemed discreditable and even unprincipled. It is well known that cowards often hide behind the claim that their conduct is within current standards. At times this is most intolerable, for example, when a civil society has descended into barbarism—as happened in Russia and much more so in Germany, in the dark days in the first half of the twentieth century. However rare such cases hopefully are, and however unlikely it hopefully is that our society (whatever it happens to be) is not likely to become barbaric, the very possibility of barbarization renders the criterion of the civic tradition insufficient, as misapplying it has a distinctly barbarizing effect.

The error behind the admission of the civic traditional standard as adequate is general and common: It is the confusion of a criterion with a touchstone.[2] For example, the criterion for a piece of metal being gold of a sufficient degree of purity is traditionally a matter of specific gravity. The matter of specific gravity is difficult. The touchstone simplifies matters: A piece of matter is proven to be gold of a sufficient degree of purity by a mark left on it by a touchstone that scratches it. But suppose white gold (platinum) passes the touchstone test. We will not decide that therefore platinum is gold, but rather that the touchstone does not distinguish gold from platinum. Similarly sour taste was for ages the test for acidity (= sourness) and then some sweet acids were found (e.g., Prussian acid). At times characterizations have to be altered under the pressure of discoveries, like the discovery of very light metals.[3]

The air of paradox raised by a mode of conduct socially accepted but judged immoral disappears when we note that the comparison of an item of conduct with what is accepted in civic society is often a mere touchstone rather than a criterion.

This is not the whole picture: There is the matter of compliance with moral standards and the matter of compliance with legal ones. And the legal standards are obviously the less demanding. For example, it is legally permissible to lie, except for specific cases (such as lying with the intent to defraud and lying under oath). The legal standards are generally limited to severe violations and to received notions. Thus, English law condones the medical use of magic, for example, in societies where it is endorsed, but not in societies where it is known to be useless or worse—simply because it may be an excessive demand on practitioners to be so much better informed than their peers.

Let us move, then, from the legal standard to the standard accepted by the scientific tradition. What is this standard? The question splits into two: What is the legal standard and what is the moral standard received in the scientific tradition? The legal standards are two, and perhaps only one. The first is of exotericism, namely of openness to all, though on the condition that access requires some prior training; the second is that scientific experiment is repeatable. Following Descartes, Robert Boyle, the father of modern chemistry and of the modern scientific etiquette, declared that alchemy is to be ignored because its recipes are esoteric.[4] Now violation of scientific etiquette often reaches courts of law, and this standard is applied to any claim for scientific status for any find. In what follows this standard will be endorsed with no debate. Admittedly, objections were raised to its application to psychiatry, both on account of the confidentiality of the material involved and on the claim that human conduct, especially pathological conduct, is too complex to be repeatable. These objections are not serious. As to confidentiality, if it is betrayed by science, then it is betrayed every time a report is published on any psychiatric encounter. Moreover, unfortunately, psychiatrists in certain positions betray confidentiality regularly with no qualms.[5] As to complication, there is no reason to suppose that nuclear physics is more or less complex than psychiatry. If it is true that psychiatry cannot offer repeatable empirical information, then it is better to admit so and to refrain from demanding for it the status of an empirical science; only repeatable evidence can claim for psychiatry the status of an empirical science.[6]

So much for the legal requirement within the scientific tradition. The more problematic requirement is the moral one, namely, that proper individuals speak and act knowledgeably. It is not clear what it is to be knowledgeable. The standard view of it in modern societies is that the knowledgeable is in possession of scientific proof. Except that we do not know what scientific proof is. The fact is that this matter is regularly contested both in general (philosophical discussions) and in many particular examples (of scientific controversy). This fact led to a suggestion of a very useful touchstone:[7] Whenever experts agree, received expert opinion is binding. This touchstone is particularly lovely because it includes a clear-cut limitation: When experts disagree, doubt is appropriate. Nevertheless, it is not limited enough, as it is not a criterion as to who the experts are. Already tradition relies on experts, except that these are traditional experts whose expertise is validated by tradition. The expertise here discussed is allegedly scientific, but in cases of scientific controversy this is question-begging. Not only do we not know what is the makeup of science, we know less what is the makeup of scientific expertise. Even when common sense tells us that we can take a certain group of people as experts, common sense also tells us that for all we know they can become barbarians. Even if it is most unlikely that the group in question will become barbaric, the very possibility of it becoming one exhibits the defect of the touchstone in question. Moreover, not having any touchstone invites the experts to become barbarian out of sheer (short-term) self-interest. And we do not want to tempt the experts even when we know that they will not be tempted, of course. Moreover, the question is, is the unanimity of a group of experts based on science or on self-interest to begin with? In the case of psychiatry, it is uncontested that the unanimity achieved by the efforts of the authors of the current authorized psychiatric vocabulary (DSM-IV) is based on the lowest common denom-inator, not on scientific investigation, on the search for respectability rather than the search for the truth that should render the profession respectable.[8] This would be inconceivable were there a clear and uncontested criterion of scientific validity. To repeat, only a minimal criterion for scientific validity is generally recognized, namely the claim that science is more or less open (has no trade secrets) and the claim for the empirical character of scientific experiment in the form of repeatability (where the second claim is additional or implied in the first claim).

Perhaps some elaboration on the current situation in received professional opinion may be useful. In recent decades the philosophy of Thomas S. Kuhn has won popularity—especially among the sciences with dubious credits, of course—just because it offered a touchstone for the scientific character of a discipline, and one that is easier to comply with than by presenting the genuine article. A discipline is scientific, says Kuhn, if and only if it is in possession of a paradigm and its membership follows it unanimously. Before one knows what a paradigm is, one may notice that it is a remarkable suggestion, since the touchstone is proposed that makes no distinction between a good and a poor paradigm. Of course, a touchstone proper distinguishes pure pieces of gold from the less pure ones, and purity is the asset required. Yet Kuhn's paradigms, whatever they are, are themselves neither touchstones nor tested by any touchstone: The touchstone is the unanimous adherence of researchers to it, and certainly this holds for parapsychology no less than for psychology. Can it be that in his opinion as long as all researchers share a paradigm their product is pure science?[9]

One can hardly attribute all this to sheer oversight. Kuhn offered his criterion this way quite intentionally, of course, since differentiating between good and poor paradigms will require a new touchstone, and Kuhn declares this not possible: It takes experts to comprehend a paradigm, and it takes leaders to propose it, he says, following the esotericist theory of science of Michael Polanyi.[10] Since science can, and at times does, undergo revolutions, the goodness of a paradigm is not a matter of a fixed criterion: Any idea is good as long as it is upheld by the scientific leadership, they declared. And so, according to Polanyi and Kuhn, what matters is the command of the scientific leadership, not any specific idea. The reason for that, they say, is that there must be coordination between researchers, that this coordination requires control, and that the best arrangement is when the scientific leadership controls the research of the rank and file. Even were this true, the control of the leadership should count as a necessary condition, not as a sufficient one; it would condemn the psychiatric manual (DSM), perhaps as it is a result of a compromise rather than of leadership proper, but it should not declare all well-coordinated research scientific. Moreover, even while admitting that coordination is required and that it is done by the leadership, control is better not in the hands of the leaders, since democratic control is generally more reliable (as other forms of control are conducive to corruption) and more in the spirit of the scientific tradition. It is an inconsistency of the Polanyi-Kuhn philosophy that it is traditionalist yet it relinquishes the most central concern of the scientific tradition for openness and for democracy.

It is clear in any case that the admission of the lowest common denominator of a research tradition as a paradigm is not what Kuhn has in mind. Rather, he prefers a biparadigm discipline, he says under pressure. Under more pressure he even admits multiparadigms. He clearly suggests that properly controlled a multiparadigmatic field will evolve to become monoparadigmatic. This is no guarantee, especially since it is the paradigm that is used for the coordination of research, so that there is no coordination between paradigms, unless a superparadigm is postulated: There is nothing to prevent the disintegration of a discipline.

An example will illustrate this disintegration. When Hans Küng was deprived of his status as a cardinal, he was appointed professor in Tübingen's theology faculty. His colleagues there complained vociferously: Adding a dissenter to their faculty of theology, they said, would deprive it of its scientific status! They were totally unconcerned with the presence of non-Catholic theology elsewhere; it was the presence of a Catholic dissenter that they deemed a threat. (Needless to say, parallels in psychotherapy easily spring to mind: The diverse schools in the field, as in theology, are more concerned with heresies than with the existence of competing schools.)[11] Moreover, Küng is an advocate of Kuhn's views, whereas his colleagues cannot be accused of familiarity with them, let alone assent to them, and yet they do and he does not apply these very views consistently to their own case. This is an eye opener: The futility of any effort to use Kuhn's theory to distinguish between the putative scientific status of physics and of theology may be the reason Küng likes it, but the same futility is a prominent defect of this theory—so much so that it demolishes it entirely. The reason it is popular despite this defect is, perhaps, that it offers a cheap way to acquire scientific status. This is stressed here not as a complaint but as an illustration of the view that what commands respect does not always deserve respect—not even in the commonwealth of learning.[12]

So much for the two initial criteria for propriety, the standard accepted in the community at large and the standard accepted in the scientific community. The third and last criterion for propriety mentioned above is due to the Romantic tradition; it suggests that individuals behave properly when they act in accord with their best sense of mission and inner conviction. This is a dangerous idea and one that facilitated the deterioration of European society into the state of barbarism. It need not be discussed here beyond the observation that however dangerous it is, at times it is a sign of virtue, especially when one lives in a barbarian society and rejects its mores. In a civilized society the defects of the law require democratic campaigns for their reform. In emergency, when the process of legislation is too slow, one is in a tough position, since the right thing to do is too demanding: One may feel bound to violate the law and stand trial.

The corollary from this is obvious. There is no single criterion that is satisfactory; they are all open-ended. This is not to dismiss them. We use them within limits and with good results; we present each of them in different wording and debate these critically; we try constantly to improve each of them; and we regularly attempt to bring them together. Thus, we try to render the customary scientific through research, to develop a proper sense of propriety through education, and to develop our educational system so as to render it scientific. What exactly this means is not clear, though some suggestions are rather obvious. Classical individualist philosophy takes it for granted that actors are autonomous and that the propriety of their action is rooted in their ability to justify their actions rationally, namely, scientifically. Yet there were two schools of thought about the scientific justification of informative ideas, the one that found certainty in scientific intuition and the one that found certainty in scientific evidence. And there were two schools of thought about the justification of moral ideas, the ethics of intentions and the ethics of consequences. The advocates of ethics of intentions criticized the ethics of consequences, observing that these are often beyond actors' control; and the advocates of ethics of consequences criticized the ethics of intentions, observing that the way to hell is paved by good intentions. All this is in clear violation of common sense and is based on the idea that common sense is no substitute for rational, scientific justification. Today we take propriety to be recognizing one's duties, taking them with due care, and trying one's best to do what is expected of one, and do it as well as can be reasonably expected. Propriety is thus no longer taken to be justified either by good intentions or by favorable outcome or by any other single criterion. Rather, propriety is taken to be bona fide, a matter of good intention with no violation of accepted codes unless circumstances seem to call for it, and with no disregard for what is known to be the likely undesirable consequences of one's action. It is a common precept that good intentions are invoked by attempts to avoid likely ill consequences of one's actions, by attempts to avoid unreasonable risks—though without raising expectation of assurance of success, of course.

RESPONSIBILITY

What characterizes a responsibility is its being a special kind of duty: It is a duty freely undertaken and the undertaking in question is rather open-ended. Let me take this slowly.

The following observation is all too clear, yet regrettably it requires restatement: Responsible conduct is proper and irresponsible conduct is improper, yet, strictly speaking, one can behave properly without ever raising the question of responsibility. Proper conduct is possible without ever accepting any responsibility, since in a civilized society the conduct of citizens is deemed improper only if they break the law and irresponsible only if they violate a responsibility which they themselves have freely undertaken. This observation is not quite true, as the law does not forbid lying except in well-specified cases (particularly, lying in an attempt to defraud or lying under oath). It holds only to the extent that the law does represent publicly recognized morality, especially in the case of the acceptance of responsibility: Neither the law nor morality demand the acceptance of responsibility; they both demand that one discharges those responsibilities that one has freely undertaken.

The last sentence is criticized, and from the fact that some parents are responsible, some not. Now to the extent that responsible parenthood is required by law, it may be deemed more a matter of propriety than responsibility, akin to the duty to pay a debt: A debt is the outcome of an undertaking—to return a loan or to make a gift—it is hardly a matter of responsibility. Therefore, to know to what extent parenthood is a matter of responsibility we may wish to inquire into the question, what makes an undertaking a responsibility?

An undertaking to make a gift is scarcely a responsibility but the undertaking to represent a client is. The reason is technical: There is hardly a problem when one offers to make a gift, but when one undertakes to represent a client the promise is too open-ended. Thus, when a representative makes a mistake, this raises the question, was the mistake responsible or negligent? There are standards of responsibility in many but not all cases. What is clear is that once one has discharged one's undertaking properly, then one has discharged one's responsibility. The requirement, then, is for proper discharge not of one's duties but of one's undertaking, and of an undertaking that is pretty open-ended. Consider, then, parental duties. It is not clear to what extent parenthood is a matter of choice. To the extent that it is, and to the extent that the duties it incurs are open-ended, it incurs parental responsibility. (Of course, open-endedness itself may be rather open-ended, but this is scarcely problematic.)

This idea, of responsibility as open-ended, can be generalized to include also open-ended duties to oneself. Through self-neglect one may easily become a public nuisance. The duty to avoid being a public nuisance is the duty to take proper care of oneself. We may call that duty a responsibility to oneself. In this sense, the responsibility to oneself is a form of duty, the duty to avoid becoming a burden on society; responsibility to society at large may be deemed a civic duty, namely, the duty of a citizen *qua* citizen: A civic duty may count as a civic responsibility, then, if and when it becomes too open-ended to be simple and clear-cut. Yet we will view this as not quite correct as long as we wish to distinguish between duties and responsibilities as those that are given and those that are freely undertaken. There is no objection to this usage, as long as it is clear that the civic responsibilities involved are not to any particular individual or institution other than the law or to society at large.

Nevertheless, responsibility to oneself is the exception, as this responsibility is taken for granted; it is hardly ever a legal matter, because when one betrays it one does not sue oneself: One may be charged with improper conduct as specified by some law, but in modern society such laws are disdained and abolished sooner or later, since they are paternalist, designed to ensure that citizens follow good judgment in their own interest. Responsibility to oneself also requires that one does not abuse drugs or attempt suicide; both alcohol consumption and attempted suicide were criminal in the United States for a while, but it was deemed wise to decriminalize them; the abuse of other drugs is still illegal, and either on questionable paternalist arguments or in order to defend the young.

Responsibility to oneself is important nevertheless, as it is a matter of selfesteem. The absence of responsibility to oneself also is a strong motive for the irresponsible acceptance of responsibility to the public at large or to friends and relations or the irresponsible acceptance of parenthood. But the matter of responsibility to oneself still is a matter of morality or psychology, not of the law. The law makes responsibility different from civic duties or the duties or responsibilities of a citizen *qua* citizen; legally responsibility, to repeat, is a matter of undertaking toward others. It is not always clear toward whom, especially in matters of legal complication that will be ignored here altogether, in matter of political affairs or other public affairs, which will likewise be ignored here, and in cases of the mentally incompetent, whether minors, mentally deficient, disabled or disturbed. What is to be done with individuals belonging to these categories is a difficult question. Usually they are appointed guardians. In the case of the mentally incompetent, then, the duties to oneself are transferred from them to those who volunteer to act as their guardians, and the guardians are responsible to the state to represent properly the interest of their charges. There is then the problem, who belongs to which category? Who is a minor? Who is mentally disturbed? Of these categories the one that concerns us here is that of the mentally disturbed. Who is mentally disturbed? The responsibility of psychiatrists is not only to their patients, but also to the state that requires from them to certify individuals as mentally incompetent as well as to the appointed guardians of their mentally incompetent patients.

These matters present psychiatry with the responsibility of the medical profession to the state and to patients, except that the service of the psychiatrists to both the state and their patients is problematic and that psychiatric patients are problematic as well. The rules of responsibility require that psychiatrists admit the difficulty they have here, but it is the leadership of the profession that is chiefly irresponsible, as it sanctifies the silencing of this matter, thereby enabling members to act irresponsibly without violating accepted norms.[13]

Responsible Leadership

Little is said in the literature on responsibility, by philosophers or by psychologists. In psychology the conspicuous case is that of Jean Piaget. He spoke of the growth of individual moral autonomy—at the age of 12, incidentally; he did not touch upon responsibility, much less upon its growth. The reason is that individualist ethical theory took responsibility to be a part of moral autonomy and the outcome of free undertaking to others. Responsibility was first introduced as a special category only by thinkers who rejected individualism and spoke of the responsibility of political leaders in the Romantic vein. The most Romantic political leadership was Nazi, of course, and their regime began in 1933, but it started in earnest a few months later, when its Führer freely and readily accepted personal responsibility for some shocking cold-blooded murder of some of his closest colleagues; this (political) responsibility, he said, he undertook only toward the nation and its history—thereby rejecting the classical individualist view of responsibility as to individuals and the classical legal view of responsibility as prescribed by law.

This is not to endorse the classical individualist view of responsibility. Historically, responsibility is much older than autonomy, as all societies have some leaders, and they normally show some sense of responsibility, yet autonomy was invented in the Mediterranean basin somewhere in the first millennium B.C. And, of course, political leaders may be responsible to groups most of whose members are not autonomous at all. The current view of political leadership in tribal society was first advocated by Sir Edward Evans-Pritchard and quoted by Ernest Gellner: The African tribal aristocrats are trained to self-reliance and authority; yet their fellow tribespeople are not autonomous and do not aspire to be autonomous. Empirically, then, the responsibility of political leaders to their people is not that to autonomous individuals.[14]

Classical philosophers viewed traditional European leadership, aristocracy and clergy alike, with a cynical eye. Hence the popularity of Machiavelli as the first political scientist who only appeared a cynic because of his scientific detachment, a view shared by Sir Francis Bacon, Jean-Jacques Rousseau, and almost every thinker in between. Today we take it for granted that the historical facts are more complex, that some kings and some popes acted responsibly in their own lights, some not. This, indeed, is the datum which students of responsibility should not ignore.[15]

The question still is, what responsibility do leaders undertake when they agree to lead? The famous theory of leadership of Elihu Katz and Paul Lazarsfeld presents one sort of leadership that is clearly important in democracy, and that can hardly be justly treated from the viewpoint of classical political theory: It rests on the evident fact that some citizens have influence on their neighbors' opinions. When a new situation occurs that invites the opinion of the citizen, it is most natural to consult a wise neighbor, and one who functions in the position of a wise neighbor is, by definition, an opinion leader.[16] Now does the position of opinion leader entail any responsibility? It seems difficult to find any duty that is entailed by opinion leadership. Of course, an opinion leader may easily betray trust and, say, disseminate disinformation. This is at times directed by central political organizations, which may subtly suggest to their followers to subtly manipulate their peers in some specific manner decided upon by public relations officers of these organizations. This is not in any way a responsibility of the opinion leader: Manipulating people and disseminating disinformation is immoral and at times also illegal.

This is not the whole story. In some countries professional organizations, such as dental or medical ones, suggest to their memberships in periods prior to significant and emotionally charged elections to be careful about conversing with patients for fear of exploiting their influence when unwittingly acting as opinion leaders. Yet it is questionable that the professional organizations that issue these warnings are concerned with the autonomy of the individual voter. More likely they are concerned with the damage that the profession may suffer from its members' freely and unwittingly acting as opinion leaders. And indeed, whatever the merit or demerit of the suggestion is, acting as opinion leaders consciously is certainly preferable to doing so unwittingly.

The question remains as to influential members of the community, whether aristocrats or professionals: Do they have some special duties, and if so, are these responsibilities to the public? Are these responsibilities moral or professional or legal? This question is not merely a thought experiment. A few thinkers, including the famous novelist and essayist Aldous Huxley and the leading philosophers Michael Polanyi and Karl Popper claimed that scientists do have a special responsibility. Moreover, Huxley suggested that a professional oath be instituted for scientists, akin to the Hippocratic oath. Popper agrees and he issued the slogan *sagesse oblige*.[17] Yet the Hippocratic oath was abolished in most countries just because it is either an oath to maintain one's responsibility, and then it is redundant, or else to transcend it, and then it is immoral, as it may easily be read to be the undertaking to take care of the interest of the patient beyond what one has legally undertaken. This attitude is paternalist; it permits and demands of physicians to act in the interest of their patients even if against the explicit instructions of the patients themselves. Though paternalism is still extremely popular, it is quite beyond debate, as it is clearly both immoral and illegal. Still, this should be said against it now, before it is dismissed without further discussion. When the clergy act paternalistically, they claim privileged knowledge, and they have a mandate from their religion, from their tradition, perhaps even from their congregation. This does not exculpate their conduct, but it makes it understandable. When physicians (psychiatrists or somatoiatrists) do so, they have no privileged knowledge, since they often know at most only the medical aspects of their patients' interests, and they have no mandate, and they use pathetic paternalist arguments in attempts to extricate themselves out of some narrow corner or another. All paternalist excuses are unacceptable, but they are outrageous when used to cover up for some faults. Still, the fact is that professional individuals are able to use paternalist arguments because they are opinion leaders, and this demands some further discussion of the responsibility of the intellectuals in modern society.

Responsible Science

Public discussion on the responsibility of the scientist is new, because science was traditionally admired as the quest for knowledge and seen as the domain of autonomous individuals; despite widespread expectations that it transform society (for the better), its social and political dimensions were not noticed. As a social or political affair science began to be noticed only after World War II, with the recognition of the role of science in the military. This became too conspicuous to ignore after Hiroshima, with the advent of governments' involvement on a large scale in applied scientific research and the rise in social status of the professional scientist to a position of very high esteem. The shift in concern is symbolized by the strange competition between Harry S Truman and Robert J. Oppenheimer about the responsibility for Hiroshima. During the one conversation that took place between them, Oppenheimer expressed a sense of guilt about Hiroshima; afterwards Truman expressed contempt for this expression, saying the bombing of Hiroshima was his doing and so his responsibility, not Oppenheimer's. Still, the debate over the guilt occupied much public interest ever since.

I choose as an example for that Erik Erikson's *Insight and Responsibility*, because the title of the book comes as close to the matter of the responsibility of the scientist as possible and because Erikson is a leader of a whole school in psychology and in psychotherapy, and because he is a fairly popular writer. Despite its title, however, the book says nothing about responsibility, and its subject index refers to responsibility about a dozen times, referring to less than one line for every twenty pages. One of these lines says, obviously, we must now learn to accept the responsibility of not having as many children as possible. True, but too little; the other references say less on responsibility. In particular, there is no discussion there of responsible leadership or even of responsible delegates.[18]

We no longer demand of responsible actors, especially leading actors, to hold uncontroversial views; on the contrary, democracy assumes that the political leader represents the views of one party. This is not to say the democratic leader need or even may ignore the view of the opposition party. This is why there is a sizable and stubborn opposition; for example, the democratic leader can hardly declare a war without a national consensus.[19]

The fact that a democratic leader is responsible to the nation as a whole, the majority and the minority alike, while being a representative of the majority party, is a major item in political life within every democracy. It conflicts flatly with the idea that one must act on scientifically verified opinion, which is the traditional individualist moral philosophy still irresponsibly preached by many a philosopher and by most scientists—if and when they at all take cognizance of matters outside the sphere of their narrow expertise.

Of course collectivist ethics permits political leaders to be responsible and act as they find fit. But also it permits and even demands that the political leader serve the general will of the nation. How the political leader knows what the general will is and how best it is served is a matter I need not enter into here.[20]

The commonwealth of learning was always nearly amorphous since the views it endorsed were largely that action is justified only by rational or scientific proof. If anywhere this view were ever applicable, its place surely is the commonwealth of learning. Only in almost amorphous society—in traditional science (not in contemporary science), in the world of fashion, and in street gangs leadership grows spontaneously; and the worlds of fashion and of street gangs are not exactly rational. Yet the strict justificationist code of science imposes on its practitioners ever narrowing constraints of professional expertise constrained by full rational, scientific proof.[21] And so the scientific leadership tries to shun public activity, yet when forced out of their shells they do so with a vengeance, pretending that they act not as powerful leaders but on their views which, they allege, are fully justified. It follows that the people, even within the scientific community, who do not share their views are just knaves and fools. Yet during the tragic Vietnam War the pseudoscientist, irresponsible, self-appointed spokesperson of the scientific community in the United States, Professor Noam Chomsky of the celebrated Massachusetts Institute of Technology played on all traditional prejudices of his peers and claimed his case was as clear as the greenness of grass, clearly implying that his opponents were knaves and fools: "My view is that the grass is green," he brashly declared.

I do not wish to deny his charge that the advocates of the Vietnam War (on both sides) acted irresponsibly. I think that as the result of the utter failure of singer Joan Baez to organize a protest movement against the atrocities of Pol-Pot, it is by now commonly agreed that Chomsky's conduct was no less irresponsible than that of his adversaries, and considering his academic mantle I for one would say he was more irresponsible as the destroyer of the ivory tower, of the last bastion of credibility. And so, to conclude, let me say, since responsible leadership is permitted to hide behind the book but only up to a point, and since when the book's defects are pointed out it becomes increasingly irresponsible to ignore them, especially when the criticism is offered along accepted lines, by the book, especially by the book of political democracy and by the book of scientific integrity, doubtless the most becoming role of women and men of science is to act as critics—a role quite traditional, through the Middle Ages and the Enlightenment, to the dissidents in East Europe prior to the demise of the Soviet Union.

The ivory tower is their proper place—the place of the detached critic. But for this, little more need be said: The democratic canons of criticism should be spelled out and discussed in detail. And so also the canons of the community of science should be spelled out and discussed in detail; they are agenda, and must be taken as agenda for any scientific leader who feels the brunt of our recent double and triple fiasco, of the poor roles science has played in recent decades, in the Holocaust, in Hiroshima, in the Cold War, in Vietnam and in Cambodia, not to mention the defense of the conduct of the Soviet Union by so many intellectuals until its very collapse.

The next battle concerns the population explosion, industrial pollution, poverty, and the propagation of nuclear weapons (the four P's). To fight it we need all the credibility we can amass. It may be the last chance.[22]

Responsible Expert Services

The services that psychiatrists offer the state or institutions or individuals are expert professional services and fall under the rubric of professional etiquette. Professional etiquette is a complex matter, as its official purpose is to secure responsible conduct of professional experts to their clients, yet it is all too often the means by which to keep a professional organization closed and elitist and protect professional interests even at the public's expense. It is well known that this holds particularly true of the legal and medical professional organizations. One need hardly say that the elitist attitude may serve the elite's interest, but only in the short run. In the long run openness is advantageous to all. This makes elitism rather irresponsible. This is by no means peculiar to the psychiatric profession.

But since psychiatry is in more need for improvement, its need to open up its closed clubs is even more urgent than that of the medical profession at large or of other medical subprofessions.

What are the requirements from responsible experts that differ from those of any nonexpert? First and foremost, the claims for expertise are claims that invite higher than usual levels of responsibility. It is therefore the prime responsibility of experts to delimit their expertise very clearly: First and foremost experts are aware of the limits of their expertise, and their responsibility to their public as experts is to make this known whenever it is relevant. Unfortunately, experts—all experts—are tempted to claim omniscience. They tend to claim so both in their own interest and in the interest of their customers and in the public interest. Yet this is an error on every count.

The situation becomes quite difficult when the customer requires, and even insists on the requirement, that the expert takes over all responsibility and pretends to be omniscient. That this is the customer's relinquishing of responsibility is obvious, and that customers often find responsibility too much of a burden just because of the situation in which they are customers of experts—legal, medical, or any other—is equally obvious. But it is nonetheless wrong and unwise for customers to relinquish responsibility just because it is too heavy a burden, especially since it is in such moments that responsibility is important. When experts accept the role of the omniscient agent they ask for trouble that may appear later on as unpleasant complaints, litigation, and so on.

Usually, when the burden is really too heavy and the customer must stay in charge, there is the possibility of calling the help of other experts, especially the help of expert psychiatrists. This is difficult when the initial service is psychiatric. Not that a psychiatrist who requires the aid of a colleague should have trouble getting it; but the service the colleague should perform is the one the original expert should have performed and failed.

Yet the complication of matters this way is at least in part merely technical. What it amounts to is that customers may become (for a while at least) mentally incompetent, and then the usual procedures should take place, and none of them permits experts to take charge without customers first being declared mentally incompetent and appointed guardians to represent them to experts. At times this is impossible. Then emergency conditions take effect. This too is a mere technicality. What is more problematic is different. It is that expert psychiatrists do not know when an individual under tremendous stress is mentally incompetent. Responsibility requires admission of inability, because experts, we remember, are obliged to report the limits of their own expertise.

How is this limit decided? When do experts know what they can responsibly undertake and what not? The standard answer, we remember, is that all and only what is given to scientific proof is known. This answer, we remember, does not tell us what is proof. The question, what is scientific proof, is, finally, highly controverted. Where are we to go from here?

We are here to do what science always does: We are here to observe. Professional etiquette tells us what is responsible professional conduct and so we should be able to report what it is.

What is taken as responsible professional conduct in expert scientific society? Here we have come full circle to our starting point. So let us accept some simple observations and follow some simple rules.

Let us assume that we do need some radical change in the psychiatric profession to stop the increasing complaints against it as irresponsible—either by rebutting these charges or by admitting them and rendering it more responsible or by a mixed strategy. Let us assume that this will not be undertaken by the profession as it is now, that there will be no radical change in the psychiatric profession without some radical intellectual and organizational change in it. Let us further assume that the profession should accept only the very minimal standards required of a scientific enterprise. Let us agree that these include openness, including the practice of admitting criticism without defensiveness, the limitation of claims to those that can be supported with no serious controversy, particularly the limitation of the claim for the status of empirical science only to cases when the evidence in question is repeatable. (No repeatability, no second opinion!) This minimal list already includes so much that there is no hope that the profession as construed these days will endorse them. What then should one do to render the profession more responsible?

Clearly, what one can and should do first is to undertake to act as a responsible individual within the accepted system. This includes the effort to study and publicize in every possible manner the extant criticism of the profession, of different theories, and of the professional organization. To be effective such attempts must sooner or later find their organizational expression, preferably within the extant professional bodies. But the motto of the study should be, "*We are not on trial.*" This should do for now.

ENDNOTES

1. The strongest wholesale condemnations of psychiatry today are those of Thomas S. Szasz. See his *The Myth of Mental Illness: Foundations of a Theory of Personal Conduct* (New York: Hoeber-Harper, 1974); *Law, Liberty and Psychiatry: An Inquiry into the Social Use of Mental Health Practices* (New York: Macmillan, 1963), and later writings. The most ambitious critique is perhaps that of Adolf Grünbaum. See his *The Foundations of Psychoanalysis: A Philosophical Critique* (Berkeley: University of California Press, 1984) and my review of it in my *The Gentle Art of Philosophical Polemics* (La Salle, IL: Open Court, 1988). The latest condemnation, written in a vivid popular style, is that of Jeffrey Mussaieff Masson. See his *Against Therapy: Emotional Tyranny* (New York: Macmillan, 1991). He shares with Szasz the view that there is no such thing as mental illness and that therefore the profession is fraudulent, and that the worse offense of the profession is to the autonomy and the dignity of the patient. Grünbaum's claim is utterly divorced of any direct considerations of this kind; his claim is that psychoanalytic theory is unscientific, implying, perhaps, that all psychiatry is, and concluding that treatment is so unreliable that it should not be supported by medical insurance; his direct concern is entirely with "scientificity." Unfortunately, he does not even allude to what this is, to what he thinks scientific character amounts to; he uses a new and unexplained terminology and he overlooks both the demand for repeatability and the distinction between scientific theory and scientific technology.

For a critical discussion of the contribution of Szasz see N. Laor, "The Autonomy of the Mentally Ill: A Case Study of Individualistic Ethics," *Phil. Soc. Sci.,* 14 (1984), 331–49; see also Y. Fried and J. Agassi, *Paranoia: A Study in Diagnosis* (Dordrecht: Kluwer, 1976).

It is hard to say what description of a practice is an adequate characterization, much less what critique of it is just. If there is any document that the profession recognizes as an adequate characterization of it, then surely it is DSM IV, which exhibits agreement for the sake of agreement while disregarding both scientific etiquette and patient interest; see N. Laor and J. Agassi, *Diagnosis: Philosophical and Medical Perspectives* (Dordrecht: Kluwer, 1990), final chapter.

2. The popular idea that every deduction is explanatory has as a corollary the claim that all touchstones are

explanatory (all metal scratched by a touchstone is gold, this piece of metal, etc., therefore, this piece of metal is gold). This claim is absurd. Hence this popular idea is absurd. It is advocated by all positivists (including the "logical positivists"), and inherently so, since positivism requires that metascientific characterizations should not be metaphysical, and thus that they should be logical, yet there can be no logical distinction between a criterion and a touchstone. The doctrine advocated by Karl Popper in his classic *Logik der Forschung* (1935) is somewhat better, since it involves testability, and testability is more a matter of the logic of a researcher's situation than can be characterized within pure logic. Still, it is also positivist, as it frankly shuns metaphysics, and is therefore also unsatisfactory. This leads to the (general) question, how can metaphysical considerations be allowed into metascience without commitment to any specific metaphysics? By relativizing satisfactoriness to any given metaphysical doctrine. For more details see my *Science in Flux* (Dordrecht: Kluwer, 1975).

(Positivists can tighten their requirement from a satisfactory explanation: They can do so by smuggling their own metaphysics, which is mechanistic, while declaring it obligatory, namely a part of logic of science. See below.)

3. See the discussion of this point in A. J. Paris's life of Sir Humphry Davy (1838), apropos of Davy's discovery of light metals (sodium, potassium) and the question this raised as to whether these deserve to be viewed as metals. (Niels Bohr suggested in 1913 that hydrogen is a metal too.) The discovery of isotopes refuted the identification of gold by its specific gravity. Later, the discovery of the neutron led to the identification of any element by the number of protons in its nucleus. All this does not invalidate the traditional touchstone, though its use was superseded.

4. René Descartes, *Discourse on Method,* sixth part, fourth paragraph; Robert Boyle, "On the Unsuccessful Experiment," in his *Certain Physiological Essays,* and preface to his *The Skeptical Chymist.*

5. On the instituted disloyalty and betrayal of patient confidentiality see Thomas S. Szasz's already mentioned *Law, Liberty and Psychiatry,* and his "Mental Health Service in the School," *This Magazine Is About Schools* (October, 1967), 140–166, reprinted in his *Ideology and Insanity: Essays in the Psychiatric Dehumanization of Man* (M. Boyars, 1983). An outstanding example of the heartless disloyalty of professionals who are proud of it can be found in a very famous collection, G. B. Blain and C. C. McArthur, *Emotional Problems of the Student,* with an introduction by Erik Erikson (New York: Appleton-Century-Crofts, 1961). One contributor brags about his having solved the problem of protecting Harvard University from a student about to break down without violating the poor fellow's civil rights: He spied on him and caught him in a library about to throw a book on some-

one. See also my *Towards a Rational Philosophical Anthropology* (Dordrecht: Kluwer, 1977), p. 112.

6. For a discussion of the question of repeatability in the social sciences see my *Technology: Philosophical and Social Aspects* (Dordrecht: Kluwer, 1985). For repeatable facts in psychiatry, see Y. Fried and J. Agassi, *Paranoia: A Study in Diagnosis* (Dordrecht: Kluwer, 1976), and *Psychiatry as Medicine,* (Dordrecht: Kluwer, 1983), introductions to chap. 3 and conclusion.

7. This suggestion was made in Bertrand Russell, *Skeptical Essays* (New York: Norton, 1928).

8. See end of note 1 above.

9. This criticism of Kuhn's philosophy was made in great detail by both Paul K. Feyerabend, who argued that safecrackers too follow a paradigm and suffer paradigm changes or scientific revolutions the way Kuhn describes them, and by John Watkins, who showed that by Kuhn's criterion mediaeval but not contemporary theology is scientific. See their contributions to I. Lakatos and A. Musgrave, eds., *Criticism and the Growth of Knowledge* (Cambridge: Cambridge University Press, 1970). See also note 12 below.

10. For decades Michael Polanyi expressed the same views, scarcely altered, beginning with his *Science, Faith and Freedom* (1946) and his *The Logic of Liberty* (1951) to his *Knowing and Being* (1969); his *magnum opus* is *Personal Knowledge: Towards a Post-Critical Philosophy* (1958). They were all published by Routledge (London) and the University of Chicago Press.

See A. C. Crombie, ed., *Scientific Change: Historical Studies in the Intellectual, Social and Technical Conditions for Scientific Discovery and Technical Invention, from Antiquity to the Present* (New York: Basic Books, 1963), pp. 375–80, for Polanyi's judicious comments on Kuhn's "The Function of Dogma in Scientific Research," *op. cit.,* pp. 347–69; for Kuhn's indebtedness to him, see also Kuhn's response there, pp. 391–5, esp. p. 392, where Kuhn admits this—perhaps reluctantly and obliquely, but if so, then nevertheless unmistakably. Polanyi's chief criticism, namely that Kuhn's view is too fragmentary, still stands.

11. The matter of purity of schools was first discussed by Karl Popper. See his *Conjectures and Refutations* (London: Routledge, 1961). For detailed discussions of the matter, see my *Science and Society* (Dordrecht: Kluwer, 1981) and my "Minimal Criteria for Intellectual Progress," 1994, *Iyyun, 43,* pp. 61–83, where the practice of stonewalling is analyzed.

12. See note 9 above. The idea that Kuhn's view is presented in disregard to the existence of nonscience is but the application of Polanyi's critique of Kuhn's view cited in note 10 above. Polanyi's view is not open to the same critique. Yet the fact that the commonwealth of learning can be very uncritical, e.g., when Kuhn's view gains so much popularity there, is a significant critique of Polanyi's view as well. See my *Science and Society*

(Dordrecht: Kluwer, 1981) for detailed discussions of the matter.

13. It is a strange fact that the psychiatric profession refuses to admit the inevitability of conflicts between different responsibilities that one may undertake *en bloc* when becoming a psychiatrist. After all, this denial prevents the relief from some impossible burden that members of the profession suffer. The denial is common to professions that have strong guilds: They are the result of leaderships taking better care of their guilds as guilds than of the individual guild members. See my "Democratizing Medicine," in Gayle L. Ormiston and R. Sassower, eds., *Prescriptions: The Dissemination of Medical Authority,* (Westport, CT: Greenwood Press, 1990), pp. 3–22.

14. See Sir Edward Evans-Pritchard, *The Position of Women in Primitive Societies and Other Essays in Social Anthropology,* p. 127, quoted in Ernest Gellner, *Cause and Meaning in the Social Sciences* (London: Routledge, 1973), p. 149.

15. There is a surprising absence of discussion of responsibility in the literature. The first significant discussions of responsibility are probably those of Max Weber; the first significant discussion of responsibility in the philosophical literature is in Popper's works. Much of what is known about responsibility is to be found in biographical and narrative literature; I should mention here as token examples the case histories of Aristides de Soussa Mendes and of Raoul Wallenberg, as well as Rudyard Kipling's short story, "The Man Who Would Be King."

16. See Elihu Katz and Paul Lazarsfeld, *Personal Influences; the Part Played by People in the Flow of Mass Communication,* with foreword by Elmo Roper (Glencoe, IL: Free Press, 1955).

17. See my discussion of this in my *Technology: Philosophical and Social Aspects* (Dordrecht: Kluwer, 1985), final sections.

18. See Erik Erikson, *Insight and Responsibility: Lectures on the Ethical Implications of Psychoanalytic Insight* (New York: Norton, 1964).

19. See my "The Logic of Consensus and of Extremes," in F. D'Agostino and I. C. Jarvie, eds., *Freedom and Rationality, Essays in Honour of John Watkins, Boston Studies*, Vol. 117 (Dordrecht: Kluwer, 1989), 3–21.

20. See my *Towards a Rational Philosophical Anthropology* (Dordrecht: Kluwer, 1977).

21. See my *Science and Society* (Dordrecht: Kluwer, 1981).

22. See my *Technology: Philosophical and Social Aspects* (Dordrecht: Kluwer, 1985).

CHAPTER 23

THE BEHAVIOR THERAPISTS' DILEMMA:

Reflections on Autonomy, Informed Consent, and Scientific Psychology*

Jon Ringen

A new doctrine concerning informed consent to therapeutic interventions has been articulated in case law during the past two decades. The legal judgments and their interpretations incorporated in recent codes of professional conduct make it clear that understanding the new doctrine of informed consent requires a satisfactory conception of autonomous (or self-determined) choice or action. Efforts to articulate such an account encounter unresolved and problematic tensions between current conceptions of science-based therapeutic practices and current conceptions of the ethical and legal principles that constrain these practices. In what follows, consideration of the radical behav-

*An early version of this paper was presented as an invited contribution to the Symposium on Philosophical Foundations of Behavior Therapy at the 23rd Annual Convention of the Association for Advancement of Behavior Therapy. A later version was the basis for an invited talk given to the Program in Literature, Science, and the Arts at the University of Iowa. The Center for Advanced Studies at the University of Iowa graciously provided resources that facilitated research and writing for this and other projects and, thereby, introduced a welcome measure of efficiency into my (recently past) life as a commuting spouse. Thanks also to Eric Hockett for valuable constructive criticism.

iorist conception of behavior therapy will be shown to provide a useful perspective from which to approach these tensions. It illuminates issues which influential discussions of these tensions fail to address, and it suggests a general framework for understanding both modern natural science and the ethical and legal principles that describe and protect liberty and self-determination. It also highlights what is distinctive about radical behaviorism and the conception of the natural sciences by which it is inspired, and, as a consequence, poses important questions about what kind of understanding is required for the development of better (e.g., more effective and more humane) behavior therapy.

A deep tension is sometimes said to exist between two features of modern clinical psychology (see Dworkin, 1981, 1988; Macklin, 1982). On the one hand, it has been argued (e.g., Skinner, 1971; compare Kalish, 1981) that scientific considerations support radical behaviorism as the most appropriate framework for understanding and facilitating the development of effective behavior therapy. On the other hand, an increasingly significant ethical and legal constraint on therapeutic practice, the doctrine of informed consent, enjoins behavior therapists (along with practitioners in the other helping professions such as psychiatry, nursing, internal medicine, and, hopefully, the law) to acknowledge (and act in ways that respect) the autonomy of those who come to them for help (for discussion see Faden & Beauchamp, 1986; Lidz et. al., 1984). *The behavior therapists' dilemma* describes a widely accepted diagnosis of why these two aspects of modern clinical psychology are in tension, namely, that either radical behaviorism is false or human beings never act autonomously. If this statement is true, it poses a real dilemma. It requires a choice between alternatives which many contemporary behavior therapists would find it difficult to defend. It is worth considering in more detail what this dilemma is and how it might be avoided. To that end, it will be useful to briefly describe the contexts from which each "horn" of the dilemma emerges.

Two events from the early 1970s can serve as useful points of reference. The first is the 1971 publication of B. F. Skinner's *Beyond Freedom and Dignity*. The second is the 1972 legal judgment in the case of *Canterbury v. Spence*. Some brief remarks about each of these events provides useful background.

Faden and Beauchamp (1986) summarize the essentials of the *Canterbury* case as follows:

> ...the patient underwent a laminectomy for severe back pain. After the laminectomy, the patient fell from his hospital bed, and several hours later suffered major paralysis. He had not been warned that a laminectomy carried approximately a 1% risk of such paralysis. A second operation failed to relieve the paralysis, and an appeals court held that risk of possible paralysis should have been disclosed before the first procedure. (p. 133)

The justification for the finding concerning risk disclosure focused on self-determination.

> True consent to what happens to one's self is the informed exercise of a choice, and that entails an opportunity to evaluate knowledgeably the options available and the risks attendant upon each. The average patient has little or no understanding of the medical arts, and ordinarily has only his physician to whom he can look for enlightenment with which to reach an intelligent decision. From these almost axiomatic considerations springs the need, and in turn the requirement, of a reasonable divulgence by physician to patient to make such a decision possible. [1]

This much just reaffirms a long-standing legal concern with self-determination. But the *Canterbury* decision went beyond this to articulate a new standard of risk disclosure, thus:

> The context in which the duty of risk-disclosure arises is invariably the occasion for decision as to whether a particular treatment procedure is to be undertaken. To the physician, whose training enables a self-satisfying evaluation, the answer may seem clear, but it is the prerogative of the patient, not the physician, to determine for himself the direction in which his interests seem to lie. To enable the patient to chart his course understandably, some familiarity with the therapeutic alternatives and their hazards becomes essential. [2]

The court argued:

> Respect for the patient's right of self-determination on particular therapy demands a standard set by law for physicians rather than one which physicians may or may not impose upon themselves. [3]

Faden and Beauchamp (1986) succinctly describe the new doctrine emerging here:

> The extent of the disclosure required is to be measured exclusively by a lay reasonable person standard of what is material to the patient's decision rather than a professional standard based on customary practice. To the *Canterbury* court, the weighing of risks and benefits for the patient is not an expert skill to be measured through a professional standard because it is not intrinsically a professional judgment. (p. 136)

In sum:

> *Canterbury* reaffirmed that self-determination is the sole justification and goal of informed consent, and established the patient's needs for information rather than the physician's practices must form the basis of any adequate standard of disclosure. (p. 137)

This feature of the *Canterbury* case had a significant impact. According to Faden and Beauchamp (1986):

> Case law has stimulated philosophers, physicians, legislators, social scientists, legal commentators, and many others to reflect on the adequacy of present practices of obtaining the consents of patients (and subjects). The law contributed the term "informed consent" and set others on the road to conceiving of the social institution of con-

sent rules as a mechanism for the protection of autonomous decision making. (p. 142)

Physicians have heretofore considered the physician–patient relationship by beginning from the patient's submission to the physician's professional beneficence. The law enlarged that perspective by emphasizing instead that patients voluntarily initiate the relationship and have the right to define its boundaries to fit their own ends. The goals sought by patient and physician were generally the same; but when they differed, the law highlighted for medicine the validity of autonomy concerns. (pp. 142–43)

Thus, the *Canterbury* case sparked widespread discussion of informed consent in medical ethics and focused attention on respect for patient autonomy in decisions concerning therapy.

Two points deserve emphasis here. The first point is that the informed consent doctrine defended in the *Canterbury* case puts constraints on the therapeutic intervention process. It requires disclosure of risks and benefits that meet the reasonable person standard of disclosure. The second point is that these constraints are justified as ways of enhancing patient autonomy (or self-determination). This is *one* aspect of the context in which behavior therapists work. Another aspect is suggested by themes in B. F. Skinner's *Beyond Freedom and Dignity*.

Skinner (1971) argues that the protection of human autonomy (which is a salient feature of the American political and legal tradition and which presumably is exemplified in *Canterbury v. Spence)* is an obstacle to the development of a useful science and effective technology for changing behavior:

Almost all our major problems involve human behavior, and they cannot be solved by physical and biological technology alone. What is needed is a technology of behavior, but we have been slow to develop the science from which such a technology might be drawn. One difficulty is that almost all of what is called behavioral science continues to trace behavior to states of mind, feelings, traits of character, human nature, and so on. Physics and biology once followed similar practices and advanced only when they discarded them. The behavioral sciences have been slow to change partly because the explanatory entities often seem to be directly observed and partly because other kinds of explanations have been hard to find. The environment is obviously important, but its role has remained obscure. It does not push or pull, it *selects*, and this function is difficult to discover and analyze. The role of natural selection in evolution was formulated only a little more than a hundred years ago, and the selective role of the environment in shaping and maintaining the behavior of the individual is only beginning to be recognized and studied. As the interaction between organism and environment has come to be understood, however, effects once assigned to states of mind, feelings, and traits of character are beginning to be traced to accessible conditions, and a technology of behavior may therefore become available. It will not solve our problems, however, until it replaces traditional prescientific views, and these are strongly entrenched. Freedom and dignity illustrate the difficulty. They are the possessions of the autonomous man of traditional theory, and they are essential to practices in which a person is held responsible for his conduct and given credit for his achievements. A scientific analysis shifts both the responsibility and the achievement to the environment. (pp. 24–25)

On Skinner's view, a scientific understanding of human behavior shows that human beings are not autonomous. This is the prescientific view he thinks should be given up.

It is important to distinguish two separate aspects of Skinner's remarks. The first is a point that many people, especially those in disciplines like medicine and psychology, will find very compelling. The second is Skinner's defense of the behavior therapists' dilemma.

The compelling point is a widely (but not universally) accepted view of relations between basic scientific research and clinical therapeutic practice. On Skinner's view, effective treatments for behavioral disorders are most likely to come from a scientific approach to both the understanding of human beings and the understanding and evaluation of therapy. The general point Skinner is making here is one that is widely taken for granted in medicine: *Basic scientific research* can identify causal processes involved in the problems (disease, injury) for which people seek help. *Clinical research* can identify and assess the effectiveness of various treatments/therapies for these problems. At the most general level, behavior therapy is an approach to psychotherapy that takes this point for granted (see, e.g., Goldfried & Davison, 1976; Kalish, 1981; Kazdin & Wilson, 1978). The general point here is a familiar one: Knowledge of cause-effect relationships is what allows the prediction and control of disease and effects of treatment. From the perspective of professional ethics, the *principle of beneficence* (Faden & Beauchamp, 1986, pp. 9–13) makes such knowledge essential to members of the helping professions like medicine (including psychiatry) and clinical psychology: Members of the helping professions need effective ways of treating those it is their professional duty to help. The history and current practice of medicine suggests that science can provide the basis for such treatment by identifying the cause-effect relations involved in disease, trauma, and therapeutic intervention. This suggests a second constraint on therapeutic interventions. Call it the principle of causal determination: Intervention should be guided by scientific knowledge of the cause-effect relations involved in the problem at hand. This constraint is just a reflection of the familiar assumption (shared by behavior therapists and practitioners of clinical medicine and clinical psychology) that the problems presented in the clinic are a result of the natural causal processes that scientific investigations aim to discover.

So the context in which behavior therapists work includes two general constraints on therapeutic intervention in the helping professions. The first constraint, the doctrine of informed consent, arises in the context of the law and professional ethics. The existence and value of human autonomy are said to justify the doctrine of informed consent. The doctrine enjoins therapists to help in ways that respect this value. The second constraint, the principle of causal determination, arises in the context of modern science and its technological applications. Past success in achieving scientific understanding and the subsequent development of effective science-based technology are said to justify this principle. Therapists are enjoined to help in ways that are guided by a scientific understanding of the causal processes involved in human biology, psychology, and social relations. These two constraints provide the context in which the behavior therapists' dilemma arises. Behavior therapists, like psychiatrists and clinical psychologists and other members of helping professions are enjoined to intervene in ways that satisfy both constraints. Skinner's argument in *Beyond Freedom and Dignity* entails that these two constraints cannot both be satisfied. This is the behavior therapists' dilemma. On Skinner's radical behaviorist account the most promising scientific approach to understanding human beings has shown (and, in a certain sense, must show) that human beings are not autonomous. If this is right, then one can't reasonably accept both that human beings are autonomous and that a scientific understanding of human beings is

possible. It is of considerable interest whether Skinner is right about this general conclusion, but the behavior theorists' dilemma does not raise that issue directly. It raises a more restricted question, namely, whether behavior therapists must choose between radical behaviorism and a conception of human beings as capable of real self-determination. Discussion of this more restricted issue sidesteps the controversial (but interesting and important) issue of whether radical behaviorism *is* a promising approach to the understanding of human beings. In addition, it focuses attention on one of the few Skinnerian theses that have become part of conventional wisdom, namely, that radical Skinnerian behaviorism is incompatible with a conception of human beings as autonomous. An examination of this thesis clarifies both what radical behaviorism is and the conception of autonomy and self-determination embodied in the legal, ethical and political practices exemplified by the doctrine of informed consent. This examination highlights issues typically ignored in discussions of the compatibility or incompatibility of autonomy and causal determination. It also suggests a sense in which Skinner and conventional wisdom *may* be wrong in accepting the behavior therapists' dilemma.

A number of considerations make acceptance of the behavior therapists' dilemma at least prima facie plausible. This can be seen from a relatively straightforward comparison of the basic tenets of radical behaviorism with the basic features of an influential conception of autonomous action.

There are two basic features of radical behaviorism which are important for understanding the behaviorists' dilemma. Radical behaviorism is deterministic and it is antimentalistic. The deterministic thesis has already been mentioned. Radical behaviorists maintain that human behavior is completely determined by antecedent causes (or, at least, as determined as other natural phenomena). The antimentalistic thesis is simply the thesis that mental states (like beliefs and desires), feelings (like pains, etc.), and traits of character (like being intelligent or rational or calculating) are not among the *causes* of behavior. The deterministic thesis is not distinctive of radical behaviorism; it is endorsed by virtually every defender of scientific psychology. Among contemporary scientific psychologists, the antimentalistic thesis is distinctive of defenders of radical behaviorism. Defense of the antimentalistic thesis is roughly what divides radical behaviorists (and eliminative materialists) from contemporary cognitivists. Radical behaviorists share with eliminative materialists the view that mentalism in scientific psychology is a candidate for replacement by better scientific conceptions in roughly the way that the phlogiston account of combustion, calcination (e.g., rusting), respiration, and smelting was replaced by the modern account in terms of the uptake and loss of oxygen. The issue raised by *Beyond Freedom and Dignity* is whether the deterministic and antimentalistic theses are incompatible with the conception of self-determination required by the justification of informed consent as a means of protecting autonomy. The distinctively radical behaviorist's concerns are raised by the anti-mentalistic thesis.

Faden and Beauchamp (1986) propose a useful analysis of the concept of autonomy required by the doctrine of informed consent. The main features of their analysis are:

A. x acts autonomously only if
1. x acts intentionally
2. x acts with understanding, and
3. x acts without controlling influences. (p. 238)

There are at least two questions about the analysis that are relevant to assessing the compatibility of radical behaviorism and the kind of autonomy that the doctrine of informed consent is said to protect. The first question is whether this analysis describes what the law and professional ethics concerned with informed consent is or should be designed to protect.[4] The second question is whether radical behaviorism is consistent with the view that people (sometimes) act autonomously in this sense. Both are worth discussing, but the second is more germane to the issues raised by Skinner's arguments and by the behavior therapists' dilemma.

Skinner argues that autonomy is incompatible with any complete scientific understanding of human beings. Part of his argument is a version of a familiar argument that has also been presented by many others: According to scientific accounts, human beings are just complex physical systems whose behavior and capacities are the effects of complicated causal interactions, which it is the business of science to discover. The story here is the familiar one involving the emergence of complex replicating molecules from the primeval soup, the evolution by natural selection of distinct biological species, and the process of individual con-

ception, development, and learning unfolding in each case in ways in which what occurs at every point in time is completely causally determined by the preceding events and states.

Many people worry that if this general scientific conception of human beings were correct, then people could never act autonomously. This worry can be connected directly with the account of autonomous action being considered. That account of autonomy requires that autonomous acts be free of controlling influences. The scientific account of human action requires that every event is completely causally determined, so there are no acts that are free of determining causal influences. The conclusion is that the causal determinism involved in the scientific account of human action is incompatible with the account of autonomy and self-determination that legal, political, and ethical arguments require.

The main worry here is that if the scientific account is true, there would be no basis, in fact, for making the distinction between autonomous and nonautonomous acts, which the law, ethics, and a democratic political tradition require. This incompatibilist view entails that one can't consistently accept scientific determinism and the traditional conception of human beings as acting in a self-determining way. The reason is that if determinism is true, no human act is, in the relevant sense, free of controlling influences.

If this incompatibilist view is correct, then it is not just behavior therapists (and radical behaviorists) who are faced with a dilemma. Any psychotherapist who accepts determinism faces a dilemma as well, namely, either a scientific understanding of human action is impossible, or there is no autonomy of the sort informed consent requires.

Traditionally, scientific psychologists and their defenders have argued that there is a way out of this dilemma. They argue that scientific determinism and autonomy are compatible. Proponents of this kind of compatibilism argue that self-determination does not require a distinction between events that are completely causally determined and events that are not. All that is required is a distinction between two kinds of causes of behavior: those that are controlling influences and those that are not. The basis for that distinction is said to lie in the first two conditions in the description of autonomous acts: that the acts be intentional and done with understanding. The main idea here is that one can distinguish acts that are *caused* by the agent's own intentions, formed with appropriate understanding of the action and its consequences, and acts that are not caused in this way. In the latter case controlling influences may be present: Agents may be forced to act in violation of their own intentions (or alternatively, to form intentions that are not their own in the sense that on reflection the intentions do not coincide with what the agent wants). An example of this is the well-worn "your money or your life" scenario. Actions performed under such conditions conflict with second-order intentions and fail to be authentic in the sense of Dworkin (1981).

Alternatively, agents' circumstances may be such that they don't understand their actions or the consequences of these actions. For example, in cases germane to the doctrine of informed consent this would include the agents not having the expertise or mental capacity to understand what others do understand and agents being given inadequate information. In the latter case, something significant to the agents' intentions may be withheld or overlooked by those providing the information. A lot remains to be done in clarifying the distinctions required here (see Dworkin, 1988, for a useful beginning), but, for the purposes at hand, it is sufficient to focus on the central idea: that the required distinction is essentially that between acts caused by adequately informed (and authentic) intentions and acts not caused by such intentions.

Many compatibilists argue that this is the main distinction one needs to distinguish autonomous acts from acts that are not autonomous. Acts can be autonomous even if the intentions and understandings that guide these acts are themselves completely causally determined and not self-determined. This form of compatibilism is widely accepted as defeating the psychotherapists' dilemma. It does not, however, defeat the behavior therapists' dilemma. An examination of why this is so highlights the distinctiveness of radical behaviorism and the conception of natural scientific understanding radical behaviorism embodies.

The main difference between the behavior therapists' dilemma and the psychotherapists' dilemma is that the former is tied to the status of radical behaviorism. Because this is so radical behaviorists cannot accept the form of compatibilism just described, which many cognitively oriented therapists defend. Radical behaviorists (and eliminative materialists) reject mentalism. That is, they reject the thesis that mental states are among the causes of behavior. Informed intentions of the sort com-

patibilists require simply are certain types of beliefs and desires. They are identified by compatibilists as causes of autonomous choices and actions, and so the compatibilists are committed to exactly the kind of mentalism that radical behaviorists reject. Radical behaviorists are faced with the same kind of problem that mentalistic compatibilism aims to solve, namely, to specify what distinguishes acts that are free of controlling influences from those that are not. The radical behaviorist must do that in some way that does not rely on *mental states or capacities* as *causes* of autonomous acts.

Skinner and others (Dworkin, 1988) have suggested that *this* problem is simply insoluble: An autonomous act is an act caused by informed intentions. If mental states are not among the causes of behavior, then there are no autonomous acts. If this is right, then the behavior therapists' dilemma is unavoidable even if mentalistic compatibilism is correct.

The widely heralded "cognitivist revolution" and the flourishing of mentalistic cognitivism in the sixties, seventies, and early eighties (Gardner, 1985) has often been taken as evidence that the tensions described by the behavior therapists' dilemma pose no real dilemma, after all. At least, they pose no dilemma that confronts scientific psychology. Cognitivists argue that mentalistic approaches to scientific psychology are the most promising and so conclude that radical behaviorism is unacceptable on scientific grounds. Behavior therapists who persist in defending radical behaviorism still must deal with the dilemma, but, the argument goes, there is nothing in science that poses the dilemma, and science suggests that radical behaviorism can be reasonably rejected. In this context, the conclusion that radical behaviorists cannot avoid the behavior therapists' dilemma might be presented as a reason for preferring contemporary cognitive psychology to radical behaviorism. Dworkin (1988) alludes to such reasons. Specifically, mentalistic cognitivism allows therapists to be scientific and to have a basis for distinguishing autonomous and nonautonomous acts. This view appears to be a part of current conventional wisdom. Viewed from this perspective, *Beyond Freedom and Dignity* seems to presuppose and defend outmoded science. If this is correct, then the main point of the behavior therapists' dilemma is moot. Radical behaviorism is not appropriately described as a promising scientific approach to understanding effective therapy, and mentalism is not appropriately described as a pre-scientific mode of understanding.

There is, however, more to be learned from the behavior therapists' dilemma than this piece of conventional wisdom allows. First, Skinner's remarks about the environment acting to *select* behavior rather than to "push or pull" suggests an alternative to the current conventional view of the relative merits of radical behaviorism and classical cognitivism. Second, there is a way of understanding the antimentalism of radical behaviorism which is both consistent with Skinner's arguments against mentalism and which avoids both horns of the behavior therapists' dilemma.

Skinner's remarks allude to a feature of radical behaviorism that has gotten remarkably little attention in the philosophical and psychological literature. Skinner's radical behaviorism links antimentalism with a nonmechanistic form of causation, namely *selection by consequences*, as exemplified in the process of natural selection. On Skinner's view, operant conditioning constitutes an instance of selection by consequences that operates in producing behavioral adaptation during the lifetime of organisms. Skinner argues (e.g., 1969, 1971) that operant conditioning stands in opposition to mentalism in psychology in precisely the way that natural selection stands in opposition to vitalism in biology (for discussion, see Catania & Harnad, 1984; Ringen, 1986). From this perspective, the cognitivist revolution in psychology appears in relation to radical behaviorism rather like the resurgence of vitalism that led to the "eclipse of Darwinism" in the 1920s and 1930s (see Bowler, 1983; Catania, 1987, 1992). The decline of classical (mentalistic) cognitivism, the continued flourishing of work on classical and operant conditioning, and the emergence of nonmentalistic forms of cognitive neuroscience encourage attention to formulating a new synthesis in psychology which consolidates the radical behaviorists' natural science approach to psychology in the way the new synthesis in biology did during the second half of this century. It remains to consider how this perspective illuminates the behavior therapists' dilemma.

Here is a proposal: The antimentalism of radical behaviorism is simply the thesis that mental states such as informed intentions are not *efficient* causes of behavior. The short argument for this proposal is that mental states such as plans, desires, informed intentions, and so on make essential reference to goals and so are more reasonably treated as final causes than efficient causes. This argument and its implications deserve fuller discussion than they have yet been accorded and than is possible here (for more detailed discussion see Ringen, 1993a, b, c). It is, however, appropriate here to note why the proposal is germane to a discussion of the behavior therapists' dilemma. The proposal is of interest for at least two reasons. First, it suggests an explanation of the persistent antimentalism of radical behaviorism, namely, the traditional view that since the time of Galileo natural science has been rightly concerned with efficient, not final causation and so mentalistic explanations have no place in scientific psychology. Second, it suggests a way of avoiding the behavior therapists' dilemma—radical behaviorists *need* have no objections to attributing informed intentions to individuals as long as it is not claimed that such intentions are efficient causes, or that references to such intentions constitute scientific explanations of behavior. Both of these suggestions raise a range of controversial issues that badly need to be discussed. Here it is sufficient to briefly address one of the issues most central to resolving the behavior therapists' dilemma, namely, the relations between efficient causal accounts of behavior and mentalistic explanations in terms of beliefs, desires, or informed intentions. The issue is whether the two types of accounts are rivals in the sense that a mentalistic account, construed as an account in terms of final causation, would be displaced by a complete efficient causal account. (For discussion, see Taylor, 1964, 1967; Noble, 1967). It is worth taking seriously the suggestion that they are not: that is, that a complete efficient causal account of behavior is not incompatible with the attribution of final causes such as goals, plans, or intentions. The view is not the widely held one that teleological explanation is just a form of efficient causal explanation. It is that these are two distinct forms of explanation, but they are not rivals in the sense that one rules the other out or that one is more fundamental than the other. Perhaps Aristotle's doctrine of final causation (historically, one of the main objects of caricature and criticism by defenders of the modern scientific conception of intelligibility) may be usefully interpreted in this compatibilist way. Furthermore, various artifacts and other naturally occurring systems seem to be both completely causally determined and goal directed in the relevant senses. Rosenbleuth and Wiener (1950) provide a classic statement of this view. Homing torpedoes, tomahawk missiles, and the spawning migration of salmon all seem clear examples of goal-directed systems that are completely causally determined. From this perspective, there seems no a priori reason to think human behavior is any different (for relevant discussion see Dennett, 1984), except perhaps in degrees of intelligence (e.g., range and speed of adaptability).

The modern scientific conception of *nature* as a system of efficient causal processes has perennially seemed in tension with the conception of *human nature* embedded in traditional religious, ethical, and political values (Burtt, 1951). This latter conception attributes to human beings a capacity for self-determination which in recent legal doctrine and guidelines for professional therapeutic practice has come to be identified with the capacity for forming and acting on appropriately informed intentions. The behavior therapists' dilemma presents the issue of determining whether, and if so, how a natural scientific understanding of such a capacity for autonomous choice and action is possible. Conventional wisdom has it that such understanding is not possible unless informed intentions are among the efficient causes of behavior identified by scientific psychology. This leads many radical behaviorists to conclude that science has shown (or will show) that human autonomy does not exist. It also leads many others to conclude that radical behaviorism simply cannot be correct. The alternative suggested here is that conventional wisdom errs in misconstruing informed intentions as efficient causes. They are, rather, more akin to final causes, which do not have a place in the modern scientific conception of nature. If this is correct, we need an account of how the efficient causal explanations of biological and psychological phenomena are related to the mentalistic conceptions that are the stock in trade of our moral, legal, and political traditions. No such account has been given here, but there seems no reason to conclude that the former need displace the latter and, hence, there seems no reason why radical behaviorists need find the behavior therapists' dilemma a challenge to the consistency of behavior therapeutic practice. The issue is not whether informed intentions are in fact among the efficient causes of behavior—it is whether they are efficient causes at all. From this perspective, it appears that to understand the capacity for autonomous action we need to clearly identify the range and speed of adaptability to changing circumstances that intelligent systems such as human beings can exhibit. And we need to provide causal accounts of how this capacity is exhibited in various artifacts and other naturally occurring systems. Such accounts may occasion revision of traditionally held conceptions about self-determination. For example, they may clarify the extent to which the capacity for informed consent and other self-directed intelligent action deteriorates in rapidly changing circumstances, and they may even help identify the conditions under which the development and exercise of appropriately informed intentions is either facilitated or inhibited. However, there seems to be no a priori reason for concluding that there can be no informed intentions or autonomy if mentalism finds no place in science. Folk psychology may, indeed, be here to stay, but its role is not to contribute to the natural scientific project of providing causal (e.g., mechanistic or selectionistic) explanations of behavior or of the processes that constitute effective therapeutic intervention.

ENDNOTES

1. Quoted in Faden and Beauchamp (1986), pp. 133–134.
2. Quoted in Faden and Beauchamp (1986), p. 134.
3. Quoted in Faden and Beauchamp (1986), p. 135.
4. In the literature one finds some concern that, in fact, neither the law nor professional practice implement informed consent in a way that really enhances autonomous authorization of treatment by a patient. The concern is that informed consent procedures simply provide legally valid evidence of consent, which can relieve a practitioner from liability for harm of the sort that some form of therapy may put a client at risk. For discussion see Faden and Beauchamp (1986) and Lidz et al. (1984).

REFERENCES

Bowler, P. (1983). *The eclipse of Darwinism: Anti-Darwinian evolution theories in the decades around 1900.* Baltimore: Johns Hopkins University Press.

Burtt, E. A. (1951). *The metaphysical foundations of modern physical science* (rev. ed.). New York: Humanities Press.

Catania, A. C. (1987). Some Darwinian lessons for behavior analysis: A review of Bowler's *The eclipse of Darwinism. Journal of the Experimental Analysis of Behavior,* 47, 249—257.

Catania, A. C. (1992). *Learning* (3rd ed.). Englewood Cliffs, NJ: Prentice-Hall.

Catania, A. C., & Harnad, S. (1984). Canonical papers of B. F. Skinner. *Behavioral and Brain Sciences*, *7*, 473–724.

Dennett, D. (1984). *Elbow room*. Cambridge: MIT Press.

Dworkin, G. (1981). Autonomy and behavior control. In T. Mappes & J. Zembaty (Eds.) *Biomedical ethics*. New York: McGraw-Hill.

Dworkin, G. (1988). *The theory and practice of autonomy*. New York: Cambridge University Press.

Faden, R., & Beauchamp, T. (1986). *A history and theory of informed consent*. Oxford: Oxford University Press.

Gardner, H. (1985). *The mind's new science*. New York: Basic Books.

Goldfried, M., & Davison, G. (1976). *Clinical behavior therapy*. New York: Holt, Rinehart, and Winston.

Kalish, H. (1981). *From behavioral science to behavior modification*. New York: McGraw-Hill.

Kazdin, A., & Wilson, G. (1978). *Evaluation of behavior therapy*. Cambridge, MA: Ballinger.

Lidz, C., Meisel, A., Zerubavel, E., Carter, M., Sestak, M., & Roth, L. (1984). *Informed consent: A study of decision making in psychiatry*. New York: Guilford Press.

Macklin, R. (1982). *Man, mind, and morality: The ethics of behavior control*. Englewood Cliffs, NJ: Prentice-Hall.

Noble, D. (1967). Charles Taylor on teleological explanation. *Analysis*, *XXVIII*, 96–103.

Ringen, J. (1986). The completeness of behavior theory: Review of *Behaviorism, science, and human nature* by Barry Schwartz and Hugh Lacey. *Behaviorism*, *14*, 29–39.

Ringen, J. (1993a). Adaptation, teleology, and selection by consequences. *Journal of the Experimental Analysis of Behavior*, *60*, 141–148.

Ringen, J. (1993b). Critical naturalism and the philosophy of psychology. *New Ideas in Psychology*, *11*, 153–177.

Ringen, J. (1993c). Dennett's intentions and Darwin's legacy. *Behavioral and Brain Sciences*, *16*, 386–390.

Rosenbleuth, A., & Wiener, N. (1950). Purposeful and nonpurposeful behavior. *Philosophy of Science*, *17*, 318–26.

Skinner, B. F. (1969). *Contingencies of reinforcement*. New York: Appleton-Century-Crofts.

Skinner, B. F. (1971). *Beyond freedom and dignity*. New York: Alfred A. Knopf.

Taylor, C. (1964). *The explanation of behaviour*. London: Routledge and Kegan Paul.

Taylor, C. (1967). Teleological explanation—A reply to Denis Noble. *Analysis*, *XXVIII*, 141–143.

CHAPTER 24

PROFESSIONAL CODES OF ETHICS AND ONGOING MORAL PROBLEMS IN PSYCHOLOGY

Karen Strohm Kitchener

The American Psychological Association (APA) has recently revised its professional ethical code (APA, 1992). The revision of the code attempts to provide standards of conduct that more specifically address frequent ethical issues that arise in practice, research, and teaching than have former codes. These standards are enforceable and psychologists may be held accountable for failing to adhere to them. Although an attempt was made in the revision to write the standards in clear and behavioral terms (Nagy, 1989), they have been criticized for being less precise and overly dependent on legal qualifiers (Bersoff, 1994; Koocher, 1994). On the other hand, the code also identifies six more general principles that serve as a statement of the underlying ethical values for psychology. These principles are to be considered aspirational goals for psychologists as they attempt to identify an ideal course of action or ethical stance. The format of explicit standards and statements of values provided an initial attempt to address a criticism of earlier codes (Sinclair, Poizner, Gilmour-Barrett, & Randall, 1987).

By defining aspirational goals, a dimension was added that earlier codes ignored: the basic or fun-

damental principles on which the ethical practice of psychology is based. The principles are intended to act as the foundation for ethical decisions if more precise guidance is not included in the standards themselves. In essence four of the principles—competence, concern for others' welfare, professional, and scientific responsibility, and social responsibility—identify the psychologist's responsibility to benefit and not to harm those with whom they work. For example, if psychologists did not comply with the principle requiring them to be competent, the public could not benefit from their services nor could it depend on their research. Ultimately, they might harm those whom they intended to serve. The principle of concern for others' welfare is a positive statement of psychologists' responsibility to contribute to the well-being of the individuals and groups with whom they are working while social responsibility requires a similar concern about society and the community. Professional and scientific responsibility requires that psychologists be accountable for their professional behavior.

It is interesting to note that "social responsibility" has been elevated to a general principle in this edition of the Ethics Code. Minor mention was made about social responsibility in the 1981 code and its amended version in 1989 under Principle 1f (APA, 1981, 1990), i.e., "psychologists know that they bear a heavy social responsibility because their recommendations and professional actions may alter the lives of others." In general, the 1981 and 1990 versions of the code focused on psychologists' ethical responsibility to the individuals and groups with whom they directly worked. The addition of social responsibility to the general principles in the Ethics Code implies that psychologists have a broader responsibility to contribute to human welfare and intercede when they are aware of social policies that affect it in a negative way.

"Integrity" and "respect for people's rights and dignity" are the other two general principles. Respecting individuals' rights and dignity implies that psychologists have a fundamental responsibility to respect others' liberty to choose their own course of action and thoughts. This includes respecting others' lifestyles, their privacy, their right to make decisions about people with whom they share their confidences, and so on. The psychologist's responsibility to adequately inform research participants, therapy patients, supervisees, and others about the activity in which they are being asked to engage follows from the responsibility to respect other's rights and dignity. In order to make adequate decisions about their own lives, people must have adequate information on which to base those decisions.

The concept of integrity might be translated to mean what others (Beauchamp & Childress, 1989; Kitchener, 1984; Ramsey, 1970) have called "fidelity." Ramsey (1970) argued that "fidelity" or faithfulness is a central ethical concern for all helping professions since it involves issues such as keeping promises and truthfulness. These concerns are echoed in the principle of integrity as it states that psychologists are "honest, fair and respectful of others" and that they do not make statements that are "false, misleading, or deceptive" (APA, 1992). As I have argued elsewhere (Kitchener, 1984), these issues arise when psychologists enter into a voluntary relationship with a client, research participant, student, supervisee and so on.

> By the very fact that two individuals freely consent to participate in a relationship, an ethical commitment which involves certain obligations for both parties is implied. To some extent obligations to be faithful derive from the respect due to autonomous persons (e. g., if people wish to be treated as autonomous agents, they must respect others' autonomous rights). Lying, for example, is disrespectful of anothers' right to choose freely based on accurate information. Similarly, not fulfilling a contract (e. g., to respect confidentiality) disregards the other individuals' choice to enter into a relationship that has set boundaries. (p. 51)

Multiple relationships that cross boundaries and distort the contract between psychologists and those with whom they work further exemplify a lack of integrity since they involve a betrayal of trust between a psychologist and the person with whom he or she entered into a relationship. In essence, if psychologists have no integrity or are untrustworthy, no meaningful relationships between them and others could exist.

Despite criticism of the 1992 code, it is worth while noting that the concept of not harming others has been stated explicitly while it was missing in earlier versions (APA, 1981, 1990). Further, it has been elevated to a standard that is enforceable. Specifically, Standard 1. 14 (APA, 1992) states, "Psychologists take reasonable steps to avoid harming their patients or clients, research participants, students, and others with whom they work, and to minimize harm where it is foreseeable and unavoidable." Because the maxim to avoid harm is in the enforceable section of the code and since the principles focusing on benefiting others are in the aspirational section of the code, it suggests that not harming others is a more stringent ethical responsibility than is helping them.

Ideally, the ethical standards in conjunction with the principles ought to guide psychologists' actions when they are faced with ethical decisions. However, in addition to the criticisms that others have raised (Bersoff, 1994; Koocher, 1994; Peyton, 1994) there remain several ethical issues that are either not addressed or about which the code offers contradictory advice. Three examples will be used to illustrate the limits of the revised code; one from therapy, one from teaching, and one from research. They include the limits of confidentiality, multiple role relationships in academic settings, and deception in research. While the scope of this chapter does not allow for a thorough discussion of these issues the fundamental problems facing the profession in each area will be identified.

LIMITS OF CONFIDENTIALITY

Since the initial code of ethics for psychologists was written in 1955, confidentiality in practice and research has been a cornerstone of psychologists' ethical responsibilities. Similarly, since the earliest codes were written there has been recognition that psychologists' obligations to respect confidentiality is not inviolate. In fact, in one of the earliest versions of the code psychologists were allowed to break confidentiality when "there is clear and imminent danger to an individual or to society" (APA, 1959, p. 280). In the most recent version of the ethics code (APA, 1992), further exceptions have been allowed in Standard 5.05a. These include when it is mandated by law; when the client, patient, or other is at risk of harm; in order to provide needed services to the patient or client; in order to obtain professional consultation; and in order to obtain payment for services.

The realities of the 1990s, however, are that real confidentiality may be more of an exception than a rule, particularly when an individual is seen in an institutional setting. Secretaries and other staff have access to confidential information. Individuals, anonymously or not, are discussed at case conferences or staffings. Computerized data on clients may allow individuals in unrelated positions in a company or an institution access to records and testing data. Insurance companies and their multitude of employees often have access to diagnoses, treatment plans and, sometimes, even detailed case histories. Similarly, managed care settings often require peer review of diagnoses and detailed treatment plans. The situation becomes further complicated when psychologists are employed by the military or by a firm that expects information to be provided to management on problematic employees.

Additionally, clients are discussed with supervisors and in training seminars. Illustrative cases are used in articles, books, and lectures. As an example of how such material can lead to a breach of confidentiality, in one unfortunate instance a member of an audience recognized her sister as the person the psychologist was using as an illustration despite the fact the identity of the person in the case had been masked.

Further, the legal limitations to confidentiality grow. State laws now require psychologists to break confidentiality if they have reason to suspect child abuse (Heins, 1983). Since *Tarasoff* and because of the accumulation of related case law, there has been pressure on psychologists to notify authorities when their patients are potentially dangerous and some states have legalized breaches if there is an imminent danger to an identifiable third party (Wise, 1978). With the advent of AIDS, there is increased discussion about whether the so-called "duty to warn" extends to potential sexual or needle partners of those who are HIV positive (Melton, 1988; Lamb, Clark, Drumheller, Frizzell, & Surrey, 1989).

On the other hand, clients or patients, when asked, appear unaware of the real limits of their confidentiality. Based on a study of high school students, undergraduate psychology students, and former clients at a mental health and a university counseling center, Miller and Thelen (1986) found that 69% believed that everything revealed in a therapy relationship was confidential and 74% believed that there should be no exceptions to confidentiality. In other words, there is a substantial gap between what people believe is and ought to be the case regarding confidentiality in therapy and the reality regarding the confidentiality of information.

In light of the real limits of confidentiality it is time to ask: What does confidentiality mean in current psychological practice and what are the profession's ethical obligations to patients and research participants? This is especially true at a time when the profession has taken a substantially new position in the 1992 ethics codes in regards to confidentiality. Earlier versions of the code allowed psychologists to breach confidentiality only in the service of the client or society. In other words, psychologists were allowed to take action in the best interests of the client or to protect others.

Additionally, the new code allows psychologists to reveal information about their clients in order to obtain service fees. This disclosure is limited to the minimum that is necessary to obtain payment and by the fact that psychologists are required by Standard 1.25 to have an agreement early in the relationship about the payment and billing arrangements. One would presume this would include the information that confidentiality might be broken to obtain payment.

It may be argued that psychologists have the right to reasonable compensation for their work and that when clients fail to pay their bills they have broken the implicit or explicit contract to which they consented when they entered treatment. On the other hand, the inclusion of this exception to confidentiality in the Ethics Code remains another example of how the concept of inviolate confidentiality has been superseded with a much looser concept of protecting a client's or patient's privacy.

Beauchamp and Childress (1989) argue that a professional rule like confidentiality can be justified by the principles it entails and the consequences that derive from it. From a consequentialist perspective, in psychology confidentiality is intended to protect the unauthorized disclosure of private information to third parties, and, thus, allow a client to trust a therapist with information that would permit the therapeutic relationship to proceed. Typically, in therapy this includes not only the specific information disclosed to the psychologist but the fact that the person is in therapy at all since it remains the case that for many clients seeking help is a stigma both socially and professionally. If, by contrast, the profession would establish a rule that made it mandatory to disclose all illegal activity to the police, such a rule would very soon undermine the trust that is essential for therapy to proceed.

From a principled perspective, the psychologist's duty to protect confidentiality derives from several sources. First, if we assume that people are autonomous and have the right to make decisions about their own lives, then one of those decisions includes deciding with whom secret information about themselves is shared. Autonomy, of course, does not imply license to do anything that one chooses if one's actions will infringe upon the autonomous rights of others to make decisions about their own lives. Thus as autonomy is limited so is the expectation that others will keep one's confidence if the information shared reveals an intention to infringe on the rights or life of others. It is because of this limitation on autonomy that the majority opinion in the *Tarasoff* case ruled that the psychiatrist had the responsibility to warn Tatania Tarasoff of his client's intention to kill her. This principle is underscored in the current code by Principle D: respect for people's rights and dignity. This principle suggests psychologists ought to honor people's privacy, confidentiality, self-determination, and autonomy.

Further, several people (Beauchamp & Childress, 1989; Bok, 1983; Kitchener, 1984) have argued that basic issues of fidelity or faithfulness provide added support to the responsibility to keep confidences. The trust between human beings that allows for human interactions and social obligations depends on assumptions of trust and loyalty, particularly when interactions involve private information that may leave one person vulnerable. Failure to uphold the obligation to keep silent may unavoidably wound the person whose confidences have been broken. In the current code, the concept of fidelity is reflected in Principle B: integrity, which states that psychologists should be honest, fair, and respectful of others. Respect for others includes keeping promises like the promise of confidentiality.

As Bok (1983) points out, in a professional relationship where there is an explicit promise to keep confidence the potential for harm is even higher and the obligation to keep confidence even stronger than in ordinary relationships. In this case, the harm derives not just from the information that is revealed but also from breaching the assumption of trust in professionals and in promise keeping. Ultimately, such breaches can undermine the profession and people's willingness to share their secrets with professionals whether in a research or clinical setting.

This is exactly the problem in cases that involve clients who report engaging in acts that could potentially harm a third party, such as child abuse, unprotected sex with a naive partner when the client has AIDS or the HIV virus, or threatening another's life. When the professional reports what the client has revealed with the expectation of secrecy, it undermines confidence in the profession. In the long run the social costs may also be great because people in need of help won't seek it. Bok (1983) argues:

> Society therefore gains in turn from allowing such professional refuge, the argument holds, in spite of the undoubted risks of not learning about certain dangers to the community; and everyone is better off when professionals can probe for the secrets that will make them more capable of providing the needed help. (p. 233)

This is not, however, to argue that professional confidentiality should be inviolate. It is to remind psychologists that there may be serious long-term consequences to the individual, the profession, the community, and to the fabric of human relationships if psychologists take their responsibility to protect confidentiality too lightly. This is particularly true because of client expectations about confidentiality (Miller & Thelen, 1986) and as articulated in the opening of this section, because the threats to confidentiality are so numerous. As Beachamp and Childress (1989) argue, confidentiality is a prima facie obligation and one who chooses to breach it must provide an ethical argument for breaking it stronger than the one for keeping it.

Clearly there are arguments for breaking confidentiality when the life of another person is at stake or when the well-being of a child who has no ability to fend for him or herself is at risk. On the other hand, psychologists are already on a so-called "slippery slope" in regards to revealing confidences. Providing private information about clients to insurance companies in return for benefits was an initial step. Allowing psychologists in the military or working for institutions to reveal client information for the good of the organization is another. Allowing psychologists to break confidence to ensure bills are paid is the most recent. None of these can be justified by the welfare of the client or patient or the threat of harm to the autonomous rights or life of others. Although they may be ethically justifiable they are not included in the common understanding of confidence keeping. It may be that to respect client's rights and dignity and to have integrity in their relationships psychologists practicing therapy will have to have more thorough discussions with their clients or patients at the outset of treatment about expectations and the realities of confidentiality in the modern world.

As has been noted earlier, not taking reasonable steps to avoid harm is a sanctionable offense under the new ethics code (APA, 1992). If psychologists do not take informing their clients about the possible reasons for breaking confidentiality seriously, they may find themselves censored by the association for not doing so and for causing their clients harm by the omission of information. Further, they may face legal consequences since courts have upheld clients' or patients' rights to have this kind of information in advance (Pope and Vasquez, 1991).

MULTIPLE RELATIONSHIPS

Although there has been considerable discussion in psychology of the potential harmful effects of multiple relationships—particularly sexual ones—between therapists and their clients, less attention has been paid to the multiple relationships between faculty members and students. The exception to

this is the prohibition in the most recent APA Code (1992) of engaging in sexual relationships with students in training whom psychologists have responsibility for evaluating or over whom they have direct authority. This standard would, for example, prohibit psychologists from engaging in sexual relationships with students in their classes, with advisees, with students they are supervising in research or practice and with students whose comprehensive exams they must assess. Since in most psychology graduate programs students are evaluated yearly by the faculty as a whole, in reality this would also prohibit sexual relationships between faculty and most current graduate students. Since the profession has taken such a clear position on this issue, it will not be dealt with here. Rather the focus will be on nonsexual, nonromantic relationships between faculty and students.

There are many nonsexual multiple relationships that exist between faculty and students by the very nature of an academic setting. Faculty serve as advisers for students who are in their classes. At the graduate level, they hire students as research or teaching assistants and these same students are in their classes and/or are advisees. Sometimes faculty co-author publications with students—students they are evaluating in other contexts.

Based on the social–psychological literature (Kitchener, 1988; Kitchener & Harding, 1990; Secord & Backman, 1974), we know that different roles carry with them different expectations and obligations and that a single individual may occupy several roles simultaneously. For example, a department head in a university graduate program may be responsible for both promoting the development of students and terminating them. Similarly, the role of a clinical supervisor involves the expectation to help the supervisee develop professionally and an obligation to evaluate the same person's adequacy against an external standard. In essence these multiple obligations are mirrored in the Ethics Code (APA, 1992) in Principle E: concern for others' welfare and Principle F: social responsibility. These principles imply that, on one hand, psychologists should contribute to the development of students, but that this must be balanced against their responsibility to the community not to graduate incompetent psychologists.

In terms of role theory, Secord and Backman (1974) argue that failure to act in accordance with role expectations can lead to frustration, confusion, anger, and disgust on the part of the person whose expectations haven't been met. Because the role of a psychology faculty member carries with it multiple expectations and because faculty are required to play many roles, when they or the student are unclear about which role they are playing, the student can experience considerable distress.

To some extent, the role of the faculty member carries with it unrealistic expectations about being knowledgeable and wise; thus, students may be unable to adequately or objectively evaluate the feedback or recommendations of a psychology faculty member and to reject them when they are not in their best interests (Kitchener, 1992). In addition, the relationships between faculty and students are asymmetrical in the sense that faculty have the responsibility to make decisions about the success or failure of students who are enrolled in educational programs; thus, faculty wield very real power over the outcomes of students' lives and careers. As a result of the power differential and role expectations associated with being a university or college faculty member students may be unable to make reasonable decisions about the appropriateness of entering into dual relationships with faculty.

When it is a faculty member who fails to meet role expectations, the problem is exacerbated by the position of power and authority that faculty member holds. Students may feel betrayed and such betrayal may weaken their trust in others in similar positions of authority and may lead to skepticism about the potential benefits of engaging in educational activities in general. The power differential also leaves open the potential for faculty to exploit students and students, because of their relative powerlessness, have little opportunity for retribution. Take the case of a faculty member who publishes a student's idea or paper under the faculty member's name as an example (see Goodyear, Crego, & Johnston, 1992, for other examples). The student may both be afraid of complaining and unclear to whom to take the complaint.

The difficulty students have in acting as their own advocates may be an outgrowth of the implicit contract between students who enter into a college or university program and the faculty members who are engaged to teach in it (Chambers, 1981; Kitchener, 1992). Students make decisions about entering into undergraduate or graduate programs based upon promises made in bulletins and descriptive materials about the nature of the educational experience. Those materials imply that in return for attending, paying money, and abiding by the rules of the institution—if the student is sufficiently able—he or she will benefit from the educational experience and will not be harmed by it. Thus, when they enter into relationships with faculty, students do so with the assumption that they will not be harmed by those relationships and with the expectation that faculty will act with their interests in mind.

Because of the potential for role confusion and the resulting emotional turmoil that can arise when multiple role relationships between faculty members and students go awry or because of the potential for students to be exploited, it is necessary to ask: Should nonsexual, nonromantic dual role relationships between faculty and students be professionally limited or controlled? Despite the potential problems enumerated above, I believe the answer to this question is a qualified "no."

In general the answer is "no" because the role of the faculty member is inherently ambiguous. The role includes both the responsibility to help the student develop in an educational sense and it involves some quality assurance for the public. Although the ambiguity of this role may sometimes be difficult for students to manage, there is little within our current educational system that can be done to avoid it. On the other hand, faculty members need to be clear with students and, perhaps, honest with themselves that evaluation is a part of every relationship with every student. The responsibility to evaluate does not disappear even with very good students. Diluting the appearance of this responsibility, for example, by being "pals" with students may unjustly obscure the real nature of the relationships. When faculty have to evaluate students negatively, students may feel betrayed to have their "friend" act against what the student perceives to be in his or her best interests.

Additionally, the answer to the question must be "no" because many of the same multiple roles that have potential for harming students because of their ambiguity or because of the potential for exploitation also contain in them seeds of powerful learning. Students who are employed by a faculty member on a grant or who co-author an article with a faculty member have the opportunity to benefit beyond anything they could normally experience or learn in the classroom. The on-the-job experience may allow them to express their own ideas and/or lead them into career opportunities that they would otherwise not have. Last, informal out-of-class contacts with faculty have been related to students' intellectual development (Pascarella & Terenzini, 1991), which is an important goal of higher education.

For positive experiences to occur, however, when they engage in multiple relationships with students, faculty members must aspire to help the student benefit from the relationships and at minimum ensure that the student is not exploited. The importance of avoiding exploitation is codified in Standard 1.19 (APA, 1992), which states that psychologists "do not exploit persons over whom they have supervisory, evaluative or other authority" and Standard 1.14 (APA, 1992), which requires that psychologists avoid harming those with whom they work. In addition, because the faculty–student relationship is inherently asymmetrical, it is the faculty member who must remain clear about the potential for role confusion and must clarify his or her roles for students. This clarification can reduce the potential for the misunderstanding and frustration that can accompany role confusion and minimize the potential for harm.

The new APA Ethics Code (APA, 1992) offers faculty some additional guidance under Standard 1.17 when engaging in such relationships. This standard acknowledges that multiple relationships may not always be avoidable and then offers the following three guidelines for psychologists to follow when they are not:

1. Psychologists should remain aware of the potential harmful effects of such relationships and refrain from entering them if the relationship may limit their objectivity or if the other party might be harmed or exploited.
2. Psychologists must refrain from taking on new obligations if preexisting relationships would create the risk of harm.
3. If a potentially harmful multiple relationship arises, the psychologist must attempt to resolve it with regard for the best interests of the affected person and in a way that complies with the remainder of the Ethics Code.

There is little doubt from this standard that the burden of responsibility for clarifying the relationship and remediating harm lies with the psychologist.

DECEPTION IN RESEARCH

Probably the most debated ethical issue in psychological research involves deception (Baumrind, 1985, 1990; Diener & Crandall, 1978; Fisher & Fryberg, 1994; Kelman, 1972). Baumrind (1985) distinguishes between intentional and uninten-tional deception, defining intentional deception in research to include "withholding information in order to obtain participation that the participant might otherwise decline, using deceptive instructions and confederate manipulations in laboratory research, and employing concealment and staged manipulations in field settings" (p. 165). By unintentional deception she appears to mean the difference between full disclosure of all the information regarding a psychological study and the information that a reasonable person would want in order to make an informed decision about participating. In the second case, she argues there will always be some degree of difference between what the researcher intends to communicate and what participants in research understand about the nature of the study.

What Baumrind (1985) calls unintentional deception has not been seen as ethically problematic by those writing in the field (Baumrind, 1985; Beauchamp & Childress, 1989; Diener & Crandall, 1978; Keith-Spiegel & Koocher, 1985). Rather, by using a reasonable person standard for what is revealed to the research participants, the participants can make a decision about whether participating or not participating is in their best interests. In other words, the participants themselves can decide whether the risks are reasonable and whether they are willing to donate their time for the pursuit of knowledge.

By contrast, intentional deception has been seen as ethically problematic. Three concerns seem paramount (Baumrind, 1985, 1990; Diener & Crandall, 1978). First, deception interferes with an individual's ability to make an autonomous decision about participation. Central to the concept of autonomy is the idea that a person is free of personal limitations as well as influences of others that would interfere with his or her ability to make meaningful choices (Beauchamp & Childress, 1989). If critical information about the consequences or nature of participation in a psychological study is withheld or deliberately distorted then a person cannot reasonably give consent to participating. To reiterate a point made earlier, Principle

D: respect for rights and dignity (APA, 1992) suggests that psychologists should respect others' autonomy.

Second, deception inherently involves lying to respondents or deliberately distorting the truth. Again, as noted earlier, Principle D: integrity says that in science as well as practice and teaching psychologists should be "honest, fair and respectful of others." Although there are some circumstances in which lying or deception might be ethically justifiable, e.g., to save another's life, the question is: Does the outcome of a particular study involving deception justify lying?

Truth telling is central to the fabric of human communication and social interactions (Baumrind, 1990; Ramsey, 1970). People make decisions about how and whether to interact with, to follow, or to trust others based on what has been revealed to them. I have argued elsewhere on the grounds of utility that lying and deceit can have serious consequences for both the relationship between professionals and the public as well as for the profession itself (Kitchener, 1984). (See also Baumrind, 1990.) If it becomes known that participants are commonly deceived in psychological research, then the participants in that research may feel no obligation to be truthful in their responses to the research, thus nullifying the research itself (Baumrind, 1985). Further, it may lead the public to distrust psychologists in general, thus undermining the effectiveness of the profession.

The third problem with deceptive research involves the ethical justification for doing research in the first place. At a fundamental level a central ethical justification for doing research on humans is beneficence or doing good (Veatch, 1987). Although there are many kinds of "goods" that can arise from research, including knowledge for knowledge's sake, the maxim implies at least that research participants not be harmed. Further, as argued earlier, the current code implies that the responsibility to avoid harming patients, clients, or research participants (See Standard 1.14) is a stronger obligation than is the social or scientific responsibility to benefit others. Avoiding harm is particularly important in psychology where research involves few earthshaking breakthroughs that may have long-term positive benefits for humankind.

The concern is that some participants report being harmed by deception research and others report that they would anticipate being harmed if subject to such conditions. Subjects feel harassed, distressed, embarrassed, humiliated, ashamed, and

so on after the research and some of these feelings may extend beyond any attempt to debrief them (Baumrind, 1985; Fisher & Fryberg, 1994; Keith-Spiegel & Koocher, 1985; Wilson & Donnerstein, 1976). It is ethically problematic even if only some participants are harmed, if they have not had the opportunity to freely decide that they are willing to risk harm in order to make a scientific contribution.

In the most recent version of the APA Ethics Code (1992), the profession has attempted to address some of the problems regarding deceptive research. In particular, a statement has been added requiring that: "Psychologists never deceive research participants about significant aspects that would affect their willingness to participate such as physical risks, discomfort, or unpleasant emotional experiences" (Standard 6.15b, APA, 1992). In other words, psychologists must always provide participants with enough information about the study that they can make a reasonable decision about the risks involved for themselves, and, therefore, make an informed choice about participating. In Standard 6.12 the code allows researchers to dispense with consent only after considering other regulations and institutional review board requirements and after consulting with peers. Even then consent can be eliminated only in rare cases, for example, naturalistic observations, archival research, and anonymous questionnaires. This implies that consent cannot be avoided in deception research, which at least superficially addresses the first concern with this research paradigm.

On the other hand, the problem may not have been addressed as well as it initially appears. As Kelman (1972) has pointed out, often those who are asked to participate in psychological research are disadvantaged or powerless. Their position in the social structure or organization may leave them believing that they do not have the option of refusing to participate. The role of the researcher involves an implicit expertise that potential research subjects may not believe that they have the knowledge to question. They may believe, for example, that the researcher would never really do anything that might harm them, thus warnings to the contrary in consent forms may not be sufficient.

In addition, the participant's powerlessness and naivete implies a danger that researchers may misuse their power in an improper fashion. Thus, a researcher may undermine the usefulness of the consent procedure by implying that it is an unnecessary nuisance. The new standards in the APA Code can function as they were intended to function only if the researcher takes the process of consent seriously and emphasizes that the potential participants should also do so. If participants are students receiving course credit for participation, the researcher needs to recognize that course credit can motivate students to participate in activities that may not be in their best interests or to fear revealing their real concerns to investigators (Fisher & Fryberg, 1994).

Although the code addresses in a more ethically defensible way the rights of subjects to make accurate decisions about participating in research, it does not address the core issue in deception research—that it involves deliberately lying to participants or manipulating their beliefs about the situation they are encountering. In other words, the core of this experimental procedure remains an ethical embarrassment to psychologists. Further, a substantial minority of participants in deception research find it distasteful (Wilson & Donnerstein, 1976; Fisher & Fryberg, 1994); thus, for this minority violating the trust which is central to human relationships is potentially harmful.

Social-psychologists have been urged to consider alternative experimental procedures. In fact, the Ethics Code requires that psychologists only use deception when it is justified by "the study's prospective scientific, educational or applied value" and when "equally effective alternative procedures" are not feasible (Standard 6.15a, APA, 1992). However, similar requirements in earlier codes did not lead to a reduction in deception research studies (Adair, Dushenko, & Lindsay, 1985), thus the likelihood of psychologists abandoning this paradigm without further restrictions being imposed is slim.

If deception research does harm participants and since Standard 1.14 requires psychologists to take steps to avoid harming others and to minimize harm when it is foreseeable and unavoidable, then it may be that some social-psychologists could be sanctioned for engaging in a common research practice. It may be that the profession will come to the point of requiring that all research participants be warned that psychological research may involve deception and that they risk being deceived if they are involved in any psychological study. It is unlikely that such a statement would keep people from participating in research; however, it would warn them that the researcher may not deal with them truthfully.

CONCLUSIONS

Despite criticism the new psychology Ethics Code (1992) has clarified some of the psychologist's responsibilities to clients, students, and research participants and it identifies a set of values that help psychologists think about their ethical responsibilities when no specific standard addresses the issue. No code can, however, solve all of the ethical issues for a profession. The problem of how to describe confidentiality in a clinical setting is an ongoing problem with which individual psychologists and the profession as a whole will have to continue to struggle, just as the issue of whether deception research can ever be done ethically is a long-term problem for social-psychology.

Similarly, no code can legislate "goodness." It can say that psychologists should not exploit others whether they are research participants, students, or clients and that harming them is wrong. The fact that this code has such clear statements about avoiding harm and exploitation are important ethical milestones in the profession since they were not included in earlier versions (Kitchener, 1984). Professional ethics codes cannot, however, act as a conscience for the individuals who are engaged in research, teaching, and clinical practice. Ultimately, the well-being of those with whom psychologists work will depend on how seriously psychologists take their ethical responsibility to treat others with care.

In fact Nodding (1984) argues that while ethical principles and ethical codes are useful, they are limited and can under some circumstances be used to rationalize both ethical and unethical behavior. Ultimately she suggests that a caring attitude lies at the heart of all ethical behavior. As she puts it, "Everything depends, then, upon the will to be good, to remain in caring relation to the other" (Nodding, 1984, p. 103).

While the profession is responsible for supporting fundamental human values and making its stance public in an ethics code, the individual is responsible for acting on the code. At minimum, Nodding's work should remind psychologists that ethical codes are not and never can be inclusive of all ethical considerations. Tightening standards will never remove from psychologists the burden of making tough ethical decisions nor will standards suffice if psychologists treat others and their lives with disdain.

REFERENCES

Adair, J. G., Dushenko, T. W., & Lindsay, R. C. L. (1985). Ethical regulations and their impact on research practice. *American Psychologist, 40,* 59–72.

American Psychological Association (1959). Ethical standards of psychologists. *American Psychologist, 14*(6), 279–282.

American Psychological Association (1981). Ethical principles of psychologists (Rev. ed.). *American Psychologist, 36,* 633–638.

American Psychological Association (1990). Ethical principles of psychologists (Amended June 2, 1989). *American Psychologist, 45*(3), 390–395.

American Psychological Association (1992). Ethical principles of psychologists and code of conduct. *American Psychologist, 47*(12), 1597–1611.

Baumrind, D. (1985). Research using intentional deception: Ethical issues revisited. *American Psychologist, 40,* 165–174.

Baumrind, D. (1990). Doing good well. In C. B. Fisher & W. W. Tyron (Eds.), *Ethics in applied developmental psychology: Emerging issues in an emerging field* (pp. 17–28). Norwood, NJ: Ablex.

Beauchamp, T. L., & Childress, J. F. (1989). *Principles of biomedical ethics.* Oxford: Oxford University.

Bersoff, D. N. (1994). Explicit ambiguity: The 1992 Ethics Code as an oxymoron. *Professional Psychology: Research and Practice, 25,* 382–387.

Bok, S. (1983). *Secrets: The ethics of concealment and revelation.* New York: Random House.

Chambers, C. M. (1981). Foundations of ethical responsibility in higher education. In R. H. Stein & M. C. Baca (Eds.), *Professional ethics in university administration* (New Directions in Higher Education, No. 33, pp. 1–12). San Francisco: Jossey-Bass.

Diener, E., & Crandall, R. (1978). *Ethics in social and behavioral research.* Chicago: University of Chicago.

Fisher, C. B., & Fryberg, D. (1994). Participant partners: College students weigh the costs and benefits of deceptive research. *American Psychologist, 59,* 417–427.

Goodyear, R. K., Crego, C. A., & Johnston, M. W. (1992). Ethical issues in the supervision of student research: A study of critical incidents. *Professional Psychology: Research and Practice, 23*(3), 203–210.

Heins, M. (1983). The necessity for child abuse reporting. In D. Ganos, R. Lipson, G. Warren, & B. Weil (Eds.), *Difficult decisions in medical ethics.* New York: Alan R. Liss.

Keith-Spiegel, P., & Koocher, G. P. (1985). *Ethics in psychology.* New York: Random House.

Kelman, H. C. (1972). The rights of the subject in social research: An analysis in terms of relative power and legitimacy. *American Psychologist, 27,* 989–1016.

Kitchener, K. S. (1984). Intuition, critical evaluation, and ethical principles: The foundation for ethical decisions in counseling psychology. *The Counseling Psychologist, 12*(3), 43–55.

Kitchener, K. S. (1988). Dual role relationships: What makes them so problematic? *Journal of Counseling and Development, 67,* 217–221.

Kitchener, K. S. (1992). Psychologist as teacher and mentor: Affirming ethical values throughout the curriculum. *Professional Psychology: Research and Practice, 23*(3), 190–195.

Kitchener, K. S., & Harding, S. S. (1990). Dual role relationships. In B. Herlihy & L. B. Golden (Eds.), *Ethical standards casebook.* Alexandria, VA: American Association for Counseling and Development.

Koocher, G. (1994). The commerce of professional psychology and the new Ethics Code. *Professional Psychology: Research and Practice, 25,* 355–361.

Lamb, D. H., Clark, C., Drumheller, P., Frizzell, K., & Surrey, L. (1989). Applying *Tarasoff* to AIDS-related psychotherapy issues. *Professional Psychology: Research and Practice, 20,* 37–43.

Melton, G. B. (1988). Ethical and legal issues in AIDS related practice. *American Psychologist, 43*(11), 941–947.

Miller, D. J., & Thelen, M. H. (1986). Knowledge and beliefs about confidentiality in psychotherapy. *Professional Psychology: Research and Practice, 17*(1), 15–19.

Nagy, T. F. (1989). Revision of *The Ethical Principles of Psychologists*: APA Task Force's progress report—Three years later and ready for review. Paper presented at the annual meeting of the American Psychological Association, August 11–15, New Orleans.

Nodding, N. (1984). *Caring: A feminine approach to ethics and moral education.* Berkeley: University of California.

Pascarella, E. T., & Terenzini, P. T. (1991). *How college effects students.* San Francisco: Jossey-Bass.

Peyton, C. R. (1994). Implications of the 1992 Ethics Code for diverse groups. *Professional Psychology: Research and Practice, 25,* 317–320.

Pope, K. S., & Vasquez, M. J. T. (1991). *Ethics in psychotherapy and counseling: A practical guide for psychologists.* San Francisco: Jossey-Bass.

Ramsey, P. (1970). *The patient as person.* New Haven: Yale University.

Secord, P. F., & Backman, C. W. (1974). *Social psychology.* New York: McGraw-Hill.

Sinclair, C., Poizner, S., Gilmour-Barrett, K., & Randall, D. (1987). The development of a code of ethics for Canadian psychologists. *Canadian Psychology/Psychologie Canadienne, 28*(1), 1–8.

Veatch, R. M. (1987). *The patient as partner.* Bloomington, IN: Indiana University.

Wilson, D. W., & Donnerstein, W. (1976). Legal and ethical aspects of nonreactive social psychological research: An excursion into the public mind. *American Psychologist, 31,* 765–773.

Wise, T. P. (1978). Where the public peril begins: A survey of psychotherapists to determine the effects of *Tarasoff. Stanford Law Review, 31,* 165–190.

CHAPTER 25

A CRITICAL EXAMINATION OF THE ETHICAL PRINCIPLES OF PSYCHOLOGISTS AND CODE OF CONDUCT*

William O'Donohue
Richard Mangold

The American Psychological Association's (APA) Ethics Code (1992) is an influential document that has a great number of profound consequences. If it is used as it is intended, then psychologists rely upon it for "decision rules to cover most situations encountered by psychologists" (APA, 1992, p. 1599). Thus it becomes a comprehensive guide for action that influences the professional behavior of psychologists by defining ethically obligatory, permissible, and impermissible behavior as well as the "higher" aspirations of psychologists. Regulatory bodies also rely upon it to define behavior that is sanctionable. The code (APA, 1992, p. 1598) itself recognizes that "Psychologists and students, whether or not they are APA members, should be aware that the Ethics Code may be applied to them by state psychology boards, courts, or other public bodies." The content of the code can result in actions such as whether psychologists can continue to be licensed, are subject to civil actions, or can

retain membership in the American Psychological Association. Thus, it also functions to define whether a nonpsychologist has been mistreated by defining impermissible professional behavior. Finally, the Ethics Code has consequences concerning the public's perception of the profession of psychology. For example, the code can be scrutinized by the public and conclusions can be made regarding the degree to which the field has its own self-interest or the public's interest in mind.

Given the range of behavior subsumed under the code and the magnitude of consequences of the Ethics Code, it is particularly important that the code be accurate in its assertions about what is ethical and what is unethical. Errors of failing to proscribe some unethical behavior or incorrectly identifying a behavior as unethical when it is in fact ethical can result in serious harm to individuals (either clients or psychologists) as well as damage to psychology's public image. O'Donohue, Fisher, and Krasner (1987, p. 395) have stated, "They [ethical codes] are not beyond criticism: They are not revealed truth or epistemologically incorrigible

*The authors would like to thank Sol Feldman and Karen Strohm Kitchener for their comments on an earlier version of the manuscript.

statements, although sometimes it seems that they are treated as such." It is important to critically examine the code for two principal reasons: (1) Criticism is essential to the growth of knowledge (Lakatos & Musgrave, 1970; Popper, 1965) and hence the improvement of the code; and (2) the Ethics Code takes on an authoritative role in distinguishing ethical and unethical professional conduct. In these official inquiries the code itself is not questioned, but rather a derivative question is addressed: Is some behavior consistent or inconsistent with it? However, at some point it becomes important to ask the prior question: How good is the Ethics Code or a particular ethical principle itself?

This chapter will examine four major questions regarding the quality of the Ethics Code: (1) What is the Ethics Code supposed to do, and is it doing this? (2) What is the quality of the assumptions concerning the nature of morality that are embedded in the Ethics Code? (3) To what degree are the ethical principles mere authoritarian pronouncements as opposed to rational, well-grounded and reasoned conclusions? and (4) To what degree is the Ethics Code consistent with a science of human behavior? However, for purposes of setting an appropriate context for this inquiry a brief history of the APA ethics codes will be presented.

HISTORY OF THE ETHICS CODE

The American Psychological Association was formally established in 1893 but it was not until 1938 that the APA established an ethics committee, eventually adopting an ethics code in 1953. This code was five years in development and involved a unique and quasi-empirical approach in its creation. The APA asked its members for input regarding actual cases involving ethical matters and received one thousand cases to begin their work. From this, the first Ethical Standards of Psychologists (APA, 1953) was developed. The Ethical Standards of Psychologists was 171 pages in length and included sections on ethical standards and public responsibility in client relationships, in teaching, in research, in writing and publishing, and in professional relationships. One of the major drawbacks of this first code was its length. Since 1953 the Ethics Code has been revised seven times (American Psychological Association, 1958, 1963, 1968, 1977, 1979, 1981a, 1992). It is not altogether clear what factors have prompted the revisions or the timing of these revisions.

The current revision, called the Ethical Principles of Psychologists and Code of Conduct (herein called Ethics Code; APA, 1992) was the first major revision in twelve years. It consists of an introduction, a preamble, six general principles (A–F), and specific ethical standards. The six general principles include competence, integrity, professional and scientific responsibility, respect for people's rights and dignity, concern for other's welfare, and social responsibility.

It is important to recognize that there are other APA guidelines for dealing with ethical matters. However, it is also unclear how these documents relate to one another (e.g., Is one superordinate?). The other guidelines include the General Guidelines for Providers of Psychological Services (1987), Specialty Guidelines for the Delivery of Services by Clinical Psychologists, Counseling Psychologists, Industrial/Organizational Psychologists, and School Psychologists (1981b), Ethical Principles in the Conduct of Research with Human Participants (1982), and Standards for Educational and Psychological Tests (1985). The APA has encouraged the development of casebooks that demonstrate examples of behaviors that are ethical and unethical such as the Committee on Professional Standards—Casebook for Providers of Psychological Services (APA, 1983). In addition, different divisions within the APA, such as the clinical, counseling, industrial/organizational, and school psychologists have had the opportunity to expand their own expectations of behavior for members of those divisions (APA, 1981b) while other major APA boards, task forces, and committees have dealt with ethical matters relevant to their own mandates.

FUNCTIONS OF A PROFESSIONAL CODE

In order to understand the scope and impact of the ethical code it is important that we are aware of both its explicit and implicit functions. In other words, what are the possible functions of the Ethics Code and how does it safeguard the public as well as the professional?

A "profession" has been defined by the American Heritage Dictionary (Morris, 1970) as "a body of qualified persons of one specific occupation or field." There is presumptively a body of theory, knowledge, and skills that is utilized by the members of the profession in the performance of their profession. As a result members of society sustain a different relationship with a professional than with a nonprofessional. It is reasonable to expect professionals to be trustworthy, competent, and to cause no harm by their professional behavior. In light of this, professionals and professional organizations, including the APA, have developed mechanisms to balance their own self-interests against the interests of the people with whom they provide services. Ethics codes can be described as moral guides to self-regulation. Ethics codes can also be described as principles specifying the rights and responsibilities of professionals not only in their relationship with the client but with other professionals as well. To this end, the APA's Ethics Code appears to have the same primary goals as the ethics codes of many other professions.

The APA states explicitly that "The Ethical Code is intended to provide standards of professional conduct that can be applied by the APA and by other bodies that choose to adopt them.... Whether or not a psychologist has violated the Ethics Code does not by itself determine whether he or she is legally liable in a court action, whether a contract is enforceable, or whether other legal consequences occur. The results are based on legal rather than ethical rules" (p. 1598). In the preamble, the Ethics Code states further that it "is intended to provide both the general principles and the decision rules to cover most situations encountered by psychologists. It has as its primary goal the welfare and protection of the individual and groups with whom psychologists work. It is the individual responsibility of each psychologist to aspire to the highest possible standards of conduct.... the Code is intended to provide both the general principles and the decision rules to cover most situations encountered by psychologists" (p. 1599). Further, "each psychologist supplements, but does not violate, the Ethics Code's values and rules on the basis of guidance drawn from personal values, culture, and experience" (p. 1599). This last point is particularly interesting as it indicates that the APA considers its professional ethical code as superordinate to other ethical commitments and therefore it should override a personal or cultural ethical commitment in cases in which these are inconsistent with the Ethics Code.

An important question becomes, Do professionals have a morality of their own, which is distinct and perhaps even inconsistent with ordinary morality (i.e., universal moral principles that apply to all humans)? Freedman (1978) has argued that professional morality (i.e., the morality attached to

a professional role) is different from, and can conflict with, ordinary morality. Freedman maintains that professionals are "more constrained by their professional values than are non-professionals and, conversely, take into less account those considerations which ordinarily apply" (p. 1). Freedman provides an example of the differences in confidentiality as experienced by the medical professional and the layperson. On the one hand, breaches of confidentiality have potentially more serious consequences for the professional, the assumption being that anything divulged during the process of disclosure is strictly private because confidentiality is crucial to enhancing full and accurate communication and such communication is essential for the appropriate functioning of the profession. On the other hand, during ordinary discourse, the individual must explicitly request that information be kept confidential and violations of any promise are regarded as less serious, as confidentiality and completely open communication are less essential to these interactions. This indicates that confidentiality is a "stronger value in professional morality than in ordinary morality. Thus, professional morality with its different hierarchy of values can lead professionals to resolve value conflicts in different ways than ordinary morality would recommend" (O'Donohue et al., 1987, p. 394). Thus part of the function of an Ethics Code may be to explicate these departures from ordinary morality.

In addition to the argument suggesting that there are primary differences between professional and ordinary ethics, one could argue that Ethics Codes serve to preempt external policing. That is, by allowing professional organizations to police themselves these organizations can escape the usual ways in which ordinary oversight mechanisms (e.g., legislation and law enforcement) might deal with a problem. For example, sex scandals involving congressmen and minors in the recent past were judged by their peers to be violations of congressional ethics and were dealt with by filing "letters of reproach" against those congressmen involved. Ordinary policing of these individuals might have required them to face criminal charges and perhaps even prison sentences. Furthermore, the incidence of ethical violations among psychologists including sexual involvement with clients and harassment continue to be a major concern (Hall & Hare-Mustin, 1983). One might rightly question whether or not professional organizations can in fact police themselves. Thus another possible function of an ethics code may be to preempt external oversight by real or illusory internal policing.

Perhaps one of the drawbacks to "policing ourselves" is that we are not fully protected by those processes that are intrinsic to American law. One might question the extent to which individuals' rights are in fact safeguarded or the individual is extended appropriate due process during ethical inquiries.

In sum, although the APA explicitly states that the Ethics Code should serve as a guideline for professional behavior it is unclear exactly what broader functions the code is attempting to serve. If it is to outline departures from ordinary morality and to claim that these override personal morality than it would be useful to explicate arguments for this. If it is to preempt external policing then a careful review of the arguments against external policing needs to be made. External policing (such as making proscribed acts illegal and subject to civil or criminal litigation) may in fact allow greater safeguarding of rights and may result in a more just judicial process. These possibilities should not be ruled out a priori.

THE ETHICS CODE AND ETHICAL THEORY

In this section we will examine the relationship between the Ethics Code and ethical theory. When the code states that some act is unethical, what general ethical standards are being relied upon to make this claim? The broader ethical theory that is implicit in the APA's code is important because it has direct implications for three critical issues: (1) for precisely understanding what an ethical standard may mean; (2) for evaluating the Ethics Code—if the implicit ethical theory is problematic then it may be the case that the Ethics Code is flawed; and (3) for identifying relevant issues for determining whether an ethical standard has been violated. For example, if the broader ethical theory holds that an act is bad only when a person intends bad consequences, then ascertaining the individual's intentions can become critical in ethical investigations. On the other hand, if the broader ethical theory evaluates the moral worth of an action only by a consideration of the act's consequences relative to other possible acts, then only actual consequences and the possible effects of alternative acts need to be assessed. Conversely, if an individual is to have a fair opportunity to defend his or her actions, then the ethical premises of the

ethical code must be clear. Without this, the grounds for indicating that an *ethical* violation (as opposed to, say, a violation of organizational procedure) has occurred is unclear. Moreover, a legitimate ground is not open upon which to base a defense: "My actions were not unethical in some fuller sense implied by the code or principle." Thus, it appears important to both potential defendants and to potential complainants that they fully understand the content and exact nature of the ethical principles and to do this, we claim, involves an explication of the ethical premises and assumptions involved in the Ethics Code.

It is difficult to answer questions concerning the underlying ethical theory that is relied upon by the code because the code itself is silent on this issue. There is no explicit mention in the code regarding what general standards were relied upon to produce the specific ethical pronouncements contained in the code. Moreover, the language it uses to express ethical standards is somewhat unusual and puzzling. It uses the indicative mode ("Psychologists do not engage in sexual intimacies with current patients or clients," p. 1605) rather than one that uses the language in which ethical statements are usually made—"ought," "must," or "should." However, it is clear that the code does not intend these to be simple indicative claims. For example, it would be absurd to argue that the ethical standard quoted above is not true because some psychologists do in fact engage in sexual intimacies. This kind of "facts of the matter" is not relevant to this normative claim (or other normative claims). Rather, this claim and other ethical claims deal with what should be the case. However, it is unclear why the APA has chosen this indirect form of ethical language rather than the more straightforward "Psychologists *should not* engage in sexual intimacies with current patients or clients."

Although the code does not explicate the general ethical theory upon which it is based, it appears clear that certain candidates can be ruled out. For example, this is not a theologically based ethical code. No appeals appear to be made concerning issues such as "Whatever God wills is what ought to be done." This is not surprising given the secular nature of psychology. Moreover, this code does not appear to rely upon ethical relativism. The code views itself as applying to all psychologists (or at least all those practicing in North America). It makes no appeal that this code is not relevant to different groups of individuals. This is interesting because internally the code (APA, 1992, p. 1601) suggests that there are situations in which differences in "age, gender, race, ethnicity, national origin, religion, sexual orientation, disability, language or socioeconomic status" necessitate that psychologists make certain adjustments or special treatments. However, it appears to view professional ethics absolutistically and therefore as equally applicable to all psychologists regardless of these differences among psychologists.

Important to an issue that we will discuss below—on the compatibility of science and morality—the Ethics Code is not based upon ethical nihilism. Ethical nihilism suggests that there is nothing that is morally right or morally wrong. This is obviously not relevant in that a nihilist cannot consistently produce an ethics code. Relevant to the next issue we discuss—justifying an ethics code—the code is not based on ethical skepticism, that is, that it is impossible to know what is ethically right or ethically wrong. The code also is not based on ethical egoism (each person ought to act to maximize his own good or well-being).

Two influential ethical theories that may function as the general ethical grounds of the code are utilitarianism and deontological ethics. Eyde and Quaintance (1988) have interpreted the previous version of the code as subsuming Kantian deontological ethics. Kant (1943) suggested that the highest good was a good will. Kant rejected the notion that an act was good because of its consequences: "the good will is not good because of what it effects or accomplishes or because of its adequacy to achieve some proposed end" (p. 49). Thus Kant believed that when a person acts with a good will the person acts out of respect for moral laws. The moral law is embodied in Kant's categorical imperative, which may be stated in two forms, which Kant took to be equivalent: (1) Act only according to that maxim by which you can at the same time will that it should become a universal law; (2) Act so that you treat humanity, whether in your own person or in that of another, always as an end and never as a means only. From the categorical imperative Kant thought that specific duties can be derived.

In this view the Ethics Code would be an attempt to derive from the absolute moral law the duties a psychologist holds by virtue of being a psychologist. One criticism of Kant's deontological theory is that it is difficult to derive specific duties from his categorical imperative. However, it would be useful if the APA ethics committee would indicate

the extent to which the Ethics Code is based upon an account of a psychologist's duties. It would be useful to ascertain whether these duties have been accurately enumerated and it is also important because it indicates the irrelevance of an act's consequences in a deontological ethical theory in ascertaining the ethics of certain behaviors.

A utilitarian theory in direct contrast to a deontological theory judges the ethical worth of an act by the act's consequences. Utilitarian theories differ according to what kind of consequences are of importance (e.g., happiness vs. pleasure). Utilitarian theories also differ to the extent to which they believe that the consequences of each individual act need to be considered separately (i.e., act utilitarianism), as opposed to the belief that acts fall into some broad classes and therefore rules can be constructed regarding which classes of acts generally have better consequences (i.e., rule utilitarianism). Given the fact that the Ethics Code consists of general rules, it seems reasonable to believe that if the code is based upon a utilitarian theory it is based upon rule utilitarian theory. Otherwise it would simply need to indicate that each act needs to be considered in a casuistic manner.

But if the code is based upon a utilitarian ethic it is not clear what kinds of consequences the Ethics Code considers in judging the moral worth of actions. For example, John Stuart Mill (1863) criticized Bentham's (1838) version of utilitarian ethics on the grounds that Bentham failed to distinguish between the quality of a pleasure. Mill thought that it is better to be Socrates unsatisfied than a pig satisfied. Thus, in order to have a clearly workable utilitarian ethic it is not only important to specify what kinds of consequences are morally relevant but also to specify a weighing of these consequences. (A weighing of consequences to clients vs. consequences to others might also be necessary.)

Finally, there are indigenous psychological theories of morality and the relationship between these and the APA's Ethics Code is also unclear. Kohlberg (1981) has arguably the most influential psychological account of morality. Kohlberg has claimed to have found culturally universal stages of moral development. There are six developmental stages that fall within three moral levels (preconventional, conventional, and postconventional or autonomous). Two issues are of concern here. First, Kohlberg's theory is at least partly deterministic. That is, the extent to which one advances along these stages is determined at least in part by the quality of one's environment (e.g., schooling, parenting, models). Thus, could a legitimate defense against a moral failing be that one has been a victim of one's poor environment and therefore has not developed morally as one should? The second and more serious issue is that in Kohlberg's conception the highest stage of moral development is characterized by individual principles of conscience. Moreover, these principles are not concrete but abstract, general, and universal. The second level of moral development, on the other hand, is oriented to obeying authority or concrete rules. The question becomes, does the APA's concrete Ethics Code influence one to behave in a manner in which psychological theory itself indicates is a lower stage of moral reasoning?

In summary, it is not clear in what account of morality the Ethics Code is grounded. This is problematic for several reasons but particularly because it vitiates the process of fair ethical inquiries. It is recommended that the ethical grounds of the code be explicated and defended in order both to better understand the code and its application as well as to expose it to the light of criticism so that improvements can be made.

EVIDENCE, ARGUMENT, AND THE ETHICS CODE

Apparently the APA believes that it has discovered how psychologists *qua* psychologists should behave. How can we defend these ethical judgments? By what method were these ethical claims produced? To what degree are these claims warranted by evidence and argument?

Because of the authoritative and regulative role of the code, it may be useful to very briefly argue for the possibility of error in the code. Three considerations are relevant here. First, the code itself has undergone seven previous revisions (American Psychological Association, 1953, 1958, 1963, 1968, 1977, 1979, 1981a, 1990). Thus, the possibility of flaws perhaps is uncontroversial even to the APA itself. However, admittedly, there might be some ambiguity in this matter. The APA can of course argue that its code has always perfectly tracked the ethics but the revisions were necessary because the underlying ethics changed. However, no such argument has been advanced and since morality commonly has been viewed as being fixed, the first interpretation seems more plausible.

(It is interesting to note the issue of the ethical responsibilities of the APA toward individuals who have been judged as engaging in unethical behavior by a previous code, e.g., barter arrangements and certain cases of therapist–client sexual contact, but whose behavior would no longer be judged unethical by a revised code.)

Second, the Ethics Code is not based upon an allegedly infallible procedure but rather a human product (and a committee at that!). Thus, unlike certain systems of theological ethics, which posit ethical standards as emanating from an infallible god, there is no reason internal to the code to believe that the Ethics Code is epistemologically incorrigible.

Third, other professional organizations have devised their own ethics codes and these in many respects are different from the APA's code. This inconsistency raises the question of which is right. For example, the ethics code of the Association for the Advancement of Behavior Therapy (1977) contains the following: "B. Has the choice of treatment methods been adequately considered? 1. Does the published literature show the procedure to be the best one available for that problem?" In contrast the APA Ethics Code (APA, 1992, p. 1600) states, "Psychologists rely on scientifically and professionally derived knowledge when making scientific or professional judgments or when engaging in scholarly or professional endeavors." Although the general drift of the codes is similar, the APA's Ethics Code seems to be looser because it renders a decision as ethical as long as the decision was based upon scientific and professional knowledge. (In fact in the previous standard, p. 1600, "Maintaining Expertise", the code states that the professional should "maintain a reasonable level of awareness of current scientific and professional information.") The AABT code is much more rigorous in that it requires specific knowledge, i.e., a rather thorough knowledge of the scientific outcome literature regarding the most effective treatment, and does not appear to countenance the relevance of "professional knowledge." However given these inconsistencies, both cannot be correct and therefore it raises the possibility that the APA Ethics Code is not correct.

The question becomes, Are the assertions of the Ethics Code correct? This unfortunately is a very difficult question to address as the code itself simply makes assertions without any appeals to evidence or arguments. If we take the hallmark of rationality to be the explicit consideration of all relevant evidence, arguments, and counterarguments in arriving at a conclusion, then the code does not appear to be a document within the rational tradition. Rather, the document as presented simply appears to be a series of bald, undefended, unargued, authoritarian fiats. If we as psychologists want to be rational and to form our beliefs on the basis of argument and evidence, then the Ethics Code appears to present us with serious problems.

As a case in point the Ethics Code now states, "Psychologists do not engage in sexual intimacies with a former therapy patient or client for at least two years after cessation or termination of professional services" (p. 1605). The question becomes, Is this ethical standard correct? In evaluating this claim one is immediately confronted with the (unanswered) question considered in the previous section, i.e., what ethical premises and theories underlie this claim? Therefore one is in the unfortunate position of guessing what is the relevant ethical premise upon which to construct a possible argument. If one adopts a utilitarian ethical standard, then one needs to examine data concerning the effects of sexual intimacies on former patients. However, the Ethics Code does not cite data nor is there any companion document that provides the evidence and argument. Questions arise such as: What evidence or arguments resulted in this change from previous ethics codes? What evidence is there that the passage of two years is relevant to the effects of sexual intimacies on former clients? How good is this evidence? Is there any contrary evidence? How good is the total body of evidence in supporting the notion that after two years the net amount of happiness relative to the net amount of pain renders this sexual contact as ethically permissible?

In summary, because the Ethics Code does not argue or cite evidence but rather simply asserts, it provides no acceptable warrant for its assertions. Epistemologically its acceptance relies upon an authoritarian appeal (Because the APA says so!) rather than upon an epistemology that recognizes the importance of defending one's claims by arguments, and the importance of evidence and critiques of counterarguments and opposing positions. It is suggested at a minimum that the APA prepare a companion document to provide evidence and arguments in defense of these now bald assertions.

THE ETHICS CODE AND PSYCHOLOGICAL ACCOUNTS OF HUMAN BEHAVIOR

What is the relationship between the factual claims of science—*is* statements—and the normative claims of ethics—*ought* statements? There are several basic schools of thought on this important issue. One school is that of ethical naturalism, which asserts that ethical claims can be derived from factual claims. Skinner (1971) provides an example of this when he attempts to define "what is morally good" with the empirical matter of "what is reinforcing."

This attempt has been criticized on many grounds, but one that strikes at the heart of ethical naturalism is G. E. Moore's (1960) naturalistic fallacy. This fallacy states that one cannot define ethical terms such as "good" or "what ought to be done" in terms that are purely factual, descriptive, and nonevaluative. Moore (1960) has argued that this is fallacious because this would make many open and debatable questions closed and trivial. As Moore states, "Whatever definition be offered, it may always be asked, with significance, of the complex so defined, whether it is itself good" (p. 19).

For example, if we follow Skinner's suggestion and define good as that which is reinforcing, when we ask is x good we need to ask is x reinforcing. However, if we ask the seemingly open and debatable question, "is that which is reinforcing good?" our question becomes (using the definition) the closed and trivial question, is that which is reinforcing reinforcing? Although the first question seems worth debating, the second question does not. Thus, Moore presents some reasons to believe that moral terms cannot be defined in terms of nonevaluative natural properties.

The second school of thought on the relationship between science and morality is that these two are incompatible. For example, Carl Hempel (1965) also argues that science cannot establish objective standards of right and wrong. According to Hempel, at best science can provide us with instrumental judgments of value. That is, science can only tell us which means are instrumental for bringing about certain ends. Hempel illustrates the relevance of science for normative ethics by involving Laplace's demon—a perfect scientific intelligence that knows all the laws of nature, everything that is going on in the universe at any given moment, and can calculate with infinite speed and precision from the state of the universe at any particular moment its state at any other past or future moment:

> Let us assume, then, that faced with a moral decision, we are able to call upon the Laplacean demon as a consultant. What help might we get from him? Suppose that we have to choose one of several alternative courses of action open to us and that we want to know which of these we ought to follow. The demon would then be able to tell us, for any contemplated choice, what its consequences would be for the future course of the universe, down to the most minute detail, however remote in space and time. But, having done this for each of the alternative courses of action under consideration, the demon would have completed his task; he would have given us all the information that an ideal science might provide under the circumstances. And yet he would not have resolved our moral problem, for this requires a decision as to which of the several alternative sets of consequences mapped out by the demon as attainable to us is the best; which of them we ought to bring about. And the burden of the decision would still fall upon our shoulders; it's we who would have to commit ourselves to an unconditional (absolute) judgment of value by singling out one of the sets of consequences as superior to the alternatives. (pp. 88–89)

Kant (1943) has claimed that "ought implies can." That is, to meaningfully claim that someone ought to do x is to imply that he could do x. Thus, it is contradictory to assert that someone ought to do something that the person cannot do: It is wrong to claim that Jane ought to have jumped 18 feet in the air without any aid when Jane simply cannot do this.

Science has been considered by some as a search for universal laws. All general scientific laws state impossibilities. Newton's second law, for example, states that it is impossible for any two objects to behave differently than to be attracted to each other in direct proportion to their masses and in inverse proportion to the square of the distance between them. Thus a deterministic universal scientific law states that it is impossible for the entity to behave in any other way.

Thus, if human behavior can be subsumed under deterministic scientific laws (as many would as the goal of scientific psychology), then this same behavior falls outside the purview of morality. The prominent psychologist B. F. Skinner (1971, p. 101) clearly realized the incompatibility of a scientific determinism and morality:

> In what we may call the prescientific view (and the word is not necessarily pejorative) a person's

behavior is at least to some extent his own achievement. He is free to deliberate, decide, and act, possibly in original ways, and he is to be given credit for his successes and blamed for his failures. In the scientific view (and the word is not necessarily honorific) a person's behavior is determined by a genetic endowment traceable to evolutionary history of the species and by the environmental circumstances to which as an individual he has been exposed. Neither view can be proved, but it is in the nature of scientific inquiry that the evidence should shift in favor of the second.

It is also important to realize that this incompatibility is held not only by radical behaviorists but also by other psychological determinists, e.g., biological determinists (perhaps the early Freud and many physiological psychologists).

An interesting aspect of this incompatibility is illustrated in the dispositions of ethical violations. At times violators of the Ethics Code are required to enter into psychotherapy. But, then, how are we to understand this: Is psychotherapy an application of scientific principles for the treatment of moral failings?

Therefore the question arises to what extent is the Ethics Code consistent with the science of human behavior or its regulative principles? If morality implies human agency—the freedom to make choices—and if a science of human behavior (or at least some influential versions of it) presumes determinism—the impossibility to behave otherwise—then to what extent does it make sense to have an ethics code for psychologists?

CONCLUSIONS

We conclude that the full functions of the Ethics Code are unclear; that the ethical theory or premises upon which the code is based is not explicit and is poorly understood; that since no evidence or arguments for the claims within the code are provided it is epistemologically undefended; and that it is inconsistent with influential scientific accounts of human behavior.

This is a most unfortunate state of affairs for the public as well as for psychologists. These problems raise such profound questions about the status of the code that in its current form it should not be regarded as an acceptable document upon which psychologists can guide their actions or evaluate the actions of others. Admittedly these problems are not easily resolved and some of them directly involve difficult and fundamental philosophical issues. However, we suggest that this is not an artifact of our arguments but rather an inevitable consequence of being involved in the types of complex activities that comprise the profession of psychology.

Thus, these need to be addressed by adequately consulting the relevant literature. Although it is beyond the scope of this chapter to present and argue for concrete proposals, one possibility deserves mention. The prominent philosopher of science Sir Karl Popper (1992) has recently provided an interesting and somewhat radical proposal for professional ethics based on his epistemological fallibilism. Popper (1992, pp. 201–202) suggests the following ethics code:

> 2. It is impossible to avoid all mistakes, or even all those mistakes that are, in themselves, avoidable. All scientists are continually making mistakes. The old idea that one can avoid mistakes and is therefore duty bound to avoid them, must be revised: it is itself mistaken....
>
> 5. We must therefore revise our attitude to mistakes. It is here that our practical ethical reform must begin. For the attitude of the old professional ethics leads us to cover up our mistakes, to keep them secret and to forget them as soon as possible....
>
> 6. The new basic principle is that in order to learn to avoid making mistakes, we must learn from our mistakes. To cover up mistakes is, therefore, the greatest intellectual sin....
>
> 9. Since we must learn from our mistakes, we must also learn to accept, indeed accept gratefully, when others draw our attention to our mistakes. When in turn we draw other people's attention to their mistakes, we should always remember that we have made similar mistakes ourselves. And we should remember that the greatest scientists have made mistakes. I certainly do not want to say that our mistakes are, usually, forgivable; we must never let our attention slacken. But it is humanly impossible to avoid making mistakes time and again....

Thus, Popper calls for a radical new orientation to ethical mistakes based on his notion of the inevitability of errors in human knowledge and conduct. This might provide an interesting epistemological grounding for the construction of the code as well as providing useful guidelines for the broader aims of the code. However, additional work is required regarding identifying acceptable ethical standards to define a "mistake" as well as understanding what is legitimately subject to ethical evaluation (human agency) and what is outside the purview of moral discourse (determined behavior).

REFERENCES

American Educational Research Association, American Psychological Association, and National Council on Measurement in Education. (1985). Standards for educational and psychological tests. Washington, D. C.: American Psychological Association.

American Psychological Association. (1953). Ethical standards of psychologists. Washington, D. C.: American Psychological Association.

American Psychological Association. (1958). Standards of ethical behavior for psychologists. American Psychologist, 13, 268–271.

American Psychological Association. (1963). Ethical standards of psychologists. American Psychologist, 18, 56–60.

American Psychological Association. (1968). Ethical standards of psychologists. American Psychologist, 23, 357–361.

American Psychological Association. (1977). Ethical standards of psychologists. APA Monitor, March, 22–23.

American Psychological Association. (1977). Ethical guidelines for the delivery of human services. Washington, D. C.: American Psychological Association.

American Psychological Association. (1979). Ethical standards of psychologists. Washington, D. C.: American Psychological Association.

American Psychological Association. (1981a). Ethical principles of psychologists. American Psychologist, 36, 633–638.

American Psychological Association. (1981b). Specialty guidelines for the delivery of services by clinical (counseling, industrial/organizational, and school) psychologists. American Psychologist, 36, 639–681.

American Psychological Association. (1982). Ethical principles in the conduct of research with human participants. Washington, D. C.: American Psychological Association.

American Psychological Association. (1983). Casebook for providers of psychological services. American Psychologist, 38, 708–713.

American Psychological Association. (1987). General guidelines for providers of psychological services. American Psychologist, 42, 712–723.

American Psychological Association. (1990). Ethical principles of psychologists (Amended June 2, 1989). American Psychologist, 45, 390–395.

American Psychological Association. (1992). APA council adopts new ethics code. APA Monitor, October, 5–7.

American Psychological Association. (1992). Ethical principles of psychologists and code of conduct. American Psychologist, 47(12), 1597–1612.

Association for Advancement of Behavior Therapy. (1977). Ethical issues for human services. Behavior Therapy, 8, v–vi.

Bentham, J. (1838). The works of Jeremy Bentham. London: Hutchinson.

Eyde, L., & Quaintance, M. (1988). Ethical issues and cases in the practice of personnel psychology. *Professional Psychology: Research and Practice, 19,* 148–154.

Freedman, B. (1978). A meta-ethics for professional morality. *Ethics, 89,* 1–19.

Hall, J., & Hare-Mustin, R. (1983). Sanctions and the diversity of ethical complaints against psychologists. *American Psychologist, 38,* 714–729.

Hempel, C. G. (1965). Science and human values. In C. G. Hempel (Ed.), *Aspects of scientific explanation.* New York: Free Press.

Kant, I. (1943). *Kant's groundwork of the metaphysic of morals.* London: Hutchinson.

Kohlberg, L. (1981). *Essays in moral development.* New York: Harper and Row.

Lakatos, I., & Musgrave, A. (Eds.). (1970). *Criticism and the growth of knowledge.* Cambridge: Cambridge University Press.

Mill, J. S. (1863). *Utilitarianism.* London: Hutchinson.

Moore, G. E. (1960). *Principia ethica.* New York: Cambridge University Press.

Morris, W. (Ed.). (1970). *The American heritage dictionary of the English language* (pp. 1044–1045). New York: Houghton Mifflin.

Nielsen, K. (1967). Problems of ethics. In P. Edwards (Ed.), *The encyclopedia of philosophy.* New York: Macmillan.

O'Donohue, W., Fisher, J. E., & Krasner, L. (1987). Ethics and the elderly. In L. Carstensen & B. Edelstein (Eds.), *Handbook of clinical gerontology.* New York: Pergamon.

Popper, K. (1965). *The logic of scientific discovery* (2nd ed.). New York: Harper & Row.

Popper, K. (1992). *In search of a better world.* London: Routledge & Kegan Paul.

Skinner, B. F. (1971). *Beyond freedom and dignity.* New York: Alfred A. Knopf.

INDEX

Abrahamsen, A., 92, 189, 191
abstract objects, 267–8
abstraction, reflective, 72–4
action (representation), 181
activation process, 210, 211
Acuna, C., 214
Adair, J.G., 369
adaptability/adaptation, 198–9, 229
adjustment path (value), 327, 329
Adler, Alfred, 279, 284
adrenergic system, 209
affirmative stimulus meaning, 99–100
agency theory, 199–200
agnosia, 213–14
Ahumada, A., 214
Alexander, R.D., 333
Alford, D.J., 304
Alston, W.P., 228
altruism, selfishness and, 333–6
Amari, S.-I., 197
American Psychological Association, 61, 291, 317–19,
    361–70, 371–9
Amit, J., 197
Amundson, R., 122
amygdala system, 210, 211, 215
analogic synthesis, 101–2
analytic truth, 130–2
analytical behaviorism, 111
analyticity, 99–101, 104, 136, 163
Anderson, J.A., 209
Anderson, J.R., 162, 166, 175
anger, 85–9 *passim,* 213
Anna O. (case study), 301
anomalous monism, 105
anthropocentrism, 135–6, 265–8
anthropomorphism, 269
antimentalism, 355, 356, 358
antinaturalism, 22–3, 184, 185
Antony, L.M., 5, 8
appearance, potentiality and, 219–22
Aristotle, 19, 21, 38, 90, 93, 129, 150, 222, 228, 236,
    267, 358
Arkes, H., 41

Armstrong, D.M., 138
arousal, 210, 211, 215
Arrowood, A.J., 231
articulation of values, 322–4, 326, 327, 337
artificial intelligence, 90, 93, 158, 161–2, 164, 168, 173,
    176, 182, 184, 186–97, 199, 245, 254
Ashby, W.R., 211
associationism, 177
Astrom, K.J., 191
asymmetric dependency, 178–9, 181
attentive consciousness, 210–13
attribution, 277
Austin, G., 55
Austin, J., 266
autonomous individuals, 345–7
autonomy, 364
    behavior therapist dilemma, 352–9
auxiliary interpretive strategies, 335–7, 337
Azrin, N.H., 109

Bachrach, H., 291–3, 297, 301
Backman, C.W., 366
Bacon, F., 35, 113, 151, 346
BACON program, 61, 170
bad theories, 8–9, 249
Baez, Joan, 347
Ballard, D.H., 190
barbarism, 341, 342, 343
Barchas, J.E., 209
Barker, P., 51
Barlow, D., 300
Barnard, S., 155
Barndon, J., 190
Barnes, B., 30, 37
Baron, R.M., 322
Barrett, P.H., 60
Barsalou, L.W., 249
Bartley, W.W., 23, 35, 305, 308, 310–14
Barwise, J., 128, 249
basal forebrain systems, 209–10
basal ganglia, 210, 211, 214
Baumrind, D., 367–8
Beauchamp, T., 353–4, 356, 362, 364–5, 367

Bechtel, W., 92, 189, 191
Beck, A.T., 304
Beekman, G.J., 211, 222
Beer, R.D., 193, 197
behavior, 111–12
   mechanistic, 149–55
behavior therapists' dilemma, 318, 352–9
behaviorism, 66, 79–80, 160
   folk psychology and, 254–5, 264–9
   linguistic, 126–39
   opposition to Cartesianism, 81–94
   psychological epistemology, 108–22
   Quine's contribution, 96–106
   radical (Skinner), 79, 126, 141–8, 358
Beitman, B.D., 280
Bekesy, G. von, 213, 222
beliefs, 12, 54
   desires and, 257–60, 262, 296, 321, 325–6
   irrational, 280, 304–14
   supernatural, 134, 264–5
Bell, A.G., 61
Bell, Daniel, 44, 45
beneficence principle, 354–5
Bentham, Jeremy, 375
Ben–Ze'ev, A., 230, 233, 236, 239–40
Bergin, A., 292, 293, 295
Bergström, L., 100–1
Berkowitz, L., 42, 56
Berman, A., 211
Bernard, M.E., 306, 307–8
Berth, E.W., 71
Bickhard, M.H., 175–9, 181–2, 190, 193, 196, 198
Binswanger, L., 134
biological approach to brain, 158, 207–22
biological behaviorism, 79
biology, evolutionary, 91, 93, 113–14
Bios, 151–2, 153
Black, J., 170
Blanco, M.I., 212–13
Block, N., 176
Bloor, D., 30, 37–8, 40
Boas, F., 40
body–mind relation, 82–4, 93, 97, 105, 116, 152, 157, 164
Boehme, G., 35
Bohm, D., 186, 220
Bohr, N., 220
Bok, S., 364
Boring, E.G., 86
Bossomaier, T., 197
bounded rationality, 166–7, 171
Bowler, P., 358
Bowling Green group, 50, 51
Boyd, R., 4
Boyle, R., 341
Bracewell, R.N., 209, 221
Bradshaw, G.L., 52, 60, 61, 67

brain, 116, 275
   biological approach, 158, 207–22
   in Cartesianism, 89–92
   philosophy of mind, 99–105, 142–5
Brandt, Richard, 294–7
Brannigan, A., 45
Brentano, F., 83, 211, 212, 216
Breuer, Josef, 287, 301
Brewer, W.F., 53, 54
Bridgman, P., 84, 87, 102
Brillouin, L., 220
Brody, B.A., 214
Brody, N., 301
Bromley, D., 273
Brooks, C.V., 215
Brooks, R.A., 193, 196, 197
Broughton, J.M., 68
Brown, H.I., 4, 24, 31, 188, 199, 310, 311
Brown, J.R., 38
Bruner, J., 266
Bucy, P.C., 211
Buehler, K., 35
Buller, D.J., 91
Bunge, M., 216
Burkitt, A.N., 197
Burtt, E.A., 150, 359
Button, G., 40

Campbell, D., 2, 43, 46, 74, 312
Campbell, F., 221
Campbell, R.L., 176–7, 181, 190, 193, 196, 198
Canguilhem, G., 40
Cannon, W., 209
Canterbury case, 353–4
Cantril, H., 235
Cardozo, S.R., 304
Carey, S., 53, 244, 247
Carley, K., 45
Carlson, W.B., 60, 61
Carlton, E.H., 221
Carnap, R., 35, 96, 111, 116, 163
Cartesian dualism, 211–12
Cartesian linguistics, 89–90
Cartesian materialism, 90–3
Cartesianism, 80, 81–94
Cartwright, N., 249
Case, T., 185
Catania, A.C., 135, 358
Cattell, R.B., 66
causal counterfactual, 136–7
causal determinism, 355, 356
causal explanations, 358
causal hypothesis, 298–9
causal meanings, 150–1
causal patient, 136
causality, 114–15

causation, 135–9, 150–3, 268
causes/functions (difference), 86–9
cerebral cortex, 209–11, 213–14
Chalmers, D.J., 190
Chambers, C.M., 366
characterization, 228
Charness, N., 167
Charniak, E., 244
Chassan, J., 300
Chater, N., 188, 248, 254, 276–7
Cherian, S., 193, 197
Cherniak, C., 23, 24
Chew, G., 220
Chi, M.T.H., 53
children (conceptual changes), 53–4
Childress, J.F., 362, 364–5, 367
Chinese Room, 163–4
Chinn, C.A., 53, 54
Chipman, S., 218
cholinergic system, 209
Chomsky, N., 40, 74, 80, 89–90, 93, 98, 127, 130, 177,
    254, 347
Christensen, W., 200
Christiansen, M., 254
Chubin, D., 45
chunking mechanisms, 165–6
Churchland, Patricia, 272, 276
Churchland, Paul, 158, 186, 188–90, 197, 248, 270–4
Ciaranello, R.D., 209
Cicchetti, D., 43
circularity, 9–13, 29–31
civic responsibility, 344–5
civic tradition, 340–1
Clark, C., 363
Clement, J., 58
clinical psychology and philosophy, 279
    irrational beliefs, 304–14
    psychoanalysis, 281–7
    psychoanalytic therapy, 291–302
COAST program, 52
code of conduct, 371–79
codes of ethics, 361–70
cognition
    computational theories, 160–71
    typical emotions, 158, 227–8, 235–8
cognitive abilities, 20, 22–8, 29, 31
cognitive adaptation, 193
cognitive approach (psychology of science), 50–62,
    66–75
cognitive behavior therapy, 292, 294–6, 299, 302, 305,
    312
cognitive dissonance, 133–4
cognitive errors, 304
cognitive psychology, 357
    of science, 3, 66–75
    of scientific knowledge, 69–74
cognitive revolution, 80, 357–8

cognitive science, history and, 60–1
cognitive science and psychology, 157–9
    computational theories, 160–71
    computationalism (problems), 173–82
    folk psychology, 159, 243–78
    naturalized cognitive science, 184–200
    neurobehavioral science, 207–22
    typical emotions, 227–41
Cohen, L.J., 40
Collett, P., 40
Collingwood, R.G., 121
Collins, H., 41, 46
Collins, R., 44
commonsense, folk theories and, 246–9
commonsense knowledge, 134
commonwealth of learning, 347
communal conception of human nature, 333–7
communal service, 328–9, 335, 337
comparative concern (emotion), 230–2
compatibilism, 356–7
competitive rivalry, 231
complex of values, 331, 332
complexity, 23, 252–3
computational science, 91
computationalism, 51, 261, 262
    cognition theories, 160–71
    problems with, 158, 173–82
computerized tomography scans, 221
computers
    epistemology for, 162–4
    philosophy of mind and, 217–19
    psychology of science and, 51–3
    rationality and, 23–4, 26, 28
Comte, A., 35, 38, 39
con–sequences/consequences, 214–15
conceptual analyses, 122, 264–9, 276
conceptual nervous system, 115, 116
concomitant variation, 137, 138
confidence estimates, 215
confidentiality, 341–2, 363–5, 373
confirmation bias, 22–3, 30
conformity, 231–2
connectionism, 53, 67, 92, 94, 158, 162, 174, 176, 182,
    187, 189, 191, 196, 254
consciousness, 229–30, 236–7
    attentive, 210–13
    narrative, 214–15
    objective, 213–14
consequences, ethics of, 344
constructional realism, 219
constructivism, 41, 46–7
contagion model of knowledge, 45
contingencies, 41, 265
    linguistic behaviorism, 127–9, 135
    of reinforcement, 110–12, 115, 117, 141–8
control, 277
    intelligence and, 192–6

control (*cont.*)
  prediction and, 142–3, 144
  system, 191, 192
cooperation, 231
Copernicus, 81, 282
correspondence forms, 158, 174–7
correspondence theory of truth, 36, 129
counterempiricism, 253, 254
counterfactual reasoning, 55–6, 58
Craighead, W.E., 307
Crandall, R., 367
Crawford, T., 306–8
creative marginality path, 328–9
creativity, 72–4, 169–70
Crego, C.A., 366
critical rationalism, 280, 305, 310–14
Critical Realist movement, 185
critical reflection, 327
Cunningham, D.K., 304
Cunningham, M., 192–4, 195, 196
cybernetics, 160, 173, 187, 192
CYC project, 182

Dakin, S., 231
Danziger, K., 46
Darden, L., 53
Darley, J.M., 276
Darwin, Charles, 45, 60, 73, 83, 113, 114, 134, 210, 282
Daugman, J.G., 221
David, C., 281
Davidson, D., 40, 105, 257–8, 259–60
Davies, M., 254
Davison, G., 295, 354
Dawkins, R., 333, 334
DAX–MED task, 54, 56
Dayhoff, J., 209
deception in research, 367–9
deduction, 20, 24, 26, 27, 30
Deep Thought chess program, 168
definitions (behavioral), 86, 110
delimiting oppositionality, 154
De Mey, M., 50, 67, 70
democracy, 147, 148, 346, 347
Democritus, 185
Dennett, D.C., 159, 188–9, 215, 259–61, 263, 276, 278, 360
deontological ethics, 375
depression, 336
Derr, P., 87
Descartes, R., 12, 21, 36, 82, 89–92, 96–7, 184, 211, 238, 310, 341
descriptions (rationality), 19–20, 29
descriptive epistemology, 6
desires, 257–60, 262, 296, 321–3, 325–6, 334–5, 337
De Sousa, R., 237
Deutsch, K., 44, 45
Dewan, A.M., 219

Dewey, J., 113
Diener, E., 229, 232–3, 237, 367
differentiation, 179–80
DiGiuseppe, R., 305, 310
dignity, 147, 148
Dineen, F., 40
Dirac, P.A.M., 220
direct observation, 117–18
discourse of values, 320–2, 325
discovery, 44, 45, 56
disjunction problem, 177–8, 179
dispositional properties, 138–9
Dixon, R.M.W., 278
Doherty, M.E., 50, 57, 59, 66
Donnerstein, E., 42, 56
Donnerstein, W., 368, 369
Donovan, A., 57
dopaminergic system, 209, 214
double-conditional theory of therapy, 284
dream theory, 283
Dretske, F., 253
Dreyfus, H.L., 191
Dreyfus, S.E., 191
Drumheller, P., 363
Dryden, W., 304, 305
dual-space search, 54, 55–6, 61
Duhem, P., 285
Dunbar, K., 54–9 *passim,* 61
Durkheim, E., 40
Dushenko, T.W., 369
Dworkin, G., 352, 357
Dyke, C., 186
dysfunctional thinking, 304

Earman, J., 188
Eccles, J.C., 211
ecological psychology of cognition, 67
ecological validity, 4, 56–60
Edelman, G.M., 194
Edelson, M., 286–7, 300, 301
effects, individuation by, 252
effort process, 210, 211
ego, 282
ego strength, 292–4 *passim,* 297
egoist values, 323–4, 332, 334–7
Eigen, M., 196
Einstein, A., 42, 59, 87, 168–9, 216, 285
Ekman, P., 234
eliminationism, 6, 7, 8, 257
eliminative materialism, 215–16, 243, 244–55, 264, 355–6
elitism, 348
Ellis, A., 280, 304–10, 312–14
Ellsworth, P.C., 237
Elster, J., 37
emergent representation, 181
emotions, 209–10

typical, 158–9, 227–41
empathy, 101, 103, 106
empiricism, 23, 72–3, 111–12, 127, 132, 136
    logical, 22, 157
    Quine's view, 96–9, 104, 106
encodingism, 158, 174–9, 181–2
energy (dematerialization), 220
entities of folk theory, 249–52
envy, 228, 230, 235, 236
EPAM program, 160, 165–7
epicycles, 244, 250, 253, 254
episodic process, 215
epistemic norms, 1–2, 19–20, 22–3, 29, 31, 69
epistemic subject, 70–1
epistemology, 1–3, 130, 184, 274
    for computers, 162–4
    evolutionary, 2, 23–4, 43, 312
    genetic, 3, 66–75
    naturalized, 4–5, 8–13, 69, 97
    normativity (abandonment), 4–14
    philosophical, 109–11
    problems of, 21–2
    psychological (Skinner), 109–11
    Quine's approach, 96–9, 101, 104
    rational–emotive therapy, 280, 304–14
    social, 2, 33–47, 50
equal effectiveness thesis, 299–300
equilibration, 69, 71–2, 74
equilibrium paths (value), 326–32
Ericsson, K.A., 167
Erikson, E., 347
errors, 59, 177, 312, 313
Erwin, E., 287, 298, 299, 301
eternal sentences, 100
ethical naturalism, 377
ethical nihilism, 375
ethics, 80, 145–8, 310, 343–4
ethics and psychology, 1, 19, 317–18
    behavior therapists' dilemma, 352–9
    codes of ethics, 361–70
    critical examination, 371–9
    responsible psychiatry, 339–49
    values (formation), 319–38
ethnomethodology, 245, 266
Euler circles, 153, 154
evaluation, 268, 314
    typical emotions, 227, 236–40
    of values, 321, 325, 331
Evans, R.J., 194
Evans-Pritchard, E., 345
evidence, 2, 4, 6, 9, 104
evolutionary biology, 91, 93, 113–14
evolutionary epistemology, 2, 23–4, 43, 312
experimental simulations, 56–60
experimental social epistemology, 41–7
experimentation (therapeutic), 297–301
experts/expertise, 342, 348–9

explanandum/explanans, 253
explanation (definition), 151–3
external validity, 42
externalist psychology of science, 68
extremists (philosophy of mind), 215–16
extrinsic systems, 213
Eyde, L., 375
Eysenck, H.J., 291

faculty members–students (multiple relationships), 365–7
Faden, R., 353–4, 356
fallibilism, 96–8, 305, 311–12
false representation, 181
falsificationism, 34–5, 51–2, 54–9
familiarization process, 215
Faraday, M., 57, 60, 61, 169
Farmer, J.D., 194
Farris, H., 54–5
fast Fourier transform (FFT), 221
Faust, D., 22, 40, 67
Fay, A., 54, 55–6
feedback mechanisms, 218
feelings, 213
    typical emotions, 227, 236–43
Fehr, B., 228
Feigenbaum, E.A., 182
Feigl, H., 219
Feist, G.J., 51
Feldman, J.A., 189
Feldman, M., 295
Festinger, L., 133
Feuerbach, L., 287
Feyerabend, P.K., 54, 112
fidelity (integrity), 362, 364
Fine, A., 38, 298
Fisch, R., 66
Fisher, C.B., 367, 368, 369
Fisher, J.E., 371
Fisher, S., 291, 301
Fiske, A.P., 336
Fitness, J., 228
Fleschig, P., 213
Fletcher, G.J.O., 228
Flores, F., 249
Fodor, J., 74, 88, 90–3, 159, 175–8, 186, 188, 190, 208, 244, 246, 248, 253–4, 260–3, 269, 278
folk psychology, 46, 141, 158, 215, 243
    conceptual analysis, 264–69
    falsity of theories, 244–55
    implications, 275–8
    survival of, 270–5
    underwritten by science, 256–63
Fontana, D., 277
Forbes, M., 298
Ford, K.M., 188
Forster, M., 190

Foucault, M., 35, 40
Fourier transform, 220–1
frame problem, 188
Frank, J., 299
free association, 284, 286
free will, 151, 152, 268, 278
Freedman, B., 373
Freedman, J.L., 229
freedom, 147, 148
Freeman, W., 196–7, 222
Frege, G., 129, 266, 311
Freud/Freudian theory, 68, 149, 212, 251, 279–87,
    291–2, 302
Frijda, N.H., 228–9, 234, 238
Frizzell, K., 363
frontolimbic forebrain, 214–15
Fryberg, D., 367, 368, 369
Fuller, S., 2, 34, 36–7, 39, 41, 43, 45–6, 50, 56, 60, 67
functional analysis, 87–8, 93
functions/causes (difference), 86–9
fundamental attribution error, 41
Furnham, A., 244

Gabor, D., 221
Galanter, A., 215
Galileo Galilei, 38, 82, 113, 114
Gall, F.J., 207, 208, 215
Garcia, R., 73
Garcia-Rill, E., 209
Gardner, H., 357
Garfield, S., 292
Garfinkel, H., 245, 266
Gasking, D., 121
Gay, P., 286
Geertz, C., 35
Gellner, E., 281, 282–3, 284–5, 345
general naturalized intelligence theory (GNIT), 187,
    189, 191–7, 199
generalizations, 247–51, 261, 262
generic oppositionality, 154
genetic epistemology of science, 3, 66–75
genotypes, 197
Gentilini, J.M., 304
Gentner, D., 247
Georgopoulos, J.C., 214
Gestalt psychology, 52–4, 66–7, 160
Ghiselin, M., 334
Gholson, B., 2, 50, 66, 67, 68, 72
Gibbard, A., 295
Gibson, J.J., 67
Gibson, R.F., 13
Giere, R.N., 2, 50, 67
Gill, M., 212
Gilmour-Barrett, K., 361
Glass, G., 291, 299, 301
Glymour, C., 35
goal consistency (rationality), 309

Gödel, Kurt, 23
Goldberg, A., 299
Goldfried, M.R., 280, 354
Goldiamond, I., 127
Goldman, A.I., 5, 34, 69, 276
good, theory of (Brandt), 294–7
Good Old–Fashioned Artificial Intelligence (GOFAI),
    158
good theories, 8–9, 249
Gooding, D., 51, 60–1
Goodman, N., 249
Goodnow, J., 55
Goodyear, R.K., 366
Gorman, M., 42, 52, 54–6, 59–61, 67
GPS program, 160
Granny psychology, 262, 278
Green, D.G., 196
Greenberg, R., 291, 301
Greeno, J.G., 61
Greenwood, J.D., 276–8
Grice, P., 266
Grieger, R.M., 304
Grillner, S., 209
Grossberg, S., 189
grounds, 2
Grover, S.C., 66
Gruber, H., 60, 61, 70
Grünbaum, A., 280, 284–7, 298–301
Guha, R., 182
Gunji, Y.–P., 197

Ha, Y.–W., 51, 52, 54, 55
Haack, S., 7
Habermas, J., 68
Hackett, E., 45
Hacking, I., 250, 252
Hahlweg, K., 23, 198, 199
Hall, J., 373
Hamburg, D.A., 209
Hammond, K., 41
Hanson, N.R., 112
Hanson, S.J., 197
hard disjunction, 154
Harding, S.S., 365
Hare-Mustin, R., 373
Harnad, S., 176, 358
Harman, G., 295, 296
Haroutunian, S., 74
Harper, R.A., 307–8
Hart, K.E., 304
Hartog, J., 214
Hastorf, A.H., 235
Haugeland, J., 158
Hawley, A., 43
Hayes, J.P., 244, 245, 246
Head, H., 213
Hebb, D., 108, 115, 151

'heed concepts', 267, 276
Heesacker, M., 304
Hegel, G.W.F., 37
Heilman, K.M., 212, 214
Heins, M., 363
Heisenberg, W., 220
Hempel, C.G., 79, 87, 111, 116, 318, 378
Heppner, P.P., 304
Heraclitus, 185
Herder, J.G., 40
Hermans, H.J.M., 213, 214
hermeneutic psychoanalysis, 286–7
Hersen, M., 300
Hersh, N.A., 214
Hilgard, E.R., 212
Hineline, P.N., 81
Hinton, G.E., 189–90, 209
hippocampal system, 210, 211
Hippocratic oath, 346
Hiroshima, 347, 348
historical biology, 298
history, 60–1, 273
   of ethics code, 372
   individuation by, 250–2
Hittner, J.B., 304
Hobbs, J.R., 170
Hochschild, A.R., 236, 237
Hocutt, M.O., 90
Hodges, B.T., 322
holism and cognitive dissonance, 133–4
Holland, J., 67, 193, 249
Holmes, C.L., 169
hologram, 221
Holyoak, K.J., 67, 249
Holz, W.C., 109
Holzkamp, L., 68
Holzman, P., 287
homeostasis, 218
homology question, 103
homosexuality, 295
Homskaya, E.D., 214, 215
Hooker, C.A., 23, 185, 186, 188, 190, 194–5, 198–200
Horder, J., 233
Horgan, T., 189
Hornik, K., 189
Houts, A.C., 50, 66, 67, 68, 72
Hughes, D.G., 155
Hull, C., 79, 108, 116, 119, 133, 152, 161
'human essence', 46
human nature, 359
   communal conception, 333–7
   criterion (equilibrium), 331–2, 335, 337
   individualistic conception, 333
human sciences, naturalistic
   reconstruction of, 36–41
Hume, D., 19–20, 22, 138
Husserl, E., 212

Huxley, A., 347
hypothetical mechanism (theory), 108, 112, 115–22
hypothetico-deductive confirmability, 284

identity, 84, 105, 219
implicit definition, 179–80
in-principle arguments, 177
incoherence (encodings), 176
incompleteness theorem, 23
indeterminacy of translation, 102–4
individual (epistemic subject), 70–1
individual creativity, 328
individualist view, 333–7
individuation, 250–2
induction, 35, 102–3, 113, 188
inferences, 119, 170
information
   misinformation, 130, 132–4
   processing, 67, 160–2, 171, 189, 196, 209, 213
informed consent, 318, 352–9
inner states, 142, 146
innovation, 43, 44–5
inside-out philosophy, 81
insight (in computation), 168–9
instability (emotions), 232–3
instantiations, 222, 261
instrumentalism, 159
instruments (role), 118–20
integrity, 362, 364
intellectual property, 39
intelligence, 193–8
intensionality, 83, 106, 129, 130, 276
intensity, emotional, 233, 236, 237
intention, 210–12, 236–8, 257–63, 343–4, 357, 358–9
intentional inexistence, 211–12, 216
interactivism, 158, 179–81
internalist psychology of science, 68–9
interpretation of behavior, 111–12
interpretivists, 42
introspection, 83–4, 87, 89, 91, 105, 106, 116, 161, 184
intuition, 167–8, 184
invention, 44
irrational belief, 280, 304–14
irrational desires, 296
is/ought confusion, 6–7, 19–20, 145, 146, 147, 377
isomorphism, 128, 129, 218
Ito, K., 197
Ito, M., 211
Izard, C.E., 232

Jacob, F., 57
Jacobs, S., 305
James, W., 209, 210, 211, 219, 273
Janik, A., 40
Jantsch, E., 186
Jaynes, J., 212
Jenkins, J.M., 233, 234

Jensen, J., 293
John, E.R., 208
Johnson, C.R., 197
Johnson, S., 197
Johnson-Laird, P.N., 52
Johnson-Laird, W., 24
Johnston, M.W., 366
judgement, 25, 27–8
Jung, C., 212–13
justification, 6, 56, 119, 149
    epistemology and, 4, 7–9, 12, 14, 23, 44–5
    logic of, 24–7
    rationality, 310, 311

Kagan, J., 229
Kahneman, D., 24, 84, 230, 231
Kaiser, M.K., 247
Kalish, D., 309
Kalish, H., 352, 354
Kant, I., 20, 21, 36, 310, 375, 378
Kaplan, C.A., 168
Karmiloff-Smith, A., 244
Katz, E., 346
Kaufer, D., 45
Kauffmann, S.A., 197
Kazdin, A., 292, 298, 300, 354
Keith-Spiegel, P., 367, 368
KEKADA program, 52, 61, 169
Kelman, H.C., 368
Kelso, J.A.S., 209
Kempen, H.J.G., 213, 214
Kepler, J., 52, 53
Kim, J., 5–6, 9
Kimpers, T.P., 51, 58
Kitayama, S., 333, 336
Kitchener, K.S., 362, 364–6, 368–9
Kitchener, R.F., 1, 67, 69, 71, 110, 113, 119, 121
Kitcher, P., 34, 248
Klaaren, K.J., 237
Klahr, D., 54, 55–6, 61
Klayman, J., 51, 52, 54, 55
Kliegl, R., 291
Kline, M., 23
Kline, P., 291, 301
Knonow, A., 214
Knorr-Cetina, K., 41
knowledge, 33, 44–5, 113, 132, 354
    –claims, 23
    problems of universals, 134–5
    psychology of, 67–70
    scientific, 10–13, 31, 59–60, 67–74, 134, 355
    sociology of, 34–41, 59, 67, 68
Koch, S., 2, 157
Kohlberg, L., 317, 375–6
Kohn, R., 336
Kohonen, T., 189
Koocher, G.P., 367, 368

Kornblith, H., 2, 34
Kosso, P., 4
Kovecses, Z., 228
Krasner, L., 371
Kreboizen (placebo therapy), 298
Krebs, Sir Hans, 52, 169
Kripke, S., 253
Kruger, L., 211
Kubie, L.S., 66
Kuhn, D., 247
Kuhn, T., 35–6, 112, 137, 198, 342
    psychology of science, 52–5, 60, 66
Kulkarni, D., 52, 56, 169
Küng, H., 343

Lacey, H., 323, 332
Laird, J.E., 182
Lakatos, I., 35, 54, 56, 59, 285, 372
Lakoff, G., 195, 228
Lamb, D.H., 363
Langley, P., 51–3, 67, 162, 170
language, 22, 39–40
    folk psychological, 270–5, 277
    games, 40
    learning, 89, 99, 101–4, 106, 163–4, 170
    linguistic behaviorism, 80, 126–39
    machine, 217–19, 222
    mentalist, 86, 90–3, 104–5, 141, 216
    natural, 126–7, 143–5, 163, 170–1, 245–6, 253–4,
        264, 266–7
    philosophy of (Quine), 99–104
    of rational thinking, 143–5
    of thought, 269, 276
Laplace, Marquis de, 150, 377–8
Larkin, J., 58
Larsen, R.J., 229, 232, 233, 237
Lashley, K.S., 116, 208, 209
Latané, B., 276
Latour, B., 38, 41, 59, 60
Laudan, L., 23, 35, 54, 56–7, 317
Laudan, R., 57
law statements, 137
Lazarsfeld, P., 346
Lazarus, R.S., 228, 233, 235, 237, 239
leadership (in psychiatry), 339, 345–7
learning
    commonwealth of, 347
    by computers, 165–6
    language, 89, 99, 101–4, 106, 163–4, 170
    logical (theory), 153–5
    naturalized cognitive science, 188–91, 193–7
    skills, 25–7
Leibniz, G.W., 37, 184, 221
Lemos, R., 296
Lenant, D.B., 182
Leslie, A.M., 244, 277
Levine, D.S., 209

Lidz, C., 353
Lindberg, D., 21
Lindgren, K., 189
Lindsay, R.C.L., 369
Lindsley, D.B., 209
linear thinking, 167
linguistic behaviorism, 80, 126–39
linguistics, 39–40, 106, 145, 246
    Cartesian, 89–90
    control myth, 268–9
    of folk psychology, 264–5
Loar, B., 257
local vector control, 194–6
Locke, John, 22, 36
locus of control, 277
Loewer, B., 177, 178
logic, 309
    deductive, 20, 24, 26–7, 30
    of identity, 84
    of justification, 24–7
    system of, 29–30
logical behaviorism, 111, 141
logical empiricism, 22, 157
logical learning theory, 80, 153–5
logical positivism, 22, 79, 279, 317
logicality of computation, 165–7
Logos, 151–2, 153–4
Lowe, C.F., 145, 147
Luborsky, L., 299
Luria, A.R., 214, 215
Lyddon, W.F., 304
Lynch, J.C., 214
Lyons, L.C., 304
Lyons, W., 228, 239

McAvoy, T.J., 191
McCarl, R., 182
McCarthy, J., 168, 244
McCarthy, R.A., 208, 214
McClelland, J.L., 67, 162, 189, 209, 254
McCloskey, M., 247
MacCorquodale, K., 113
MacCulloch, M., 295
McDermott, D., 244
McFarland, D.J., 211
McGinn, C., 276, 278
McGuinness, D., 209, 210
Mach, E., 113–15, 211
Machiavelli, N., 346
machine language, 217, 218–19, 222
MacIntyre, A., 326
MacKay, D.M., 211
Macklin, R., 352
McLaughlin, B., 188
MacLean, P.D., 209
McNeil, M., 215
macrostructure, 138

Maes, P., 193, 197
Maffie, J., 4
Magoun, H.W., 209
Mahoney, M.J., 51, 58, 66, 80, 304–5
Malan, D., 292
Malsburg, C. von der, 197
manifestation of values, 322–3, 326–7
Mannheim, K., 37, 38, 67
Mar, G., 309
Marcelja, S., 221
Marglin, S., 324
Margolis, H., 334
Markus, H.R., 333, 336
Martín–Baró, I., 327, 329, 337
Marx, Karl, 37, 157
Marxism, 281
materialism, 152, 185
    Cartesian, 90–3
    scientific dualism, 216–17, 219–20, 222
mathematical models, 186
Matson, W.I., 81, 82, 83
Matthews, B.A., 135
Mauthner, F., 40
Maxwell, J.C., 60, 61, 220
meaning, 22, 99–101, 104, 110, 152
    Churchland's treatment, 273–4
    precedent, 153–4, 155
mechanism/mechanistic behavior, 80, 82, 149–55,
    165–7
Medin, D.L., 244
Medlin, B., 185, 267
Meehl, P., 113, 279, 298
Mehalik, M., 61
Meja, V., 38
Melton, G.B., 363
Melzack, R., 238
memory, 170–1, 191–3, 195, 207–8, 211, 212
Memphis State group, 50
Mendel, G., 45
mental images, 163, 164
mental model, 52, 53, 61
mental states, 90–1, 105, 116–17, 141, 142, 188, 238,
    253, 261–3, 267, 358
mentalism, 258–9, 269, 318, 356–9
    scientific dualisms, 216–17, 219–20, 222
mentalist language, 86, 90–3, 104–5, 141–2, 216
mentalistic explanations, 115–16
metaethical issues, 294
metaphysics, 1, 21, 39, 54, 82–3, 114, 157, 184–5
metarules, 27
metascience, 50
metastable states/structures, 198
metatheory, 1, 157
microstructure, 137–8
Mill, J.S., 42, 110, 137, 375
Miller, A.I., 70
Miller, D.J., 363, 364

Miller, D.T., 230, 231
Miller, G.A., 215, 218
Miller, N., 120
Miller, T., 291, 299, 301
Millikan, R.G., 250–2
Milner, P., 210
mind
 –body relation, 82–4, 93, 97, 105, 116, 152, 157, 164
 –brain connection, 158, 207–22
 emotion and, 209–10
 folk psychology, *see main entry*
 philosophy of, 104–5, 142–5, 215–22
 see also brain; cognitive science and psychology
Minsky, M., 188, 215, 249
Mishkin, M., 213
misinformation, 130, 132–4
Mitroff, I.I., 58
Mittlestaedt, H., 211
Mitwelt, 134
Monod, J.–L., 57
Montague, R., 309
Moore, G.E., 377
moral autonomy, 345
moral problems in psychology, 361–70
morality, 147, 310, 344, 373–9
 ought/is confusion, 6–7, 19–20, 145, 146, 147, 377
Morris, S., 52
Morris, W., 372
Morse code, 175, 177
Mos, L.P., 152
motivation, 209–10
 typical emotions, 227, 236–40
motor equivalence, 208
Mountcastle, V.B., 214
Moxley, R.A., 85, 87
multiculturalism, 329
multiple relationships, 362, 365–7
Murdock, M., 301
Murphy, G.L., 244
Musgrave, A., 372
Mynatt, C.R., 50, 51, 57, 66

Nagy, T.F., 361
narrative consciousness, 214–15
narrative defense, 257
narrow AI theory, 158, 184, 187–92, 196–7
native informant, 162–3
nativism, 82, 102–4, 176
natural language, *see* language
natural science, 9–11, 97, 114, 359
 of intelligent systems, 184–200
natural selection, 358
naturalism
 abandonment of normativity, 4–14
 epistemology, 2, 4–5, 110, 158
 nonnormative, 5, 6–14
 Quine's view, 96–8

radical (Skinner), 108, 121, 122
 reconstruction of human sciences, 36–41
naturalized cognitive science, 184–200
NAVLAB system, 164
necessity (rationality), 309–10
negative stimulus meaning, 99–100
Neimeyer, R.A., 50, 66, 68, 72
Nelson, R.E., 307
Nelson, R.J., 187
Nerlich, G., 321
Nersessian, N.J., 60, 61
Neu, J., 240
Neumann, E., 212
neural network, 67, 162, 186, 209
neurobehavioral science, 207–10
neuropsychology, 210–15
neutral monism, 158, 219
new Cartesianism, 90–3
New Eleusis task, 52, 55
Newell, A., 60, 158, 160–2, 175, 182
Newton, I., 38, 45, 150–1, 284, 309–10, 311, 378
Nisbett, R., 22, 24, 40, 67, 84, 244, 249, 278
nnets theory, 189–92, 194–6
Noble, D., 358
Nodding, N., 369
nominalization, 267–8, 277
nonmachines, 149–55
nonnormative naturalism, 5, 6–14
Norcross, J.C., 280
Nordahl, M.G., 189
normative epistemology, 19–20, 22–3, 29, 110–11
normative issues, 1–2
normative scope of social epistemology, 34–6
normativity, abandonment of, 4–14
norms
 epistemic, 1–2, 22–3, 29, 31, 69
 of rationality, 19–20, 29
novel sentences, 127–9, 130, 133
Nowak, G., 53
Nowotny, H., 67

Oaksford, M., 188, 248, 276–7
Oatley, K., 228, 232–3, 234, 238
objective consciousness, 213–14
objective observation sentences, 132
objects, 21–2, 181
 abstract (generation of), 267–8
Oblon, M., 61
observation, 28, 111–12, 116
 sentences, 100–1, 103
 theories, 117–20
occasion sentences, 100
O'Donohue, W., 312, 371–2, 373
Olds, J., 210
ontogenesis, 197, 198
ontology, 53, 97–8, 129, 138

of folk theory, 245–6, 250–4, 276
operant conditioning, 358
operational definitions, 84–5
operationalism, 109, 110, 118
opinion leaders, 346
Oppenheim, P., 87
Oppenheimer, R.J., 347
oppositionality, 154–5
O'Rorke, P., 52
Ortony, A., 230, 239
Oscar-Berman, M., 214
Osgood, C.E., 267, 268
ostension, 101, 102, 106
ought/is confusion, 6–7, 19–20, 145, 146, 147, 377
outside-in philosophy, 81

pain, 21–2, 132, 142, 143, 146–7
Palmer, S.E., 175
pan-critical rationalism, 280, 305, 310–14
Papez, J.W., 209
paradigms, 35, 52–4, 137, 194, 292–3, 342–3
parallel distributed processing, 67, 174, 189, 198, 209
Paranjpe, A., 277
Paras, K.C., 304
parsers, 170
Parsons, T., 269
partiality (of emotions), 235–6
Pascarella, E.T., 367
paternalism, 346
pattern recognition, 179
Paulus, P., 45
Pavlov, I., 79, 85, 115
Peacocke, A.R., 196
Pearson, K., 113
Peirce, C.S., 35, 84–5, 87, 214
Penfield, W., 213
Penfold, H.B., 194
perceived change, 228–30
perception, 21–2, 173–4, 210
Perner, J., 244
Perry, J., 128, 249
personal values, 321–30, 333, 336
phenomenology, 216, 269
phenotypes, 197, 198
philosophical epistemology, 109–11
philosophical naturalism, 199–200
philosophy
    behaviorism in, 79–80
    falsity in folk theory, 244–55
    of language, 99–104
    natural sciences of intelligent systems and, 184–200
    practical (Skinner), 145–8
philosophy and clinical psychology, 279
    irrational beliefs, 304–14
    psychoanalysis, 281–7
    psychoanalytic therapy, 291–302
philosophy of mind, 104–5, 142–5

neurobehavioral science and, 215–22
philosophy of science, 38–9, 51–4
    linguistic behaviorism, 126–39
    origins of, 134–5
phlogiston, 250, 252, 254, 356
phrenology, 208
physical objects, 21–2
physical skills, 25–6, 27
physical symbol system hypothesis, 158, 161–4, 171
physicalism, 96, 97, 98, 109, 158
Physikos, 151–2, 153
physiological mechanisms, 115, 119
Piaget, J., 67, 181, 192, 317, 345
Piatelli-Palmarini, M., 74, 194
Pickering, A., 39–74
picture theory of meaning, 128–9
Pinch, T., 54, 59
Pines, A., 247
Place, U.T., 89, 126, 128, 130, 245, 266–7, 269, 276–8
placebo hypothesis, 287, 298–301
Plantinga, A., 253
Plato, 222, 267, 309
pleasures (values), 334
Pohl, W.G., 214
Poincaré, H., 113, 114
Poizner, S., 361
Polanyi, K., 324
Polanyi, M., 47, 342–3, 347
Pollack, J.B., 189, 190
Pollock, J., 37
Pope, K.S., 366
Popper, K., 36, 60, 74, 145–6, 185, 346, 372, 379
    falsificationism, 35, 51–2, 54, 56
    psychoanalysis, 279–80, 283–5
Port, R., 197
Porter, T., 47
positivism, 42
    logical, 22, 79, 279, 317
    Skinner on, 108, 112–15, 120, 122
possibility criterion, 330–2
posterior cerebral convexity, 213–14
potential interaction, 180–1
potentiality and appearance, 219–22
Potter, J., 245
power, 33, 35, 329–30
    relations, 46, 332
Powers, W.T., 192–4, 195
pragmatism, 35, 84–5, 113, 181, 285
precedent meaning, 153–4, 155
predicate expressions, 267–8
predication meaning, 154–5
prediction and control, 142–3, 144
Pribram, K.H., 208–16, 218–19, 221–2
Price, H.H., 138
Priestley, Joseph, 38
Prigogine, I., 186
primitive suggestibility, 132–4

Prince de Broglie, L.V., 220
Prioleau, L., 301
problem solving, 191–2, 198, 312
process theory, 186–7
professional ethics, 361–70, 374–9
professional etiquette, 348, 349
Proffitt, D.R., 247
property rights, 324, 331
propositional attitude, 261–2, 269
propositions, 109, 130–1, 134
propriety, 340–4
prototype analysis, 158, 191, 227–8
proximal cause, 88
psychiatry (responsibility), 318, 339–49
psychoanalysis, 280, 281–7
psychoanalytic therapy, 280, 291–302
psychodiagnostic approach, 66
psychodynamic therapy, 301–2
psychogenetic epistemology, 74
psychological account of behavior, 377–8
psychological epistemology, 2, 74
    Skinner, 66, 80, 108–22
psychological investigation (values), 332–7
psychologism, 110, 122
psychologists, 371–9
psychology
    behaviorism in, 79–80
    cognitive science and, *see main entry*
    ethics and, *see main entry*
    folk theories and, 243–54
    of knowledge, 67–8, 69–70
    rationality and, 19–31
    of scientific knowledge, 67–74
    social epistemology and, 33–47
psychology of science, 1–3, 50–62
    cognitive psychology, 66–75
psychometric approach, 66
psychopathology, 305
psychotherapy, 378
punishment theory, 109
Putnam, H., 6, 7, 90, 250, 253
Pylyshyn, Z., 188, 190

Quaintance, M., 375
qualification, lack of, 309–10
quality space, 102
quantum theory, 185–6, 187, 200
Quin, Y., 168
Quine, W.V., 2, 5–14, 36, 37, 162
    behaviorism, 79–80, 84, 86, 96–106, 109, 120, 131,
      141

Rachman, S., 299
radical behaviorism, 79, 126, 141–8, 352–9
radical naturalism, 108, 121, 122
Radnitzky, G., 23, 311
Rajamoney, S., 52

Ramsey, P., 362, 368
Randall, D., 361
random variation, 311
rational-emotive therapy, 280, 304–14
rational beliefs, 306
rational thinking, 143–5, 147–8
rationalism, 82
    pan-critical, 280, 305, 310–14
rationality, 167, 377
    accounts of, 304–14
    bounded, 166–7, 171
    naturalized epistemology, 19–31
reality/realism, 37–8, 229, 326, 328
recognition process, 167, 170–1
Reeke, G.N., Jr., 194
Reese, W.L., 151
reflective abstraction, 72–4
reflective equilibrium, 331
reflex (conceptual analysis), 109
reflexivity, 29, 31
reflexology, behaviorism and, 85
Reichenbach, H., 149
Reid, T., 232
Reiner, R., 20, 23
reinforcement theory, 110–12, 115, 117, 141–8
Reitz, S., 215
relativism (psychoanalysis), 292–7
relativistic theory, 185–7, 216
religion, 287, 295
representation, 82, 158, 174–82
repressed wishes, 296
repudiation theory, 105
research, deception in, 367–9
resignation path (equilibrium), 327–8
responsibility (in psychiatry), 318, 339–49
Revlin, R., 54–5
Rey, G., 177, 178
rhetoric, 44, 45
Ricardo, David, 44
Richards, G.D., 274, 276, 277
Richie, D.M., 176, 181
Richman, H.B., 166, 167
Riegel, K., 68
rights, 320, 324, 331, 365
Ringen, J., 110, 122, 358
rivalry, 231–2
Robinson, D., 208
Robinson, F., 211
Robinson, P., 298
robots/robotics, 26, 164, 196
Robson, J., 221
Roe, A., 66
Rogers, C., 292
Rogers, M.E., 304
role expectations/confusion, 365–7
Romantic tradition, 341, 343–4, 345
Roos, L., 214

Root, M., 258
Root-Bernstein, S., 46
Rorer, L.G., 305
Rorschach test, 295, 297
Rorty, R., 264, 275
Rosch, E., 228
Rose, J.E., 213
Rosenbleuth, A., 358
Rosenbloom, P., 181
Rosenwein, R., 60
Ross, L., 22, 24, 40, 84, 244
Rouse, J., 35
Rousseau, Jean-Jacques, 346
Royce, J., 2
RPT task, 55, 56
Rubin, Z., 235
Ruch, T.C., 211
Ruff, R.M., 214
rules, 24–8, 115, 144, 336
    of language, 89–90, 127, 128
Rumelhart, D.E., 67, 162, 189, 209, 254
Runes, D.D., 150
Russell, B., 96, 128, 219, 311
Russell, J.A., 228, 278
Rychlak, J.F., 149–55 passim
Rychlak, L.S., 155
Rycroft, C., 277
Ryle, A., 292
Ryle, G., 79–80, 82, 84, 111, 266–7, 276, 277

Sachs, D., 287
Sakata, H., 214
Saltzman, E.L., 209
Samarapungavan, A., 53
Sapir, E., 40
Saussure, Ferdinand de, 40
Schachter, D.L., 245
Schachter, S., 213
Scherer, K.R., 234
Schiffer, S., 248
Schinbrot, T., 197
Schmitt, F., 34
Schroedinger, E., 220
Schuldenfrei, R., 323
Schulenberg, D., 52
Schumacher, J.A., 185
Schwartz, B., 323–4, 327, 332, 336
science
    epistemic status, 10–13, 31
    folk psychology and, 256–63
    genetic episemology, 3, 66–75
    morality and, 377–8
    problems of universals, 134–5
    psychology of, 1–3, 50–62
    Quine's behaviorism, 97
    responsible psychiatry, 346–8
    social ecologies of, 41–5
    sociology of, 67–9
    and technology studies, 36–7, 40–1, 45
scientific creativity, 72–4
scientific determinism, 356, 378
scientific dualisms, 216–17, 219–20
scientific knowledge, 10–13, 31, 59, 60, 67, 69–74, 134, 355
scientific law statements, 137
scientific laws, 309–10, 378
scientific method, 47, 311
scientific psychology
    behavior therapists' dilemma, 352–9
    folk psychology and, 246–50, 252–3, 276–8
scientific tradition, 340, 341–3
scientists, 53–4, 58–9
    psychology/sociology of, 67–8
scotoma of action, 213
Scriven, M., 108
Searle, J.R., 149, 163–4, 217
Secord, P.F., 365
selection, 43, 45
selection by consequences, 358
selective retention, 312
self-consciousness, 276
self-determination, 353–7, 359, 364
self-interest, 342, 373
self-organization and intelligence, 196
self-reflexivity, 7, 8, 14
selfishness, 333–6
Seligman, M.E.P., 336
semantic differential, 267, 268
semantics, 90, 99–101, 106, 127, 130, 132, 187–8, 261, 267
Sen, A., 321
sensory equivalence, 208
sensory stimulations, 12, 13, 100, 130
sentences, 99–102, 127–9, 130, 133
sentiments, emotions and, 234–5
sequacious meaning-extension, 153–5
sexual intimacies (ethics), 374, 376–7
sexual relationships (faculty members–students), 365–7
Shadish, W., 46, 50, 66, 67, 68, 72
Shannon, C.E., 213–14
Shapere, D., 23
Shapin, S., 45
Shapiro, D. and D., 299
Sharafat, A., 211, 222
Shaver, P., 228
Shepard, R.N., 218
Sherrington, C.S., 115
Shimoff, E., 135
Shimony, A., 6–7, 9–10
Shinn, T., 50, 67
short-circuit argument, 121, 122
Shrager, J., 51–3, 55, 67
Sidman, M., 212
Siegel, Harvey, 8, 10, 29, 298

signs (linguistic), 127–8
Siklossy, L., 162, 163
Silverman, E.S., 304
similes (of private experience), 269
Simon, H.A., 52, 56, 60, 67, 152, 158, 160–3, 166, 168–9
Simonton, D.K., 51, 72
simpliciter, 99
simulating social epistemology, 59–60
Sinclair, C., 361
Singer, B.F., 66
Singer, T.E., 213
single-subject designs, 109, 300–1
single cause myth, 268
Skarda, C., 196–7
skepticism, 11–13, 24, 251, 292–7
skills (in justification logic), 25–8
Skinner, B.F., 2, 128, 254, 265, 292, 312, 317
   behavior therapists' dilemma, 352–8
   radical behaviorism, 66, 79, 84–9, 101, 126–7, 135, 138, 141–8, 358
   theory of theories, 80, 108–22
Skinner, R.D., 209
Skinner Box, 85
Skorupski, J., 110
Slovic, P., 24
Smith, B.C., 175, 261, 275–6, 277
Smith, C.A., 228, 235, 239
Smith, D., 304
Smith, L.D., 113, 122, 312
Smith, L.S., 2
Smith, M., 291, 299, 301
Smolensky, P., 188, 190, 191
SOAR project, 182
social comparison (emotion), 230–2, 241
social ecologies of science, 41–5
social epistemology, 2, 33–47, 50
social groups, 306–7
social institutions, 323–4
social psychology of science, 67
social responsibility, 361–2
social transformation, 329–32, 335, 337
social values, 320–1, 324–5, 332–3
socialization processes, 321
Society for Philosophy and Psychology, 62
sociology
   of knowledge, 34–41, 59, 67, 68
   of science, 67–9
   of scientific knowledge, 67, 68
Socius, 151–2
soft disjunction, 154
'soft psychology', 278
solipsism, 83, 91, 93
spatial frequency, 221
speciesism doctrine, 82
'specific' therapies, 287
Sperry, R.W., 217
Spevack, A.A., 215

Spinoza, B., 135, 228, 230, 235, 284
spontaneity (in computation), 165–6
Spurtzheim, G., 207
Srinivas, K., 190
Staats, A.W., 152
Stalin, J., 235
Stampe, D., 253
standing sentences, 100
Stapp, H., 220
Staszewski, J.J., 166, 167
Stearns, S.D., 189, 191
Stehr, N., 38
Stengers, I., 186
Sterelny, K., 157
Stevens, A., 247
Stevens, S.S., 211
Stich, S., 215, 244, 273
Stiles, T., 301
Stilson, S.R., 155
stimulus–response behaviorism, 85, 141
Stolk, J.M., 209
Strawson, P., 266
Stroud, B., 8, 12–13, 29
structuralism, 70, 88
students–faculty members (multiple relationships), 365–7
substance theory, 185–6
Suci, G.J., 267
suggestibility, primitive, 132–4
summaries (role of theory), 112–13
supernatural beliefs, 134, 264–5
surplus meaning objection, 120–1
Surrey, L., 363
survival value, 307
Swartberg, M., 301
symbol, 158, 160, 173, 181–2
   physical system, 158, 161–4
   -tokenings, 253–4
   synonymy, 99–101, 104, 110
   syntax, 90, 127, 188, 261
   synthetic truth and, 130, 132
   synthetic truth, 130–2
   systemfailure error (SF), 59
Szasz, T., 287, 319
Szentagothai, J., 211
Sztompka, P., 42

'talking cure', 301
Tannenbaum, P.H., 267
Tarasoff, Tatania, 364, 365
Tarski, A., 129
Taylor, C., 320, 321, 337, 358
Taylor, R., 232
Taylor, S.E., 307
teleological behaviorism, 79, 149, 150–1, 152, 154
teleosponsivity, 153, 154–5
Terenzini, P.T., 367

Terveen, L., 177, 179, 181–2
Thagard, P., 53, 67, 249
thalamus/thalamic gate, 210–11, 214
Thatcher, R.W., 208
theism, 287
Thelen, M.H., 363, 364
theories, Skinner's theory, 108–22
theory-immunization, 285
therapeutic outcomes, 280, 292–7
Thompson, N.S., 87
Thorndike, J.L., 85
thought, language of, 269, 276
Tienson, J.L., 189
Tjeltveit, A., 293
Tolman, E.C., 79, 113, 116, 161
Toulmin, S., 35, 40, 43
Touretzky, D.S., 189, 191
transcendental psychology, 184
transduction, 179, 182
transference resolution, 292, 293
transformations, 221, 222
    from below, 329–32, 335, 337
translation, indeterminacy and, 102–4
Troxell, W.O., 193, 197
Truman, H.S., 347
truth, 38–9, 129–32, 268
Tukey, D.D., 54
Turing machine, 23, 24, 188
Turner, M.B., 157
Turner, S., 46–7
Turner, S.H., 304
Tversky, A., 24, 84
Tweney, R.D., 50–2, 54–7, 59–61, 66, 67
2-4-6 task, 51–2, 54–9 passim, 61

Ukhtomski, A.A., 208
Ulasevich, A., 155
unconscious processes, 210–13
universal law statements, 137
universal linguistic control myth, 268–9
universal Turing machine, 23, 24, 188
universals, problems of, 134–5
utilitarian theory of ethics, 375

vacuous explanations, 121, 122
Valenstein, E., 212, 214
Valentine, E.R., 276
van Gelder, T.J., 197
van Loon, R.J., 213, 214
Vasquez, M.J.T., 365
Veatch, R.M., 368
Verba, A., 162
verbal behavior, 246
verbal propositions, 277
verbal protocols, 160–2, 169
verbal responses, 110–11, 118
Verstehen, 101, 276

volition, 210, 211
Vosniadou, S., 53, 54

Waddington, C.H., 211
Wallace, D., 182
Wallach, L., 332
Wallach, M.A., 332
warrant, 2, 4, 5, 6
Warrington, E.K., 208, 214
Wason, P., 24, 51, 55, 56, 59
Watson, J.B., 79, 84, 104, 273
Wattenmaker, W.D., 244
Weaver, W., 213
Weiskrantz, J., 212
Weizsacker, E. von, 220
well-being, 333–6, 369
Wellman, H.M., 244, 277
Wertheimer, M., 66, 67
West, C., 327
West, L., 247
Wetherall, M., 245
Whellan, T., 129
White, H., 44
Whitely, J.M., 306, 307
Whitley, R.D., 68
wide AI theory (WAIT), 158, 187–91
Widrow, B., 189, 191
Wiener, N., 358
Wigner, E., 185, 220
Wilkins, J., 274
Williams, R.N., 155
Willshaw, D., 209
Wilson, C.L., 209
Wilson, D.W., 368, 369
Wilson, G.T., 299, 354
Wilson, T.D., 237
Wilson, T. de C., 278
Winch, P., 40
Winfree, A., 197
Winkler, R., 196
Winograd, T., 249
Wise, T.P., 363
Wittgenstein, L., 38, 40, 79–80, 96, 128, 133, 141, 266
Wollman, N., 155
Wolpe, J., 296
Woods, P.J., 304, 310
Woolfolk, R., 292
Woolgar, S., 41, 50, 67
Woolsey, C.N., 213
Wright, J.J., 214
Wrong, D., 35
Wundt, W., 40, 184

Yao, X., 189

ZBIE program, 163–4, 170
Zytkow, J.M., 52, 67